The Great Ideas

Man

Mathematics

Matter

Mechanics

Medicine

Memory and Imagination

Metaphysics

Mind

Monarchy

Nature

Necessity and Contingency

Oligarchy

One and Many

Opinion

Opposition

Philosophy

Physics

Pleasure and Pain

Poetry

Principle

Progress

Prophecy

Prudence

Punishment

Quality

Quantity

Reasoning

Relation

Religion

Revolution

Rhetoric

Same and Other

Science

Sense

Sign and Symbol

Sin

Slavery

Soul

Space

State

Temperance

Theology

Time

Truth

Tyranny

Universal and Particular

Virtue and Vice

War and Peace

Wealth

Will

Wisdom

World

Four medieval portraits of the great poet, Dante Alighieri, whose 700th anniversary is celebrated this year: by Signorelli, *top left;* Gaddi, *middle;* Giotto school, *top right;* Michelino, *bottom.*

The chief imagination of Christendom,
Dante Alighieri, so utterly found himself
That he has made that hollow face of his
More plain to the mind's eye than any face
But that of Christ.

—W. B. Yeats

THE

GREAT IDEAS

TODAY

1965

WILLIAM BENTON *Publisher*

ENCYCLOPÆDIA BRITANNICA, INC.

Chicago · London · Toronto · Geneva · Sydney · Tokyo

THE GREAT IDEAS TODAY 1965

Editors in Chief Robert M. Hutchins

Mortimer J. Adler

Executive Editor Otto Bird

Managing Editor Philip W. Goetz

Associate Editor Paul Carroll

Art Director Denis Fodor

Picture Editor Bonnie Abiko

Layout Artist Howard Baumann

Contributing Editor Milton Mayer

Contributors

Adolf A. Berle, Jr.   Yale Brozen   John E. Smith

Jeremy Bernstein   Arthur Larson   Stephen Spender

Kenneth E. Boulding   George Gaylord Simpson   Robert Theobald

LIST OF ILLUSTRATIONS

LIST OF ILLUSTRATIONS

LIST OF ILLUSTRATIONS

CONTENTS

A NOTE ON REFERENCE STYLE

In the following pages, passages in *Great Books of the Western World* are referred to by the initials 'GBWW,' followed by volume, page number, and page section. Thus, 'GBWW, Vol. 39, p. 210b' refers to page 210 in Adam Smith's *The Wealth of Nations*, which is Volume 39 in *Great Books of the Western World*. The small letter 'b' indicates the page section. In books printed in single column, 'a' and 'b' refer to the upper and lower halves of the page. In books printed in double column, 'a' and 'b' refer to the upper and lower halves of the left column, 'c' and 'd' to the upper and lower halves of the right column. For example, 'Vol. 53, p. 210b' refers to the lower half of page 210, since Volume 53, James's *Principles of Psychology*, is printed in single column. On the other hand, 'Vol. 7, p. 210b' refers to the lower left quarter of the page, since Volume 7, Plato's *Dialogues*, is printed in double column.

Gateway to the Great Books is referred to by the initials 'GGB,' followed by volume and page number. Thus, 'GGB, Vol. 10, pp. 39-57' refers to pages 39 through 57 of Volume 10 of *Gateway to the Great Books*, which is James's essay, "The Will to Believe."

PART ONE

Work,
Wealth,
and Leisure

INTRODUCTION

Automation has become a major topic of economic controversy. Like any major economic question, automation involves more than economics. A high level of unemployment has persisted since the end of World War II. Our economy can now produce greater wealth with fewer men than at any time since man has had to work for a living. This fact gives rise to a whole series of questions: What will people do if there are not enough jobs? How will they obtain an income? Can income be divorced from work? What will people do with their ever increasing free time? How are work and wealth related to leisure and to the pursuit of happiness? Such questions as these are now becoming meaningful for the many, not just for the few. It is no wonder then that we find ourselves in a new situation, and far from knowing all the answers, we do not know whether we are asking the right questions.

A symposium exploring these problems has to take into account the fact that there are different approaches to them. Mr. Yale Brozen is associated with the group at the University of Chicago identified with the neoclassical or traditional liberal position in economics (characterized by its opponents as "conservative"). Mr. Adolf A. Berle has been known for his eloquent and forceful analysis of public and government responsibility in matters of economic and social policy since the early days of the Roosevelt "Brain Trust." Mr. Robert Theobald, for the purposes of our symposium, is perhaps best known for sponsoring and promoting the idea of a guaranteed annual income. Mr. Arthur Larson, who served as a special assistant to President Eisenhower, is widely known for his vigorous statement on public policies in *A Republican Looks at His Party*.

The symposium focuses on two questions that circumscribe the economic aspects of the topic. One deals with the facts of the situation: Does automation produce massive unemployment? The other question raises a more general problem of policy: How will incomes be provided if there are not enough jobs? Mr. Brozen and Mr. Theobald were asked to direct their attention primarily to the first of these two questions, and Mr. Berle and Mr. Larson to the second. Yet it was understood from the start that what each contributor had to say might also bear on the whole range of topics being discussed.

Our contributors disagree about the meaning of automation. Is automation a new form of technological change utterly different from any that has occurred before? To this, Mr. Brozen replies "No," while Mr. Theobald voices a strong "Yes." In fact, the latter claims that even the word "automation" is a misnomer, since the computer now replaces managers and decision-makers as well as "hands"; he accordingly prefers the more comprehensive "cybernation," from the Greek word for steersman or manager (*kybernetes*). There is also disagreement concerning the effect of automation. Is it producing more or fewer jobs? It is not just that accurate figures on unemployment are difficult to obtain. The concept of unemployment, and so, too, of full employment, is inherently vague: Who is to count as a member of the labor force? Full employment certainly does not mean that every man, woman, and child holds a job. Economists even talk of "over-full employment."

Unemployment, however defined, at 5 percent of the labor force is too high, when jobs constitute the only source of income for most workers. But our contributors disagree about its cause: Is it primarily the fault of technological change or of uneconomic measures promoted for social and political purposes? Automation is undeniably responsible for some displacement of workers, especially among the young and unskilled. But what should be done to overcome it?

The approaches recommended by our contributors for solving the problem of the "employable" unemployed are, with one exception, complementary rather than opposed. Mr. Brozen advocates greater freedom in employment practices so that jobs that would be unprofitable at the minimum wage rate might be opened to the young and untrained. Mr. Berle notes that there is much work that needs doing that cannot be profitably organized into jobs and, hence, depends on public initiative. Mr. Larson shows how a national program to promote more widespread ownership of business and industry could provide workers with a source of income other than wages.

The exception concerns the relation of work and income. Mr. Berle expressly asserts that income cannot be divorced from work without disastrous moral and social effects, and Mr. Larson presupposes that shares in ownership would be earned by work. In contrast, Mr. Theobald not only defends the social benefit of the minimum wage rate and other social welfare legislation but also proposes that government guarantee an annual income to all, even without work. This, although admittedly at a minimal level, would effectively divorce income from work.

Such a proposal is, indeed, radical and new. In fact, it is sometimes asserted that economic change is now so rapid that the wisdom of the past has become obsolete. Yet President Johnson in one of his first pleas for the Great Society found it apropos to quote Aristotle: "Men come together in cities in order to live, but they remain together in order to live the good life" (cf. GBWW, Vol. 9, p. 446a). Our very affluence makes it important to understand the meaning and function of wealth and happiness and of work and leisure. On these subjects, as on almost all that concern thoughtful men today, the wisdom of the past is still relevant. It is therefore appropriate that this symposium conclude with a distillation of what *Great Books of the Western World* has to say on wealth and happiness, work and leisure.

Automation

YALE BROZEN

Extensive experience as a consultant to business corporations and government agencies augments the teaching career of Yale Brozen, Professor of Business Economics in the Graduate School of Business at the University of Chicago. In addition to serving the American Telephone and Telegraph Company and General Motors Corporation, Professor Brozen has been a consultant to the President's Materials Policy Commission, the State's Attorney Office in Cook County, Illinois, the Anti-Trust Division of the U.S. Department of Justice, the National Association of Manufacturers, and the National Science Foundation.

Born in 1917 in Kansas City, Missouri, he was educated at the Massachusetts Institute of Technology and the University of Chicago, from which he received his Ph.D. in 1941. In World War II he was a training administrator of the U.S. Army Signal Corps Radar Training Program. Professor Brozen has lectured at the Illinois Institute of Technology, the University of Minnesota, and Northwestern University, in addition to being Visiting Professor in Economics in 1954 at the Escola de Sociologia e Política in São Paulo, Brazil, and in 1964 at Rikkyo University in Tokyo. At the University of Chicago, he heads the Research Management Program, teaches in the Executive Program, and directs the summer program on Recent Developments in Applied Economics for professors of economics. His textbook, Workbook for Economics (1946), is widely used in universities in the United States and abroad. Dr. Brozen lives with his wife and son in Chicago.

4

and Jobs

At the accession of George III (1760), the manufacture of cotton supported hardly more than 40,000 persons; but since machines have been invented by means of which one worker can produce as much yarn as 200 or 300 persons could at that time, and one person can print as much material as could 100 persons at that time, 1,500,000 or 37 times as many as formerly can now earn their bread. . . .

And yet there are still many, even scholars and members of Parliament, who are so ignorant or so blinded by prejudice as to raise a pathetic lament over the increase and spread of the manufacturing system. . . . There are persons who regard it as a great disaster when they hear that 150,000 persons in our spinning works now produce as much yarn as could hardly be spun with the little hand-wheel by 40,000,000.

These people appear to cherish the absurd opinion that if there were no machines, manufacture would really give employment to as many millions as now; nor do they reflect that the whole of Europe would be inadequate for all this work; and that in that case a fifth of the whole population would need to be occupied with cotton-spinning alone! Both experience and reflection teach us just the contrary; and we should certainly maintain that, if we still had to spin by the hand-wheel today, cotton manufacture would employ only a fifth of the present number.

From Edward Baines' *History of the Cotton Manufacture in Great Britain*, 1835.

The mathematician who developed much of the logic underlying computer design predicted, in 1949, that the United States faced "a decade or more of ruin and despair." He forecast wholesale unemployment because automation, he felt, would abolish jobs on an unprecedented scale.[1] Despite his expectations, the number of persons gainfully occu-

---

1 Norbert Wiener, *The Human Use of Human Beings: Cybernetics and Society* (Boston: Houghton Mifflin Company, 1950), p. 189.

5

pied in civilian pursuits increased from 59 million in 1949 to 63 million in 1955.

In 1955 a parade of witnesses testified before the U.S. Congressional Subcommittee on Automation that intolerable unemployment was a looming problem unless automation was used wisely and well. Since 1955 the number of persons with jobs in the United States has increased from 63 to 71 million—a record number. In addition, 4 million persons now hold second jobs—an increase of about 2 million.

During this period in which the number of civilian jobholders increased by 12 million and the number of jobs by 14 million—the period predicted to be "a decade or more of ruin and despair"—real wage rates and per capita income also increased. The average hourly income of factory workers in 1949 was $1.80 (measured in 1964 dollars). The average hourly income of factory workers now is $2.55 (exclusive of fringe benefits), a more than 40 percent increase. Since the typical workweek is essentially unchanged (39 hours in 1949, 40 hours now), this has meant a rise of more than 40 percent in the weekly and annual income of the average factory worker. The wage rate and annual income of typical nonfactory workers rose almost 35 percent in this same period. There has been a remarkable rise in the wage income of the average worker at the same time that the total number of people with jobs has increased.

WHY IS AUTOMATION ALARMING?

In the face of these data, why do some cry that doomsday is coming? What is it about automation that causes alarm? Why is it that workers asked about their attitude toward mechanization feel no threat, yet appear frightened when asked about their feelings toward automation?

The hallmarks of automation, to distinguish it from mechanization or automatic methods, are its sensing, feedback, and self-adjusting characteristics. Because it senses changing requirements and adjusts without human intervention, it presumably does away with the need for human attendants or human labor. This is very frightening indeed to those who depend upon jobs for their livelihood.

Fear of automation can be traced to four sources. One is based upon the assumption that there is a fixed amount of goods that buyers want. Any new method that enables us to turn out more goods per man-hour will, it is believed, enable us to turn out the fixed amount of goods and services with fewer men. If a man helped by an automatic machine can produce twice as many widgets per hour as he formerly did, then, presumably, only half as many hours of work will be available for each man to do. If workweeks are not shortened, only half as many jobs could, it is asserted, be provided in these circumstances. President Kennedy once used this sort of logic when he said "that approximately 1.8 million persons holding jobs are replaced every year by machines."

The second source of fear springs from the idea that automation or cybernation is something more than the latest stage in the long evolution of technology. Automation is said to be so different in degree that it is profoundly different in its effect. Automated machines controlled by computers do not simply augment muscle power as previous machines did. They replace and outperform human intelligence. In the future, machines will not only run machines; they will repair machines, program production, run governments and even rule men. Union leaders will collect no dues and businesses will have no customers because, presumably, there will be no production workers required. Human beings will, it is believed, be made as obsolete by these machines as horses were by the tractor and the automobile.

The third source of fear is our greater awareness of the workers displaced by automation than of the other unemployed persons. Among the more than three million unemployed are several thousand persons laid off because their skills are not usable by concerns installing automated processes to replace previously used technology. Presumably, there are no job opportunities open to them since they possess only obsolete skills. Others who are laid off or who are among the unemployed because they have voluntarily quit their jobs are less worrisome because their skills are not obsolete, and they will have new jobs in a few weeks.

A fourth source of fear is the high incidence of joblessness among the unskilled. It is felt that the unskilled are unemployed because automated production reduces the demand for unskilled workers. Any increases in the demand for labor occurring because of automation are believed to be concentrated on highly skilled workers.

IS THE ALARM JUSTIFIED?

Automation causes displacement. Some people do become unemployed because of it, although most firms retrain and place employees in new jobs when eliminating old jobs.[2] Yet, automation does not itself

2 There is no single source that provides a census of the retraining done when new technology is installed by business firms. The U.S. Bureau of Labor Statistics studied the experience of 20 major firms converting to electronic accounting and found that only 0.03 percent of the 2,800 employees involved in the operations affected by the installation of computers were laid off. (*Adjustments to Introduction of Office Automation*, Bulletin No. 1276 [Washington, D.C., 1960].) Employees who needed retraining to hold jobs with the application of new technology were retrained by these firms.

In eight companies intensively studied by the Stanford Research Institute, seven of which installed automation equipment, not one person was laid off. All persons displaced were retrained, often for higher paid positions. ("Expectations and Realizations of Automation," *Stanford Research Institute Journal*, No. 2, 1964, p. 13.)

R. Conrad Cooper testified, on March 28, 1961, before the Subcommittee on

KITCHENS, 1875 AND 1965
Women still devote time to kitchen work

create unemployment. The number of men jobless is not greater than it would have been if no automation had occurred.

It may seem paradoxical to argue that automation causes displacement but does not cause unemployment. Many observers point to specific persons unemployed as a result of this phenomenon. They fail, however, to point to the unemployed who found jobs because of automation. They fail to recognize those who would have joined the jobless if new technology had not been developed and applied.

Although automation has displaced some employees, the total number unemployed is smaller today than it would have been without automation, given the present wage structure. There are, certainly, some people now among the unemployed who would still have jobs but for these innovations. However, a still larger number today have jobs that they would not have had, had it not been for automation.

Unemployment and the Impact of Automation of the House Education and Labor Committee, that the replacement of the South Chicago Works of the United States Steel Corporation affected 1,346 employees. Of these, 71 percent were retrained and 8 percent were transferred to other departments. The others retired, quit, were discharged for violation of plant rules, etc. Only one employee was laid off. Similar instances are detailed in other testimony before congressional committees and in published literature. See G. P. Shultz and A. R. Weber, "Technological Change and Industrial Relations," *Employment Relations Research* (New York: Harper & Brothers, 1960). For a national analysis of employer efforts in training and retraining, see J. Mincer, "On-the-Job Training: Costs, Returns, and Some Implications," *Journal of Political Economy*, LXX (Supplement: October, 1962), 50-79.

Yale Brozen

Although we may grant that automation differs from other kinds of technology, we should not blind ourselves to history to the point of saying it is completely new. Perhaps the earliest automated device was the pressure cooker, invented by Denis Papin in 1679. He originated a pressure control that is still one of the most widely used regulators. Despite this automated device, cooks are still extensively employed and housewives still find it necessary to devote time to their kitchen work. Although homemakers may spend less time in the kitchen, this has simply freed them to do more of other kinds of work, such as better educating their children and decorating their homes.

During the eighteenth century, several types of automatic regulators were applied to windmills. An automatic, card-programmed loom was devised by Jacquard over 150 years ago. An automatic flour mill was built in 1741. Eighteenth-century steam engines were controlled by governors that had sensing, feedback, and resetting characteristics which are the hallmarks of automation. Despite increasing automation in the last two centuries, employment has risen continually.

In terms of a very recent type of automation, the use of electronic data-processing equipment, a United States Department of Labor study of large firms that introduced such equipment concluded that:

> Despite the reduction in labor requirements for the tasks performed by the computers, total employment of the offices as a whole rose. Over the four years from December 1953 to December 1957, total office employment at 17 of the offices studied increased an average of 7 percent. This increase,

STEAM ENGINE AND GOVERNOR   1862 DRAWING OF SWISS JACQUARD LOOM

Hallmark   *Card-programmed loom devised*

of automation   *over 150 years ago*

however, was less than the 15 percent rise reported for clerical and kindred workers in the Nation as a whole. In 6 of the 17 offices, the increase was greater than 15 percent; in 7, less; and in 4 there was a decrease. Although the immediate effect of electronic data processing suggests some retardation in the growth of office employment, particularly part-time work, the experience of some offices suggests the possibility of expanding employment in new areas of office activity to handle information which had previously been uneconomical to acquire.[3]

This experience of increasing office employment despite reduced labor requirements per unit of output is a specific instance of what has been going on generally in our economy. From 1919 to 1962, man-hours required per unit of output in the American economy dropped by 67 percent, yet total number of jobs rose from 42 to 68 million (*see* Figure I). The tripling of output per man-hour did not reduce the number of jobs by two-thirds as those who believe in a fixed amount of work available would predict.

One group which subscribes to the fixed-lump-of-work philosophy has

3 U.S. Bureau of Labor Statistics, *Adjustments to Introduction of Office Automation*, Bulletin No. 1276 (Washington, D.C., 1960), p. 4.

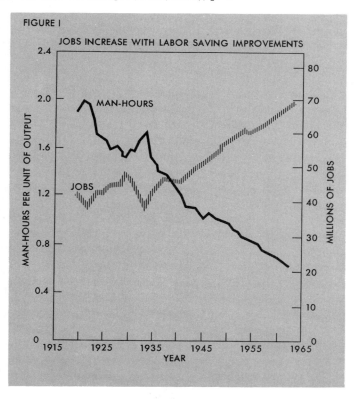

FIGURE I

JOBS INCREASE WITH LABOR SAVING IMPROVEMENTS

SCHOOLROOMS, NEW YORK 1886, CHICAGO 1965
Increasing the scale of educational activities

pointed with alarm to the 1960–63 annual rise in output per man-hour of 3.6 percent. It has said that this exceeds the long-term average annual rise of 2.4 percent from 1909 to 1963 and the average annual postwar rise of 3 percent. This, it is claimed, indicates that the pace of technological change is accelerating and will create a great unemployment problem.

The more rapid rise of output per man-hour from 1960 to 1963 was accompanied by an increase in the number of civilian jobs from 67 to 69 million. An even more rapid rate of increase in output per man-hour from 1949 to 1953, amounting to 4 percent per year, was accompanied by an increase in civilian jobs from 59 to 62 million. On the other hand, a slowed rate of increase in output per man-hour from 1953 to 1954, when output per man-hour rose by only 1.8 percent, well below the long-run average rise of 2.4 percent, was accompanied by a drop in employment from 62 to 61 million. It would seem that a more rapid rise in output per man-hour should be welcomed as a means of creating jobs more rapidly than they can be destroyed by other factors at work in our economy.[4]

The primary effect of automation is not a reduction in the number of jobs available. Rather, it makes it possible for us to do many things that

4 A study by S. Fabricant for the prewar period found that "trends in unit labor requirements have been negatively correlated with trends in man-hour employment in different industries" (that is, decreases in hours of labor per unit of product—increases in output per man-hour—have been correlated with increased employment while increases in hours of labor per unit of product have been correlated with a decline in employment). (*Employment in Manufacturing, 1899-1939* [New York: National Bureau of Economic Research, 1942].)

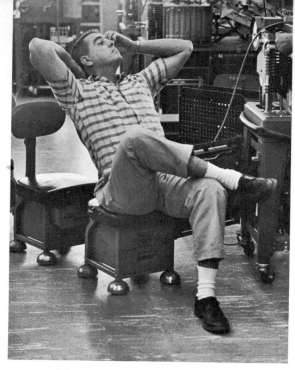

MACHINE TENDER IN THE SIXTIES
*Automation turns machine operators
into machine tenders*

otherwise could not and would not be done. Automation enables us to earn larger incomes and lead fuller lives. It will, in the future, literally make it possible to travel to the moon. It saves lives through the aid it gives doctors. By controlling traffic signals in response to traffic flows and reducing traffic congestion, it adds hours to the free time of commuters every week. It helps scientists, with the aid of high-speed data processing, to develop new knowledge that otherwise would not be available in our lifetimes. We are increasing the scale of educational activities because mechanization, automation, cybernation, or whatever we choose to call our new technology, makes it possible to do more than we could formerly. With the coming of automation, men are able to do more and have more. Both great and mundane activities are being enlarged.

AUTOMATION AND TYPE OF JOBS

Technological change does tend to alter the nature of work. We know from experience that automation in the factory turns machine operators into machine tenders and maintainers. This has already occurred in the textile industry, to name one example. Upon walking into the loom room of a modern mill, the first impression is that of a vast space filled with busy machinery and no people in sight. (Yet employment in textile mills totals nearly 900,000 workers.) Controls on individual machines enable one man to supervise a dozen or more looms. The chemical and petroleum refining industries use automatically controlled, continuous processes. (They, too, provide employment on a large scale amounting to more than one million jobs.) Instead of men running to distant points in a refinery to twist valve wheels, they now monitor instrument panels.

The effect of automation has been to increase the relative number of maintenance men, engineers, office employees, production control specialists, and other nonmachine operators that are required. (These are the people the U.S. Bureau of the Census calls nonproduction workers.) This is simply a continuation of a trend that has been going on for decades. In 1899 only 7 percent of the manufacturing industry labor force consisted of persons other than production workers. Today 26 percent of manufacturing employees are nonproduction, or indirect, workers (*see* Table I). Since 1939 production worker employment in manufacturing has increased 65 percent, while that of other workers has increased by over 160 percent.

In addition to changing the balance among occupations in a given industry such as manufacturing, technological progress is also changing the balance among industries. Only a century ago, fifty out of every one hundred workers toiled on farms producing the nation's supply of

TABLE I

GROWTH OF INDIRECT WORKER EMPLOYMENT IN MANUFACTURING, 1899–1963 (In Thousands of Persons)

Year	Total	Production Workers	Indirect Workers	Indirect Workers (Percent of Total)
1899	4,850	4,502	348	7
1919	9,837	8,465	1,372	14
1939	9,527	7,808	1,719	18
1959	16,675	12,603	4,072	24
1963	17,035	12,586	4,449	26

Sources: U.S. Bureau of the Census, "Historical Statistics of the United States, Colonial Times to 1957" (Washington, D.C., 1960), p. 409; "Manpower Report of the President" (Washington, D.C., 1964), pp. 226–28.

food and fiber. Only two to three out of every one hundred workers were producing educational, medical, recreational, and other services which contribute to a richer, fuller, healthier life. Today, the number of workers in these life-enriching occupations is relatively five times as great (*see* Table II). Those toiling on farms have been reduced to one-sixth their former number. They now direct machines instead of using animal power and their own muscles. The quality of life has been improved and brute toil has been reduced because technology has increased our incomes to the point where we can afford these services and these machines.

TABLE II

**DISTRIBUTION OF THE WORK FORCE IN THE UNITED STATES
1870–1960**

Industry	1870	1900	1930	1960
Extractive Industries	52.3%	40.7%	24.3%	9.9%
Agriculture	50.2	37.4	21.5	8.3
Mining	1.6	2.6	2.5	1.1
Forestry and Fisheries	0.5	0.7	0.3	0.5
Fabricating Industries	23.5%	27.8%	29.2%	31.8%
Manufacturing	17.6	22.0	22.8	24.5
Construction	5.9	5.8	6.4	7.3
Specialization Aiding Industries	11.4%	17.0%	26.4%	31.9%
Trade	6.1	8.6	13.1	17.7
Finance, Insurance, and Real Estate	0.3	1.1	3.1	4.3
Transportation and Public Utilities	5.0	7.3	10.2	9.9
Personal Service Industries	10.1%	10.5%	13.1%	15.2%
Domestic Service	7.3	6.0	5.4	3.7
Personal Service	2.0	3.5	5.3	6.3
Government (not elsewhere classified)	0.8	1.0	2.4	5.2
Life-Enriching Industries	2.6%	4.0%	7.0%	11.1%
Education	1.5	2.2	3.4	5.0
Other Professions	1.1	1.8	3.6	6.1

Sources: U.S. Bureau of the Census, "Historical Statistics of the United States, Colonial Times to 1957" (Washington, D.C., 1960), p. 74; United States Department of Commerce, "Survey of Current Business," July, 1961; G. J. Stigler, "Trends in Employment in the Service Industries" (Princeton: Princeton University Press, 1956).

Yale Brozen

Those who are concerned about unemployment should welcome rather than fear automation. If it were not for the technical advances of the past decade, unemployment, at present wage levels, would be above the astronomical levels of the early 1930's. Alternatively, if real wage rates were at levels consistent with full employment using the same technology as that available a decade ago, wage rates would be lower by about $8.00 a week (or 20 cents an hour) than they are now.

Technological change has created more jobs than it has destroyed. The number of civilians at work in 1964 is 10 million higher than a decade ago. A number of forces, including advances in technology, created 60 million additional jobs during the past decade. Fifty million jobs, however, were destroyed by various causes (primarily by the upward movement of wage rates). The 60 million new jobs created and the 50 million jobs destroyed left a net gain of 10 million positions.

This does not mean that 60 million separate individuals changed jobs in the last ten years either in the sense of shifting to a new employer or shifting to a different job with the same employer. In any given year, 8 to 10 million persons voluntarily quit their jobs and take jobs with other employers. Often, it is the same people who again quit their jobs to move to still other positions.[5] Also, the typical firm trains people for one set of positions, and then retrains the same people a few years later for new jobs. The average employee at General Motors Corporation, for example, is retrained six times in ten years. People in the American economy are astonishingly mobile and adaptable.

The net result of automation and other job-making forces at work in the economy during the past decade can be displayed in the form of graphs representing the demand for labor. Figure II, drawn to represent a hypothetical demand for labor in 1954 and 1964, roughly approximates the situation existing in labor markets in those two years. In 1954 average earnings were approximately $2.05 per hour (1964 dollars) and 61 million persons were gainfully occupied. In 1964 average earnings were $2.55 an hour and 71 million persons were gainfully occupied.

If wage rates had risen to $2.55 an hour with no change in the demand situation (that is, if the demand curve showing the number of men who would be employed at various wage rates in 1964 were the same as that shown in Figure II for 1954), the number of men gainfully occupied would have dropped to 36 million. What actually happened, of course, is that the demand for men shifted between 1954 and 1964. It did not

---

5 The average employee spends only 4.6 years with the same employer. (H. R. Hamel, "Job Tenure of American Workers, January 1963," *Monthly Labor Review*, October, 1963, p. 1145.)

remain static. As a consequence, wage rates and employment both rose.

The primary causes of the shift in demand were an increased quantity of capital available to assist each worker in doing his job, a rise in the average level of skill, and improvements in techniques of production (and design of products). The net result of these forces was a shift in the demand for labor to the position shown for 1964. If no increase in wage rates had occurred (and all other factors developed in the manner in which they did), there would have been 121 million jobs available. An increase of 60 million over the number of jobs available in 1954 would have occurred.

Since 121 million persons were not available to fill jobs, employers would have been confronted by extreme labor shortages. During the decade, employers in most industries did find themselves short of labor from time to time. They offered higher rates to attract the additional people they wanted. Wage rates in these industries were, in effect, successively bid up by employers. In some industries, unions and employers agreed on wage increases through collective bargaining rather than employers unilaterally bidding higher rates to attract employees. The net result of these wage rate increases (including the raising of minimum wage rates by statute) was to destroy 50 million jobs, leaving a net increase of 10 million positions.

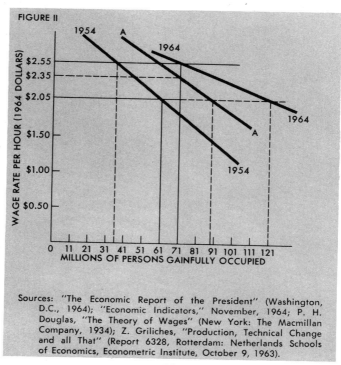

Sources: "The Economic Report of the President" (Washington, D.C., 1964); "Economic Indicators," November, 1964; P. H. Douglas, "The Theory of Wages" (New York: The Macmillan Company, 1934); Z. Griliches, "Production, Technical Change and all That" (Report 6328, Rotterdam: Netherlands Schools of Economics, Econometric Institute, October 9, 1963).

Curve A in Figure II is drawn to show what the 1964 situation might have been if no additions to technical possibilities had occurred. Without technological change, the number of jobs at the 1954 wage rate would have increased to only 89 million, a 28 million increase. Under these circumstances, wage rates could have risen by only 30 cents, instead of by 50 cents, and still have left the rate of demand sufficiently high to provide 71 million jobs (*see* Curve A, Figure II).[6] The net effect of the mélange of technological changes that occurred in various industries in the decade preceding 1964 was to make it possible for those at work to earn about $400 per year more in 1964 than they could have earned if no new technical possibilities had been developed.

COULD THE RESULT OF AUTOMATION BE DIFFERENT?

This specific outcome was the result of the balance among the kinds of technological change that occurred. If different sorts of new techniques had been developed, it is conceivable that the demand for labor could have shifted in a way that would have required a wage decrease to provide the 71 million positions available in 1964. Categorical statements that a given result will always follow from even a given type of automation cannot be made, much less that the result would be the same for all types of automation.

A type of automation that, let us say, has the effect of reducing the amount of labor required per unit of product, without changing capital, material, or skill requirements, will have different results depending on the responsiveness of product sales to price decreases. If sales are very responsive to a price decrease, the introduction of this type of automation will result in a large increase in sales. With a large increase in sales produced by the cost reductions resulting from automation, the industry will hire more people. On the other hand, if sales of the product are somewhat unresponsive to a price decrease, the industry will use fewer people because of automation.

The different effects on employment can be illustrated. Suppose that a new technique reduces the amount of labor required per unit of product from one hour to nine-tenths of an hour. If the industry was producing 1,000 units of product per week, its labor requirements were 1,000 hours per week (or 25 men working a 40-hour week). With a reduction in the labor input required, let us suppose that the price of the product falls

6 These figures are approximations indicating magnitude and direction of the effect of technological change. They are based on the measurement of the amount of technological change (Z. Griliches, *op. cit.*) and the elasticity of demand for labor (P. H. Douglas, *op. cit.*; H. G. Lewis, *Unionism and Relative Wages in the United States* [Chicago: University of Chicago Press, 1963], and S. P. Sobotka, Profile of Michigan [New York: The Free Press of Glencoe, 1963]).

by 7 percent and sales rise by 20 percent. (It is assumed that product price falls less than 10 percent despite the 10 percent reduction in labor required per unit because the cost of materials, power, and equipment remain unchanged.) With an increase in sales to 12,000 per week, the industry will now require 1,080 hours of labor per week (or 27 men working a 40-hour week). More men will be hired despite the reduced labor requirement per unit of product.

If, on the other hand, sales increase by only 3 percent in response to a 7 percent reduction in price, total sales will not rise sufficiently to maintain employment in the industry. With an increase in sales to 1,030 units per week, the industry will now require only 927 hours of labor per week (or 23 men). Two men will lose their jobs in this industry, or two quits or retirees will not be replaced.

However, the fact that an automating industry uses fewer people, if it does, does not necessarily mean that fewer jobs will be available in the economy as a whole at prevailing wage rates. The product of the automating industry sells at a lower price after automation than that for which it would otherwise sell. If sales do not increase markedly and provide more jobs, or at least rise enough to maintain the number of jobs, those buying the product must be spending less of their incomes for it than they formerly did. The leftover income will be used to purchase more of other products. The increase in sales of other products will provide job openings which will absorb people released from the automating industry. These released people may be absorbed with no cut in wage rate or may obtain higher wage rates.

Whether this specific result follows the introduction of a new technique in an industry whose sales are not very responsive to price depends on the capital–man ratios in the automating industry relative to other industries. If the automating industry's capital requirements are reduced by automation along with its reduced manpower requirements, additional capital will become available to other industries as well as additional manpower. If the amount of capital released from an automating industry is large relative to the number of men released, other industries will increase their employment by a greater amount than the number of men displaced. In these circumstances, unemployment will drop or wage rates will tend to rise despite the displacement of men by automation.

A major part of the new techniques developed in the past decade has the characteristics and effects just described. An illustration of this type of automation is provided by the installation of electronically operated, computer controlled, railroad classification yards. The Conway yard now in operation on the Pennsylvania Railroad is an instance of this sort. An investment of $34 million was made at Conway, Pennsylvania, and nearby points to automate the classification of freight cars. Because of the more rapid handling of cars with the facility, it saved the equivalent of 13,000 freight cars. The same amount of freight can now be moved with $100 million less investment in rolling stock. The net saving in capital investment in railroad equipment as a result of this facility amounted to nearly $70 million. The labor saved in moving the same quantity of freight amounted to 200 men.

Freight service was improved by saving time required to classify freight cars. Also, with the cost saving, the price of freight service was reduced. (Since 1958, the average price of a ton-mile of railroad freight service has dropped from 1.46 to 1.31 cents despite increased wage costs.) As a result, the volume of freight moved on railroads is higher now than it otherwise would be. For every one percent saving in rail manpower required to move a given volume of freight, railroads manage to obtain about three-fourths percent more business than they would otherwise have. The net result has been a one-fourth percent decline in employment on railroads for every one percent saving of manpower required to provide a given volume of freight service. This, however, has not increased the amount of unemployment in the nation, as may be seen from the following facts:

The investment in the Conway yard displaced 200 men and released $70 million in capital. With the volume of freight service increasing by the amount discussed above, 150 men and approximately $5 million in capital were reabsorbed in other railroad departments. A net displacement of 50 men occurred along with the release of over $60 million of capital. The additional supply of capital made available to other industries increased the number of jobs available by about 400. (This figure is based on the relations prevailing in the past decade. In general, we can expect a little more than half the capital becoming available to be used for modernization—for economizing on labor and materials—and less than half for expansion. Approximately one man is released for each $35,000 of modernization investment and one man is required for each $18,000 of expansion investment.)

In terms of the proportions in which capital was used in the 1950's, the released $60 million was used to pay for $34 million of modernization and $26 million of expansion. Modernization to this extent released about 1,000 men and expansion of this amount required about 1,400 men. The net increase of 400 jobs outside the rail industry absorbed 350 more men than the number released by the construction of the Conway yard. Hence, the result of this type of automation was decreased unemployment despite lower rail employment.

In railroading and coal mining, the employment decline would have been much greater, given the increases in wage rates that occurred, but for automation. The reduction of costs following automation made it possible for railroads to retain markets that would have been lost to trucks, buses, pipelines, barges, and airlines. Cost reduction in coal mines

U.S. AUTO PRODUCTION LINE: 1921 AND . . .
Automation of the . . .

made it possible for coal to retain markets that would otherwise have been lost to oil, gas, waterpower, and atomic energy. By retaining their markets, railroads and coal mines have been able to provide more jobs than would have been available if they had not been able to minimize through automation their rise in costs and prices. The Studebaker plant in South Bend, Indiana, might still be operating today if the company could have automated sufficiently to reduce costs to the level where the plant would be viable.

ECONOMIC AND UNECONOMIC AUTOMATION

Much of the automation going on in the American economy is an adaptive response to changing prices of labor and capital. As we increase the stock of capital, productivity rises and wages increase. As wage rates increase, it pays the individual firm to introduce techniques that were not previously economic. From the point of view of a single business, the wage rise makes the introduction economic and forces it. From the point of view of the nation, the rise in the quantity of capital makes the introduction possible and desirable.

"Detroit automation" typifies this variety of technological change. It is little more than carrying automatic manufacture a step further: transfer equipment is used to move work from one automatic machine tool to another, and these tools are interconnected to obtain high utilization. The technique was first used in 1927 by Morris Motors Limited of England. The method was technically, but not economically, successful at that time.

Since 1927, wage rates have risen, and machine tools have become more expensive. When real hourly wage rates doubled their 1927 level, the

. . . 1965
. . . *Detroit variety*

saving in direct labor costs for operating machinery, transferring work, and building machine tools was sufficient to justify the investment in transfer equipment and interlock controls.

Automation of the Detroit variety, resulting mainly from a rise in wage rates, has different consequences depending on the cause of the rise in the wage rate. A wage rise forced by an increased demand for labor on the part of other industries (as a consequence, let us say, of an increased supply of capital), leading to economies in the use of labor by the auto industry and a decrease in its use of people, does not result in unemployment. If auto wages rise to prevent an unwanted loss of labor to other industries, those who do leave will be men taking jobs elsewhere. Joblessness among the people leaving the industry does not occur since they are being bid away by rival employers. Automation, introduced to economize on labor in these circumstances, is economic for both the firm and the nation.

Wage rates increased by raising floors set by a minimum wage law (such as the Fair Labor Standards Act), by administrative action (such as that permitted by the Walsh-Healey Act and the Davis-Bacon Act), or by negotiated agreements between employers and unions, produce very different employment results. To the extent that higher rates result from these actions than those that would be set in free markets, the resulting automation releases manpower to inferior, alternative uses. The released men may either remain unemployed or move to less productive, lower paid, alternative jobs. Automation in these circumstances is not economic from the point of view of the nation, although it is forced on the firm by the overpricing of labor.

The experience of coal miners illustrates the effect of the overpricing of labor in causing uneconomic automation and a loss of jobs. Bituminous coal mining employment dropped from 384,000 in 1945 to 168,000 in 1960. This more than 55 percent decrease in number of jobs is directly attributable to the 163 percent rise in coal mining wage rates which occurred in this period. Wage rates in coal mining were already 18 percent higher than manufacturing wage rates in 1945. By 1960, despite a rapid rise in manufacturing wage rates, coal mining rates were 39 percent higher than manufacturing rates. The consequence was (and is) a depressed employment situation for the Appalachia region despite an increase of 550,000 in manufacturing jobs in this area. If labor costs in coal mining had increased at the same rate as those in the nation, there would be at least 80,000 more coal mining jobs available today, and Appalachia would not be a depressed area.

WHY IS THERE HIGH UNEMPLOYMENT AMONG THE UNSKILLED?

The situation of the operation of elevators in Chicago provides another example of unemployment caused by arbitrarily determined wage rates and the resulting uneconomic automation. There is a high incidence of unemployment among male juveniles in Chicago. Many of these boys would be happy to accept jobs as elevator operators at $1.25 to $1.50 an hour. The elevator operators' union, however, imposes a minimum wage rate of $2.40 an hour for operators in downtown Chicago buildings. In this circumstance, owners of these buildings find it economic to spend

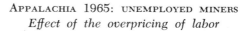

APPALACHIA 1965: UNEMPLOYED MINERS
Effect of the overpricing of labor

$40,000 per elevator to automate their lifts and make them self-operating. The tax, insurance, depreciation, maintenance, and interest costs of automating an elevator amount to $8,000 per year. It did not pay, therefore, to automate when two shifts of operators cost only $5,000 per year. The union has driven the two-shift cost of operation to $10,000 per year. The result is elevator automation, a drain of capital from expansion of production where it would provide more jobs, fewer jobs for elevator operators, and problems of unskilled teenagers finding tasks to keep themselves occupied. The decreased demand for unskilled teenagers, resulting from the high minimum wage rates set on jobs that they might take, forecloses the opportunity for the acquisition of personal characteristics and skills which would equip them for more productive, better paying jobs in later years.

There is a growing concentration of unemployment among unskilled workers not only because of the high minimum wage rates for newly hired workers set by union-employer agreements, but also because of the successive increases in statutory minimum wage rates by congressional amendment of the Fair Labor Standards Act of 1938. In 1949 the minimum wage rate set by federal statute was $0.40 per hour. At that time, average earnings of manufacturing industry employees were $1.38 an hour. The minimum wage has been increased several times since 1949, reaching $1.25 in September, 1963. By then, average earnings of manufacturing industry employees were $2.47 per hour. Thus, compared with the hourly wage of workers in manufacturing, the minimum wage has risen from 29 percent in 1949 to 51 percent in 1963.

It is hardly surprising that unemployment among the unskilled increased with this rapid rise in the minimum wage. In absolute terms, the statutory minimum wage has been more than tripled since 1949. In relative terms, it has been raised to 176 percent of what it was in 1949. The growth in unemployment among teenagers from 595,000 in 1949 to 979,000 in 1963, or from 17 percent of all the unemployed in 1949 to 25 percent of the unemployed in 1963, should have been expected. To the extent that teenagers are inexperienced, unskilled workers, they are the ones who have been priced out of the labor market by the rise in the minimum wage rate.

Increasing the price of unskilled workers so greatly, relative to that of skilled workers, unduly penalizes the hiring of the unskilled. It is fortunate that the proportion of the work force that is unskilled has been diminishing (*see* Table III). Otherwise, the unemployment problem would be more severe than it is, given the increases in minimum wage rates that have occurred.

The decreasing number of unskilled workers available and increasing demand for them has caused a rise in their money wage rates by 66 percent between 1949 and 1963 in occupations not covered by the wage law.

TABLE III

**EDUCATIONAL ATTAINMENT OF EMPLOYED PERSONS
18 YEARS OLD AND OVER, 1952–62**

Years of School Completed	1952 (Thousands)	1952 (Percentage)	1962 (Thousands)	1962 (Percentage)
Less than 8	11,612	19.7	8,494	13.3
8–11	21,706	36.9	20,426	32.0
Less than 4 years of high school	33,318	56.5	28,920	45.3
High school 12	15,876	27.0	20,688	32.4
College 13–15	4,950	8.4	6,981	10.9
College 16+	4,766	8.1	7,350	11.5
4 years of high school or more	25,592	43.5	35,019	54.8
Total employed	58,910		63,939	
Median school years completed	10.9		12.1	

Sources: D. F. Johnston, "Educational Attainment of Workers, March 1962," "Monthly Labor Review," May, 1963, p. 508.

The rise would have been greater but for the fact that the increase in the statutory minimum wage (and the minima set by union-employer agreements) foreclosed many jobs to unskilled workers and increased the number seeking work in the exempt occupations. This increased the supply of workers competing for the exempt jobs and held down the wage rise which would otherwise have been greater for these people.[7]

The doom criers who are alarmed about automation say that "a permanently depressed class is developing in the United States."[8] If there is such a class, it is caused by legislation such as the Fair Labor Standards Act, not by automation. The data on income received by the poorest 20 percent of the population do not indicate, however, that they are becoming worse off. From 1949 to 1962 average family income of the poorest

7 Y. Brozen, "Minimum Wage Rates and Household Workers," *Journal of Law and Economics,* October, 1962; D. E. Kaun, *Economics of the Minimum Wage: The Effects of the Fair Labor Standards Act* (Ph.D. dissertation, Stanford University, 1964); J. M. Peterson, "Employment Effects of Minimum Wages, 1938-50," *Journal of Political Economy,* LXV (October, 1957), 412–30.

8 R. Theobald, "The Threat and the Promise of Cybernation," *Main Currents,* September-October, 1964, p. 5.

20 percent of the population rose by 60 percent in current dollars or by 28 percent measured in constant dollars.

AUTOMATION AND FREE TIME

Normally, the average workweek tends to fall as income per hour rises. It has been found that workers tend to decrease their preferred workweek by 2 to 3 percent for every 10 percent rise in hourly earnings.[9] As productivity increases because of automation and other reasons, and wage rates rise, we should expect the average workweek to fall.

Yet, in the post-World War II period, the average workweek has shown little tendency to decline despite a marked rise in real hourly earnings. A major reason for this lies in the fact that people were spending less time at work in the late 1940's than they wished. Employers have been penalized for employing people more than 40 hours per week or 8 hours a day. The Fair Labor Standards Act passed in the 1930's forces employers to pay a 50 percent penalty for employing people longer than these specified periods. The workweek was arbitrarily shortened, then, despite the wish of people to work longer hours in order to earn higher incomes.

We appear to be nearing the point in pay levels at which the statutory straight-time workweek is approximately the preferred workweek for a majority of employees. If this is the case, and past relationships between preferences for income and free time prevail, employers will soon find that they will have to shorten hours of work in order to attract the employees they desire. If productivity and wage rates continue to follow the same trend as in the past decade, the average workweek will tend to fall two to three hours in the next decade.

The fall in the average workweek will not necessarily take the form of shorter hours in the weeks when people are actually at work. It may take the form of longer annual vacation periods or a "sabbatical" leave of several months every decade (or some longer-than-a-year interval).

CONCLUSION

If no technological change had occurred in the past decade, the number of jobs available could have grown as it has from 61 to 71 million only at the price of restricting increases in wage rates. Wage rates could have been increased by only 30 cents per hour or $600 per year instead of $1,000 a year. With this restricted wage increase and automation, the number of jobs would have grown to 91 million instead of 71 million

---

9 T. A. Finegan, "Hours of Work in the United States: A Cross-Sectional Analysis," *Journal of Political Economy*, LXX (October, 1962), 452–70.

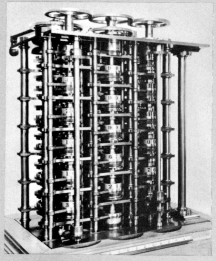

CHARLES BABBAGE'S DIFFERENCE ENGINE

HOLLERITH'S MACHINE USED IN 1890 CENSUS

COMPUTERS: A COMING OF AGE

The engines and devices on this page all have some significance in their own right. Together, they show the evolution of the computer which has evoked a variety of human emotions, ranging from fear to idolatry. Charles Babbage's 1885 Difference Engine (*above, left*) merely sought to make accounting easier by speeding up multiplication; the 1965 NASA computers (*below*) oversee the intricate functioning of giant rockets. This evolution has wrought a revolution that affects not only accountants and rocket specialists but, more broadly, all men, and now even space itself.

EARLY IBM CARD-PUNCHING MACHINE

PUNCHER FOR HOLLERITH MACHINE

COMPUTER AREA AT GODDARD SPACE FLIGHT CENTER

(*see* Figure II and compare the number of jobs at $2.35 on Curve A and Curve 1964). In effect, technological change has created 20 million jobs in the past decade.

Since employers could not find 20 million additional persons to fill these jobs, they have bid against each other for the available work force. The net effect, then, has been an additional rise in annual earnings of the typical worker of $400 in the past decade above what he would otherwise have received if no new inventions had been made.

Instead of castigating automation for causing unemployment, we should be inviting more automation to help solve the present unemployment problem. The overpricing of labor in industries such as coal mining and the setting of high minimum wage rates by statute for unskilled labor has caused unemployment because many workers are not productive enough to be employed at these wage rates. With more technological advance, productivity would be increased. The men presently priced out of the market would be employable if their productivity were increased, and it would be by technical progress.

At present, employers are tending to hire fewer of the less skilled, less educated people because of the high minimum wage rates set by laws, by governmental administrators (under the discretionary authority granted by the Walsh-Healey Act, the Davis-Bacon Act, and the various prevailing wage rate laws passed by state legislatures), and by agreements between unions and employers. At these rates, less skilled personnel are not sufficiently productive to be employable. Adaptation to automation would be easier if the wage structure were less rigid. It could take place, then, by the acceptance of lower wage jobs by some individuals as well as by attaining higher skill levels.

Individuals are doing much of the adapting required within our present wage and tax structure by staying in school longer. The proportion of 16- and 17-year-old youths in school has increased from 75 to 88 percent in the past ten years. The median level of education has risen from 10.9 to 12.1 years in the past decade (*see* Table III). Also, people are acquiring the special skills in demand. Further, employers are providing retraining for a majority of their own employees directly affected by automation. They are minimizing displacement by letting attrition of their work force take place through retirements and quits rather than layoff when the number of employees must be reduced. The amount of reduction would be minimized, however, if wage rate increases were less precipitate.

In short, the unemployment problem with which we are faced is not a result of automation and will not be worsened by automation. Automation should be welcomed as the means of alleviating poverty and undoing the damage done by bad wage laws and improper union-employer agreements. It should not be feared as a job destroyer. It is a job creator.

Jobs for the

A Public

ADOLF A. BERLE, JR.

Of Adolf A. Berle, Jr., legal and economic scholar, practising attorney, and Chairman of The Twentieth Century Fund, Supreme Court Justice William O. Douglas said recently: "He is one of a select group who have given close attention for some decades to the critical question, 'Whither are we going?'" Born in 1895 in Boston, Mr. Berle was graduated from the Harvard Law School at the age of twenty-one. After serving as an army lieutenant in World War I, he practiced law in New York City. Since 1927 he has taught at Columbia University, where he is now Professor Emeritus of Law. A member of President Franklin D. Roosevelt's New Deal "Brain Trust," he has had a distinguished career of public service. Among the public offices that he has held are those of Chamberlain of the City of New York, Assistant Secretary of State of the United States, and Ambassador to Brazil. In 1961 he served as Chairman of President Kennedy's Task Force on Latin America, and the same year as Special Assistant to the Secretary of State. In addition to being on the board of directors of various corporations, Mr. Berle is a consultant to The Center for the Study of Democratic Institutions. He is the author of many books on American economic organizations, including: The American Economic Republic *(1963),* Power Without Property *(1959),* New Directions in the New World *(1940),* Tides of Crisis *(1957),* The Twentieth Century Capitalist Revolution *(1954), and, with* G. C. Means, The Modern Corporation and Private Property *(1932). The father of three children, he lives with his wife in New York City.*

Displaced:
Responsibility

Forecasts by economists, scientists, and technical experts indicate the existence and growth of a problem new in history. Consumption of goods and services will increase at a substantially greater rate than the increase of population; it has been doing so, in fact, for the past half century. Production of goods and services will likewise increase, also more rapidly than population. The rate could readily be 5 percent annually compounded. At that rate, present production would roughly double in fifteen years. But, due to increased mechanization—automation, in the current phrase—demand for labor will not increase proportionately to production, to the growth of population, or to the growth in labor force. Consequently, without some added element, the result will be steadily growing unemployment—this in the face of brilliantly growing prosperity. The number of persons annually added to the labor force will not find jobs waiting for them.

Present figures indicate that these estimates are not without base. At the opening of the fourth quarter of 1964, the economy of the United States was producing at a new high, turning out goods and services at the rate of $618 billion per year. The personally received income of individuals, approximating a rate of $500 billion annually, gave the United States record-breaking consuming power, both in gross amount and per capita. Yet, in face of these facts, 5.2 percent of the American labor force remained unemployed and the percentage had not significantly changed for some time. Increase of production and consumption did not and apparently will not reduce this backlog significantly. Forward estimates, indeed, suggest a slow but steady rise in this percentage of unemployed labor force.

Projected for, say, fifteen years, this situation would become extremely serious. Assuming that the labor force (presently about 74 million) has then increased to more than 90 million; assuming also that the percentage of unemployed has slowly risen from 5.2 to 7.2 percent, the result would then be about 6.5 million unemployed Americans. This is the most moderate calculation. Many observers forecast an accelerated increase in production by machine, and more rapid increase in the numbers and percentage of unemployed. This factor might lead to an unemployed labor force of 10 percent or more—that is, from nine to ten millions of unemployed. Obviously, if mechanization or automation scores a really dramatic breakthrough, the results might be even greater. Bluntly, much of the labor capacity of America will simply not be needed to produce the capital goods and the food, clothing, shelter, and other consumers' products that, with services, supply the wants of the American population.

Hence our problem. What happens when men and women do not work, not because they cannot, or do not wish to, but merely because their work is either unnecessary or (more probably) not met by job-opportunity?

Obviously, they cannot be left to starve. They, therefore, will have to have an income. The practical question is thus posed: Where will the money come from, and on what terms will it be paid to them?

These questions must be combined with a second problem, no less pressing. These people will also have to have "work." Participation, tasks

UNEMPLOYMENT IN APPALACHIA,
HARLEM, UTICA
*These people will have to have
a sense of usefulness*

with possibility of achieving something, giving a sense of usefulness, are
essential to living. The experience of Great Britain after World War I,
which supported a substantial fraction of its labor force through distribution of doles, avoided wholesale homelessness and starvation and even
the grosser forms of misery. But a segment of Britain's population decayed
under that regimen, and the social results were almost calamitous. Our
problem is thus a double one. Incomes must indeed be provided, but
simultaneously some function must be assigned to the recipients.

The present mass of unemployed in the United States fluctuates around
5 percent of the American labor force. This totals about 74,000,000 so that
between 3,750,000 and 4,000,000 are unemployed. To this number must
be added another fluctuating number of individuals not in the labor
force—that is, considered unemployable—who are on relief. This adds
1,000,000 to 1,250,000 more to our figures.

Better statistics would break down these figures into "permanent" unemployed or relief recipients, and "transitionally" unemployed or relief
cases. It would be found that recipients of relief not reckoned as unemployed labor force ("unemployables") tend to be permanent; this has
been the experience of New York City with its relief problems in Harlem
and elsewhere. Of the 3,750,000 "unemployed" ("employable"), a hard
core remains more or less permanently out of work. A larger number
fall out of work, later find new jobs, fall out of work again, again find

employment. At the top of the statistical bloc are individuals who become unemployed for a time between jobs or in readjustment, but once readjusted do not reappear on unemployment rolls.

This transitory quality of the total leads some to say that there is no real permanent problem, and to maintain that this whole load of unemployed-plus-relief recipients is really a frictional and transitional problem. In part this is true, but not wholly so. The measure of truth in it was demonstrated by the experience in the United States in 1939–40. Then, a large carry-over of unemployed from the depression of 1933 still existed. Pressure of war work suddenly created a forced market for labor of all kinds. Most of the supposedly "permanent" unemployed then did connect with jobs, and most passed permanently into normal employment.

But this suggests two considerations. First, the absorption of both permanent and frictional unemployed was due to the massive enlargement of the labor market created by the defense needs of the state. Second, without such massive intervention, a continuous load of several million Americans, in varying degree of permanence, will fall into the limbo of unemployed. While the plight of the transitionally unemployed is neither as grave nor as frightening as those of the permanent or semipermanent unemployed, it is none the less bitterly unhappy for the individuals and dangerous for the state and the community. The problem may be alleviated but is not removed by classifying part of it as "transitional." The measures needed may be different for permanent, semipermanent, and transitionally unemployed. But the fundamental remains unchanged. All of them must have income from some source; all of them must be given opportunity to participate, presumably through work.

UNFULFILLED NEEDS IN OUR SOCIETY

The deficiency, existing and estimated, is a lack of "jobs." A job may be defined as a more or less regular task, under stated conditions of work, and carrying a predictable amount and stated rate of pay.

"Work" may be defined as individual labor, effort, or occupation required to satisfy a need or want. Work does not crystallize into jobs unless, through private or public organization, someone is prepared to assume responsibility for meeting the need or want, and to organize and employ individuals, under stated conditions and pay, to satisfy it. For this purpose, it is immaterial whether the want is for service—say, cleaning the streets or teaching at a university, or for goods—be they buildings, automobiles, or shirts. Unless the need or want is connected through individual, private, or public enterprises, organized to satisfy the want and to employ individuals in doing so, jobs will not result. If, as suggested, there is a double need, first to supply income to this growing segment of unemployed and second to assign them tasks, our problem is to organize the work as well as the finance—the former to provide the tasks, the latter to pay for them.

All calculations and statistics made thus far have been on the basis of jobs as they are currently conceived and organized under our present system. No census (so far as the writer knows) has yet been made of needs or wants (requiring work to satisfy them) but *not* organized into jobs under our present system.

Yet it is clear that, while the number of jobs is indeed inadequate now and likely to be more so in the future, there is *not* a shortage of unsatisfied needs and wants. These exist but under present organization they merely go unsatisfied. The current commercial (private sector) economy and the current public sector economy simply do not meet many needs and wants which are obvious and visible, and whose usefulness is beyond debate. Even a cursory glance suggests the vast area of work that ought to be done is not being done and hence is not crystallized into available jobs.

For example, the current teaching load in primary and secondary schools runs about thirty pupils per teacher—in many areas it is more. There is no dissent among parents and educators that far more effective education would result if the teaching load were reduced to fifteen or ten pupils per teacher. Bluntly, there is immediate need for double or treble the number of teaching jobs now in existence. The need will become even greater as the American school population increases, and in the next few years it will increase more rapidly than the general population will.

The most casual glance at any American city indicates that the most elementary work of caretaking and cleaning up is inadequately done. There is immediate need—certainly there is want—for a great deal more city caretaking, cleaning up, junk disposal, and the like, that must be done to reach the standards considered civilized by, say, the Germans or Austrians. As in the case of our inadequate school staffing, though the work is there to be done, the jobs are not.

Illustrations could be multiplied almost without number. If we had an adequate census of the work now required to satisfy the wants or needs that are now unsatisfied, we would discover that a far larger number of jobs would have to be created to satisfy these needs and wants.

If to these wants we add the work required for urban reconstruction, for rehabilitation of rural areas, for depollution of waterways and air, and a host of similar needs, we discover two interesting facts. First, our estimate of the amount of work wanted or needed would vastly increase in both the private and the public sectors. Americans have the highest personal standard of living in the world—measured by their consumption. Yet the standard of living one encounters when he goes out into the street—the level of aesthetics, cleanliness, and so forth that he is forced

Needs in Manhattan, Harlem, . . .
Vast areas of work . . .

to put up with in his city or town—is far lower than that expected and received by most Western Europeans. Second, there is complete inadequacy of systematic organization to meet known and recognized deficiencies in these standards—let alone to raise them.

Apparently, therefore, our problem is not lack of needs and wants to achieve simple, and definite, and wholly accepted ends. Certainly it is not lack of manpower. Were we to connect the manpower with the needs and wants, reducing them to jobs, the problem would be minimized. Indeed, it might largely disappear.

ORGANIZING THE NEEDS INTO JOBS

This permits elaboration of a line of attack. Let us, therefore, state a principle:

Wherever there are unfilled needs or wants, there are potential jobs for the men and women now or later to be unemployed. These needs or wants may be met either through private (nonstatist) enterprises employing men and women and selling their product or service for profit, or through public organization—provision by the state, the communities, or by public corporations or enterprises, paid for by public funds.

If the principle is adopted, the problems involved become clearer. In fact, there are three.

The first is the problem of defining the need or want, and bringing into being an organization to meet it. The second is assuring that the unem-

34

ployed manpower shall be adequately educated and trained to fill jobs
and thereafter obtain them. The third is the problem of finance.

It will be noted that this principle severely limits the supplying of
income *without* assigned tasks or responsibilities or work. We have done
this not because it cannot be arranged—as will presently be seen—but
because assignment of income with no responsibility or task means con-
demning the recipient to an unwalled poorhouse in which he rots. This
was the English experience at the time of the dole.

There is, nevertheless, a hard-core or irreducible number of people
who will need income, but who cannot accept responsibility or perform
work of any kind. We have long accepted certain categories of such
recipients. Small children and aged people are recognizably in that
category. These are provided for now, though not perhaps as well as
they should be. Further, in any labor force there will always be a certain
number of sick or maladjusted who are physically or congenitally unable
or unwilling to accept the discipline required to meet any responsibility.
(Some of these become incurable beggars, drifters, vagrants, alcoholics,
drug addicts, or otherwise irresponsible.) Little can be done about this
hard core until medical and psychological techniques can cure those not
incurable and, upon cure, social organization can provide them with

. . . RURAL VIRGINIA, AND LOS ANGELES
. . . that ought to be done

THE HANDICAPPED
A certain number unable to meet responsibility

some sort of task. Probably we shall have to live with this hard core for a considerable period of time. Of the present group of unemployed, perhaps two million (more or less) are thus "unemployable." We do not know how to make them "employable." Since this group cannot be allowed to starve, provision has to be made for them—indeed is being made now in one fashion or another.

In consequence, we have thus three groups: (a) children, the chronically sick, and the aged, whose right to be supported is already recognized; (b) the undisciplined and chronically maladjusted who are supported because they cannot be allowed to starve; finally (c) a very much larger group presently employable or capable of being made so, for whom no jobs exist now or in prospect. This last group is the number one problem, since its number will probably increase as long as our current organization of work into jobs does not now, and in future is not likely to, produce enough jobs to occupy their time, or provide them with income.

The main line of attack thus must be the organizing of existing and growing wants and needs into jobs, to which these employables and potential employables may be put.

A problem emerges at once. Many of these potential employables are not now sufficiently educated or trained to be put to work even if jobs existed for them. Certainly this is true of a very large proportion of them. Current statistics already show that, of the unemployed, a large number are illiterate—a larger number in fact than statistics show. American public-school education has become devastatingly inadequate in a number of areas. Many adults who have been through grade schools and even halfway through high school are literally unable to read and write. The proportion of men drafted for service into the United States Army but rejected because of substantial illiteracy is not only high but shocking. There is reason to believe that a large proportion of these people can be made literate. There is at least reason to hope that the effectiveness of the public school system in the great cities—for example, New York and Chicago—and in the backward states of the Union, notably the Deep South, can be improved.

To be employable, an individual must be skilled as well as literate. Literacy only establishes a base. The effect of increased mechanization is the progressive elimination of the need for "unskilled" labor—most (though by no means all) work that can be done by an unskilled laborer can be done better and more cheaply by machine. This argues a need for further training in skills. But machines also are progressively displacing semiskilled and even highly skilled labor. This is the precise effect of "automation." Consequently there is need for training above the literacy level—training in skills—which also creates a base permitting the individual to change from one skill to another. (Attack on this problem of vocational education has been made, though it must be admitted the results are not yet impressive.) Meanwhile, support of men and women who are either illiterate or, though literate, unskilled has to be provided during their period of education and training. At this stage, the responsibility or task assigned them in response to any income they receive must be their *obligation to become trained*, through agencies or in centers or other institutions provided for that purpose.

Already it can be said that within a relatively short time—say, six or seven years—few individuals who do not have at least a respectable high-school education will be "employable." Even today, the child who "drops out" from school below that level is likely to fall into the category of unemployable.

This has led some to a conclusion believed by this writer to be unjustified. The contention is frequently made that if all the present unemployables and all children now in school are brought to the level of high-school graduates, they will then be employable and will thereupon be employed. At present, in fact, most high-school graduates are employed. Yet given the pace of mechanization, it seems unlikely that when all unemployed individuals have become high-school graduates, and all schoolchildren have completed high-school training, they will thereupon find jobs. I see no basis for the assumption advanced by some that high-school training for everyone will mean that everyone will be employed. Without some change in the organization of affairs, there still will not be enough jobs to go around. To convert an unemployable into an employable by education does not mean, as far as I can see, that he will automatically be employed. He is even less likely to be employed as the mechanization process accelerates in the future. It is, therefore, false to say that the cause is solely defective education. Added education is essential. But, by itself, education will not solve the problem. Greater organization to meet needs and wants will also be essential, even to employ educated individuals.

Nor is the conclusion warranted that more rapid growth of the American economy will by itself resolve the situation. Up to now, many economists (among them as able a man as Gunnar Myrdal) have assumed that mere growth at a greater percentage rate per annum will, if high enough, provide sufficient jobs to employ the entire employable labor force. These economists ascribe the relatively high unemployment rate in the United States to the fact that until 1962 the American economy expanded only at the rate of 3½ to 4 percent annually—whereas in Europe annual growth rate had to reach 5 percent even to be acceptable, while to bring about full employment it should reach 6 percent or if possible 7 percent per annum. Given that rate of growth, it is thought, there would be no unemployment.

This conclusion may have been warranted in the decade from 1940 to 1950, and perhaps during most of the decade from 1950 to 1960.

RURAL KENTUCKY SCHOOL
HOUSE, 1965

*There is reason
to believe . . .*

Adolf A. Berle, Jr.

. . . that a large proportion of these people can be made literate

But I do not see that, without some change in organization, it is true in the United States today. Increase of the gross national product of the United States is currently proceeding at almost 5 percent, and it is not adequately reducing the proportion of unemployed. With accelerated mechanization and automation, greater increase—say, to 6 percent or even 7 percent annually—will not change that fact *unless* a part of that growth is steered into channels calculated to make more jobs. Increase along the present lines is at least partially accomplished by mere mechanization—that is, by more production with less employment.

Unquestionably a greater or more rapid expansion of gross national product will be needed. But to meet the problem of unemployment, a substantial part of that expansion must take place in services provided by human beings. These will run the entire gamut, from street cleaning and home care to teaching, music, acting, and the fine arts. As noted, there are already wants and needs for a great deal of such service. Any rise in the aesthetic standards and demands of the American public will presumably push the aggregate of these unfilled wants and needs to far higher levels. But organization of these needs into available jobs is inadequate now, and no significant increase of organization is in sight.

FINANCING THE JOBS

Let us now assume that the American community has squarely confronted the problem, has ascertained the presently unfilled needs and wants, and has worked out methods of organizing for their satisfaction. Let us assume that it also has confronted, organized, and commenced the massive process of education and training, bringing present unemployables into employable shape, and has organized channels for connecting them with the work of satisfying unfilled needs and wants as rapidly as they become adequately educated and trained. It then has before it the easiest of the three problems: that of finance. This must include: (a) the cost of surveying, planning for, and organizing satisfaction of the unfilled needs and wants presently ascertainable; (b) the task of staffing the top level of the organizations to fill those wants; (c) the cost of placing the employables in those jobs as soon as possible after their training; and (d) the cost of paying for the work as it is done.

Costs of a continuing government operation of this kind can be met only by: (a) taxation, federal or local; (b) collection of charge for the work done; (c) long-term borrowing by federal or local units; or (d) short-term borrowing by federal or local units.

The first two methods place a charge on the current earnings of everyone. Basically, they take purchasing power from individuals and corporations, transfer it to one or another agency of the state, and, through these agencies, apply it to the cost of organizing, training, and eventually to paying the individuals who otherwise would be unemployed or unemployable.

The third method—long-term borrowing—essentially does the same thing. Bonds are issued by the federal government or local agencies, they are paid for by already accumulated savings, and the proceeds are used for these purposes. This is more expensive: the bonds must also bear interest. The fourth method—short-term borrowing—basically means increasing the supply of bank-created money through the mechanism of the commercial banks. This carries with it the risk of inflation if currency-credit supply is thereby increased more rapidly than the increase of production of goods and services.

For practical purposes use of any, or any mixture, of these methods can be effected only through the federal government, though in marginal amounts the resources of states, municipalities, and local agencies are available. The federal government alone has the adequate taxation base through its income, corporation, and excise taxes. Long-term borrowings in the volume needed probably would be possible only by direct use of federal credit—that is, issue of federal bonds or through federal guarantee of local securities which is also use of federal credit. Short-term borrowing in this volume obviously could be carried on only by the federal government, a large part of whose debt now consists of short-term borrowings more or less continuously renewed. We may, therefore, conclude that the financing problem, whether through taxation or borrowing, will devolve on the federal government.

At this point, it is necessary to make a rough estimate of the probable cost of the operation. This can only be a sophisticated guess. There is no past experience. If we assume that there are now about four million unemployed, and if we further assume that initially two million of these are permanently unemployable (for reasons of health or otherwise) the dimensions appear. The hard-core two million will always be on some sort of relief or dole as they are now—a cost presently being paid through local relief or otherwise. The remaining two million, also being supported by relief or other arrangements, pose the immediate problem. If nothing is done, apparently this number will rise, possibly sharply. They now receive some income—estimate it about $700 per family (not per individual). If each individual in this group were to receive, let us say, the equivalent of $3,500 per year, the individual expense would be about $7 billion annually, to which another billion would have to be added for the cost of operation. Part of this might be recouped through savings of current relief expense. In the present situation $7.5 billion annually would be a substantial attack on the problem. If met by direct taxation without recourse to any kind of borrowing, we should expect an addition of $7.5 billion to the federal budget.

This, of course, is not an impossible figure. The country has found it quite practical to afford about $4 billion annually for foreign aid; and a very large amount for romantic adventures such as moon-shots and space exploration. Further, gross national product of the United States (estimated to reach $659 billion for the year 1965) is currently increasing at the rate of over $30 billion annually. Diverting somewhat less than one-third of the annual increase in American product to the goal of training, putting to work, and providing income for Americans displaced by the march of science and machines is not a great burden. It would entail no direct sacrifice; every American would be rather richer at the end of each year than he was at the beginning. He might, of course, be still richer if the burden of financing income for the displaced were not imposed on him—unless, perhaps, he was displaced himself, which becomes increasingly possible. Straight federal taxation for this purpose is, therefore, not a grievous sacrifice. Basically, failure to do it means that the human cost of advancing technology is borne through the misery and decay of the people displaced—unless, of course, they are to be shot as soon as displacement occurs.

There is little reason to suppose that very much of the program could be financed by commercial charges for the services or products generated by these new jobs for the displaced. The greatest needs and wants currently unfulfilled are not now being filled by the private sector—that is, by business—precisely because they are not of the kind which can be sold for a price at a profit. Doubling or trebling the facilities of the public school system, for example, is an absolute necessity from the human point of view—but schools never were and cannot be operated on the profit system. Certain kinds of municipal or rural services —depollution of the air, and of rivers and riverways, and the like—might perhaps be charged in some fashion to the surrounding property owners or inhabitants, but such charges would produce effects very similar to those of direct taxation.

Long-term borrowing—that is, tapping savings—is always possible in federal finance. It can and should be resorted to under some circumstances, as part of a general policy of debt, budget, and fiscal management of the federal government. In the writer's view, borrowing should not be resorted to for the specific purpose of providing incomes. It should remain a tool of the federal government in handling its fiscal policy. Specific jobs of work in certain kinds of public work projects—road building, bridge building, recreation facilities, and so forth—sometimes are capable of being financed by a charge for service. Tolls can be charged for roads, for admission to recreation parks, and so forth. But at most, these will be in the nature of windfall contributions. They cannot be counted on to carry the main load.

Short-term government borrowing can be indulged in only with the greatest caution. Unquestionably getting wanted or needed work done does add to the general well-being of the United States. In fact it will contribute substantially toward increasing its gross product. But the operations we are discussing will add only indirectly to the current supply of goods and services and hence do not provide a sound basis for increasing the currency-credit supply. It may be added that there probably is less danger than some suppose—the actual increase in production and floating supply of goods and services has been growing with sufficient rapidity to allow for cautious increase in the supply of currency and credit, even without an increase in the supply of goods and services. Short-term borrowing, nevertheless, ought not to be relied on; or, if used at all, it should be used as part of the total federal fiscal policy—that is, for financing entire operations of the federal government rather than as a separate tool for operations providing incomes for those who have none.

It must be foreseen that, if the forecasts are accurate, the task of providing income for the technologically displaced will grow. If we take $7.5 billion as the immediate target cost, we must assume that it is likely to double at the end of a decade. This need not cause dismay. It is a reasonable assumption that the gross national product of the United States will continue to increase through that decade at an average rate of $30 billion a year—much faster, in fact, than the burden we are asking the federal government to assume. If ten years from now the burden has doubled or even trebled—has become, let us say, $15 billion or even $22.5 billion annually—by that time the gross national product will have increased by $300 billion annually. Our gross national product ten years from now is likely to be approaching a trillion dollars—annually —as against $659 billion for the year 1965. If the private sector activities which provide most of this pay the cost through taxation there is reasonable certainty that they will be quite able to do so—and still be more prosperous than ever before. It may also be added that the displacement of men which constitutes our problem is a direct result of the private sector system; it has no real right to complain if it is asked to contribute to the costs of solving a problem it has itself created and is unable to meet.

In blunt fact, the cost of supporting the displaced will be an item anyhow, unless the country adopts the unthinkable policy of arranging for their swift death. They will, in any case, be a charge on the community by way of relief; or on private charity financed through voluntary contributions of individuals or corporations. Their elementary need for food, clothing, and shelter will be paid for out of gross national product by business and individuals, through taxes or contributions, in any event. The cost may be minimized initially by adopting the dole or relief system and supporting some millions of Americans in involuntary idleness to rot rather than undertaking the task of converting unfilled needs and wants into jobs and directing the displaced towards these jobs. Yet some, at least, of the supposed savings of the dole or relief method are illusory. Any considerable portion of the population rotting in idleness and frustration rapidly adds to community costs, for defense against crime, maintaining health, and preventing a spreading social poison from corrupting entire regions.

I am convinced that, over the long run, the proposed solution is the cheapest as well as the best. When unemployed are converted into employables and are assigned work, each individual begins to discover possibilities within the private sector. Part of the cost will be recouped by the private sector: two million Americans and their families on relief cannot be a market for goods. Possessing income and a job, they provide such a market. The addition of, let us say, between $7 and $10 billion to their individual purchasing power will at once be reflected in added demand for goods and services sold through private sector and regular market channels: presumably at a profit. Through taxation, the federal government will recover at least part of the cost that we here suggest should be borne through federal financing. The initial $7.5 billion, though it probably will rise, is the gross cost. A substantial part will come back to the federal government through regular tax channels because of the added business and private sector markets and earnings created by supplying that market.

A second and presumably auxiliary method might also be mentioned. During the depression of 1933, Mr. Harry Hopkins and Mr. Henry Wallace evolved a "food-stamp plan." In effect, this gave to the poorest sectors of the population capacity to buy at half price the surplus food the government was accumulating. Such surpluses exist now and, through a "food-stamp plan," can be made available directly to the qualified individuals. This principle is repeated in the federal Food Stamp Act of 1964. There are, of course, difficulties in this process. It does reduce the increased market for private sector business that would other-

Images of

JOB CORPS TRAINING

BREADLINE IN NEW YORK, 1930's

The image of poverty, as conveyed by these pictures, is not unfamiliar to Americans. Appalachia may be the contemporary image of it, but there was also the misery of the 1902 famine (*right*) and the depression of the thirties (*above, right*). Progressively, the image of poverty has been overlaid with the vision of public intervention in the relief of such poverty. It may have amounted to no more than the presence

FARMERS BUILDING A WPA BRIDGE: *Converted into employables*

wise be created. (Individuals who can buy food at a 50 percent discount will not buy commercially offered food at twice the price.) The impact of such plans on private producers ought to be kept within bounds. Discount selling to specific population groups can only be an expedient of marginal usefulness.

Poverty

NEW YORKERS IN LINE FOR COAL DURING 1902 STRIKE: *Idleness and frustration . . .*

of a policeman keeping order in a coal line as in the 1902 picture (*above*). But by the thirties it had become more massive, in part through the presence of the Works Projects Administration (*below, left*). If today's Americans are less accustomed to the spectacle of misery, they have become all the more accustomed to expecting government intervention such as the Job Corps (*above, extreme left*) as a guard against misery's obtrusion.

COAL LINE DURING 1902 STRIKE: *. . . adds to community costs*

Work, Wealth, and Leisure

In some circles the trend toward displacement by machines has been projected to an extreme point. The day may come, they believe, when, let us say, 20 percent of the employables of the United States can produce all goods and services that the United States can readily consume. There will then be, they think, no "work," still less jobs, for 80 percent of the population. Then, it is suggested, the problem will become that of distributing income generally, without either providing or requiring work of any kind in exchange. The wage conception will be outdated; the nexus between work and income will be cut. An individual assured of everything he needs to live in reasonable comfort would be left to find a meaningful life after his own fashion. He might contemplate the stars, recite poetry, play chess or other games—or merely loaf. The task of education in that case would be to develop his capacity to provide such a life for himself quite separate from his income. The income, presumably, would be a direct payment to him by the state, taken by taxation of private industry or by nationalization of all industry.

This conception was embodied in the now famous report of the so-called "Ad Hoc Committee" in New York. (See "Cybernation, Unemployment and Freedom," page 49.) Despite its visionary quality, the conception cannot be dismissed lightly. At present it is clearly impractical. The underlying structure of customs, of habits, and social institutions for any such arrangement does not now exist. Levels of education and culture permitting individuals to find and make their own ways of life and civilization have yet to be reached. History has indeed occasionally furnished examples of tiny "leisure classes" which for brief periods were fertile and useful. But there is no example of a whole population living in leisure. The nearest analogy (it is not too close) may be that of Rome in the fourth century A.D. Then a substantial percentage of the population apparently did live without work. The results were anything but inspiring, and in any case below the nonworking sector was a great slave population.

Yet if productive capacity increases during the next century as it has during the past forty years, a base may exist for a wholly different civilization. When mechanization makes it possible for, say, 20 percent of the population to furnish everything wanted or needed by the whole population, just such problems will be raised and may be solved. Then, of course, any kind of a job would be a luxury. Interesting work rather than money or profit would be the greatest prize. Comfort without work would be the common lot.

As a distant possibility, therefore, the Ad Hoc Committee's suggestion that receipt of income should be separated from work cannot be entirely disregarded. It may be noted, however, that, unless human nature changes, some group would have to assign that income on some basis, administered by some social machinery. This would suggest either a social economic dictatorship, or a complete consensus by all hands, given effect by some political machinery representing that consensus. Neither institution is at present in sight.

All this is a fascinating intellectual exercise, but today comes under the heading of science fiction. A century from now the problem may indeed emerge. Yet, to this writer, it seems unlikely. The present situation, in fact, is not that there is not enough work to be done but that it is not organized so that it provides jobs. Further, as civilization progresses, wants and needs are likely to increase: standards of individual and collective living will rise. The immediate crisis does not arise from lack of needs or wants whose satisfaction requires work. It proceeds from the fact that, increasingly, needs and wants are of a kind not readily satisfied through private sector business and operations, because private enterprise cannot satisfy them. Their satisfaction cannot be made to yield a monetary profit in conventional sense. Education, beautiful cities, unpolluted rivers, first-rate architecture in middle- and low-income housing, creditable and widely diffused culture including theatre, music, painting, the arts—to take only a few—are not being undertaken by the private sector. No one has seen a way to offer such satisfactions and charge for them through the price-and-profit system. This is equally true of public health, personal services for the elderly, even of adequate nursing for the sick at home or in hospitals. The private sector, sparked by a price and profit mechanism, does not, or at least does not yet, know how to supply these needs and wants. Business, like the public, must therefore accept the fact that the state must do so.

Cybernation,

ROBERT THEOBALD

One of the three conveners of the Ad Hoc Committee on the Triple Revolution which submitted its findings in 1964 to President Johnson, Robert Theobald is a British economist who lives and works in the United States. He gained prominence with his controversial book Free Men and Free Markets *(1963). In that book and in previous publications, he introduced the thesis that he continues to explore in the following essay: namely, that because there will not be sufficient jobs for the unskilled after the impact of cybernation in industry and in services, the government will have "to provide every individual with an absolute constitutional right to an income adequate to allow him to live with dignity," regardless of whether or not he holds a job.*

Born in 1929 in Madras, south India, Mr. Theobald was graduated with a Master of Arts degree in Economics from Cambridge University, England. He has done postgraduate work on economic growth at Harvard University. In 1957 he left the Organization for European Economic Cooperation and came to the United States, where he has been a consultant for the United Nations and The Center for the Study of Democratic Institutions and a lecturer before a wide variety of organizations. He now lives with his wife in New York City and divides his time between writing and consulting and lecturing on both sides of the Atlantic. Among his other publications are: The Rich and the Poor *(1960) and* The Challenge of Abundance *(1961), as well as two overseas investment handbooks,* Profit Potential in the Developing Countries *and* Business Potential in the European Common Market.

48

Unemployment and Freedom

W e are now entering a new era whose requirements are as different
from those of the recent industrial age as those of the industrial
age were different from the agricultural era. In the agricultural era,
human skill was combined with human and animal power in a system
which provided a minimal standard of living for the vast majority of the
people and a leisured existence for a small elite. In the industrial age,
which we are now leaving, human skills were combined with machine
power to provide great wealth for a few, a reasonable standard of living
for most, and abject poverty for those unable to find a place within the
productive system. Today the cybernated productive system is emerging—
an innovation in productive techniques and organization based on machine power and machine skill, that is, on the combination of automated
machinery and the computer.

Cybernation is already manifesting the fundamental characteristics of a
production revolution: the development of new productive techniques and
the subsequent appearance of new principles of organization; a localized
beginning and the appearance elsewhere of the same revolutionary productive complex; a complete reordering of man's relationship to his environment and a dramatic increase in total energy.

The beginning of the cybernation revolution is localized here in the
United States and now in the 1960's. We must recognize, however, that
although the problems posed by the cybernation revolution are part of a
new era in the history of all mankind, they are first being faced by the
people of the United States and their early successes or failures will have
a continuing effect on the course of the revolution.

The development of cybernation will bring about many fundamental

49

changes in the organization of the socioeconomic system. The computer will become far more efficient than a human being in carrying out all repetitive physical and mental tasks. Already we know that it is possible to replace almost all production workers with cybernated systems in which computers control machines. The computer is also proving more economical than white-collar workers in the carrying out of repetitive mental tasks, with computer systems replacing office workers, bank clerks, accountants. Even the functions of middle management, such as inventory control, are proving susceptible to computerization.

These are, however, primitive developments. In the near future we will see that the computer can take over any structural task: that is, any task where the decision-making rules can be specified in advance. For example, the computer has already been used to design machinery and bridges and to analyze stock portfolios. Computer system applications now at the near-completion stage of planning include the granting of many types of bank loans and the process of odd-lot trading on Wall Street. This last application is perhaps particularly noteworthy for it will replace a group of professionals whose median income is around $50,000 a year.

The computer will force man's mind out of the repetitive productive

TEXAS OIL REFINERY AND CONTROL CENTER
The cybernation revolution is a new era in history

system just as surely as industrial machinery forced out man's muscle. The initial introduction of computer systems is a response to a need to increase economic efficiency or to rationalize operations; but as computer systems become fully operative, a drive emerges toward the reorganization, for purposes of compatibility, of interacting systems and institutions. The greater the number of areas of computer application, the greater the force behind this drive and the more rapid the elimination of job opportunities.

This reality has not been perceived by many economists who are still examining the effects of automation, rather than cybernation. Automation is properly described as the use of advanced machinery *not* involving computers: and it is automation which has so far been predominant in industrial and service reorganization. Automation sets up few drives toward system-linkage and therefore does not make the goal of full employment impossible. However, cybernation—the combination of advanced machinery with the computer—produces ever stronger drives toward system-linkage, which make it necessary to use ever more complex machine, rather than human, communication and control methods, and thus inevitably destroys the possibility of full employment.

At the same time as the computer is eliminating the possibility of full employment, it is producing a drive toward unlimited productive power. This drive results from combining what is in effect unlimited energy with the control and communication system of the computer and the activities of those involved in research and development. While this drive toward unlimited productive power is still denied by most economists, it is fully accepted by those most closely associated with production—the manufacturer and the farmer. Americans now expand their production, both within America and abroad, just as fast as they are able to increase profitable sales.

There is no longer any effective limit to our productive abilities: we have passed beyond the dismal science of traditional economics. U Thant, secretary-general of the United Nations, expressed this reality in the following words: "The truth, the central stupendous truth, about developed countries today is that they can have—in anything but the shortest run—the kind and scale of resources they decide to have. . . . It is no longer resources that limit decisions. It is the decision that makes the resources. This is the fundamental, revolutionary change—perhaps the most revolutionary mankind has ever known." This is the true meaning of the word abundance: not that goods and services are already available and waiting to be used, but that we possess the potential to call forth enough to meet our material needs.

These drives set up by cybernation, which will eliminate the mind of man from the productive system and make possible unlimited production, highlight the challenge we face. We shall be able to produce everything

600-LINES-A-MINUTE COMPUTER PRINT-OUT WHEEL
These devices will eliminate the mind of man

we need, using only a small fraction of the time of those available to work. Continuation of the present socioeconomic system will result in an ever higher level of unemployment, with the unemployed being deprived both of a decent standard of living and of opportunities for meaningful activity. Appropriate evolutionary changes in our socioeconomic system, however, would allow us to achieve a society where every individual and family would have an income adequate to ensure a dignified life and where each individual would be able to develop meaningful activity for himself.

THE UNEMPLOYMENT SITUATION NOW

In recent years it has been possible to produce all the goods that people and institutions have been willing and able to buy without employing all those who wished to find a job: in the United States the unemployment rate, seasonally adjusted, has remained around or above 5 percent of the civilian labor force, according to Department of Labor statistics.

This average unemployment rate conceals marked variations for various classes of workers. Thus the unemployment rate for workers with less than eight years education is more than six times as high as that for the college graduate with over sixteen years of education; the unemployment rate for Negroes is twice as high as that for whites, regardless of occupation, educational level, age or sex; the unemployment rate for teen-agers is around three times the national average, the unemployment rate for Negro teen-agers around five times the national average, and the unemployment rate for Negro teen-agers in the ghettos is often ten times the national average—that is to say, over 50 percent; finally, the unemployment rate in the depressed areas is often three times or more the national average.

These figures, while serious enough in their manifest implications, drastically underestimate the true extent of the unemployment problem. They do not take into account underemployment or featherbedding. In addition, they ignore the fact that many who would like to take up full-time work can only find part-time jobs.

Also, present methods of calculating unemployment rates—a person is normally counted as unemployed only if he has actively sought a job recently—ignore the fact that many men and women who would like to find jobs have not looked for them because they know that there are no job openings that they are able to fill. Unfortunately, little research has yet been done in this area, but the few available studies suggest that the number of people who have ceased to look for work because of the lack of suitable job opportunities is substantial.

For example, Charles Killingsworth, professor of economics at Michigan State University, is carrying out an extensive survey of the national unemployment position of those with least education. Killingsworth stated in a paper given before a conference on automation and cybernation called by the International Labour Office in July, 1964, that in 1950 "the unemployment rate for the poorest-educated group was four times the rate for the most-educated group: by 1962, the real rate for the bottom group was twelve times the rate for the top group." Killingsworth arrived at these conclusions by taking into account—as the official Department of Labor unemployment figures do not—changes in the percentage of individuals with various levels of education officially reported as looking for work in 1950 and 1962. Killingsworth showed, in effect, that a substantial number of less-educated potential workers were no longer being counted as unemployed.

Similar observations have been made with regard to youth unemploy-

SOUP FACTORY CHEF AT WORK, 1965
Make possible unlimited production

HARLEM TEEN-AGERS
Unemployment ten times the national average

ment: although the official unemployment rate for teen-agers has remained relatively constant since 1960, there are a substantial and growing number of young Americans who are neither in school nor employed. It has been estimated officially by the Department of Labor that 750,000 young Americans between the ages of 16 and 21 are neither in school nor at work. It is this growing amount of concealed unemployment which has caused many researchers to conclude that the true rate of unemployment is roughly double the rate shown in the official statistics at the present time. This means that over 7 million people would like to find jobs as opposed to the 3.8 million shown in the official statistics for 1964.

The average official unemployment statistics therefore no longer indicate the extent or nature of the unemployment problem. In addition, it is now clear that repeated failure to find employment is resulting in self-devaluation as well as loss of confidence and interest in all types of work for an ever growing number of people. Failure to secure a place in the national job structure can increasingly be seen as affecting not only the individual's attitude to performing work for wages, but also his atttitude toward the carrying out of tasks on his own behalf, that of his family, and, indeed, his community. The massive increase in welfare agency case loads reflects not only rising levels of joblessness among the unskilled, but also profound psychological changes resulting from this self-devaluation. The chronically unemployed become the inactive.

Present employment and welfare regulations also reinforce the individual's initial reaction of self-devaluation, which then often becomes a downward trend, irreversible not only in economic but also in social and psychological terms. The older worker calls himself "retired": his social security status would be affected if he took some employment. The worker in his prime years is forced onto relief: in most states the requirements for becoming a relief recipient bring about such fundamental alterations in an individual's situation that a reversal of the process is always difficult and often totally infeasible.

The recent apparent stabilization and even downward drift of the unemployment rate to around 5 percent is therefore misleading. It is a reflection of the discouragement and defeat of people who cannot find employment and have ceased to look for a job rather than a measure of the economy's success in creating jobs for those who want to work. Formerly

HARLEM YOUTH
*Young Americans neither
in school nor employed*

55

when an individual lost a job he was a jobless worker who could expect, and could be expected, to find a new job when and where economic conditions made this possible. Today, however, the pace of technological, economic, and social change is so fast that the content and context of work are continuously altering to such an extent that a low-skilled individual who loses his job often loses with it his validation as a member of the labor force: he sees that both the economy and society are moving forward in time and technological complexity, while he remains rooted in skills that were productive in the past. Thus, today's unfavorable unemployment picture not only reflects large-scale human distress, but also indicates a new factor in the economic situation: in the past, unemployed workers were basically a reserve of manpower and skills—a commodity always ready for use; today, unused manpower and skills are a rapidly *deteriorating* commodity.

What then of the future? Many authorities are now arguing that the current unemployment problem is only the forerunner of an infinitely more serious situation. They base this argument on two factors: the spread of cybernation; and the significant increase in size of the labor force which is now occurring and will continue in the second half of the 1960's. In the twelve-month period ending June 30, 1965, the number of people reaching the age of 18 rose almost one million to 3.8 million and will con-

EMPLOYMENT RELOCATION CENTER IN NEW JERSEY
Over 7 million people would like to find jobs

tinue at this higher level. During the 1965 to 1975 period, the total labor force is expected to expand from 79 to 93 million at an annual average rate of 1.4 million.

It was this combination of factors which led the Research Institute of America, a management advisory firm, to conclude (December 27, 1963): *"The moment of truth on automation is coming*—a lot sooner than most people realize. The shattering fact is that the United States is still almost totally unprepared for the approaching crisis."[1]

THE ARGUMENT OF THE NEOCLASSICAL ECONOMIST

Although workers replaced by cybernation are deeply concerned and although many manufacturers of cybernated equipment anticipate that cybernation will force major changes in the socioeconomic system, few economists agree with this evaluation of the situation. Most economists argue that new technological systems represent no more than an extension of past technological trends which can be dealt with using already developed policies. Although almost all economists would agree that unemployment has been allowed to persist at excessive levels over recent years, they maintain that enough jobs can be developed for an indefinite period into the future to ensure that everybody who wants to find employment will be able to do so.

There are, however, two major schools of thought about the methods which could be effective in providing jobs and reducing unemployment. The neoclassicists, represented by Yale Brozen in this volume, argue that the main cause of excessive unemployment in recent years has been the use of union and societal power to push wages above the "economic" level. The economists of the Johnson administration disagree: they claim that recent unemployment has resulted from a failure to increase the demand for goods with sufficient rapidity.

Let us take up these two arguments in turn, reviewing Yale Brozen's first. Brozen essentially argues that the demand for labor and the supply of labor should be brought into balance by allowing wages to find their own level: that if there is no interference with market forces, wages will vary in such a way as to ensure that everybody who is looking for a job will be able to find one. Thus, Brozen argues that the elevator operator's union has deprived many workers of jobs by raising wages so high that it is now more economical to install automatic elevators than to continue to use manually operated elevators. Essentially all economists accept the validity of Brozen's argument that the effect of raising wages is to make the use of machinery more attractive. The labor unions are therefore

1 The existing confusion in terms is illustrated by the fact that the word "automation" is used here in the sense in which I use "cybernation" in this article.

confronted with an increasingly serious dilemma. Every time a union succeeds in raising wages, it also increases the likelihood of management using machines rather than men. Although the increase in wages benefits those who keep their jobs, it will damage the interests of those who lose their jobs because they have been priced out of the market.

Brozen also points out, again quite correctly, that society confronts a similar problem with respect to minimum wage policies. During the years since World War II, society has increasingly accepted the concept that every worker should be paid a wage which will allow him an adequate minimum standard of living. As Brozen shows, the minimum wage was only 29 percent of manufacturing employees' hourly earnings in 1949 but rose to a level of 51 percent in 1963. At the existing level of $1.25 an hour, the minimum wage is so high that potential employers cannot afford to hire many workers whose employment might be economically advantageous if minimum wages were lower. But Brozen does not deal with the implications of the fact that even a minimum of $1.25 is so low that many workers receiving it still live below the poverty line.

Brozen's argument about the effect of wage rates is, therefore, correct in theoretical economic terms: it is even possible that if wages could, in fact, be made to vary in accordance with the demand and supply of labor it would be possible to achieve full employment following his prescription.

CAPE KENNEDY SCENE
Machine systems do not get tired

However, neither the worker, nor the unions, nor society in general would accept the prerequisite of a decrease in wage rates. Thus Brozen's simple solution, while not necessarily "economically" impossible, cannot be put into effect for political and social reasons.

Brozen's solution, however, is not only socially and politically unacceptable, it is also impracticable in anything but the shortest run. His argument does not take into account the fundamental implications of the new technology. In addition to the often substantial direct economic savings that would result, the use of automatic machinery also appears more attractive than men for a wide range of noneconomic reasons. Machine systems do not get tired, they can carry out a particular task with a continued precision which cannot be demanded or expected of a human work force; they are incapable of immorality, they do not lie, steal, cheat or "goof off"; they do not claim that their rights as human beings are being violated by factory work practices; they are not class conscious; above all, they are not vocal in their criticism of management, and they do not go on strike.

THE APPROACH OF THE JOHNSON ADMINISTRATION

Government economists are recognizing that new equipment is developing so fast that there is a growing loss of jobs through continuing obsolescence of human skills and that skilled individuals must, therefore, be prepared to undergo retraining frequently and to change their jobs several times during their lives if they are to be able to compete with machine systems. But, while there is increasing stress on the need for retraining of the skilled and also on the problem of the untrained and the ill-educated, most emphasis is still directed to the overall unemployment problem.

Most economists who are presently active in developing economic policy on employment and unemployment believe that the approach proposed by Brozen is impracticable. They accept the fact that wages cannot be drastically lowered in an attempt to secure minimum unemployment; they put forward an alternative approach which calls for the implementation of policies designed to ensure rapid expansion in the demand for goods, thus creating additional jobs.

The source of the theories and policies now being applied by the Johnson administration is generally assumed to be John Maynard Keynes, the eminent British economist. It is indeed true that Keynesian analysis is being used. While continuing to uphold the validity of some neoclassical economic theory, Keynes refuted the assumption, currently still upheld by Brozen and his colleagues, that generalized unemployment is impossible because the demand for labor and the supply of labor will be brought into balance by wages finding their own level. Keynes proved in

The General Theory of Employment, Interest and Money, written during the depression and published in 1936, that it was possible for growing and continuing unemployment to occur in modern conditions because effective demand for goods would not necessarily rise as rapidly as the potential supply.

Basing themselves upon this undeniably accurate Keynesian analysis, government economists are proposing policies which they claim would lead, if adopted, to a sufficiently rapid increase in demand to ensure minimum unemployment. It is, however, important to recognize that a drive toward minimum unemployment is not the *only* policy proposal which can be derived from an interpretation of Keynesian analysis: society could equally well decide that it no longer wished to channel the quasi-totality of its efforts toward the goal of minimum unemployment, but rather desired to seek a new social order which would allow us to take full advantage of the potential of emerging abundance and our ability to eliminate toil.

Economic analysis should not be the deciding factor in the choice between these policies: we must make it in terms of our social goals. In order to determine what we wish to do we must first understand why the administration argues that minimum unemployment is not only feasible, but also desirable. Walter Heller, as chairman of President Kennedy's Council of Economic Advisers, put forward the accepted view in his testimony before the Senate Subcommittee on Employment and Manpower: "Clearly, we need not fear that the increasing productivity associated with even a speeded-up rate of technological progress will founder upon a contradiction between our needs and our ability to satisfy them. As people continue to receive the extra incomes which our enlarging production can generate they will also continue to buy the enlarged output—for private and public consumption and investment."

It is on the basis of this unproved and, indeed, unprovable value judgment, which is increasingly challenged by other social science disciplines, that America mobilizes much of its domestic efforts to ensure minimum unemployment. Continued acceptance of the desirability of minimum unemployment, however, sets up certain constraints which are still little understood. Given our present economic system, internal economic stability is possible *only* if the amount people and institutions are willing and able to buy rises as fast as the amount we are able to produce: it is essential that effective demand keep up with potential supply. This necessity follows from the fact that the viability of our present scarcity-oriented socioeconomic system is based on a very simple relationship: it is assumed that it is possible for the overwhelming proportion of those seeking jobs to find them and that the incomes received from these jobs will enable the jobholder to act as an adequate consumer.

The successful functioning of the *present* socioeconomic system is therefore *completely* dependent on an ability to provide enough jobs to go around; a continuing failure to achieve this invalidates our present mechanism for income distribution. It is for this reason that businesses of all sizes, economists of all persuasions, and politicians of all parties try to keep effective demand growing as fast as potential supply: to encourage those who are still able to act as adequate consumers because they are still obtaining sufficient incomes from their jobs, to consume more and more of the kind of products that the economic system is presently designed to produce.

This need to keep demand and supply in balance makes it impossible to channel the existing drive toward unlimited productive power for the good of society. The ever more powerful drive of technology toward unlimited production and the elimination of the mind of men from the productive system increasingly force the adaptation of the individual to the needs of the socioeconomic system. The process of adaptation is already far advanced. At the present time, the individual in his work role is considered to be as geographically and occupationally mobile as may be necessary to maximize production: in his role as consumer his social status is already gauged by his willingness to expend his resources of time and money in a manner most favorable to absorbing whatever the productive system is currently turning out.

Man is no longer controlling the drives of the technico-economic system: rather, he is being dominated by them. The effort to attain minimum unemployment is perhaps the most important factor operating to prevent control of these technico-economic drives. It is therefore urgent that we displace our commitment to the goal of minimum unemployment from its primary position in our order of priorities.

Those who believe in minimum unemployment policies will not be convinced by this line of analysis. They will not be willing to give up the attempt to keep demand growing as fast as supply, and thus create enough conventional jobs, until they are convinced that it will necessarily fail. However, it is now clear that the effect of cybernation in developing abundance and eliminating jobs will inevitably come to exceed our capacity to create jobs. How can we be certain of this? Government economists argue that every time the demand for goods increases, the number of people employed to produce them also *necessarily* increases. While this relationship has generally held true in the past, the development of the computer ensures that it will not be valid in coming years. In the relatively near future, those who need to expand their plants to meet created demand will choose to buy machines rather than to hire men: the machines they buy will be produced predominantly by other machines. The new machines purchased will be so much more efficient than earlier machinery that large numbers of organizations now using older machinery and hence employing many men will be forced to close down: they will be too inefficient to compete.

The process can be summarized as follows: Created demand will lead to purchases of highly efficient and productive machine systems which need few men to control them, that is, to the installation of cybernation; these new machine systems will be so efficient that older automated machine systems still requiring significant amounts of human activity for their operation and control will no longer be able to compete, and the organizations using them will be priced out of the market. Thus, in the relatively near future, a policy of forcing rapid increases in demand in order to increase employment opportunities will actually lead to the opposite result: it will raise unemployment rather than lower it. It is the certainty of this development which should lead the Johnson administration to reconsider its present policies *now*. The urgency of reconsideration is increased by the fact that the drive to minimum unemployment is involving so much of our energies, both analytical and practical, that we are failing either to observe or to take effective action to counter certain existing major unfavorable trends within the socioeconomic system.[2]

There is already evidence which strongly suggests that the impact of cybernation is causing a reversal of a long-run historical trend. It seems no longer true that an ever larger proportion of Americans are entering the increasingly abundant society, and we can anticipate that there will be a larger proportion of the population who will be poor in 1975 than in 1965, unless we change the socioeconomic system. Perhaps the most clear-cut evidence of this development is to be found in the fact that there has been a very rapid increase in the welfare case load even during the highly prosperous first half of the 1960's. For example, New York City added almost 6,000 welfare cases monthly during 1964. January, 1965, saw a new, but predictable, phenomenon—a strike of New York City welfare workers.

Willard Wirtz, secretary of labor, summarized the effect of current trends in his 1963 year-end message: "The confluence of surging population and driving technology is splitting the American labor force into tens of millions of 'haves' and millions of 'have-nots.' In our economy of 69 million jobs, those with wanted skills enjoy opportunity and earning power. But the others face a new and stark problem—exclusion on a permanent basis, both as producers and consumers, from economic life. This division of people threatens to create a human slag heap. We cannot tolerate the development of a separate nation of the poor, the

---

2 Our failure can be traced, in large part, to the fact that Keynesian analysis explicitly excludes those factors which are of most importance in present conditions. "We take as given the existing skill and quantity of available labor, the existing quality and quantity of available equipment, the existing technique." (J. M. Keynes, *The General Theory of Employment, Interest and Money* [New York: Harcourt, Brace & Co., 1936], p. 243.)

unskilled, the jobless, living within another nation of the well-off, the trained and the employed." The social programs of the Johnson administration, particularly those implemented under the rubric of the "War on Poverty," while more than a mere Band-Aid approach, only alleviate the symptoms of society's ills; they do not attack the fundamental causes of society's sickness.

The implications of cybernation are far-reaching, and for this reason are destructive of the validity of many existing patterns of socioeconomic analysis. The initial setting up of computer systems can be explained, at least in part, by traditional economic analysis: it represents an attempt to increase efficiency through a rationalization of operations. But, as we have already seen, when computer systems become fully operative, they set up a drive toward the reorganization, for purposes of compatibility, of interacting systems and institutions. The greater the number of areas of computer application, the greater the force behind this drive becomes, with a consequent trend toward the emergence of a total computer system organized for maximum efficiency in terms of the immediate, defined task.

Within such cybernated computer systems, there will be little place for men. Only a relatively few top decision-makers will be required to ensure production. If, therefore, we allow present trends to continue, we will see the rapid development of a new type of organization of the socioeconomic system, within which incomes and nonwork time would vary in inverse proportion. Starting at the bottom of the scale, there would be a great number of totally unemployed workers subsisting inadequately on resources derived from heavily bureaucratized government schemes designed merely to ensure physical survival; the greatest proportion of the population would work considerably shorter hours than at present and would receive wages and salaries which would provide for necessities and even some conveniences, but would not encourage them to develop a meaningful pattern of activity; and a small number of people with the highest levels of education and training would work excessively long hours for very high salaries.

ECONOMY, SOCIETY, AND THE INDIVIDUAL

Cybernation is destroying the central assumptions underlying most existing economic analysis and policy proposals. These are still based on the contention that realities are represented by a series of past observations transformed into fundamental economic "knowns" by the passage of time. Prominent among these economic "knowns" are the assumptions that the official unemployment statistics represent the true unemployment picture; that a continuing increase in demand will continue to improve the unemployment position; that unemployed workers represent a nondeteriorating, ever available labor reserve; and that it is feasible to require skilled individuals to undergo retraining as often as it is necessary for them to remain economically competitive on a day-to-day basis with machine systems.

Besides the problems arising from the mismatch between reality and the supposed "knowns," the observation, analysis, and interpretation of socioeconomic events and conditions are defective because of the existence of a considerable number of unknowns and gaps in our knowledge. Many of these are capable of being filled through the use of already existing economic techniques, methods, and approaches. Prominent among these economic "unknowns" are: real unemployment and underemployment figures; current real labor needs, both in quantity and types of skill; which jobs are liable to be taken over by machine systems, both in the near and more distant future; which of society's current unmet or undermet needs can be provided for by a restructuring of the work so that it can be carried out within the private enterprise system; which needs should be provided for through tax-financed federal, state, or local governments, and which should be provided for through tax-rebate-financed organizations, such as the nonprofit institutions; which of the already known societal needs cannot be met by institutions organized according to industrial-age approaches; and what kind of new institutions are needed and how are they to be financed—for purposes of financing, what is an institution?—is an individual an institution?

The foregoing "unknowns" are not included in conventional economic analysis, which, consequently, does not cover large new areas of primarily economic problems. In order to be effective in finding solutions to these new problems created by the emergence of cybernation and abundance, new methods of financing and work-organization are needed in areas where the market mechanism was formerly an efficient operating force.

It has become apparent that our economy is curiously deficient in financial mechanisms enabling the individual to act as an institution, self-directed and alone responsible for his activities. Isolated examples of the individual as an institution do already exist: the independent rich and those receiving grants or fellowships. These individuals are able to act outside of the constraints typical of the industrial-age, market-oriented, task-structured system. In contrast to industrial-age generalized time-patterning, their work often requires them to adopt a highly idiosyncratic rhythm of activity and inactivity. This manner of working is, therefore, not amenable to remuneration according to present economic criteria and mechanisms; if alternative mechanisms are not forthcoming, society will not be able to benefit from the talents of those who are capable of acting in this way but who lack financial support.

There are two other societal groups—the low-skilled unemployed and those being educated or trained—where the need for new mechanisms of distributing income is immediately obvious from a humanitarian standpoint. Unfortunately the economic advantages to society do not become apparent if conventional methods of economic analysis are used. Again, the task-structured industrial-age economic model is not applicable; a one-to-one correlation between current expenditure and current returns cannot be demonstrated. What can be established, and recently has begun to be understood, is that the failure to find new ways of financing those being educated and the failure to maintain the low-skilled unemployed as bona fide members of society are resulting in large and growing allocations of economic resources for costly rehabilitation programs of inadequate scope and size.

I have proposed elsewhere that we develop a new principle of income distribution appropriate to the era of cybernation:[3] a guaranteed annual income. Although designed to meet the immediate need of underwriting the activities of creative individuals and improving the methods of financing the educational system, it also provides an economic principle for solving the social and cultural self-devaluation of the unemployed. This is a *general* economic principle, applicable to every member of society. It underwrites the status of the recipient as a member of society, rather than a mere economic mechanism which enables a human being to remain alive even though society has virtually ceased to regard him as one of its members. We will need to provide every individual with an absolute constitutional right to an income adequate to allow him to live with dignity. No government agency, judicial body, or other organization whatsoever should have the power to suspend or limit any payments assured by these guarantees.

The guaranteed income is essential if we are to preserve our goal of individual freedom. It is not merely one possible solution to the problems of cybernation which can be compared with many others: on the contrary it is the prerequisite to the other policies which must be developed to deal with existing problems. There is, in American society today, a vast amount of human energy which cannot be employed because of a lack of

---

3 I have discussed the justification as well as suitable techniques for the introduction of the Guaranteed Annual Income in *Free Men and Free Markets* and also in a speech given before the International Association of Personnel in Employment Security on June 30, 1964, which was reprinted in *The Congressional Record* July 8 and in *Vital Speeches*, August 1. The idea of the guaranteed annual income is an old one. In the last two years, however, it has received support from a variety of groups and individuals who have cited a wide range of reasons for their support. Among those who have proposed this scheme or closely related variants are Milton Friedman, a conservative economist; the Delegate Assembly of the National Association of Social Workers; and Charles Reich, a lawyer. The guaranteed income was also proposed by an ad hoc group of 32 individuals in a document entitled *The Triple Revolution* (*New York Times*, March 23, 1964). It discussed the cybernation, weaponry, and human rights revolutions.

available resources: the provision of a guaranteed income will lead to cultural, social, and political advance on an unprecedented scale.

For society at large, and especially for those creative individuals now shackled by its absence, the provision of a guaranteed annual income is in a situation analogous to that of the granting of limited liability to companies at the time of its introduction in the nineteenth century. Limited liability was introduced to encourage risk-taking by those investing in companies. The concept of a joint venture was replaced by the concept that the stockholder's liability for company debts no longer put a lien on his total wealth, but only on the amount he invested in the company. Limited liability was a precondition for the taking of risks: it did not ensure risk-taking or innovation, but it did make them possible, thus allowing the economy and society to benefit from the self-interested acts of individuals.

Similarly, a guaranteed income provides the individual with the ability to do what he personally feels is important. This allows risk-taking and innovation in areas where the existing and emerging needs of society are not being met by an otherwise efficiently functioning free enterprise market system. The minimum income is not mediated through the offices of any other individual or organization within the market system and, therefore, does not bring with it built-in pressures for the recipient to continue doing that which is already being done through the market system.

Turning to a consideration of the effect of a guaranteed minimum income on those now unemployed or threatened by unemployment, we must recognize that the upbringing and education of much of the present population has limited their horizons so severely that they cannot fully benefit from the potential abundance which their own work has created. Society crippled these people in order to get them to produce efficiently. As their productive efforts are no longer required, society must not only provide them with rights to adequate incomes, but must also provide new types of activities which will give them a sense of satisfaction from their lives.

This can be done only through new types of organization. The provision of a guaranteed income will greatly simplify the problem of providing new work roles for individuals who will not have to be paid wages. We can anticipate the organization of what I have called "consentives": productive groups formed by individuals who will come together on a voluntary basis, simply because they wish to do so. The goods produced by these groups will not compete with those mass produced by cybernated organizations: the consentive will normally produce the "custom-designed" goods which have been vanishing within the present economy.

This type of productive unit will continue far into the future, for the use of a man's hands is one of the most satisfying ways of spending time.

MUSEUM SCENE
We must develop creativity

Nevertheless, the proportion of the population spending most of its time in production will decline as education in its fullest sense takes an ever more central position and other activities seem more challenging.

The guaranteed income will, perhaps, have its greatest importance in the development of education. In the very near future, we will recognize that a mere extension of the period of education will not be enough. We will need major changes in concepts of education to meet the new challenges. We must face up to the fact that today's school and university were designed to serve the requirements of the passing industrial age. If we are to educate for the future, we must find ways to develop the creativity and to enlarge the capacity of the individual to think in terms of his own uniqueness.

The conclusion of this essay can be briefly summarized. It is inevitable that there will be far more "unemployment" in the future than there is today, but we will come to perceive unemployment as favorable rather than unfavorable. The individual and society fear unemployment today for two reasons: first, because it usually involves the receipt of an inadequate income; second, because it threatens cessation of all activity which seems meaningful and it encourages antisocial activity. When we provide adequate incomes to all and develop each individual's uniqueness so that he himself knows what he wants to do, unemployment, which will then be redefined as the condition of *not* holding a job, will be seen as highly desirable. Paradoxically, therefore, economists can best serve society by directing their organizational effort and their professional skills toward "minimum employment" rather than "full employment."

67

Patterns of

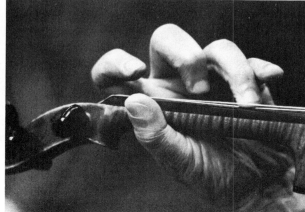

Non-Work

As patterns of work change, so, inevitably, will those of non-work. Some of the familiar free-time pursuits shown on this page may endure: poetry reading, music making, boating, reading, golfing, and merely lolling in bed. But change may be afoot if, for example, the pattern of "consentives" (Theobald) actually emerges or longer vacations become a pattern (Brozen) or if the forces freed from work in which the incentive is profit are put to work on projects in which the incentive is not profit but the service of the common weal (Berle). Whatever the specific shape of the new patterns, the general prospect would seem to be for new, large solutions for the new, large problem, and some of them may take forms as unexpected as in the picture at top left which shows ladies in retirement in California taking a communal ride on their tricycles.

Progress
Key to a

ARTHUR LARSON

A former Director of the United States Information Agency, Arthur Larson is Director of the Rule of Law Research Center at Duke University. From 1954 to 1961 he served in various administrative capacities in the Eisenhower administration: Undersecretary of Labor, Director of the USIA, and Special Assistant and Special Consultant to the President. At present he is consultant to President Johnson on international affairs. Mr. Larson was born in 1910 in Sioux Falls, South Dakota. After study at Augustana College and the University of South Dakota Law School, he went to Oxford as a Rhodes Scholar; he received from the university a Master of Arts degree in Jurisprudence in 1938 and Doctor of Civil Laws in 1957. He practised law in Milwaukee, Wisconsin, for four years and then taught law at various universities, being appointed Dean of the University of Pittsburgh School of Law in 1953. Among his eleven published books, the best known is A Republican Looks at His Party *(1956). Other books include:* The Law of Workmen's Compensation *(1952) in two volumes, considered a leading treatise in the field and regularly cited in the appellate courts;* Know Your Social Security *(1955; rev. ed. 1959);* What We Are For *(1959); and* When Nations Disagree: a Handbook on Peace Through Law *(1961). The father of two children, Mr. Larson lives with his wife in Durham, North Carolina. An accomplished amateur musician, Mr. Larson's interests include musical composition—organ, string, choral, and vocal—performing on the classical guitar as well as on ancient instruments, and the collecting, arranging, and performing of folk music.*

Sharing:
Private Property Economy

Unemployment raises a specter in the minds of most workers. It does so mainly because it means the cessation of income. If it were not for the close connection between work and income, unemployment would not arouse the fear that it does, nor would the effects of automation be a matter of such concern.

Employment, however, is not the only source of income. In making this statement, I mean to exclude expressly public financial assistance that is unrelated to employment; that is to say, all forms of the dole. But aside from both work and the dole, there is a potent source of income in investment and the ownership of productive property. Usually, of course, investment as a source of income is thought of as the prerogative of the favored few. This article, in proposing a national progress sharing program, will argue that it is now feasible as a possibility for the many and not just for the few.

A progress sharing program is a program based on the principle that wage earners should obtain income-producing capital so that a significant and increasing part of their regular income consists in the return on capital investment.

Measures are already in effect working toward this end. Two main plans can be distinguished. One, called "equity sharing," enables workers to build up a substantial holding of shares in the corporation for which they work. The other, called "deferred profit sharing," is considerably more widespread and consists of a plan for the workers to build up a fund invested in a diversified portfolio of stocks in which they own shares. The most publicized of recent plans is a combination of the two called the "progress sharing plan," which was adopted by the American

PROFIT SHARERS GEORGE ROMNEY (AMERICAN MOTORS)
AND WALTER REUTHER (UAW), 1961
Most publicized of recent plans

Motors Corporation and the United Automobile Workers in 1961.

In this article, the term "progress sharing" will be used, for convenience sake, for any one and all of the three types of plans. It will not be limited to the third plan, combining both equity sharing and profit sharing.

It is difficult to estimate the number of plans already in force in the United States that would fall within these categories (*see* Fig. 1). About forty thousand deferred profit sharing programs of all kinds are already in operation in the United States, and they are being initiated at the rate of about five thousand new programs a year. There are, in addition, an estimated sixty thousand cash profit sharing plans which could be converted to deferred plans without much difficulty. For some years there has been a strong trend toward deferred profit sharing plans, equity sharing plans, and stock purchase plans, all of which are immediately relevant to the present discussion. In 1960, one out of five companies on the New York

Stock Exchange made available some kind of stock acquisition plan for all its employees. One out of every five companies with fifty or more employees has either a cash, deferred, or combination profit sharing program. We are, therefore, talking about something that is by no means radical or untried.

Indeed, the first profit sharing plan in the United States is believed to have been established as early as 1794 by Albert Gallatin, later Secretary of the Treasury under Presidents Jefferson and Madison.

Profit sharing plans on a large scale spread rapidly in the last two decades of the nineteenth century and received new impetus in the period 1910–29. The Great Depression halted this surge, but a phenomenal growth in profit sharing began in 1939 and has continued since, aided by favorable tax legislation resulting from a Senate Finance Subcommittee report that year. The report concluded with this point-blank statement: "We believe it [profit sharing] to be essential to the ultimate maintenance of the capitalistic system."

PROGRESS SHARING AND UNEMPLOYMENT

A progress sharing program can contribute to the solution of the problem of unemployment.

If we assume that, because of the complexity of the problem, part of the solution must take the form of distributing the available work to minimize

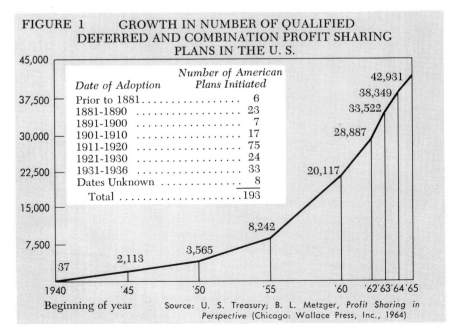

FIGURE 1   GROWTH IN NUMBER OF QUALIFIED
DEFERRED AND COMBINATION PROFIT SHARING
PLANS IN THE U. S.

Date of Adoption	Number of American Plans Initiated
Prior to 1881	6
1881-1890	23
1891-1900	7
1901-1910	17
1911-1920	75
1921-1930	24
1931-1936	33
Dates Unknown	8
Total	193

Source: U. S. Treasury; B. L. Metzger, *Profit Sharing in Perspective* (Chicago: Wallace Press, Inc., 1964)

unemployment, the progress sharing idea acts directly upon the problem. The difficult part of the task is not that of spreading the work more widely. This could be done to a considerable degree by simply shortening the workweek. Indeed, this is the solution most often put forward by organized labor. But, in this case, what happens to the income levels of those who go on the reduced week? When organized labor proposes, for example, a thirty-five-hour week, the intention is emphatically not to accept the equivalent of a loss of five hours pay per week. If the workweek were reduced to thirty-five hours from forty hours, or perhaps even lower, with no reduction in weekly pay, the per hour labor cost would necessarily be sharply increased—perhaps by 12 or 15 percent for a start. The implications of such an increase on prices and the resultant self-cancelling wage-price spiral are by now familiar.

The progress sharing plan would meet this difficulty by offsetting the loss of wages due to reduced work hours by the gain of income from capital. This would not come about suddenly, but neither would the effects of automation be felt overnight. If national progress sharing were put into effect soon enough, and with enough of the parallel devices to augment workers' stock ownership (to be discussed later), there should still be time to build the capital estates of workers at such a rate that the gradual increase of income from capital would be at least roughly in phase with the gradual loss of wage income from reduced hours of work. This gradual reduction of the workweek can be accomplished in orderly fashion by the kind of provision—by no means unusual—adopted in the contract between the Chemical Workers Union and Burroughs, Welcome & Company in Tuckahoe, New York:

> Each workday is reduced, effective at once, by ten minutes. A year hence, another ten-minute reduction becomes effective and, in 1966, a third ten-minute segment is cut off, reducing the present 40-hour week to 37½ hours by July 1, 1966.

A progress sharing program would also act indirectly upon unemployment in that it would stimulate economic activity and facilitate an overall increase in rate of growth. There are several reasons for this. One is that the income from capital would become a reasonably steady source of purchasing power, widely distributed, in the hands of people whose income normally returns to the purchasing stream almost immediately. As the plan reduced unemployment, the spreading of available work would increase purchasing power in the hands of those now unemployed.

Furthermore, if the higher return to labor, which seems to have become almost routine in the periodic labor negotiations, took the form of equity sharing rather than of rigid higher per-hour wages, the relative flexibility inherent in the equity sharing procedure would be a force for offsetting recurrent recessions. Fixed labor charges, crystallized in binding union contracts, cannot be reduced by reducing the hourly wage, and hence, when business falls off, the company whose labor cost is a large proportion of the cost of the product is left with no alternative but to lay off part of its work force. This, in turn, reduces the purchasing power of those who thus become unemployed, which reduces the demand for products and thus occasions further layoffs. This is the familiar downward spiral which had much to do with producing the Great Depression of the 1930's and which, although more recently checked by a variety of stabilizing devices, still to some extent operates during recessions. Under an equity sharing arrangement, fully accepted on all sides, this would not happen because the portion of return to labor represented by the sharing of profits would absorb the first beginnings of the downward movement, which in the past have triggered the cycle of layoffs, reduced purchasing power, and further layoffs.

Another factor, less tangible but perhaps most potent of all, is the economic benefit that would flow from giving the worker the motivation that goes with gaining a share in the fruits of his own production (*see* Fig. 2). The improvement in work performance and morale has probably been the most immediate reason, from the point of view of employers, for the

FIGURE 2
PRINCIPAL REASONS FOR ESTABLISHING PROFIT SHARING PLANS

	Frequency of Mention—By Type of Plan			
PRINCIPAL REASONS	*Total— All Plans*	*Cash*	*Deferred*	*Combi- nation*
Incentive (to increase efficiency, profits, quality, and the like)......	53	17	32	4
Employee Security (general security, retirement benefits, death benefits, and the like)....................	49	2	44	3
Partnership (to promote loyalty, interest in company, good relations, and the like)........................	45	18	23	4
Attract/Hold Competent People.....	43	6	34	3
To Reward Employees and Give Them Opportunity to Share in Company Growth	39	14	24	1
Tax Advantages	11	—	9	2
Economic Education	8	4	3	1
Flexibility in Compensation........	3	2	1	—
Other reasons	4	1	3	—
Number of Objectives Listed*......	255	64	173	18
Number of Companies Answering....	125	37	80	8

Source: Profit Sharing Research Foundation survey using Dun & Bradstreet's representative sample of profit sharing companies of small or medium size (employing 500 or less).
*Objectives listed, of course, exceed the number of companies answering as many companies mentioned multiple reasons for plan installation.

upsurge of profit sharing plans in the United States. The Profit Sharing Research Foundation has published studies documenting the improvement in production resulting from profit sharing in hundreds of companies. The attitude of workers toward their work, far from being a nebulous element economically, can be a decisive one.

HOW PROGRESS SHARING CAN BE ADVANCED

The national progress sharing program is essentially private in the sense that the mechanisms, institutions, and persons actually carrying on the program are nongovernmental. If the program is to succeed, private persons must put it into effect through business corporations, labor unions, associations, and research organizations. A good example of the way in which nongovernmental measures can contribute to widespread adoption of suitable progress sharing plans is the formation of the Council of Profit Sharing Industries in 1947, to promote the practice of profit sharing in the United States, which was followed in 1951 by the establishment of the Profit Sharing Research Foundation to carry on research studies on profit sharing. This organization, which is now under the directorship of Mr. B. L. Metzger, was originally directed by Mr. J. J. Jehring, who is continuing his work in this field through the Center for Productivity Motivation of the University of Wisconsin. The function of such research is not only to supply business and labor with reliable facts on the advantages of profit sharing but also to help tailor progress sharing plans to the requirements of particular companies by drawing upon the rich variety of experience that has already been amassed in the use of different types of plans.

However, as is usually true when the object is to achieve a rapid and widespread alteration in the private economy, there is an important place for a coordinated set of governmental actions designed to facilitate this change. Five main categories of actions can be distinguished: tax measures, credit measures, governmental services, the revision of estate taxes, and action to require full distribution of earnings.

Considerable tax incentives for profit sharing of the deferred type are already in existence. Among the tax benefits to the company and to the employees of a qualified plan are the following:

> Up to 15 percent of the total compensation paid into the plan for the employees by the employers is deductible for income tax purposes, and this 15 percent may be spread over more than one year, in order to average out profits and losses.
> Trust funds are exempted from paying taxes on their growth from year to year, and taxes are paid only when benefits are received.
> Payment of the capital share of the fund is taxable at the capital gains rate of 25 percent when received in a lump sum, and at ordinary rates when received in installments.

There is no estate tax on the employee's share in the fund when it passes to his designated beneficiary (as distinguished from his legal estate).

The present law needs some overhauling. A number of loopholes have appeared which tend to emphasize the use of these plans for the benefit of management groups (*see* Fig. 3). The cure of this would lie in making more exacting requirements to insure that, if a plan is approved at all, it must apply equally to all employees of the particular corporation.

Another change designed to shift the stress from executive compensation to broad equity sharing by employees would be to increase the 15 percent limit of tax deductibility to, say, 20 percent, while at the same time placing a ceiling on the total amount that any individual could accumulate on the tax-deductible basis under the particular plan. This ceiling should be quite high, since, as indicated at the outset, the object is to build up estates that will provide significant amounts of current income. On the other hand, the unlimited use of the tax-deductible privilege in connection with very high executive salaries tends to tie up too much capital in these individual accounts. The raising of the 15 percent figure to 20 percent would hasten the creation of significant capital estates for the person with lower earnings. The possibility of abuse at higher income levels would be forestalled by the proposed ceiling. Above the ceiling, any profit sharing distribution would have to be in cash and would be taxable as ordinary income.

There would also be an advantage in requiring that the yearly earnings from a deferred profit sharing trust fund be paid out at least annually in cash to the participants. The reason for the suggestion is to get the income

FIGURE 3

PERCENT OF PROFIT SHARING PLANS COVERING SPECIFIC TYPES OF EMPLOYEES

TYPES OF EMPLOYEES Percent of Profit Sharing Plans Covering Specific Types

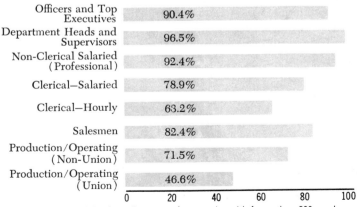

Officers and Top Executives	90.4%
Department Heads and Supervisors	96.5%
Non-Clerical Salaried (Professional)	92.4%
Clerical—Salaried	78.9%
Clerical—Hourly	63.2%
Salesmen	82.4%
Production/Operating (Non-Union)	71.5%
Production/Operating (Union)	46.6%

Source: Dun & Bradstreet's survey of companies with fewer than 500 employees.

from these large and growing accumulations of capital into the channels of consumption. One of the primary reasons for these proposals is to obtain income to supplement wages. A large proportion of profit sharing plans of the deferred type, and of other related schemes, have not had this purpose at all but have been preoccupied with providing security for a later time. In effect, they have been substitutes for, or supplements to, more conventional types of pension plans. But emphasis should be at least as much upon current income as upon the security of owning a capital estate. This major purpose would be defeated if these plans were converted into quasi-pension plans by the withholding and plowing back of earnings of the capital fund itself.

It is obvious that it takes a large amount of capital to produce a really worthwhile addition to current income. It is therefore necessary to supplement the profit sharing concept with other measures under which the wage earner can acquire stocks through his own purchases. Hundreds of such stock purchase plans are in effect by private agreement, and they characteristically contain some special feature making it cheaper and more attractive for the employee to buy stock than it would be for an outsider.

The most constructive measure that the government could adopt would be to provide credit for the acquisition of stocks in somewhat the same way that credit is provided for purchase of farms and of homes. The policy of encouraging widespread ownership of farms produced not only the Homestead Act (1862) but more recently the Farm Credit Administration and the Farmers Home Administration of the Department of Agriculture. The federal policy of encouraging private home ownership is reflected in the establishment of the Federal Housing Administration and in the elaborate credit arrangements under which families may purchase homes with very small down payments and repay their loans at low interest rates over long periods. Indeed, as Kelso and Adler point out in their book, *The Capitalist Manifesto*, our society has developed credit practices under which automobiles, expensive household equipment, and other consumer items can be financed on liberal credit terms—but no such credit facilities are available to the wage earner who wants to acquire capital stocks.[1]

In this book, and in a later book, *The New Capitalists*, Kelso and Adler develop some of the detailed features of such a plan—including a name for the FHA-type corporation that would oversee it: the Capital Diffusion Insurance Corporation (CDIC).[2] As Kelso and Adler add, there is at least

---

1 Louis O. Kelso and Mortimer J. Adler, *The Capitalist Manifesto* (New York: Random House, Inc., 1958), p. 228.

2 *Ibid.*, p. 241, and *The New Capitalists* (New York: Random House, Inc., 1961), p. 59.

one factor making credit financing of equity stocks a more favorable proposition than similar financing of homes, automobiles, and consumer goods. The equity stock itself produces income which can be used to help pay for the capital cost of the stock.

Various other detailed arrangements would add to the effectiveness of the program. A loan insurance program, similar to that of the Federal Housing Administration for mortgage loans, could be worked out to cover loans for the acquisition of equity stocks. Interest upon such loans should be deductible for income tax purposes. This would not be out of line with the present general deductibility of interest payments. Some complications would be encountered, such as the prohibition in the laws of many states against corporations extending credit on the security of their own stock. However, with the feature of loan insurance, it should not be difficult to devise plans for attaining the desired result even under such statutes.

A third way the government can help is to develop an array of governmental services to further the rapid adoption of progress sharing plans.

The Danish Act of April 10, 1957, offers a good precedent for the promotion of profit sharing and establishment of social funds. Under this statute, a committee of ten members is appointed, representing employers, employees, and the public. The tasks of the committee, as set out in section 2 of the Act, are as follows:

1. At the request of business managements, to guide the companies in drawing up rules for profit sharing in connection with the establishment of social funds, for instance, by assisting in the drawing up of regulations, etc.
2. To make applications to companies to encourage them to introduce profit sharing in connection with the establishment of social funds, or to improve or promote existing schemes.
3. To consider reasonable applications from joint committees or other representatives of employees or workers in commercial and industrial enterprises in respect of such initiative.
4. To draw up and publish standard rules for profit sharing schemes and social funds, and otherwise spread general information on the subject.
5. To watch labor conditions at any time and to make applications to the Minister for Economy and Labor or to organizations of workers, employees, and employers in cases where the Committee finds that an alteration of ruling laws, regulations, common practice, etc., would be desirable in order thereby to promote the introduction of or extension of already existing profit sharing schemes in connection with social funds.

It should be noted that this act stops far short of any kind of governmental compulsion. But it definitely puts the government on the side of encouraging profit sharing plans, and supplies promotional, educational, and planning services.

Work, Wealth, and Leisure

A special government committee in the Netherlands[3] made a study and report on profit sharing and specifically rejected the idea of a statutory obligation to enforce the system of profit sharing. The committee gave a number of reasons, but the principal one appears to be that profit sharing will work only if the participants are psychologically ready for it.

This being so, one of the government's most important functions would consist in conducting educational programs for labor and management to prepare the way for systems of this kind. In addition, the government's services should include acting as watchdog over the funds, regulating them through reporting, auditing, and the like, and generally performing services for them similar to those performed for insurance companies, banks, and similar institutions.

Finally, the government should set an example by devising trust programs applicable to government employees, along the lines of the "saving-sharing" programs now being applied to hospitals and other nonprofit organizations.

The revision of estate taxes is also needed in order to bring them in line with the new objective. Present estate and gift taxes, in general, are steeply graduated according to the size of the donor's estate. As a result, the bulk of a very large estate is apt to go either into governmental treasuries in the form of taxes or into tax-exempt foundations. If, however, an overriding national policy is adopted favoring the creation of individual estates in the hands of workers, a fundamental change in the method of calculating the estate tax should be adopted, as argued by Kelso and Adler.[4] The amount of the estate tax should be graduated not according to the size of the donor's estate but according to the size of the estate of the recipient. At the level where it is determined that a capital estate is no more than adequate to perform the function of maintaining a decent standard of living for the particular recipient, there should be no estate tax at all. This would have two effects. The estates being built up by the measures already suggested would not be diminished when passed along. Moreover, testators with large estates would have an inducement to favor distribution of their estates among a number of recipients who are able to receive the bequest tax-free because of their individual situations.

This proposed change would involve some problems of administration, but these would not be insuperable. Because of the peculiar relation of the federal estate tax to the corresponding taxes of the states, it would be possible to bring about this change by federal legislation. This makes it a particularly straightforward proposal for a national program. There is

3 Interim report of the committee established by decree of the Minister of Social Affairs and Public Health on June 15, 1948.
4 *The Capitalist Manifesto*, pp. 194 ff.

nothing radical about this proposal. On the contrary, it is a great deal more democratic and sensible than the present state of affairs into which we have drifted, with its curious mixture of half-confiscatory taxes and proliferating exemptions.

In considering possible proposals, the final question is whether corporations (or at least those which have achieved a certain stage of maturity) should be compelled to distribute their earnings in the form of dividends rather than be allowed to retain them and plow them back into the business, as many corporations now do to a large extent.

Retained profits have for years been the largest single source of capital for American corporations. Cumulative totals of sources of capital funds from 1947 to 1956 show that retained profits accounted for $88.1 billion of capital, while stock issues provided only $21.5 billion. Long-term debt accounted for $51.9 billion, short-term debt $47.5 billion, and other sources $13.0 billion. For the sake of completeness, it should be added that the other very large source of capital, in the technical sense, is provision for depreciation, which amounted to $102.9 billion. Thus, the two "internal sources" of capital—retained profits and provision for depreciation—amounted to $191 billion, while all external sources added up to only $133.9 billion.

The full distribution of earnings would facilitate stock purchases on credit. Obviously, the faster earnings are paid out to a purchaser who is relying on those earnings to help pay for his stock, the sooner substantial stock holdings will be built up. The other principal consideration is the effect this move would have in encouraging and facilitating the financing of small businesses which need venture capital. When the management of a large corporation retains most of the year's profits and uses them for expansion, it is preventing full and open competition for available capital. Over the years, the practice has developed of paying out to the common stockholders a dividend merely large enough to keep them reasonably contented, with the rest of the profits being retained for capital. Of course, in the process, the individual stockholder's share becomes worth that much more, and, consequently, he has not really been deprived of a financial right. What he has been deprived of is the right to make his own decision on whether he would prefer to have his earnings reinvested in the same company or invested in some other company. If compulsory distribution of profits were adopted, there would be much more capital available for small, experimental, and adventuresome young businesses.

A related line of action would take the form of simplifying and reducing the expense of the issuance and transfer of stock. Particularly if the preceding suggestion were in any degree adopted, it would become important to streamline the stock issuance process, since new issues, particularly in small amounts, would become a much more prominent part of the capital-supplying source.

An argument against the full-distribution theory is that a certain amount of retained earnings is reasonable and desirable in the interests of efficiency. Moreover, the all-out prohibition of retained earnings is so drastic a departure that to make it a part of the overall program might seriously prejudice the chances of its adoption.

The best course might well take the form of a compromise measure under which the amount of allowable retained earnings would be limited in some degree without being altogether eliminated.

WHY PROGRESS SHARING SHOULD BE ACCEPTED

Historically, the impetus for profit sharing has come mostly from managers and owners. Under today's conditions, with the growth of the professional managerial group, there is no reason why managers should not promote widespread increase of profit sharing. Experience in hundreds of plans has built an impressive record of improved motivation of workers, reduction of waste in materials, elimination of costly work practices, smoother adjustment to technological dislocations, and generally increased quality and efficiency of workmanship. Moreover, since a large proportion of corporate executives are themselves enjoying the benefits of profit sharing and stock acquisition plans, they are scarcely in a position to resist the extension of this type of benefit and motivation to wage earners. The professional managers, if they do question progress sharing, would be more apt to do so as the custodians of the interests of stockholders.

The source of concern for the stockholder is the partial dilution of the value of shares that might result when they are distributed to employees without any corresponding payment in cash. The only answer to this fear is a demonstration that the improvements in efficiency, productivity, motivation, and stability resulting from such a plan more than offset the dilution in share values. Such studies as have been made appear to demonstrate that plans of this kind definitely benefit the stockholder. The Profit Sharing Research Foundation has published two volumes of studies entitled *The Stockholder and Employee Profit Sharing* (1960).

In these studies the fourteen largest department-store chains in the United States were analyzed in detail, seven of which were profit sharers and seven non-profit-sharers. The study concluded that "there was a positive correlation between the presence of an employee profit sharing plan and superior financial performance from the point of view of the stockholder." Taking the year 1952 as a base, with the figure 100 as the starting point, the index of earnings per common share for profit sharers rose by 1958 to 155.4 compared with 110.8 for non-profit-sharers. A few other comparative figures for 1958 are as follows:

	Profit Sharers	Non-Profit-Sharers
Net Income to Net Worth	11.36%	6.93%
Net Income to Sales	3.31%	2.43%
Company Earnings per Employee	$687.00	$461.00

The study of the sixteen largest food-store chains in the United States, which included eleven profit sharers and five non-profit-sharers, led to the same conclusion. In 1958 the index of earnings per common share, with 1952 equaling 100, was for the profit sharers 219.3 and for the non-profit-sharers only 168.5.

The other key items, corresponding to the table above, came out as follows in 1958:

	Profit Sharers	Non-Profit-Sharers
Net Income to Net Worth	13.83%	11.59%
Net Income to Sales	1.41%	1.15%
Company Earnings per Employee	$615.00	$408.00

On the part of organized labor, the endorsement of profit sharing by Walter Reuther and other officials of the United Automobile Workers in 1958 is the most significant indication of a new attitude toward these plans. As recently as 1949, the UAW-CIO Facts for Action attacked profit sharing with all the familiar labor arguments: workers would suffer losses in time of low profits or company losses; profit sharing is uncertain compared with fixed fringe benefits; the idea that workers could be made capitalists in any significant degree was scoffed at; the specter of the "speedup" was invoked; finally, and most fundamentally, collective bargaining and traditional union-management relations would be affected.

Basic to this concern is the assumption that profit sharing creates a conflict of interest in the individual worker. As long as labor-management relations were conceived of as a power struggle, many labor leaders were not anxious to see union members acquire a financial stake in the company itself. Obviously, if union strategy appeared to call for a protracted strike, and if the individual worker realized that this would not only eliminate the profits in which he hoped to share but even reduce the value of his existing stock holdings, the worker would think twice about voting for such a strike. On this view of labor relations, it is to the advantage of the union official to foster the idea that all good things come from the union, and that when the worker's lot is improved it is to the union and the union alone that the worker should be grateful. This pattern becomes confused when the worker begins to see benefits reaching him directly as a result of his participation in company progress.

For union officials to abandon this view for the one presently held by such an outstanding labor leader as Walter Reuther requires acceptance of the fact that labor relations are entering into a new phase in which the role of unions and labor officials must rise above that of mere line officers in a running battle with management. As early as 1958, Walter Reuther said in a statement printed in the *New Republic* (July 21, 1958):

> You take this profit sharing idea. This has frightened a lot of people because they don't understand why we proposed this. The profit sharing idea was not a demand; it was a mechanism. In the profit sharing scheme we're trying to find a rational means by which free labor and free manage-

FIGURE 4
EMPLOYEES' ATTITUDES TOWARDS PROFIT SHARING

(expressed in response to the question:
"Which . . . are the most important advantages
in making your company a good place to work?")

Advantages	GROUP	
	NON-UNION PROFIT SHARING EMPLOYEES	UNIONIZED PROFIT SHARING EMPLOYEES
Steady Employment	87%	87%
Profit Sharing Plan	85%	82%
Pension Benefits	80%	74%
Sickness and Accident Benefits	76%	69%
Hospital and Medical Insurance	72%	74%
Liberal Vacations	68%	68%
Good Pay Rates	61%	55%
Recreational Programs and Facilities	37%	23%

Source: Opinion Research Corporation, Executive Summary.

ment, sitting at the bargaining table, can attempt to work out in their relationship practical means by which you can equate the competing equities—in workers and stockholders and consumers.

The change of union attitudes toward profit sharing is spreading to other unions, as shown by the profit sharing agreements between the Saramar Aluminum Company and the United Steelworkers of America, and between the Emerson Electric Manufacturing Company and the International Union of Electrical Workers. Profit sharing is under serious study in other highly unionized industries, such as the missile industry, aircraft industry, and steel industry (*see* Fig. 4).

In general, the change in attitudes observable among labor union leaders may in part be attributable to the growing sense of union security. At a time when unions were fighting for their existence, or struggling to achieve and establish a level of bargaining power roughly equal to that of management, it was not surprising that some labor leaders viewed with apprehension anything that would detract from the undivided loyalty of union members. Although in some areas and some industries the struggle has not entirely passed out of this phase, for the most part the unions no longer need to conduct their affairs as if they were engaged in a continuous fight for their lives. They can move forward with confidence to the devising and executing of schemes that frankly rest upon the proposition that ultimately the surest guarantee of the worker's well-being is the well-being of the enterprise in which he is employed.

As word spreads of the success of such plans, it would be surprising if workers generally did not take the initiative in pressing for progress sharing. There are stories of impressive fortunes built up by ordinary employees under some of the older profit sharing plans. Every now and then we read in the papers about some little old lady who, as a result of staying with the Sears, Roebuck Plan during her working life, left an estate of several hundred thousand dollars. Under the Joslyn Plan, of the Joslyn Manufacturing and Supply Company of Chicago, which has been active for about forty-seven years, a typical account of an average employee would look like this:

Member's Contribution	$ 6,800
Company Contribution	20,883
Interest Earned by Fund	89,393
Total	$117,076

This estate has been built up under a plan in which the amount of sharing is about 15 percent of the wage. Within this 15-percent limit, which is the tax-deductible limit, it is not uncommon to find funds where, after fifteen years, the earnings, plus the annual profit share, plus the increase in value of the fund during the year, have been larger for one year than the employee's take-home pay for that same year.

From the wage earner's point of view, the decisive argument will be the success of these plans in improving the lot of the worker. The record at this time is a convincing one. The phenomenal rate of growth of the plans, and the very low termination rate—less than 2 percent of all plans in existence in 1961—provide objective proof of success. It is also possible to demonstrate that the adoption of profit sharing plans, far from cutting into other types of benefits, is more likely than not to be accompanied by better employee benefits than those in non-profit-sharing enterprises, including such benefits as production incentives, Christmas bonuses, thrift plans, and pensions.

On the whole, the reaction of workers who have participated in these plans resembles that of an old workman in a story told by Sir Geoffrey Shakespeare when introducing the Duke of Edinburgh for a talk at the British Industrial Co-Partnership Association. Sir Geoffrey said:

> A very great industrialist, the late Sir Malcolm Stewart, who was pioneering in co-partnership from the turn of the century, told me that when he started on a profit sharing scheme in the London Brick Company, he went down to Stewartby . . . to see how it had been received. He met an old workman, and he said to him: "Tell me, how do you like this profit sharing?" The old workman replied very gravely and in almost biblical phraseology: "Sir, surely goodness and mercy have followed me all the days of my life, but this is the first blinking time they have caught up with me."

THE AMERICAN CONCEPT OF LABOR RELATIONS

The progress sharing idea in fact represents a return to the indigenous American concept of labor relations.

The concept of a class struggle, developed by Marx and others to describe conditions observed in England, Germany, and elsewhere on the continent of Europe, never did fit the American scene. There were many reasons for this. One was the essential agrarian character of the American economy at a time when these theories were being developed. Another was the generally classless nature of the American society. Rising from poverty to success was the rule, rather than the exception, in the picture that Americans had of their society.

Then when the industrial phase began to gain momentum in the United States, the frontier was once more extended, and an economic factor was introduced into the equation which was completely overlooked in the calculations of Marx and such European economists as David Ricardo. As Bernard Dempsey, S.J., has demonstrated, the availablity of the option of striking out and making one's living and perhaps one's fortune on the frontier introduced a new determinant into the wage calculation.[5] The economic return to labor was no longer the result of a sheer supply-and-demand bargain between employer and employee. If this bargaining process drove the wage below a certain point, the wage earner always had the option to head for the frontier, where he could make his own way with a combination of capital (in the form of land) and personal labor applied to this capital to make it productive. The result was what Dempsey has called the "frontier wage," rather than a wage that was the inexorable product of the class struggle and the "iron law of wages."

Closely related to this factor is the American tradition that the key to improvement of the lot of the workingman is to increase, through greater production, the total stock of goods to be shared. Writers on economics such as Marx and his predecessors seemed to be preoccupied with distribution. One gets the impression that Marx conceived of the economic problem as if there were a more or less fixed quantity of goods to be distributed and that the problem was to take this stock of goods away from the capitalists and redistribute it more equitably to the proletariat. The American idea is well summarized in the words of a contemporary of Marx, Abraham Lincoln: "Let not him who is houseless pull down the house of another, but let him labor diligently and build one for himself." In short, the way to achieve not only equality but also prosperity for the worker is to have two houses where only one existed before. Because this greater production could only be achieved through the mutual effort of employer and employee, and since a market for this greater production could only be created by widespread purchasing power and good wages, the most accurate American concept of labor relations was that of the mutuality of ultimate interest of employer and employee.

The direct carry-over from the American frontier situation to the present proposal for progress sharing has been well developed by Father Dempsey. In place of the geographical frontier, we now have the frontier in our industrial society represented by organizational arrangements that will produce similar motivations and opportunities. Specifically, when workers own capital shares in industrial production and are entitled to share in the profits of the enterprise, we have again the combination of capital and direct opportunity to make capital productive that was present in the agricultural homestead.

PRIVATE PROPERTY AND DEMOCRACY

One of the most persistent themes running through the writings of John Adams, Thomas Jefferson, and other founders of American

---

5 Bernard W. Dempsey, *The Frontier Wage: The Economic Organization of Free Agents* (Chicago: Loyola University Press, 1960).

democracy is the idea that real democracy is possible only when individuals are substantial owners of property. For example, John Adams wrote to James Sullivan on May 26, 1776:

> Is it not equally true, that men in general, in every society, who are wholly destitute of property, are also too little acquainted with public affairs to form a right judgment, and too dependent upon other men to have a will of their own? . . . Harrington has shown that power always follows property. This I believe to be as infallible a maxim in politics, as that action and reaction are equal, is in mechanics. Nay, I believe we may advance one step farther, and affirm that the balance of power in a society, accompanies the balance of property in land. The only possible way, then, of preserving the balance of power on the side of equal liberty and public virtue, is to make the acquisition of land easy to every member of society; to make a division of land into small quantities, so that the multitude may be possessed of landed estates. If the multitude is possessed of the balance of real estate, the multitude will have the balance of power, and in that case the multitude will take care of the liberty, virtue, and interest of the multitude, in all acts of government. I believe these principles have been felt, if not understood, in the Massachusetts Bay, from the beginning. . . .

Ownership by the worker of a share in the industry of which he is a part has effects that are personal, national, and international.

There are personal effects because ownership of a share in what he is operating and producing once more restores to the worker, at least in some degree, the identification with his product that was lost when the handicraft was replaced by the factory. Psychologists have written of the alienation of worker from product that resulted, and of the evils that have flowed from this alienation. The worker who sees no connection between his efforts during working hours and any consequences of interest to himself is alienated indeed: the largest part of his life is meaningless; he is little better than a machine going through motions, working on someone else's product for someone else's profit. Whether he works well or badly, whether he contributes his human ingenuity to improve the work or not, whether he sets himself the standards of a craftsman or a hack, are all a matter of indifference, so long as he does enough to keep his job.

The national impact of progress sharing on political democracy lies in the close relationship between responsible citizenship and the ownership of property which was emphasized by the Founding Fathers, as already noted.

The third facet, that of the international significance of this proposal, lies in the fact that the achievement of the optimum combination of private enterprise and ownership by all Americans would demonstrate to the world that the American system can really deliver the kind of benefits that international communism promises but never produces.

The equating of ownership of capital by the state with ownership by individual persons is a major fallacy of communism. Marx had nothing against capital as such. Indeed, he stressed that it was from capital that the good things flowed which should belong to all workers. What he overlooked was that the only reliable way to get the benefits of capital into the hands of workers was literally to give them the capital itself directly and personally.

Putting capital in the hands of the state, as a sort of trustee for the workers, changes little: government officials, managers, and bureaucrats take the place of private capitalists, managers, and employers, while the worker remains as alienated as ever from the real benefits of ownership.

There is no reason to assume that the American private enterprise system has reached its optimum form. Indeed, there are forces at work, most conspicuously the impact of automation on employment, which promise to compel changes of some kind for better or for worse. The question is not whether changes are going to occur but whether inevitable change is to be the product of intelligent control of observable forces, rather than the random effect of these forces blindly working themselves out. Progress sharing offers a rational solution to some of the more urgent problems.

WEALTH AND HAPPINESS
IN
GREAT BOOKS OF THE WESTERN WORLD

Wealth is the principal concern of Adam Smith in *The Wealth of Nations* and of Karl Marx in *Capital*. But the interest of both authors is focused on the production and distribution of wealth, not on the nature of wealth and its relation to happiness. Smith expresses the ordinary notion of wealth when he notes that "every man is rich or poor according to the degree in which he can afford to enjoy the necessaries, conveniences, and amusements of human life" (GBWW, Vol. 39, p. 13a). Marx voices the promise of an industrial society when he says that it "creates those material conditions which alone can form the real basis of a higher form of society, a society in which the full and free development of every individual forms the ruling principle" (GBWW, Vol. 50, p. 292d). We can obtain some measure of the extent to which these conditions have already been satisfied from Smith's description of "the very meanest person in a civilised country":

> Compared, indeed with the more extravagant luxury of the great, his accommodation must no doubt appear extremely simple and easy; and yet it may be true, perhaps, that the accommodation of a European prince does not always so much exceed that of an industrious and frugal peasant as the accommodation of the latter exceeds that of many an African king, the absolute master of the lives and liberties of ten thousand naked savages (GBWW, Vol. 39, p. 6c–d).

Smith was writing this at the dawn of the industrial era, considerably before the appearance of what Professor Galbraith calls "the affluent society." If there was affluence then, compared with other times and places, he would find an undreamed-of abundance in the wealth that is now produced by industry operating under advanced technology.

The production and distribution of wealth is obviously no longer the problem it once was. But the proper use of wealth and its place in the pursuit of happiness still remains the problem that it has always been. It has become even more pressing now that more people enjoy greater wealth than ever before. For this reason, what the moralists, the theologians, and the philosophers have to say is more widely relevant today than it was in the past.

WEALTH: A MEANS, NOT AN END

For Aquinas, the happiness of this life remains at best imperfect when compared with the happiness that awaits us in heaven. Not everyone shares his faith and hope. Yet the place that he assigns to wealth in the

90

ADAM SMITH   JOHN STUART MILL   KARL MARX

pursuit of happiness would be generally recognized. Although it is necessary as a means, it cannot constitute the essence of happiness, and for the
reasons that Aquinas offers in discussing the question, "Whether man's
happiness consists in wealth":

> It is impossible for man's happiness to consist in wealth. For wealth
> is two-fold, as the Philosopher (Aristotle) says, natural and artificial.
> Natural wealth is that which serves man as a remedy for
> his natural wants, such as food, drink, clothing, conveyances, dwell-
> ings, and things of this kind, while artificial wealth is that which
> is not a direct help to nature, as money, but is invented by the art
> of man for the convenience of exchange and as a measure of
> things saleable.
>
> Now it is evident that man's happiness cannot consist in natural
> wealth. For wealth of this kind is sought as a support of human na-
> ture: consequently it cannot be man's last end, but rather is
> ordered to man as to its end. Therefore in the order of nature,
> all such things are below man, and made for him, according to
> Psalm 8.8: *Thou hast subjected all things under his feet.*
>
> And as to artificial wealth, it is not sought save for the sake of
> natural wealth, since man would not seek it except that by its means
> he procures for himself the necessaries of life. Consequently much
> less does it have the character of the last end. Therefore it is im-
> possible for happiness, which is the last end of man, to consist in
> wealth (*Summa Theologica*, GBWW, Vol. 19, p. 616a–b).

Just as it would be generally admitted that wealth is at best only a
means to happiness, so, too, it would be admitted and emphasized, at
least by philosophers, that wealth holds the lowest place among the
necessary means. Thus Plato writes:

> The care of riches should have the last place in our thoughts. For
> there are in all three things about which every man has an interest;
> and the interest about money, when rightly regarded, is the third

91

and lowest of them: midway comes the interest of the body; and
first of all, that of the soul (*Laws* V, GBWW, Vol. 7, pp. 694d–695a).

To place wealth in the lowest place is one way of noting that there are
things that it cannot help us to obtain. To place it below the goods of both
body and soul is to claim that there are qualities of body and soul that
wealth cannot provide. Among these are certainly a sound body and a
sane mind. The fact that these are frequently beyond the reach of any
amount of wealth shows its limitations.

Wealth, as Adam Smith emphasizes, "does not consist in money, or in
gold and silver; but in what money purchases, and is valuable only for
purchasing" (GBWW, Vol. 39, p. 186b). This is to claim that wealth is not
merely the wherewithal for obtaining the goods that are needed for life
and the good life, but rather these goods themselves. Wealth consists of
the economic goods of life—those external conditions, such as food,
shelter, health and the means of protecting and preserving it, education,
and time free from toil. Our society today is affluent in that the great
majority of people possess wealth in this sense of the term. This
does not mean that everyone owns productive property so as to be
independently "wealthy," but rather that the level of the general
welfare, measured by the goods enjoyed by the citizens, is higher than
ever before.

Yet even when it is identified with economic goods, or welfare, and
not merely with money, wealth still remains a means. This becomes obvious once we reflect that our huge educational system, representing vast
wealth in our society, can never provide more than an opportunity and
occasion for learning and understanding—that is, the conditions that a person needs for the pursuit of knowledge. Knowledge itself is a personal
achievement, not something that can be bought.

WEALTH AND INDEPENDENCE

Although it may be modest, the place that wealth occupies in the pursuit of happiness is, nonetheless, a real and necessary one. How
necessary it is may be seen by investigating the contribution that wealth
can make to the development of the individual. On this subject, John
Stuart Mill is especially eloquent when he treats "of individuality as one
of the elements of well-being." He writes:

> If it were felt that the free development of individuality is one of the
> leading essentials of well-being; that it is not only a co-ordinate
> element with all that is designated by the terms civilisation, instruc-
> tion, education, culture, but is itself a necessary part and condition
> of all those things; there would be no danger that liberty should be
> undervalued, and the adjustment of the boundaries between it and

ALEXANDER HAMILTON   IMMANUEL KANT

social control would present no extraordinary difficulty. But the evil
is, that individual spontaneity is hardly recognised by the common
modes of thinking as having any intrinsic worth, or deserving any
regard on its own account. . . . It is the privilege and proper condition of a human being, arrived at the maturity of his faculties, to
use and interpret experience in his own way. It is for him to find out
what part of recorded experience is properly applicable to his own
circumstances and character. . . .

He who lets the world, or his own portion of it, choose his plan
of life for him, has no need of any other faculty than the ape-like one
of imitation. He who chooses his plan for himself, employs all his
faculties. He must use observation to see, reasoning and judgment
to foresee, activity to gather materials for decision, discrimination to
decide, and when he has decided, firmness and self-control to hold
to his deliberate decision. And these qualities he requires and exercises exactly in proportion as the part of his conduct which he
determines according to his own judgment and feelings is a large
one. It is possible that he might be guided in some good path, and
kept out of harm's way, without any of these things. But what will
be his comparative worth as a human being? It really is of importance, not only what men do, but also what manner of men they
are that do it. Among the works of man, which human life is rightly
employed in perfecting and beautifying, the first in importance
surely is man himself. Supposing it were possible to get houses built,
corn grown, battles fought, causes tried, and even churches erected
and prayers said, by machinery—by automatons in human form—it
would be a considerable loss to exchange for these automatons even
the men and women who at present inhabit the more civilised parts
of the world, and who assuredly are but starved specimens of what
nature can and will produce. Human nature is not a machine to be
built after a model, and set to do exactly the work prescribed for

it, but a tree, which requires to grow and develop itself on all sides, according to the tendency of the inward forces which make it a living thing (GBWW, Vol. 43, pp. 294a–295b).

In the essay *On Liberty*, in which this passage occurs, Mill is arguing for liberty of opinion and action and for toleration of difference. He does not inquire into the material conditions of such liberty. Yet a good case can be made out for the claim that some measure of economic independence is absolutely essential for the liberty and individuality that Mill extols.

"In the main," Hamilton points out in *The Federalist*, "it will be found that a power over a man's support is a power over his will" (GBWW, Vol. 43, p. 219a). With dependence upon another for one's livelihood, there is always the possibility of being intimidated from doing, or even expressing, anything that might jeopardize its continuance. For this reason, it was generally held by the American Founding Fathers, as Professor Larson has noted in his essay, that a wide distribution of productive property is essential for a healthy and independent democracy.

The economic independence that ownership of productive property secures is used by Kant to distinguish active from passive citizenship:

> The apprentice of a merchant or tradesman, a servant who is not in the employ of the state, a minor (*naturaliter vel civiliter*), all women, and, generally, every one who is compelled to maintain himself not according to his own industry, but as it is arranged by others (the state excepted), are without civil personality, and their existence is only, as it were, incidentally included in the state. The woodcutter whom I employ on my estate; the smith in India who carries his hammer, anvil, and bellows into the houses where he is engaged to work in iron, as distinguished from the European carpenter or smith, who can offer the independent products of his labour as wares for public sale; the resident tutor as distinguished from the schoolmaster; the ploughman as distinguished from the farmer and such like, illustrate the distinction in question. In all these cases, the former members of the contrast are distinguished from the latter by being mere subsidiaries of the commonwealth and not active independent members of it, because they are of necessity commanded and protected by others, and consequently possess no political self-sufficiency in themselves (*The Science of Right*, GBWW, Vol. 42, p. 437a–b).

If complete happiness involves the full development of the individual, participation in political life, such as Kant's active citizen enjoys, would seem to be essential. Kant agrees with the Founding Fathers that for such activity property is the necessary material basis.

The connection between property and happiness is further illuminated by Aristotle's consideration of slavery. The chattel slave differs from the free man in being utterly without property. He does not own even himself, since as an individual he belongs to another. For this reason, according to Aristotle, he lacks the very possibility of happiness. "No one assigns to a slave a share in happiness," Aristotle writes, and then adds, "unless he assigns to him also a share in human life" (*Nicomachean Ethics* X, GBWW, Vol. 9, p. 431c). What the slave lacks, and what, in Aristotle's view, makes him a slave, is precisely independence and, also, along with it, the leisure that is needed for the pursuit of virtue and a life of political activity. For this reason, when in his *Politics* he comes to present his conception of the best society, he demands that the citizens "should be the owners of property" (*Politics* VII, GBWW, Vol. 9, p. 533c).

WEALTH—BUT NOT TOO MUCH

Although wealth or property is necessary for complete happiness, Aristotle argues that one must avoid excess in the acquisition of external goods:

> But, being a man, one will also need external prosperity; for our nature is not self-sufficient for the purpose of contemplation, but our body also must be healthy and must have food and other attention. Still, we must not think that the man who is to be happy will need many things or great things, merely because he cannot be supremely happy without external goods; for self-sufficiency and action do not involve excess, and we can do noble acts without ruling earth and sea; for even with moderate advantages one can act virtuously (this is manifest enough; for private persons are thought to do worthy acts no less than despots—indeed even more); and it is enough that we should have so much as that; for the life of the man who is active in accordance with virtue will be happy. Solon, too, was perhaps sketching well the happy man when he described him as moderately furnished with externals but as having done (as Solon thought) the noblest acts, and lived temperately; for one can with but moderate possessions do what one ought. Anaxagoras also seems to have supposed the happy man not to be rich nor a despot, when he said that he would not be surprised if the happy man were to seem to most people a strange person; for they judge by externals, since these are all they perceive (*Nicomachean Ethics* X, GBWW, Vol. 9, p. 433c–d).

Aristotle thus agrees with both More and Thoreau, in the works reprinted in Part IV of this volume, that wealth can become not an aid but an obstacle to the pursuit of happiness. It does so when it interferes with leisure; the rich, "hindered by the care of their property . . . are thereby prevented from taking part" in the political life of their community (*Politics* IV, GBWW, Vol. 9, 492c). On this view, the main function of wealth is to provide the security and freedom to pursue the activities that contribute most directly to happiness: not just politics, but all those liberal activities in which men can find their fulfillment. In this, Aristotle, no less than More and Thoreau, would agree with the statement of Tawney that if a man has important work to do, and enough time and income to enable him to do it properly, "he is in possession of as much happiness as is good for any of the children of Adam."[1]

1 *The Acquisitive Society*, reprinted in *The Great Ideas Today 1962*, p. 480d.

NOTE TO THE READER

The whole of Chapter 99 of the *Syntopicon* is devoted to the idea of wealth. All of it, and especially the introduction, will be illuminating to any reader interested in the subject. But for the subjects dealt with in this symposium some of the topics and subtopics are more immediately informative than others.

The elements and different kinds of wealth are dealt with in the passages referred to under WEALTH 1. The kinds, uses, and ownership of property are discussed in the passages cited under WEALTH 7. Discussions of the right to property and the question of economic justice can be found by consulting LABOR 7b and JUSTICE 8.

On the relation of wealth to happiness, the reader should see WEALTH 10 which deals with the moral aspects of wealth and poverty. WEALTH 10a provides references on the nature of wealth as a good, its place in the order of goods, and its relation to happiness, while WEALTH 10b deals with the question of the limits to the acquisition of wealth. HAPPINESS 2b(1) might also be consulted for discussions of the relation of the goods of fortune to happiness. The contribution of wealth to the general welfare is considered in the texts pointed out under STATE 7a.

Wealth and property in relation to different forms of government is the subject of WEALTH 9f, which lists references to the bearing of wealth on democracy. What discussion there is in *Great Books* on the issues between capitalism and socialism can be located by consulting DEMOCRACY 4a(2).

The symposium as a whole bears on the question of economic progress. Progress in both economic efficiency and justice is the subject of WEALTH 12. PROGRESS 3 is devoted entirely to economic progress, considered under three subtopics: the increase of opulence in 3a; the improvement of the status and conditions of labor in 3b; and man's progressive conquest of the forces of nature in 3c.

FURTHER READINGS

BERLE, ADOLPH A. *The Twentieth Century Capitalist Revolution*. New York: Harcourt, Brace & Co., 1954.
———. *Power Without Property: A New Development in American Political Economy*. New York: Harcourt, Brace & Co., 1959.
———. *The American Economic Republic*. New York: Harcourt, Brace & World, Inc., 1963.
DEMPSEY, BERNARD W. *The Frontier Wage: The Economic Organization of Free Agents*. Chicago: Loyola University Press, 1960.
FRIEDMAN, ROSE. *Poverty: Definition and Measurement*. Washington: American Enterprise Institute, 1965.
GALBRAITH, JOHN KENNETH. *The Affluent Society*. Boston: Houghton Mifflin Co., 1958.
HECKSCHER, AUGUST. *The Public Happiness*.
New York: Atheneum Publishers, 1962.
KELSO, LOUIS O. and ADLER, MORTIMER J. *The Capitalist Manifesto*. New York: Random House, Inc., 1958.
———. *The New Capitalists*. New York: Random House, Inc., 1961.
MYRDAL, GUNNAR. *Challenge to Affluence*. New York: Random House, Inc., Pantheon Books, Inc., 1963.
STRACHEY, JOHN. *Contemporary Capitalism*. New York: Random House, Inc., 1956.
THEOBALD, ROBERT. *The Challenge of Abundance*. New York: Clarkson N. Potter, Inc., 1961.
———. *Free Men and Free Markets*. New York: Clarkson N. Potter, Inc., 1963 (New York: Doubleday Anchor Books, 1965).

WORK AND LEISURE
IN
GREAT BOOKS OF THE WESTERN WORLD

Work and leisure are always thought of as opposed to each other. If one is at work, he is by that very fact not at leisure. A leisure class is a class that does not work, and does not have to work. As an extension of this same way of thinking, work becomes identified with activity as such, and leisure then comes to mean free time, that is, a period of time in which one does not have to do anything. Hence also, by a still further extension, leisure gets to mean idleness. Work is then equated with being occupied or employed, and leisure with being unoccupied or unemployed. We thus face the paradoxical conclusion that as society provides more leisure for more people, it also produces more unemployed.

Such a conclusion is as uncomfortable as it is paradoxical. A society in which the great majority of the people had literally nothing to do would be a bored society, not a great society. Hence, it is not without significance that many people are now calling for a reexamination of the meaning and nature of work and leisure. Toward such a reexamination, the *Great Books*, especially those written by the ancients who were privileged to belong to a leisure class, can make a distinct contribution. In particular, they enable us to make and develop a threefold distinction between: (1) leisure and free time; (2) leisure and subsistence-work; and (3) leisure and play.

LEISURE AND FREE TIME

The first distinction is illuminated by the following passage from Aristotle's *Politics*, where he is discussing the best society:

> The whole of life is further divided into two parts, business and leisure, war and peace, and of actions some aim at what is necessary and useful, and some at what is honourable. And the preference given to one or the other class of actions must necessarily be like the preference given to one or other part of the soul and its actions over the other; there must be war for the sake of peace, business for the sake of leisure, things useful and necessary for the sake of things honourable. . . . For men must be able to engage in business and go to war, but leisure and peace are better; they must do what is necessary and indeed what is useful, but what is honourable is better (*Politics* VII, GBWW, Vol. 9, p. 538a–b).

Leisure, in this passage, is grouped with peace and with actions that aim at the honorable; it is identified as that for the sake of which business and compulsory or useful actions are done. Happiness itself, for Aristotle, consists in activity. The same is true of leisure. In fact, leisure is one of the main constituents of a happy life. The active character of leisure, in Aristotle's view, is more prominent in the original Greek than in the English translation. To contrast leisure with "business" connotes too readily that leisure is merely not being busy—"business" being the positive notion of which leisure is merely the negation. But in Aristotle's Greek, it is the other way round. "Leisure" is the positive term (*scholé*), and its opposite is "nonleisure" (*ascholé*), which is here translated as "business."

Aristotle's view would stand out more clearly if "leisure" in English were a verb as well as a noun, as it is in Greek. Thus it is perfectly natural for Aristotle to talk about the "activity of leisuring" and to claim that "to leisure is better and more perfect than to nonleisure." He may sometimes use "leisure" (*scholé*) as a noun to mean time free from work. But there is no implication that leisure is a mere privation, mere lack of occupation, or idleness. In fact, the sense is all the other way. Leisure is highly active. As we shall see, he wants man "to leisure well" (*scholazein kalos*). For him, there would be nothing paradoxical, as there is for us, in speaking of "leisuring long and hard" and being "tired and worn out from leisuring."

Leisure, for Aristotle, is honorable or noble, whereas work, he says, is "useful and necessary." Yet he also maintains, as we shall see, that leisure, too, is a necessary activity. Obviously, work and leisure must be necessary in two different ways. In fact, we can distinguish three different ways in which an activity may be necessary for us. Some activities are absolutely necessary and cannot be omitted or eliminated, given the kind of creature man is; such are the biological activities of eating, sleeping, and the like. Other activities are necessary but can be eliminated, provided other ways are available for achieving the same result; such is the work of producing food, shelter, and all the economic goods that we need for life. This is work that can be escaped if we possess sufficient wealth or productive property to obtain the necessary goods without working. Finally, some activities are necessary not for life, but for the good life; these might be said to be morally necessary, whereas the previous activities are biologically or economically necessary.

Aristotle, in the passage quoted above, is evidently distinguishing leisure from those activities that are economically necessary—the activities we must engage in just to remain alive. We are not free to do them or leave them undone. Time spent on such compulsory activities is not free time.

Leisure, in contrast, occupies our free time. We pursue it in the time that remains free after we have met the necessary demands of living. This fact helps to explain why leisure is sometimes confused with free time it-

ARISTOTLE   VIRGIL   SAINT THOMAS AQUINAS

self. Free time is a condition for leisure. If we had no free time, if all our time were consumed in satisfying merely the biological and economic needs of the body, we would not be able to engage in leisure activities.

The fact that leisure is dependent upon free time is no reason, however, for identifying the two. Thoreau went to Walden Pond to reduce his work to a minimum and found that working six weeks a year was sufficient to provide him with food and shelter. But he did not so drastically reduce his work merely in order to do nothing. He reduced his work load because he had more important things *to do*. Being at leisure was for him anything but being inactive, as his account of life at Walden eloquently testifies.

LEISURE AND SUBSISTENCE-WORK

Leisure is not opposed to work as inactivity to activity. What, then, is the basis of the opposition between them? To answer this question, it is helpful to consider the simplest form of work. Perhaps the simplest (if not, in fact, also the original) form of work is that of a man working with his hands to provide for his daily sustenance. According to Aquinas, manual labor can be understood as standing for "all human occupations by which man lawfully gains a livelihood." This labor may have subsidiary aims, such as supplying a remedy for idleness, a curb of concupiscence, or a surplus for almsgiving, but its main purpose, according to Aquinas, is to provide food to sustain life (GBWW, Vol. 20, p. 667a, c). We might well name this form of work after its primary end and call it subsistence-work.

In the past, subsistence-work has always been associated with toil and drudgery. The *Georgics* of Virgil, for example, are devoted to celebrating the life of the farmer. That life, as Virgil pictures it, has its delights. But work is not one of them. Although not without its satisfactions and com-

99

pensations, work is usually described as hard and painful, a laborious drudgery. "Work has conquered all," he declares, but it is only as "remorseless and under the spur of harsh necessity" (GBWW, Vol. 13, p. 41a, lines 145-146). Virgil's adjective here is the Latin word *improbus*, and this means not only remorseless and persistent, but also insatiable, bad, and disliked. Labor is usually associated with what is hard and painful, and with what one would gladly avoid if one could, along with disease, and sad old age, and death (*ibid*. p. 69a, lines 67-68). Labor appears with the same associates in the *Aeneid*, where it is shown on the outskirts of the "ghostly realms of Dis," accompanied also by grief and care, fear, and famine, and loathly want (*ibid*. p. 218b, lines 274-276).

Virgil's description of subsistence-work offers further means of distinguishing it from leisure activity. The drudgery lies not only in its being hard and strenuous, but even more in its being recurrent and repetitive; it has to be done over and over again. For this reason its compensation lies not within the activity itself, but in its extrinsic product or result. All these characteristics are caught and summed up in the famous lines in *Georgic* I in which Virgil declares that except for "patient toil," all things, "by fate impelled, speed on to the worse, and, backward borne, glide from us, just as an oarsman rowing his boat against the current, need but relax his arms a moment and with headlong force the current sweeps him down the hurrying tide" (*ibid*. p. 42b, lines 200-203).

Work in the sense of subsistence-work is obviously an evil, and it is not difficult to understand why men should see in its necessity a sign of punishment for some ancient wrong or sin. As Aristotle notes: "That in a well-ordered state the citizens should have leisure and not have to provide for their daily wants is generally acknowledged, but there is a difficulty in seeing how this leisure is to be attained" (*Politics* II, GBWW, Vol. 9, p. 465c). For him, as for the ancient writers in general, such work should be left to slaves, so that the citizens might be free to devote themselves to leisure activities.

In one place in his *Politics*, Aristotle declares, with prophetic insight, that slaves would no longer be necessary if men possessed automatic machinery: "If every instrument could accomplish its own work, obeying or anticipating the will of others, like the statues of Daedalus, or the tripods of Hephaestus, . . . if, in like manner, the shuttle would weave and the plectrum touch the lyre without a hand to guide them, chief workmen would not want servants, nor masters slaves" (*ibid*. p. 447b-c).

We now do possess automated slaves, and nowhere have the results been so dramatic as in agriculture, the basic work of subsistence. We have learned how to produce increasing quantities of food with ever decreasing numbers of men, who thus have been released for other pursuits, and even those still engaged in the production of food have little of the pain and drudgery that once characterized the work of the farmer.

GBWW on Work and Leisure

Leisure, as we have seen, is not to be confused with free time. It is an activity or use of free time. In this it differs from subsistence-work. Leisure is like such work in being a serious activity. To further characterize it, we need to see how it differs from other free activities, that is, from other uses of our free time. Here again Aristotle merits consideration. As already noted, he regards work, or "business," as a means, serving leisure as an end. Hence, for a fuller understanding of leisure, we need to consider activities that are pursued as ends, *i.e.*, intrinsically worth doing for their own sake. He provides an analysis of such activities in the following passage from the *Ethics*:

> Those activities are desirable in themselves from which nothing is sought beyond the activity. And of this nature virtuous actions are thought to be; for to do noble and good deeds is a thing desirable for its own sake. Pleasant amusements also are thought to be of this nature; we choose them not for the sake of other things; for we are injured rather than benefited by them, since we are led to neglect our bodies and our property. . . . Happiness . . . does not lie in amusement; it would, indeed, be strange if the end were amusement, and one were to take trouble and suffer hardship all one's life in order to amuse oneself. For, in a word, everything that we choose we choose for the sake of something else—except happiness, which is an end. Now to exert oneself and work for the sake of amusement seems silly and utterly childish. But to amuse oneself in order that one may exert oneself, as Anacharsis puts it, seems right; for amusement is a sort of relaxation, and we need relaxation because we cannot work continuously. Relaxation, then, is not an end; for it is taken for the sake of activity (*Ethics* X, GBWW, Vol. 9, p. 431a–c).

Aristotle is not denying here that a person may subjectively and in his own mind pursue amusement or play for its own sake, without thinking of any further purpose. Men play golf and cards and go to the movies without needing any further justification than the activities themselves. They do so for the pleasure they obtain from them, and pleasure is itself an end of action needing no further justification.

Play, however, is not only and wholly an end. It also serves as a means; in fact, we need it as a means because of the weakness of the flesh. Aristotle is pointing this out when he notes that play and amusement perform a therapeutic function. We are incapable of working or "leisuring" continuously and must turn aside, from time to time, for relaxation, recuperation, recreation. Play for such purposes is therapeutic and a means to other activities.

Yet Aristotle's main reason for not identifying leisure with play lies elsewhere; the point is not that play is a means as well as an end, whereas leisure is wholly an end. Play is not serious enough, Aristotle claims, to count as the end of life. He expands upon this point in another text in which he also further develops the meaning of leisure:

> Nature herself, as has been often said, requires that we should be able, not only to work well, but to use leisure well; for, as I must repeat once again, the first principle of all action is leisure. Both are required, but leisure is better than occupation and is its end; and therefore the question must be asked, what ought we to do when at leisure? Clearly we ought not to be amusing ourselves, for then amusement would be the end of life. But if this is inconceivable, and amusement is needed more amid serious occupations than at other times (for he who is hard at work has need of relaxation, and amusement gives relaxation, whereas occupation is always accompanied with exertion and effort), we should introduce amusements only at suitable times, and they should be our medicines, for the emotion which they create in the soul is a relaxation, and from the pleasure we obtain rest. But leisure of itself gives pleasure and happiness and enjoyment of life, which are experienced, not by the busy man, but by those who have leisure. For he who is occupied has in view some end which he has not attained; but happiness is an end, since all men deem it to be accompanied with pleasure and not with pain (*Politics* VIII, GBWW, Vol. 9, p. 543a–b).

Thus, according to Aristotle, it is by "leisuring well" that we enjoy happiness. In fact, leisure, for him, *is* happiness. Happiness is a serious activity and, hence, not to be equated with play or amusement. Not the playboy, but the virtuous man is the happy man. For Aristotle the virtues include both the moral and intellectual excellences that develop and perfect both the individual and society, including the activities of love and friendship. They might be called simply the goods of the spirit and of civilization.

To identify leisure with virtuous activity, in Aristotle's sense, implies that it is obligatory, but obligatory morally, and not physically, as subsistence-work is. Play or amusement is not obligatory or necessary in a moral sense, although it may be necessary physically, in that we are so constructed as to be incapable of continuous serious activity. It is simply desirable.

The meaning of leisure is thus clarified by comparing and contrasting it with work and play. Leisure is like both work and play in being an activity, a use of time, and not just the absence of doing anything. It is like work, and unlike play, in being both serious and necessary. But it is not necessary in the same way that work is. Work, understood as that which is needed for our subsistence, is physically necessary, necessary to support life; leisure activity is morally necessary, indispensable for the good life.

In fact, work, as distinguished from play, can be considered as having two forms: subsistence-work and leisure-work. The first of these has its compensations outside of itself, in its product or reward; it is also a compulsory or unfree work which, because of its drudgery, should be lessened as much as possible; and, in fact, is being eliminated through the use of machinery. The second (that is, leisure-work) is intrinsically rewarding and would be pursued even without extrinsic compensation; it is an activity of our free time. In these two respects, leisure is similar to play and opposed to subsistence-work.

The way our life is organized today makes it extremely difficult to find activities that exemplify one and only one of these three kinds of activity. Most work for most people is a combination of subsistence-work and leisure-work—in some respects intrinsically satisfying and yet something for which we also receive an extrinsic compensation. So, too, our play and amusement is often mixed with leisure activity, since it involves both love and friendship. Yet the mere fact that our experience compounds work, play, and leisure is no justification for confusing these important parts of life as though they were not profoundly different from one another.

Once we have succeeded in clarifying and distinguishing them, we can see the relation of work and leisure, on the one hand, to wealth and happiness, on the other. Subsistence-work is pursued for the sake of the economic goods that it obtains. But wealth consists in economic goods, understood broadly as covering whatever is needed to maintain life. Both work and wealth are sought as means to an end beyond themselves. That end, in the most general and also the most ultimate sense, is happiness, and happiness is achieved in and through leisure activity.

NOTE TO THE READER

The whole of Chapter 44 of the *Syntopicon* is devoted to LABOR. All of it, and especially the introductory essay, will be of interest to anyone seeking to further his understanding of work and leisure. LABOR 1*b* collects references to discussions in the *Great Books* dealing with labor, leisure, and happiness. The pain of labor and its social necessity are the concerns of topics 1*c* and 1*d*. Passages on the nature of work and the kinds of work can be found by consulting LABOR 2 and 3.

Further references to what *Great Books of the Western World* have to say about the pleasures of play and diversion are cited under PLEASURE AND PAIN 4*d*.

All the writers in the foregoing symposium deal with the question of unemployment. References to what the *Great Books* have to say on this subject may be found in LABOR 7*e*.

Automation is a very recent development. Even the word is only a few years old. Yet automation itself is but the most recent effect of the impact of science on human life. On this subject, the *Syntopicon* provides references in SCIENCE 1*b*(2) and WEALTH 6*e* and 8*c*.

It might also be noted that both More and Thoreau, in the works reprinted in Part IV of this volume, have much to say that bears directly on work, play, and leisure.

FURTHER READINGS

ANDERSON, NELS. *Work and Leisure*. London: Routledge & Kegan Paul, Ltd., 1961.

ARENDT, HANNAH. *The Human Condition*. Chicago: University of Chicago Press, 1958.

BELL, DANIEL. *Work and Its Discontents* (1956). Reprinted in *The End of Ideology*, rev. ed. New York: Collier Books, 1962.

FRIEDMANN, EUGENE A. and HAVIGHURST, ROBERT J., *et al. The Meaning of Work and Retirement*. Chicago: University of Chicago Press, 1954.

GRAZIA, SEBASTIAN DE. *Of Time, Work, and Leisure*. New York: The Twentieth Century Fund, 1962.

KAPLAN, MAX. *Leisure in America: A Social Inquiry*. New York: John Wiley & Sons, Inc., 1960.

LARRABEE, ERIC and MEYERSOHN, ROLF (eds.). *Mass Leisure*. New York: Free Press of Glencoe, 1958.

LEVENSTEIN, AARON. *Why People Work*. New York: Collier Books, 1964.

PIEPER, JOSEF. *Leisure, the Basis of Culture*. Translated by A. DRU. New York: Pantheon Books, 1952.

STEERE, DOUGLAS VAN. *Work and Contemplation*. New York: Harper & Bros., 1957.

Contemporary Aspects of a Great Idea

Milton Mayer

On Death

Death is the one idea that has no history. Human experience has affected every other, not just in the exact sciences or in mathematics, but in every field. Justice, Love, State, World, even Man, even Life, have something fundamental to be said about them that was not (and could not have been) said of old. Only Death stands unmoved by man's relentless compulsion to know.

The paper-thin bibliography of the subject is eloquent testimony to the invincibility of our ignorance. We do not know what to say about Death because we do not know what to think about it, and we do not know what to think about it because we do not know what it is. Of all the ideas Mark Twain says the Greeks stole from us, this is the one they stole entire. It is the only area of human wonderment in which there is intellectual despair, all the deeper in view of the stupendous advances that have been made in medicine and its related fields. Every day's paper tells us of the millionaire attended by the most eminent physicians and dead at fifty, or forty, or thirty—so far short of the biblical three score and ten.

One explanation of the limited discussion of Death is that it is generally viewed as a negation of an idea—the idea of Life—rather than an idea in itself. And even in this respect it is singular. There are other ideas (Ignorance, for instance, or Evil) that as negations appear to stand to their opposites (Knowledge, Good) as Death appears to stand to Life; but the appearance is deceptive. Ignorance, for example, has the character of remediable deprivation, Evil of having an at least arguable existence of its own. But death—except in theology and (in a technical sense) in law and medicine—is commonly regarded as an irremediable deprivation, possessed of no trace of existential reality.

But it is easier than that to explain the rarity of death *qua* death in the tradition of metaphysical, moral, and philosophical discourse. All such discourse requires a starting point which in death is missing: the report of common experience. We may acknowledge the validity of the modern physiologist's assertion that "it is impossible to define life without death";

but death is impossible to describe, much less define. The enigma of the one enigmatizes the other. Here is the most important of all the facts of life, and we cannot begin a discussion of it. And because we cannot begin a discussion of it, our discussion of life is balked.

We can ruminate and speculate and dream—and how persistently even the most prosaic man dreams of it—but we cannot think of death. Death belongs to the poets. Whoever writes of it writes poetry, however ably or ineptly he writes it, however pretentiously he lards his poetry with empiricism. Dante, Shakespeare, Milton, Goethe; Hawthorne, Melville, Tolstoy, Mann—these are our foremost authorities on death, along with the little child with the unanswered question, "Where do we go when we die?"

What is death? Why, death is a "fell sergeant" and "an end of woes," a "curse" and a "cure," a "veil," a "gulf," a "valley," an "old nurse," and a "drunken sleep"; an "untimely frost" and a "dearest friend"; yes, and a "wall" and a "doorway," and a "night" and a "daybreak." What is death? Death is "cold," it is "grand," it is "abhorred," it is "soft," it is "lovely," "easeful," "delicate," "stealthy," "foul," and "fiendish." Say you Yea or say you Nay, you say it to the poets who scrutinize it as nearly as a man can, who burn their candles and their wits to search it, smell it, taste it, embrace it, and at last be embraced by it.

Ours is the Age of Man, Man the Knower, Man the Doer, Man the Master. All the greater, then, his frustration. There are certain limited conditions under which he can prolong life for weeks or months or even, on occasion, years; *this* is on the whole new. There are still broader conditions under which he can fend off the environmental predisposition to early death that is due to dietary deficiency. There are very broad conditions under which he can reduce or eliminate suffering. But Death still comes. The confidence that stubborn cancer will yield its secret abounds, that Death will yield *its* is heard nowhere. The Greek philosopher's tidy assertion that "Man is the measure of all things" is far less arrogant now than in the fifth century before Christ, but Death comes. Man is the measure of all things, but Death is the measure of Man.

The Age of Man has had a profound and novel effect upon the traditional conditions of Death, and this in three spectacular ways. Longevity, secularization, and total war distinguish us from all of our forebears in their availability to the general run of men. And this availability is both cause and effect of the sudden flowering, at the end of the eighteenth century, of the biblical plea for the dignity of the individual and the sanctity of every least human life. The privileged bones of the past rattled their protest—though Death itself doubtless chuckled— when the authors of the American Declaration of Independence proclaimed the inalienable right of man to life.

But social reformation, diverting man's awe from providence to progress, was largely nonreligious, and even antireligious. Expressions like "reverence for life" found a flamboyant response. It may be doubted that men were becoming more reverential toward other men than they had been, but there was no doubt that in the advanced societies they were transferring their worship from the Living God, Whose handiwork was Life and Death, to the Living Man, whose handiwork was A Better Life.

The promise of man's sufficiency in the temporal order necessarily vitiated his sense of subsistence in the eternal. By the end of the last century the schism between intellectualism and fideism had become a dogma: The thinker was the skeptic, and the devout were the unregenerate (or stubborn) victims of ancient superstition. It wasn't Marx, but Man, who rejected faith as a kind of utopiate and identified secularism with civilization. There is not much current quarrel, in the advanced cultures, with the verdict of Karl Jaspers, the contemporary German philosopher: "The traditional religions are becoming untenable to an increasingly large number of people: almost all dogmas and revelation in its exclusive claim to absolute truth are disbelieved. The *de facto* unchristian lives of the majority of Christians is a criticism to which it is impossible to close one's ears."[1]

More than one paradox attended the assertion of human dignity. The Industrial Revolution reduced the once independent contractor—even the miserable farm tenant—to the status of a disposable appendage to the machine. The "junk heap" of worn-out and cast-off and interchangeable men rose alongside the mountainous profession of respect for the status

1 *The Origin and Goal of History* (New Haven: Yale University Press, 1953), Part II, chap. 2.

MILTON MAYER

Milton Mayer claims "in all modesty to know as much about death as any man alive." As a journalist in Chicago from 1925 until 1937 he reported on executions, murders, and suicides. From 1937 to 1947 he taught at the University of Chicago and, after that, became a free-lance journalist. His articles have appeared in many magazines, and a collection of them was published in 1964 under the title What Can a Man Do? *In 1964 he became Professor of English at the University of Massachusetts. Mr. Mayer was born in 1908 in Chicago. His time is divided between Amherst, Massachusetts, and Carmel, California, and frequent trips to Europe.*

of man as man. Now, with automation, he can be "got rid of" altogether, occupationally consigned to death; and with the computer, he loses the personal recognition that even the house slave of old enjoyed, his very name; he is identified like a corpse in the morgue.

Still, this tagged and numbered man enjoyed a stupendous increase of goods, leisure, and mobility, even if these mass-produced and mass-distributed blessings contributed to the effacement of the individual personality in which dignity resides. Life was sweeter. Man's resistance to morbidity—to the expectation of a hard life and a hard death—was stiffened. And then came the cataclysmic turn, exactly fifty years ago. Its name was Verdun.

For a hundred years, beginning at Waterloo, the doctrine of the dignity of man was ascendant while the grotesque indignity of death went on claiming a man at a time (and once in a while a large or small batch). We may assume that man's impertinent claim to dignity was an affront to the ancient Enemy. But we may also assume that the Enemy was too old a hand at the game to spend a century of evenings sitting by his ice-cold fire and nursing a pique. If he would bring modern man to heel, he would have to modernize his own procedures and unobtrusively retool. At Verdun he unveiled his own assembly line for mass production.

Two million strapping young men—the apotheosis of Life—had been driven into a colosseum without spectators and handed the triumphant product of the Age of Man, the machine gun, and set at each other's throats at a distance too great for the distinction of persons or the bestial dignity of the two combatants in the Roman arena. One million of them dutifully killed the other million, and when the million were dead a few hundred yards of mud and blood had changed hands a half-dozen times and the world acknowledged Death as the winner. Mass man had met his mass master and human dignity its indignification.

Nothing like Verdun had ever happened before; the most devastating of all prior calamities was the Great Plague of Europe, which killed a fourth of the people of that continent in the fourteenth century. But its twenty-year toll was "only" some 25 million lives; Verdun's over twenty years would have been of the order of 220 million. And Verdun was man's own willing and man's own contrivance and man's own doing—a point of which (we may be sure) Death took judicial notice for future reference. When it was all over on Armistice Day (now Veterans Day), and the lark, still bravely singing of life, was able again to make itself heard, there were eight and a half million bits and pieces of soldiers who could be counted (if not found); they were numbered. But so handsome was the reaper's swath in those four years that the numberless civilians are forever assessed at a variable ten to twenty millions.

Was Verdun man's surrender to death? Would life ever recover from its macabre commitment there? Did modern man—the most modern man

of all, the German, the Frenchman, the Englishman, the American—
want to kill and die? Had death overtaken life?

Sigmund Freud reflected somberly on the condition of civilized man
and the status of the elemental lust to kill in the progress of civilization:
"When the frenzied conflict of this war shall have been decided, every
one of the victorious warriors will joyfully return to his home, his wife
and his children, undelayed and undisturbed by any thought of the
enemy he has slain either at close quarters or by distant weapons of
destruction. It is worthy of note that such primitive races as still inhabit
the earth, who are undoubtedly closer than we to primitive man, act
differently in this respect, or did so act until they came under the influence
of our civilization. The savage—Australian, Bushman, Tierra del Fuegan—
is by no means a remorseless murderer; when he returns victorious from
the war-path he may not set foot in his village nor touch his wife until
he has atoned for the murders committed in war by penances which are
often prolonged and toilsome. . . . Behind this superstition lurks a vein of
ethical sensitiveness which has been lost by us civilized men."[2]

Nothing like Verdun had ever happened before. But something like it,
and even more congenial to Death, was to happen again, and that within
a generation: At Auschwitz, modern mass man built a machine for killing
masses of innocents and in that one installation killed four million of
them (and another two million elsewhere). This mass extermination of
the unarmed mass by men stripped of every trait but massiveness was a
long, long stride from Verdun. Death had never done better. But before
the stench of the secret ovens could offend the nostrils of the rest of the
civilized world the Nuclear Age began in Asia. August 6, the city of
Hiroshima: twenty of its two hundred doctors able to attend the dying,
and 1,650 of its 1,750 nurses killed or maimed; and August 9, the city of
Nagasaki: six hundred of its eight hundred medical students killed, and
forty-four of its forty-seven hospitals destroyed.

Death no longer "struck." Man struck—one man attached to an unseen machine touched a button and hadn't even to see what he'd done.
Modern Death had only to set the computers, read the numbers, and
affix the tags.

Alexander conquered the world and died for want of a four-day dose
of drugstore antibiotics; more justification for twentieth-century
man's defiance of the Last Enemy than helpless Alexander had. But
twentieth-century man with his antibiotics seemed to have lost Alexander's will to live. What were the Civil War's 600,000 dead to the
Second World War's 60 million? Or to the Third World War's 600
million?

2 *Thoughts on War and Death*, GBWW, Vol. 54, p. 764c–d.

On Death

Has the Bomb changed man's attitude toward death? Political scientist Hans J. Morgenthau says that it hasn't—we go on "thinking and acting as though nothing of radical import had happened"—*but that it has changed death itself*: "The significance of the possibility of nuclear death is that it radically affects the meaning of death, of immortality, of life itself. . . . [Nuclear destruction] destroys the meaning of death by depriving it of its individuality." The prospect that death can at last be inflicted upon the whole of mankind suggests the ultimate irony of the Organization Man: Let's all go together and nobody will be out of step with anybody else.

With the end of mankind a ready possibility—even a probability of considerable weight—the meaning of death is indeed transformed. It not only loses its individuality, as Professor Morgenthau points out, but its sociality. Men think of dying meaningfully for home and family, or for country, or for liberty or glory or morality . . . or dignity. But all of these values are outlawed by the assurance that to attempt to defend them by thermonuclear means is at once to destroy them. Human dignity presupposes a human race and a human measure. A nonhuman world—a dead world—would honor equally the patriot and the traitor. It would be a world of homogeneous heroes, or, equally, of cowards and fools; a world in which death, like Macbeth's life, would signify nothing.

A few years ago the *Journal of Gerontology* (January, 1961) published a symposium on "death attitudes." The contributors agreed that there was a prevalent rejection, among modern Americans, of the thought of dying. Death, said sociologist Robert L. Fulton, has become "an infringement upon our right to life, liberty, and the pursuit of happiness. . . . I would say that as never before we choose to disguise it and pretend that it is not the basic condition of all life." True, more and more people die old. But true, too, more and more people die in hospitals or "rest homes," and die alone.

Modern death isolated in the drugged asepsis of the hospital is one of the symbols of existentialism, that shapeless "philosophy" which finds each individual alienated from all the rest. None of existentialism's exponents (including the celebrated Frenchman Jean-Paul Sartre) has attempted, or is likely to attempt, a systematic statement of this "new" view of life and death—a view which seems to combine the more inclement aspects of Antisthenes' Cynic, Epictetus' Stoic, and Plotinus' Sage with the sorrowing sighs of Ecclesiastes.

Man's existentialist struggle to escape from the meaninglessness of life ends in the absurdity of death, and estrangement from his kind is the dominant condition of both. "Man," says Sartre, "is alone, abandoned. . . ." Alone, abandoned . . . in his human dignity.

Animal psychologists are fascinated by the occasional behavior of a mouse cornered by a cat. The game, as the cat sees it (and who knows?—perhaps the mouse, too), has gone on until the cat is bored with it. The mouse seems to sense that his time has come. The cat sits back on his haunches and stares at his victim. And the mouse proceeds to preen himself sedately, like a fop before the mirror. He smoothes his coat and his whiskers with his forepaws—and takes his exquisite time about it. The cat seems to appreciate the gesture, and never moves a muscle. At last the mouse's preparation is finished, and he faces the cat. He is ready for death, with dignity.

IMMORTALITY

Immortality is the hinge on which death turns. If man survives death, death is one thing (as, indeed, is life); if he doesn't, it's another. The most eminent modern theorist of death opens his discussion of the subject with the statement that "the problem of the survival of death by human persons is an empirical problem for which we have no empirical evidence. It is a question of fact, and of fact in time, for which there are no antecedent probabilities one way or the other. Human survival is neither probable nor improbable, because we have to aproach it through those same questions of world order which include the basis of probability."[3]

This logic is hard to take. But it is irrefutable. The atheist who accuses the believer of wishful thinking or superstition is a victim of pot-and-kettle complaint. And the agnostic, or skeptic, has his own troubles: Apart from the worldly calluses of fence-sitting, he just might land in that unenviable vestibule in which Dante found the trimmers, rejected by both Heaven and Hell.

The idea of immortality, then, and therefore the idea of death, is an idea only by extension, or courtesy. In the first and controlling instance it is "only" a transcendental belief. It depends, not partly, but wholly, on one's world view or creed or "philosophy of life." If, says Hocking, men "believe that the universe has a unity and a dominating purpose, or makes on the whole some sort of sense, they are prone to conclude that the minds of men must be able somehow to carry on their adventure. If they adopt the view that human life and consciousness are episodes in a world which as a whole has no purposive structure, but is in its last analysis plain physical fact, they are bound to consider survival both meaningless and impossible."[4] Death, and death alone, is at once a totally objective and a totally subjective reality. It is the one idea be-

---

3 William Ernest Hocking, *The Meaning of Immortality in Human Experience* (rev. ed.; New York: Harper & Brothers, 1957), p. 3.
4 *Ibid.*, p. 23.

longing to the order of indisputable events about which we can know nothing of significance without knowing the individual who has the idea.

Modern man's not so remote ancestor always demonstrated an ardent preoccupation with worldly survival—except for the martyrs and ecstatics —but the hoped-for salvation of his soul always took an unchallenged, if matter-of-fact, place in his matter-of-fact life. His religion held him comfortably in its matrix; it was a system, before the rise of the nation-state, larger, more meaningful, and *more* comprehensible than worldly associations; indeed, all such associations had their center of gravity in his religion. John Dewey says that "the thing new in history, the thing once unheard of, is that [the church has become] a special institution within a secular community."

Paul Tillich, the Protestant theologian, insists that the "tragic conse-quences . . . are no reason for giving up the attempts to discover and the obligation to express truth," and one such consequence may be that "science has undercut the cosmic frame within which man has seen him-self in biblical literature and ecclesiastical teaching, namely, as the bearer of the history of salvation for the universe, as the *only* creature in whose nature God could become fully manifest, and as he who will experience his own historical end as the end of the universe." Can he die—and live— with this downgraded picture of himself and his situation? Or does the spread of the new "theologies," Fascism, Nazism, Communism, prove that he can't, that his hunger for meaning will not tolerate the loss of his divine status unrequited? Must he have *something* more to live and die for than the ant has?

In his *Psychoanalysis and Religion*, Erich Fromm assures us that "the psychoanalytic cure of the soul aims at helping the patient to achieve an attitude which can be called religious in the humanistic though not in the authoritarian sense of the word. . . . It is [the] process of breaking through the confines of one's organized self—the ego—and of getting in touch with the excluded and disassociated part of oneself, the unconscious, which is closely related to the religious experience of breaking down individuation and feeling one with the All. . . ." But existentialism, often called "the philosophy of death," confronts the downgraded, "excluded and disassociated" part of man more simply. In the works of Sartre and Camus, and in the earlier writing of Heidegger, conscious man, conscious of his being alone, must first of all achieve "freedom-toward-death" to achieve his liberation from the terror that is quite real and quite con-scious at the apogee of the Age of Man. Once he accepts the proximity— and absurdity—of death he can achieve an "authentic existence," and only then; still alone, but unterrified, able, in effect, to produce himself, his essence, through his existence.

Whether man rushes into the Church or the Communist party, whether the recent American "religious revival" or the totalitarian innovation simply means that he has to go somewhere, anywhere, in his new situation and come to terms somehow, anyhow, with the lost intelligibility of death and the new persuasion of finitude, he is faced with the challenge of Sartre's play *No Exit*, whose characters are in Hell in this life. The Hell, of one kind or another, is plain enough; but the corollary of Heaven in Palm Springs or Miami is harder to come by. Is "the farce of life" a painful farce and nothing more?

Ancient man—and his God—projected the possibility of a richer worldly existence than that. Hell on earth and Heaven thereafter were not the exhaustive alternatives of the pre-post-Christian man. Christ assured his followers that the Kingdom of God was within them. And before Christ the Greeks argued that happiness was possible in this life through the harmony of the soul achieved (like the harmony of the state) through the habitual virtues of its components; such was the message of Plato's *Republic*; and Aristotle went further and maintained that *blessedness* (the highest form of happiness, which Christianity reserves to the next world) was achievable here and now through the gods' gift of good fortune to the man of transcendant goodness. If the prescientific possibilities of life are real, death even in the Age of Man, even as the end of the "biochemical entity," may still crown something more than a farce.

BURY THE DEAD

Death is no laughing—or even crying—matter. It is deadly serious, and always has been. Its seriousness is veiled in war or in mass catastrophe, where the event that causes death is more traumatic to the survivors than death itself; Verdun's million, or the hundred thousand of a flood or an earthquake or a bomb, are far easier to cope with than the spectacle of a simple funeral procession on the road. Solemnity seems to involve the contemplation, not of windrows of dead men, but of one: If he, then I.

We repress the attendant exultation—he, but ah, not I. We repress it partly because we know that we ourselves are next, but partly because this is the one occasion, of all of life's, in which it is as privately as it is publicly scandalous to indulge the *Schadenfreude* that takes comfort in the misfortune of another. Whoever rejoices at another's death—let the victim be his or the public's worst enemy—vastly discredits himself. And the sense of the most awful subhumanity attaches to the desecration of a dead body. The methodical conversion of slaughtered Jews into needed soap—whatever else it is—is less horrifying to us than the jubilant mutilation of a dead Mussolini or the festive depravity of a lynch mob. We find antiquity's nadir on the field of Troy, where the dead body of Hector, gratuitously stabbed by one Greek after another, is fastened head down to a chariot and dragged through the dust; and the perpetrator is glorious Achilles, beloved of the gods.

Man alone celebrates death, and celebrates it with luster; he alone is "splendid in ashes and pompous in the grave." He alone disposes of his own cadavers, and does so ritualistically. Why? The ritual of burial appears so early, so universally, and so persistently in human history (and prehistory) that its existence, says Joseph Wood Krutch, "may be one of the criteria for distinguishing between men and mere half-men, and some sort of respect for his dead may have been part of the nature of man for as long as there has been man to have a nature."[5] Custom?—Whence the custom? Ego-satisfaction?—Whence the ego-satisfaction? Piety, fear, guilt, grief, honor, ostentation, "wishful thinking"?—Whence all of them that they should take this ubiquitous form in man alone?

Not in his physiology, for many other creatures are more adept by nature at burying. Not in his imagination or his memory, for many of the other creatures are just as imaginative and most of them more retentive. Not in his respect for another's life; in his disrespect for it he outstrips most of the creatures of earth, and the ancient Scythians (so Herodotus takes the trouble to inform us) strangled their dead king's concubine, his cupbearer, his cook, his groom, his lackey, and his messenger and buried them with him, and on the first anniversary of his death strangled fifty of the best of his attendants (with fifty of their most beautiful horses) to mark the occasion. What is there, then, in man that calls for the *decent* burial of his corpses? "It is," Patrick O'Donovan wrote in the *London Observer* on the occasion of Winston Churchill's funeral, "a gesture, made over and over again by Christians and Communists and humanists and the unconcerned. It is a proud half-conscious assertion that man is not an animal that dies alone in a hole."

Here is an oddity—if nothing more—of cosmic proportions. Supernaturalist and naturalist are *in practice* agreed with the "half-conscious assertion." The denier of immortality and its affirmer might both be expected to reject utterly the importance of the dead body, but they both accept it. The affirmer of immortality, through the Church, pays ponderous and elaborate homage to the worthless clay, and the denier does the same. The atheist materialist ideologues of the Soviet Union restored the lost art of mummification to the inert matter that was once Lenin and Stalin, and to house it reared a structure that more closely than any other mausoleum compares with the pyramids of Egypt. "For political purposes," you say; but in that case the politics were in head-on collision with the ideology. And when the *soul* of Stalin was disgraced, his *body* was thrust from the shrine and cast into the ground. These atheists, forbidding

5 *Human Nature and the Human Condition* (New York: Random House, Inc., 1959), pp. 177–78.

a hallowed burial to the *body* that once housed a villainous *soul*!

Man the burier seems to be saying, "You can't do this to *me*." Man the mourner, too. Anecdotes recur—going back to Patroclus' horse, which wept over his body—of the grief of lower animals, especially of dogs for their masters, birds for their mates, and mother monkeys, horses, and cows for their young; but its incidence usually suggests so simple an explanation of the loss of the food source or the incomprehension of the "loved one's" failure to respond or return. Though the lower animals "manifestly feel pleasure and pain, happiness and misery"—this is Darwin —the notion of bereavement among undomesticated animals generally yields to the account of the pair of starlings one of which "was shot in tLe morning; by noon a new mate was found; this was again shot, but before the night the pair was complete; so that the disconsolate widow or widower was thrice consoled during the same day"[6]—but, then, Darwin had not heard of Hollywood.

Just as man's acknowledged or unacknowledged belief in immortality (or resurrection) ought to relieve him of concern for the disposal of a corpse, so ought it to relieve him of the burden of bereavement; and, conversely, bereavement ought to pervade the lives of the survivors in the lower species of animal which show no sign of such belief. Why mourns man, and not the starling? If there is not immortality or resurrection—yes. But if there is—what more is there to say than, "The Lord giveth. The Lord taketh away. Blessed be the name of the Lord"? "Towards the dead person himself we take up a special attitude," says Freud. "We suspend criticism of him, overlook his possible misdoings, issue the command: *De mortuis nil nisi bene*, and regard it as justifiable to set forth in the funeral-oration and upon the tombstone only that which is most favourable to his memory. Consideration for the dead, who no longer need it, is dearer to us than the truth, and certainly, for most of us, is dearer also than consideration for the living."

Our attitude toward death (he adds) "has a powerful effect upon our own lives. Life is impoverished, it loses in interest, when the highest stake in the game of living, life itself, may not be risked. . . . It is an inevitable result of all this that we should seek in the world of fiction, of general literature, and of the theatre compensation for the impoverishment of life." But "this conventional treatment of death" was being swept away by the World War (not yet known as World War I): "Death will no longer be denied; we are forced to believe in him. People really are dying, and now not one by one, but many at a time, often ten thousand in a single day. Nor is it any longer an accident. . . . Life has, in truth, become interesting again; it has regained its full significance."[7]

---

6 *The Descent of Man*, GBWW, Vol. 49, p. 479b–c.

7 *Op. cit.*, p. 762a–d.

Those words were written in 1915; just thirty years later two hundred thousand died in a single day. "Life has, in truth, become interesting again." Freud was a better psychologist than the visiting Englishman who asked recently, "Why are you Americans so interested in death?" It is life that is interesting to Americans, so interesting that a large proportion of their $2 billion annual expenditure on funerals[8] goes into gussying up the corpse. In his essay "The Doctor and Death,"[9] August M. Kasper says that the average American's outlook on life and death changed in the first quarter of the present century: "With great optimism we embraced science and reason. Sin went out the window, and with it, its wages— death. Sickness became preventable and curable, and its companion, death, seemed equally vulnerable to our attack, an attack which was largely an elaborate denial of death." The undertaker—now a "grief therapist"—undertook to demonstrate that what is isn't, and what isn't is, and society to "hustle the dead off the scene" (in the words of anthropologist Margaret Mead) "without an opportunity for young and old to realize that death is as much a fact of life as is birth."[10]

Amiable old Death, making his door-to-door rounds with the fidelity of the Fuller Brush Man, finds his wares indisposable: "Nobody here but us live ones." What is this bent on the assuagement of grief, and the belief that it can be assuaged by rouging the earthly remains of its object? Death is a grievous reality. Sympathy, yes; but assuagement, "therapy"? Whoever purports to peddle it in the marketplace would seem to do so with intent to defraud; he cannot deliver the goods to sober men and women.

The scandal of American (and Canadian) funerary practices erupted with the sensational publication of Jessica Mitford's *The American Way of Death* in 1963, but the small "protest" segment of society had been fighting them for several years with funeral societies offering burial as low as $150 (compared with the private undertaker's average of close to $1,500) and cremation even lower. Church opposition to cremation may be theologically dubious, but that of the undertakers' lobbies (which have achieved restrictive legislation in many states) is economically intelligible: "A funeral is not an occasion for a display of cheapness. It is, in fact, an opportunity for the display of a status symbol which, by bolstering family pride, does much to assuage grief."[11]

8 Estimated by Jessica Mitford, *The American Way of Death* (New York: Simon & Schuster, Inc., 1963). The total costs of personal expenditures (tuition, books, living expenses) for *all* higher education in America are around $1.9 billion (pp. 40–41).

9 *The Meaning of Death*, ed. H. Feifel (New York: McGraw-Hill Book Co., Inc., 1959), p. 259.

10 *Male and Female* (New York: William Morrow & Co., Inc., 1949), p. 365.

11 *National Funeral Service Journal* (August, 1961), quoted in Mitford, *op. cit.*, p. 22.

The sumptuous funeral was opposed ineffectually by Solon in Greece and by Constantine in Rome; but only the general acceptance of monotheism overcame it to any significant extent. Among the Jews the simplest burial was the rule—it still is in modern Israel—and was handled by the synagogue. Christians of course rejected the show and splendor of this life in their disposal of the dust of their dead. In early America—as in Europe—burial was wholly a family matter. Expensive funerals are still a rarity in Europe (where the American "open casket" is unknown) except for funerals of state, in which the ceremony is profoundly political, demonstrating the majesty and continuity of royalty or rule.

The ancients associated funeral rites with propitiation of the gods—a likely heritage of the primitive fear of spectral vengeance—and in modern burial the scarcely separable roles of debt and guilt undoubtedly play a part in the disposition of the survivors to have their dead "live it up." Gratitude, never fully expressed or expressible, takes the common form of gifts, and, in unprogressive societies without armament races or drag races, children still bury their parents (rather than parents their children) and piety tends to persuade the distraught to empty benevolence. Guilt, too; we all mistreat one another, by neglect if in no ruder way, and we seize a "last" (which we know is an after-last) occasion to relieve ourselves.

There is no real mystery about the lavish American funeral, and much democracy of a kind. We are still, even now, more restrained than the Scythian kings with their strangled concubines and cupbearers and cooks in their tombs, but in the society which considers every man a king, and in which the generality of men have a comparatively princely income, it is not unnatural that the fashion of the blooded mighty should become the fashion of the bankrolled many, and both gratitude and guilt encumber the dead with baubles and baggage. The sociological motivation is more readily acceptable than the religious: What, in a nominally Christian country, has a procession of Cadillacs or an "impermeable casket" got to do with the Gospel of Christ crucified *and risen?*

Denominational dogma segregates the suicide and the unrepentant from sacred ground, and the bodies of these sinners (unless their survivors have money) share the shame of the unforgivable paupers in potter's field. Beyond that one dogma, the Church as a whole says nothing in the matter—and it is the Church whose hope is the soonest possible permeability of *every* casket come the Last Day. The Eternal Flame must be extinguished *before* the promise of Eternity is realized, and Perpetual Care is impossible until the last caretaker is gone; but men will have Parian marble to commemorate the spirit, though the marble begins its perishing as soon as the flesh it anchors, and the imperishable spirit (if not its commemorators' cash) has eluded the grasp of the speediest undertaker.

119

On Death

Men want to live on, in their children, in their friends, in the memory of men. And they will sacrifice everything to do it, their lives included. Take immortality away from them, and they will die for the closest thing to it they can get. Leave them their belief in the genuine article and they will still die for its substitute. The gods told Achilles before Troy that "if I stay here and fight, I shall not return alive but my name will live for ever: whereas if I go home my name will die, but it will be long ere death shall take me";[12] and he debated the matter and stayed. But in Hades he changed his mind: "I prized that wretched chimera, glory, higher than life. I had not yet experienced how affairs stand here. . . . We are all immersed in the same darkness, without the least preference or distinction."[13]

But we are speaking here as mortals, unlike Achilles, and fame is our immortality. But how much fame is worth one's life? A few hundred million have heard of Homer's Achilles, but billions in the past three thousand years have not. But (says Francis Bacon) to achieve the immortality to which man's nature most aspires you want to be not a warrior but a writer like Homer, whose verses have continued "without the loss of a syllable or letter."[14] Ah, but as many have never heard of Achilles as have never heard of Homer. How much shall I give—my life, or how much less?—to be famous in Greece but not in Rome, in Rome but not in Europe, in Europe but not in Asia or Africa or America? Or in a crossroads village, when ten will speak of me a thousand years from now, when only nine in all the world remember the name of the man whom millions remembered the day after he died?

The duration is as much the essence of my mortal immortality as its spread is. How long do I want my fame to last? Why, forever, of course. But this is the chanciest of all worldly enterprises, requiring me to invest everything I have with no certainty whatever of a dividend or (should there be one) of its size or continuity. Worse yet, I shall have no enjoyment of it. A man once called upon fame to comfort him "by a solemn assurance, that when the little parlour in which I sit at this instant shall be reduced to a worse furnished box, I shall be read with honour by those who never knew nor saw me"[15] and that man, Henry Fielding, enjoyed a very small fame, and then his *Tom Jones* was made into a movie, and I doubt not that more people read his words (or at least heard them) in two nights than in two centuries.

12 GBWW, Vol. 4, p. 61b.
13 Lucian, *Dialogues of the Dead* (Chicago: Great Books Foundation, 1948), p. 92.
14 *Advancement of Learning*, GBWW, Vol. 30, p. 28a.
15 GBWW, Vol. 37, p. 273b.

Undying fame is sometimes cited as a suggestive, if shadowed, evidence of the existence of the real thing, but this just-as-good substitute is terrible trouble to pursue and most unsurely got. It sometimes seems that its best guarantee is notoriety won by an unrelieved life of consummate wickedness. Mark Twain—that unlicensed poet—serves up the verity in a yarn of old New Orleans about a bloody pirate who reformed and was at last elected alderman of the city; but "to-day the loyal and generous remember only what he was, and charitably forget what he became."[16]

History does even better by the point than the humorist. Consult your encyclopaedia and your history book—but consult them in vain—for the name of the man whose life was the most eminent as well for the greatness of his virtue as his power, who saw his country victorious under his command and whose honors and triumphs brought him to the happiest possible end of a life which, so far as human life may be, had been full of all that is good and honorable; a man whose riches were nobly acquired and nobly dispersed to the needy, a man juster than Solon himself, a man profoundly beloved and even more profoundly mourned by the greatest city in all history. Atrocious Nero lives on everywhere, but who, outside of Italy (and perhaps in it), remembers that Poplicola whose praises I have sung on no less authority, and in no other's very words, than Plutarch's?[17] There is more immortality in burning Rome than in saving it.

An end to all of them, Achilles with Homer, Poplicola with Nero, the poet with the peasant. But is there no hint at all of their survival, then, outside of divine revelation? There is a hint, and more than one; a hint within nature and experience, and a peculiarly hard one to document. There is a persistent hint of actual communication from and with the dead.

There is no end of instances of biological "revival," more every day,[18] but no report from the revived to confirm even Hamlet's fear that the dead might dream. Cryobiology, the science of life at low temperatures, is developed to the point where human tissue and whole organs, and even whole animals, have been frozen and revived, and last year Robert C. W. Ettinger of Detroit published *The Prospect of Immortality*,[19] in

---

16 *Life on the Mississippi* (New York: Bantam Books, 1945), pp. 299-300.

17 GBWW, Vol. 14, p. 86a–d.

18 On July 13, 1964, Dr. Charles Drew of Westminster Hospital in London performed a nine-hour heart operation on Robert Macklin, 41. For two hours and twenty-two minutes, with the patient's body temperature reduced from 98.6°F. to about 50°F., there was no pulse, no breathing, and no blood flow. "In every accepted sense of the word," Dr. Drew is quoted as saying, "Macklin was physically dead. . . . There was no life whatsoever." The operation was successful (*National Enquirer*, November 22, 1964).

19 Garden City, N.Y.: Doubleday & Co., Inc., 1964.

which he argues that freezing will preserve human life in suspension indefinitely; he does not report any takers among the living, but he makes the more attractive suggestion that quick-freezing immediately after death offers the distant prospect of the cure of the mortal affliction by future undiscovered medical procedures.

It is hard to resist a reference here to God's Frozen People; Mr. Ettinger's proposal has encountered the intensely self-conscious jocularity that always greets frauds, incompetents, and wise men alike in respect to "cheating death" or communicating with the dead. So the claims of psychic research, or parapsychology, are generally hooted at by professors of the established sciences. Though most "occultists" are naturalists, they are regarded as supernaturalists by naturalists in other fields, and most psychologists[20] spurn psychic research as neuroticism—or charlatanry —in spite of the assertive warning of their great colleague, Carl Jung, that "anyone who has the least knowledge of the parapsychological material which already exists and has been thoroughly verified will know that so-called telepathic phenomena are undeniable facts. . . . The ideas and doubts of theoretical physicists in our own day should prompt a cautious mood in psychologists, too. . . ."[21]

Nor is Jung alone in insisting that the door be left open to the procedures whose validity, if it is ever demonstrated, will affect the life of man more profoundly than all the breakthroughs of science together. William James was one of the founders of the American Society of Psychical Research and was fully convinced of the reality of psychic phenomena (though he admitted that his years of study of them had left him "baffled"). Reports of psychic experiments were "simply howled down" in James's day, and it is still almost impossible to make a career of parapsychology. But we are hard put to ascribe victimization or fraud to such moderns as Sir William Crookes, inventor of the tube with which X rays were discovered (and president of the Royal Society), astronomer Camille Flammarion of the French Academy of Science, physicist Sir Oliver Lodge, and the inventor of the incandescent lamp, Thomas Edison; all of whom, along with Sir Arthur Conan Doyle, were satisfied as to the genuineness of spirit communication.[22] According to the *Encyclopædia Britannica*, it *appears* that there *may be* "a strong prima facie case for

---

20 "Some people go to a psychologist. Others come to see me," says Madame Frederika, one of the fifty thousand practicing clairvoyants in France. There is reported—in the *New York Times*, December 28, 1964—to be one practitioner of "occultism" to every 120 Parisians, compared to one physician for every 514 and one priest for every 5,000. A French statute of 1895, still on the books, illegalizes interpretation of dreams or forecasts of the future.

21 "The Soul and Death" in *The Meaning of Death*, op. cit., pp. 13–14.

22 S. Ralph Harlow, *A Life After Death* (Garden City, N.Y.: Doubleday & Co., Inc., 1961), pp. 25–27.

some communication from human spirits that have survived death"; and Alexis Carrel, "quite unconvinced" by spiritualist claims, nevertheless concluded that "it is far from being unreasonable that some part of human personality may escape death."[23]

The possibility that there are actual sense perceptions stimulated interiorly by the brain or the nervous system, can be discountenanced by easy scoffers, but not by those who know that we know little of the human subconscious. What we call sensory hallucination may be real in an order of reality we cannot yet reach. "Parapsychologists are convinced that ghosts and apparitions are psychic creations, not spirits wilfully wandering in the world of the living, or somehow separated from a living body and straying about erratically in some other place."[24]

Mankind as a whole (taken over the whole of its history) disagrees on the last point: Ghosts exist, and are spirits of the dead, and there are seven distinct kinds: (1) Wrongdoers, especially murderers, who cannot rest away from the scene of their crime; (2) their victims, haunting the wrongdoers; (3) carnal creatures, so enamored of the bodily appetites that they cannot survive death without carrying about some semblance of their bodies; (4) those who, troubled over the unfinished worldly business they left behind them, come back to take care of it; (5) those who foresee trouble for their loved ones and wish to warn them; (6) the unburied; and (7) the maladjusted dead clinging to the places of their worldly habitation.

Of course you and I do not believe in ghosts; only primitive peoples believe in ghosts, such as the inhabitants of present-day England. "Few Britons think ghosts are purely imaginary," the *New York Times* reports in the fourteenth year of the second half of the twentieth century. "Even the Church of England takes the official position that ghosts are possible. . . . One fifth of them, according to a recent survey, appear in daylight. More than half are middle-aged. Five per cent are children. And, as would be expected of a nation so universally fond of man's best friend, two per cent of ghosts are believed to be dogs." The best antidote is, of course, exorcism by "bell, Book, and candle," occasionally conducted by church officials.[25]

However little mortal man knows of death and the dead—Carrel says, "We are as ignorant of death as we are of life"—he may think he knows a little something about dying. He has seen and studied the performance under a variety of conditions, and often under the optimum conditions

---

23 "The Mystery of Death," in *Great Adventures in Medicine*, ed. Samuel B. Rapport and Helen Wright (New York: Dial Press, Inc., 1952), p. 855–56.

24 F. S. Edsall, *The World of Psychic Phenomena* (New York: David McKay Co., Inc., 1958), p. 111.

25 *New York Times*, September 23, 1964.

of a hospital and an operating room. We don't know how men die with their boots on, but physicians say that those who die with them off, as most of us do, find it "always easy at the last." It "is almost always preceded by a perfect willingness to die. . . . All competent observers agree that except in imagination there is no such thing as death agony. . . . The final flutters of a failing heart pump an ever-diminishing supply of blood. . . . After an interval of peace, the oxygen starvation that goes with failing circulation takes its toll on the brain. The patient may hear the ringing of nonexistent bells or see the flashing of nonexistent lights. He may feel a slight restlessness. Gradually he drifts into darkness, without pain, without sensation. The final blacking out which precedes death is in no wise different from falling asleep."[26]

We lay this body down every evening, and, what is more, we can come pretty close to knowing the last wakeful instant (though not the first or any other instant of sleep). We are stretched out prone and prostrate a third of our lives—"dead to the world"—in something like rehearsal for the long run. We actually court sleep, and at some point in the day we prefer its emptiness to the fullness of being awake; but, lest we let the analogy carry us away, be it said that we "know" that we shall awaken and that the worst bad dream will end. We have always slept . . . and always awakened. Montaigne wonders if this is a foretaste. (But he does not ask whether we shall hate to get up on the Last Day, and do it as bad-naturedly as on every other.) We are well practiced in sleep, but "in dying, which is the greatest work we have to do, practice can give us no assistance at all. A man may by custom fortify himself against pain, shame, necessity, and such like accidents, but, as to death, we can experiment it but once, and are all apprentices when we come to it."[27] It has been thus up to now. Will it always be? Carrel points out that there are two kinds of mysteries: those we can conquer and those that that are forever beyond our reach, the Unknown and Unknowable. "There is a frontier between these two worlds, a wall that we will never climb. On which side of this wall is death located? We do not know. To find an answer to this question will be a long and difficult task. How-

---

26 O. A. Battista, "What Happens When You Die," *Science Digest* (May, 1964). Within a few minutes of circulatory stoppage, the oxygen starvation of the human brain at ordinary temperature is (as far as we now know) functionally irreparable; this, determinable by electroencephalogram, is death, and not (as Harvey discovered three hundred years ago) the cessation of the "heartbeat," which may be restored by artificial respiration, heart massage, massive blood transfusion, or drugs. Soviet scientists are reported to have used refrigeration successfully to extend the survival of brain function to as much as an hour after anoxia (the deprivation of oxygen). *See* William Harvey, *The Motion of the Heart*, GBWW, Vol. 28, pp. 276d–277d; *San Francisco Chronicle*, June 24, 1964, report of American Medical Association convention; and "The Reversal of Death," *Saturday Review*, August 4, 1962.

27 *Essays*, II, 6, GBWW, Vol. 25, p. 176d–177c.

ever, in the course of a few hundred years, science may be capable of ascertaining whether or not death is to remain forever a mystery."[28]

There are some things we are pretty sure we know about being dead. It involves no pain of a sensible nature. (And no pleasure.) If there is spiritual torment or ecstasy, it is of a kind that the spirit does not know on earth, for the spiritual torments and ecstasies which we indulge here are all dependent upon corporeality, from which the responses of the five external senses and the two internal senses of memory and imagination are inseparable. Thus death, barring bodily resurrection, would seem to be eternal rest, as advertised; at least from worldly pleasure and worldly pain. The man being tortured to death, or the man on the scaffold, or the man in terminal illness with great pain likelier than not prefers death by, so to say, *dis*preferring life. Not release, but only release from present horrors; nor liberation, but only liberation from the present conditions. "Whatever it is, it can't be worse than this"; the sooner 'tis over, the sooner to sleep. But there are men who know to a certainty when the thief cometh, men condemned by man's law to die at a given hour of a given day; as a newspaperman, I have known a few such men, and I think of none who wished they were dead that day rather than the next.

They, like the rest of us, perhaps the dying, too, to the last split second of consciousness, think that a reprieve is not impossible. How long a reprieve? An hour's, a day's, or a year's, or a hundred, but a reprieve. Abdul was sentenced to death, and on his last day he sent a message to the Caliph: If the Caliph would grant him a thirty-day reprieve, he would teach him to fly. "You must be mad," said Abdul's friend, "to make such an offer." "Look," said Abdul, "in thirty days, the Caliph might die, or I might die, or, who knows? I might teach him to fly."

Is death ever itself a desideratum, or does it only seem so under apparently hopeless conditions? Is it wished for more commonly in "backward" societies, where labor is unrelieved and suffering irremediable, or in "advanced" societies which, by reducing labor and suffering, perhaps weaken their will to endure it? Is the poor man's desire for death a case of sour grapes, as the Stoic says, and only the rich man's genuine? The Green Pastures may or may not be green; we paint them here and their verdure depends upon the brownness of those we are grazing.

Modern man is acutely anticipative, perhaps the first in all history really to accept the ancient dictum that "this, too, shall pass away." Motion has hold of him, including the motion of the neon sign on the wall of a California cemetery that flashes the words, "Rest in Peace," "Rest in Peace," "Rest in Peace," on and off. He thinks that there will be a big change any day now—and there usually is. But the great change in his

28 Carrel, *op. cit.*, p. 849.

life, and the end of all change, is unchanged: Death.

In his habituation to change, and his anticipation of it, he comes to love change and pursue it. The great change (if it is change he wants) is still death. Now a man who is worth very much as a man has always been, if not reckless, indifferent to his life; the frontiersman of science and discovery and money and fame and revolution and religion and love. But the persistent fascination of Homer's Ulysses is his daredeviltry for daredeviltry's sake, his aimless adventure, his taking a gander at the Cyclops for kicks. A man who risks his life should risk it with an intelligence that comprehends both the value of the end and the choice of the means. But we seem to see something more often now—or is it only that we who see it are getting old?—than we ever did before: a whole breed of Ulysseses, playing "chicken" on the highways and racing cars on the ice.

If we are setting a lower value on life than those before us—or those around us whose lives are poorer than ours—we are making the most radical of all changes. This is not to say that it may not be the right change; those before and around us may have overvalued life and therefore tended it more carefully (within their much more limited abilities) than it deserves. Modern man's valuation, not of death, but of life, is not necessarily wrong, and the spread of secularism may be a blessing in its liberation of him to look at life (which he knows) entirely apart from death (which he doesn't).

Passing strange, if life should be losing esteem among the very people who have access to its blessings in measure undreamed of; unless, of course, what we take to be blessings are not blessings at all. But the fact is that the devaluation of life—if we may judge by their indulgence in murder, manslaughter, war, alcoholism, suicide, and "the pace that kills" at work or play—is the world's highest in those societies that enjoy the widest spread of comfort, leisure, diversion, and a splendid living standard. The speculation on the paradox is abundant enough, ranging in form from man's inability to survive without the perpetual challenge of hardship to his inability to maintain the *persona*, the sense of individual identity, against the depersonalization of the machine and its products.

Man does not really believe the old and honorable guff about the individual's dying and the race's living on. He rejects the sociologically popular and pernicious doctrine of the "social organism," and rightly, both as a man and a citizen. He senses its denial of the free man, the Crusoe, if not the God, within him. He knows what it is to live alone with *his* consciousness, so often isolated from his neighbor's or his countrymen's; to be glad or guilty or fearful or troubled or satisfied when no one else is, not even the companion of his bosom. He has his own sore throat, his own grudge, his own pleasure of a sunset or a book.

I will not be a leaf of a tree—or a tree that cannot be seen for the forest. Is *my* life to be oozed not of *its* meaning but of *mine*? Am I to know the man next door only by the color of his door and be known by mine? Am I to be tagged with a number, and then another number, and then another number, as a dog is tagged or a tin can? Are all those around me to undergo the same homogenization? At some point I am one with my wall-to-wall carpet and my automatic transmission and my Disposall (which has already eliminated my garbage man). My life has become so comfortable as to be imperceptible to me. I am bored—to *death*—and death's shares rise ineluctably as life's fall. They are the only two issues offered, and I buy into the one as surely as I sell off the other.

THE LOVE OF LIFE

These meditations (or vaporings) compel us to the trickiest question that man has any competence to try to answer: Is life becoming cheaper or dearer in our time? The answer, on the evidence, would *seem* to be: dearer. Certainly so, if we are becoming more secular. The believer in immortality does not need Euclid to tell him that seventy years are nothing compared with eternity; but the nonbeliever may be expected to hold those seventy years dearly as being all that he has or ever will have.

On this showing, the answer to the tricky question is monstrous easy. But it fails to satisfy, partly, perhaps, because of some contrary signs, in greater part because it fails to inspect the question closely. What is the currency we are to use to measure cheapness and dearness? What makes life meaningful (and meaningless) to us? What do we want "out of" it that we can or can't get? Wealth? Health? Fame? Power? Private influence? Friends? Love? Variety? Excitement? Steadiness? Quietude? Intelligence? Beauty? Virtue? Or some or all of them (or still others, such as suffering, sorrow, sacrifice) and in what combination? "Happiness" tells us nothing until we have said what will make us happy (or what we think will); no more does "the full life"; for life may be full of any or all of these things (and of years besides) and utterly empty of others we value higher (or come, at a date too late, to value higher), or it may be short and sweet.

How cheap or dear do we hold another's life as against our own? We all kill men, directly or indirectly, advertently or inadvertently. As sovereign members of an organized society we execute criminals, and if, in war, we do none of the bombing, we are all accessories in providing the weapons and the will. Some of our neighbors are in want. A little farther away some of our fellow citizens starve; still farther away, hunger's toll takes some ten thousand human beings every twenty-four hours. And our charity, domestic and foreign, does not affect our living standard. Of course, those with whom we are at war we tend to think of as sub-men, who "don't understand anything but force"; wild beasts, by nature or corruption the enemies of humanity. First we demote them from manhood in sufficient degree to justify our killing them in conscience.[29] Few men otherwise ever kill a man or condone his killing.

The believer in immortality should, in reason, value his own life lower than the disbeliever does his (but the other's no higher); but the case is infrequently encountered historically, except among the relatively few religious martyrs. The self-immolation of Buddhist monks in Vietnam astonishes us as roundly as the behavior of the early Christians astonished the Romans; though the modern psychoanalytic jargon may relieve us of a little of our astonishment by substituting "martyr complex" for "martyr."

Killer of self or another, man is a killer, and Freud thinks that his lust to kill is older than love; primitive man "liked to kill and killed as a matter of course." The public executioner may send a real or affected shudder through us, but his post is never vacant for want of applicants. In seventeenth-century England more than two hundred crimes were capital—including the stealing of a handkerchief by a "malicious" seven-year-old. But for all the rigor of the penalty, crime did not decline (nor has it yet), and the abandonment of the death penalty by the Netherlands a hundred years ago has been followed by most of Europe and by a few American states. (The tendency to substitute life imprisonment is increasingly strong in most others, especially in the North and the West).

The causes of the trend (apart from the failure of deterrence) are not clear. What is perhaps clearer is man's rejection of his own image as a killer except in war and in play (including prizefighting, against which legislation is urged with some small ardor). Either he does not like to kill, or he is ashamed of liking to (or of being seen liking to); or, with the growth of understanding of the unconscious, he is afraid to stimulate his own bloodlust by doing so. Public execution was always an occasion of general degradation.

But if (as Arthur Koestler says in his *Reflections on Hanging*) there is "a spoonful of sadism at the bottom of every human heart," a "little Stone Age man inside us," we may still want men killed and even to be in on the killing. Newspapermen know to what lengths some men (unrelated to the case) go to find a way to be admitted to an execution. The mob that waits outside a prison when a notorious execution occurs—and that cheers when the hearse comes out the prison gates, as it did in the

---

29 Q. (Asked on television of a South African mercenary in the Congo): "Wally, how do you feel when you're out there fighting? How do you feel about killing anyone?" A.: "The first time I felt a bit squeamish, but after that it was like, well, I'd done a lot of cattle farming, you know, and killing a lot of beasts, it's just like, you know, cattle farming, and just seeing dead beasts all over the place. It didn't worry me at all" (ABC-TV, December 9, 1964).

Lindbergh-Hauptmann case in 1936—undoubtedly contains a fair number of persons who would like to be in immediate attendance. And if we do not want to see others killed, or kill them, it may still be possible that we want them dead (though we may repress the wish or sublimate it by deciding that they would be "better off").

Still, the closed execution and the use of humane instruments to perform it seem to testify to man's progressive effort to control his blood-lust, as do the conventions (however widely breached) for the treatment of prisoners of war. Even stronger testimony is the modern repudiation of torture. Torture to bring about death with maximum pain was the common practice of our savage ancestors. These savages had a wisdom we civilized have lost: Like us, they wanted to inflict the worst possible punishment on their enemies. But whether death (above all, a quick death) was in fact punishment, they knew no more than we do. What they did know was that pain was punishment, and for centuries the art of torture, like all human arts, was steadily refined by man's admirable ingenuity.

Torture, not as punishment, but as a device to obtain criminal confession or testimony, is still practiced everywhere, though it is forbidden by the law of most civilized societies. But there is not much evidence, outside of the statutes, that civilized societies as a whole are disturbed by the quiet employment of "a little" torture in criminal cases or war, and almost no evidence that modern man has any compunction against the "blind" or "saturation" bombing of helpless civilian populations. Even the Nazi practice of genocide, in the wartime slaughter of the Jews, cannot be shown actually to have outraged an "outraged" world (or the mass of the German people, themselves wartime sufferers). But the world sentiment toward *mercy* killing is different.

The practice of euthanasia on mental and physical defectives, either at birth or afterward, is traceable, like all killing, to man's beginnings, and its advocacy, especially for the dying (with their own permission or, *in extremis*, without it), but also in cases of hopeless monstrosity at birth, is considerable among modern secular humanitarians. But the churches in the Western world are adamant against it.

The prima facie argument against euthanasia is easy enough: We cannot *know* that the dying, even in the last extremities, will in fact die. Nor can we *know* that either mental or physical defectiveness is, or will be, incurable. But the religious position more accurately reflects the general unease. The Commandment reads, "Thou shalt not kill." True, there is exegesis to substitute "murder" for "kill." But John Locke's contention that men, as God's handiwork, "are His property . . . made to last during His, not one another's pleasure," as it challenges capital punishment, war, and suicide, challenges euthanasia, too. If Locke is right, man, including the exegetist, is, and always has been, wrong; dead wrong.

On Death

How cheap—or dear—was life held in the past compared with the present? The historical inference would seem to be irresistible: In the ages of primitive or nonexistent medicine, sanitation, drainage, and disinfection, of murderous labor conditions, and of implacable and recurrent plague, epidemic, famine, flood, and fire, men could not have valued life anything as highly as we do. But wait.—Why isn't the opposite as likely to be true? Why wouldn't the very hazards of life make it that much more precious? If a man anticipates no more than thirty years on earth—the life expectancy of ancient Rome—why wouldn't he hold each of those thirty, and each day and hour of them, dearer than we do with an expectancy of almost seventy?

But we may turn the argument on itself yet again. Up to (and into) the present century, 20 to 40 percent of all infants born alive died during their first year, and three out of four of all deaths were those of children under twelve. Only two of Thomas Jefferson's six children survived infancy; Edward Gibbon was the only one of seven siblings to do so; more than half of Judge Samuel Sewall's fifteen children in the Massachusetts Bay Colony were lost. And this was the fact of death among the favored few; in the Dublin Foundling asylum, 45 babies survived of 10,272 admitted between 1775 and 1796; a mortality rate of 99.6 percent. Small wonder that even the relatively prosperous New England colonial, not to say the suffering masses of most of the rest of the world, rejoiced mightily in death's approach and yielded himself "with unaffected cheerfulness."

We do know that suicide in the past was much rarer than it is now, in spite of the hardness of life, and in spite, too, of the fact that the early religions, unlike ours, did not undertake so sternly to dishearten its indulgence. We know, too, that among primitive peoples of our own era it is almost unknown, and that the suicide rate among the traditionally oppressed, such as the American Negro, is only a fraction of that of their "happier" countrymen. But we know something, in addition, about past man's evaluation of *another's* life than his own. It was lower far than ours.

In and out of the dangerous trades—the workers called them deadly, not dangerous—wage-labor was a mercilessly used commodity like any other. And from the beginning of time the conqueror had been deemed to have the right to the life of the conquered. At his discretion he might spare his enemy's life (which, however, remained forfeit) and enslave him. Whole populations went into chains (unless they were put to the sword), and their care was strictly a matter of their animal worth to their masters. On these counts, at least, modern man respects human life in a way that his early forebears did not.

The modern anomaly is the apparent reversion to the ancient—and pre-ancient—indifference to other men's lives in war. Mass slaughter by remote control came in with artillery and the aerial bomb; we do not need to go to the trouble or the unpleasantness of lopping off a hundred thousand heads one at a time. And, far from there being a general revulsion of mankind, the acceptance of streamlined massacre seems to be suddenly universal. It would be a reckless philosopher of history who would say today that the rising esteem for another's life that preceded our own time was secure. The earnest observer sees all about him the triumphant recognition of mortal worth, above all in the acknowledged right to medical care (which as recently as a century ago was reserved to the rich); and he sees all about him the acknowledgment, even the embrace, of total war, and the rising tide of crimes of peacetime violence.

The last of the tricky questions involving the value of life is no easier than the others: How cheap or dear do we hold an old man's life, a young one's, an infant's? I was once (when I was very young) engaged in a discussion of the fate of Socrates, at the point of his refusal to escape from the death cell. I argued that he had made a simple calculation to achieve immortality at the expense of a few more years of life. After all, he was an old man; why should he mind dying? "Young man," said an old man in the group, "you have never been an old man." I am older now, and I think I know what the old man meant.

Bright youth; or should we say dazzling and dazzled youth? Try to tell the young, as Hegel does, that "the nature of finite things as such is to have the seed of their passing away as their essential being; the hour of their birth is the hour of their death"; only try. Death is impossible to the young. Their lives are charmed, and what we call their deaths; movie star James Dean—even John F. Kennedy—"had it made." Impossible, and, more important, unimaginable. For how far away is youth from the years of childhood in which you are dead, bang, bang, every day in cops and robbers, cowboy and Indian? What has death to do with the world of cheerleaders, hot rods, plunging halfbacks, and all-night sessions with the books or the band? Ask rather what has it *not* to do with the middle-aged twisters and drinkers, fighting the wearisome fight, and the losing fight, to recapture the dead and gone reality of youth.

The young understand death well enough; what they don't understand is the necessity to look both ways before crossing the street. They understand death well enough, but not the necessity to brush their teeth. They understand death well enough, but not the necessity to apportion their time and treasure their days, their hours, their minutes. Why shouldn't they be prodigal of them?—They have "all of life" left. Death is too far in the distance to be seen on the clearest day. On the clearest day—and all days are clear—they see the day. The past was childhood and done with; the future is age and afar. The present, the now, is bubbling, effervescent. Youth, youth.

Youth is rising to command, to take over. The future belongs to it—

not it to the future. It is climbing the hill of life with such strides as middle age takes on the other side and hobbled senility dreams of. The summit, the peak of man's power, is above the clouds, invisible, but it is there, and youth will be there with it and fasten its standard to it. And there it is, sure enough. Just see what man does at the peak of his power, lord of the universe. And there he flails about him for a few years, say, from thirty to forty. And then, one day or, likelier, one night, a disconsolate vision. . . .

Maybe it is only a crick in his back or a stitch in his side that doesn't disappear, and he has to lie abed a few days and still it doesn't disappear; or it disappears, and reappears. Maybe a classmate, a friend his own age, is suddenly dead: "Joe?" "Why, I saw Joe last Thursday, and he was as healthy as I am." *And so he was.* Somewhere between thirty and forty (or, if he is a little less introspective, before forty-five), he realizes that he will die. It doesn't dawn on him—it comes much less perceptibly than the dawn. But it comes. Its mark is wistfulness.

The wistfulness will sharpen, little by little, until it stabs him again and again, more and more frequently. His children—and hers—are grown. The house is too large. A smaller house, then, and then a smaller, until, one day, he asks himself, "Will this be the last one?" And then, one day, his wife sees a new overcoat she thinks he'd like to have, and for the first time in his life it occurs to him that the coat he has will . . . will last. Another beachhead or two established. He who had known so many illnesses and accidents as incidents, events, misfortunes one *recovers* from is told by the doctor, "You'll be all right if you take it a little easier. . . ." And now, when his friends ask him how he is, he says, with careful affability, "Hanging on, hanging on." And to himself, "Why, I've got thirty . . . twenty . . . ten good years in me yet."

Now he knows. Life is fading slow away.

Our ancestors expected to die when their "time" was come, and their time was come at whatever age above thirty-five or forty they were stricken by illness or, as was so often the case, by malnutrition. At forty, said Montaigne in the sixteenth century, and what he said was as true in the first half of the nineteenth, "we are pretty well advanced; and since we have exceeded the ordinary bounds, which is the just measure of life, we ought not to expect to go much further . . . we should acknowledge that so extraordinary a fortune . . . is not likely to continue long."[30] It is not that we do not expect nowadays to die at forty, or at fifty, or at sixty, but rather that we do not *expect* to die.

For medicine, in the past one hundred years, above all in the past twenty-five, has done one wonder after another. The "killer" diseases of

30 Essay, I, 57, GBWW, Vol. 25, p. 157a–b.

the old have been beaten further and further back. The great killers nowadays, heart disease, cancer, and stroke, are not in the first instance the diseases of age at all, but of middle life. These three afflictions account for 71 percent of all American deaths, and we read headlines daily like "Surgeon General Forecasts Era of Hope in Ending Disease," and we accept the hyperbole because we have seen the validity of so many previous hyperboles in medicine. What then, if we must die of *some* thing *some* time, shall we die of? Old age?

But we no longer know where to put the finger on old age, not in the era of Senior Citizenry. There are too many active, even strapping men in their eighties to be seen in every community. Nor do they die of *old age*. Our forefathers would have been incredulous, as we are not, to hear that "There is no known case of death from old age. No pathologist has ever established at the autopsy table that a person dying of natural causes had body tissues correct and adequate in every way except that they had worn out in the process of aging."[31]

Man's life span, in contrast with his life expectancy, has not lengthened much. What has happened, in addition to the past century's spectacular reduction of infant mortality, is that more people are living out the life span of the biblical three score and ten. Once a man reaches fifty or so now, his expectancy is almost exactly what it was one hundred fifty years ago—about twenty-five years. As far back as the human record goes, some few men have always lived to be one hundred or even one hundred twenty; more and more are now living to that age. In well-fed societies the percentage of the population over sixty-five will continue to grow and their life expectancy, once they have reached that age, rises steadily. The population is exploding at both ends.

We do not know the limit of human life or if there is one. We know that aging is an accumulation of bodily changes that increases one's chances of dying *of disease*, but we do not understand the nature of the changes themselves: why, for instance, a canary, which is about the same size as a mouse and has a much higher metabolic rate, *i.e.*, lives "faster," should live six to seven times longer than the mouse.

But age we do, canary, mouse, and man, and for a man to grow old, above all in an age of youth and mobility and tempo, is to take on a kind of settled melancholy. I am "on the shelf," and the shelf itself grows bare. I am less and less urgently necessary, less and less often sought. I am not wanted *badly* by anyone except my true love (while she or he lasts). I may not be a nuisance to others, only a bit of a bother. Or I may be a nuisance and know that they would be better off with me out of the

31 "Healthy Added Years" by Edward L. Bortz, President, American Geriatrics Society, in *1961 Britannica Book of the Year* (U.S.A.: Encyclopædia Britannica, Inc., 1961), p. 67.

way. And I, too, sinking more and more of what I have into staying alive. I surrender myself to the high priesthood of the doctors, who hold the keys of life and death. And between the doctor and the undertaker, the confrontation of either's bills is enough to discourage the confrontation of the other's. And so my substance—and my grandchildren's—is surrendered for another week or two of a life that no one values much.

When society was relatively stable and knowledge relatively unchanging, the wisdom of the aged was profoundly prized, and when West finally met East, it turned out that age in the Orient was not only respected for its wisdom but revered as a bridge to holy ancestry. But the tempo of technological change in the past two hundred years or so has accelerated to the point where elder statesman Herbert Hoover, an engineer by trade, had to say of satellite television, "I belong to a generation that just doesn't understand all that." It is no longer an open question whether the old are old fogies. It is a fact. And it will be from now on: Each generation of us in our dotage will belong to a generation that just does not understand "all that."

THE LOVE OF DEATH

That living should grow no more perfect with our practice of it—and, unlike all of our other undertakings, be most difficult when we have had the most practice of it—is enough to touch every satisfaction with conscious or unconscious unease, every joy with evanescence. The agreement of the thoughtful men of all times is general, if not universal: Life is hard, *la vie est dure, ernst ist das Leben.*

Let us be plain and say that life is a bowl of seedless cherries; that we bring into it with us a long train of sorrows in our do-it-yourself kits; that its persistent, and likely increasing, pains outweigh its pleasures, that its enjoyment is nothing to the grind of labor. A sweet-sour affair at its probable best, with the sour quantitatively and qualitatively predominant.

There are passages of joy, and others of contentment, and others of rest; occasions (and not a few) when the gods and the muses bestow nepenthe and even nirvana, for a day or a night, or a week or a month or two; but they are occasions, and they pass and leave us with envy and pride tormented, ambition dismayed, humiliation sustained and recalled, betrayal suspected, loss and the fear of loss suffered; withal a perpetual irritation that boards the boat with us in the frenzied seizure of a holiday from it. The monotony alone persuaded Francis Bacon that "a man would die, though he were neither valiant nor miserable, only upon a weariness to do the same thing so oft over and over"; and a great university president of our own time to answer a young man's question as to the aim of life by saying, "The aim of life is to get through it."

Or let the gods smile more incessantly than their wont, and let the middle years be a continuum of delights; what do they bring, every day closer, than the time of incapacity of those delights, of subsidence of every appetite and the bitterness at their recollection? Recall, or try to recall, in misery ecstasy; Francesca and Paolo were condemned in Dante's Hell to suffer nothing worse than this. The slow, but ever accelerating, increment of incapacity, to be capstoned and concluded by the absolute disappointment and frustration that alone puts an end to disappointment and frustration. The physical torments may be ameliorable, but not the "mental"; for them no sedative is surcease.

It is likely, these days of modern medicine, that I shall know for some months or years that I am a "terminal case." The term approaches; there is no fooling me, nor do I want to be fooled. This ten-cent bowl of clay will outlast me, this peck of potatoes, this bulb will bloom, this grass will grow, this tree, this house, this puppy, yes, this day will break . . . I shall not be here, or anywhere. And my life?—A succession of lumps with just enough respite to make them bearable and, how many (a dozen? two dozen?) more than compensatory splendors from beginning to end?

See how the thorn outlasts the rose. Great Goethe at seventy-five assayed the course of his existence as "nothing but pain and a burden . . . perpetual rolling of a rock that must be raised up again forever"; he had not, he insisted, had as much as four weeks of genuine well-being. And who was greater or more successful than he, unless it was Martin Luther, who, when the Electress Dowager said to him, "Doctor, I wish you may live forty years more," replied, "Madame, rather than live forty years more, I would give up my chance of Paradise."

Still, we hang on, *for dear life.* At any and every cost, we hang on. We lower our sights, cut the cloth to fit the condition, and hang by an ever slenderer thread. With Faust we plead, "Stay—thou art so fair." What, then, of life's derogation by Goethe and Luther? Can they be right? It would seem not, for even in modern America, with its high suicide rate, only one person in ten thousand takes the advice of the Roman Stoics and unencumbers himself of life; and of these few some several do so in derangement or panic and not in settled determination.

Proof enough of the life instinct, if (as Goethe and Luther insist) the bargain is a bad one *and still we cling to it.* Did not Satan say of Job, "All that a man hath will he give for his life," and the Lord reply, "Save his life"? Did not the first psychologist, and every psychologist since, say that self-preservation is the first law of nature? But then life is good, no matter how bad, and better than death however good. But the "first" law of nature yields to another law of nature, the law of death. Some men won't, and no men can, preserve their lives outside the super-natural condition that "he who would save his life shall lose it, but he who loses it for my sake shall find it."

There is one way left to save the primacy of self-preservation. The impossibility of preserving life is an impossibility only up to now. We cannot say, because all men have died, that all men will. A nice point—as the lawyers say—but a point, to be taken ever more seriously as the character and operation of the organic system are ever more seriously investigated.

The obstacles to eternal life on earth are not theological (as witness the doctrine of the resurrection). Augustinian theology, among others, suggests that preternatural man in the Garden was corporeally immortal and lost his immortality.[32] But natural man, born of woman, is no longer innocent; he is only ignorant, knowing only enough to know that he is not innocent. But he is not content to be ignorant, and his presumption (that got him into trouble in the first place) knows no end. He has no hesitation to take hold of the tree of life and convert it into knowledge, pulp, or plastics. The Man in Black may be willing to wait for the return of the Second Adam to be born again; not the Man in White.

Death is the failure of a system or, more precisely, a system of systems. Every part of the organism depends upon every other, and accident or disease, if it is serious enough, cannot be localized. The special difficulty —and this is the central distinction between the living organism and the inorganic system—is that the parts are in constant motion. We don't know if, at some point, nature, the master mechanic, finds it just too expensive to keep the old bus going. We have supposed so.

So strong has the supposition always been that irreversible chemical changes are assumed to be responsible for man's embryonic development, his growth, his decline, and his death. These changes—which we don't understand—are supposed to constitute a kind of mechanism. As man turns his intellectual engines on death, and looks for its causes, he bethinks him of every possible kind of "antibody." Is there, for example, a "death hormone" produced (like other hormones) by the organism, that kills us either by its own action or by activating what we now take to be the causes of death? In reporting this hypothesis, one writer must be credited with the understatement of the ages when he says that a drug designed to counteract that hypothetical hormone "would be of considerable interest."

Fifty years ago Freud was "astonished to find how little agreement exists among biologists on the question of natural death," and it is a pretty fair guess that he would be at least as astonished today. As we learn more about the causes of the "causes" of death, and attack those causes, with some success, we wonder more and more often whether man without whiskey, whipped cream, war, and a few other ancient and modern conveniences would have to die. This is not to suggest that

32 *The City of God*, GBWW, Vol. 18, pp. 357a–377a.

the "noble savage" of Rousseau lived forever, for the wild animals do not; he would have to be able to protect himself against accident, infection, and (hardest of all) against other men in addition to his being protected against his own tastes and passions. But take a man's whiskey, whipped cream, and war away from him—Winston Churchill went to a resplendent ninety on some such diet—and it is not certain that he would be interested in living very long, or at all.

It is only loose (if highly respected) talk to say that death is natural and that you will die as sure as you are born. Whom are we talking about and to? There are thousands of kinds of living creatures that die and thousands that don't die and live on, as far as we know, forever. The living immortals are the untold number of almost all the classes and orders of Protozoa, the unicellular (or, to be zoologically more particular, noncellular) animalcules almost all of which reproduce by fission, or a splitting or division of the "mother" into two or more "daughters." Given access to temperate water and not too much salt—and, of course, food, but they are not at all choosy—they are immortal in the sense that they go on living and never die. (Of course they lose their personalities when they divide, but, despite their constitutional versatility, they don't seem to have had much personality to begin with.)

Assume the hypothesis that human life as we now know it might be extended indefinitely. The world would be untenantable in no time; with no infant mortality, and even without a rising birthrate, the population would double every generation. The consumer burden of the very first generation of the nonproductive aged would starve out the race; unless, in that very first generation, the hard-pressed young reverted to primitivism and killed off their parents. But these cataclysms might well be reckoned the least of the scheme's disadvantages.

It is the prospect of death that gives life its form and its meaning, that gives love its poignancy, that occasions concern and kindness and aid and consolation in the human heart. And time; as Heidegger points out, we really know time because we know we are going to die. Without this passionate realization of our mortality, time would simply be a meaningless movement of the clock. For man, strictly speaking, is not in time like a boat on a flowing river; time is in man. It is not time that marches on, but we.

Love, and kindness, and time; and biography, the shape of life. Without death we should never have the measure of a man. We should not know what a good or a bad, successful or unsuccessful, happy or unhappy human life was, or what we might do to achieve the one and avoid the other. We should have no models of childhood, youth, maturity, old age, or the whole of life seen as a whole, because there would be no whole. Even now, as life expectancy rises to a modest seventy, we are witnessing an increasing formlessness, with the dislocations of protracted adolescence and suppressed senility, with childish thirty-year-olds at one end and childish sixty-year-olds at the other; with television advertisements for soapsuds in which the mother's hands cannot be told from the daughter's. The generations blend and merge, with parents and children "chums," and the delinquency of the too-long young is traced to the delinquency of the not-soon-enough old.

Love, kindness, time, biography; and progress. There would be a geriocracy—the tyranny of the old bores whose grip on power and prestige could not be shaken, and whose wealth could not be subjected to the redistribution of death. They would, even as we, mere octogenarians and nonagenarians, "belong to a generation that just doesn't understand all that"; and what they did not understand they would not encourage. And they would be hated for their domineering uncomprehension.[33] An end, to be sure, to recklessness and to ruinous abandon; but an end, too, to discovery and exploration and experimentation and invention and the daring that carries the race to new horizons.

Don't we live long enough on the whole? What would most of us do with more time? When men lived to be thirty or so, men did great things at thirty or so—Jesus, Alexander, Mozart, Napoleon; and when they live to be seventy or so they do not do many more great things than these. What do we do with the time that Jesus, Alexander, Napoleon, and Mozart did not have? Why, we kill time.—But only in our spare time, we say.—But if we have time to spare, what do we want more time for?—To spare? What we would do with more time is probably what we have done all along. So we lose the great efforts of a Dr. Tom Dooley at thirty-four or of a T. S. Eliot at seventy-six; but we lose the vile efforts of others who, like them, might live on; and the empty efforts of most. Would we *dare* to have time without end?

Old Faust in his closet says, "I long for death, existence I detest," but Mephisto the traveling man replies from the eternal experience which polls the opinion of the race: "And yet Death never is a wholly welcome guest." And I, too, though I have been told that there have been men who wanted to die, and have heard some say so themselves, have never known one, not one, of whom I was sure that he would not want to live tomorrow, or ten minutes from now; unless he was dying just then, and in excruciation.

---

33 Nobel Prize-winning geneticist Hermann J. Muller of Indiana University, asked about the "prospect of immortality" through freezing, thought that it should be more readily possible in the future "to use both genetics and methods of treatment of the developing individual as well as improved educational methods to produce better people than to reform revived individuals whose past was in an earlier age. . . . It seems to me that we would be extremely selfish in a misguided way to want to intrude upon these later generations. Moreover, I think they would quietly wipe us away, and we, of course, would never know the difference. I would not blame them a bit for this" (*Science News Letter*, June 20, 1964).

We conscious mortals have everything to lose by dying—we speak here as mortals for whom death is the end—and nothing to gain by dying. We conscious mortals——. But what of us *unconscious* mortals, every one of us, whose unconsciousness is of the proportions of the iceberg beneath the surface?

"We do not assert," Freud writes of the death instinct, "that death is the only aim of life; we do not overlook the presence of life by the side of death. We recognize two fundamental instincts, and ascribe to each of them its own aim." But the life instincts, the erotic or sexual, are the younger and, in the end, the weaker of the two. They "are always trying to collect living substance together into ever larger unities, [while] the death instincts which act against that tendency . . . try to bring living matter back into an inorganic condition. The co-operation and opposition of these two forces produce the phenomena of life to which death puts an end."[34] The winner: Death, the "self-destructive tendency."

The death instinct is not the *wish* to die, but the *need* or *necessity*. We know what it is to wish consciously to die, and the ambivalence that attends it. Death's praise, too, and life's dispraise are not manifestations of the death instinct at all; they are Freud's "intelligent striving."

The death instinct is unconscious. Here is *ennui*—the French noun, for which we have no precise counterpart—that a man feels consciously. He is simply tired, tired of "it all," and he knows it. Here is the French adjective *blasé*—again we have no precise counterpart—which the man feels, and knows he feels, who is not merely tired of it all but thinks that he has seen and known it all and has, in the American vulgate, "had it." But even to act out these sentiments in the form of suicide is not the death instinct.

Indeed, suicide, under extreme provocation of one kind or another of suffering, may be the recourse of what Freud calls the "part instincts" of self-preservation against what is felt to be destroying the self. But purposive suicide, "getting it over with," is probably the smallest proportion of all self-destructive patterns of behavior. The forces of adventuresomeness may be destructive or constructive, and they may inspire the daredeviltry (or self-sacrifice) that is sure or almost sure to be fatal, death being the one adventure the daredevil hasn't had. We approach the death instinct a little closer in the "accident-prone" person or the man who is drinking himself to death.

The Freudian hypothesis is, in effect, that every human being is a suicide. Without knowing it, we are trying harder to die than to live. Death is the only cure for what ails us all. We don't want to go back to the living womb, to a sheltered life; what we want to go back to is the biblical dust. It is all right for a sentimentalist like Tennyson to say that

---

34 *New Introductory Lectures on Psycho-Analysis*, GBWW, Vol. 54, p. 851b–d.

"no life that breathes with human breath / Has ever truly longed for death," but a hard-boiled old hand like Satan ought to know better than to say that "all that a man hath will he give for his life." On the contrary, say the Freudians; you are taking man's *word* for it; he will, in fact, give all that he has to die.

The Freudians have many common folk with them these recent days. We see that the preparation for the possible world war that will end the world—and every preparation for world war has always before been validated—is the leading activity of every great government. President Johnson solemnly says that the United States can "deliver" six hundred missiles and the Soviet Union only two hundred—and just as solemnly adds that the population centers of both nations would be destroyed. But man, and man everywhere, sits in the midst of this gathering doom and says, "What can a man do?—Nothing." He may be right or wrong; he is probably right. But that is not the point. The point is that man, not as an individual, but as a species, has got to this point; to the point of what the philosopher Herbert Marcuse of Brandeis University calls "the exalted acceptance of death." Is man saying, "Better dead than red (or white, or blue)," or is he saying, without knowing it, simply, "Better dead"?

THE FEAR OF DEATH—WHO'S AFRAID?

The long habit of living," says Sir Thomas Browne in his *Urne-buriall*, "indisposeth us for dying." Life is a habit, and every habit binds us the tighter the longer we practice it. Twentieth-century man should, on this count, be more indisposed for dying than his ancestors, for he has more of the habit of living by some thirty years per man. And the habit of gung-ho, or living it up, which was once confined to the few, is nowadays extended to the many.

But there is little doubting that, as machinery has replaced bodily exertion, man's life has been becoming progressively less physical and crude and progressively more mental and esthetic. Those who deplore the whoop-and-holler of modern culture tend to ignore the much more stupendous spread of education and the arts. The Old Adam is still there, beating the drums; but the Egghead is cooking on a scale beyond the wildest hopes of those who first thought that man was more than an incorrigible brute.

Modern, mental man probably pays more attention to death than the physical man of yore. That is, he probably thinks about it more; though the physical man of yore (and of now) was (and is) probably more fearful of the sure deprivation of the more obvious long habit of corporeal activity. Mental man has found a thousand ways to conceal the indelicacies of life. But dying is nearly always indelicate and undignified.

Its ugliness mocks every beauty real and cosmeticked. Every disguise and pretense falls in inexorable ruin as he proceeds, little by little, to the indistinguishable condition of the cave man and the composer of the *Ode on a Grecian Urn*. In the process he must be "attended to," the continent man incontinent, the temperate man intemperate, the esthetic man unesthetic; the operator operated, the manipulator manipulated, the proud man prone and lowered.

And he does not bear pain as well as he thought he might—or, in any case, he is afraid that he won't. He may comport himself like a child, utterly incapable of the advice he admired when Marcus Aurelius pointed out that the complaints of the body are *its* complaints, not his. Man is not nearly so stolid as the lower animals which suffer pain without analgesics or any other comfort; so, it would seem, the further his civilized life is from theirs, the less stolid. Besides, the ubiquitous and effective pain-killers of our time relieve him of the habit; only a masochist would have a tooth out without novocaine.

But by the same token the physical pain of dying is minimized. The painless extraction of teeth has been extended to the painless extraction of people. These days we may die happily forever after, under constant, increasing sedation. We have not yet had a treatise entitled "Dying Can Be Fun," but we know that it need not be agony. Then, too, life seems to prepare itself, perhaps for death, but in any case for dying: It releases us, little by little, from the needs that, little by little, become incapable of fulfillment. We have been letting our old friends go, our old interests unclutch as we develop what Lewis Mumford calls an "inner deafness and blindness" to the coming and going of captains and kings and the crises of personal, social, and political life. Fatigue brings its own relief. Time loses its urgency, and the hand that can still turn the calendar leaves it unturned. This is the "providential amnesia" of common medical observation, the gradual withdrawal to the point where, as Hazlitt says, death only consigns the last fragment of what we were to the grave.

And still we are afraid to die. Give me my choice, to die tonight in an airplane crash or ten years from now in long lonely pain, and I will try my cunning and say, "Make it fifteen . . . make it twenty. . . ." We live always with both death and dying, and modern medicine gives us increasingly longer notice of the appointment; types of cancer and cardiovascular diseases that only a generation ago carried a man off on the instant or in three months have so far yielded to research that their progress may be restrained for ten years or twenty and, in the direst of them, for many months. Death sits longer at our bedside than it did before, and makes itself at home; it can wait.

Men, says Epictetus, are disturbed not by the things that happen but by the opinions about the things. "Death," he adds airily, "is nothing so terrible . . . the opinion about death, that it is terrible, is the terrible thing." But Santayana, in our own time, insists upon looking at the matter in a different way entirely: "The radical fear of death . . . is the love of life. . . . Nothing could be more futile, therefore, than to marshal arguments against that fear of death which is merely another name for the energy of life. . . . [If] the love of life were extinguished, the fear of death, like smoke rising from that fire, would have vanished also."[35] Precisely the opposite, says Plutarch (b. A.D. 46), taking issue with Santayana (b. A.D. 1863). "It is fear of death, not craving for life," says our ancient Greek, "that makes a fool hang on to his body and wind himself about it. . . ."[36]

Plutarch and Santayana cannot agree. Can you and I?—Hardly. But we can agree on some subsidiary issues involving the nature of the fear of death. We can agree that we see death as an everlasting kind of night. Night and the unknown . . . the *dead of night.* The time of helplessness, when our blinded senses deceive and disarm us against the enemy; the time of stealthy disaster and all despair, "the prisoner's hour." This dread of the dark—so readily seen in childhood, so hollowly defied later on—is intensified by darkness' silence. The racket of the day reassures us; now the world is spectral still. The dead of night.

But perhaps the greater terror arises in our impossibility to imagine incorporeality, the nonpossession of the body with its senses. Nonsensitivity is inconceivable. We cannot imagine not being hurt. The worms, the sharks, the buzzards torment us while we live, as they will not when we are dead and they have their way; and thus the hospital eye banks (and now kidney banks) beg the sensitive living for their senseless organs and the medical schools beg for cadavers, and there are not enough; we are afraid of being hurt when we know that we won't be. We have seen ourselves cut and sutured and we have known that "it" doesn't hurt under anesthetic; *but neither seeing nor knowing is believing.*

The terror of the endless dark and the terror of being chewed or nibbled or torn to pieces are terror enough; but the ultimate terror is that death means that I shall be no more; not you, or he, or they, but *I.* Your death, his, and theirs I can bear, however hardly; mine I cannot. The whole world is a procession that passes, and I alone in the reviewing stand. I love others, and some most dearly, and my goodwill to the rest is enormous. But I *can* live without them all—only not without myself. No; not without that self-knowing knower whose consciousness that he is, and that he is he, is all there is. Before me all was only report and record; after me, too. While I *am*, reality is. The world began when I

35 "Lucretius," GGB, Vol. 10, pp. 381a–382a.
36 "Contentment," GGB, Vol. 10, p. 279a.

was born. It ends when I die. And die I do, and this is unbearable; and
I shall bear it.

HOW TO DIE

Dying takes some doing. Why shouldn't we try to figure out how
best to do it, if we are going to have to? It would seem that the
Boy Scout has the heavier assignment; he is expected to be prepared
for every contingency. We have only to prepare ourselves for a certainty.

The easiest way, beyond a doubt, is to believe that it isn't going to
happen; the next easiest, to be steeled; easiest of all, to be assured that
we'll be all right when it's over with. A painful operation, but a minor
one. So we are back, at the end, where we started: Dying, like death,
turns on the survival of death. What is a little fear, a little pain, a little
loss, or even a great deal of all of them, when we know that they are
transitional to everlasting glory?

But the rub is that the believer in immortality, no less than the nonbeliever, dies a *mortal* death, and mortal man is weak. The historical
literature of death is, however, persuasive on the point that the believer
is at least a little likelier to die easy than the nonbeliever. But the record
is replete with the instances of nonbelievers who carried the thing off
with as much aplomb as the devout. There is a case to be made that
the mundane virtues that carry us well through life carry us well through
the mundane exertion of dying.

The moral virtues enable men to resist the pleasures of this life and bear
its pains (not the least of which is the pain of resisting pleasure). The
agnostic and atheist view of dying puts great store by these virtues, and
with considerable weight. For we know that virtues are habits (as are
vices), and that virtues (and vices) are formed by repetition of the acts
of which they are the habit; the more often we do a thing, the easier
it is to do it (and the harder it is not to). He who has the habits of
fortitude, temperance, justice, and wisdom is not likely to lose them of a
sudden; they have become his settled disposition, "second nature." Thus
he should be equable in his contemplation of the loss of the pleasures of
life, and of the pain of its leaving. Let him but be virtuous, and a philosopher; enough. He requires no crutch, and no goad; no hope of heaven,
no fear of hell. He has been able to live, and live exemplarily, without
religion. Why should he not be able to die without it?

The man who believes in immortality is generally pessimistic about
man, the nonbeliever optimistic. The one usually accepts the hope of
divine bliss and the fear of divine retribution as the necessary tension to
which original sin reduced us all. The other cannot believe that a grown
man must "become as a little child" in the sense that his righteousness
must be induced by the promise of bubble gum and the threat of bumps;

what more, under such conditions, is righteousness than calculation? Israel Zangwill makes the point in his story of the wise man who, upon being informed by the Lord that he would not go to heaven, said, "At last I can do good without fear of reward."

After the eager and ecstatic death of the primitive Christians who believed themselves saved, the history of the Church showed a precipitate decline in the hope of heaven and a precipitate rise in the fear of hell. Piety among nonecstatics seems to be more effectively enjoined by the promise of punishment than it is by the promise of reward. For a great many centuries Protestants no less than Catholics painted the horrors of damnation in vivider colors than the joys of salvation. The result was a dread of death so strong that many writers (some of them on some sort of sampling basis) have maintained that it is deeper among believers than nonbelievers; a paradox, but far from an impossibility.

The modern Church tends to reexamine some of its dogmas, and its consideration of eternal damnation may in part reflect its long concern with the apostasy of men and women who simply cannot stomach the traditional outlook. Among the eminent believers who have taken a hard look at the matter is none other than Pierre Teilhard de Chardin, the Roman Catholic theologian (and paleontologist) whose *The Phenomenon of Man* and *The Divine Milieu* have made so great an impact on the world in the past few years. In the latter work he writes: "Of all the mysteries which we have to believe, O Lord, there is none, without a doubt, which so affronts our human views as that of damnation. . . . We could perhaps understand falling back into inexistence . . . but what are we to make of eternal uselessness and eternal suffering? . . . You have told me, O God, to believe in hell. But You have forbidden me to hold with absolute certainty that a single man has been damned." Here is a new look, indeed, one that goes so far as to ask whether Hell is anything more than eternal death and the deprivation of the beatific vision of God.

Immortality does not follow from God's existence, in any case; and still less the personal immortality that seems to be peculiarly rooted in Western individualism. Herbert J. Muller in his *The Uses of the Past* argues that the modern Westerner rejects the anonymous immortality of the World Soul offered by Hinduism and Platonism because "John Smith not only wants to live forever—he wants to be forever John Smith, hanging on to everything except his warts; and in a heaven' swarming with Smiths he still wants to be set apart, or even catch the eye of the Super-Smith." Theologian Paul Tillich (among others) points out that the Bible does not speak of the "hereafter" or of the "life after death."[37] What it does speak of, and with repeated precision, is what follows

37 "The Eternal Now" in *The Meaning of Death, op. cit.*, pp. 32–33.

least of all from God's existence, namely, the resurrection of the body.

"Far be it from us," says Augustine, "to fear that the omnipotence of the Creator cannot, for the resuscitation and reanimation of our bodies, recall all the portions which have been consumed by beasts or fire, or have been dissolved into dust or ashes, or have decomposed into water, or evaporated into the air." True, resurrection of the body is much further from man's comprehension than immortality of the disembodied soul, for the main and simple reason (as Penrod would say) that the perishing of the body is abundantly familiar to us. But the doctrine of corporeal resurrection *of the dead* is bounteously grounded in the New Testament wonder of the Second Coming, the Last Judgment, and the Second Death of the unredeemed, as the immortality of man's soul is not.

The Creeds recited in nearly all the Western Churches sustain the resurrection and fortify the faithful in the harder of the two doctrines. But the harder is at the same time the easier, for it pictures man as he knows himself, and at least appears to circumvent the metaphysical difficulties of separability of soul and body and the independent existence of the soul. A New Jerusalem of *people*—however crowded by space-occupying bodies—makes less of a demand upon our imagination-circumscribed piety than a gathering of even the blithest spirits.

The assemblage of my dust is no mean miracle, and is second in splendor only to the Creation itself. In the course of a long and peripatetic life I have left a fingertip here, an earlobe there, and teeth and hair everywhere. I have even had the disconcerting experience of falling among cannibals who, having severally consumed *and assimilated* morsels of me, fell out among themselves and were dispersed to the ends of the earth. The credulity of the credulous seems to be sore taxed by the doctrine of hale-and-hearty resurrection, as witness the prevalent religious opposition to cremation.

Why is cremation, the proper burial of ancient Greeks (and of ancient and modern Hindus), frowned upon? If, to be sure, the bones and dry dust of my decomposed body are snugly ensconced in one place, I suppose that they are easier reassembled *if it is men who are doing the reassembling.* But it is God, to Whom all such things are equally easy. Why then undertake to keep me from the quick clean fire? Because—I am told—the disposition of my dead body is no more the proper business of men than the disposition of my live one by suicide. But see how the faithful, with the sanction and cooperation of the Church, embalm me and perfume me and preserve me, even with stout caskets and still stouter caskets around the caskets; is not this a disposition of the body, with as much attempted interference in God's work as cremation itself, and much more lost trouble and lost money besides?

Nature shows us its winnowing ways on every hand, as it did in the Scripture on the seed's need to fall to the ground and die in order to be reborn or to fructify the life-bearing earth. We are not seeds (or leaves or trees). But we are bodies, and the more we get to know about bodies, including falling bodies, the more difficult it is to cling to the belief in their arising. Modern man, including the modern man of faith, grows increasingly ambivalent toward the tradition of death which he inherited. Nor is there any sign that the current religious revival (if there is one) is reducing the ambivalence fed by the increase of scientific knowledge.

Nowhere is the ambivalence plainer than in India, between Gandhi and Nehru. In his *All Men Are Brothers*, the Mahatma said that the living faith in God "sustains us in life, is our one solace in death." Truth is God, and "even the atheists who have pretended to disbelieve in God have believed in Truth. The trick they have performed is that of giving God another, not a new, name. . . . You may pluck out my eyes, but that cannot kill me. But blast my belief in God, and I am dead." His successor and disciple, dying sixteen years later as the prime minister of India, declared that he did not want any religious ceremonies performed for him after his death: "I do not believe in any such ceremonies, and to submit to them, even as a matter of form, would be hypocrisy. . . ." *But* he asked that his ashes (should he die abroad) be sent back to Allahabad and "a small portion of them thrown into the Ganges"; and so the unbelieving Pandit joined the believing Mahatma in the everlasting flow of the sacred river.

We believe in immortality, said William James, because we believe that we are *fit* for it, that, apart from reward and retribution, we believe that our life somehow deserves it. "Can things whose end is always dust and disappointment be the real goods which our souls require?" Let man have faith and hope and "his days pass by with zest; they stir with prospects, they thrill with remoter values. Place round them on the contrary the curdling cold and gloom and absence of all permanent meaning which for pure naturalism and the popular science evolutionism of our time are all that is visible ultimately, and the thrill stops short, or turns rather to an anxious trembling."[38]

There is an anxious trembling in the world today. Whatever may have been man's psychic estate when his atmosphere was faith and hope, the deliquescence of that faith and hope does not by itself, or even with the increase of knowledge, appear to have met his most dire needs; at least not yet. And Freud's most famous colleague, C. G. Jung, says, "As a physician I am convinced that it is hygienic—if I may use the word—to discover in death a goal towards which one can strive; and that shrinking away from it is something unhealthy and abnormal which robs

[38] *The Varieties of Religious Experience* (New York: Modern Library, 1936, pp. 136–39.

the second half of life of its purpose. I therefore consider the religious teaching of a life hereafter consonant with the standpoint of psychic hygiene. When I live in a house which I know will fall about my head within the next two weeks, all my vital functions will be impaired by this thought. . . . Among all my patients in the second half of life—that is to say, over thirty-five—there has not been one whose problem in the last resort was not that of finding a religious outlook on life. It is safe to say that every one of them fell ill because he had lost that which the living religions of every age have given to their followers, and none of them has been really healed who did not regain his religious outlook."[39]

In the foxhole where we all die, today's nonbeliever may be tomorrow's believer; maybe not. In either event each of us will, some time soon now, join the great majority, and it is not unbecoming (for the flesh is weak) to wonder whether some of the sting can be taken out of the procedure. If Death cannot be cheated, maybe he can be talked into taking it a little easy; and, again, maybe not. It wouldn't seem so, for the art of dying graciously is nowhere advertised, in spite of the fact that its market potential is greater than gracious living's.

Those who know, *i.e.*, every one of us, are almost all agreed that the best way to die is not to shuffle and lag but to be hurrying to do something useful (or something *else* useful), or at least something urgent that preoccupies the putative victim. This is a happy concatenation that is hard to arrange: but ever easier, it appears, in the more civilized industrial societies. Sudden death by violence is standard front-page fare these days. It frightens us, as the long list of death notices among the want ads do not; but the fear is probably the product of the spectacularity.

Sudden death is unanticipated, and anticipation is almost certainly the hardest part of dying. But we encounter an occasional dissent on the point. The famous last words of the dying may not have been their last words, nor their last thoughts. But an occasional doomed man, usually a writer, undertakes to make a written record. To be sure, the record, whenever it ends, ends a moment too soon to be satisfactory, but it does tell us something; all the more, if the writer is dying, as most of us do, of natural causes. The most recent, novelist Thomas Bell, a professing atheist, in his account of his last months, registered an eloquent exception to the prevailing view: "Those who drop dead in their tracks . . . have missed dying altogether. And dying—not death . . . but dying—must surely be placed high among the two or three supreme human experiences. It's one I would willingly forgo for another twenty years. Since I can't, I may as well make the best of it by regarding it as an opportunity, an

39 *Modern Man in Search of a Soul* (New York: Harcourt Brace & Co., Inc., 1933), pp. 128–129, 264.

uncommon one, but by no means unique. . . ."[40]

We are told (by the Greek tragedians) that man learns through suffering (and by the idiomatic Christian that you can't get to heaven on roller skates). And it may be that a man can learn a little something useful by suffering the sense of dying, and even that the longer he attends its school the more he will learn both about the conduct of this life and the demeanor of its close. What is indicated, on this hypothesis, is a lifelong expectation, and a conscious expectation, of death.

Why shouldn't the tried and true recipe for old age be tried for dying? Why not avoid going glumly and idly into the one as into the other? The fewer hours you have left, the fewer you have to be idle. Now you may know the measured urgency whose knowledge is denied to youth. On his ninetieth birthday Justice Holmes said that "to live is to function. That is all there is in living. . . . 'Death plucks at my ears and says, Live— I am coming.'" You will not finish your work; no man has. Your stamp collection, your reading, your music, your chess game will not be complete; no man's has. But you will have made death hustle for you; you will have been moving, he will have to catch you on the fly. And like Lady Mary Wortley Montagu, the eighteenth-century English wit, you will be able to die saying, or at least knowing, "It has all been very interesting"; with the accent on the *all*.

Remember that thou shalt die; why not practice doing it in the death of others? A somber business, sitting with the dying; but to be somber is not the same as to be morbid. We learn by seeing and feeling, and not just by doing. See men die, and feel it, then. Best of all, perhaps, see yourself dying, once in a while, of a bump or a lump, during those hours, or days, or weeks, before the doctor comes and says, "I've got good news for you"; whoever has had *this* experience has practiced dying as has no one else but the man who has been told, "I've got bad news for you."

"He who should teach men to die would at the same time teach them to live." But dying is self-taught, and he who having learned it should teach it is unavailable. We are told that the thing for a man to do, when he finds himself with a lemon, is to make lemonade out of it. We do *not* know that there are *no* worse things than dying. We do know that it would be nice to be rid of the blemishes of this life and we know (unless we are fools clear out to the rind) that we shall not be in this happy case while we live. The Great Frederick of Prussia found a French name for his palace, *Sans Souci*; and there, care-ridden, misanthropic, and lonely, he died. Man's mad vanity is mocked by life. Death takes us down a peg or two, too, and cuts us and our furnishings to size; probably not a bad thing for most of us, and maybe the best thing that ever happened to any of us. Who knows?

[40] *In the Midst of Life* (New York: Atheneum Publishers, 1961), p. 123.

Milton Mayer

BIBLIOGRAPHY

BELL, THOMAS. *In the Midst of Life.* New York: Atheneum Publishers, 1961.

BOWERS, MARGARETTA K., *et al. Counseling the Dying.* New York: Thomas Nelson & Sons, 1964.

BROWN, NORMAN O. *Life Against Death.* Middletown, Conn.: Wesleyan University Press, 1959.

CARREL, ALEXIS. "The Mystery of Death" in *Great Adventures in Medicine*, ed. SAMUEL B. RAPPORT and HELEN WRIGHT. New York: Dial Press, Inc., 1952.

CONRAD, BARNABY (comp.). *Famous Last Words.* Garden City, N.Y.: Doubleday & Co., Inc., 1961.

DUNNE, JOHN S., C.S.C. *The City of the Gods: A Study in Myth and Mortality.* New York: The Macmillan Co., 1965.

FARBEROW, NORMAN L. and SHNEIDMAN, EDWIN S. (eds.). *The Cry for Help.* New York: McGraw-Hill Book Co., Inc., 1961. (Book deals with suicide)

FEIFEL, HERMAN (ed.). *The Meaning of Death.* New York: McGraw-Hill Book Co., Inc., 1959.

HABENSTEIN, ROBERT W. and LAMERS, WILLIAM M. *The History of American Funeral Directing*; revised edition. Milwaukee, Wisc.: National Funeral Directors Association, 1962. (Much broader than its title would indicate, this book deals with various attitudes on death from the time of the Egyptian pharaohs.)

HARMER, RUTH MULVEY. *The High Cost of Dying.* New York: Crowell-Collier Press, 1963.

HOCKING, WILLIAM ERNEST. *The Meaning of Immortality in Human Experience*, including *Thoughts on Death and Life*; revised edition. New York: Harper & Brothers, 1957.

MITFORD, JESSICA. *The American Way of Death.* New York: Simon & Schuster, Inc., 1963.

PELIKAN, JAROSLAV. *The Shape of Death.* Nashville, Tenn.: Abingdon Press, 1961.

RAHNER, KARL. *On the Theology of Death.* New York: Herder & Herder, Inc., 1961.

SCHACHTEL, HYMAN JUDAH. *The Shadowed Valley.* New York: Alfred A. Knopf, Inc., 1962.

SPARK, MURIEL. *Memento Mori.* Philadelphia: J. B. Lippincott Co., 1959.

SULZBERGER, CYRUS. *My Brother Death.* New York: Harper & Row, 1961.

TROISFONTAINES, ROGER. *I Do Not Die.* New York: Desclee & Co., 1963.

ULANOV, BARRY (comp.). *Death, A Book of Preparation and Consolation.* New York: Sheed and Ward, Ltd., 1959.

WAUGH, EVELYN. *The Loved One.* Boston: Little, Brown and Co., 1948.

WERTENBAKER, LAEL TUCKER. *Death of a Man.* New York: Random House, Inc., 1957.

WHITE, ROBERT W. (ed.). *The Study of Lives*, chap. 4 and 9. New York: Atherton Press, 1963.

NOTE TO THE READER

In the *Syntopicon* the idea of death is joined with that of life to form Chapter 48. The reader interested in pursuing further the themes explored by Mr. Mayer will find abundant material in the passages cited under the various topics into which that chapter is divided. LIFE AND DEATH 6 deals with the life span and the life cycle, and what *Great Books* has to say about the human life span may be found by consulting the passages cited under 6b. The transition from life to death and its causes is the subject of Topic 7.

The major themes of Mr. Mayer's essay turn about the concern of the living with life and death, which is the subject of LIFE 8. Passages dealing with the various funeral rites that men have practiced may be found by consulting Topic 8d. The love of life is discussed in the texts cited under 8a, and the love of death in those under 8b. The fear of death and the practice of dying, discussed in the final sections of Mr. Mayer's essay, provide the subject of Topic 8c, and the interested reader can find extensive discussions of this subject by consulting the passages that are cited there.

Immortality, Mr. Mayer writes, is "the hinge on which Death turns"; belief in personal immortality affects one's view of death. Chapter 38 of the *Syntopicon* is entirely devoted to the idea of immortality, and the very first topic brings the two ideas together under the heading, *The desire for immortality: the fear of death.* The chapter as a whole will be of interest and profit to anyone desiring to pursue further his study of immortality.

A REVIEW IN PICTURES

On Death

OF THE PRECEDING ESSAY BY MILTON MAYER

Death is the one idea that has no history. It is the idea that punctuates all the other ideas, and thus it has endured, without development or synthesis, through the ages. What has changed—and therefore has a history—is the way of dying, as distinct from the Idea of Death. In its own way, the picture suggests all this: the array of grave markers in the New York City cemetery commemorates the individuality of death that was the pattern of the past; behind grave markers, the skyscrapers loom like giant monuments to the new, massive form of dying to which the pictures of Verdun, Belsen, and Hiroshima (*following pages*) bear silent witness. But in the end, there remains now, as ever, the one idea that has no history.

Continued

GERMAN SOLDIER'S SKELETON, 1916
The grotesque indignity of death

VERDUN PILLBOX
He would bring modern man to heel

AND HUMAN DIGNITY ITS INDIGNIFICATION

CONCENTRATION CAMP, 1945
Depriving death of its individuality

HIROSHIMA, 1945
So handsome was the reaper's swath

Continued

FATHER DUFFY'S MONUMENT, NEW YORK
Man's mad vanity is mocked by life

How much fame is worth one's life? Manolete the matador (*right*) fought for fame in his suit of lights and achieved fame. Mussolini bullied his way to fame in his black shirt and achieved notoriety. Father Duffy achieved fame twice over—once as Chaplain of the "Fighting 69th" in World War I and then as the Broadway Priest. But death blurred the image of the fame of all three. The end transformed the lithe matador into a frail form on the sand. The bluff dictator ended up resembling a carcass in a slaughterhouse. Pigeons roost on Father Duffy's monument in Times Square. The quest for undying fame actually may be the quest for immortality, but, whatever the quest may be, it is, as stated in the preceding essay, clearly *terrible trouble to pursue and most unsurely got.* Yet, all men, in their own way, keep seeking immortality and keep sympathizing with the seekers who merely die in the process. Mourning is many things, but, among them, it is the expression of such sympathy, the begrudging of death. Skippy, the dead spaniel elaborately buried by humans (*following page*), lives on as a human declaration that it shouldn't happen, even to a dog. A bird's attendance on its dead mate is seen as grief, resentment of death, in the eyes of the human beholder. It matters not that birds usually "mourn" even more briefly than Soviet leaders, who buried Stalin with pomp on one day and reviled him on the next. Stalin is dead, the party lives on, was the meaning—just as the royal mourners could reflect that, though George VI was dead, the dynasty lived on. The pictures on the following pages demonstrate predictable human reactions to death: it shouldn't happen to dogs, it can't happen to parties (or dynasties), and it was unfairly imposed on the old Spanish villager mourned by the women. *Man the burier seems to be saying, "You can't do this to me."*

AND THEY WILL DIE FOR THE CLOSEST THING

MANOLETE APPLAUDED (LEFT) AND GORED (RIGHT)
Fame is our immortality

MUSSOLINI AS DICTATOR (LEFT); AS CORPSE (RIGHT)
*There is more immortality in burning Rome
than in saving it*

Continued

DOG'S GRAVE
Splendid in ashes and pompous in the grave

BIRD WITH DEAD MATE
Darwin had not heard of Hollywood

A GESTURE, MADE OVER AND OVER AGAIN BY CHRISTIANS AND COMMUNISTS AND HUMANISTS AND THE UNCONCERNED.

PARTY LEADERS CARRYING STALIN'S COFFIN
*I saw Joe last Thursday and he was
as healthy as I am*

QUEENS AT FUNERAL OF KING GEORGE VI
Death is no laughing matter

DEATH IN A SPANISH TOWN
In no wise different from falling asleep

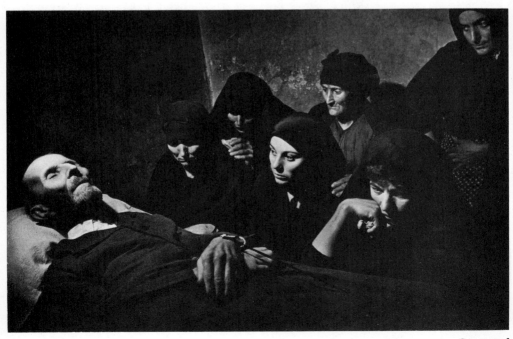

Continued

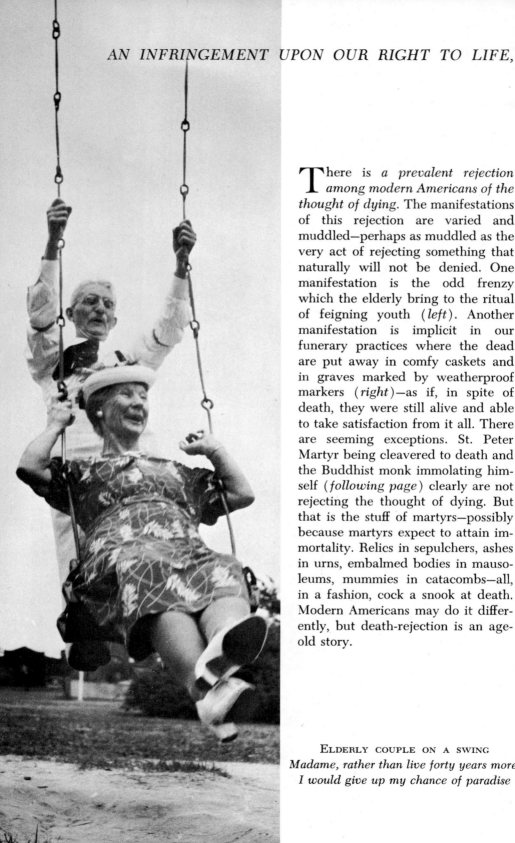

There is *a prevalent rejection among modern Americans of the thought of dying.* The manifestations of this rejection are varied and muddled—perhaps as muddled as the very act of rejecting something that naturally will not be denied. One manifestation is the odd frenzy which the elderly bring to the ritual of feigning youth (*left*). Another manifestation is implicit in our funerary practices where the dead are put away in comfy caskets and in graves marked by weatherproof markers (*right*)—as if, in spite of death, they were still alive and able to take satisfaction from it all. There are seeming exceptions. St. Peter Martyr being cleavered to death and the Buddhist monk immolating himself (*following page*) clearly are not rejecting the thought of dying. But that is the stuff of martyrs—possibly because martyrs expect to attain immortality. Relics in sepulchers, ashes in urns, embalmed bodies in mausoleums, mummies in catacombs—all, in a fashion, cock a snook at death. Modern Americans may do it differently, but death-rejection is an age-old story.

ELDERLY COUPLE ON A SWING
Madame, rather than live forty years more,
I would give up my chance of paradise

GRAVE-MARKER SALESMAN
Gratitude and guilt encumber the dead with baubles and baggage

CEMETERY BILLBOARD IN CALIFORNIA
Rest in Peace! Rest in Peace! Rest in Peace!

Continued

"ST. PETER MARTYR," D. 1252
*Dying is nearly always
indelicate and undignified*

SUICIDE OF BUDDHIST MONK IN VIETNAM, 1963
Dying takes some doing

BODIES OF LENIN AND STALIN IN RED SQUARE MAUSOLEUM
As much aplomb as the devout

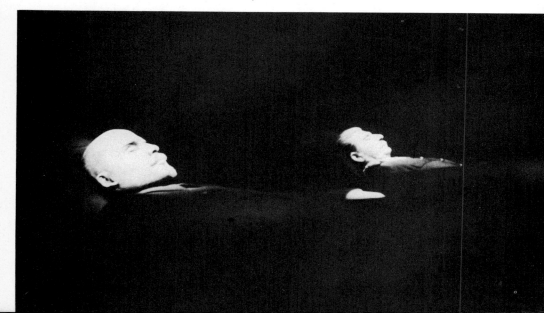

"FOR POLITICAL PURPOSES," YOU SAY.

Skeleton Chapel of the Capuchins, Rome
Ponderous and elaborate homage

Couple in Mexican catacombs
Nowhere is the ambivalence plainer

Continued

WE HAVE ONLY TO PREPARE OURSELVES

Death is impossible to the young, and, apparently, almost everyone feels too young to die. The result is a procession of scrambled and paradoxical patterns: the lad below blinks at the bright sunlight though the pall of death is all about him. The Japanese politician is caught in a tableau of death-rejection (*above, right*) as is the soldier (*below, right*) —even though the soldiers and the politicians of Verdun, the concentration camps, and Hiroshima contrived new ways of making men die. Birds are thought to mourn as briefly as Communist leaders. Oldsters feign youth, and youth could not care less. Man knows that all ideas have undergone change with the passage of history—bar one . . .

BELSEN CONCENTRATION CAMP, 1945
Ernst ist das Leben

FOR A CERTAINTY

JAPANESE ASSASSINATION
*What is a little fear,
a little pain*

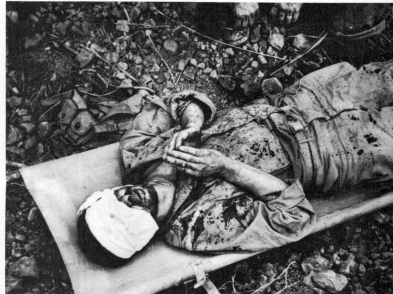

WOUNDED U.S. SOLDIER, OKINAWA, 1945
*In the foxhole where we all die, today's
nonbeliever may be tomorrow's believer*

Continued

DEATH IS THE ONE IDEA
THAT HAS NO HISTORY.

PART THREE

The Year's Developments in the Arts and Sciences

Literature: Stephen Spender

Philosophy and Religion: John E. Smith

Social Sciences: Kenneth E. Boulding

Biological Sciences: George Gaylord Simpson

Physical Sciences and Technology: Jeremy Bernstein

Literature

STEPHEN SPENDER

Ever since he published his first poems and criticism in the early 1930's, Stephen Spender has contributed to contemporary English and American literature as a poet, critic, editor, translator, and lecturer. Born in 1909 in London, he was graduated from University College, Oxford, in 1930. Mr. Spender first achieved recognition as a member of the group of young Oxford poets— including W. H. Auden and Louis Macneice—who introduced a fresh dimension of social and political commentary into English verse. From 1939 to 1941 he was co-editor, along with the critic Cyril Connolly, of the influential literary journal Horizon. *After World War II, Mr. Spender served as counselor in the Section of Letters in UNESCO. In 1953 he was a founder of* Encounter, *the monthly magazine of literature, criticism, and political opinion, and he continues as its co-editor. After lecturing at various American universities, he was appointed Visiting Professor in English at Northwestern University in 1963. In recognition of his service to English letters, Mr. Spender was made a Commander of the British Empire in the Honour's List on the Queen's birthday in 1962. Among his more than twenty books are:* Collected Poems *(1955), an autobiography* World Within a World *(1951), and the collections of critical essays,* The Creative Element *(1953),* The Making of a Poem *(1955), and* The Struggle of the Modern *(1963). He makes his home in London with his wife, the concert pianist Natasha Litvin, their son, and their daughter.*

In an immense essay on the year's fiction for 1914, Henry James, after surveying the current parade of novelists, ended with a phrase about a young novelist just discernible in "the dusty rear." This was D. H. Lawrence. Although Lawrence had published *Sons and Lovers* the year before, James deserves credit for noticing Lawrence at all. (Perhaps he had been told about Lawrence by H. G. Wells, on one of their walks near James's home at Rye, England.)

A writer reviewing the year's harvest of imaginative writing is aware that he may well leave unnoticed the most significant novel or book of poems. I only have to contemplate the essay which lies ahead to remember the editor who rejected Rimbaud's *A Season in Hell*, and Gide's rejection, while acting as a publisher's reader, of the first volume of Proust's *Remembrance of Things Past*. I should explain that I have not read all of what other writers may regard as the year's most significant books; I have chosen to write about a few books, hoping that they best represent the general climate of imaginative writing in 1964.

This having been said, by way of exorcism, I have to remark that the past year was not a very exciting one in fiction, and in poetry it was a sad year. We saw the passing away of one great poet in the main line of the tradition, T. S. Eliot, and one extraordinary, admirable, and much-loved eccentric figure, Edith Sitwell. Add to this that one of the most striking books of poetry to appear was *The Far Field*—the posthumous collection of Theodore Roethke, who died in August, 1963—and there is the feeling of the great poets of the first half of this century moving into the shadows.

Later in this essay, when I turn to poetry, I shall attempt to determine the meaning that Eliot had for other poets who, as long as he was alive, went on thinking of him as the great, unsleeping center of consciousness for poets, forever aware of the problems of writing poetry in an age which seems antipoetic. I shall try also to sum up the impression made on her time by Edith Sitwell: a distinct and clear one, though off-center, in fact almost by definition eccentric.

We may well remember 1964 as the end of an epoch rather than a year of outstanding positive achievement. One novel seemed to be a potential landmark: Saul Bellow's *Herzog*. With its massive documentation about the hero's life, the attempt to cross a wasteland of nihilism and arrive at a positive attitude toward the present age, it reads like the last of a series of works of self-examination projected into fiction. In this it bears a resemblance to another edifice of self-examination set up in 1964: Arthur Miller's drama *After the Fall*, in which the playwright also attempts a massive summing-up of moral positions over several years, making great quantities of public and private dirty linen still dirtier in the process. But it is scarcely necessary to say that apart from their troubled consciences, Saul Bellow and Arthur Miller have little in common; and what they do have demonstrates the superiority of Saul Bellow who, with all his richness of humor, his intensity of living, his ebullience, yet has an immense refinement. Throughout his searchings, the center of Bellow's conscience is his own soul, and, possibly, God. Miller's final court of appeal is a committee of liberal intellectuals, each with three or four divorces behind him, nursing stricken consciences about their leftism during the 1930's and still more about their anti-communism during the McCarthy era.

The low tension of the year under review is demonstrated by the fact that the novelists whom one regards as carrying the torch of the Novel like a sacred cause, did little more than carry on. C. P. Snow in *The Corridors of Power* discouraged even the most ardent fans of his fictional hero Lewis Eliot, and it seemed fitting that the appearance of this volume in a long series of Grand Soap Opera coincided with the disappearance of the author into those very Whitehall corridors. Another serial writer, Anthony Powell, was much more encouraging. His *The Valley of Bones*, the first in a new sequence which begins the second part of *The Music of Time*, takes the reader up to the beginning of World War II, which provides Powell with a new cast of characters drawn from a Welsh regiment, who are very fresh blood indeed. Powell's admirers may agree that he is best when writing about school and university, and for him, as for many others, the war provided a stimulus like that of going back to school.

The French novelist and critic Alain Robbe-Grillet suggested nearly a decade ago that the novel is dying because it has failed to advance as an art form, but if this were true, it would be more so of the French and English than of the American. For the Novel (with a capital *N* this time) draws nourishment from two distinct sources: first, art, that which in

the novelist corresponds to the renewal of language, the invention of
form and idiom in the poet, and which is, hence, the realization of his
inmost moral sensibility, his values—this is what Henry James calls
the creation of "interest" in the novel; and second, what James calls
"saturation" in the material of actual life which surrounds the novelist
when he is writing and provides his subject matter.

In the essay on *The Younger Generation of 1914,* from which I quoted
above, Henry James writes:

> Nothing is further from us, of course, than to undervalue the particular
> acquainted state, that of saturation and possession, however it may have
> been brought about; for it represents on behalf of the novelist, as that of
> any painter of things seen, felt, or imagined, just one half of his authority,
> the other half being represented, naturally by the application he is inspired
> to make of that advantage.

Of his contemporaries, James points to Arnold Bennett and H. G.
Wells as the masters of "saturation" to the exclusion of "interest," so
that regarding Bennett, he writes:

> When the author of *Clayhanger* has put down upon the table, in dense un-
> confused array, every fact required to make the life of the Five Towns
> press upon us and to make our sense of it, so full fed, content us, we may
> well go on for the time in the captive condition, the beguiled and amused
> condition, the acknowledgement of which is in general our highest tribute
> to the temporary master of our sensibility.

Of course, at the end of the same paragraph, James is protesting:
"Yes, yes; but is this *all?* These are the circumstances of the interest—
we see, we see; but where is the interest itself, where and what is its
centre and how are we to measure it in relation to *that?*"

The division of the Novel into the "saturation" and the "interest" does
suggest that in most novels these proportions are unlikely to be exactly
observed. What it usefully makes one see, however, is that in certain
writers, in certain countries, in certain times, one aspect is likely to
predominate. Where the surrounding state of history is immensely interesting, this material seems to press its claims upon the novelist: "Describe
me! Deal with me! Be swamped by me! Forget about Henry James and
his special 'interest'!" Thus to James, the Russians are the supreme
examples—particularly Tolstoy—of the novel saturated at the expense
of the significant art. One notices that the Russian who was nearest to
James was Turgenev, who lived a great deal of his life in Paris, and who
was, like James and Joyce, the great practitioner of the novel in exile.

The English novelists Bennett and Wells, whom James was attacking
in this article, were preoccupied with kinds of life hitherto undealt with
by novelists—Bennett's five industrial towns in the English Black country,

and Wells' new men, the scientists. To them, interest lay more in using their narrative skill to point to what was alive than in inventing life and its values through art.

If the interest in surrounding life is overwhelming, the novelist is more concerned with using the novel as a vehicle, like a train or bus, for conveying this life than with making a simulacrum in which characters and values are invented for the sake of the artistic form which is life perfected by the Godlike artist.

The characteristic of American life is to overwhelm. Thus, the great American novelists, so long as they remained in America, have been novelists of "saturation." It is only when they have gone to Europe, like Henry James, that they have thought of "interest" as being the result of artistic form. The great poetic-aesthetic novels of the twentieth century were all written in Europe, or by Europeans. The great American novels of the same period, like European novels in the nineteenth century, are saturated with material.

BELLOW IN SEARCH OF HIMSELF

In 1964 the American novel seems to be beginning to correspond to the Russian novel in the nineteenth century. *Herzog* has very much the look of a novel like *Oblomov*, with a hero a real "character," a "card," funny but tragic, foolish but clever, a bungler and cuckold, but basically so wise that the world surrounding him seems his creation and he its God.

At the beginning of *Herzog*, Moses Herzog surveys the ruins of his life. His wife Madeleine has left him for her lover Valentine Gersbach. His adult-education lectures in New York are a fiasco—incoherent not only to himself but to his students. Herzog has given up his job and wanders from place to place, sleeping on a mattress without sheets, getting up at all hours of the night to write down random thoughts such as *"Death— die—live again—die again—live."* He is seized with a passionate desire to clarify himself to himself. Above all, he writes letters endlessly, fanatically, to the newspapers, to people in public life, to friends and relatives, and at last to the dead, his own obscure dead, and finally the famous dead. As far as the "story" goes, this episodic novel is simply a round of visits by the narrator in search of his past.

Herzog is a subjective book about a subjective man—a solipsist almost. But the egocentricity is atoned for by the fact that what Herzog discovers about himself is the bundle of spiritual and physical qualities which makes every living person an instrument through which the world is experienced. The difference between Herzog and the other characters is the intensity of his consciousness that he is such an instrument.

This consciousness, upon which behavior is dress like the transvestite's, is the center of Herzog, out of which come his letters to all those figures

SAUL BELLOW

Herzog can do no wrong . . .
he can only be wronged

past and present, living and dead. These letters are desperate attempts to communicate in rhetorical fantasy on the level of Herzog's religious consciousness. Following them, we see Herzog move from real despair into condemnation of the easy existentialist despair which is characteristic of the culture he represents: the armchair drivers through the infernos of Dante, Kierkegaard, or Kafka. In a letter to Professor Mermelstein, Herzog writes:

> I venture to say Kierkegaard meant that truth has lost its force with us and horrible pain and evil must teach it to us again, the eternal punishments of Hell will have to regain their reality before mankind turns serious once more. I do not see this. Let us set aside the fact that such convictions in the mouths of safe, comfortable people playing at crisis, alienation, apocalypse and desperation, make me sick. We must get it out of our heads that this is a doomed time, that we are waiting for the end, and the rest of it, mere junk from fashionable magazines. Things are grim enough without these shivery games.

Herzog's letters risk stealing the interest from the rest of the book, especially since there is no point of view except that of Herzog himself. His wives, mistresses, brother, daughter, parental family, lawyer, psychoanalyst, and his friends the Sisslers at Martha's Vineyard are foils, serving to dramatize himself to himself. All the same, the observation, accuracy, and humor of scenes and portraits is so great that they do balance the impressive weight of the letters. In fact, their somewhat two-dimensional quality is an advantage. They become documentation to the evolving central essay of a thesis inseparable from lessons lived by the hero.

Good writing is vital writing; and life is always funny as well as tragic: in fact, the more vitality, the funnier it is. Most sadness is simply negative, the expression of lack of life. Even at their most tragic, Shakespeare and Tolstoy conceal within the sad tree of wintry language the sap of humor. Considering all that has happened to him, it is funny that Lear should be able both to howl and to say: "Howl! Howl! Howl!" And there is no funnier, more tragic scene in literature than in *War and Peace* when Pierre rushes into a building in Moscow to rescue a child, who, as he holds it in his arms, promptly bites him (GBWW, Vol. 51, pp. 528c-530b).

Bellow's writing has the tragedy through which the funny sap always runs. I do not mean by this that there are not also stretches of deliberate comedy, farce even. Bellow is nearly always funny about women, so much so that one suspects Herzog not of misogyny but of a neurosis I have never heard named: that of regarding women as ridiculous, particularly when they are American or Americanized, injected at birth, as it were, with pretentious ideas. The conversation and amorous action that go with the "shrimp Arnaud and salad . . . cheese and cold-water biscuits, rum-flavored ice cream, plums from Georgia, and early green grapes," served by Herzog's over-sympathizing, rapaciously understanding mistress, Ramona, make high comedy indeed.

This is a book which exists within a language, packed, textured, and rich, with which Bellow can do anything he likes. Since the language itself seems to dissolve into its muscular stream all problems of form, it may seem carping to suggest that it is not without faults as a novel.

The most serious criticism to be made arises from the novel's special achievement: its realization of the total subjectivity of Herzog. For although Herzog represents a subjectivity which is common to all human beings, the novel scarcely provides a point of view from which one can see him objectively. For example, his qualifications are so eminently those of the sensibility of the writer of the book —who is also both literary genius and academic and must share with Herzog his considerable erudition—that it is difficult to believe in Herzog the worldly failure with only $600 to his name. A mind scarcely distinguishable from Herzog's own is secretly writing his hero's success stories in all those letters that do not get posted. This criticism implies that like other American writers (preeminently Mailer) Bellow runs the risk of making a success of attacking success. None can suspect that he does this through lack of integrity, a secret acceptance of the standards which Herzog despises. The fault is an artistic one: that of not having created any other character in the novel as convincing as Herzog. The very essence of Herzog's integrity is that of Bellow himself.

I do not mean that Bellow does not make Herzog absurd: but then to be absurd is to be existential, to be completely self-conscious. The point is that Herzog's consciousness is of a kind to undermine that of every other character in the novel. His attitude toward women is an example of this. The reader is never in a position to judge whether Herzog has not after all on his side wronged Madeleine, Ramona, and the other women in his life. And even if it were made to appear that he had done so, the point of view from which one would understand this would be Herzog's consciousness, explaining what it was in the woman which had caused Herzog to wrong her. Herzog is subject; all the other characters are object. His way of being wrong is always righter, because more fully conscious, than anyone else's way of being right. Essentially, Herzog, like the Hebrew prophet whose first name he bears, can do no wrong: He can only be wronged.

It is strange that *Herzog* should appear in the same year as two parallel works that have much the same characters and situations. One of these is Arthur Miller's play *After the Fall*, whose hero is a Jewish intellectual with bad wife-trouble and a conscience which tells him that everything is wrong with American society; and that while he must confront the public evil he must also come to terms with himself and if possible get a better-model wife. Seeing Arthur Miller's hero identify himself with the wrongs of recent history and run through an assortment of glamorous women, while vicariously suffering the horrors of Auschwitz, misgivings that I felt only very faintly about the success story of Herzog-Bellow became formulated in my mind as a question: "Is this the cure for the disease, or is it merely a more subtle form of the disease?" The disease being, of course, sales talk, money, vulgarity, conformism to the standards set by money, violence, worship of success, success, success. . . .

MAILER'S AMERICAN MELODRAMA

With Norman Mailer, both the standards he attacks and those he defends become equally ludicrous: It is as if James Bond were to conduct a crusade against violence. *An American Dream* appears heralded by publicity announcing that the author heard that Dostoevsky wrote novels for serial publication in magazines against deadlines: so, in his pugilistic manner, Mailer took on the Russian challenge and wrote a chapter of his novel every month for *Esquire*, and on several occasions, like Dostoevsky, he delivered the copy only hours before his deadline.

An American Dream is the story of an extroverted, much more violent Herzog who carries his hatred of the female species and his grudge against society into action. Like Herzog, Stephen Rojack is also a professor. But of course Mailer's hero is not *just* a professor. Like Jack Kennedy, with whom he has double-dated, he is a war hero. In the course of capturing a German position he has, with quite lascivious pleasure, shot one of the enemy. As he fires at the soldier with his "great bloody sweet German face," he feels toward him the resentment he would feel for a homosexual, "a sweet young faggot." After returning from the war, Stephen Rojack marries Deborah, a lusty Irish-American heiress. At the time of the opening of the novel, he has, like the hero of *Herzog*, parted company from his wife; but Deborah and Stephen, like Madeleine and Herzog, cannot altogether relinquish one another. They play out in memory and sometimes in actual scenes the old, violent quarrels.

Early in *An American Dream*, such a meeting takes place at Deborah's apartment. In a particularly sordid scene, Deborah taunts Stephen, says that she no longer loves him, boasts of acts she commits with other lovers. Stephen strikes her face, then strangles her. He goes downstairs and makes love to Fräulein Ruta, Deborah's German maid. Fortified by this act, he returns to his wife's room, pushes her out of the window, and calls downstairs to the maid: "Ruta, get dressed, get dressed quick, Mrs. Rojack has killed herself."

The rest of the novel is taken up with Stephen Rojack dealing coolly enough with various situations which arise as the result of his wife's death and embarking on another love affair (it is real love this time, though it ends in disillusionment) with Cherry, a nightclub singer.

One consequence of the death is, of course, that the police arrive on the scene. This gives Norman Mailer another opportunity to take up the Dostoevsky challenge, and he writes some interviews with the police which compete with those of the public prosecutor with the murderer in *Crime and Punishment*. Forensic pathology is fascinating, and Mailer exploits the opportunities of showing that the police obtain ample evidence from Deborah's corpse that she must have been strangled before being thrown over the balustrade. A weakness of the novel is that the murder, so far from being a perfect crime which murderer and detective could argue about, is, in the light of modern scientific analysis, transparently obvious, so that the long drawn out arguments between Rojack and the detective Roberts are superfluous. Or perhaps they occur because the police enjoy dragging out conversations with a war hero, ex-congressman, professor, and television star.

Finally, Rojack evades trial, not because the police are persuaded by his arguments that they would do wrong to prosecute him, but on account of intervention from above. Wealthy, influential Oswald Kelly, Deborah's father (who had, incidentally, seduced her when she was fifteen), exercises pressure to save Stephen. By confessing to the seduction of Deborah, Kelly also appears to help Rojack's conscience by demonstrating that he is worse than Stephen. By ruining Deborah, Kelly has also ruined the Rojack marriage; he is responsible for the qualities in Deborah which cause Stephen to murder her. Thus, Kelly is ultimately responsible for everything. He is the Devil from one of Stephen's television lectures in which he had whimsically explained that the world is the battleground

NORMAN MAILER

Inclination to
Make Your Flesh Creep

of a war between God and the Devil, which the Devil may win.

The best scenes in *An American Dream* are incidental to the main story and are amusing. Extremely funny interviews occur between Rojack and the men responsible for employing him respectively at the television studio and the department of the university where he works. It is in these comic scenes that Mailer shows that if he could drop his role of first public prosecutor of the whole American way of life, he might write a satiric comedy perhaps almost of the first order of Peter de Vries' *Reuben, Reuben.*

In spite of his pretensions, Mailer has no standing as a moralist. But he is Dickensian when he allows himself to write simply out of his saturation in material, such as when he is describing the nightclub where Cherry works, or her Negro lover Shago.

An American Dream is written in a high-pressured style which again brings us back to James Bond, although Ian Fleming is far more lucid and less pretentious. Mailer's style can attain a pitch of incoherence passing the border line of the incomprehensible:

> After a black night of drink and a quarrel beyond dimension, she lost the baby, it came brokenly to birth, in terror, I always thought, of the womb which was shaping it, came out and went back in again in death, tearing by this miscarriage the hope of any other child for Deborah.

The general level of hysteria is pitched so high that, reading this, one can almost believe Mailer means that the baby left Deborah's womb and then reentered it in order to die there, having in a brief moment of reflection during its sojourn in the outer world decided to regard it as a

175

sepulcher. Such an idea would, after all, be hardly more absurd than attributing to it a dislike of Deborah which caused it to emerge.

On the whole, *An American Dream* must be considered a symptom of the conditions from which it emanates and which the writer sets out to attack. It is possible that the characters he invents would behave in the ways and with the motivations which he attributes to them. Perhaps America is like this. But Norman Mailer has not made his novel credible either on the level of naturalism or on that of prophetic vision. As a description of real circumstances, it is no more, no less, credible than *Dr. No* or *Goldfinger*. On the level of imaginative insight it only comes to life in the scenes of satiric comedy. Perhaps Mailer's basic fault is that he tries too hard to make the reader's flesh creep by overpainting his American nightmare.

Indeed, if the Fat Boy in *The Pickwick Papers* had emigrated to America and his descendants had inherited and transported there the ancestral inclination to Make Your Flesh Creep, one of these descendants might well have looked exactly like the photograph of Norman Mailer on the dust jacket of *An American Dream*.

"MUST THERE ALWAYS BE A RED BRICK ENGLAND?"

The traditional concern of American novelists has been to define some kind of American—the Bostonian, the New Yorker, the Southerner, the Midwesterner, the American in Paris, the American Innocent Abroad; and now the Jew as an American, the Negro as an American; tomorrow perhaps the Puerto Rican as an American.

Contemporary English novelists, by contrast, seem concerned not so much with defining the Englishman (who is, like the English Channel, rather taken for granted) as the historic situation within which the English find themselves. If one were to sum up the English attitude it would be somewhat as follows: "Here we are, the English, just the same, in a changed world. On second thoughts, a weeny bit changed ourselves. Quite a new class of people seem to be walking about on the streets. But aren't they after all rather like characters we used to read about in novels by Arnold Bennett and H. G. Wells? And, of course, they don't really alter anything. There's still the Royal Family and Oxford and Cambridge and London and the House of Lords—and there's always Us!"

But the Us, nevertheless, find themselves in a new situation: the welfare-state society with its new towns and new universities, the setting for novels by Angus Wilson, David Storey, John Braine, Keith Waterhouse, and others. The irony of the situation described in Angus Wilson's novel of life in a new town—*Late Call*—is that it is only the old lady, Sylvia Calvert, who experiences a change of heart as a result of the new circumstances of living in the new town. Her son, the headmaster and committeeman with a social conscience, remains stuck in the attitudes of the 1930's. Her grandchildren are out for themselves, impervious to all but the opportunities for enjoyment which their surroundings offer. At best, it seems they will develop into the members of a new middle class whose social ambitions are confined to everyone having a car, a television set, a washing machine, and a refrigerator.

Angus Wilson is himself of the generation of the 1930's. He takes a more charitable view of the welfare-state England than do younger novelists like Keith Waterhouse and David Storey. Keith Waterhouse's hero in *Jubb* regards the town in which he lives—with its committees, its housing estate officers, its planned community living—simply as a strategic area for carrying out his plans for waylaying women. The view of English provincial life in David Storey's *Radcliffe* is even more brutal; and it is unrelieved by the tolerance for sexual eccentricity which alleviates the gloom of Waterhouse's picture.

The cause of the somewhat cynical attitude of writers like Kingsley Amis, John Osborne, Allan Sillitoe, John Braine, and others toward welfare-state England may be that they are analyzing the effects of a wider situation of England upon the limited aims and achievements of a country that is supposed to have had a social revolution. The wider situation is the general decline of England's position in the world.

One has the impression of a country that takes two steps backward for every step forward. Add to all this the fact greatly advertised by John Osborne that although there has been since World War II a much advertised English social revolution, it has scarcely altered the general structure of a population whose interests seem equally divided between the activities of the Royal Family, betting pools, bingo, and other such escapist occupations. The image of a society with wider opportunities is imposed upon that of the old class structure.

There is also an awareness of American achievement against which the English are constantly measuring their own society. This may find expression as resentment of America or it may take the form of simply ignoring it. There is little or nothing about anything except the immediate English provincial scene in *Jubb* and *Radcliffe*: but then there is little about London, either.

Angus Wilson in *Late Call*—his very carefully drawn study of the life of members of an English middle-class family in a new town—sketches in two episodes the ambivalent attitude of the Calverts to Americans. The first takes place in a dining car, where Sylvia Calvert and her husband Arthur find themselves seated opposite an American couple, the Hoppners. A conversation begun by Arthur Calvert on a note of false cordiality continues with his trying to put across an anecdote about his snubbing an American colonel during World War I. The Hoppners are frozen to silence, and the conversation ends with a near row—an international storm in a British Railways Restaurant teacup. Arthur Calvert, himself an ignoramus, regards the Americans as uncultivated, when, in fact, they are far better educated and more sophisticated than the Calverts—something which Sylvia Calvert has the good sense to realize.

The second encounter occurs toward the end of the novel, when Mrs. Calvert, desolate with her own family, takes to going for lonely walks. Caught in a storm on one of these excursions, she rescues a small American girl, who takes her to the farmhouse where her parents live. The Egan family with their sympathy, understanding, and freshness, save Sylvia Calvert from despair. Angus Wilson beautifully indicates the double role of America in the lives of his characters. Americans are spoken of sometimes with envy and patronizing contempt—an attitude which has scarcely been revised since before World War I—but also they are regarded as life-giving restorers and comforters.

Late Call is an admirably planned novel. The prologue describes the adventure of two small girls during the hot summer of 1911—Myra, the daughter of a lady holidaying at a farm, and the farmer's daughter, known to Myra's rather grand but consciously broadminded and sensible mother, Mrs. Longmore, as the "little Tuffield girl." The tough, elder country girl leads the lady's daughter astray, causing her to lose her hat in a stream, tear her clothes, and run barefoot through the fields. This—a scandal to Mrs. Longmore—is one of Wilson's most poetic inventions.

The second chapter opens more than fifty years later. The "Tuffield girl" is now Mrs. Sylvia Calvert, a competent woman, manageress of a seaside hotel, and married to Capt. Arthur Calvert, a seedy survivor from the Western front, who has been shot through the lungs and who boasts in old-timer's war slang of his exploits, drawing on a fund of stories to illustrate his own coolness in difficult situations. The main part of the story begins with Mrs. Calvert leaving, on account of ill health, the job which she has had for many years as manageress of the hotel and which has enabled her to pay off her husband's gambling debts. Her son Harold—headmaster of the comprehensive school at Carshall, an English new town, and whose wife Beth has recently died—invites his mother and her husband to come and live with him and his three grown children.

The novel has little story except the unfolding, stage by stage, in the mind of Sylvia Calvert of the character of her son, her three grandchildren, and various other people in their lives at the new town. By means of incident built upon incident, Mrs. Calvert gets to know her son and grandchildren. Wilson depicts, stroke by stroke, scenes illustrating her reactions on first seeing the room with yellow curtains and tubular furniture allotted to her and Arthur in her son's house; her dismay at Harold's demonstration to her of working the elaborate electric cooker; her difficulties in fitting her own furniture into their new room; the party given by Harold for them; the typing she does for a welfare committee—and so on. Harold Calvert lives a routine of school and committees; he believes in the ideal of an enlightened and rational community which Carshall represents. He conducts a crusade against the local authorities—beyond whom looms the Ministry—to prevent a strip of land, which he considers an integral part of the concept of Carshall, from being built over. "Committee" is the key to Harold Calvert's personality.

As Mrs. Calvert gets to know more of this world for which she has exchanged her independence, she experiences a sense of desolation. She takes to going for long walks alone in the country that is not far from Carshall. There she recovers gradually the memory of that first escapade which forms the prologue to the novel, and which has somehow come to seem the most significant experience in her life.

At the end of the novel, she has rediscovered the sources of her inner strength, thanks partly to the American friends whom she meets in the neighborhood. She is able to confront the death of her husband from a stroke, the nervous collapse of her son, the flight of one grandson to a life of homosexual freedom in London, and the breaking up of the rest of the family. She has become surprising to herself.

Late Call is scattered with sharp characterizations of the kind of people whom Angus Wilson observes with a very clear eye and an ear for every inflection of their speech. Angus Wilson is the one living novelist capable of creating Dickensian minor characters. There is Miss Bulmer, the Welfare Officer, who in a wonderful scene breezes in on Sylvia Calvert and tells her that she is not facing up to the excitement and fun of life in Carshall, and who, seeing a performance of *Look Back in Anger*, says of the establishment in Jimmy Porter's attic: "What a household! Oh! It's a clever enough play. But a decent social worker could have cleared up the whole mess in a day and a half." Other memorable characters include the homosexual waiter, Wilf Corney, Muriel Bartley the social worker, and speech-making Jock Parsons, the corporation's public relations officer.

In spite of these characters and of certain outstanding scenes, *Late Call* seems a bit monotonous, perhaps because the thoughts of Sylvia Calvert, which are the string connecting other characters and incidents, read like an accurate report of her thinking without convincing the reader that here are the thoughts themselves. A typical example of her thinking is the following, as she walks through Carshall Town Centre:

Her purchases made, she watched the metal arms of the fountain jerkily dropping their loads of water; it was clever but you couldn't say that it played. Staring into the basin, she wondered what sort of supervisor they could have that would let it silt up with chocolate wrappers and ice-cream cartons like that. She looked for a while at the twisted bronze called "Watcher" that Beth had so admired. Although it was difficult and modern, you could admire the way the metal had been twisted so cleanly.

And so on, for another page. This is thinking accurately deduced from Mrs. Calvert's character and the situation of her walking in the Town Centre. But it is how she would have thought she thought if she had gone home and reported her meditations to her husband or a friend. It just misses the quality of the unexpected which is real thinking. And when one has read a good many pages of this kind, one begins to feel that in *Late Call* Wilson is often being conscientious more than excited. A good deal of the book is written as though he felt a duty to write a novel about a new town. Little of the rest of the novel lives up to the spontaneous and imaginative writing of the prologue about the two children lost in the countryside.

Another novelist who seems to have written a book partly out of a feeling that he should make some strong imaginative statement about the situation of life in an English provincial town is David Storey in his new novel *Radcliffe*. The result is quite the opposite of *Late Call*. Angus Wilson's novel seems too careful, too contrived, too much under control; David Storey has written a study of life in the industrial north of England which makes up in violence and overemphasis for what is perhaps an uncertain grasp of the subject.

Radcliffe presents the relationship between two men: Leonard Radcliffe, the last of a line of squires and aristocrats; and Victor Tolson, a working man whom Leonard first met at the school to which he was sent as a result of the decline in the Radcliffe family fortunes. Victor Tolson and Leonard Radcliffe are drawn together by a sadomasochistic homosexual relationship, which is immensely fortified by being a metaphor—in Leonard's mind and perhaps also vaguely in Tolson's—for the attraction of pure spirit (Leonard Radcliffe, the failed artist) to impure physiology (Victor Tolson). The Yorkshire landscape, superimposed on a Brontesque heritage and the satanic mills of industry, acts demonically upon the minds of both protagonists. An orgastic fusion of Leonard's and Victor's relationship happens when they share a tent during a job of putting up marquees for a contractor, but their relation rapidly disintegrates into horror and revulsion; and after a scene in which Tolson tricks Leonard into eating a sandwich spread with excrement, the novel ends with Leonard murdering Tolson and then going insane.

The excessive violence of this book comes strangely from the author of *This Sporting Life*, a scrupulous account of the life of English rugby footballers, which proves once and for all that the epithet *sporting* has come to signify precisely its opposite.

All the same, *Radcliffe* adds considerably to the witness of other writers that the result of social change in the provincial towns of England has been to loosen upon society a flood of half-educated people, bred from the industrial ugliness, who have little reverence for life and can only make a mockery of love, which they regard as dirt. The mockery and obscenity of their fellow workers is the cause of the destruction of the relationship of Victor Tolson and Leonard Radcliffe.

Radcliffe must be counted, I think, an ambitious failure. Storey has tried to bring all his gifts and experience to bear upon a large subject matter: the countryside in which the ruined Radcliffe manor stands adjacent to the industrial landscape and the new building estate; the decadence of the old family embodied in Radcliffe tragically drawn to the brute insensibility of the uprooted countryman who retains his physique but who has become corrupted by the town, embodied in Tolson. In his descriptions of the threatening, sinister landscape. Storey has drawn on the associations of northern England with the Brontës and with the baroque novel. A writer who made a reputation as a painter before he turned to the novel, Storey also hangs this novel with a number of vast word-paintings of weather and scenery. Finally, a Lawrentian vision of the dark gods of sex casts a glow over the people and places in his novel.

Perhaps *Radcliffe* is an attempt to get away from the near-routine novel, play, and film of postwar England which caused an American reviewer recently to sigh: "Must there always be a Red Brick England?" If so, the attempt is to be applauded, the failure respected for its courage.

The Jealous God by John Braine is a reminder of the kind of depressing picture of life in a northern industrial town which Storey may be trying to get away from. The God referred to is God as worshipped by the Church of Rome who forbids birth control, who names sexual intercourse outside matrimony a mortal sin, and who does not recognize divorce.

In Protestant and perhaps also in Catholic countries, there is a widely accepted view that although Catholicism imposes very strict rules regarding sex, Catholics are not puritans because the Church recognizes the sensual life as a condition of living in the body and merely imposes rules upon the body. Sins of the senses are admitted in the confessional. Puritans, however, tend to treat the desires of the body as though they had no right to be recognized by the pure spirit. Thus, puritans are inhibited, Catholics are merely repressed. Early in the present century, George Moore, who was a Protestant, wrote a number of novels and stories exploiting this idea that Catholics enclosed free-ranging sensual thoughts within rigidly repressed bodies. John Braine's new novel is within this conventionally literary view of Catholicism.

His hero, Vincent Dungarvan, is a thirty-year-old schoolteacher who lives in a northern industrial town with his mother, who wishes him to be a priest. Obsessed by fantasies about girls, he has never slept with a woman.

In the public library near his home, he meets Laura, who seems superior to any girl he has met. He enters into conversation with her, they meet at tea shops, espresso bars, and other meeting places characteristic of postwar provincial England. Before making love with Laura, Vincent experimentally seduces his henna-haired sister-in-law Maureen. Being a Catholic, he feels no puritan guilt, although he knows it to be against the rules. Conscious of sinning, he does not feel remorse about the sexual act.

Vincent and Laura now start having an affair. After this has gone on for some time, Vincent discovers that Laura has been concealing the fact that she has already been married. When they come to a showdown about this, she tells him that she divorced her husband because of his "unnatural" sexual demands. Also he hated the prospect of having children, whereas Laura does want children. Before long she starts reproaching Vincent because his Catholicism prevents him from marrying a divorced woman.

Perhaps because John Braine makes no serious effort to solve the problems of understanding created by the relationship between Vincent and Laura, melodrama takes over in the second half of *The Jealous God*. Laura's ex-husband Robert returns to her. Vincent meets him in a tea shop and knocks him down. Maureen writes an anonymous letter telling Laura about Vincent's affair with her. Conveniently, Robert commits suicide, Vincent and Laura fall into one another's arms, and presumably will achieve parenthood. The rules of the jealous God have been obeyed.

A weakness of the novel seems to be that the motivation and behavior of Vincent and Laura are too schematic in relation to the kind of characters they supposedly are: intelligent and open people who discuss things and give each other Rilke's *Duino Elegies*. Although their attitudes are understandable, their behavior is more stupid than one would expect, given the type of people they are shown to be. Neither in life nor in fiction do facts explain and excuse behavior completely. In *The Jealous God*, the fact that Laura's husband made demands on her which she regarded as unnatural could not be her only reason for leaving him, since later she went back to him. She may have resented Vincent's Catholic scruples, but if she loved him she would at least have made a great effort to understand them—to love him for them even. And if she was incapable of understanding what was deepest in him, his religion, then the happy ending of the novel, occasioned by the suicide of her ex-husband, could not have solved the problem of their relationship, which was to understand why, without Robert dying, Vincent could not marry Laura. The problems of their relationship have not been resolved by the death of Robert which enables them to marry. The situation with which the novel starts has not been altered within the consciousness of the characters. All that has happened have been some more or less accidental external changes which put Vincent on the right side according to the rules of Catholic matrimony.

Apart from the espresso bars, the housing developments, the social clubs, and the house in which Maureen and Vincent's brother live—all of which are excellently described—the England of Roman Catholicism, in which a son is sacrificed to his mother and withheld from other women, seems very little changed since the beginning of the century.

A novel in which even the external changes that have taken place are minimal is Elizabeth Taylor's slight but telling, beautifully written *The Soul of Kindness*. The heroine, Flora, is an upper-class English woman, living gracefully and with the beauty of a Botticelli angel whom her husband, mother, and friends adore. She seems the center of their lives and to be forever thinking of ways of helping others.

In fact, Flora is profoundly selfish; her real sin in life is to act out a role in which she is spared from all unpleasantness by being surrounded by people who adore her and are grateful to her. The action of the book centers on the way in which Flora nearly ruins the life of her younger brother Kit, by forcing on him the image she has formed of him as an actor of genius with a brilliant career. Actually, Kit is an agreeable mediocrity, but by encouraging him to have ambitions which her husband and everyone else realize are too high for him, Flora pushes Kit to the edge of suicide. When the consequences of her selfishness are brought home to her by Elizabeth—a scruffy Bohemian painter who has always loathed Flora—her world, for the time being, collapses.

Flora seems easy game for a writer as skillful as Elizabeth Taylor at scoring up niggling moral points against her character. But it makes pleasant reading and shows the selfishness which may be involved in overestimating others. Apart from this, *The Soul of Kindness* describes an upper-class English life—carried on in the country and London by Flora as hostess and by her husband Richard in his business—which is almost as gray as the England of Wilson, Waterhouse, Storey, and Braine. In her portrait of Flora, Miss Taylor neatly supplements the picture of life in welfare-state England in the new towns and the industrial provinces with one of conservative families carrying on with unobtrusive helpful selfishness, the same as ever.

The general view of England in all these novels is of a society which has undergone profound historic changes which have produced only superficial or negative changes in people's behavior and thinking. The generation which has produced these changes—that of Angus Wilson's Harold Calvert—and which still goes on producing them (Harold S. Wilson's government might be Harold Calvert's), although it exercises a limited power and schoolmasterly moral authority, does not speak into the heart of a younger generation. It is accepted as the inevitable stick which succeeds the chewed-up conservative carrot.

Drab English disillusionment is not as recent as it looks. It is a mood, induced by World War I, of an England dulled by losing her position in the world. During the thirties among the intellectuals and under-graduates of the Left, there was a partial awakening from it, corresponding to the movement of the anti-nuclear bomb youth which lasted for a short time in the 1950's. But is was in the 1930's that W. H. Auden, one of the leading rebels, epitomized England as "this country where no one is well," and, in fact, for the young intellectuals of the 1930's, the impulse was at least partly to go abroad, to go to Spain and support the Republicans, to attend international congresses in France, *to get out of here.* This rejection of England on account of a feeling that it was a society gone dead goes back to D. H. Lawrence, who left England, but who never ceased to give his reasons for doing so.

It was Kingsley Amis who, in the 1950's, before his long spells in Portugal and America, wrote his "Let's hear no more about abroad," a remark as characteristic of its time as Auden's of the feeling of the 1930's. Part of the grittiness of the work of some of the writers here discussed may be the result of their grim determination to stick it out in England.

Christopher Isherwood, perhaps more than any other, even of his generation, must, in the eyes of Kingsley Amis, represent "abroad." Only two early novels are laid in England. The stories and novels upon which his prewar reputation is based were those written about Berlin in the late 1920's and 1930's. Even after Isherwood left Hitler's Germany he did not return to England but wandered from country to country until, finally, he settled in America in 1938.

There is a certain amount of England in *A Single Man.* George, the hero, is an English expatriate who lectures in a California college, the San Tomas State College, outside Los Angeles. Occasionally he goes and takes dinner with another English expatriate, Charlotte, who, as she gets drunk, becomes nostalgic about England. Missing the England of the Cotswolds, Elizabethan architecture, and asking George to admit he loves it, misses it, wishes to be back there, is an important part of her frustrated emotional life. But George is completely rooted in California. What he misses is not England but his recently dead American friend, Jim, with whom he shared a house looking over the Pacific coast, on a street called Camphor Tree Lane. *A Single Man* is about missing Jim, about being middle-aged and a homosexual with feelings of persecution in a society where it is important to conform. It is also about American youth in a Western college. The role of youth in the novel is to refresh the dry roots of George's life: mockingly, withholdingly, bitchily, that is just what the student Kenny does on the occasion of a wild evening spent with George, first at a bar, then on the beach, then at his home, where nothing happens.

The action of *A Single Man* is confined to a single day. George gets up from bed, thinking of his body, his life, not as a person, but as *it,* the machine that will take over. He looks in the glass and sees not so much a face "as the expression of a predicament." The predicament is middle age. And so, we follow him through his day. On the freeway, driving to the college, in the hallucinated state of mind which overtakes the solitary

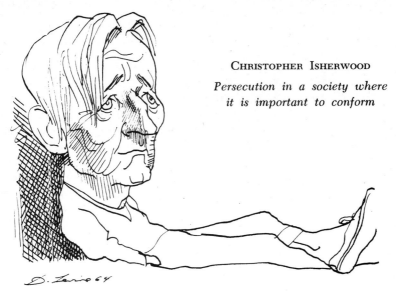

CHRISTOPHER ISHERWOOD

*Persecution in a society where
it is important to conform*

driver, he becomes the prey of his hates and fears. He sees on the edge of the beach "a huge, insolent high-rise building which will contain one hundred apartments . . . growing up within its girders." He thinks it would be amusing "to sneak into that apartment building at night, just before the tenants moved in, and spray all the walls of all the rooms with a specially prepared odorant which would be scarcely noticeable at first but which would gradually grow in strength until it reeked like rotting corpses." We see him in the classroom delivering a lecture on Aldous Huxley's novel *After Many a Summer*. This scene—perhaps the central one in the book—is a dazzling example of the professor who is a "character" and the students who cut him up, in their act of deriving nourishment and entertainment from one another which is more significant than the lecture itself. At his best, Isherwood has a gift for describing a sense of human behavior as though it were something different, intenser, more spectacular, like the gyrations of tropical birds in a vast, golden cage. Here is George exercising the spell that involves them all:

> Slowly, deliberately, like a magician, he takes a single book out of his brief-case and places it on the reading desk. As he does this, his eyes move over the faces of the class. His lips curve in a faint but bold smile. Some of them smile back at him. George finds this frank confrontation extraordinarily exhilarating. He draws strength from these smiles, these bright young eyes. For him, this is one of the peak moments of the day. He feels brilliant, vital, challenging, slightly mysterious and, above all, *foreign*.

Here without employing Angus Wilson's method of reported interior thinking, which proves soporific with Mrs. Calvert, Isherwood gives an impression of George's thoughts bouncing round the walls of eyes, like a ball in a tennis court. At the end, after dinner and many drinks with Charlotte, and the flirtatious scene in the dark by the ocean, when Kenny persuades George to stand on his shoulders, helping him over a railing with a drop of eight feet below it onto the beach—George goes home to bed. Isherwood provides us with alternate endings. Either George goes to sleep and starts another such day tomorrow or he dies—he might just as well do so. "Cortex and brain stem are murdered in the blackout with the speed of an Indian strangler."

The California which Isherwood describes in *A Single Man* is not essentially more encouraging than that of Wilson's or Storey's England. In some ways, it is worse. The destruction-by-construction proceeding in the English new town is at least under some kind of control. That on the Pacific coast is the invasion of a concrete and girdered jungle, which is still, however, a tremendously energetic and varied growth. From Balzac onwards, the novel has thrived on societies which resemble jungles rather than drab, but orderly, public gardens.

TRADITIONAL *vs.* UNDERGROUND NOVELS

None of the novels so far discussed (even when, as with *Herzog* and *Late Call*, the action covers fifty years or more) is what earlier in the century was called a saga, like John Galsworthy's *Forsyte Saga*, a narrative carried forward over a span of several generations, against a background of contemporary history.

Two novels published this year belong to this honorably academic tradition: *The Rector of Justin*, by Louis Auchincloss; and *Full Fathom Five*, by John Stewart Carter. Both novels have received considerable and merited attention. If they were simply Royal Academy pictures in the manner, say, of that portrait of the Sitwell family by John Singer Sargent which is reproduced in Edith Sitwell's autobiographical volume *Taken Care Of*, I would be inclined to leave two examples of a respectable genre to their respectful public. But each of these books is intensely interesting in its way and deserves attention.

The Rector of Justin is the portrait of Dr. Frank Prescott, headmaster and founder of a New England Episcopalian boys school. When the book opens, in September, 1939, the headmaster is an octogenarian, approaching dignified retirement. We see him through the journal of Brian Aspinwall, a devout, young teacher with ambitions to be a priest and, as the book proceeds, a growing desire to write the biography of the Rector. Brian is an earnest and decent young man who has gone to the school in a spirit of devotion, prepared to give of his best to teaching, and honored to be working with Dr. Prescott.

Brian Aspinwall is no fool. He is truthful with himself and with others. The reader is made aware of this early. For Brian, though admiring, cannot fail to state the truth. So he notes in his journal that the headmaster is a hearty authoritarian with an invalid wife more intelligent than himself. Dr. Prescott, Brian soon learns, approves of "hazing"; he seems to care more for discipline than for fair play in the school; he prefers breaking up a hundred Davids and Jonathans of friendship to risking one case of sodomy; he is scornful when he learns that his wife and Brian Aspinwall share an enthusiasm for Henry James's *The Ambassadors*, of which he says that "it has nothing whatever to do with life on this poor planet of ours." In fact, Prescott, alas, is no progressive; he would not qualify to be president of Bennington or Sarah Lawrence College.

Nevertheless, *The Rector of Justin* is not just another debunking novel about a Victorian prig (Frank Prescott studied at Balliol College, Oxford, under its most famous master, Benjamin Jowett). Although Prescott is shown to be a bully, a hypocrite, and a play actor, he is also a scholar, responsible to himself and to others, one who truly cares for the values of civilization, a man of God, who also has a sense of humor. Few characters in modern fiction have been portrayed so completely in the round. At the end, the reader is able to form his own opinion of the Rector. If one is a fanatical believer in progressive education, one will probably dislike him; if one suspects that small human animals should occasionally be put in their places, one will read this novel with an open mind.

Part of the complexity of this subtle novel is that Auchincloss reminds us how men in responsible positions, like wines, have vintages: in one year, Dr. Prescott is excellent for his pupils; in others, he is a menace. The Rector succeeds with some pupils, and some members of his family, and fails with others. Is his daughter right in regarding him as a bigoted puritan? Her crudely sophisticated, psychology-versed reaction makes her appear unsympathetic, but that she is so may be her father's fault.

One can read *The Rector of Justin* with a sense of relief—even after *Herzog* (which is a more interesting book)—because Auchincloss gives an objective picture of a section of life, and because the various narrators who carry forward the story have minds sharply and clearly distinguished from the writer's own. Dr. Prescott is a solid, three-dimensional character about whom one can have various opinions, as though one were at the school. One does not feel that the author is laying traps to involve us in a confessional autobiography.

Another novel in which a great deal of conscious art is applied, this time in the attempt to produce a Jamesian academy family portrait, is John Stewart Carter's *Full Fathom Five*. This is about various members of a great Chicago family (with grandpapa, the baron robber, buried in a great black marble vault) who have developed a grand style of living, built themselves a mansion filled with beautiful objects, and, some of them—notably the narrator's father, who is a doctor, excellent with his poorest patients—taken to good works. All this has disappeared at the time when the narrator is writing, largely because the plutocratic culture described was entirely dependent on the rich having a great many servants. Also, the depression had made most of the characters poorer.

There is no continuous story, though there are some extended anecdotes. Carter's method is Proustian and owes a great deal to other writers, notably to F. Scott Fitzgerald. The narrator, who, like André Gide in *Les Faux Monnayeurs*, is a poet and also the novelist-writing-this-novel, is occupied in a voyage of self-discovery which necessitates his understanding his forebears, relations, and *their* relations. More importantly, he is discovering himself as a writer while creating their characters.

Full Fathom Five consists of three sections, each section being a study of one main character—the first, when the narrator is still a child, is a description of his Uncle Tom. This relationship between an older man, who is still young, and a very young boy is subtle and revealing. Later, when Uncle Tom fails in his marriage and his wife explains to the narrator that the reason he fails is because he is innocent (by which she seems to mean not that he is a clumsy or inadequate lover but that he does not belong enough to the world), one sees how the attraction between the uncle and the boy was that of mutual innocence. The second section is about the involvement of the narrator's grandmother, mother, and Cousin Corinne with a world-famous tenor, the counterpoint to these relationships being that of the tenor, the performing artist, with the narrator, the creative artist. And the last, and perhaps the most interesting section, describes the narrator's father in his living and his prolonged dying, a doctor and healer who recites poetry when he wishes to express his feelings.

There is a great deal in this novel to be grateful for, yet it is overladen with the writer's awareness of what he is writing about and how he is going about it. Well before the end, this self-consciousness oppresses the reader like a groaning conscience. Carter's devices would be justified if they had the result of objectifying the situation of a poet both living his life and turning it into his poetry. To make an artist a character in fiction does indeed present special difficulties, because the reader is left wondering how good the artist's work is. (It is a popular fallacy that there is such a thing as an artist without art, but, in fact, this is not the case; the art is the standard by which we judge artists.)

It may seem strange to introduce William Golding into a section of this essay discussing novels which seem to belong within a high academic convention. William Golding is a writer of great originality, but to be original does not prevent a writer fitting into a convention. There is indeed a place within the traditional academy for works which seem at first glance eccentric but later are seen to be affirmations of traditional attitudes written in a style which tends toward the classical. The fable and the parable at once surprise and delight with their oddity and at the same time are seen to be profoundly traditional. Within this tradition are *Gulliver's Travels*, *Rasselas*, *Robinson Crusoe*, *Dr. Jekyll and Mr. Hyde*, *A High Wind in Jamaica*, and *Animal Farm*. There is something about such works which seems to make them take place in a no-man's-land between childhood and maturity. No one seems quite to know which kingdom they belong to—that of the children in their heaven or the grown-ups in their purgatory. Sometimes a book which has been written—perhaps as a political pamphlet—for adults becomes annexed by children.

William Golding is obviously a writer to whom the above remarks apply. Add to them that, among the characteristics of such works, one is that they should be admirably and simply written.

Golding's novels are variations on the Fall of Man. *Lord of the Flies* is, of course, his most celebrated. In his latest novel, *The Spire,* he writes a fable of the Fall which takes place in medieval England. Joycelyn, the dean of a cathedrel (identifiable with Salisbury) which is in process of being built, has a vision in which he is told, with his good angel standing behind him, that he must order the master mason to erect a great spire surmounting the cathedral nave. But the shallow foundations on which the cathedral rests are shingly and incapable of sustaining a spire. Golding invokes all the forces of his visionary prose poetry to describe the boiling perturbation of the shingly soil in a great pit under the structure, resulting from the strains and stresses imposed on the foundations and the surrounding soil by the weight of the spire's construction. Obsessed with his fanatical vision, Jocelyn forces first the master mason and then, when he decamps from the site, a crew of workers who are publicans and sinners—rabble collected from highways and byways—rapists, thieves, and drunkards—to go on adding

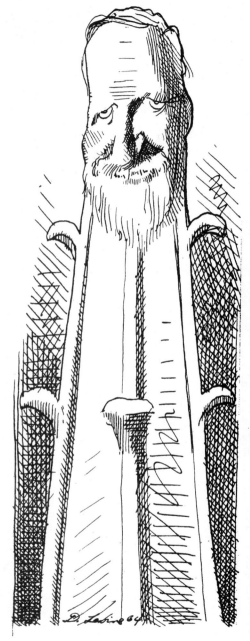

WILLIAM GOLDING

A sculptured model made in prose

189

to the octagonal spire, tier by tier. At last, when the spire is completed, the inevitable anticipated disaster occurs: it collapses, bringing down Jocelyn in its fall.

This is a novel without dénouement, only a kind of postscript in which Jocelyn comes to learn the nature of the devil which he mistook for his angel. From the start, the reader, like most of the builders of the spire, who call it "Jocelyn's Folly," knows what is bound to happen.

The gains resulting from sacrifice of a story are poetic and imagistic. The spire is a sculptured model made in prose which Golding puts before the reader, who can, as it were, walk all round it and observe it from every side. The novel develops processionally like a series of scenes over the arch of a church porch. There is a sequence, but the catastrophic end is held within the same glance as the false vision which is the beginning.

Here, as in his other novels, at his best Golding is a prose poet of gusty exhilaration. There are wonderful descriptions of how the weather felt to the workmen laboring on the roof of the cathedral like sailors on a mast, with the great deck of Salisbury Plain seen below. Nevertheless, this novel reads like the end of a set of variations on a single theme. One feels that Golding must find a new myth: there is danger of the Fall of Man becoming a cliché of his imagination.

Another enterprise in a grand convention of some Royal Academy of Letters, sustained through 1964, is a new volume which is the first in the second part of Anthony Powell's sequence *The Music of Time*. *The Valley of Bones* brings Powell to the outbreak of World War II, and provides him with a new set of characters—an energetic crew of soldiers taking over from the rather tired and frayed London socialites who were the leads in his first half-dozen volumes. Anthony Powell is a very English writer and the subject of the first part of his series is rooted in Eton and Oxford and English town-and-country upper-class life. He deals convincingly with friendship and early love affairs, and he has created at least one original comic character, Widmerpool, at Eton, a universally derided figure of fun. Subsequently, Widmerpool remains crude, but he develops that stubborn contempt for those who are his superiors and acquires a grasp of their weaknesses, which gives him a kind of power over them. He has that determination which, in the long run, is impressive and might result in his eventually becoming a conservative prime minister. Widmerpool is perhaps the only one of Anthony Powell's characters in the early part of the series who really develops. The rest undergo changes certainly, but they are all of a kind which tend to make their characters become fainter and more set. The limitations of *The Music of Time* are that Powell can only generalize sententiously about life, and that he does not understand politics. A reader of *The Acceptance World*, the volume devoted to the 1930's, could read with amusement the scene in which a good many of Powell's characters are seen walking on a hunger march through Hyde Park as sympathizers with the unemployed, but unless he already knew a good deal about the period, he would not derive the slightest understanding of what the 1930's, and their hunger marches, were all about.

One feared that Powell's series was going to die of inanition—starved of life and also of any sense of surrounding history. *The Valley of Bones* comes then as an immense relief. It gives one the curious feeling that by way of the war and contact with soldiers, Powell has found his way back into the world of *A Question of Upbringing*, not Eton, but a school, nevertheless, with all its responsibilities and irresponsibilities, its characters who are self-caricatures, its freedom within a very crude and square framework of discipline. The time is the outbreak of war, and the scene is Wales, country of the Arthurian legends. The narrator, Nicholas Jenkins, is an officer in a company whose sergeant major is called Cadwaller, his commanding officer Rowland Gwatkin, reminding Nick of:

> . . . When Rowland brave, and Olivier,
> And every Paladin and peer,
> On Roncesvalles died.

In portraying the characters of officers and men in this company, Anthony Powell's feeling for history, which is literary and picturesque, and not at all political, seems actually an advantage, where it was a weakness in *The Acceptance World*. For, in fact, once war broke out in England itself, for those who served in the war, politics ceased to matter, except to the politicians. What mattered was the sense of England itself. The war was Shakespearean. One reason why Churchill seems great—whatever mistakes in strategy and politics he may have made—is because he seemed to embody the English past in its landscape, and its poetry.

However, *The Valley of Bones* describes a period before Churchill became prime minister, that of September, 1939, and the "phony war." In portraying his Welsh peasants (now most of them bank managers or miners) become a patriotic army, Powell subtly suggests the world of the Welsh Fluellen and his army in Shakespeare's *Henry V*. It is a comedy of soldiers who might, when there is fighting, become heroes, but who, during the period of the "phony war," most of them, become mild failures: Sergeant Pendy who, after being efficient and reliable, suddenly loses all heart and commits suicide on account of news he has heard from home of his wife's infidelity; Captain Bethel, the peacetime hanger-on of theatrical troupes, who allows it to be thought that he is an international rugby football player and brother of a V.C., and who is exposed as a drunken bungler. The most subtly drawn portrait is that of Captain Gwatkin, an officer whose efficiency and high sense of duty are undermined by a streak of temperamental folly, which causes him to become completely disoriented through the havoc wrought on his heart by Maureen, the local tart, whom he romantically imagines to be an angel in human guise. Owing to this deterioration, Gwatkin forgets to inform his fellow officers of the significance of the code word "Fishcake," an omission which is discovered by the colonel, with disastrous results.

The soft-hearted Gwatkin is superseded by Kedward, a tougher, more realistic type, and the set of preliminary tests of character, which form the subject of Powell's novel, is concluded with the end also of the phase of the "phony war."

There is comedy and pathos in *The Valley of Bones*, but there is, above all, the truth of army life which makes soldiers curiously timeless. Here is a moving passage in which Popkiss, the chaplain, reads the relevant passage from *Ezekiel* which gives the title to the volume:

> Thus saith the Lord God unto these bones, and say unto them, O ye dry bones, hear the word of the Lord. Thus saith the Lord God unto these bones; Behold, I will cause breath to enter into you, and ye shall live. And I will lay sinews upon you, and cover you with skin, and put breath into you, and ye shall live. . . .

"Popkiss paused, looked up from his Testament, stretched out his arms on either side. The men were very silent in the pitch-pine pews."

It will be seen in the next volume whether Powell has not found his real subject in the officers and men of the war.

At the other extreme of the spectrum from the academic is the writing from the underground. When one opens "little" magazines and books published often by obscure publishers containing underground writing, one has the impression of an avant-garde, and, indeed, there is a certain common area of avant-garde and underground writing. I should define the avant-garde writers as searching for new forms, and the underground writers as seeking to free themselves of all inhibitions in order to realize without conscious thought or art their individuality in their writings. Sometimes the avant-garde writer, in his search for new forms, also draws on the material of his unconscious mind or seeks to stimulate the flow of images through drugs. But there is an essential difference between a poet like Rimbaud and writers like Henry Miller, William Burroughs, or the beat poets, in that Rimbaud was seeking through the disintegration of his personality to use his poetic sensibility as the medium through which an objective poetry could realize itself. The underground writers are seeking to express themselves. The standard by which we judge Rimbaud's work is not his biography, interesting though this is; the standard by which we judge Henry Miller, William Burroughs, or Jack Kerouac, is themselves. In their writing, they are forever telling us that they are so and so, that they did such and such. If we discovered that Miller had never had sex or that Burroughs had never taken drugs, their work would have no significance, because they themselves have made its meaning identical with their experience. As Alexander Trocchi writes in *Cain's Book*:

> For a long time now I have felt that writing which is not ostensibly self-conscious is in a vital way inauthentic for our time. For our time—I think every statement should be dated.

By "self-conscious," he obviously does not mean that the writer should be conscious of his art but that he should be conscious of himself, that he should aim at a total subjectivity in his writing so that it becomes identical with himself in his life, so that the terms on which the reader accepts him are those of believing in this total sincerity.

Underground writing springs from the feeling that in the modern world all values approved by the society in which we live—whether society means government, education, criticism, or established reputations—are hypocritical and "square." The only true values are those internal ones of the writer's own being which should remain utterly unaffected by the outside social values: the underground writer writes out of what happens to his body. As far as possible, he tries to establish a direct connection between his sensual experience and his writing, so that no critical correcting or censoring—the result of outside standards—comes between his poetry or prose and his experience of his own being. Because the writer is true to his own nature and to nothing else, therefore, the reader—who has, as it were, implicitly taken an oath to be true in the same way—can have confidence in him. No one cares a damn what T. S. Eliot "did," but the writing of Henry Miller would become false if one discovered he did not do the kind of things described in *Tropic of Cancer*. Conversely, Miller's ideal reader of him is one who does the same things.

A great deal of moral fervor—whether or not it is misguided—goes into underground writing and the activities which are considered as identical with the writing itself. When William Burroughs or Alexander Trocchi start defending their drug addiction or attacking those who look askance at it, they adopt the moral tone of a mid-Victorian novelist discussing the conditions in which children in the nineteenth century work in factories. The situation has been analyzed by Michael Polanyi in a recent essay "On the Modern Mind" (*Encounter*, May, 1965):

> Since ordinary decent behaviour can never be safe against the suspicion of sheer conformity or downright hypocrisy, only an absolutely a-moral, meaningless act can assure man of his complete authenticity. All the moral fervour which scientific scepticism has released from religious control and then rendered homeless by discrediting its ideals, returns then to imbue an a-moral authenticity with intense moral approval. This is how absolute self-assertion, fantasies of gratuitous crime and perversity, self-hatred and despair are aroused as defences against a nagging suspicion of one's own honesty.

The ultimate moral standard by which all other standards are judged is the unredeemed individual. The good is that which gives him the most intense realization of his sensual being, taken to be his true self. Everything is false that goes beyond the self that can taste, enjoy, experience. Thus, in the fiction of the underground, the reader is always conscious of the sensual presence of the writer, who is concerned with measuring all things by the scale of his own physical being.

Effects that might extend beyond the writer writing—the writer not concerned with making art but concerned only with being himself for the sake of the reader who, reading the words, must also be himself—are distrusted, avoided, disliked.

This is perhaps to oversimplify. Underground authors like William S. Burroughs and Alexander Trocchi avoid trying to write "literature" because they do not consider it literature anyway; or, conversely, because they think the writing which derives from an addiction in relation to which the writer himself is but the pen, is true literature, and everything else that is being written false.

Nova Express by Burroughs, written in a style which seems remotely to parody science fiction, is about an imaginary country, where the Nova police hunt out the Nova mob of junkies, dopies, criminals, etc. Its style consists largely of nightmare images strung together on parenthetic dashes. Thus: "Along canals of terminal sewage—the green boy-girls tend gardens of pink flesh—Amphibious vampire creatures who breathe in another flesh—double sex sad as the drenched lands of swamp delta to a sky that does not change—Where flesh circulates stale and rotten as the green water. . . ." Here Burroughs seems to have fallen into the trap of writing bad poetry, a most dangerous thing to happen to a prose writer who has been compared (by Kerouac) to Swift. Poets realize how boring poetic material in the raw can be: how essential it is to avoid monotony, to use various devices to provide variety and interest.

Jack Kerouac, in *Desolation Angels*, describes meeting in Tangiers an American writer called Bull who has written a book called *Nude Supper* "all about shirts turning blue at hangings, castration, and lime," about whom he says:

> You may talk to me about Sinclair Lewis the great American writer, or Wolfe, or Hemingway, or Faulkner, but none of them were as honest [as Bull], unless you name . . . but it aint Thoreau either.

Honesty, then, is the criterion. Honest about what? Not about what goes on outside you, nor even about what goes on in the mind, but honest about your entrails, and honest about whatever unconsidered, uncensored, unreflecting stream of expressions comes out.

Kerouac's book is an example of the required honesty. It asks of the reader firstly that he should be Kerouac's spiritual companion on Desolation Peak in northwestern Washington. This is Kerouac at his best, alone amidst nature and pouring out prose poems partly about his surroundings, partly his reminiscences, which at their best recall Whitman. As writing, this gets a bit tedious, but since what we are asked to consider, after all, is not writing but life, or life become identical with the writing, then Kerouac translated into snowy mountains is Kerouac at his best.

After 120 pages, however, Kerouac, thinly disguised as a character called Jack Duluoz, descends from the heights to San Francisco, and now we are among the beatniks with their beards and blue jeans; their stage properties of the bed and bottle in the pad; their ritualistic parties; their cult of an incommunicable witless slang with which they wish to communicate with everybody; their resort to alcohol, drugs, and sex, which they regard as Aladdin lamps supposed, after rubbing, to produce the genie of spontaneous utterance; their pretentious anti-intellectual streams of ideas; their name-dropping acquaintance with God, Christ, Buddha; their air of superiority over everyone who is disciplined, intelligent, industrious, humble; their total incapacity to enter into any real interchange of conversation; the tendency of all their activities toward the brawl, the prayer meeting, or the sexual orgy (all and any of which they regard as interchangeable); their lives forever verging on a nonstop party where everyone is proving to everyone else (down to stripping off the last inch of clothing) how natural he is and how spontaneous. Everyone here is a genius, but no one says anything interesting. Describing a poetry reading given by a poet called Merrill Randall (learning the trick of Kerouac's witless transpositions, I assume this to be Randall Jarrell), Kerouac relates how he hears a line or two, then hurries from the room because "in it I hear the craft of his carefully arranged thoughts and not the uncontrollable involuntary thoughts themselves, dig. . . ." and it is revealing that in his clumsy attempt to parody a line of "Merrill Randall," he can produce only a line of pure Kerouac:

> "The duodenal abyss that brings me to the margin
> consuming my flesh."

So "uncontrollable involuntary thoughts" become the criterion by which everything is judged. This is so unreliable a standard that Kerouac's world is one in which people are totally lost, unable to do anything except try to live up to the act of self-conscious spontaneity which is the common pretense of the group. Finally, on many occasions, one does not know whether Kerouac approves or disapproves of the things done and said by his uninvented characters. We are told, for instance, that in Tangiers, "Bull goes arm swinging and swaggering like a Nazi into the first queer bar, brushing Arabs aside and looking back at me with: 'Hey what?' I cant see how he can have managed this except I learn later he's spent a whole year in the little town sitting in his room on huge overdoses of morfina and other drugs staring at the tip of his shoe too scared to take one shuddering bath in eight months. So the local Arabs remember him as a shuddering skinny ghost who's apparently recovered, and let him rant. Everbody seems to know him, boys yell 'Hi!' 'Boorows!' 'Hey!'" Reading this one has an ashamed certainty that unless there was an awareness of the American fleet at the back of the boys' minds, they would fling "Bull" or "Boorows" into the harbor.

And yet, with all this, we are assured that Kerouac is an apostle of love. "His mysticism and religious yearning are . . . finally ineradicable from his personality . . . If critics were to give grades for humanity, Kerouac would snare pure A's each time out," writes Seymour Krim in an incredible introduction. This is a world in which it is assumed that you only have to go around saying that you love everyone for it to be accepted that you are a mystic and a saint. And to point out the difficulties involved in loving anyone is regarded as square. The difficulty of the position of utter spontaneity is that it removes all basis for self-criticism.

THE YEAR'S POETRY AND THE DEATH OF ELIOT

I shall conclude with some remarks about books by half a dozen poets published this year, because although perhaps no volume has been published which offers work strikingly new, it is possible, I think, to suggest a clearer picture of the present state of poetry than of the novel.

Before doing this, however, it seems right to consider what meaning the recent deaths of two poets, T. S. Eliot and Edith Sitwell, should have for us. Their deaths mark, I think, the end of an epoch. They also have a bearing on the immediate present of poetry and its future.

Many books have been written analyzing T. S. Eliot's poetry and criticism. Their multiplicity does not in itself explain, however, why his name and work were so much a lodestar and touchstone for so many of his contemporaries. W. B. Yeats may have been a greater poet and D. H. Lawrence more of a genius, but there was some quality in Eliot which seemed absolute. One reason, I think, for Eliot's centrality is that his achievement did not seem dependent on a philosophy or mystique which were private to him, his especial patent. Obviously, Yeats with his séances and his system of esoteric symbols, his study of remote Neoplatonist philosophies, barricaded his talents behind a high fence. Lawrence's insistence on sexuality and love, which at times seems to embrace the reader, is ultimately excluding because when looked at closely it is a compound of social and sexual snobberies which pay tribute to Lawrence, the miner, married to Frieda von Richthofen, the baroness. And Robert Graves's White Goddesses are for Robert Graves alone and serve to show that no one but himself has a muse.

Eliot is central and accessible partly because, despite the difficulty and complexity of some of his views, his sources are stated, his position— at once modern and passionately traditional—is open. Intellectually, he is formidable, and in his poetry, inimitable; but one knows what he read, what he believed, his ideas about poetry, the tradition to which he belonged. Moreover, despite his awareness of his own gifts, the sensibility behind the poetry, the person disappearing deliberately into the impersonal expression, is humble; that is to say, he is a bewildered and searching, religious man. He may be aware that he is a historic figure, he may be a royalist and a reactionary, but he also knows that he is equal with others in the eyes of God.

Eliot was the example of the poet who is not so much consciously modern as aware of the problem of one who would have been a poet at any time, having to invent form and idiom to suit the modern situation. He was modern without being modernist. His technique is advanced without being in the least avant-garde. It is difficult to think of any other writer (unless perhaps Joyce) who is so conscious of having a timeless vocation which, nevertheless, has to express itself within the conditions and limitations of this particular time. Eliot might be regarded as the twentieth century's answer to Matthew Arnold's argument, in *The Function of Criticism*, written at the end of the nineteenth century, that "important" poetry may become impossible at a time when those values within the surrounding culture upon which poetry formerly subsisted are no longer present; and, therefore, it may be a more urgent task to write criticism establishing values which will make a future poetry possible than to attempt great poems. Eliot, as it were, built critical awareness into his poetry. The reader discovers in the poem the values which support its culture. In T. S. Eliot, critical consciousness of the problem of writing poetry in a fragmented society is inseparable from the act of writing the poem. The conflict between a tragic awareness of the destructive forces and an intellectual determination to construct something affirmative upon their denial is the basic drama of his work, both poetry and prose.

Three distinct stages are evident in his development. The first— that of *Prufrock and Other Observations* (1917)—when, despite his avoidance of arty bric-a-brac effects, romantic nostalgia, and also despite his self-mocking irony, he nevertheless falls back on the aesthetic vision of a past life lost, which compensates for the loss. Prufrock, who dares not eat a peach, but who has his vision of the mermaids "singing each to each," bears marked resemblance to Strether, James's hero in *The Ambassadors*, who does not live his life, but who has his vision. What was new in the early Eliot was not the aestheticism but the intensity of his disgust at modern life and his intelligent transfusion of a Baudelairean sensibility into English poetry.

In the second phase of his development—that of *Gerontion* (1920) and *The Waste Land* (1922)—Eliot is no longer content with the aesthetic posture. He now confronts the deeper tragedy of modern man: he finds himself imprisoned in a history which makes it impossible for him to believe what his ancestors believed which gave their lives meaning. History:

> Gives too late
> What's not believed in, or if still believed,
> In memory only, reconsidered passion.

Probably the immense appeal of Eliot for many of his contemporaries was that he expressed the confrontation of the significance of believing with the impossibility of believing with a depth of imaginative insight which balanced the affirmation of belief against the negative horror of a world without belief. He went beyond the Jamesian position of expressing the situation of the artist forced to find the meaning of life in the invention of values in art, to a statement of the despair of religious man in a world which had undermined the premises of belief.

In his later poetry, Eliot resolved the problem of belief undermined by modern history, by postulating man in eternity, existing on the most important level of his consciousness outside the limitations of historic time. *The Waste Land* envisions what has happened to consciousness as the result of living within the "unreal cities" that survive from a fragmented civilization and await their destruction. In the *Four Quartets* (1943), the same consciousness affirms that it inhabits an eternal city which is the point of intersection on this earth of historic time and eternity.

The immediate importance of Eliot for his contemporaries was that he stated the relation of the living, whose tradition has become fragmented, with the dead, who lived within that tradition, not just didactically, but as apocalyptic vision. *The Waste Land* is like a blinding flash of lightning which suddenly reveals the reader to himself in his true historic situation, here in the present, a prisoner cut off from the significant past. Eliot could express the destructive forces of the present with as great an intensity as he could realize the values of the past. He focused even the squalid materialism of the present within a vision of the whole of civilization. The passages of squalor in *The Waste Land* are an affirmation because they are seen as having significance within the vision of the whole civilization.

I suspect that in the near future, Eliot's work—particularly his criticism—will recede somewhat. The young will be puzzled at the almost hypnotic hold it had over his contemporaries. His limitations will count against him: his identification of the politically reactionary with the traditional—in particular, his anti-Semitism—his indifference in most of his work to average sensual living, a certain lack of vitality which shows in his very intermittent poetic output, and, more significantly, in his apparent failure to enjoy life. His critical intelligence was at the center of things in the 1920's; it will be less so in the 1970's. Eliot will, in fact, fall back into the tradition, and it is impossible to surmise at this point where he will take his place. It remains true, however, that he expressed certain ideas and feelings with a vividness and a clarity equaled only by the greatest poets.

No reputation could be more different from Eliot's than that of Dame Edith Sitwell. Eliot's relations with other people were careful and correct, although, to those who knew him personally, it is clear that they were tinged with warmth, considerateness, and affection. Dame Edith's were impulsive, uncalculating, all fire or all ice. During her last illness, she wrote a conversational, scrappy, whimsical autobiography—*Taken Care Of*—which reveals a good deal about her character and tells very little of real fact about her life. It is not only polemical but, in passages, vitriolic, not only at times devastating to others but also to her own reputation for charity, tolerance, and good sense. This is a pity because she had all these qualities, even if they were rather unevenly distributed.

There is something breathtaking about the fact that not the deaths of her imagined enemies, nor her own approaching demise, nor her conversion to Catholicism, could prevent her remarking in her preface:

> I trust that I have hurt nobody. It is true that, provoked beyond endurance by their insults, I have given Mr. Percy Wyndham Lewis and Mr. D. H. Lawrence some sharp slaps. I have pointed out, also, the depths to which the criticism of poetry has fallen . . . but I have been careful, for instance, not to refer to the late Mr. Edwin Muir (Dr. Leavis's spiritual twin-sister).

The title of the book, *Taken Care Of*, implies a settling of accounts. But there is little method in it. Its arrangement reminds one of an old-fashioned desk with pigeonholes out of which stick, more or less randomly, a great many scraps of paper—letters, poems, pages from journals, cuttings, accounts paid and unpaid. A reader like myself who was fond of Dame Edith and who admired in her qualities here not consistently revealed—generosity, splendid courage, toughness combined with tenderness, complete lack of self-pity, wit, and an aristocratic habit of independence displayed in dress, manner, appearance, and grand style—will read this book with more concern for the harm she may be doing herself than that which her often unfair attacks will do to others. But then, while writing this, I am conscious of her scornfully reading what I have just written: I hear her laugh, I see her shrug her shoulders. It is a pleasure, in fact, to quote some lines of an amusedly admiring review from *The Times Literary Supplement*:

> One thinks of some grand ship of the line going down in flames, but with its flags still flying, and its deck guns firing to the last.

Her last work cannot then be considered a testimony. It does, however, provide material for meditating on her achievement and her personality. In everything she was that most unfashionable of persons in an age in which even the new poetry and the new criticism have become the new conformism—she was an original. She had an extremely original childhood among her extremely original family where she suffered extremely original tortures at the hands of a doctor instructed by her father to correct her stance. The account of her childhood is the most moving part of the book and explains the streak of childishness which was apparent even when she had attained world fame: as when, for example, she would have her correspondents address their letters to "Dame Edith Sitwell, D.B.E.; D. Litt; Litt. D."

This book illuminates the nature of her transmogrifying talent. Everything and everyone that moved her intensely tended to turn into some fantastic or grotesque image in her inner world. In her memory, her past resembles some mythical garden in which the same scenes continue to be played by the same distorted figures from her childhood and youth. Apart from admitting that she herself could not have been an altogether attractive child, the picture she presents of her parents and family relations and the elderly inhabitants of a boardinghouse, where she once stayed, are uncorrected by afterthoughts or later impressions. She writes about her own childhood as though she were still a child and she brings the same childish vision to scenes and people occurring long after she was grown up.

One sees, too, that her poetry was the direct result of a distorting process which she applied to her experience. Her poems are largely transcriptions of a special interior world, one which is much like a caricaturist's. *Gold Coast Customs* is her best work because it is the one most explicitly caricature. Her poetry has qualities which go back to the eighteenth century—not to the Age of Enlightenment, but to the visionary, spiritually disturbed period of Christopher Smart, Blake, and cartoonists like Rowlandson, Richardson, and Gilray. It is interesting to learn that among her earliest reading was the poetry of Pope. And it is with one aspect of Pope that she seems to identify: not the Pope of transparent lucidity and sustained intellectual flight, but the Pope of grotesque imagery; the Pope tender to his friends and caricaturing his enemies as bugs to be pinned into the pages of his satires; the Pope who, however many of his victims he persecuted, always—though without self-pity—regarded himself (his frail body supported by that iron cage which perhaps in Edith Sitwell's mind corresponded to those iron braces she was made to wear during her childhood) as the supreme victim.

One other voice from the generation now passing into the shadows was heard in 1964. It was that of Ezra Pound in an interview with Grazia Livi, published in *City Lights Journal*. Here is an extract:

E.P.: I have lived all my life believing that I knew something. But then a strange day came and I realized I knew nothing. Yes, I knew nothing. And thus words became devoid of meaning.

G.L.: Perhaps they lose their meaning because new elements are being introduced with vital force into the life of Man. I speak of the growing mechanization and of its mad and anti-poetic influence on humanity.

E.P.: Yes, that too. But at the same time I believe that all of this is transitory. I think there is a germinal force in humanity that will outlive mechanization. In short, I believe that some part of man's consciousness will remain in spite of everything, and will be strong enough to persevere against the force of unconsciousness.

G.L.: But through what medium? Perhaps through art? Once you wrote in *The Spirit of Romance*: "Art is a fluid moving above or over the minds of men . . ."

E.P.: Oh, the medium! I don't know anything anymore. I have even forgotten the name of that Greek philosopher who said that nothing exists and that if anything did exist it would be unknowable, and if it could be known, it would be uncommunicable.

G.L.: According to you, then, the contemporary world is nothing but a shipwrecked magma [*sic*] for which no road of salvation exists?

E.P.: No—it is something else: the contemporary world doesn't exist. For nothing exists which is not in rapport with the past and the future. Thus the world of today exists only as fusion, as a curve in time. But I repeat: I know nothing now. I have arrived too late at the greatest uncertainty. . . .

G.L.: If a "world of the present" doesn't exist so much less does a contemporary man exist!

E.P.: Exactly. There is no contemporary man. There exists only a man who is able to possess the growing consciousness of error. . . .

This remarkable interview, very moving in itself, is perhaps the last message from the last representative of the great generation of writers moving into the shadows.

Readers need not be reminded of the immense if fragmentary achievement of Ezra Pound—of the indebtedness of nearly all living modern English and American poets to him—in order to disagree with his self-condemnation, but this interview does seem to put finis to a period of imaginative writing in this century, and it reminds us at the end of this article that perhaps the most important literary events of 1964 were portents of a period coming to an end more than that any writers were "making it new."

One should put here with the poets rather than the novelists the fine new novel of one notable survivor—Samuel Beckett's *How it Is*. The hero—"I"—is a soliloquizing voice brooding over his past and present condition in this strange novel; he is one of Beckett's inhabitants of Dante's *Purgatorio*: passing eternities in a swamp of mud, addressing himself to another of the damned called Pim, who is perhaps the hero's alter ego.

SAMUEL BECKETT

Marvelous things emerge from slime

Beckett is the poet of boredom and monotony. Unlike his masters, Dante, Baudelaire, and Joyce, who knew a similar acedia, he makes little attempt to vary his material and its presentation. All the same, marvelous things emerge from this slime. *How it Is* achieves a simplicity of pure evocativeness which has the quality of a testament, as in this passage, where "I" is remembering the woman in his life:

> the flowers on the night-table she couldn't turn her head I see the flowers I held them at arm's length before her eyes the things you see right hand left hand before her eyes that was my visit and she forgiving marguerites from the Latin pearl they were all I could find

> iron bed glossy white two foot wide all was white high off the ground vision of love in it see others' furniture and not the loved one how can one

> sitting on the foot of the bed holding the vase bile-green lute the feet dangling the flowers between the face through them that I forget what it was like except intact white as chalk, not a scratch or my eyes roved there was a score of them

The outstanding characteristic of the masterpieces of the period which now seems drawing to a close is that their authors dramatized a picture of modern life, technological and scientific, against an intellectual and spiritual vision of a past, which they considered a unified culture. Nearly everything which in the language of the technologists, sociologists, economists, and planners is regarded as progressive, was categorized by these writers as evidence of fragmentation—the breakdown of values which in the past had given life spiritual meaning. In the work of the writers whom we think of as modern, progress was regarded as heresy. The self-imposed obligation of the poet or novelist was to concentrate with all the forces of soul and intellect on a vision of the significant past with which to confront—as with some dazzling shield—the disruptive values, but he had to use weapons of modern form and idiom in order to fight against these values for the envisioned past.

Writers like Proust, Eliot, Pound, Joyce, and Yeats were participants in a vast act of invocation of the past, in order that the ghosts of Homer, Virgil, Dante, the Elizabethans, might walk through the galleries of their works, giving to the modern poets (as Virgil gave strength to Dante) the power to hurl back into the mouths of the heretics of progress the accusation that it was they—the technologists—who were the hollow men. The nemesis of these writers—and that which makes it perhaps impossible for younger writers to continue in their line—is that they were nostalgic. Their attitude toward the present was determined by their immersion in the past. Ultimately, nostalgic positions are self-defeating: first, because it is impossible to live in the past without romanticizing it; and second, because the inventions of modern forms and idiom cannot be based exclusively on hatred of the present. In the long run, artists have to accept the present in order to go on developing a modern idiom.

Perhaps one reason why poets writing today seem "minor" compared with the great figures of the recent past is that their virtues are negative. Reading a dozen or so volumes of poetry published in 1964, it strikes me that their greatest merit is that they are not nostalgic. This means abandoning the high themes of great mythologies and histories which we associate with Pound, Yeats, and Eliot. All the same, what looks like a negative retreat from a position of exalted arrogance in which the poet hurled down mythical thunderbolts from past times at the cringing present may be a very solid gain.

A year in which new volumes have been published by Robert Lowell, Randall Jarrell, Philip Larkin, John Berryman, Donald Hall, and a posthumous volume by Theodore Roethke, cannot be written off as neglible for poetry. Moreover, these poets have certain characteristics in common which may be more important for poetry than if one were able to hail a new "movement." Lowell, Jarrell, and Hall are extending with great confidence areas of language peculiar to each of them.

Lowell has achieved a very great directness. What moves him in the poems in *For the Union Dead*—and it may be something so personal as to seem incommunicable or even trivial—becomes illuminated and powerful by the force of his caring. He is a virtuoso at giving the casual, the travel note, the marginal incident tremendous force. He does so because he can interpret every surface as the unexpected skin of the earth which might become the point of seismic weakness through which there breaks the earthquake. One is aware, under every line he writes, of something alarming, the possible occasion of madness or violence. For instance, at Buenos Aires:

> In my room at the Hotel Continentál
> a thousand miles from nowhere,
> I heard
> the bulky, beefy breathing of the herds.
>
> Cattle furnished my new clothes:
> my coat of limp, chestnut-colored suede,
> my sharp shoes
> that hurt my toes.
>
> A false fin de siecle decorum
> snored over Buenos Aires
> lost in the pampas
> and run by the barracks.

A good deal of what I have written above would apply also to John Berryman's 77 *Dream Songs* which won the Pulitzer Prize last year. These apparently casual stanzas written in a six-line form, which is an original invention like that of Pound's *Hugh Selwyn Mauberley*, are never so light as not to be ominous. Berryman has invented a character—related, at several removes, to Pound's Mauberley and to Eliot's Prufrock—called Henry, who is accompanied by his unappeasable and mocking shadow, Mr. Bones. Henry's natural mode of discourse is that phase of drunkenness when nothing seems serious, but things might at any moment get dreadfully serious. Henry is a scoffer and self-scoffing, but his scoffing is, of course, the ironic mask which covers a dream. He can be lucid and also very obscure and incoherent. A good deal of the book has to be read to get any sense of its quality, which a quotation cannot convey. All quotations can do is to give an idea of the stanza:

> The glories of the world struck me, made me aria, once.
> —What happens then, Mr. Bones?
> if be you cares to say.
> —Henry, Henry became interested in women's bodies,
> his loins were & were the scene of stupendous achievement.
> Stupor. Knees, dear. Pray.

A difficulty (which Berryman does not avoid) is that the invention of a catchy stanza may achieve too great facility in using it, and this tends to self-parody, not always deliberate. The complete mastery of the controls of the medium leads the poet into the danger of getting out of control because the stanza becomes a vehicle for near-automatic writing.

Randall Jarrell and Donald Hall are also poets who in their new volumes have thrust their inventions much further than previously. *The Lost World*, by Randall Jarrell, is childhood; and the title poem of the book is the recovery of this world—"O arms that arm, for a child's wars, the child!" In a way which is slightly reminiscent of the narrative poems of Robert Frost, Jarrell makes a language entirely out of closely observed and highly relevant facts around a situation which creates a character. The surface factual truth of the events in the narrative coincides with the deeper imaginative truth of character and situation, so that the reader accepts whatever material Jarrell introduces on the level of imaginative truth and does not ask: "Is this poetic?" Indeed, the more Jarrell can make his language out of unpoetic-seeming material, the more one is delighted. In "A Night with Lions," the lion with which the boy in the poem plays is the Metro-Goldwyn-Mayer lion; and as the boy captures it for his childhood, Jarrell captures it for his poetry and for our enjoyment.

One's reservations with Jarrell are entirely on the grounds of sentiment. Childhood is a dangerous subject for a poet who, like Jarrell, always loves what he writes about but, at times, does not distinguish between loving and being besotted with it. For this reason, I preferred the poems about adults to those recovering lost childhood. Much the best poem in the book is "Next Day," the soliloquy of a middle-aged woman grieving over the loss of her youth. It is expressed with a tautness and wonderful clarity of imagery which quite avoids self-pity:

> When I was young and miserable and pretty
> And poor, I'd wish
> What all girls wish: to have a husband,
> A house and children. Now that I'm old, my wish
> Is womanish:
> That the boy putting groceries in my car
> See me.

Randall Jarrell is sometimes too warm to avoid being embarrassing. Donald Hall risks the opposite danger: of being too cold. His poems have a very beautiful clarity, and in this volume, *A Roof of Tiger Lilies*, he never fails to present the roads and villages of an English or American countryside so that the reader has the impression of seeing, with detachment, exactly the scene described:

> A Roman road took us from the village of Bradwell-
>   on-Sea through marshy crop farms down to the shore
>   on a ridge which was so gradual
>
> my friend had to point it out. Yet in a tidal flood
>   the road is a strip of dry land in a plain
>   of water. Now the sloping meadows
>
> erupted with the lean daffodils of March. We walked
>   tilting our bodies against the Northern wind.

Yes, one sees it all so clearly and beautifully, as though one was there. But isn't the economy of means a little too simply artful? And on this walk, doesn't one find oneself giving little nods of approval? Yes, the way the lines run from one to the next without any pause at the end of a line conveys beautifully the feel of walking. And the stanzas which also run

The End of

EDITH SITWELL

She was an original

THEODORE ROETHKE

Something about him half-Ariel, half-Caliban

EZRA POUND

Growing consciousness of error

on (like crossing a ditch or hedge of the spaces between them) seem very nice, too. Yet when I read poetry which seems *pleased with itself*, I can imagine in one of those houses which the friends pass by on their walk how "Little Jack Horner/ Sat in a corner/ Eating his Christmas pie/ He put in his thumb/ And pulled out a plum/ And said, 'What a good poet am I!' "

An Epoch

The faces on these pages are familiar as the link connecting the tradition of past generations with modern expression. Dame Edith, the mercurial, Eliot, the ascetic (*below*), Pound, the romantic, Roethke, the nature mystic, were all poets who seemed to share the judgment that it was worth infinite travail to translate the remembrance of things past into the idiom of the present. But of late the past has seemed to be retreating at an accelerated pace, and its remembrance and translation become ever harder. The last of the quartet's survivors, Ezra Pound, resigned saying, "words became devoid of meaning." It was the adieu from a *generation now passing into the shadows*.

On the other hand, if one can set aside the slight irritation caused by Hall's deliberateness, this is an extremely agreeable book to read, besides which there is much to admire in his technique.

No Jack Hornerism occurs in Philip Larkin, who is, in *The Whitsun Weddings*, a poet of impeccable but unobtrusive technique and, moreover, one of the best poets writing today. Philip Larkin, who lives in Hull, where he is librarian at the University, never leaves England; he is probably less influenced than any other English poet of his generation by American poetry. His writing indeed takes up the development of English poetry before the influence of Pound and Eliot had been felt, and looks as if it would have been exactly as it is, had they never written. The poet who seems nearest to Larkin is Edward Thomas—the friend of Robert Frost when he was in England in the 1910's—a rather neglected writer whose nature poems have a clear and pure exactitude like that of the early work of Frost. Although intensely English, Larkin's development runs parallel with that of Americans like Jarrell and Hall, in that the form and language seem fitted very closely to experiences which seem actual and literal, rather than dreamy and romantic. In fact, he depends less on having a heady temperament than the Americans (notably Lowell and Berryman), some of whom tend adroitly in their poetry to substitute for the romantic the picture of the neurotic always close to breakdown and madness. Larkin's reservations are those of a man of ordinary tastes who likes to lead an average life, without being ironic about it. He is extraordinary, it is true, in that his vocation has singled him out, condemned him literally to singularity, a fate which he contemplates ruefully in "Dockery and Son." In this poem, he visits the college where twenty years previously he was an undergraduate and learns from the dean that his contemporary, Dockery, now has a son at the college. Returning home on the train, he reflects:

> Well, it just shows
> How much . . . How little . . . Yawning, I suppose
> I fell asleep, waking at the fumes
> And furnace-glares of Sheffield, where I changed,
> And ate an awful pie, and walked along
> The platform to its end to see the ranged
> Joining and parting lines reflect a strong
>
> Unhindered moon. To have no son, no wife,
> No house or land still seemed quite natural.
> Only a numbness registered the shock
> Of finding out how much had gone of life,
> How widely from the others. Dockery, now:
> Only nineteen, he must have taken stock
> Of what he wanted, and been capable
> Of . . . No, that's not the difference: rather, how

Convinced he was he should be added to!
Why did he think adding meant increase?
To me it was dilution. Where do these
Innate assumptions come from? Not from what
We think truest, or most want to do:
Those warp tight-shut, like doors. . . .

These reflections never stray over the kind of thoughts that any bachelor
might have. They have intensity but there are after all intensities of the
commonplace, intensities of repression, inhibition, resentment, virginity.
What is extraordinary is the expression itself, and Larkin seems to remind
us that a poet's exceptional quality lies in his power to use language, and
in the vocation which this imposes on him, more than in his being unlike
"ordinary" people. But do we quite accept this? Larkin is probably the
best English poet writing today, and it is not his fault that one feels a bit
grudging that our best poet is someone who by implication tells us that
a poet is just an ordinary chap with extraordinary language at his
command, and a sense of dedication which prevents him entering and
enjoying the consolations of ordinary lives.

The late Theodore Roethke was very far from being an ordinary
person either in his poetry or his life. His posthumously published
volume, *The Far Field*, reminds us that he is the poet of a unique
world. Born of a family of Michigan flower gardeners, he impresses
on us that he was brought up in greenhouses, a world of orchids,
roses, ferns, newts, slugs, steamy heats, and mildewy soils. Divided
between the roses and the mud, he has something about him half-Ariel,
half-Caliban. In physical appearance, as well as behavior, he had the look
of someone earthbound and at the same time leaping, a dancing and singing bear. In these last poems he is conscious of dying, and in the last poem
in the volume, "One More, the Round," he surely writes his epitaph:

What's greater, Pebble or Pond?
What can be known? The Unknown.
My true self runs toward a Hill
More! O More! visible.

Now I adore my life
With the Bird, the abiding Leaf,
With the Fish, the questing Snail,
And the Eye altering all;
And I dance with William Blake
For love, for Love's sake;

And everything comes to One,
As we dance on, dance on, dance on.

The picture I have given here is rather orchestral, of poets playing
different instruments in a symphony which has the common theme of

poetry in our time. If the year's events are to be properly commented on, note must be taken of a discordant voice: that of Karl Shapiro. On the dust jacket of *The Bourgeois Poet,* the publishers say, evidently with the authority of Shapiro himself: "All these poems are in a form . . . which Mr. Shapiro has been using more frequently in recent years—a form in which he eschews not only rhyme, but versification as well. It is his belief that these two traditional attributes of poetry are non-essential and artificial impediments to the poetic process." Translating this into the language of ordinary common sense, all this amounts to is that Shapiro has, for the time being at any rate, stopped writing poetry and devoted himself to small stretches of prose, fables, journal notes, and aphorisms. I should add that Shapiro does not write what are called "prose poems," or if he is attempting to write them, they are a form in which he is totally ungifted. Here is an example of his writing:

> What kind of notation is in my *Time* file for my life, especially my death? Will they say I died, O God? If they don't say I died how can I die? There it is fine and relevant to die, an honor so to speak, interesting as divorce.

For Shapiro, it may be a necessary phase of his development that he should write anonymous, colorless slabs of prose. What is distressing is that he appears to think that his is a path other poets should follow. In recent criticism, and also in some of these notes, he attacks colleagues (including all French poets) for use of rhyme, versification, and for other qualities in their work which are commonly held to distinguish poetry from prose. Shapiro should ask himself—Would he really be happier if his contemporaries did what he is doing and produced arid, little squares of rhymeless, formless writing which they peddled as essential poetry? Would he not feel that his patent is being infringed?

Robert Lowell is perhaps the only poet who seems concerned with writing great poetry, making affirmations which either come out of a highly stimulated subjective excitement or attempt great statements about the human condition. The general achievement of poetry today is a varied and serious discourse about a great many experiences and ideas which have been made accessible to discussion in poetry owing to the great development of the medium—the deliberate abolishing of standards which separate a poetic subject matter from a nonpoetic one. Poets can write about anything in poetry. This is a gain, but perhaps the result of it is that they tend too easily to write about whatever immediately strikes them, without achieving much intensity. The accessibility of commonplace objects to poetry has encouraged too many commonplace poets. What we seem to need is a kind of poetry in which all the poet's experiences are available as imagery and observation, but in which the level of the discourse is itself high.

BIBLIOGRAPHY

FICTION:

AUCHINCLOSS, LOUIS. *The Rector of Justin.* Boston: Houghton Mifflin Co., 1964.

BELLOW, SAUL. *Herzog.* New York: The Viking Press, Inc., 1964.

BRAINE, JOHN. *The Jealous God.* Boston: Houghton Mifflin Co., 1964.

BURROUGHS, WILLIAM S. *Nova Express.* New York: Grove Press, Inc., 1964.

CARTER, JOHN STEWART. *Full Fathom Five.* Boston: Houghton Mifflin Co., 1965.

GOLDING, WILLIAM. *The Spire.* New York: Harcourt, Brace & World, Inc., 1964.

ISHERWOOD, CHRISTOPHER. *A Single Man.* New York: Simon and Schuster, Inc., 1964.

KEROUAC, JACK. *Desolation Angels.* New York: Coward-McCann, Inc., 1964.

MAILER, NORMAN. *An American Dream.* New York: The Dial Press, Inc., 1965.

POWELL, ANTHONY. *The Valley of Bones.* London: William Heinemann, Ltd., 1964.

STOREY, DAVID. *Radcliffe.* New York: Coward-McCann, Inc., 1964.

TAYLOR, ELIZABETH. *The Soul of Kindness.* New York: The Viking Press, Inc., 1964.

WATERHOUSE, KEITH. *Jubb.* New York: G. P. Putnam's Sons, 1964.

WILSON, ANGUS. *Late Call.* New York: The Viking Press, Inc., 1965.

POETRY:

BECKETT, SAMUEL. *How it Is.* New York: Grove Press, Inc., 1964.

BERRYMAN, JOHN. *77 Dream Songs.* New York: Farrar, Straus & Giroux, Inc., 1964.

HALL, DONALD. *A Roof of Tiger Lilies.* New York: The Viking Press, Inc., 1964.

JARRELL, RANDALL. *The Lost World.* New York: The Macmillan Co., 1965.

LARKIN, PHILIP. *The Whitsun Weddings.* New York: Random House, Inc., 1964.

LOWELL, ROBERT. *For the Union Dead.* New York: Farrar, Straus & Giroux, Inc., 1964.

ROETHKE, THEODORE. *The Far Field.* New York: Doubleday & Co., Inc., 1964.

SHAPIRO, KARL. *The Bourgeois Poet.* New York: Random House, Inc., 1964.

SITWELL, DAME EDITH. *Taken Care Of.* New York: Atheneum, 1965.

NOTE TO THE READER

Throughout his evaluation of current fiction and poetry, Mr. Spender exercises standards of critical judgment. For a discussion of principles of literary criticism, the reader can consult the references cited under POETRY 8 in the *Syntopicon.* Further examination and practice of literary criticism can be found in essays in Volume 5 of *Gateway to the Great Books*: Saint-Beauve's "What Is a Classic?" pp. 65-75; Arnold's "The Study of Poetry," pp. 19-41; Schiller's "On Simple and Sentimental Poetry," pp. 155-211; and Virginia Woolf's "How Should One Read a Book?" pp. 5-14.

Commenting on American literature, Mr. Spender notes: "The traditional concern of American novelists has been to define some kind of American." Examples of this characteristic of American authors can be seen in the fiction in *Gateway to the Great Books*: Hemingway's "The Killers," Vol. 2, pp. 169-77; Fitzgerald's "The Diamond as Big as the Ritz," Vol. 3, pp. 397-431; and Melville's "Billy Budd," Vol. 3, pp. 31-98. Other aspects of the question, What is an American?, are examined by De Tocqueville, "Observations on American Life and Government," GGB, Vol. 6, pp. 564-690, and De Crèvecoeur, "The Making of Americans," GGB, Vol. 6. pp. 546-59.

Discussing Saul Bellow's *Herzog,* Mr. Spender observes that "Even at their most tragic, Shakespeare and Tolstoy conceal within the sad tree of wintry language the sap of humor." In Plato's *Symposium,* GBWW, Vol. 7, p. 173c-d, Socrates argues that this mixture of comedy and tragedy is the mark of the great writer. Implications of Socrates' position are examined in the introductory essay on POETRY in the *Syntopicon,* GBWW, Vol. 3, p. 406b-c.

T. S. Eliot is at once "modern and passionately traditional," Mr. Spender observes. The relationship between a contemporary author and literary tradition are examined by T. S. Eliot in his essay "Tradition and the Individual Talent," GGB, Vol. 5, p. 404-11. Another major point made about Eliot is concern with the problems of belief. Additional discussions of this problem can be read in passages cited in the *Syntopicon* under GOD 6c(2), KNOWLEDGE 6c(5), RELIGION 1-1b(3), TRUTH 4a, and WILL 3b(3).

Philosophy

JOHN E. SMITH

"*Professor John E. Smith is admirably lucid,*" *wrote* Newsweek *in a review of his book* The Spirit of American Philosophy *(1963),* "*and he has succeeded in making the thought of the classic American philosophers accessible to any willing and reasonably sophisticated reader—which is no mean feat.*" *Professor Smith, of the Department of Philosophy at Yale University, is a specialist in American philosophy and the philosophy of religion. Born in 1921 in Brooklyn, New York, he studied at Columbia University and the Union Theological Seminary and took his Doctorate in 1948 from Columbia. After seven years of lecturing on philosophy and religion at Vassar and Barnard Colleges, Professor Smith joined the Yale faculty in 1952, and in 1961 he was appointed departmental chairman. In 1960 he was the Dudleian Lecturer at Harvard University and in 1963 the Suarez Lecturer at Fordham University. He received an honorary degree from the University of Notre Dame in 1964. During 1965 he was visiting lecturer at the University of London. His books include* Royce's Social Infinite *(1950),* Reason and God *(1961), and a critical text and introduction to Jonathan Edwards'* Treatise Concerning Religious Affections *(1959). Professor Smith is married and lives in New Haven, Connecticut.*

and Religion

The most important question in philosophy today is, what is philosophy itself? What is the nature and function of the philosophical enterprise?" With these words, John Dewey concluded his last public lecture before a special assemblage of students and colleagues at Columbia University well over a decade ago. That his words were not only accurate but prophetic as well has been made clear by the development of philosophical thinking since that time. Therefore, a large part of an understanding of philosophical developments some fifteen years after mid-century must be achieved by attending to the efforts of philosophers to come to a decision concerning the nature and aims of their own enterprise. It may seem odd that a discipline should nearly exhaust itself in discussion about what it ought to be, but that is the current state of affairs, and we would be neglecting much that is important if we failed to record the fact. For the future of philosophy it is essential to discover how this situation has come about and what positive suggestions are being made for the recovery of philosophy in the years to come.

For a variety of reasons, philosophy and philosophers have been caught in an extended crisis—one must say "extended" because its roots are found in the eighteenth century, if not earlier—brought on by perplexity, uncertainty, and, in extreme cases, even despair, over the nature and prospects of philosophy, its aims, its proper subject matter, and the methods it should employ. One result has been an almost exclusive preoccupation on the part of philosophers with the reflexive question as to what philosophy can and should be. Embarrassment in the face of the natural sciences and their unquestioned prestige has led many philosophers to avoid making any claim whatever to *truth* or to knowledge with regard to their conclusions. Some have supposed that philosophy adds no new knowledge but is merely an analytic clarification of what we already know, functioning as a sort of map showing us the connections between the various languages that have been developed for expressing the knowledge gained from other sources. Others have come to regard philosophy as confined to study of what is called the logical structure of the statements expressing the results of investigation in the natural sciences. Others have preferred to limit philosophy to an analysis of the meanings conveyed in ordinary language, so-called, and most recently this approach has been extended to include the special languages of religion, law, ethics, and so on. In some cases the lack of clear bearings by which to steer a philosophical course had led to resignation and abandonment of philosophy altogether as a legitimate enterprise. Moreover, the insistence of philosophical questions has shown itself in the fact that they continue to be raised by literary critics, intellectual historians, and theologians, even when philosophers have ceased to take them seriously.

As Mortimer Adler points out in *The Conditions of Philosophy*, modern and contemporary thought, in contrast with the dominant philosophical climate of the ancient Classical world and the Middle Ages, have been pervaded with critical self-awareness and uncertainty. The contrast is between a direct, confident, straightforward attempt to pose and resolve philosophical problems on the one hand, and an uncertain self-scrutiny that leads to the postponement of these problems in the face of a host of preliminary questions such as: Is philosophical knowledge possible at all? Where Plato would have raised the question of the good life or the nature of the soul and attempted to give an answer, most modern philosophers have felt the need of asking first whether such questions can be answered. In comparison with the tradition of "critical philosophy" illustrated in the thought of Locke and Kant in the seventeenth and eighteenth centuries and in our own day by such analytic philosophers as G. E. Moore and Wittgenstein, Plato and Aristotle in the ancient world and Duns Scotus or Aquinas in the Middle Ages approached philosophical problems with a reasonable assurance about the importance and autonomy of philosophy. As a result, these earlier thinkers were able for the most part to identify philosophical questions and to attack them directly much as the historian or mathematician might do in their own domains. This is not to say that Plato or Aquinas paid no attention to the question of the nature of philosophy or that neither one of them had anything to say on the subject. It is rather that they did not regard such reflection as central nor, in their view, did it exhaust their concern as philosophers. They went ahead on the assumption that philosophy is a legitimate study and that it has distinctive problems of its own which no man can afford to neglect. In consequence, they were led to think thoughts that have become a permanent part of the intellectual heritage of the West.

Modern philosophers have been less sure of their ground and have for some time been considering "second-order" questions, largely about philosophy itself. Many philosophers have begun with the sense that philosophy has to be defined and defended against its critics before the problems of philosophy can be discussed. Second-order questions have come to dominate the scene so that, for example, instead of raising the question of the good—the question of what men ought to be and to do—attention is shifted to such considerations as: What sort of predicate is meant by the term "good"? How can we verify moral judgments? What does the ordinary man mean by the term "good"? These questions are believed by many philosophers, especially professional ones, to be the only legitimate questions for philosophy. Hence, it is often said that, as regards philosophical ethics, for example, the philosopher should make no moral evaluations but should concern himself instead with the meaning of such judgments after they have been made by others and with the sort of language in which moral judgments are expressed.

In order to understand what sort of response is currently being made to the state of affairs just described, three things are necessary: first, the need to reflect in more detail the present stage of the continuing debate about the proper business of philosophy, especially the clear signs of dissatisfaction that appear against the view that philosophy should be confined to critical or second-order questions alone; second, the need to make clear the positive proposals that are being advanced for the recovery of philosophy in the future; third, the need to take note of the philosophical contributions that are being made by those who, not being content to identify philosophy with the debate itself, have continued to pursue philosophical problems directly on the basis of more or less settled convictions about the importance of philosophical thinking. In carrying out the third part of this program we shall be able to report on current work in the philosophy of religion, the history of philosophy, the philosophy of science, developments in existential philosophy, and in the fields of religious ethics. For we must not lose sight of the philosophizing that is actually going on at a time when so much intellectual energy is being expended over the question whether philosophy is possible at all. And, as will become clear, one of the most interesting developments now taking place is the renewed interest in philosophical discussion of the religious issues, including new light on the ancient and perplexing question of the relation between philosophy and theology.

THE PROPER BUSINESS AND FUTURE OF PHILOSOPHY

The dominant position, at least in academic philosophy, over the past twenty-five years has been some form of analytic or linguistic philosophy, according to which the proper business of philosophy is the analysis of language, the meanings expressed through it, and the uses to which it can be put. This way of thinking has come primarily from British philosophers of the twentieth century, including G. E. Moore, A. J. Ayer, Gilbert Ryle, and Ludwig Wittgenstein, although the line of thinking represented can be traced back to the fourteenth century and the "Terminism"—concern for the proper language and arrangement of terms in expressing knowledge—associated with William of Ockham. In addition, the analytic approach has been powerfully represented in Continental philosophy by the logical positivists of the Vienna Circle under the guidance of Rudolf Carnap. More recently the outlook has established itself in America where it has come to dominate the academic scene.

No single description of what is meant by "linguistic" philosophy would satisfy all its proponents, and indeed the expression itself has been attacked as inaccurate or misleading, largely because of the difficulty that attaches to explaining exactly what is meant by "linguistic." The fact is that the philosophy of analysis embraces a cluster of positions, each with a special emphasis. Despite this variety, all are committed to the general thesis that philosophy cannot be oriented toward "reality," or "being," or "God," but must be confined to the study of our language or the symbolic devices we use in *expressing* what we want to say. Stating the point in terms proposed by Adler in *The Conditions of Philosophy*, we may say that, according to the analytic or linguistic approach, philosophy deals entirely with "second-order" questions. And these are questions that have to do with, for example, the logical conditions for raising questions, or, more freely expressed, talk about talk. So conceived, philosophy has no subject matter of its own that would permit the raising of "first-order" questions after the fashion of history or mathematics.

An increasing number of philosophers are raising their voices in protest against what they take to be the trivializing of philosophy in the linguistic approach. Some of those joining in the protest were themselves trained in the analytic approach so that the signs of unrest do not stem entirely from external sources. Analytic philosophers are most meticulous in their thinking, and the whole movement has been remarkably self-contained in the sense that few analytic philosophers have ever learned anything from nonanalytic philosophers. One consequence of the minute scale upon which analytic philosophers have conducted their researches is shown in their tendency to describe what may be no more than a minor change in outlook as a "revolution" in philosophy. Perhaps where the scale of thought is so limited even the slightest shift either in doctrine or emphasis is bound to appear as a major displacement.

In the most summary form, it can be said that three features serve to define the linguistic approach to philosophy: first, philosophy is supposed to restrict itself to the study of language, its structure and uses; second, philosophy is supposed to concern itself primarily with clarification and interpretation of statements whose truth or falsity is grounded elsewhere, rather than with the debate between alternative philosophical points of view; third, philosophy is supposed to consider second-order questions such as the problem of how we know and what questions we are equipped to answer. Above all, philosophy is not to be thought of as an enterprise that deals directly with reality or that has unique questions of its own; instead, it is to focus on the language used to express what is known or believed outside of philosophy. The final word is that philosophy has neither autonomy nor method of its own.

Two recent volumes, very different in character, make it plain that the analytic conception of philosophy does not go unchallenged and also that a considerable portion of the criticism is coming from within the ranks of those brought up under the influence of that conception. One of these volumes, *Clarity Is Not Enough* (edited by H. D. Lewis of King's College, University of London), is a collection of essays by many hands in which different aspects of linguistic philosophy are subjected to searching criticism. The other volume, *The Conditions of Philosophy* by Adler, is a clear and spirited attack aimed at all who would identify philosophy with second-order questions and clarification of meaning, and an equally spirited defense of philosophy as an autonomous enterprise with aims, questions, and a method of its own. The two volumes taken together furnish an excellent insight into the present state of the response to the analytic conception as well as some clues about the future prospects of constructive philosophy. If the whole debate seems somewhat academic, we must remember that the analytic conception of philosophy is entrenched in most American universities so that the majority of young students electing to study philosophy may find that they will never be introduced to the high road of constructive philosophy that stretches all the way from the Greeks to Whitehead.

Clarity Is Not Enough is important as a whole for the striking coincidence of opinion it expresses as well as for the particular points made by the individual contributors. As the title of the volume (borrowed from the first essay by H. H. Price) suggests, a central contention expressed by most contributors is that the clarification of what other people say, whether they be so-called ordinary people or experts in a field, is not a sufficient task for philosophy. The place of importance accorded philosophical studies in the traditional curriculum of university education, says Price, is not a place that philosophy could ever have attained if it had always been identified with the analytic approach. "If philosophy is only clarification," Price asks, "does it deserve the place it has had in a liberal education?" And, he continues in partial answer, "it acquired that place on the strength of a claim to be much more than this."

Price is willing to allow that being clear about what we are saying and attempting to make our questions plain before we attempt to answer them is *part* of the philosopher's business, but he says, "I do not think that it is the whole of his task . . . certainly clarification is not all that the educated public demands." And in saying that philosophy must be more than analysis aimed at clarifying, Price is claiming that the "more" must take the form of metaphysics. He makes two points in criticism and correction of the analytic approach to philosophy. First, he complains that analytic philosophers have paid too little attention to "pre-verbal" and "non-verbal" thinking, concentrating instead on "full dress" language that is precise and well-formed already, having been standardized for some special purpose. Second, and as a corollary, Price points out, as Whitehead had done some decades ago, that not everything philosophically worth saying can be said in the language we already have at hand. To say something novel, to introduce a fresh perspective based on new insight, may lead us to break through the familiar and well-worn discourse to which we have become accustomed.

In spelling out further what philosophers must do, Price adopts a novel position with regard to the truth or falsity of metaphysical doctrine. On the one hand, he does not believe that the statements of such doctrine can be either true or false, but he does hold that the arguments for these statements can be true or false. This conclusion is bound up with his view of metaphysics according to which it is the aim of the speculative philosopher "to produce a unified conceptual scheme under which all the known types of empirical fact may be systematically arranged." This scheme is likened to a map in that it involves a world of fact to be represented and some principle of projection or interpretation in terms of which the representation is possible. Thus, for example, the "map" of most medieval philosophers was theocentric, representing all reality in relation to God; the map of many modern philosophers, such as Hume or Kant, has been anthropocentric, representing all reality in relation to man and his nature; and again the map of some more recent philosophers, like Henri Bergson or Whitehead, has been biocentric, representing the cosmic process in relation to life and its functions.

Some indication, however, of how strong the clarification view of philosophy is can be seen from the fact that it reappears even in the constructive position of a philosopher who criticizes it. For, after defending the significance of metaphysics understood in the sense of a map of reality, Price goes on to interpret it as one more form of clarification—"synoptic clarity" in distinction from the "analytic clarity" of the analytic philosophers. Once again the claim is that the philosopher's task is not "to give us new information about matters of fact" but to make things comprehensible. The domain of fact is sealed off, as it were, as something already determined or known apart from philosophy; the work of the philosopher adds no new knowledge.

Another paper in the collection, "Misleading Analyses" by Errol

John E. Smith

E. Harris, though written several years ago, is important because it focuses very clearly the criticisms that can be advanced against the method used by some linguistic philosophers to dispose of metaphysical thought by branding it "misleading" or the cause of illusions. By considering some typical examples, Harris shows that no one (except, perhaps, philosophers themselves, who should know better) is ever really misled by supposedly "misleading" metaphysical theories or doctrines unless they approach such theories with a metaphysical position of their own which they are not acknowledging. Thus Ryle, for example, claims that philosophers, in making such statements as "Virtue is its own reward," are guilty of taking "universals" (in this case, Virtue presumably) to be "objects," to which Harris replies:

> No sane person who at all understands the difference between universals and particulars could think that one was the same as the other. No sane person ever imagines that Unpunctuality or Virtue is a person like Jones or Smith, even though some allegorists have so depicted them. If we are not apt to be misled by allegories, why should we be by the grammar of ordinary language?

Harris considers the charge put forward by some that phrases like "the thought of . . ." or "the idea of . . ." have misled us into believing that there really are such entities as thoughts, ideas, judgments, and other presumably bogus entities. Those who make this charge propose to eliminate these "mental" elements by a proper "analysis" of what we "really mean" (that is, what we would have to mean if we were to agree with the philosophical assumptions of the one making the analysis) when we describe our thinking processes and habits. Harris' reply here is that there is no proposal regarding the use of language enabling us to ignore the fact that when we do think of taking a trip, or reflect on the solution of some problem, we are thinking of "something" and not just engaging in an "act of thinking." If so-called mental entities are really spurious or illusory, the device of changing our way of speaking so as to refer to mental "events" or "activity" instead does not solve any problem. Harris' general conclusion is instructive:

> First, the allegation that philosophers . . . are confused by the forms of ordinary language and misled into the formulation of absurd theories is not proven. In fact, the errors imputed to the philosophers are errors they have not made and are such as would be committed only by the intellectually deficient. Secondly, the imputation of these errors to the allegedly misleading character forms is itself the result of confusion . . . Thirdly, the attempt to show that some traditional philosophical problems are only apparent, and arise only from the way in which we talk about certain matters, fails because the problems remain however we choose to alter our way of speaking, so long as we continue by our words to refer to the same subjects.

219

Other noteworthy criticisms of the linguistic conception of philosophy and the dissolution of philosophical problems come from Brand Blanshard in "The Philosophy of Analysis," from Lewis in "Mind and Body," and even from Ayer in "Philosophy and Language." Blanshard is critical of all views that "would demote philosophy to the position of a critique of language." He attacks clearly and vigorously the reduction of knowledge to sense perception and the relegation of reason to the position where it can do no more than clarify meanings already in mind. In addition, he objects to the thesis that philosophy as such is not involved in determining the truth or falsity of any statement but is instead restricted to making clear what is meant by statements whose truth is otherwise known. Nor is Blanshard altogether happy about Moore's defense of commonsense beliefs on the ground that, for Moore, there are beliefs we can know to be certain before we can be said to know what they mean!

In the course of examining the relation between mind and body—one of the master philosophical problems since Descartes separated the two completely—Lewis shows how a philosopher's view of the relationship can be wholly determined either by his acceptance of a certain method for treating the problem or by his acceptance of the verifiability theory of meaning. That is to say, if a philosopher allows as evidence only what can appear to sense and in sense experience, his view of the self, its consciousness and thought processes, will be very different from what would be advanced by a philosopher not committed in advance to such a view. Lewis argues that linguistic philosophers ignore fundamental distinctions rooted in a wide range of fact available to all in favor of their technique of analysis that is alone supposed to be adequate for philosophical thinking. Lewis considers, for example, the attempt of P. F. Strawson, in his book *Individuals*, to eliminate the usual distinction between body and mind by rearranging our language so that we can get along without the sharp distinction supposed by all of us to exist between our own selves and other persons. Strawson's proposal is that it is possible to "construct the idea of a special kind of social world in which the concept of an individual person is replaced by that of a group." Lewis' comment on this proposal takes us to the heart of the debate about the linguistic conception of philosophy and its role. Lewis writes:

> It is an ominous indication of where we end when, in seeking to understand human life, we resort to techniques and linguistic procedures which do not take close account of what we find the facts about ourselves to be in our own experience.

The concern here expressed over the strong possibility of either losing or distorting the facts of situations because of the emphasis on language and the use of terms, marks a recurrent theme in *Clarity Is Not Enough*. The most striking instance is found in Ayer's contribution, "Philosophy and Language." This paper, appearing as it does in a collection of essays critical of analytic philosophy, is important especially in view of the fact that Ayer's earlier book *Language, Truth and Logic* has been for some years the "bible" of classical positivism, and its succinct and uncomplicated statement of the position had much to do with establishing linguistic philosophy as the dominant form of philosophical inquiry in America as well as in Britain. Now Ayer is anxious to show that much linguistic philosophy, so-called, has not really been concerned exclusively with the study of language but rather with the factual situation behind language and with the attempt to cause us to return to the facts for a second look so as to avoid our omitting anything from our accounts of experience. That Ayer finds it important to make this point suggests a new stress on the priority of fact over language, experience over expression, even if his account of what linguistic philosophers have been doing is open to question. Ayer, at any rate, now seems interested in escaping from the prison of language or at least from allowing linguistic considerations to determine every philosophical conclusion.

There are, in fact, at least three points where Ayer seems to have modified his view in a direction that implies dissatisfaction with the linguistic view. After calling attention to the importance of emphasizing the situations to which our language must be adjusted, Ayer writes:

> The difference is between starting with the words and then looking for the facts to which to fit them, and starting with an identification of the facts and then seeing how they can best be described.

He then proposes an analogy between philosophy as properly oriented and the taking of photographs. "The interest," he says, "lies in the photographs, and not in the mechanism of the camera by which they happen to be taken." Ayer says this as if analytic philosophers, including Wittgenstein, had always accepted the point, but the fact is that such a statement represents a quite dramatic reversal. For it appears at least to teach philosophy away from second-order questions and toward concrete subject matter—that is, to the world around us rather than to our apparatus for knowing that world.

Second, in proposing a return to the facts in order to see them without philosophical preconceptions (or indeed without *any* preconceptions as to the way they *must* be), Ayer is led to question the possibility of recording facts in a way that is free of all interpretation. In a sentence that is surprising indeed when considered against the background of the positivist position expressed in his early writings, Ayer asserts: "One's account of what actually happens is governed by one's idea of what is possible." This statement is surprising, not only because of the difficulty of saying what could be meant by "possible" on positivist assumptions, but because it suggests an abandoning of the view that would reduce all meaning to present or actual fact. For as soon as we begin to speak about what is possible, we suggest at once a more comprehensive order of things that takes us far beyond the reporting of sensible facts.

Third, Ayer goes on to argue that more attention be paid to the conceptual frameworks through which we seek to apprehend the world as well as to the categories we require and the assumptions we have to make. For some time now, linguistic philosophers have stressed "doing" philosophy as they say, which means making analyses of specific terms as opposed to the formulation of the general principles that lie at the root of their thinking in the form of assumptions and presuppositions. Now it appears that the new appeal to the facts, insofar as the facts themselves are dependent on the concepts we require for expressing them, will also mean a new awareness of what Kant called the a priori elements that are present in every philosophical interpretation.

Clarity Is Not Enough represents criticism of the linguistic view of the nature and function of philosophy from within, since many of the contributors have been associated with that type of philosophy at one time or another. A much more systematic and sustained critique of the linguistic conception from a different perspective is to be found in Adler's *The Conditions of Philosophy.* This work is important, not only for its diagnosis of the current philosophical situation, but also for the proposal it contains regarding the recovery of philosophy as an autonomous branch of knowledge with problems and subject matter of its own.

Adler is especially concerned over the fact that at present philosophy has, in the eyes of many, lost prestige and intellectual status vis-à-vis the natural sciences, mathematics, and historical research. He seeks to explain how this state of affairs has come about and to show how the situation might be changed through a renewal of philosophy. Commenting on the present concern of the dominant philosophical positions—analytic philosophy, logical positivism, pragmatism, existentialism, and phenomenology—Adler writes:

> If there is any one thing that all these philosophical movements have in common, it is their anxiety about the blind alleys into which philosophy has stumbled, their concern with its validity and significance, and their effort to remedy its condition and set it off on a new path toward prosperity and progress.

Modern philosophy, in Adler's view, has gone astray because philosophers generally have retreated into the discussion of second-order questions—concern for how we know and how our language functions—and have accepted mistaken views about philosophical progress, or the lack of it. Adler rejects the view, advanced by William James and held by many, that says that philosophy gave birth to all the special sciences (in many European universities, for instance, physics is still called "natural philosophy") in the sense that as soon as a technique or method was developed for dealing with a topic or subject in a precise and controlled way, a new science was born and the subject ceased to belong to philosophy. As over against this view which would leave philosophy in the end with an empty domain over which to rule, Adler believes that philosophy has its own subject matter, problems, and way of approach. In view of this fact it is illegitimate to compare philosophy with mathematics and physics as if they all represented intellectual disciplines in the same sense. Philosophy is said to be rooted in common experience as opposed to the special or abstract experience of the sciences, and philosophy is what Adler calls a "non-investigative" enterprise in that it does not begin, as physics does (physics is an "investigative" science), with deliberate, controlled observation guided by specially formulated questions. Philosophy focuses instead upon such universal experience as is open to every person in his daily life in virtue of his being alive and awake or aware.

In Adler's view, philosophy can recover itself as a reputable, intellectual enterprise if it can succeed in satisfying five conditions. First, philosophy is misconceived if it is thought to be infallible truth of a "higher" type than history and science; instead philosophy must be understood as a mode of inquiry that results in knowledge in the sense of *reasoned opinion* (for which Adler uses the Greek term *doxa*) that on the one hand does not claim finality and yet on the other is more than "mere" opinion unsupported by reasons. With regard to this first condition, Adler writes:

> The only standard of truth that is consistent with knowledge in the sense of *doxa* must eschew certitude and finality; it must allow for the judgment that one theory or conclusion is *truer* than another, or for the judgment that it is false, but never for the judgment that one theory or conclusion is *absolutely true*, rendering all other theories of the same matter necessarily false.

Second, alternative philosophical theories are to be judged on the basis of their truth value in relation to both empirical and logical criteria; there is no total discontinuity between philosophy and science that would make it necessary for truth and falsity to be confined to science alone. Third, philosophy has to be carried on in a "public" way. Here Adler is thinking of the cooperative approach to the solution of problems found in the natural sciences where many different investigators devote their efforts to the same problem. He is also attacking the view which says that, since philosophy contains no knowledge in any case, there are no genuine disagreements between different views but only the different viewpoints themselves.

Fourth, philosophy must be "relatively autonomous" in the sense that it has questions of its own which are said to be answerable "without reference to results obtained by any other discipline." Moreover, philosophy has its own method of proceeding in answering these questions. Adler's point can be seen most clearly if we consider what he calls "mixed questions" or those that involve, for example, law and philosophy or psychology and philosophy. Since it is impossible to have an exact division of labor in dealing with intellectual issues, the expert in the nonphilosophical discipline may well be thinking philosophically on the level of the layman without this fact being taken seriously, so widespread is the view that philosophical considerations can be handled by anyone equipped merely with "common sense" and "good judgment." Against this view Adler argues in behalf of expertness and special competence in philosophical analysis, although he also demands that the products of such competence not be esoteric but *continuous* with the experience and implicit philosophizing of the plain man.

Fifth, and most important among the conditions for the recovery of philosophy, is the demand that the proper subject matter of philosophy is primary questions about what is and happens in the world and not questions about how we know, think, or speak about what is and happens. This condition is aimed most pointedly at those who accept the linguistic conception of philosophy.

In order to set his proposals for the recovery of philosophy in the context of the present situation, Adler makes some comparisons between his view and rival views that he regards as incompatible with his own. First he rejects historical relativism, according to which philosophical positions are wholly self-contained and disagreement is impossible because no two positions can be talking about the same reality. Adler sees contemporary philosophy divided into two extreme and opposed positions: analytic philosophy at one end of the spectrum and existentialism at the other. Analytic philosophy does satisfy some of Adler's criteria for autonomous philosophy, but it is deficient in the crucial respect that philosophy is deprived of its own first-order questions. Existentialism and phenomenology, on the other hand, pass muster because of their insistence on first-order questions but are inadequate on all other counts. It is curious that Adler underestimates the intersubjective character of the features of human experience on which the existentialists lay stress and concludes that their approach is "private" and merely autobiographical, lacking in public experience open to all. On the other hand, he seems greatly to overestimate the "public" character of analytic philosophy by overlooking its provincialism and the fact that many analytic philosophers at present are just coming around to acknowledge the sort of criticism against their position that was made almost a half century ago by the American pragmatists.

Adler would like to deliver us from the unhappy alternative of having to choose between existentialism and the philosophy of analysis. His proposal is for a philosophy based on common experience that would satisfy the five conditions and at the same time contribute to the re-establishment of philosophy as an autonomous discipline capable of adding to our knowledge as science does. The proposal is worked out in great detail and presented with a persuasive clarity. Adler's proposal, if followed, could well have the result of bringing about conversation and debate *across* philosophical lines and between alternative philosophies. Unfortunately, this has not happened nearly enough in recent years; too many philosophers have been working harder and harder at finding more precise ways of stating conclusions taken over from the past.

PHILOSOPHICAL QUESTIONS ABOUT SCIENCE

One of the most important developments in recent years has been the serious study of the history of science. This development has served to guide discussion back to the actual situation in which scientific inquiry takes place. Instead of regarding science in the neat, well-ordered fashion in which it is presented in textbooks as a finished product, a new tendency among philosophers and historians is to view science in the making. No doubt the total involvement of science and technology in contemporary life and in its potential destruction has played an important role in producing this state of affairs. There is a new interest in understanding science as it is actually developed by investigators attacking unsolved problems. The important consequence for philosophy is that instead of trying to understand the meaning of scientific explanation, laws of nature, the construction of hypotheses, and so on, in terms of previously constructed philosophical systems, philosophers are going back to actual scientific inquiry to see what happens in order to learn what living science means. The study of past scientific discoveries is proving immensely valuable in this effort.

Three problems serve to focus the major issues. We may express them for the sake of convenience in question form. First, is there a "logic of discovery" in science and is the development of scientific knowledge a continuous affair advancing in clear steps through the detection and correction of past errors? or is the story of science a tale of revolutionary change in which a new cosmic picture replaces its predecessor, leaving no room for comparison between them with regard to their truth or falsity? Second, what is the role of *models* in scientific explanations, and how far can we go in the conquest of the unknown by likening it to the more familiar features of our concrete experience? Third, what is the status of "unobservables" or "postulated entities"—such as atoms and subatomic particles in scientific theories—and how are these related to the gross objects of ordinary experience?

Though expressed in current idiom, these questions are by no means new, and they have appeared in one form or another in the systems of past philosophers. Bacon[1] and Descartes,[2] for example, were much interested in the topic of scientific discovery, and, in fact, most philosophers of the late seventeenth and early eighteenth centuries were occupied with the problem of finding a method for gaining new knowledge rather than for systematizing the knowledge that had been passed on from the past. Lord Kelvin in the last century focused the question about models by his demand that scientific theories require mechanical models if they are to be understood. The third question was raised in an arresting way by Bishop Berkeley[3] when he attacked the "abstractions" expressed in mathematical and physical concepts as "unreal" and demanded that the familiar objects of experience be taken as the only real things in heaven and earth. A host of more recent philosophers have raised the same question—Bergson, James, Whitehead, to name but a few —and much attention has been paid to the problem of saying how the hard, enduring, colored, shaped familiar objects of ordinary experience are related to the "scientific objects" defined through atomic patterns that are devoid of these familiar features.

That the questions cited are the central ones at present can be seen at once from an examination of a remarkable volume, *Scientific Change* (edited by A. C. Crombie), which represents the result of a recent Oxford symposium on the history and philosophy of science. The contributors include specialists from the United States, Britain, Russia, as well as Eastern and Western Europe. Although the Crombie volume represents the best interweaving of philosophical analysis and the historical approach, other works meriting attention in the field are: *Logic and Language*, studies dedicated to Rudolf Carnap; *Boston Studies in the Philosophy of Science; Frontiers of Science and Philosophy* (edited by Robert Colodny), a series of lectures delivered at the University of Pittsburgh; *Philosophy of Science* (edited by Bernard Baumrin), a record of the University of Delaware seminar; J. J. C. Smart, *Philosophy and Scientific Realism*, a persistent defense of the view that the scientific picture of the world is "literally" true and the most faithful representation of the world available—Smart holds that the theories of physics are more than convenient descriptions or "constructs" whose meaning is found in the fact that they enable us to manipulate the world more successfully; and W. S. Sellars, *Science, Perception and Reality*, a series of papers aimed

---

1 *See* Bacon's *Novum Organum*, in GBWW, Vol. 30, pp. 105-95.

2 *See* especially Descartes's *Rules for the Direction of the Mind* and *Discourse on Method*, in GBWW, Vol. 31, pp. 1-67.

3 *See* the introduction to his *Principles of Human Knowledge*, in GBWW, Vol. 35, pp. 405-12.

at synthesizing the scientific outlook with a basically analytic conception of philosophy. In addition to these volumes, it is important to notice the results of a very different approach to the philosophical treatment of science contained in *The Concept of Matter* (edited by Ernan McMullin), in which a large number of contributors deal with fundamental questions, including historical studies, in the philosophy of nature.

Turning now to the first of the three questions—the nature of scientific discovery and the development of science—we can see a return of the problems that occupied the attention of Bacon, Descartes, Spinoza, Locke, and others concerned with finding a method for attacking questions of natural philosophy and metaphysics. Each in his own way believed that the discovery of the secrets of nature, of man, and of God, depends on our finding a clear and disciplined way of proceeding. As Kant was to reiterate well over a century after the death of Descartes, haphazard observations made in accordance with no rational plan can never yield reliable knowledge. Naturally, in the unbelievably complex state of modern science, there is bound to exist a host of questions concerning method and technique in scientific inquiry.

One issue especially should be singled out. It concerns the critical evaluation of what has come to be known as the "hypothetical-deductive" theory of scientific explanation upheld by such philosophers as K. R. Popper, C. G. Hempel, and R. B. Braithwaite. According to this view, we have reason to infer that a given explanatory hypothesis is probably true if we are able to deduce from it consequences that are confirmed in experimental situations. A basic question that has been raised in regard to this theory is whether it does not ignore actual inquiry and the process of discovery, reflecting instead only the *logical structure* of a completed part of science. At the turn of the century, the American philosopher Charles S. Peirce focused the issue by calling attention to the difference between *proposing* (that is, inventing) relevant and testable explanatory hypotheses, and *testing* or confirming them once they have been advanced. N. R. Hanson has taken up the Peircian theme in recent years and has become an outspoken critic of the deductive view. Hanson insists that the hypothetical-deductive interpretation does not adequately represent the creative process of discovery and that it confuses two operations that Peirce declared to be quite different from each other—namely, proposing hypotheses and testing them. Hanson sees the difference as consisting in two different logical tasks. In remarks entitled "Comments," which appear in the Crombie book, he writes:

> Imagine yourself in a logic classroom (*i.e.*, in a classroom in which logic is being taught). There are, notoriously two different kinds of question the teacher can pose. He can say: 'Here are premises P¹, P², and P³— generate from them some theorem.' But he can also say: 'Here is a theorem; find three premises from which it can be generated.' The latter

undertaking is vastly more difficult, as every mathematician and scientist knows. Being presented with an anomalous phenomenon E and then being charged to discover an H from which E follows is a different conceptual task from being given premises *If H, then E*, and E, and concluding that H is (insofar) confirmed.

Once formulated, a particular deductive argument can, so to speak, be read in both directions. Given the conclusion, we read back and see that the premises are required if we are to prove the conclusion; given the premises, we read forward and derive the conclusion from them. Hanson's point is that the actual process of discovery in science is not the same as the "timeless" logical structure of a deductive argument that has already been worked out. The process of actual discovery in science involves passing from the conclusion (some state of affairs to be explained) to a sought-for premise (hypothesis) that renders the phenomena intelligible, whereas the deductive process requires the reasoner to move from premises to conclusion when he is actually proving a theorem for the first time.

It is clear from what Hanson and others say that knowledge of the history of science is playing an important role in the dispute. The new interest in the history of science, moreover, is bringing with it new and more comprehensive questions concerning the nature of scientific development within the framework of contemporary society. Thomas S. Kuhn, in a monograph *The Structure of Scientific Revolutions*, and later in several papers, one of which, "The Function of Dogma in Scientific Research," appears in the Crombie volume, has advanced a most provocative thesis about the development of science; his view has led to considerable discussion, and not all of its implications have yet been understood. Briefly stated, Kuhn's thesis is that scientific research exhibits a threefold pattern: First, a period of more or less random and uncoordinated observation and theorizing takes place, unified only by a certain "family resemblance" among some general range of phenomena such as, for example, electrical systems. Second, a definite field of inquiry is established when someone—Benjamin Franklin in the case of electrical theory—establishes a "paradigm," which is a combination of some basic theory and relevant observations, sufficient to mark out the legitimate entities involved (that is, genuine electrical phenomena) and to indicate the sort of question that is legitimate to raise. A paradigm defines certain basic beliefs that guide and limit investigation and, as long as the paradigm holds, it functions as the scientific "dogma" of the historical period. Third, basic discoveries result when normal research *fails* to reinforce the paradigm by revealing new data that do not fit the established pattern; a scientific "revolution" occurs when it becomes necessary to put forward a new paradigm that accounts for the new phenomena.

Underlying Kuhn's threefold historical description is the basic conviction that scientific research is not simply an "open," "objective," "non-prejudiced" appraisal of the facts but an enterprise conducted by a community of inquirers working under definite historical circumstances and limited by the dominant paradigms that guide their research and determine the main outlines of their investigation. On this view, the great bulk of scientific work that occupies the majority of scientists—called by Kuhn "normal research"—is aimed at establishing the paradigm by observations. These efforts, he says, are like assembling the parts of a Chinese cube whose general outline is already known, rather than a large-scale attack upon the unknown. Discovery in the sense of establishing novel theory in a given field comes about when the appropriate paradigm is attacked, that is, when in the course of normal research, novel results are obtained that point to the need for a new paradigm. Creative insight is most needed at the point where it becomes necessary to decide whether the observations that *fail* to support the paradigm at a given time represent genuine discoveries or simply the results of research gone astray.

That Kuhn's thesis has support from the history of scientific discovery has been acknowledged even by those who do not entirely agree with it—for example, A. R. Hall, Michael Polanyi, and others. On the other hand, several features of Kuhn's theory have caused deep concern. At times Kuhn refers to the paradigm as defining the "rules of the game," and he suggests that paradigms have a merely instrumental function. He writes:

> The developmental pattern of mature science is usually from paradigm to paradigm. . . . Undoubtedly the research work that any given paradigm permits results in lasting contributions to the body of scientific knowledge and technique, but paradigms themselves are very often swept aside and replaced by others that are quite incompatible with them. We can have no recourse to notions like the 'truth' or 'falsity' of paradigms in our attempt to understand the special efficacy of the research which their reception permits.

To many philosophers such a view has seemed too skeptical because it implies an abandoning of the philosophical realism at the root of so much modern science. For that realism, every intelligible question we can frame has an answer that can be described as *the* answer no matter how difficult it may be to discover or approximate that answer. Kuhn's position suggests, on the other hand, that we do not discover the nature of the world in science but rather project a series of theories that serve to organize and limit research activities without being true or false in themselves. Kuhn's view, moreover, strikes a serious blow against the belief that scientific inquiry represents a concerted assault on the secrets of nature that is carried on by many investigators who can check each other's results because they are all intended to refer to the same universe. It is doubtful whether we can say this on Kuhn's theory because, for example, insofar as the work of Newton and Einstein took place within different paradigms, it is not clear that we can say they were both talking about the same "world." It is also doubtful whether on Kuhn's interpretation of science we are allowed to say that a new theory corrects an old one in the sense that the new theory explains more adequately the same natural phenomena that were being inadequately explained by the old theory. Despite critical questions, however, Kuhn's approach is symbolic of the new concern for approaching science through its history.

The other two problems currently under discussion by philosophers attending to the structure of modern science—the role of models in scientific explanation, and the status of the "constructs" or theoretical entities—are closely related topics. There are aspects of each question that are peculiar to it alone, but the questions tend to flow into each other in most discussions. The fact is that there are logical and methodological questions about the use of models in scientific inquiry that are largely confined to the normal work of practicing scientists, whereas the question of the status of the "microscopic entities" of theoretical physics, for example, and their relation to the ordinary objects of gross experience, involves far-reaching philosophical issues. An examination of some recent discussions, however, shows that questions about the use of models often lead on to the question of their "literal" meaning and ultimately to the same question with regard to all the abstract statements of science.

Ever since the work of Locke[4] and Kant,[5] particularly the latter, students of scientific theory have been aware of the perplexing problem that arises when we seek to understand how the basic components of scientific knowledge are related to each other. We have data of experience that come through our sensory apparatus extended by precision instruments, and we have abstract concepts such as mass, cause, gravity, plus certain mathematical and logical expressions. Scientific knowledge consists in some combination of these two elements. As Kant pointed out both in his *Prolegomena* and *The Critique of Pure Reason*, scientific knowledge of an actual world involves a synthesis of what comes to us through the senses with the categories stemming from the human understanding. To paraphrase a famous sentence of Kant's: Concepts without data of observation are empty, and data of observation without concepts and principles of interpretation are blind, brute facts that yield neither law nor understanding (*see* GBWW, Vol. 42, p. 34b).

The difficulty in saying precisely how these two components are woven together in the fabric of human knowledge can be seen from the fact that

---

4 Especially in his *Essay Concerning Human Understanding*, in GBWW, Vol. 35, pp. 83-395.

5 Especially in *The Critique of Pure Reason*, in GBWW, Vol. 42, pp. 1-250.

frequent attempts have been made to make either data of observation or theoretical concepts into the whole of human knowledge. Thus "empiricists" may regard theoretical concepts as "mere constructs" or convenient "fictions," demanding that we frame our conclusions solely in terms of actual observables, and thus avoid recourse to "nonempirical" entities or abstract terms. And on the other hand, there are "rationalists" who propose to dispense altogether with the need for observables and picturable models of the theoretical concepts in scientific explanations, proposing instead to represent states of affairs solely in mathematical terms. Others following a similar line set aside the demand for models and picturable explanations on the ground that scientific statements are purely "instrumental" in the sense that they direct operations of inquiry or show us how to manipulate nature but make no claim whatever to be "representing" the world or expressing the way it is really constituted. Both questions—that of models and the question of the status to be assigned to scientific abstractions—involve the matter of relating observational and conceptual elements to each other. Current discussion here returns to older questions in new forms.

One of the clearest and most helpful treatments of the models question has been given by Mary Hesse of Cambridge University in her book *Forces and Fields*. She writes:

> The most obvious property of a satisfactory model is that it exhibits an analogy with the phenomena to be explained, that is, that there is some identity of structure between the model and the phenomena.

A model is needed in scientific explanation because it makes a theory intelligible and testable, something that cannot be done on the basis of a mathematical formulation alone. If, for example, we regard the molecules constituting gases as if they were billiard balls, we can go on to ask whether they are rigid like billiard balls or elastic, whether they react through contact or at a distance, and so on. Since a considerable amount is known about billiard balls and their behavior, on the basis of this information we can put the important question: To what extent does the behavior of the gas molecules correspond to that of the billiard balls; what is the extent of the analogy and at what points, if any, does it fail? The foregoing illustration is a relatively simple one; a much more basic and difficult problem is brought about for contemporary science by the failure to find a single, adequate model for atomic phenomena. Stated simply, the problem is that the electron behaves like a *wave* in certain situations and like a *particle* in others. The incompatibility of the two models has led some philosophers to say that we must abandon picturable models entirely and move to the formal, mathematical level where the paradoxes of models do not arise.

Hesse regards this conclusion as unwarranted mainly because she holds that models are necessary for scientific explanation and that mathematical expressions are themselves models, not to be interpreted entirely apart from picturable elements. Moreover, she claims that while "factual description" is but one function of a model, all models are meant to express features of *actual* relationships, so that a descriptive model is one that exhibits a positive analogy and no negative analogy in all respects hitherto tested. We do encounter a paradox at the point where we hold to the "literal" significance of a model because a model is meant to be an analogy; we do not say that the gas molecules *are* billiard balls but only that they are *like* billiard balls. Hesse's proposal is to retain the "as if" in the use of a model, first as a reminder that the model might be false as a description, and secondly in order to emphasize its explanatory and not merely descriptive value.

The question of the literal, descriptive function of a model leads naturally into the larger philosophical question of the relation between scientific explanations involving microscopic elements, mathematical equations, and conceptual constructs on the one hand, and the objects of ordinary experience on the other. The contrast was dramatized some decades ago by Eddington's famous example of the two tables—the hard, solid, enduring table of ordinary experience upon which one writes, and the so-called scientific table that is mostly empty space surrounding a "dance of electrons" exhibiting patterns expressible in mathematical form. The challenge is to say how the "two" tables can be one—how the one table can *be* at once what the ordinary *and* the scientific account says it is. In recent years, especially since the emphasis on "ordinary" language and the denial that scientific language is a paradigm for all discourse, it has been fashionable to regard Eddington's problem with a wry smile, while dismissing it as illegitimate. There are signs at present that it is again being taken seriously as a problem not primarily of the nature of knowledge but rather one concerned with the nature of *things*.

Various answers have been given to the question; some have "solved" the problem by saying that there is no incompatibility; others have taken the scientific account as not expressing what the table "really" is but only as specifying a set of operations enabling us to manipulate it; still others have taken scientific explanations as "purely formal" accounts of things expressed in mathematical equations that do not require for their meaning any further reference to the objects of ordinary experience. As things now stand, there is no general consensus of opinion among philosophers about the resolution of this question.

Adler offers his solution in *The Conditions of Philosophy*, and his view, although by no means novel since it has its roots in the philosophy of Aristotle, is likely to provoke discussion that will again put the issue on the list of essential topics for philosophers. Adler's aim is to maintain a more than nominal status for the microscopic entities of science. Following the lead of some remarks by the physicist Werner Heisenberg in *Physics and Philosophy*, Adler concludes regarding the relation between the two tables (Adler speaks of chairs):

> ... there must be diverse grades of real existence which differ in the grade or degree of reality which they respectively possess. Herein lies a clue to the solution of the problem. It involves two points. (1) The reality of the elementary particles of nuclear physics cannot be reconciled with the reality of the chair as an individual, sensible substance if both the particles and the chair are asserted to have the same mode of existence or grade of being. ... (2) The mode of being of the material constituents of a physical body cannot be the same when those constituents exist in isolation and when they enter into the constitution of an actual body. Thus, when the chair exists actually as one body, the multitude of atoms and elementary particles which constitute it exist only virtually. Since their existence is only virtual, so is their multiplicity; and their virtual multiplicity is not incompatible with the actual unity of the chair.

THE IMPORTANCE OF PAST PHILOSOPHY

Philosophy has had a long history, and we are able to study it in detail because the great systems of the past have been preserved and passed down to us. Serious interest in the history of philosophy, however, is a modern phenomenon and is not to be found prior to the nineteenth century when Hegel put the history of thought into the center of things by declaring that the entire truth about reality depends on an understanding of the development of Western philosophical thinking.[6] Aristotle, it is true, had given some impetus to the study of past philosophy by his famous review of the thoughts of his predecessors at the beginning of his *Metaphysics* (in GBWW, Vol. 8, pp. 501d-506d). But although he furnished a model in this regard, he did not found a tradition. The history of philosophy, as the modern student of the subject knows it, is not an ancient enterprise, and indeed some contemporary philosophers have been decidedly against its study. For some time analytic philosophers have, with a few exceptions, written as though a knowledge of past philosophy were largely irrelevant for "doing" philosophy in the present. But even these philosophers have not neglected it entirely; they have merely located the "past" not in the period of Plato or Descartes but in the earlier decades of the present century.

A new interest in the history of philosophy is beginning to make itself felt on the current scene. It stems from those who see philosophy as deeply involved in the culture of a period and its foundations and not simply as a dialogue of ideas hovering, as it were, over the course of

6 *See* his *Philosophy of History*, in GBWW, Vol. 46, especially pp. 156c-162a.

historical events. The monumental historical and philosophical scholarship of John Herman Randall, Jr., is almost certain to transform the current situation. Randall has long been known for his interpretation of classical Greek philosophy, especially in his work on *Aristotle*, and now we have the results of his continuing studies, *The Career of Philosophy: From the Middle Ages to the Enlightenment*. The scholarship is enormous and the reading is never dull—a remarkable combination in itself.

Randall believes that each historical period has to view the past in "the novel light of its own intellectual problems, and its own emphases and importances." On this basis there is room, as he says, for a history of modern philosophy "from a perspective of American philosophizing in midcentury." Although Randall aims to show what philosophy is chiefly through exhibiting what philosophers do and the role philosophy plays in human life, he does not avoid the responsibility of articulating the view of philosophy that guides his inquiry. He writes:

> Viewed as an imaginative vision, an ultimate expression of the judgments and aspirations of human nature, a great philosophy may touch our mind with its clarified perfection, its architectonic beauty, without stirring our heart or compelling our will. But when we grasp the climate of opinion out of which that organic structure of ideas arose, when we sense the great social and intellectual conflicts that drove men to construct it, when we see it performing in the world of men that function for which it was created, then we no longer wonder at its appeal and power. And so, in ignorance of her deeds, it is idle to analyze philosophy's character. It is far wiser to tell the story of her life.

That the rewriting of history from a fresh perspective can actually serve as a means of discovering new truth is magnificently illustrated in Randall's account of the way in which the chief representatives of the Renaissance returned to the writings of the ancient philosophers and read them afresh in their own terms. He shows the extent to which the intellectual climate of modern society—its humanism and concern for science—finds roots in the world of the Renaissance. Unlike conventional treatments of this theme, Randall's analysis avoids the view that would explain the continuity between the Renaissance and the present day at the cost of thoroughly disconnecting the Renaissance from the preceding Medieval period. Textbooks have accustomed us to suppose a "benighted" Middle Ages, wholly traditional and dogmatic in outlook, that somehow came to an abrupt end and was succeeded by a "scientific" period in which knowledge abounded and none but rational explanations were allowed. We are shown instead the way in which the Aristotelian tradition was developed in the scientific studies of the Italian universities up to the Renaissance and how this development culminated in the great achievement of Galileo. In addition, and as part of the same story, Randall closes the gap between Medieval thought and the modern philosophical tradition that began with the writings of Descartes. Randall says:

> Ever since the early studies of Gilson on Descartes I have been impressed by the essential continunity between medieval and modern philosophy. The conviction has grown that seventeenth-century philosophy, in Descartes, Spinoza, and Hobbes, to say nothing of Leibniz, can be understood only as the bringing to bear of some of the medieval traditions on the interpretation and generalization of the basic ideas of the new science of nature.

This claim is made good by Randall's brilliant delineation of the three major philosophical strains in Medieval thought—the Augustinian, the Aristotelian, and the Ockhamist—and by his account of their perseverance and transformation in the succeeding centuries. The ingredients of modern philosophy are all there: the mathematical influence through the Platonic-Augustinian tradition; the concern for the natural world, its structure and forms, that stems from the organic metaphysics of Aristotle; and, finally, the roots of linguistic philosophy that lie in the "Terminism" of Ockham. Much light is thrown on contemporary philosophy. Philosophers who would otherwise seem to be without ancestors are now linked with the tradition that formed the background of their thought.

Another indication of what is currently being done to show the contemporary relevance of the insights from past philosophy is the publication of further volumes in the *History of Philosophy* being written by Etienne Gilson and his associates. Now available are *Modern Philosophy; Descartes to Kant*, written with Thomas Langan, and *Recent Philosophy; Hegel to the Present*, written with Langan and Armand Maurer, C.S.B.

For Gilson, the study of past philosophical systems and movements of thought forms an integral part of philosophy itself. Gilson writes:

> Those who take philosophy seriously must have some knowledge of its history, because philosophy is a collective enterprise in which no one can pretend to take part unless he is properly introduced. Before playing a game, one must learn its rules, must even practice for a long time under the coaching of some expert. The same can be said of the future philosopher, or of any educated man who wishes to share in a philosophical discussion without incurring ridicule. . . . Why is its history a necessary introduction to philosophy? Because philosophy is actually a continuous chain of philosophers who have conducted in the West, for twenty-five centuries, a sort of conversation on the problems the human mind can ask.

The importance of the return of first-rate historical scholarship in philosophy at present can scarcely be overestimated. For several decades analytic philosophers have opposed their "systematic" philosophy to "historical" studies with the result that there has been a decline of interest in learning from the major thinkers of the past. Or if some analytic philosophers have been concerned with the writings of previous philosophers, it is only in order to show that these thinkers conceived of philosophy as a basically analytic enterprise. Socrates, for example, has been made to appear as the first analytic philosopher because he is said to have approached problems in linguistic terms. A renewed interest in understanding past philosophers in their own terms as well as in ours will have a salutary effect on future philosophizing. A new awareness of the role that philosophy can play in expressing the intellectual basis of a culture and of the vigor it possessed when it was involved in basic issues cutting across the domains of art, morality, religion, politics, and law, may help the present generation of philosophers to overcome the academic and esoteric view that has come to dominate the enterprise.

ISSUES IN RELIGION AND ETHICS

Although much of importance in the fields of philosophical theology and ethics has appeared in recent months, the most exciting developments within the religious situation have taken place in another arena. We have come recently to speak of the "Catholic-Protestant dialogue"—colloquia and conversations taking place between scholars and theologians representing both the Roman Catholic Church and the various Protestant or Reformed churches. Largely as the result of the noble, guiding spirit of Pope John XXIII and his calling of the Second Ecumenical Council, which has already met three times and is preparing for a fourth session late in 1965, new prospects for discussion have been opened up for the first time in four hundred years.

An account of the details of the Council and its consequences for the future of the churches does not fall within the province of this article, but the fact of the development is too important to be passed over. One of the foremost theological interpreters of the Council, Dr. Hans Küng of the Faculty of Catholic Theology at Tübingen University, has written a volume, *The Council, Reform and Reunion*, in which some of the hoped-for aims, both within and without the Roman Catholic Church, are set forth. Küng raises delicate issues with vigor and candor. He does not hesitate to indicate the hopes existent on the Roman Catholic side that ecumenical conversation may lead ultimately to a reunion of Christendom through the return of the "separated brethren," nor does he shrink from emphasizing the necessity of constant renewal and reform within the confines of the Roman Catholic Church. Küng is especially concerned to make clear the special status of an Ecumenical Council:

> A diocesan synod is subordinate to canon law and has only very limited powers for reform. An Ecumenical Council is above canon law; in union with the Pope it has universal legislative authority in every field of ecclesiastical law, and can thus carry out full-scale reform throughout the entire Church.

At this point Küng makes contact with an ancient tradition expressed in the *De catholicae ecclesiae unitate* of Cyprian of Carthage in the third century, according to which the mind and will of the *whole* Church is to be made manifest in a convocation of ecclesiastical representatives with universal scope. In Küng's work there is expressed a clear and candid basis upon which dialogue seeking to penetrate the most difficult issues and sources of disagreement can take place.

In *Ecumenical Dialogue at Harvard: The Roman Catholic-Protestant Colloquium* (edited by S. H. Miller and G. Ernest Wright) we have an actual record of a series of conversations of just the sort made possible by the new ecumenical interest. This document, consisting of the addresses and papers delivered during the recent session, is especially significant because it opens with three lectures given by Augustin Cardinal Bea (President of the Vatican Secretariat for Promoting Christian Unity) on the "Unity of Christians." The discussion that followed the presentation of the main papers is also included, and it focuses on the four theses of the Colloquium: Biblical Studies; Symbol and Sacrament; *Reformatio*; and Conscience in a Pluralistic Society.

Turning now to the field of philosophical theology, the most important development is the general renewal of interest in the philosophical treatment of religious issues, including a reconsideration of the arguments for the existence of God. The extreme tension and curious interweaving of opposites in the present situation can be seen in the fact that a new demand for rational analysis and argument should make itself felt at just the time when the concern to find meaning and purpose in life through the existential approaches to religion is at its height. Actually, the current state of religious thought is even more tangled than the duality between the existential and nonexistential approaches can convey. One fact at least stands out clearly: religion is not being set aside with indifference but is once again becoming a live issue. Many people, it appears, want to believe in God's reality and yet find the stumbling blocks insurmountable. The unquestioned prestige of science and the scientific world picture together with the belief that science rules out God, have dealt a heavy blow to the possibility of an intellectual approach to religion. Many people may be willing to allow that religion is in some sense "necessary" for man, that it is useful for society, and even that some form of religion is unavoidable in practice, and yet the major difficulty is that so few seem convinced in their heart of hearts that the doctrines of the Judeo-Christian tradition can still be called *true*. Truth is thought to be the prerogative of science alone.

One way of meeting the challenge is to return to the roots and conditions of human existence in the world—the existential approach—and seek to show how man's predicament as a being involved in guilt, frustration, and evildoing can be resolved through the religious message. This way has been followed by Paul Tillich and very ably represented by him in many books that have been more widely read than might have been thought possible, considering the complexity of the issues and Tillich's massive style. But whereas Tillich has spoken successfully to the layman, he causes theologians concern largely because of his mystical conception of God as the "Ground of Being" rather than as *a* Being, and a persistent refusal to couch his thought exclusively in biblical and creedal terms. Tillich causes concern for the philosophers as well, since his thinking belongs to the tradition of ontological philosophy, the tradition of thinking about *being*, and few contemporary philosophers have the background for thinking in these terms. Moreover, despite his demand for a philosophical approach, Tillich has puzzled some philosophers by his rejection of the arguments for God as inappropriate, preferring to reinterpret them not as arguments but as statements of the way in which God is related to the human mind. The most distinctive feature of Tillich's thought is his reinterpretation of Christian doctrines in philosophical, psychological, historical, and aesthetic terms, and his claim that the convictions expressed in Christian theology represent the answers to questions that human beings raise about their own situation in the world.

A second approach to the problem raised by skepticism is found in the more rationalistic response of Charles Hartshorne, who aims at putting modern logic in the service of theological analysis and argument. He comes armed for the task with a distinctive version of the philosophy of becoming—"process philosophy," so called—stemming from the philosophy of Whitehead. More cosmologically oriented in his thinking than Tillich, Hartshorne places great confidence in the possibility of logical proof in metaphysics, and he takes the arguments for God as reinterpreted by himself and others very seriously. Hartshorne causes concern among theologians, apart, that is, from those philosophically oriented already, because of his speculative bent and the nonexistential tone of his writing. The latter trait is the main reason why, in contrast with Tillich, Hartshorne's ideas are largely unknown to the general public. On the other hand, Hartshorne's search for philosophical foundations for religion does not establish as many links with philosophers as might be expected. First, because the belief dominant among philosophers is that religion, whatever we may say about it, cannot have rational foundations, and in this regard the position of Hume still maintains itself. Second, the proponents of the formal logic Hartshorne takes so seriously are quite uninterested in seeing it used for speculative purposes.

Another position in the current spectrum is filled by analytic philosophers who deny entirely the need for approaching the religious problems in metaphysical terms and attempt instead to analyze and clarify so-called religious language within the limits allowed by the theory of experience that determines the general outlook of analytic philosophy.

It is important to notice that insofar as the analytic approach is restricted to clarification and analysis and avoids questions of critical appraisal, of truth and falsity, it can readily be combined with the content of a confessional theology developed under antiphilosophical auspices.

From the foregoing it will readily be seen that the problem of the intelligibility of religion, whether critical foundations can be found for religious insight, is the central problem of the moment. Hartshorne believes that such foundations can be found, and, in a most important but difficult book *The Logic of Perfection,* he sets forth the most exhaustive reworking of the ontological argument for the existence of God that has appeared for many a day. In the eleventh century, Anselm set out to show by rational means that God must exist. This he did by starting with the idea of God as Perfection—"that than which nothing greater can be conceived"—and then by going on to show that anyone who understands the meaning of the idea and fails to see that God so conceived must exist beyond our ideas and minds is caught in a contradiction.[7]

This argument has been the subject of discussion pro and con ever since. It has been "refuted" more often than any piece of reasoning in the history of Western thought, and yet it has a curious power of survival. It is as if we can never say for certain that it is wrong, even if there is room for doubt about its validity. Since the days of Hume and Kant, each of whom produced powerful objections to the proof, it has been customary to say that the argument fails because Anselm mistakenly thought "existence" is the same as a quality like "blue" or "short." Once we see, so the objection runs, that existence is not such a quality or predicate, we also see that existence cannot be established by logical argument alone but must be supported by evidence of another kind, namely, some actual confrontation with the thing itself.

Hartshorne is well aware of the argument's history, of its supporters and opponents together with their arguments. He offers a new form and defense of the argument, starting not where most critics have begun, with the concept of existence, but with what nearly everyone has neglected, namely, the idea of God and the concept of Perfection. For Hartshorne, God is not to be thought of as static Perfection, "absolute" and thus out of relation to the world in every respect. On the contrary, a living God, in his view, must have respects in which he transcends the finite creatures, to be sure, but also respects in which he participates in their finitude, contingency, and imperfection. According to what Hartshorne calls "Neo-classical" metaphysics that incorporates time, change, and development within the concept of reality, the Perfection that is God must embrace contingent states of affairs. God, that is to say, is not to be

---

7 Discussions of the ontological argument in GBWW can be located by consulting the *Syntopicon* under God 2c.

conceived as a "Perfect Being" set apart from the world of historical change in which we all live and suffer and to whom the novelties and tragedies of time make no difference. Hartshorne's point is that the *religious* insight of Christianity always stressed the living God who is involved in man's life and in human history, but that this conception was never used as the basis of theological doctrine for fear of introducing finitude and contingency into the divine nature. Hartshorne tries to incorporate the *religious* insight into his philosophical *theology* so that for him true Perfection has to include being related to all creatures. God is not truly understood as Perfect unless the divine nature includes knowledge of and participation in historical existence.

With this view of Perfection, plus a new way of understanding what it means to "exist necessarily," Hartshorne reformulates the ontological argument for God and concludes that the denial of theism in his form is self-contradictory and that the argument is now valid. In many ways Hartshorne's contribution represents the harvest for philosophical theology of the line of thinking that started with Bergson and reached a final culmination in Whitehead's thought. The guiding idea is that time has to be taken seriously and that reality must be conceived in dynamic terms: the true units of things are events rather than substances. The static or fixed features of things are derivative or "abstract" in comparison with the world of development and what Whitehead called the "creative advance into novelty." Hartshorne applies this way of thinking to theological problems, and the result is his conception of God as a Perfection that both includes and is related to all that happens in the temporal world. He regards his view as representative of the idea of a living God and as more in accord with the biblical picture of God than is Tillich's doctrine of God as the "Unconditioned" who is beyond the distinction of opposites.

Tillich has now completed his *Systematic Theology* with the publication of the third volume, embracing the doctrines of Life and Spirit with applications to the theology of History and the idea of the Kingdom of God. Two previous volumes have dealt with the doctrine of God as the Ground of Being and with the nature of Christ as the New Being. Tillich's theology has been developed by him in consistent fashion according to a principle called the "method of correlation."

According to this method, the Christian message is to be put forth as a set of answers or resolutions to the questions and disruptions that characterize human life under historical conditions. Theological doctrine is not simply to be proclaimed from on high, as it were, but rather its elaboration must be preceded by an analysis of the situation in which the hearer finds himself. The "existential" character of Tillich's thought is intimately connected with the method of correlation, because the analysis and diagnosis of man's situation that precede the presentation of Christian doctrine must be made from the standpoint of an existential philosophy. Only from such a standpoint can we remain sensitive to the sort of human problem for which religious insight would be a relevant solution. For Tillich, human life and its dimensions are disrupted and distorted under the conditions of historical existence. Individuals are alienated from themselves, from each other, and from the true Ground (God) of their life. A large part of Tillich's discussion in this volume is concerned with these distortions or "ambiguities," as they are called, that become manifest in man's attempt to realize himself solely on the basis of his own natural resources. Man, though created by a God who saw that all things are good, exists nevertheless in a constant tension of possibilities for evil.

Let us consider a characteristic example of Tillich's way of describing the human situation, detecting the ambiguity in it, and trying to show how the Christian answer is meant to resolve the problem. Man as a being of reason and freedom has a certain dignity and nobility that cannot be denied or suppressed. This aspect of man has long been understood, and it forms the basis of all humanistic philosophy. Though small and weak in the face of the gigantic powers of nature, man is able to chart the courses of the planets, map the inner structure of the atom, and harness some of the universe's power for his own plans and designs. Under historical conditions, however, the expression of man's unique power and dignity seems inevitably to lead to excess, to the pride or *hubris* that we associate with the human tragedy so vividly portrayed in the tragic poets and playwrights from Aeschylus to the present day. The problem is this: Is there a way in which man's greatness can be affirmed without the tragic consequences of pride? It is Tillich's contention that the Christian understanding of life makes this possible because it allows for man's self-affirmation at the same time that, in reminding man of his status as a creature, it counsels him to limit the claims he may make for his uniqueness and dignity. It is important to notice that on this understanding of the situation man is not to avoid affirming his greatness simply in order to avoid the tragic consequences of self-assertion; it is rather that in affirming himself he must at the same time be aware of the limits of his self-transcendence. An awareness of such limits is possible only by comparison with the Holy or Divine Life in which the tragedy accompanying finite, human life does not take place.

The general shape of Tillich's interpretation of Christianity is to point to the Divine Life, or "Spiritual Presence" as he calls it, as the Power that is able to overcome the maladjustments of human life as we know it. Man enters into tragic existence in the first place because he has self-transcendence or "Spirit," and he is to be rescued from tragedy ultimately by a reality who is also Spirit. Tillich uses the much-used and abused term "Spirit" in a precise way. For him it means a *unity of mean-*

ing and power; as such, it is beyond life in the biological sense and belongs only to man and to God. As Spirit, God is the Spiritual Presence in the form of Power capable of healing the broken character of historical life. Wherever meaning and power are maladjusted in human life we have tragedy and distortion; the Spiritual Presence, through the person of Christ, through the Sacraments, and through the Spiritual Community, manifests healing power in bringing meaning and power once again into harmony. God is able to overcome the distortion of human life through the channels of healing. In addition to those mentioned, there is the all-embracing medium of history through which the Divine aim is realized. History, however, though real, on Tillich's view is not ultimate for Christianity because the doctrine of eschatology, or the "last things," points to an end of history. At the end there is God, the same Who is at the beginning.

An abstract account of Tillich's position is bound to appear formidable indeed. This third volume, however, contains a wealth of concrete detail about life in its biological, psychological, moral, social, and political dimensions. Moreover, considerable attention is paid to the doctrine of the Church, both as a spiritual community and as an institution, to its relations with the individual and the social order. In a sentence full of significance for the present moment, Tillich says:

> Protestant systematic theology must take into consideration the present, more affirmative relation between Catholicism and Protestantism. Contemporary theology must consider the fact that the Reformation was not only a religious gain but also a religious loss. Although my system is very outspoken in its emphasis on the "Protestant principle," it has not ignored the demand that the "Catholic substance" be united with it . . . There is a *kairos*, a moment full of potentialities, in Protestant-Catholic relations; and Protestant theology must become and remain conscious of it.

As modern means of communication bring previously separated cultures into new relations with each other, it has become clear that the world religions cannot avoid coming into closer dialogue than has been true in the past. Thus far, apart from the not inconsiderable exchange that has taken place between Christianity and the Oriental religions as a result of long-term missionary activities, there has been little serious confrontation of the sort that would require reconsideration of doctrines on the basis of criticism from another religious standpoint. Historical and comparative studies of the major religions are on the increase and are to be welcomed, but such scholarship is not the same as close-range encounter between different faiths taking place through the life and work of those who adhere to them. It is one thing to compare this religion with that one when the person making the comparison is not personally involved in either faith, but a very different affair when it comes to exchange between actual believers. Confrontation at that level is more difficult and also more momentous, for it is only through influencing believers themselves that any lasting changes are likely to be achieved.

A very small volume by Tillich, *Christianity and the Encounter of the World Religions*, plunges us at once into the center of the problem. Tillich is unambiguous in his claim that Christians can and must seek to understand and to criticize their faith through encounter with the ideas and the spirituality of non-Christian religions. Much more is involved than the general idea of confronting a faith different from one's own. Encounter raises questions about the nature of religion as a universal fact of human life, and it calls for self-understanding. In isolation we can afford to be less clear about our aims and goals; encounter calls for a reversal of the situation and for the adherent of each tradition to become more acutely aware of the singular religion in which he stands. Tillich approaches the problem fully aware of these considerations.

He begins with the ancient task of understanding the connection between universality and particularity in religion. Christianity makes universal claims for its insights, and yet as a concrete historical tradition it appears in the limited form of a cult or church that bears many marks of the times and cultures in which it has existed. Christianity, in short, exists as "organized religion marking itself off both from other religions and the secular cultures surrounding it." A large part of Tillich's purpose is to bring Christians to an awareness of the tension between the universal truths of Christianity and the parochial character that every positive religion must assume when it becomes involved in the beliefs, customs, predilections, and prejudices of a particular culture. He seeks to accomplish his task in two ways: first, by marking out the "quasi-religions" —nationalism, communism, and liberal humanism—in order to show the peculiar critical function they perform; second, he urges the importance of initiating a dialogue between Christianity and Buddhism so as to bring Christians to an understanding of omissions in their faith. For Tillich there is truth in the criticism made by the quasi-religions against Christianity for insisting too heavily upon its own exclusive character as a special religion. On the other hand, he urges the superiority of Christianity's universal insights to these secular substitutes. With regard to the Buddhist-Christian dialogue, Tillich is convinced that Christianity has not sufficiently emphasized the "impersonal sacred" that is central to Buddhism because of the Christian concern for the personal dimension of existence.

Tillich is approaching the problem of a universal faith in a new way, and it is important to notice that he does not envisage a solution to the problem in terms of relinquishing the concrete religions in favor of a universal concept of religion that is little more than an idea. In fact, he rejects all of the most frequently proposed alternatives, in that he does not advocate a mixture of existing religions, nor the victory of one religion over all the others, nor the end of all religion in a total triumph of the secular outlook. What Tillich seeks instead is, first, that Christians will come to a new self-critical understanding of their faith in attending to the universal problem posed by the secular substitutes for religion and, second, that Christians will come to a new understanding of the other religions and quasi-religions by discovering that the universal insights of Christianity are valid above and beyond the fact that they are proclaimed as the truth of a particular religion.

One of the most important developments of recent years in the field of religious ethics is the emergence of a new concern for connecting the moral principles of the Judeo-Christian tradition with an understanding of human life as disclosed by modern psychology, sociology, political science, jurisprudence, and philosophy. The appearance of certain pressing moral and social issues—birth control, the high divorce rate, homosexuality and the law, mercy killing, to mention but a few—has had considerable influence on this new development. Dealing effectively with such issues requires detailed knowledge of the conditions of modern life, and there is an increasing awareness on the part of Christian moral theologians and philosophers that such knowledge cannot be ignored. There is, moreover, a better understanding of the insufficiency of trying to arrive at solutions merely by analyzing biblical precepts or past traditions of moral theology. To be relevant to the present situation it is necessary that Christian insights be interpreted in the light of knowledge gathered, so to speak, under nonreligious auspices.

Two recent books may be taken as representative of the new approach: H. Richard Niebuhr's *The Responsible Self* (introduction by James M. Gustafson), and Helmut Thielicke's *The Ethics of Sex* (translated by John W. Doberstein). For Niebuhr, Christian ethics is not primarily exposition of biblical principles or theological dogmas but rather a reflective effort on the part of the Christian community to criticize its own moral life. Such criticism requires, in addition to the religious insights, a general understanding of what it means to be a moral being. Consequently, Niebuhr pays attention to the positions taken by moral philosophers as well as theologians, and his work shows the influence of Aristotle and Kant as well as that of Schleiermacher and Jonathan Edwards. Niebuhr focuses on the concept of *responsibility* as a means of defining the moral dimension of human existence. In defining moral man as the being who can *respond*, Niebuhr aims at a new approach in the attempt to solve some of the problems that have faced the two classical opposite positions throughout the history of moral philosophy—the end or goal theories stemming from Aristotle, and the rule theories stemming from Kant. The responsible self is, above all, the self who responds to the encounter with God in a sense very similar to that proposed by Edwards when he spoke of man's response to God as "the consent of being to Being." Response means more than action; response includes interpretation of what we are responding to and of the particular response we prepare. Response embraces accountability and its acceptance.

The moral life in Christian perspective is response to God in three aspects—to God as Creator, to God as Judge, and to God as Redeemer. Man's response to God as Creator is to participate in the creation in the form of understanding leading to science and in the form of a maker or shaper of things from which flows the institution of civilized life. Man's response to God as Judge is to become aware of our limitations by confronting the other self and discovering the mutual dependence of all men. Here Niebuhr finds that the truth embodied in social theories of delinquent behavior depends on the fact that the consequences of human misdeeds spread throughout the human community and are often responsible for the misdeeds of others. Man's response to God as Redeemer is a life of responsible service in the understanding that, in the language of religion, we are saved and yet remain sinners to the end.

Thielicke's *The Ethics of Sex* (part of a larger work on theological ethics) represents a remarkable combination of theological principle and modern biological, psychological, and sociological analysis. He attempts to deal not only with the Christian understanding of marriage but also with intricate related problems such as birth control, abortion, homosexuality, and artificial insemination. Two basic features mark Thielicke's account as one that commands attention at present quite independently of theological commitments: his doctrine of man and his understanding of the modern sexual revolution since Freud.

The doctrine of man upon which the entire analysis is based emphasizes the polarity of man and woman with each standing equally under the grace of God. "Man" means both sexes, and the idea that the male sex is the "head" or dominant member in the partnership is set aside as running counter to the Christian understanding of the species. The reality of man can be found only where the sexes are together in mutual relationship; all problems that we identify as "sexual" in character stem from the various ways in which this mutual relation becomes disturbed or distorted. Second, full cognizance is taken of the revolution that occurred with Freud and the growth of depth psychology in our understanding of *eros* and the structure of human sexual relations. The reader, consequently, is delivered from a moralistic or prudish account couched in theological terms; instead, Thielicke seeks to understand the moral and religious issues in relation to sexual encounter as it is revealed in modern knowledge. Although limited theologically by the Lutheran perspective, Thielicke's discussion shows a remarkable appreciation for the contemporary situation and the new problems posed for theology by the powerful concern for sex in modern life. In this regard his plea for more sympathy on the part of Christians for what he calls the "worldly view" of marriage over against the strictly sacramental understanding of the relationship merits attention.

Josiah Royce once claimed that to understand the relations between morality and religion is a far more difficult undertaking than to settle the connections between science and religion. In a small but provocative book, *Morality and Beyond*, Tillich raises the first of these problems and seeks to relate the moral dimension as such to religion. He arrives at three main conclusions: first, that religion is an essential ingredient in the moral demand because religious ultimacy and the unconditional character of the moral law coincide; second, that the moral norm in the form of justice is an ingredient in religious love, otherwise love would degenerate into sentimentality; third, that the moral standpoint is not ultimate because moral law cannot motivate—only love can do that. The key to Tillich's way of reconciling the two dimensions is found in the idea that law is the form that love must assume when we are separated from it. To be commanded to perform, to require the form of obligation as the *ought* commands us, is precisely the sign that we do not perform "by nature" or from inclination and love.

EXISTENTIALISM AND HUMAN PURPOSE

We saw earlier in the discussion concerning the proper business of philosophy that the major polarity in the present situation is found in the extremes of linguistic philosophy and existentialism. In contrast to the detached form of analysis that holds sway among linguistic philosophers is the emphasis on involvement and participation in the concrete concerns of human life to be found among the philosophers of existence. We must now take note of developments in that field of inquiry, noting that the dominant concern of contemporary philosophers to settle the question about the nature of philosophy shows itself in this area as well. Existential philosophers have been no less anxious than others to define the aim of philosophy and to show that it has distinctive tasks that are not performed either by religion or science.

The type of philosophizing that is properly called existential began in the last century with the thought of the Danish theologian and philosopher Sören Kierkegaard. Kierkegaard initiated what has been called a "revolt of existence," or an attempt to drive the individual person back to an awareness of his own existence as a being with freedom and responsibilities in a world that is largely impersonal in character. Kierkegaard employed his remarkable literary skill in performing his task, and the result was a series of writings very different from the sober systematic form we usually associate with philosophy. In the course of time, existential philosophers have sought to broaden and deepen the insights of Kierkegaard's position and to bring it into more systematic form. The German philosopher Martin Heidegger has done much to accomplish this result, and more recently the work has been carried further by the French philosopher Maurice Merleau-Ponty. In an interesting short study, *In Praise of Philosophy* (translated by John D. Wild and James M. Edie), Merleau-Ponty seeks to elucidate the fundamental nature of philosophy from the existential standpoint. Like Kierkegaard, Merleau-Ponty goes back to Socrates and finds in him the model of the philosopher who is a philosopher precisely because he seeks for the mystery of his being. It is in man that the question of being becomes manifest. He writes:

> We could not have learned the meaning of the word "being" merely by considering this scenery [*i.e.*, the world]. It is in ourselves and only in ourselves that we can touch the interior of being, because it is only there that we discover a being which has an interior and which is nothing but this interior.

For Merleau-Ponty, philosophy appears more as a quest than as a fulfillment. There is a strong sense of the radical openness of experience and of the unending nature of the human quest. The point of the Socratic irony, he believes, is to force us to see that we do not possess absolute knowledge and that we must remain open to the pursuit of knowledge. To be convinced of our ignorance is a sign neither of false modesty nor self-conceit; it is a dramatic way of expressing the fallibility of all human knowledge and the difficulty of discovering who we are.

Merleau-Ponty contrasts philosophy in the sense of past traditions and schools with philosophy as creative thinking in the present. He is concerned to preserve for philosophy a special place of its own in which the extremes of "Promethean humanism" and theological absolutism can be avoided. The philosopher must free himself from the position where he is forced to take sides in the struggle between humanism on the one hand and the religious standpoint on the other. Philosophy has the aim of making us sensitive to the problematic character of our own existence, and that character is not adequately expressed either as heroic humanism or surrender to God. Merleau-Ponty regards the theological standpoint largely in terms of a divine determinism; against the view that sees man hedged in at every point by the power of God, he sounds the familiar existential note about freedom and man's incompleteness that can be overcome only in the exercise of freedom. On the other hand, in order to free man from the divine necessity we are not forced to elevate man to an absolute position such as has been done in various forms of humanism. For Merleau-Ponty, philosophy is more a search than a finding: it means a denial and transcendence of fixed positions and a continual self-reflection on man himself.

If philosophy is not to be swallowed up in theology, it must also be saved from the tyranny of history. Merleau-Ponty is critical of previous attempts, notably those of Hegel and Marx, to bring philosophy and history together in some form of identity. Philosophy as the reflective response of the philosopher to the present situation is a major factor in the making of history, and in this sense it precedes history; philosophy is never entirely encompassed by history nor identical with it.

We have our deepest insight into the present philosophical situation when we realize that, although the existential philosophers have rejected what we earlier called second intentional or critical philosophy in favor of attacking directly the question of being, they, too, find themselves uncertain of philosophy's position. Running through Merleau-Ponty's analysis is an uneasiness about the place philosophy is to occupy in contemporary life. The philosopher, he says, "limps" on the scene because philosophers generally are not clear about their task and the modern world is not receptive to reflective insight. Merleau-Ponty is troubled at the prospect that philosophical reflection is inconsistent with action and engagement in the business of life. He attacks the problem by refusing the distinction between the man of action and the man of reflection on the ground that every man embodies both. It is incorrect to think of a man of action and a reflective man as two different men; instead we are confronted with two dimensions of man himself. The proper relation between the two aspects is that of alternation: there is engagement followed by reflection and a return to engagement. But even with this solution Merleau-Ponty is not entirely satisfied, and he continues to be concerned over the fact that philosophical reflection requires distance from the scene of action in comparison with the pursuit of some "serious" endeavor, such as political activity, science, or the quest for God.

A modern reader interested in understanding what the existential approach to the world means in concrete terms and in relation to alternative philosophical positions will be rewarded by a careful reading of John D. Wild's *Existence and the World of Freedom*. One of the chief merits of this work is found in its mode of presentation: the existential outlook is itself expressed in a concrete and existential way. The position appears, therefore, less as an academic alternative than as what James would have called a "live option"—a point of view that one may adopt as a guide through the complexities of modern life.

In an attempt to find a common basis for comparing the various philosophical alternatives that confront us at the present time, Wild proposes a dramatic situation that is to serve as a model of the human predicament. We are asked to imagine a military plane with a five-man, English-speaking crew that is forced to make a crash landing on a glacial field high in the mountains. The plane is badly damaged, and there is no hope for repairs; the men emerge alive and badly battered but with their legs intact. They are able to save but two days' supply of food and a small portable radio that is in poor condition. Near the shelter which they are able to set up, one man notices what appear to be human tracks; they follow these and come to a depression which is a glacial crevice almost ten feet across. On the following day when they are better able to see, they detect a plane overhead and suppose that they have been seen. A short time later, a broken message comes over the radio, and they have the impression that a rescue party may be on the way. They are unclear, however, as to the meaning of the message. Their situation is desperate since they cannot hope to last for more than a few days in such cold.

Taking this image as a crude model of man's situation and using it as a touchstone, Wild considers five philosophical positions, their interpretation of the model, and the action that each would recommend. For the sake of convenience we may describe them as follows: 1) the rationalist view of the Greek philosophers and medieval thinkers; 2) the naturalistic philosophy based on modern science; 3) positivism; 4) the humanistic existentialism of Jean Paul Sartre and Albert Camus; 5) the religious existentialism of Heidegger, Karl Jaspers, and Gabriel Marcel. Wild's understanding of these positions and his critical assessment of their adequacy are revealed in his interpretation of their response to the image of man in the modern world.

The rationalist is a man with faith in reason and order. He believes in an independent cosmic order standing over against himself and in a rational self that comes to realization in an orderly process. Objective thinking is all important; error is willful confusion and the rejection of the dictates of reason. The rationalist has emerged from the plane wreckage with only minor cuts and bruises. Full of confidence, he is firm in his belief that the facts are clear and must be accepted. The plane observed their flight, the message indicated that help is on the way. In the meantime, unnecessary risks should not be taken. Man has freedom and is able to act in accordance with knowledge; the clear plan of action is to pay attention to what we know, strengthen our shelter, and devise a bridge across the chasm from materials to be saved from the wreckage.

The second view is represented by the man who trusts science, not universal reason but the specific findings of natural science. This man doubts the clear rationalistic universe of the rationalist, and he has further doubts about the total order that is supposed to prevail in it. On the other hand, he wants to analyze the situation and be guided by the facts alone. He does not believe in any help from beyond; there is no rescue party, and no time or thought should be wasted in thinking about help from that quarter. The facts and powers of nature must be accepted; man, however, has intelligence, and the most reasonable response is to make something like snowshoes and build a bridge across the abyss. Salvation lies in the application of scientific knowledge. Our efforts may not be successful, and nature may crush us in the end, but the reasonable thing to do is take the chance and attempt to save ourselves. Sometimes this man has a sense of tragedy in that man has limitations and his intelligence may not be sufficient. But we must continue to use the only weapon at our disposal to combat nature's might. The underlying faith of this man is that the human sciences will some day catch up with the natural sciences so that ultimately man will be able to control his own destiny as well as the forces of inanimate nature.

The third man, the positivist, emerges from the wreck with painful injuries but proceeds at once to a careful analysis of the situation. Like the naturalist, he, too, wants to apply scientific method to the solution of the problem, but he is not too enthusiastic about it and is not very confident of success. Laws governing the behavior of the elements in the situation can be discovered, and, on the basis of these, predictions can be made. Science, however, is neutral with regard to determining ends; hence any decision as to a course of action must be arbitrary. The positivist is haunted by doubts about the cogency of any solution to problems in the concrete human situation. Freedom, choice, responsibility are beyond science and cannot be understood. Positivistic man ultimately offers no solution for the human predicament; his only resource is the natural sciences and analysis of the situation.

The fourth and fifth views of life are the existential ones. Since they represent two different varieties of existentialism, it will be helpful to indicate the ground they share and then point to the particular points at which they differ. Both agree that some synoptic view of man's situation is more important in the first instance than a precise analysis of all the details. In terms of the model, before measuring the abyss or attempting to build a bridge, the total situation must be grasped in comprehensive fashion. Both agree that something must be *done* and that the time for doing it is not infinite. Both have a sense of urgency, and they believe that some concrete decision must be reached. Each is willing to accept the risk by attempting to cross the abyss, even if he loses his life.

Although the two varieties of existentialism have much in common— especially in contrast with the other positions—they differ nevertheless in some fundamental points. The nonreligious existentialism, represented by Camus and Sartre, puts radical choice at the basis of all life in the meaningful world of man and tends to exalt the individual to a point where he becomes responsible only for himself and for the world in which he lives. This man has made a choice and lives in the world defined by that choice. Like the naturalistic interpretation, this world is closed to transcendence and mystery. Beyond man there are no saving powers at work; only meaningless, alien forces. Other humans live in worlds of their own and must solve their problems for themselves.

By contrast, the way of religious existentialism is said to be "more open and flexible." This outlook embraces a greater awareness of the limitations of freedom and the possibility of its misuse. It has a sense of mystery and the conviction that freedom can be wasted if it is not exercised with a due sense of the powers other than human that limit its operation. For religious existentialism there is a greater sense of community than in the position represented by Camus and Sartre. Responsibility includes self-sacrifice and not only self-realization. Finally, there is openness to transcendence and to whatever powers beyond man there may be. Both forms retain a tragic sense and are sensitive to features of experience that do not fit into any comprehensive or rational scheme.

In *Existence and the World of Freedom*, Wild is attempting to give a more systematic form to existentialism by giving extended philosophical analyses of the basic ideas of freedom, choice, and responsibility. He very clearly shows the difference between the special or abstract fact with which science works and the concrete or "world fact" of subjective, personal experience with which the existential philosopher is concerned. Like James, whose "radical empiricism" has much in common with existential thought, Wild wants to begin where the individual person actually exists and to think as one who confronts the problems set by the human world of meaning. It is precisely from this world that we abstract when we enter the laboratory and close the door; hence for those who confine the real world to the scientific universe the world of everyday experience become irrelevant. The existential philosopher tends to reverse the relationship; the real world is the world of human life, personal relationships, and grappling with the problem of finding purpose in life. The world of fact and explanation resulting from science is but a highly selected portion of the human world, and it is completely conditioned by the objective standpoint from which it derives. The human world, however, cannot be understood from the objective standpoint but requires participation and the willingness to acknowledge the reality of subjectivity, human feelings, purposes, and aspirations.

Wild expresses the existential approach in its bearing on ethical questions and on religion. Adopting the standpoint of religious existentialism, he sets forth what he calls the pattern of existential arguments for transcendence. Over against the classical arguments for the existence of God, Wild seeks to show that the question of God is, from the religious perspective, a matter of interpreting the meaning of certain facts of lived experience. The reality of God comes to the individual not through the medium of an argument that some Being must exist but rather by a patient and careful description of the human situation, and then by pointing to the world of meaning that opens up through commitment to a transcendent reality working for the recovery of human life from its disruptions. Conviction is a matter of participation; an existential argument cannot be effective if it is viewed from an objective or non-participating standpoint.

In conclusion, Wild argues forcefully for the contribution that can be made by the existential attitude in the recovery of the humanities in our present educational system. And with this note we have come full circle in our discussion. For it will be recalled that in the debate about the nature of philosophy, we found Price, Adler, Blanshard, and others expressing concern about the eclipse of philosophy in the modern curriculum because of the failure of philosophers to deal directly with problems that arise from the full range of human experience. This concern is all the more significant at present because it represents a convergence of opinion at one point by thinkers holding very different philosophical positions on other matters. It may well be true that philosophers must disagree, but when they agree surely something of importance is at stake. The future of philosophy rests with philosophers themselves. Philosophy will recover the place of importance that it once had only if philosophers will again believe in the importance of their enterprise, stop beating around the bushes of preliminary questions, and get back to the high road of the great speculative issues.

BIBLIOGRAPHY

1. THE PROPER BUSINESS AND FUTURE OF PHILOSOPHY:

ADLER, MORTIMER J. *The Conditions of Philosophy.* New York: Atheneum Publishers, 1965.

LEWIS, H. D. (editor). *Clarity Is Not Enough.* New York: Humanities Press, Inc., 1964.

2. PHILOSOPHICAL QUESTIONS ABOUT SCIENCE:

BAR-HILLEL, YEHOSHUA, *et al. Logic and Language.* New York: Humanities Press, Inc., 1963.

BAUMRIN, BERNARD (editor). *Philosophy of Science.* New York: Interscience Publishers, Inc., 1963.

COLODNY, ROBERT (editor). *Frontiers of Science and Philosophy.* Pittsburgh: University of Pittsburgh Press, 1963.

CROMBIE, ALISTAIR C. (editor). *Scientific Change.* New York: Basic Books, Inc., 1963.

HESSE, MARY B. *Forces and Fields.* London: Thomas Nelson & Sons, Ltd., 1961.

KUHN, THOMAS S. *The Structure of Scientific Revolutions.* Chicago: University of Chicago Press, 1964.

McMULLIN, ERNAN (editor). *The Concept of Matter.* Notre Dame, Ind.: University of Notre Dame, 1963.

SELLARS, WILFRED S. *Science, Perception and Reality.* New York: Humanities Press, Inc., 1963.

SMART, JOHN J. C. *Philosophy and Scientific Realism.* New York: Humanities Press, Inc., 1963.

3. THE IMPORTANCE OF PAST PHILOSOPHY:

GILSON, ETIENNE, and LANGAN, THOMAS. *Modern Philosophy; Descartes to Kant.* New York: Random House, Inc., 1963.

GILSON, ETIENNE, LANGAN, THOMAS, and MAURER, ARMAND A. *Recent Philosophy; Hegel to the Present.* New York: Random House, Inc., 1964.

RANDALL, JOHN H., JR. *The Career of Philosophy: From the Middle Ages to the Enlightenment.* New York: Columbia University Press, 1964.

4. ISSUES IN RELIGION AND ETHICS:

HARTSHORNE, CHARLES. *The Logic of Perfection.* LaSalle, Ill.: Open Court Publishing Co., 1964.

KÜNG, HANS. *The Council, Reform and Reunion.* New York: Sheed and Ward, Inc., 1964.

MILLER, SAMUEL H., and WRIGHT, G. ERNEST, (editors). *Ecumenical Dialogue at Harvard; The Roman Catholic-Protestant Colloquium.* Cambridge: Harvard University Press, 1964.

NIEBUHR, H. RICHARD. *The Responsible Self.* New York: Harper & Row, Publishers, Inc., 1963.

THIELICKE, HELMUT. *The Ethics of Sex.* Translated by JOHN W. DOBERSTEIN. New York: Harper & Row, Publishers, Inc., 1964.

TILLICH, PAUL. *Christianity and the Encounter of the World Religions.* New York: Columbia University Press, 1963.

————. *Morality and Beyond.* New York: Harper & Row, Publishers, Inc., 1963.

————. *Systematic Theology,* 3 vols. Chicago: University of Chicago Press; Vol. 1, 1951; Vol. 2, 1957; Vol. 3, 1963.

5.   EXISTENTIALISM

AND HUMAN PURPOSE:

MERLEAU-PONTY, MAURICE. *In Praise of Philosophy.* Translated by JAMES M. EDIE and JOHN D. WILD. Evanston, Ill.: Northwestern University Press, 1963.

WILD, JOHN D. *Existence and the World of Freedom.* Englewood Cliffs, N.J.: Prentice-Hall, Inc., 1963.

NOTE TO THE READER

On all the major topics with which Dr. Smith is concerned in his essay, there is much material to be found in *Great Books of the Western World.* PHILOSOPHY is the subject of Chapter 66 of the *Syntopicon.* In addition to the introduction, the reader should consult the texts cited under the various topics in which the chapter is divided. Of most immediate relevance are the first, third, and fourth topics, dealing respectively with the definition and scope of philosophy, its method, and its uses.

Further discussions of the nature and method of science will be found in the texts cited under SCIENCE. Topic 1c is devoted to the issue concerning science and philosophy.

For the philosophical study of GOD and RELIGION, material can be located by referring to the chapters on these ideas in the *Syntopicon.* The chapter on KNOWLEDGE also contains much that bears on the same subject.

The tradition of philosophical speculation from Plato and Aristotle down to Hegel and James is extremely well represented in the *Great Books* set. Also, the interested reader should not overlook Volume 10 of *Gateway to the Great Books,* which is devoted to philosophical essays.

Social

KENNETH E. BOULDING

Economist and author, Kenneth E. Boulding has been a Professor of Economics at the University of Michigan since 1949. He has published over ten books including: Conflict and Defense *(1962),* Principles of Economic Policy *(1958),* The Skills of the Economist *(1958),* The Image: Knowledge in Life and Society *(1956),* Economic Analysis *(1941; 4th rev. ed., 1965), and* The Meaning of the Twentieth Century *(1964). A native of Liverpool, England, Professor Boulding was born in 1910. He received his Bachelor of Arts degree with First Class Honours from New College, Oxford, in 1931. From 1932 to 1934 he was a Commonwealth Fellow at the University of Chicago. Having settled in the United States in 1937, he became a naturalized citizen in 1948. Among the universities at which he has taught are: Edinburgh, Colgate, Fisk, McGill, and Iowa State College. In 1941–42, he worked as an economist in the League of Nations Economic and Financial Section at Princeton, New Jersey. With his wife, four sons, and one daughter, Professor Boulding lives in Ann Arbor, Michigan.*

Sciences

The year 1965 marks the twentieth year since the end of World War II. It is also the occasion of the fifth annual edition of *The Great Ideas Today*. Thus the time is ripe for taking a long and broad view of the social sciences. Therefore, instead of confining myself rather narrowly to the most recent developments in the field, as my predecessors in this review have done, I propose to attack the somewhat larger problem of the impact of the social sciences on society. In the course of doing this, I shall also have occasion to comment upon their latest developments.

Understanding of both the impact and the development of the social sciences requires some understanding of the methods that these sciences employ. These methods can be studied most clearly and briefly in the statistical images and the theoretical models which the social scientist constructs. In dealing with these subjects, in the first two sections of my review, I shall draw my illustrations from economics, which is the field I know best. I shall then be in a position to consider the impact of the social sciences as a whole upon public policy and recent work that is being done, especially in political science and economics. I shall conclude with a brief consideration of future developments for the social sciences.

The product of scientific activity is increase in knowledge, that is, a change in man's image of his universe which brings it closer to reality, whatever we mean by that. As we do not know absolutely what reality is, we can never be absolutely sure that any particular change in man's image of the world is, in fact, an increase in knowledge. The principal value of the scientific method is that it is a certain defense against error insofar as it produces images that are testable, and by the successive elimination of error we may hope that we are approaching truth.

Social Sciences

The social sciences are seeking knowledge about society, that is, about social systems. A social system may be defined as any pattern of events that involves the interaction of two or more persons. The study of the internal constitution and behavior of persons, with which psychology is principally engaged, is, of course, an essential prerequisite to the study of social systems, and there is clearly a continuum between, say, physiology at one end of the scale and sociology at the other, within which any boundary that we draw to define the social sciences will be somewhat arbitrary.

Insofar as the social sciences change our images of social systems, they will also change our behavior and, hence, the social systems themselves. The social system does not, as it were, "stay put" while we investigate it. It changes, sometimes profoundly, under the impact of our investigation. The social scientist, therefore, unlike the physical scientist, cannot regard himself as a detached outside observer of nature but must regard himself as part of the system that he is studying.

Man's image of himself and his society has always been the most important determinant of his behavior. We might distinguish three kinds of these images: folk images, philosophical images, and scientific images. Folk images are those created and possessed by ordinary people as a result of their ordinary experience. These serve to direct a great deal of human behavior, even among philosophers and scientists. Our images of our friends and neighbors, our behavior in the street and store and even, to a considerable extent, at work, are determined by our folk images. A child growing up in the family learns to distinguish persons, learns to identify them and respond to each differently, learns how to behave in certain situations, such as at mealtimes or in a quarrel or in the bathroom, and he does this by the process of generalization or induction from his personal experience. He projects what he has experienced in the past into the future, and he lives almost wholly in a world of what William Blake calls "minute particulars."

Philosophical images go beyond the immediate experience and generalize through reflection, meditation, poetic insights, and intuition to things beyond personal experience and even to society as a whole. There are philosophical aspects to folk knowledge, as, for instance, the learning of prejudice, stereotypes, ethnocentrism, or ideological biases. At its best, however, philosophical inquiry produces "wisdom" which distills, as it were, the experience of many men, many societies, into general propositions. Unfortunately, it is the plausibility rather than the testability of propositions which leads to their survival in philosophical discourse. Great ideas, however, such as sovereignty, freedom, responsibility, legitimacy, consensus, democracy, have enlivened men's images of their social world and have had a profound influence on their behavior.

Scientific images of society are those that are testable and that can be disproved through testing. The complaint is sometimes raised that scientific images of social systems are rather trivial and not very interesting, simply because it is precisely the important concepts that cannot be tested and hence have to be classified as philosophical. There is some truth in this, for the testing of images in social systems is very difficult because of the complexity and uncertainties of the system involved. The complexity can be visualized by reflecting on the complexity of the person himself, with his ten billion neurons, and considering that a social system is the interaction of perhaps hundreds of millions of persons. The uncertainty arises partly because of random elements in social systems themselves, which cannot be predicted. The problem of gaining knowledge about a system with mixed nonrandom and random elements is very difficult, as the random elements upset our predictions of the future and also prevent us from making secure generalizations about the past, simply because we do not know how much of the past has been random.

Even in folk knowledge and the common sense of daily life, we learn to distinguish the random from the nonrandom elements in the sequence of events. If, for instance, a man's wife flies into a rage at breakfast one morning, he does not necessarily conclude that she has ceased to love him. It may just be that she had a bad night or ate something that disagreed with her. In any human relationship, there are strong nonrandom elements of stability in the image that we each have of the other and the image that we each have of the nature of the relationship. A marital relationship, for instance, has very strong nonrandom elements in it and, if it is successful, exhibits powerful forces toward equilibrium. If events that seem to contradict this equilibrium image are interpreted as random, the image itself is not much disturbed by them.

How do we know, however, whether an event is random or not? There seems to be no easy answer to this question. If we interpret random events as nonrandom, we will build into our image of the system an order that it does not possess. The human mind has enough of a "rage for order," as Austin Warren calls it, so that we have a powerful urge to "make sense," that is, impose order, on what are, in fact, random events, or, at least, random events from the point of view of some other observer. Alexander Bavelas, a social psychologist at Stanford University, has reported orally on an experiment in which he gave to a number of subjects sets of random data—random, that is, from the experimenter's point of view—and asked them to find the rule in them. Almost without exception, the subjects were able to find rules and order in the random data given them; and what is more, when they were informed after the experiment that there were, in fact, no rules, they became quite angry and insisted that the rules that they thought they had discovered must, in fact, be true. At the other end of the scale, it is also possible to interpret an event that is not random but part of a pattern as, in fact, random and insignificant, and then we are also likely to get into trouble.

If our image of the social system has a self-confirming quality, we are in still more trouble. A young man goes to a new job, for instance, and has three or four rather unpleasant experiences in rapid succession, each of which is, in fact, quite accidental. He forms an unfavorable estimate of the job situation, of his workmates, or his employer, and, as a result, he himself behaves in such a way as to confirm his unfavorable image. We must not, of course, press this principle too far. Self-confirming images are apt to operate only over short periods, and in most social systems there are more or less objective realities which eventually impose themselves on the situation. Still, we cannot exclude the possibility that a succession of random events interpreted as a system may easily have profound and long-run effects. We may perhaps here use an analogy from the physical world. A drop of water falling on a water-shed will have a profoundly different history depending on whether a random puff of wind may blow it to one side or the other. On one side of the Continental Divide, for instance, it goes to the Pacific, on the other side, to the Gulf and the Atlantic. It is hardly possible to exclude the possibility that there are watershed systems and watershed points in the history either of a person or a society. Shakespeare's insight here is profound: "There is a tide in the affairs of men which, taken at the flood, leads on to fortune; omitted, all the voyage of their life is bound in shallows and in miseries" (*Julius Caesar*, Act IV, scene 3).

STATISTICAL IMAGES

Perhaps the most important contribution of the social sciences to the development of accurate images of complicated systems is the creation of what might be called "statistical images." There are two problems involved in the development of accurate images. One is the sampling problem, and the other is the problem of condensing, or indexing, large masses of information. The information output from any large system is always much more than any observer can possibly handle. If we try to take it all in, we will experience nothing but noise. Information always has to be filtered to produce knowledge. Thus, to make any sense out of the babble of conversation at a cocktail party, we must confine our attention to only one speaker and filter out all the rest. Or, to give another example, we can imagine the total confusion that would result if we were tuned in to all the radio waves that are passing through the room at the moment. The problem of sampling is how to set up an information filter with the least possible bias. If, for instance, we rely on neighborhood gossip for our information, we have a bias built into the information filter. We only get information through certain channels; other channels we neglect, and the channels that we select may easily have a bias in favor of scandal. Similarly, our information about other countries or other classes is heavily filtered in a way that tends to cut out information favorable to our opponents or to those who are different from us, and unfavorable to us.

In order to guard themselves against bias in sampling, statisticians have developed an elaborate technique for sampling information on a random basis. This is essentially the method of survey research. Here we have to be careful that we are taking the sample from a universe which is itself significant. If, for instance, we are sampling people to find their political views, it is not satisfactory to take the telephone directory as the universe from which to draw our sample, no matter how random the method by which we draw names from it, simply because people who have telephones constitute a biased sample of the whole population. They tend to be richer, for instance, or more involved with society than those who do not have telephones. A classic example of the failure of telephone sampling was the sad story of the *Literary Digest* in 1936, which had confidently predicted a Republican victory on the basis of a postcard poll, with names taken largely from telephone books. In the last twenty-five years the technique of sampling has developed to the point where a surprisingly small sample of a population can give us a considerable amount of reasonably accurate information about the whole. The Institute for Social Research at the University of Michigan, for instance, operates with national samples of only a few thousand people. This may be only one out of fifty or a hundred thousand of the total population of the United States, yet because of the care with which the samples are drawn, they produce surprisingly accurate results, as judged, for instance, by elections and censuses in which the samples are followed by counts involving whole populations or very large samples.

Two techniques have contributed greatly to the development of sampling in the last generation. One is the development of the method of area sampling, whereby people are selected for a sample according to their randomly selected location. This insures that it is the whole population that is sampled. Another important development is that of stratified sampling, by which members of the sample are selected according to a set of known distributions in the population. If we know, for instance, that only 10 percent of the population has incomes above $15,000, then only 10 percent of the members of the sample should have incomes above $15,000. An advantage of stratified sampling is that certain groups may be oversampled if there is special interest in more accurate information from these segments of a society, or if, for instance, these groups are such a small proportion of the total population that they might be missed in a completely random sample. Because we are sampling these subpopulations in a random way, we can correct in the overall estimates for any oversampling.

Once we have collected information from a sample, the next problem is how to condense it. How, for instance, do we extract the essential information from, say, three thousand long questionnaires? At this point the advantage of quantification—that is, the reduction of information to numerical form—becomes evident. The great advantage of numbers is that they can be added, subtracted, multiplied, and divided; and consequently, once information is expressed in the form of numbers, it is fairly easy to condense it into aggregates or averages. It is also possible to go one stage further and express the information in the form of a distribution, which tells us, for instance, what proportion of the population will fall below a given level of some numerical indicator.

A good example of the processes involved can be found in economic statistics. The gross national product is a concept now so familiar, even in political discourse, that it seems hard to realize that it was virtually unknown until the 1920's. Official data for the United States have only been available since 1929, and the "GNP," as it is familiarly called, only entered into the language of ordinary political discourse after World War II. The gross national product is the aggregate value in dollar terms of the total output of goods and services of an economy, compiled so as to avoid most double counting. For instance, we do not count the wheat and the flour as well as the bread: the value of the flour and the wheat is all supposed to appear in the value of the bread which it makes. There are some considerable difficulties in the concept as it is usually followed. Some of the activities of government, for instance, should probably be excluded and some of the activities of housewives included, but these criticisms aside, the concept has turned out to be extraordinarily useful in estimating not only the overall condition but the rate of change in the economy as a whole. The single number which results from this large process of aggregation (say the $622.3 billion that was estimated for 1964) summarizes an enormous mass of information. The gross national product in real terms consists not of a homogeneous sum of dollars but of an enormous heterogeneous mass of shoes and ships and sealing wax, of literally millions of goods and services of all kinds. Because, however, these goods and services are priced, or at least capable of being priced, we can express them all in terms of dollars, and we can add up the dollars into a total. If the gross national product rises, say from $583.9 billion in 1963 to $622.3 billion in 1964, we can be pretty sure that *something* has "risen," even though these two figures may hide a substantial change in the structure of output, with some things rising much more than others and some things even falling. If it is measured in constant prices and rises (in 1964 prices) from $595.3 billion in 1963 to $622.3 billion in 1964, we can be even more sure that some real total has risen.

Another statistical index, or family of indices, which is very useful, is that of the price level. This is in one sense an average of an enormous list of prices, or it can also be thought of as a ratio of aggregates, that is, the ratio of the total amount of money spent for things divided by a measure of the quantity of things bought. If the price level index rises, say from 100 to 120, we are again pretty sure that something has happened, and we are pretty sure of the direction, even though this information is condensed from an enormous list of prices, some of which have risen and some of which may even have fallen. There is a certain arbitrary element in the construction of an index of this kind, which cannot be avoided. If we are comparing two price lists in which some prices have risen and some prices have fallen, an index that weights heavily the prices that have risen and lightly those that have fallen will show a larger increase in the overall price level than an index that weights lightly the prices that have risen and heavily those that have fallen. It is even possible that two different indices constructed from the same two price lists may move in different directions; that is, one index may indicate that prices rose in a certain period and another index constructed from exactly the same data may indicate that prices fell. This is a difficulty, however, that is inherent in the fact that we are abstracting a small amount of highly significant information from a large information mass.

Once we have condensed a large mass of information into an aggregate or average, it is usually highly desirable to go back to what we have thrown away in the process of getting the condensed figure, and to examine the structures and distributions that exist within the aggregates and averages. Thus, in the case of the gross national product, we may wish to know its industrial composition, that is, how much was contributed by agriculture, by the defense industry, and so on. We are also interested in the distribution of income, that is, how are the claims on the total product divided among the population, and so on. Many different distributions of any given aggregate are possible, and it is usually a matter of judgment as to which are the most interesting and significant.

Demographic statistics give another example of the same problem of gain in significance but loss in information, in the course of aggregation and statistical manipulation. The most obvious demographic aggregate is the total population itself, and this is a figure of great interest. If we are told, for instance, that the United States has 185,000,000 persons, that China has 700,000,000, and that Iceland has 100,000, this tells us a good deal about these three countries. Two countries can have the same aggregate populations, however, and the significance of this number can be very different. In constructing an aggregate of population, we count each person—whatever his age, sex, income, occupation, level of literacy, religion, and so on—as one and one only, and the information thus obtained is valuable. However, we always want to go on to find out more about the population and especially its distributions. We want to break down the aggregate into a large number of subsets, for instance by age, sex, occupation, marital status, and a large number of other ways in which individuals differ from each other and are not merely counted as one. In a similar way we can see that a figure like crude birth and death rates is very useful and tells us a good deal. On the other hand, if we really want to appreciate its significance, we need to know, for instance, the age-specific birth rates (that is, how many children are born to women of different ages), and we need to know also the age-specific death rates (that is, the distribution of the total deaths by the age at death). For some purposes we may want to know the kind of families people are born into, and we may even be interested in the genetic aspects of the population: what, for instance, is the proportion of deficient children among those born.

It must be emphasized that while quantification is an enormous aid in the systematic condensation and indexing of large masses of information, it always involves a substantial loss of information, and some of the information lost is likely to be important. What this means is that quantitative information is not adequate to carry its own message. It always has to be interpreted, even if sometimes that interpretation is fairly obvious. The hoary jest that "figgers can't lie, but liars can figger" has an element of truth in it. It is very easy to use statistics in a misleading and propagandistic way, and no matter how they are used, they always have to be interpreted in terms of some frame of reference, that is, some larger image or model of the social system. Sociologist Amitai Etzioni has called attention very delightfully to what he calls the "Fully-Only" principle. We can take the same statistic, for instance that 10 percent of the people take a certain view, and we can express this by saying that "only" 10 percent take this view, or that "fully" 10 percent take this view. The inferences that we draw in the two cases are very different: one, that this 10 percent is unimportant, and in the second case, that this 10 percent is important. Any given figure, therefore, has to be the raw material for interpretation in a larger framework. Before the numerical image can be meaningful, there has to be a theoretical image, or at least some kind of model, that will indicate the significance of the figures.

THEORETICAL MODELS

The simplest model here is that which relates the figures to some norm, or normal value. If I say, for instance, that the rate of growth of the United States national product in the last fifteen years has been "only" 2 percent per annum, the inference is that it ought to have been larger, that 2 percent is dangerously low. If I say it has been "fully" 2 percent per annum, the inference is that this is quite satisfactory, even perhaps a bit too large.

The impact on society of the development, both of statistical images and of more sophisticated models of society, by which these images may be interpreted, can hardly be exaggerated. Every great advance in knowledge seems to have been the product of two different movements: one an improvement in measurement and observation, that is, essentially an improvement in statistical images, and the other an improvement in the model by which these images are interpreted. These two movements act and react on each other in a complex way, so that it is usually quite impossible to say which came first. Take, for instance, the so-called Copernican Revolution in astronomy, even more as it was later developed by Kepler and Newton into Newtonian celestial mechanics. This depended first of all on a profound restructuring of the model of the solar system from the earth-centered model to the sun-centered model and later from circular orbits to elliptical orbits; but it involved, also, a substantial improvement in the measurement of the positions of the planets, a movement which was begun before the invention of the telescope, for instance by Tycho Brahe, but was fully confirmed by the development of the telescope, which permitted much more accurate quantitative information about the solar system than had ever been possessed before.[1]

Similarly, what is sometimes called the Keynesian Revolution in economics[2] depends on a combination of a substantial improvement in the quantitative information about the economic system as a result of the development of sample surveys and national income statistics, coupled with an important reformulation of the fundamental theoretical model of the economic system itself. The essence of the change was not unlike the Copernican Revolution. Just as this represented a profound shift of perspective from a man-centered view of the universe to an abstract, system-oriented view, so the Keynesian Revolution represents a shift from the perspective of economic life as seen from personal experience to a system-oriented point of view that looks at the system as a whole. Thus, suppose we take the propositions which are central to the Keynesian analysis, that, first, from the point of view of a closed society, income and expenditure are exactly the same thing, and also that saving and investment are exactly the same thing. From the point of view of an individual, these propositions are not true at all. An individual can spend more than he gets or get more than he spends. He can save, that is, increase his net worth, without investing, that is, without increasing his holdings of real assets, simply by accumulating money or debts. Similarly, he can invest without saving if he simply draws down his cash and increases his real assets. For a society as a whole, however, every expenditure is simply one end of a transaction of which the other end is a receipt. The total of

1 Full documentation of the Copernican Revolution is contained in GBWW. The relevant texts are most readily found by consulting the *Syntopicon* under ASTRONOMY 2*b*.

2 John Maynard (later, Lord) Keynes' greatest book is his *General Theory of Employment, Interest and Money* (Harcourt, Brace and Co., 1936).

expenditures and total of receipts, therefore, are exactly the same thing. Similarly, in the absence of creation of money or national debt, the increase in the net worth of all private persons, that is, the total volume of saving, must be equal to the value of the increase of capital, which is the total volume of investment, as these are simply different ways of looking at the same thing.

The moment we make this shift from the person-oriented view to the system-oriented view of the economy, something becomes immediately clear which had been extraordinarily difficult to perceive before. The identity of savings and investment can also be expressed as an identity between the total output of a society (Y) and the sum of what is consumed (C) and accumulated (A), that is, $Y = C + A$. All this means is that everything that is produced in a given period either is consumed or it is still around and represents an addition to stocks. If we write this identity in the form $A = Y - C$, we have the identity of investment, that is, accumulation (A), with saving, which is income minus consumption. It then becomes apparent that *if* at any given level of aggregate output, the sum of consumption and what might be called willing accumulation is insufficient, that is, less than the aggregate output itself, there will be unwilling accumulations and the main impact of these is to reduce employment and total output. Under these circumstances total output will fall; as it falls, however, consumption falls again along with it, and the willingness to accumulate may likewise fall. Under these circumstances we get the familiar vicious spiral of depression, which may lead to an underemployment equilibrium, at which the society is not operating at its full capacity simply because it is not able to absorb in consumption and willing accumulation the output that it would produce at full capacity.

This was the condition of the Western world during the 1930's, and it seemed at that time to those who still thought of the economic system in essentially individual-centered terms to be an utterly inexplicable decay. The Keynesian theory gave a rough explanation of this decay and indicated the remedy. Consumption depends not so much on the total product itself as on what we call disposable income, which roughly is income after taxes. For any given level of output, therefore, lower taxes mean higher consumption, and higher consumption increases the willingness to accumulate. It may be possible also to increase the willingness to accumulate directly through manipulating the rate of interest and the loan market. To put the matter in another way, if the desire on the part of a society to save is too great relative to its existing investment opportunities, the opportunity to save can be given by increasing the national debt, which represents assets, that is, government securities, to the public.

The national debt exhibits perhaps better than anything else the contrast between what might be called the folk image of the economy and the scientific image. In the eyes of the folk image, debt is unqualifiedly bad, and it should be diminished at almost any cost. From the point of view of an individual, a debt is simply a liability. From the point of view of society as a whole, however, every debt is both a liability to one party and an asset to another. Similarly, the national debt, which is a liability to the government, is an asset to the people who hold it. Manipulating the national debt, therefore, which can be done indirectly by changing the volume of tax collections relative to government expenditures, is an easy way of adjusting the total volume of assets held by the public. The economist, therefore, sees the national debt as an instrument of overall social control, which can be used to prevent the economy from either slipping into deflation or into inflation. When the private sector is behaving in an inflationary manner, the national debt should be decreased; when it is behaving in a deflationary manner, the national debt should be increased. This idea of the national debt as a cybernetic mechanism for preventing a depression and insuring steady growth is something which depends on a sophisticated theoretical model of the economy for its perception and upon an adequate system of economic statistics for its consummation. The tax cut in 1964 represents a landmark, at least in American economic policy, as this perhaps is the first time that a deliberate tax policy was followed with the object of diminishing unemployment and not with the object of simply enabling the government to pay its bills. In the folk image, taxes are simply what the government has to collect in order that it may make expenditures. In the more sophisticated image, taxes can be a subtle but very powerful instrument of control of the overall level of economic activity and, properly managed, can prevent us from falling into depression.

Statistical images and theoretical models have had perhaps a somewhat less dramatic effect in the other social sciences than they have had in economics, though their influence has been by no means negligible. The rise of social work, for instance, as a profession has been associated with a shift in the image of poverty and crime as something purely and simply the responsibility of the poor and the evildoer, to be dealt with by private charity and moral exhortation, to an image of society in which both poverty and crime are seen as elements in a complex ecological picture with many determinants. We are, I suspect, still a long way from a real understanding of what are precisely those elements in social systems that produce poverty and crime, but we are at least moving in that direction, even if we have no great successes to report to date.

In the study of mental illness, likewise, we have come to realize that the incidence of mental illness in the whole society is not explained by the private history of each patient, valuable though this may be, and we are beginning to look for preventive and educational measures that will increase the incidence of mental health. Perhaps the most spectacular impact of sociology on the social system was the role that sociological investigation of the effects of segregation carried in the Supreme Court decision of 1954 that put segregated education beyond the pale of the Constitution. Even in the field of religion, the social sciences are beginning to create images beyond those that are derived from personal experience. It is significant, for instance, that the Information Service of the National Council of Churches of Christ in the U.S.A. would publish a report of a study of the relation of religious belief of various kinds to moral and ethical attitudes which is by no means flattering to the religious institution.[3] Studies of this kind can cause serious heart-searchings among religious leaders and induce them to consider carefully what *kind* of religion they are preaching.

Another place where the social sciences have made a substantial impact on the social system itself is in the management of organizations, whether these be business corporations, government offices, or even universities, labor unions, and churches. What is now called more generally management science, or more narrowly operations research, consists of a whole set of techniques for obtaining and processing information about an organization and its environment which will be of use to its decision makers. In operations research a mathematical model is constructed of some operation about which various decisions have to be made, such as, for instance, the routing of traffic through a tunnel or of materials through a plant; the production of a mix of different products from distillation or fractionation; or the planning of inventory. Various things about which decisions have to be made are reduced to quantitative form, and the mathematical function is derived by observation, experiment, or sometimes inspired guesswork. Then some variable is selected which is regarded as measuring the value of the operation, so that the "bigger the better," that is, the larger the magnitude of this variable, the better the operation. We then find at what values of all the decision quantities the maximand, or the quantity to be maximized, is at a maximum. In the model, at any rate, this represents the best position of the system, and the one that a wise decision-maker would choose. A special case of operations research in which all the functions involved are linear is called "linear programming." This has been applied with considerable success in maximization problems which involve a large number of variables and which, therefore, are not susceptible to solution by common-sense or rule-of-thumb methods. These techniques were developed first on a large scale during World War II, and they have had a great many applications in government, especially in national defense, and also in business firms.

3 Milton Rokeach, "Paradoxes of Religious Belief," *Information Service*, February 13, 1965.

Unfortunately, no general study has been made of the impact of operations research and similarly sophisticated techniques on management decisions, so that we really do not know how large this impact has been. It may be, indeed, that the decisions which are made as a result of operations research are not quantitatively very different from those that would be made by more informal and rule-of-thumb methods, but we cannot be sure of this, and one suspects that over the long pull the effects of these sophisticated methods of decision-making may be quite large in the avoidance of unnecessary waste. It must be emphasized, however, that no matter how complicated they may be, they apply only to part of a much larger social system. They, therefore, assist the human decision-making process, but, at least in the case of the larger decisions, they are in no sense a substitute for it.

The social sciences have made a considerable impact on management in a somewhat less quantitative way in the field of industrial relations and personnel management. Here the results both of observation and of experiment have given us some important propositions regarding, for instance, the relation between the nature of the communication system in an organization, the morale of the participants, and its overall productivity. This is by no means a simple relationship. Where morale is low, an improvement in morale almost always increases productivity, often quite substantially, and fairly simple changes in organizational structure and management methods from, say, an organization run as an authoritarian-line organization with orders from superiors to inferiors and no kickback, to an organization with more participation at all levels, has often produced quite startling results. On the other hand, where morale is high, a further increase in communication and participation may result in euphoria rather than productivity, and too much time may be spent in purely morale-building communications. Here again it is hard to assess the overall impact of changes of this kind; again taken over the long pull, however, they may be substantial.

Another example of the development of quantitative models of the social system which go far beyond what can be obtained through folk knowledge is the development of what is called input-output analysis, pioneered by Professor W. W. Leontief at Harvard University. This consists essentially in dividing the economy into a number of different segments or industries and studying the extent to which the output of each segment becomes input to all the other segments. We can then see what will be the effect of a change in one segment of the economy, for instance the defense industry or foreign trade, on all the others. This technique has been applied with some success in studying the impact of the creation of new industries in the course of economic development, and it has recently been applied to the study of the impact of disarmament on the economy.

267

THE SOCIAL-SYSTEMS CRITIQUE OF PUBLIC POLICY

In recent years there has been a rising tide of criticism in a great many fields of public policy on the grounds that decisions are mainly in the hands of people whose training is primarily in the physical sciences and engineering and who, for that reason, do not think easily in terms of social systems. No single social science can be credited with the development of what might be called the social-systems critique of policy making, but the overall impact is quite apparent. This type of criticism is noticeable in areas as diverse as flood control, irrigation, agricultural policy, public housing, urban renewal, transportation, social security, workmen's compensation, public assistance, and national defense.

It is interesting that a good deal of criticism of existing policies from the point of view of the general social systems involved has come not from the sociologists but from the geographers, who, perhaps because of their concern with overall spatial relationships, have been more open to the general social-systems point of view. There has been a good deal of criticism of our flood-control policy, for instance, on the grounds that it has been in the hands mainly of engineers, and army engineers at that, who have treated the river as an enemy, and that, hence, it has concentrated too much on dams and levees and not enough on people, zoning, and urban architecture. A flood is no problem to a river; it is, indeed, part of its way of life. If it did not have floods, it would not have a floodplain. A flood is only a problem to people, and it may be much easier to arrange things so that people conform to what the river wants to do instead of arranging things so that the river conforms to what people want to do. In practice, of course, flood control is a matter of changing the behavior both of the river and of people, and we have to conceive river and people as part of a single social system. Up to now, it must be confessed that these criticisms do not seem to have had much impact on policy, but they are so cogent that it is hard to believe that a change is not in the offing.

One could cite a number of other cases in which the failure to consider policy in terms of overall social systems leads to unexpected and frequently very unfavorable consequences. If, for instance, we conceive urban renewal as simply a matter of knocking down old buildings and building new ones that look prettier, we may easily simply transfer the problem somewhere else or, what is even worse, create what one social worker has described as "filing cabinets for live bodies," that is, localities that are neither neighborhoods nor communities, and in which, therefore, delinquency and social disorganization flourish. This does not mean, of course, that bricks and mortar are unimportant, or that architectural design and town planning are not an essential element in the building of healthy communities. Bricks and mortar and cement, however, are only the skeleton and the shell of a social system, and if we design them without reference to the social system that must inhabit them, we are almost certainly in for disastrous failures.

Another example in which the failure to regard a policy from the point of view of the social system as a whole has turned out to be unexpectedly disastrous is the movement for improved public health, as reflected, for instance, in the work of the World Health Organization. In a great many tropical countries in the years around 1950, there were highly successful campaigns for the eradication of malaria through the use of chemical insecticides, leading to the elimination of the malaria-carrying mosquitoes. The effect of this was dramatic. In many of these countries, overall mortality rates fell from somewhere in the neighborhood of twenty-five or thirty per thousand to somewhere around, or even under, ten, this often in a matter of two or three years. Infant mortality seems to have fallen even further. Birth rates, however, remained high, in some cases even increased, and as a result, not only has the overall population in many of these countries been increasing from 3–3.5 percent per annum, but this increase is heavily concentrated in the younger age groups, so that many of these countries now have more than 50 percent of their population under the age of fifteen, and the number of teen-agers entering the labor market is now almost double what it was only five or ten years ago. It is going to be extremely difficult to find places for all these teen-agers in the traditional societies of the villages. We are already seeing an explosive increase in the cities of the developing countries, some of which have been growing at rates of 12 or even 15 percent per annum. It is virtually impossible to expand employment opportunities at this rate, hence we get widespread urban unemployment, especially among young people, with its consequent dangers of social disorder and even disintegration.

Nobody is going to suggest, of course, that the reduction of mortality, especially of infant mortality, is not in itself desirable. If, indeed, a society is to have the human resources for development, it must raise its expectation of life, simply because, say, with an expectation of life between thirty and forty, people do not live long enough to make an adequate return on human investment in education and training. A developed society, therefore, practically requires an expectation of life at least in the sixties and seventies. One of the first steps toward development, therefore, should be a simultaneous reduction in both mortality and fertility. Where, however, the reduction in mortality is not accompanied by a reduction in fertility, the results can easily be disastrous. It may now be almost too late to prevent major disasters in the form of famine and social upheaval in many countries around the tropical belt. What we see here is a good example of a general principle, which is the extreme danger of concentrating on a single problem in the midst of a complex social system. The public-health specialists concentrated on a single problem, how to reduce mortality. By and large they did not regard fertility as their business. By solving one problem, however, in a partial system, they have created almost insoluble problems elsewhere. Up to a point, of course, we must have specialists, and problems must be solved piecemeal. These piecemeal solutions, however, must be made in a larger framework involving some kind of image of the general social system; otherwise piecemeal solutions may, indeed, break the larger system into pieces. There is a story of a production manager of an enterprise who said that all he wanted to do was to reduce costs, until it was pointed out to him that he could reduce costs to zero by the simple process of abandoning the enterprise altogether!

The field of economic development is a good example of an area that has received a great deal of attention in recent years, and in which the need for a general social-systems approach is widely recognized, but in which the sheer complexity of the problem and the enormous variety of cases has made any general solution very hard to find. It is widely recognized, however, that the problem of economic development cannot be solved within the framework of economics alone, even though economics has some elementary and quite essential contributions to make, such as, for instance, the proposition that if economic development requires accumulation, there must be an excess of production over consumption, or if a country fails to take advantage of certain favorable terms of trade which are offered to it, it will find development more difficult than countries which seize these advantages. It is also clear, however, that economic development is part of a much larger process of social change, and that if we are to understand it, we must understand what it is that motivates people to change, and we must understand what are the political and social institutions that encourage change, and that enable these motivations to result in action. As a result, there has been a good deal of interest, first of all in the motivations to change, in such works, for instance, as David C. McClelland's *The Achieving Society* and Everett Hagen's *On the Theory of Social Change*.

A mere study of motivation is not enough, of course. The part of the population that is motivated to change may not have the opportunity to do it, and the part that has the opportunity may not be motivated. Consequently, we cannot neglect the political structure and especially the distribution of power. This, unfortunately, seems to be a situation in which we are only wise after the event. Apart from the Marxists, who are only occasionally right, political scientists seem to have come up with remarkably little in the way of a general theory of the dynamics of power distribution. Nevertheless, we can point to economic development as an area in which the urgent needs of practice have far outrun the development of theoretical models, but where also the absence of adequate theoretical models is a severe handicap. The plain fact is that we are not being very successful in economic development, especially in the countries of the tropics, and at least part of the reason for this undoubtedly lies in the absence of adequate theoretical models and an even less adequate apparatus for collecting and processing the essential information. We have at least the beginnings of an economic information system in most countries, even though this is often quite rudimentary. We have practically no information system that will cover the psychological, motivational, ideological, and political elements of the system. A research project is now being developed, for instance, by the Department of Defense, called Project Camelot, which has as its major objective a substantial mobilization of social-science resources to study the problem of the kind of social breakdown that leads into internal war. On this subject we are starting practically from zero.

In spite of the fact that this type of criticism often seems to fall on deaf ears, and that the social sciences themselves have at most a very spotty record, at least when it comes to prediction, when one looks over the history of the twentieth century it is hard not to be impressed with signs of progress. It is particularly instructive, for instance, to contrast the twenty years after World War I, from 1919 to 1939, with the twenty years that we are just completing after World War II, from 1945 to 1965. It is not an exaggeration to say that the first period was a total failure that ended in disaster. The overall rates of economic growth, even in the developed countries, were rather low. The tropical world was still largely in the grip of colonial powers, and its development was even slower. There was a period of reasonably rapid recovery from the war in the twenties, but in the West this ended in the stock market crash of 1929 and the Great Depression of the thirties which followed it. In the Soviet Union, likewise, a period of recovery under the new economic policy was followed by the first collectivization of 1928–32, which turned out to be an even greater disaster than the Great Depression in the West, in which the Soviet Union lost half its livestock and five or six million of its people. The unemployment and disorganization of the depression years led directly to the rise of Hitler and the monstrous collapse of human decency which that represented, and the whole period ended in the bestialities of World War II, with its ruthless destruction of cities and slaughter of civilian populations on both sides.

By contrast, the twenty years from 1945 to 1965 have been relatively benign and successful, in spite of the nuclear threat and the constant menace of the Cold War. In a great many countries, the rate of economic growth has been spectacular, indeed unprecedented. Japan, out of total defeat, the loss of her empire, the destruction of her cities and her merchant marine, and the repatriation of three million overseas Japanese, went on to establish a world record for economic growth of about 8 percent per annum increase in per capita real income, sustained over the whole twenty-year period. Nothing like this has ever happened in human history before. The previous record for sustained growth before the war was about 2.3 percent per annum, attained by Japan, Sweden, and the United States from about the middle of the nineteenth century on. The case of Japan is not unique; West Germany grew at about 7.5 percent, and a number of European countries between 5 and 6 percent in this period. The United States is rather slow; indeed, in the 1950's, forty-five countries had a faster rate of economic growth than the United States, at least according to official statistics, which do not necessarily have to be believed! Even in the United States, however, growth was continuous and there was nothing like the Great Depression of the thirties. The United States achieved an enormous disarmament in 1945 without unemployment ever rising above 3 percent. Even though unemployment has tended to be uncomfortably high in recent years, running about 5 or 6 percent, we have had nothing like the disaster of the thirties. Furthermore, in the last twenty years we have seen the liquidation of nearly all the old colonial empires with the exception of the Portuguese, and even though this has created severe problems, for instance in the Congo, on the whole this remarkable transition has been achieved with little violence and to the mutual benefit of all parties. One hesitates to be too optimistic; nevertheless, it does look as if the United States and the Soviet Union are beginning to learn how to live with one another, and, even though China remains a great enigma for the future, a world war seems a good deal less inevitable in 1965 than it did in 1939.

We cannot, of course, give all the credit for the difference between these two twenty-year periods to the rising influence of the social sciences. Nevertheless, this is not a negligible factor. It is in economic policy, perhaps, that the contrast is greatest. It is an instructive exercise, for instance, to go back to the reports of the economic conferences that were held just after the first World War and to compare these with those that were held after the second. It is pretty clear that a substantial change has taken place, and that not only has our understanding of the economic system improved enormously but that also our information about it has improved. The high rates of economic growth of the last twenty-five years are by no means unconnected with the rise of Keynesian economics, of national income statistics, and of economic policies which are self-consciously directed toward what might be called a controlled market economy. It is true that a price has sometimes been paid for this in terms of inflation, but the gains are, nevertheless, substantial. One would certainly be very surprised if the Western world ever had another great depression on the scale of the thirties. The fact that the record of the controlled market economies has been distinctly better than that even of the best centrally planned, that is, communist, economies, seems to be having a marked impact on the centrally planned economies themselves, which are undergoing severe reappraisals of their economic policy and what seems to be a movement in the direction of decentralization, greater use of the market, and more individual freedom. If, indeed, we are moving into a period where ideologies can be tested by results, this would be good news for mankind.

It is still too early to say whether the development of sophisticated models and better information systems in the international system will deal with the problem of war in a way that better economic models, information, and policies have dealt with the problem of depression. Up to now, indeed, the danger of perhaps irretrievable disaster remains high. If, however, we are lucky enough to escape this for another twenty years, we may very well find that the rise of social-scientific knowledge in this field will corrode irrational nationalisms just as it seems to be corroding irrational economic ideologies. There is a race between knowledge and disaster, but in this race the longer disaster is staved off, the better chance we have of acquiring the knowledge to prevent it altogether.

DEVELOPMENTS WITHIN THE SOCIAL SCIENCES

There is a constant interaction between developments in the pure sciences and the problems perceived as important in the outside world. It is not surprising, therefore, to find that many of the developments within the social sciences themselves in the last generation have been the result of pressures generated by a sense of unsolved problems in the world outside. Where one social science tends to lag behind another, also, a sense of deficiency develops, which eventually attracts resources into it to try to bring it into line with the rest. Perhaps the most interesting example of this principle is the strong movement for the improvement of political science which has been noticeable in the last generation.

In the study of all social systems, we are constantly being brought up against the fact that the political system is at the same time one of the most important and also one of the least tractable elements in the social system when it comes to the setting up of theoretical models that are testable by refined procedures for collecting and processing information. It is hardly too much to say that it is only in the last ten years that political science has begun to move toward the kind of model construction and information collection that has long been characteristic of economics. A good deal of the stimulus here has unquestionably come from other social sciences and is a tribute to the fact that the study of social systems faces a subject matter which is so highly integrated that the specialized disciplines must be willing to learn extensively from one another if they are to function even as disciplines.

Thus, in political science, we have seen in recent years great interest in better methods of collecting information, which has come largely from political sociology, and the contacts of political science with sociologists, social psychologists, and the practitioners of survey research. Here we find, for instance, the studies of voting behavior, of opinion formation, and studies of political decision-making. In countries of regular elections, at least, political scientists have been in the curious position of having too much information about a particular moment of political behavior, namely, the vote cast in the ballot box, but very little information about all the rest of the field. The development of sample surveys of preelection behavior, for instance, by the Institute for Social Research at the University of Michigan, and also studies such as that of Professor Richard Snyder of Northwestern University on the decision-making process in the Korean crisis, all point towards substantial improvements in data collection and processing in this field.

Going hand in hand in this has been a considerable revival of interest in political theory of a fairly sophisticated kind, mainly as a result of its contacts with game theory and economics. We have, for instance, the work of Duncan Black on the theory of committee decisions, of C. E. Lindblom and R. A. Dahl and of Anthony Downs on the processes by which political decisions are made in a democracy, and by J. M. Buchanan and G. Tullock on what they call the "calculus of consent." All these attempt to apply formulations of rational behavior and optimizing concepts of decision-making, which are familiar in economics, to problems in politics. The so-called voting paradoxes have received a good deal of attention, these being situations, for instance, in which the outcome of a decision based on a voting procedure is a function of the procedure itself and the order in which matters are taken up rather than a function of the preferences of the parties. It is a symptom of the way in which the social sciences are moving toward unification that these days it is often quite hard to tell whether a book such as, for instance, Kenneth Arrow's *Social Choice and Individual Values*, is economics or political science. We could almost say that the division of the social sciences according to fields of study or according to the types of institutions studied— with, for instance, a political scientist studying states, an economist, corporations, and a sociologist, families and churches—is now breaking down, indeed has broken down. It has become clear that each social science concentrates on a certain aspect of the social system which cuts across virtually all forms of social organization, even though it may be particularly relevant to some of them. Thus the processes of decision-making are quite similar, whether they take place in a corporation, in the government, in a labor union, in a church, or in a family. If the decision has to be reached in a group or has to be accepted by a group, there are problems of compromise, accommodation, reformulation, and development of new positions which likewise take place no matter what the organization. What seems to be happening today is that besides the division according to the regular disciplines, which, to some extent at least, carves up the subject matter according to types of organizations, we seem to be getting a specialization according to certain functional processes such as decision-making, the resolution of conflict, processes of exchange, processes of threats and coercion, and so on.

Alongside these developments in political science in general, there has been a corresponding movement in the study of international systems. Part of this unquestionably is motivated by the feeling that the international system is the one which is most threatening to us today, and that unless we can solve the problem presented by the proliferation of nuclear weapons and the collapse of traditional national defense, the future looks indeed dim. As a result, there has been a certain mobilization of social-science interest in this direction which did not exist before. In the past generation it was fairly true to say that international studies were in the hands of diplomatic historians, and what might be called high-level journalists, who discussed "foreign affairs" with a certain amount of folk wisdom but with very little in the way of exact theoretical models or quantitative information. The past decade or so has seen a number of intellectual movements rather closely related and often involving the same persons, which have endeavored to close the obvious gaps and deficiencies in this field. In the first place, there has been a movement to improve the whole field of the study of international systems, first by bringing in sociologists, economists, social psychologists, game theorists, and so on, as well as political scientists, and so make the whole field multidisciplinary in character. The same sort of thing happened to industrial relations about a generation before, when it became apparent that the labor-management relationship, for instance, involved much more than economics, and that if it was to be understood and operate satisfactorily, sociology and psychology would have to be called in.

Along with the widening of the disciplinary horizons of the field, there has also come an interest in the development of mathematical models and improved quantitative information. The pioneer in both these respects was an English meteorologist, Lewis F. Richardson, whose remarkable books, *Arms and Insecurity* and *Statistics of Deadly Quarrels*, languished in microfilm for almost twenty years before they were finally published in regular form in 1960. Richardson developed a theory of arms races which he tried to test, not wholly successfully, by the application of quantitative data, and he also made important contributions toward the quantification of the history of conflict. His work often showed the marks of the gifted amateur operating in isolation, for he was at least a whole generation ahead of his time. It is, nevertheless, having an increasing influence in stimulating the present generation of researchers in this field to go beyond the folk wisdom of their predecessors as well as the folk wisdom by which the decisions in the international system are now made.

Alongside this movement for the improvement of the study of international systems has gone a closely related movement, which almost looks like the beginnings of a new science, for which the Dutch have a name. They call it *Polemologie*, that is, the science of conflict. Conflict is common to all social systems and all social organizations, whether this is economic conflict, political conflict, religious conflict, racial conflict, or international conflict. It is very hard to find any social system or any social organization that does not have conflict in it. Just as, therefore, economics abstracts from the equally universal phenomenon of exchange a theoretical system and what is beginning to be a quantitative science, so it ought to be possible to abstract a general theory of conflict from these many cases where it occurs, and it should be possible also to set up an information system which will enable us to detect where we are at any moment in any particular conflict process. Game theory is a part of this, as developed first, for instance, by John von Neumann and Oskar Morgenstern.[4] This in turn is closely related to modern decision theory. In fact, one of the standard works in the field, by Robert Luce and Howard Raiffa, is entitled *Games and Decisions.* The usefulness of game theory has been somewhat limited by the fact that its major competence had been in the field of zero-sum games, that is, games in which what one party wins, the other party loses. The extension of game theory into a general theory of conflict requires its expansion to cover the case of positive-sum games in which the total of gains and losses is positive, and these have been studied in such works as T. C. Schelling, *Strategy of Conflict,* Anatol Rapoport, *Fights, Games, and Debates,* and my own *Conflict and Defense.* There are important contributions to the theory of conflict, also, outside of game theory, as, for instance, in the economic theory of oligopoly, the theory of group dynamics (*see,* for instance, Kurt Lewin, *Resolving Social Conflicts*) and also in individual psychology, in psychoanalysis, and in the analysis of internal conflict within the person.

An important body of theory is also developing regarding what I have called "threat systems," which concerns itself with the dynamics of the way in which social systems are organized by means of threats and counterthreats. A threat relationship originates when one person or organization (call him Able) says to another (call him Baker), "You do something that I want, or I will do something that you don't want." What happens then, of course, depends on Baker's response. If Baker submits and does what Able wants him to do, a new structure of roles has been created, with Able dominant and Baker subordinate. The master-slave relationship is typical of this. On the other hand, the threat-submission

---

4 *Theory of Games and Economic Behavior* (Princeton: Princeton University Press, 1944).

pattern is also characteristic of all law enforcement and, when it is legitimized, becomes one of the most important elements in social organization. When the traffic cop says, "Pull over," we usually pull over; that is, we submit to an implied threat. If the threat is not accepted as legitimate, there may be defiance. That is, Baker says to Able, "Do your worst and see if I care." The ball is now passed back to Able. Either he has to carry out his threat, or the credibility of future threats is seriously impaired. Unfortunately, carrying out the threat is often costly. Hence, he is faced with the decision as to which of the two alternatives—that is, carrying out the threat or not carrying it out—is least costly. Another possible response to the threat is flight; Baker simply removes himself from Able's sphere of capability. Historically, this has been very important; it accounts for a great deal of human migration; and even though preachers and psychoanalysts have given this a bad press, sometimes escape is highly rational. Another possible reaction is the development of counterthreat. The system then passes into deterrence. Baker replies, in effect, to Able's original threat, "If you do something nasty to me, I will do something nasty to you." The difficulty with deterrence is that while it may operate quite successfully for a short period, it seems to have a profound long-run instability. The reason for this is that threats need to be credible, that is, believed, by the threatened party if they are to be effective, and unless they are occasionally carried out, their credibility tends to depreciate. Hence, even in a system of mutual deterrence, of which we find many examples in industrial relations, international relations, and so on, there is a certain tendency for the system to collapse into actual carrying out of threats every so often.

Along with the "pure" work in the field of conflict systems and international systems, there has been a good deal of interest in applied research in this area. Quantitatively, this is most apparent in what might be called national security research, that is, the application of sophisticated theories and models to the problem of national defense. We see this in the work of such institutions as the Rand Corporation in Santa Monica, California, and the Hudson Institute near New York City. Works that reflect this activity are, for instance, Charles J. Hitch and Roland McKean's *Economics of Defense in the Nuclear Age*, and Herman Kahn's works, especially *Thinking About the Unthinkable*. The effect of these more sophisticated approaches on actual policy is hard to determine, and its full effects may not be seen for many years. However, there does seem to be a change in the temper of the Department of Defense, for instance, in the direction of greater sophistication. Whether an institution so intimately bound up with folk images and folk ethics as the military can survive the development of sophistication without a severe crisis is another question altogether, to which I would not venture to give an answer.

There has also been a small intellectual movement in this field that has come to be known as the peace research movement, which is concerned with the application of the social sciences quite specifically to the problem of the abolition of war and the establishment of stable peace. At many points peace research and national security research overlap. In these days, certainly nobody regards war as anything but a cost to be minimized in the interest of certain other values. Nevertheless, there is a difference between those who regard it as a tolerable cost and those who regard it as an intolerable one. Or we might put the matter in another way and say that the national security research is trying to solve the problem of how to maximize national security, subject to the constraint that the probability of peace does not fall below a certain level. Peace research is asking the question: How do we maximize the probability of peace, subject to certain other values not falling below a minimum level? Thus even though the "pure" framework of international systems theory and international information collection and processing is the same for both applied fields, there are differences in values, which operate to select the problems that have the greatest interest.

We might pause to note that this difference between pure and applied research is a very general problem, which applies to all the sciences. The dominant value of pure research is curiosity, the sheer desire to know. Applied research always assumes certain other values which direct the course of the advancement of knowledge. Applied research, therefore, always implies a value system beyond that of knowledge itself, whether this is making money, increasing destructive power, or human welfare. It is a sad commentary on the human condition that such a very small amount of applied research goes to improving human welfare.

Another branch of the tree of knowledge that has shown great vitality in recent years is that of the study of information and communications. This is a field of enormous importance for the social sciences, although it goes beyond the social sciences into biology and engineering and even into the physical sciences. The pioneering work in this field was done by a happy combination of engineering and social science in the work of Claude Shannon and Warren Weaver[5] in 1949 in developing a mathematical measure of the quantity of information in a system. This measure, interestingly enough, turned out to be very similar, in fact formally identical, to the physical concept of entropy, or rather, negative entropy. As entropy is a measure of the disorder and lack of potential in a system, so information is a measure of order and potential. Another very important concept of information theory is that of the capacity of a channel of information. A unit of information is the "bit," which is short for binary unit, which is the occurrence of one event out of two equally

---

5 *The Mathematical Theory of Communication* (Urbana: University of Illinois Press, 1949).

probable potentialities that together exhaust the possibilities. Thus the information conveyed by the toss of a coin is one bit, assuming that heads or tails are equally probable. These relatively simple concepts opened enormous fields of research in practically all the sciences.

In the social sciences, information theory, like game theory, with which it is not unrelated, has perhaps been important mainly because of the problems it has suggested rather than because of those it has solved. Information theory operates at a level of abstraction below that of the content of information. It is thus ideally suited to the study of telephone engineering and even to certain abstract levels of social-systems analysis, where we are interested, for instance, in the problem of information overload in a quantitative sense, rather than the nature of the messages that the information system is carrying. Social scientists, however, cannot neglect the fact that when people communicate with each other, they at least have the illusion that they are saying something. In studying social systems, therefore, we are forced to go beyond the abstractions of information theory and to develop abstractions of content and knowledge. Knowledge, that is, the image of the world in people's minds, is an essential component of social systems. Human behavior cannot conceivably be understood without it. It is a structure of such immense richness and complexity, however, that it is not easy to reduce it to simple abstract concepts and measures. We do this in a rough way, of course, every time a teacher gives an examination and grades it. We do it in more refined ways with public opinion surveys, attitude studies, or what the sociologists call content analysis. Content analysis is an attempt to define variables which are characteristic of the content of a body of communicated material, such as a book, a newspaper, a letter, or a radio broadcast, and to measure these quantities by counting words or phrases that significantly embody them. Even though this method has limitations, it is another step toward improving our statistical images of the social system.

On the more theoretical or even philosophical level, we might almost distinguish a "communications school" of social scientists, who lay great stress on the importance of the communications network as the key concept of all social organization and of the behavior of all social systems. In the last generation, this position was represented mainly by the economist Harold Innis at Toronto, who saw very clearly the enormous importance of the communications network in the general phenomenon of economic development. In the present generation, we have social philosophers such as Kenneth Burke, sociologists such as Hugh Dalziel Duncan, whose *Communication and Social Order* is perhaps the nearest thing to a textbook in the field, with a very broad coverage, and, finally, an almost unclassifiable writer, Herbert Marshall McLuhan, also of Toronto. McLuhan's major works, *The Gutenberg Galaxy* and *Understanding Media*, are books of quite astonishing originality in which, indeed, the originality of both format and idea is so great that it may distract attention from the content. McLuhan's central theme is that it is not the content of communication that is so important in determining the pattern in the course of social systems as the form of the medium of communication itself. The types of social systems that develop, for instance, where the major medium is face-to-face conversation, are enormously different from those systems that have writing, and these, in turn, differ from those that have radio and television. He argues particularly that whereas print fragmented the world and led to the rise of national states, secular society, and scientific knowledge, television, because of its peculiarly intimate and domestic character, is going to create a very different kind of society, more organic, less fragmented, less rational in the sense at least of economic accounting, more like a great world village and less like the Greek city. He points out also that a society in which radio is a dominant means of communication is likely to be more tribal and much less rational than one dominated by print. He regards both Hitler and Franklin Roosevelt as essentially products of the brief radio age in the Western countries, and it is somewhat alarming to contemplate that most of the poor countries in the world are going through the radio age now. By contrast, television destroys the demagogue, as it destroyed Joseph McCarthy, simply because of its peculiar character as a medium. Anyone who paints with such a broad brush as this is bound to get many details wrong, and McLuhan's leaps of insight occasionally land him in a ditch. Nevertheless, this represents a line of thinking that is extraordinarily illuminating, and it is bound to have a substantial effect on the social sciences in the years to come.

We may, perhaps, summarize the present situation in the social sciences as follows. There is, first of all, a remarkable convergence of the different social sciences toward each other, and something like a unified social science at last seems to be emerging. This is not to say that the old divisions are disappearing. Economics, sociology, psychology, and so on, retain their ancient empires, but the growing points seem to be at the borders. It is becoming increasingly hard to classify either the social scientists or the works which they write in terms of the old classifications. This is happening, as I have suggested earlier, simply because the subject matter of the social sciences—that is, the social system itself—is highly unified, and pigeonholes like economics, sociology, and psychology are more a property of the social scientists than of the social system. We find economists, then, like Everett Hagen, studying the motivational implications of child-rearing. We find sociologists like George Homans and Peter Blau interpreting nearly all social phenomena through the generalized concept of exchange. We find economists like Duncan Black becoming political scientists, and political scientists like Gordon Tullock becoming economists, and even though there have been times when the interdisciplinary movement has become something of a foundation fad, it is still something that arises out of the sheer necessity of the problems.

This movement toward a unified social science has now got as far as to begin producing textbooks. We have, for instance, Alfred Kuhn's remarkable work, *The Study of Society*, which combines economics, sociology, and psychology in a genuinely integrated body of theory, using the concept of the transaction as the basic building block. There might be some danger that this movement toward the development of unified theory in the social sciences would produce a somewhat denatured and sterile eclecticism. My personal view is that we are in a period in which we are not only moving toward a more unified theory but also gaining substantial theoretical insights in many separate fields. Even in a field as old and staid as economics, we have seen significant developments in the theory of economic behavior, for instance in a remarkable work by Richard Cyert and J. G. March, *A Behavioral Theory of the Firm*. Economics has been breaking out of the formalism of maximization theory and realizing that such things as search processes and learning processes are essential to the interpretation, even, of the behavior of economic organizations like the firm. The work of the communications school referred to earlier does not fit neatly into any existing body of theory. It represents some genuinely new insights into the nature of the social system and the kind of abstractions that it is possible to make from it. We may find ourselves, indeed, with two bodies of rather integrated social theory—one revolving around the concept of the transaction and decision theory, the other revolving around the nature of media and the communications process. The task of bringing these together remains to be done.

Another movement that is characteristic of all the social sciences is the rapid development of quantification and mathematization, even in areas that have previously resisted this, such as political science. In economics, of course, the use of mathematics goes back a long way, at least to A. A. Cournot, 1838, and to W. S. Jevons and L. Walras in the 1870's. Econometrics emerged as a separate discipline in the 1920's and 1930's and continues to flourish even though there are some signs of diminishing returns. Mathematical sociology has now become a well-recognized discipline, as the appearance of a large textbook in the field indicates. The applications of mathematics to psychology have become very important in the past ten years or more, and in all the social sciences today a knowledge of mathematics is a substantial asset, and mathematical ignorance an even more substantial liability. As in any other movement, mathematization is sometimes carried to excess, and even though it is harder to talk nonsense in mathematics than it is in literary language, it seems to be quite possible to say nothing, and the mere fashion for mathematizing has occasionally done more harm than good. Still, the net gain on the intellectual balance sheet is very clear.

FUTURE DEVELOPMENTS IN THE SOCIAL SCIENCES

We may perhaps conclude this survey by taking a brief look at some possible future developments in the social sciences, at least to the point of indicating deficiencies which the future may correct. The most serious deficiency in the social sciences at present is, undoubtedly, the extreme inadequacy of its present methods of collecting data, even though these methods are undergoing rapid improvement. It was barely a generation ago that we relied even for our economic data on the accidents of tax collections and customs records, and our data collection is still very far from adequate. In other aspects of the social system, a systematic and continuous data collection has hardly begun. We can consider the parallel with meteorology. The atmosphere is a very complex system, extending over the whole surface of the globe. If we are to understand it, we must have meteorological stations collecting data continuously, spaced at reasonable intervals over the whole surface of the globe, and feeding their data into a central processing agency. We are still a long way from this ideal, even in meteorology, and it is not surprising that weather prediction is so inadequate when over large areas of the globe adequate meteorological stations are absent. Just as the globe is encircled by an atmosphere, so it is enveloped in a sociosphere. The sociosphere consists of all human beings on the earth and their relations with each other, with the organizations that they create, and with their physical environment. It is dense in New York, and thin in Antarctica, but is hardly anywhere absent. If this concept seems large to the imagination, it is no larger than the reality that we have to study. Information about the sociosphere, however, is even spottier than information about the atmosphere. A remarkable little volume has recently been published, entitled *World Handbook of Political and Social Indicators*, by Bruce M. Russett *et al.*, which brings together into a single volume a good deal of the information that is available, by countries. This is depressingly small enough, but there is even less information available by regions. What is desperately needed is a network of social data stations, somewhat analogous to meteorological stations, spaced at fairly regular intervals over the human population, say one to every ten million people, which will continually collect, process, and relay social data from which we can build up a continuing image of the succession of states of the sociosphere in all its manifold aspects. The political problems of setting up an agency of this kind are not negligible. Information, unfortunately, is rarely politically neutral, and the truth is threatening to those whose power rests on the ignorance of others. Some forms of data are obviously harder to collect than others. On the whole, however, it has been the experience of social scientists that when data are gathered in a systematic, unemotional, and scientific manner, an astonishing amount can be collected. There are also a good many different methods of collecting social data. The sample survey is only one. The sampling of the whole information process of the society as it is thrown up in the mass media, in statistical reports, and in the whole mass of printed material, can provide an enormous amount of information which can be checked and processed for internal consistency. Furthermore, the very process of collecting information would reveal the gaps and would create pressures to fill them.

A system of continuous world social data collection and processing would have an enormous impact, not only on the theoretical structures of the social sciences, which would have to adapt themselves to the accumulating statistical images, but would also have an enormous impact on the social system itself. Knowledge, as we have seen, is an essential part of the social system. Any fundamental change in the knowledge about it changes the social system itself. We might expect this impact to be particularly great on the international system. This operates at present by an information processing system which seems to be positively designed to produce misinformation. On the whole, the people who make decisions in the international system in the various countries seem to be insulated even from their own social scientists, and operate by what someone has called "club knowledge"—the kind of knowledge that is derived from gossip in clubs. A quantified and carefully sampled process of data collection in this field could hardly fail to have an enormous impact, and it would go a long way toward preventing the gross mistakes and appalling dangers that now characterize it.

THE NEW KNOWLEDGE AND THE GREAT IDEAS

The question of the relation of the enormous upsurge of new knowledge which is now taking place in all disciplines to the great ideas of the past is important and also very difficult. There are two extreme views which I think we must reject. One is that the new knowledge is so enormous and so important and so new that the great ideas of the past are really irrelevant. This is a view that regards the history of thought, or indeed almost any history, as a matter of idle curiosity, suitable for the academic specialist but quite irrelevant to the great problems of the day. At the other extreme, we find the view that in regard to social systems and the understanding of man himself at least, nearly all of what can be said has been said in the past, and that our new knowledge is merely so much busy work, which adds very little to the insights of the great minds of the ages. Thus, at a conference recently, a high official of the State Department remarked that he didn't think he had anything to learn from the social sciences; that whenever he wanted to solve a problem in international relations he went back to Thucydides and read about the Peloponnesian War!

One sets up extremes, of course, to point out that the ideal must lie somewhere between them. I must confess, however, I am much more frightened by the people who think that we are still fighting the Peloponnesian War than by people who think that anything written before they went to college can be put in the ash can. We can put the matter dramatically by pointing out that where knowledge doubles every X years, the date "X years ago" divides the acquisition of knowledge into two equal parts. The knowledge of chemistry, for instance, at least as measured by the volume of publications, is supposed to double every fifteen years. Consequently, looking at it from 1965, the date 1950 divides the history of chemistry into two equal parts. Before the scientific revolution, we might reasonably suppose that it took several hundred years for knowledge to double, in which case the voices of the ancients might have as great or even greater weight than the moderns. When, however, knowledge doubles in every generation, the present becomes overwhelmingly more important than the past, and the idea that we have to go back to the past to gain our knowledge seems almost absurd.

In the case of the knowledge of man and society, the situation is perhaps a little different from what it would be in the physical sciences. In the physical sciences, for instance, folk knowledge is quite unimportant. In our knowledge of social systems, this is not so. In spite of the rise of scientific knowledge, folk knowledge is still an important part of the total, whether we wish to admit this or not. Folk knowledge, on the other hand, does not exhibit this phenomenon of continual growth, and at this level we might very well argue that Thucydides is as relevant today as he was 2,500 years ago. Certainly, the economist who goes back to Adam Smith will often find unsuspected insights which may turn out to be highly relevant to his present problems. Similarly, the political scientist who goes back to Aristotle or Machiavelli will likewise find them discussing a world that is by no means alien to his own. On the other hand, we must recognize also that the new world of information processing and collection has opened up enormous resources which were not available to the ancients or even to those of the eighteenth and nineteenth centuries. In almost all aspects of life, the twentieth century represents a unique transition and a very sharp break with the past. An awareness of the great works of the past can protect us against the fashions and fads of the moment, and it has to be confessed that in every age there are intellectual fashions. In an age of change as rapid as this, however, the past can also become an obstacle to the understanding of the new world into which we are moving, for the siren voices of the past may persuade us that the world has not changed when in fact it has changed and changed enormously. It is now truer than ever before that "what's past is prologue,"—a place to begin but not a place to linger.

Kenneth E. Boulding

BIBLIOGRAPHY

ARROW, KENNETH. *Social Choice and Individual Values.* New York: John Wiley and Sons, Inc. (2nd ed.), 1963.

BLACK, DUNCAN. *The Theory of Committees and Elections.* Cambridge, Eng.: Cambridge University Press, 1958.

BUCHANAN, JAMES M., and TULLOCK, GORDON. *The Calculus of Consent.* Ann Arbor: University of Michigan Press, 1962.

BURKE, KENNETH. *A Grammar of Motives.* New York: Prentice-Hall, Inc., 1945; and George Braziller, Inc., 1955.

CAMPBELL, ANGUS, *et al. The American Voter.* New York: John Wiley and Sons, Inc., 1960. This is the major volume to be published from the work on preelection behavior by the Institute for Social Research, University of Michigan.

COLEMAN, JAMES S. *Introduction to Mathematical Sociology.* New York: Free Press of Glencoe, Inc., 1964.

CYERT, RICHARD M., and MARCH, J. G. *The Behavioral Theory of the Firm.* Englewood Cliffs, N.J.: Prentice-Hall, Inc., 1963.

DALZIEL, HUGH DUNCAN. *Communication and Social Order.* Englewood Cliffs, N.J.: Bedminster Press, 1962.

DOWNS, ANTHONY. *An Economic Theory of Democracy.* New York: Harper and Brothers, 1957.

HAGEN, EVERETT. *On the Theory of Social Change: How Economic Growth Begins.* Homewood, Ill.: Dorsey Press, 1962.

HITCH, CHARLES J., and McKEAN, ROLAND N. *The Economics of Defense in the Nuclear Age.* New York: Atheneum Publishers, 1965.

KAHN, H. *Thinking About the Unthinkable.* New York: Horizon Press, Inc., 1962.

KUHN, ALFRED. *The Study of Society, A Unified Approach.* Homewood, Ill.: Richard D. Irwin, Inc., 1963.

LEONTIEF, W. W. "The Structure of the U.S. Economy," *Scientific American* (April, 1965), p. 25, for a short exposition.

LEWIN, KURT. *Resolving Social Conflicts.* New York: Harper and Brothers, 1948.

LINDBLOM, CHARLES E., and DAHL, ROBERT A. *Politics, Economics, and Welfare.* New York: Harper and Brothers, 1953.

LUCE, ROBERT D., and RAIFFA, HOWARD. *Games and Decisions.* New York: John Wiley and Sons, Inc., 1957.

McCLELLAND, DAVID CLARENCE. *The Achieving Society.* Toronto: D. Van Nostrand Company, Inc., 1961.

McLUHAN, H. M. *The Gutenberg Galaxy.* Toronto: University of Toronto Press, 1962.

———. *Understanding Media; the Extensions of Man.* New York: McGraw-Hill Book Co., Inc., 1964.

RAPOPORT, ANATOL. *Fights, Games, and Debates.* Ann Arbor: University of Michigan Press, 1960.

RICHARDSON, LEWIS F. *Arms and Insecurity: A Mathematical Study of the Causes and Origins of War.* Pittsburgh: Boxwood Press, 1960.

———. *Statistics of Deadly Quarrels.* Pittsburgh: Boxwood Press, 1960.

RUSSETT, BRUCE M., *et al. World Handbook of Political and Social Indicators.* New Haven: Yale University Press, 1964.

SCHELLING, T. C. *Strategy of Conflict.* Cambridge: Harvard University Press, 1960; and New York: Oxford University Press (Galaxy Books), 1963.

NOTE TO THE READER

Professor Boulding notes that the "scientific image" of social systems is a very recent development. Yet, as he also says, the "philosophical image" as well as the "folk image" that men have of society exert great influence on human behavior. For both notions *Great Books of the Western World* is rich in material. Perhaps the easiest way of locating it is to consult the INVENTORY OF TERMS in the *Syntopicon*, under the headings: "Economics," "Political Science," and "Sociology."

What *Great Books* contains on the nature of the science of economics can be found by consulting WEALTH 9. The nature of political science as the art or science of governing is indexed under STATE 8d.

Professor Boulding discusses the methods employed by the social scientist in terms of what he calls statistical images and theoretical models. Material on both these ideas is contained in *Great Books*, although not in these terms. Statistical images are obtained from measurement, and the art of measurement is the topic of MATHEMATICS 5a. A theoretical model is, in some respects, a hypothesis, and to this subject the whole of Chapter 36 of the *Syntopicon* is devoted. The topic most relevant to this discussion is HYPOTHESIS 4.

Biological

GEORGE GAYLORD SIMPSON

One of the world's leading authorities on evolutionary theory and fossil animals, George Gaylord Simpson is Alexander Agassiz Professor of Vertebrate Paleontology at the Museum of Comparative Zoology, Harvard University. Before coming to Harvard in 1959, he was Professor of Vertebrate Paleontology at Columbia University, a position he had held since 1945, and Curator of Fossil Mammals and Birds at the American Museum of Natural History in New York City. As a staff member of that museum for thirty-two years, he published widely on extinct vertebrates, and his paleontological fieldwork took him to remote areas in Argentina, Venezuela, Brazil, and many parts of the United States. Professor Simpson was born in 1902 in Chicago. After study at the University of Colorado, he received his doctorate in 1926 from Yale University. He has received many honorary degrees, the latest being that bestowed upon him in June, 1965, by Cambridge University, England. The Meaning of Evolution *(1949) is perhaps the most widely known of his numerous publications; it has been translated into ten foreign languages. Other books by Professor Simpson include:* Tempo and Mode in Evolution *(1944),* Quantitative Zoology *(1939; revised, 1960),* The Major Features of Evolution *(1953),* Horses *(1951),* Life *(1957; revised, 1965),* Principles of Animal Taxonomy *(1961), and* This View of Life *(1964). He lives in Cambridge, Massachusetts, with his wife, the psychologist Anne Roe.*

Sciences

Biology is the study of life (Greek: *bios*, "life," and *logos*, "study"). "Life" is an abstraction definable in many different ways, but its objective manifestation is in the form of individual organisms. Biology is, then, fundamentally the study of organisms, and this was the classical orientation of the biological sciences as a whole. Most organisms, including practically all visible to the naked eye, are clearly identifiable as either plants or animals. The primary subdivision of biology, or its basic specialization, was, therefore, its separation into botany and zoology. That dichotomy is still necessary in some branches of biology and at some levels of research. It is also still followed in a number of colleges and universities. In most biological research, however, the orientation implicit in the botany-zoology division has become decidedly secondary. It is now subordinate to divisions based on levels of organization and on functions and processes.

It has long been known that there are different levels of organization in living things: from atoms through molecules, organelles (structurally and functionally distinct parts of cells), cells, tissues, organs, individuals, demes (local, reproducing populations), species, and communities (of numerous interacting species) to the world of life as a whole.[1] Biology, in its classical organismic orientation, did take all these levels into account but it centered on individuals and tended to relate the other levels

---

[1] There are complications, such as the fact that some whole individuals are single cells, but they do not seriously affect the generality of the hierarchy.

to them, both descriptively and in terms of function. But starting in the nineteenth century and up to the last few years, an additional and, one might almost say, a competing orientation has developed. This centers on molecules, and it tends to interpret other levels, up to and even beyond that of individuals, in terms of chemical and physical processes within cells and, in some cases, without regard for any supramolecular level.

The reasons for this development were both philosophical and practical. It has been claimed that the physical sciences are more basic than the biological sciences and that progress in the latter would involve the reduction of biological phenomena to physical or mechanical principles. Then, too, as a practical matter, biologists have been increasingly successful in finding the underlying chemical and physical concomitants of various vital processes. Thus they have reduced such things as digestion, energy release, many organic syntheses, and other biological events to molecular terms, which could be said, in some sense of the word, to "explain" the events.

The greatest triumph (up to now) of this reductionist approach to biology has been the determination of the structure and, although as yet only in part, the functioning of DNA (deoxyribonucleic acid), the family of molecules on which heredity, development, and intracellular syntheses largely depend. A case can be made for the claim that DNA is involved in the most basic of all biological phenomena, from the origin of life onward. Concomitantly, the revolutionary development of modern physics with relativity, quantum theory, the indeterminacy principle, etc., had reinforced its claim to be the fundamental science. The reduction of biological phenomena to those of physics and chemistry thus came to seem, in the eyes of many biologists and physical scientists, not only practicable but also the essential orientation for modern biology. Some have even maintained that explanatory theory in biology must *necessarily* be reductionist.

The brilliant successes of the biochemists and molecular biologists attracted increasing attention. An ever wider range of problems was seen as susceptible to this approach. It seemed for a time that this orientation in biology would permanently replace organismic orientation, and that it alone would lead to further important advances. This has proven to be an unnecessarily narrow and stultifying point of view. No biologist would deny that study at the molecular level is absolutely essential in biology. But it is now being appreciated again that innumerable biological problems, including the most important of all, require study at higher levels, in individuals and in populations. It is also now generally recognized that molecular biology itself is relatively fruitless and certainly is not really understood until it is related to the higher levels of organs and organisms.

In the light of these new developments, it is interesting to remember what biochemists temporarily forgot: that the biological significance of DNA itself was discovered by organismic and not by molecular biologists. As a chemical DNA was known for many years without any appreciation of its importance or knowledge of its function. It was organismic genetical experimentation that showed, first, that the principal role in inheritance is played by the chromosomes, where most of the DNA occurs, and, finally, that it is the DNA itself that constitutes genes and carries the greatest part of the message of heredity. Given that lead, the molecular biologists concentrated on DNA and found that it occurs as enormously large molecules in which four kinds of structural units are repeated in various different orders. Their arrangement constitutes (metaphorically) a code with an extremely large number of possible combinations or (again metaphorically) messages. Through a complex of intermediate steps, now also becoming fairly well known, the DNA message specifies the formation of particular protein molecules which, in turn, go far toward determining what further chemical activities will occur in a living cell. It is largely (although not quite exclusively) through these processes that development is directed. DNA in a fertilized ovum or egg, derived from parents, is the main determinant of heredity that causes development of, say, a seed into a rosebush or an embryo into a man. Moreover, in the developed bush or adult man, DNA continues to be a basic part of the physiological apparatus.

Those discoveries were exceptionally brilliant, but they solved certain problems only to bring us face-to-face with more numerous and more difficult problems. Here is where the newer orientation comes in, and reductionist molecular biology becomes not a goal in itself but a way toward more essential goals. The DNA message leads to a rosebush or a man by its reactions within a larger system, within, indeed, a developing organism as a whole. That process, still almost completely mysterious, will never be understood from any amount of knowledge of DNA alone. Its study is necessarily organismic and "compositionist," as opposed to reductionist.

There is still another aspect of the DNA molecule that requires a compositionist approach. We may take it as established that DNA does encode a message that says in effect (metaphorically, still) *Rosa* or *Homo*. But surely to understand this we must also know where the message came from; how it ever happened to be written. It is incredible, and indeed we now know definitely that it is not true, that the message simply arises spontaneously within a given molecule of DNA. How it does arise is the basic problem of evolutionary biology, which will be discussed later in some detail. Here it suffices to note that study of DNA from this point of view must be at a level even higher than the organismic: it is essentially a matter of whole populations of organisms through generations of time.

DNA is thus a striking example of the necessity for a broad biological orientation involving all levels of organization.

There are innumerable other biological phenomena that cannot be studied at the molecular level, or not exclusively there. Evolution, the most pervasive of all biological principles, is one, and not only in its relationship to DNA already noted. For humans, who have the most complex and effective nervous system ever evolved, study of that system is also supremely important. It can and must be studied at the molecular level within single nerve cells, but it will never be understood from that alone. It is indeed a *system* and can be fully understood only as such, that is, as a whole and further in its functional relationship to the entire organism in which it occurs. That leads in turn to a study of behavior, a study necessarily focused at the organismic level. Further, it then becomes apparent that for most animals comprehension of individual behavior requires a still higher level of compositionist study, for individuals normally live and behave as members of populations and of species.

In summary, this matter of levels of study and of reductionist or compositionist orientations in biology can be illustrated by a simple example. Observation may start, as it inevitably did in the history of biology, with an individual organism, say a lion. We want to "understand" and to "explain" that animal in one or another of the many senses of these words. One way is to consider the development of the lion from an egg derived from its mother and fertilized by its father. Much (but not all) of that development can be reduced to chemical processes ultimately based on DNA. Many other things about the lion can also be reduced to physical and chemical terms—its digestion of zebra meat, for example. But now, looking in the other (the compositionist) direction, what do these things mean in terms of the lion? Its digestion of zebra meat, and all the other structural and functional adaptations that enable the lion to catch and utilize zebras, mean quite simply that it is able to stay alive. Its reproductive processes are significant on a still higher level, as they maintain a continuing population of lions and the whole species *Panthera leo*. Both of these contrasting explanatory statements are scientific and true: a lion digests zebra meat *because* it has the organs, enzymes, and the whole biochemical apparatus required, and it does so *because* that keeps the lion alive and eventually permits continuation of the species. Still a third type of explanatory statement is historical rather than reductionist or compositionist: the lion exists and lives on zebras *because* it evolved from primitive ancestors and became specially adapted to its present way of life.

The reorientation of biology is not a matter of returning to a fully compositionist, organismic, and populational approach; this has never been wholly neglected, although it was for a time relatively underemphasized. Neither is it a matter of focusing on the reductionist, molecular approach; this has always been and will always be needful, but it has recently been relatively overemphasized. The desirable reorientation is a balance of all approaches. In spite of some dissenters and myopic specialists, biology today is indeed approaching such a balance. The overall view of a balanced orientation is best seen in evolutionary biology, and the rest of this discussion will be devoted mainly to that field.

THE ORIGIN OF LIFE

A pressing problem about the evolutionary history of life is how life began in the first place. This subject has had a curious history. The ancient Greeks and most Europeans through the Middle Ages and into early modern times assumed that living organisms are spontaneously generated from nonliving matter: for example, insects from mud and rats from old rags.[2] That rotten flesh could give rise to maggots seemed even more obvious. Those ideas were also orthodox tenets (if not technically dogmas) among Christian theologians, who interpreted the Bible as supporting them. The theologians attacked Francesco Redi (1626-97) for his experiments that indicated the great improbability of such spontaneous generation. Many biologists also considered the question still open until the work of Louis Pasteur (1822-95), which was so extensive and so careful that it was taken as virtually proving that living organisms arise only as the offspring of likewise living parents, a doctrine sometimes called *biogenesis*. By this time most theologians supported the view that life did not originate spontaneously (by *abiogenesis*) but was divinely created.

The scientific evidence of Pasteur and others and the doctrinal climate of opinion inhibited anything but occasional speculation until rather recently. Some biologists, including Darwin, thought that life might originally have arisen "spontaneously"—that is, by natural causes—but that there was no real evidence and no scientific way of studying the problem. Furthermore, Pasteur's "proof" of biogenesis was widely misunderstood. All that had really been established was that the spontaneous rise of living organisms under *present* conditions is extremely improbable. That has little or no bearing on the *first* origin of life under far earlier conditions, on a young earth with no previous organisms to preempt ways of life and with quite different physical and chemical characteristics of air and waters. Biologists have increasingly come to believe that although biogenesis (life only from life) is now universal, the far-distant origin of life was abiogenetic (from the nonliving by natural processes). That theory has become an active field of study.

2 Discussions of spontaneous generation in GBWW can be located by consulting the *Syntopicon* under ANIMAL 8*b*.

Fossils would provide the only direct evidence of the earliest living things, but none have been found and it is improbable that any exist in a form still recognizable. The oldest fossils clearly and definitely identifiable are less than two billion years old. That is a respectable age, but those organisms were already at a level of cellular organization comparable with present-day seaweeds. They are far beyond any merely incipient stage in the origin of life.

In the absence of direct evidence, there are still scientific ways of approaching the problem. First, we can extrapolate from our now very extensive knowledge of molecular biology and determine, within reasonable limits, how life could have arisen from the nonorganic. Second, we can reproduce in the laboratory conditions that could have existed on a primitive, prebiotic earth (that is, before life arose) and observe experimentally whether possible molecular forerunners of life actually arise under such conditions. Both approaches are currently under intensive study, and the results concur: the origin of life through known molecular configurations and processes is indeed plausible, and probable molecular forerunners of organisms do appear from nonorganic sources under experimental conditions in the laboratory.

From studies of the atmospheres of other planets and by extrapolation from the probable history of ours, it is probable that the prebiotic atmosphere of the earth contained little or no free oxygen but did contain water vapor, ammonia, methane (a simple compound of carbon and hydrogen, CH_4), carbon monoxide and carbon dioxide, and free nitrogen and hydrogen. It has been demonstrated that in such a mixture of gases the passage of electric discharges, ultraviolet light, or even (in special circumstances) simple heat can produce more complex molecules, including amino acids and nucleotide bases. The latter two compounds are building blocks for proteins and nucleic acids, respectively, which in turn are the most characteristic and indispensable molecules in living organisms.

It is, then, not only plausible but also highly probable that the primitive earth acquired a rich complex of organic but, as yet, nonliving molecules, probably, but not necessarily or exclusively, as a rich solution or "soup" in primordial seas. The precise chemical details of what followed are uncertain, not because there is no probable way to proceed from that condition to living cells, but because there are numerous possibilities, and the evidence so far does not clearly indicate a choice among them. It is, in any event, unnecessary to follow the technical chemical processes here. The really important thing from a biological point of view is that at some early stage a primitive process of natural selection could set in. For this to occur there must be molecules capable of causing the production of replicas of themselves; these molecules must vary in exact structure and composition; and some of the variations must influence the speed and efficiency of replication. Natural selection would then automatically and necessarily begin. The more effectively reproducing molecules would inevitably increase faster than the less efficient ones and ultimately at their expense.

Nucleic acids, and particularly DNA, are just such molecules: causing the production of replicas of themselves, almost endlessly variable in detail, and potentially different in efficiency of replication. Their replication depends not only on themselves but also on materials, energy, and organization in their environment. Selection would favor those that happened to be associated with such requisites for replication even if only by chance at first. Selection would then enormously favor a system that was organically bound together and organized for replication of both its DNA and the associated structures and molecules. Such a system is a living cell.

According to this view, now held in broad outline by almost all students of the subject, the earliest living systems were dependent on the presence of organic but nonliving molecules in their environment. If nothing further had happened, life would never have gotten beyond its most primitive stages and might well have become extinct some two billion or more years ago. The living systems, organisms, or cells escaping that necessity would again be favored enormously by natural selection. There were such cells: they were photosynthetic. Photosynthetic organisms, which include all our green plants today, can obtain all needed energy from sunlight and all needed materials from simple and widely available nonorganic sources: water, carbon dioxide, and a number of mineral ions.

There must have been a time when most or all organisms were photosynthetic cells. The fossil record of microscopic seaweeds up to two billion years old, previously mentioned, may date from that time. Photosynthetic organisms release free oxygen, and this produced another crucial change. Its release on a grand scale radically modified the atmosphere not only by the presence of oxygen itself (about 20 percent in our current atmosphere) but also by oxidizing and eliminating most of the ammonia, methane, and hydrogen. This led to the evolution of organisms deriving materials and energy by eating the photosynthetic organisms, and utilizing that energy by respiration involving oxygen. In other words, animal life began.

The ultimate triumph of experimental biology might be the production of an unquestionably living cell from nonorganic materials in a laboratory. In principle, there is no apparent reason why that could not be done, although the simplest living cells are so extremely, almost incredibly, complex that such a feat is technically beyond us and may remain so for a long time. The actual events by which life did arise undoubtedly took eons of time. They are now long past and unrecorded, but we are beginning to have quite clear, if not completely detailed, ideas about what happened. The spontaneous generation of the *first* living things did occur. If the conditions existing on the earth at that time were as described, that occurrence seems almost inevitable.

LIFE OUTSIDE THE EARTH

Once the origin of life is seen as a natural event and a highly probable, even inevitable, one under favorable circumstances, the thought arises that life may have originated more than once and may occur elsewhere in the universe than on earth. Present intensified interest in the origin of life is, indeed, stimulated by that possibility and by the beginning of the exploration of space. This combination is highly exciting to scientist and layman alike, and it has received a veritable flood of publicity, some responsible but much of it egregiously irresponsible. The results are both biased and confusing. It is saddening but not too surprising to observe that even some otherwise sensible scientists have made statements and proposals for which there are no sound scientific bases. For example, some "authorities" say that we *know* that extraterrestrial life exists. That is flatly false.

At present the only possibly direct evidence of extraterrestrial life is of two sorts. A meteorite that fell near Orgueil, France, in 1864, contains structures and molecules believed by some students to be of biotic origin, that is, to represent once living organisms or their products. The question cannot be considered entirely closed, but more recently it has been found (by Edward Anders and his associates) that some of the Orgueil fragments were contaminated with terrestrial biotic materials, probably deliberately so, or, in blunt words, faked. Other fragments have evidence of accidental contamination. Further, although some Orgueil fragments probably do contain genuine extraterrestrial molecules similar to those of earthly organisms, Ryoichi Hayatsu has recently shown that some, at least, of these are not compatible with biotic origin. At present, then, the supposed meteorite evidence falls far short of proof or even of reasonable probability.

The other possibly direct evidence consists of patches on Mars that seem to change color. Their infrared spectrum was believed to have bands such as might be produced by organic molecules or particularly by acetaldehyde (CH_3CHO). Now, in 1965, however, James S. Shirk and his associates have demonstrated that those bands are better explained as due to heavy water (deuterium oxide) and hence give no evidence at all on the possible presence of life. Further, W. M. Sinton, their original discoverer, has suggested that the bands are caused by the earth's atmosphere and have nothing to do with Mars, one way or the other.

Known conditions on other planets of our solar system are such that life must be virtually impossible on any of them except Mars. Even on Mars, conditions are so unlike those on earth that human life under natural conditions would be absolutely impossible and any intelligent or animal-like life next to impossible. There is no good evidence that life of any kind does exist on Mars or that conditions there have ever been such as to make the origin of life possible, still less probable. The most that can be said is that life on Mars may not be absolutely impossible.

Life, as we know it, could exist only on a planet not too different from earth. No planets outside of our own solar system are known. The universe is so enormously large that the existence of other planetary systems is plausible. Most astronomers now seem to agree that very large numbers of such systems do or may exist, but it is necessary to point out that this is not a scientific conclusion. It is speculation based on no objective evidence whatever, but on untested hypotheses about how planets might originate. If the speculation happened to be correct, then, according to current ideas of the origin of life, life probably would have arisen in some planetary systems other than ours. That nonscientific speculation still would not entail a probability that the further evolution of life elsewhere in the universe would result in anything manlike or intelligent. The evolution of man here on earth, where in fact man did arise, was not inevitable or predestined. It would be extremely improbable on any planet different from earth in any essential way, and it is incredible that no such differences would occur on planets elsewhere.

Now and in the foreseeable future, the only way we could learn of other planetary systems and of intelligent beings in them would be by receiving a radio (or analogous) message. An inexpensive watch for such a message would be justifiable, and for a time one was actually kept without result.[3] Even if the most improbable hopes for communication should finally be realized, an exchange of messages would take centuries or perhaps millions of years.

For many people the mere possibility that other intelligent beings exist somewhere in the universe is exciting, upsetting, or comforting. Yet this speculative possibility has no present biological significance. The situation is fraught with ethical, political, and scientific problems. The possibility of finding extraterrestrial life (on Mars, if anywhere) is sometimes given as a reason or justification for the space program. However, few biologists rationally believe that that extremely remote possibility, backed by no clear evidence, really warrants the expenditure of many billions of dollars for which so many better uses, scientific and otherwise, exist here on earth.

3 In April, 1965, a news report from the Soviet agency Tass claimed that Russian astronomers had detected radio waves sent by intelligent beings from outside our solar system. The report was immediately denied by the Russians themselves and on the face of it was evidently false.

THE EVOLUTION OF MAN

From the historical point of view, the origin of life, which has just been considered, stands at the opposite pole from the origin of man—one, the very first episode in the history of life, and the other, among the latest. Both happen to be among the most active and exciting fields of biological research at present. Accepting the theory of the evolutionary origin of man, anthropologists, archaeologists, paleontologists, and others have been intensely concerned with gaining increasing knowledge of the manner and concomitants of that origin. There have been many recent advances in this field of study, and interest in it continues.

All humans now living belong to a single species—a fact that should be strongly emphasized and endlessly repeated in these days of nonsensical racial strife. That species, *Homo sapiens*, is the only one extant in its genus (*Homo*) or family (Hominidae). It belongs to the same super-family (Hominoidea) as the ape family (Pongidae), and to the same suborder (Anthropoidea) as the two (sometimes reckoned as three) families of living monkeys (Cercopithecidae in the Old World and Cebidae' in the New). All of these animals, along with certain others that may be called pre-monkeys, make up the mammalian order Primates. The ancestry of man, of course, goes back to the very first manifestations of life on earth, but more particular study of that ancestry involves only the order Primates and its members.

Direct evidence of our ancestry and early relatives comes from known fossil primates, still all too scanty but considerably augmented by recent discoveries. The oldest known fossils definitely identifiable as primates come from the middle Paleocene epoch, approximately 65 million years ago. These primates differed but little from the unspecialized ancestry

GEOLOGICAL TIME SCALE		
Eras	Epochs	Approximate time since beginning, in years:
CENOZOIC (Age of Mammals. All fossils discussed in the text are from this era, and periods or epochs are not here specified for the earlier eras.)	RECENT PLEISTOCENE PLIOCENE MIOCENE OLIGOCENE EOCENE PALEOCENE	10,000 2,000,000 10,000,000 25,000,000 35,000,000 55,000,000 70,000,000
MESOZOIC		230,000,000
PALEOZOIC		600,000,000
PRECAMBRIAN	(Time of beginning unknown. Certainly over 3,000,000,000 and probably less than 5,000,000,000)	

of all the higher (placental) mammals and were classifiable among the most primitive primates as pre-monkeys (Prosimii). Their evolutionary level was approximately that of the still surviving tree shrews (Tupaiidae) of southern and eastern Asia. Only pre-monkeys are known through the rest of the Paleocene and all of the Eocene, that is, up to perhaps 45 million years ago. They were then abundant in North America and Europe. Their scarcity in Asia and absence in Africa at that time are doubtless only apparent; we simply lack evidence of their presence either because they were not preserved or because fossil deposits of appropriate age and nature have not been found. On the other hand, they almost certainly were really absent in South America and Australia.

Those diverse earliest primates included many lineages that became totally extinct but also included, as has now been fairly well established, the direct ancestors of the lemurs of Madagascar, the lorises and galagos of Africa and southern Asia, and the tarsiers of southeastern Asia. Although the latter groups are still living, they have progressed little beyond the earliest primates. They must have split off from the ancestry of monkeys, apes, and men in the Eocene at latest and probably in the Paleocene. The early pre-monkeys must also have included the actual ancestors of higher primates and hence of man, but the fossils of the connecting lineages have not yet been found. That lack is probably due to the fact that the higher primates arose in tropical areas where Paleocene and Eocene faunas are as yet practically unknown. Pending such discoveries, studies of the pre-monkeys do give a fairly clear idea of what our ancestors were like upward of 60 million years ago. Among many recent advances is the discovery, near Reims, France, of nearly complete remains of one of the earliest of all known primates.

Our scanty knowledge of the next step on the long road toward man comes mainly from the region of Al Fayyum, in the desert southwest of Cairo, Egypt. A few scraps of fossil primates have long been known from there, and quite recently our knowledge of them has been greatly increased by expeditions directed by Elwyn Simons. He has shown that these early Oligocene primates, some 35 million years old, had reached approximately the evolutionary level of the Old World monkeys. Some of them seem indeed to have been in or near the ancestry of those monkeys, but they were quite diversified and others include early gibbons and several species probably related to the enigmatic *Oreopithecus*. *Oreopithecus*, which lived in Tuscany, Italy, about 10 million years ago, was hailed only a few years past as a possible ancestor of man, perhaps filling in a long hiatus in our knowledge of that ancestry. New evidence, however, including these fossils from Al Fayyum, suggests that *Oreopithecus* represents an extinct sideline, which evolved in partial parallel to man but became extinct without achieving human status.

Other primates from Al Fayyum, still very poorly known even after the recent discoveries, seem to be very close to the common ancestry of the great apes (orangutan, gorilla, chimpanzee) and man. It is now Simons' opinion that one group of those fossils, *Propliopithecus*, formerly believed to be ancestral gibbons, is in fact the common ancestry of apes and man. The sum of this evidence (also supported by some other, less direct evidence) is that the Old World monkeys, the gibbons (lesser apes), and the great apes diverged as three distinct groups rather early, and that the specifically human line arose from that of the great apes at a later date. (A fourth, totally extinct lineage leading to *Oreopithecus* probably also diverged some time around the early Oligocene.)

The next recorded stages of ape and human evolution cover a long stretch from the Miocene into the Pliocene, more or less 20 to 10 million years ago. From that span a considerable number of mostly quite fragmentary fossils of higher primates have been found in Europe, Africa, and southern Asia. The best known is a form from the Miocene of Africa, generally called *Proconsul*, although it may not be generically distinct from some earlier named genus found in Eurasia. It was discovered about thirty years ago. Later, a nearly complete skull and various skeletal bones, as well as many jaw fragments and teeth, were found by L. S. B. and Mary Leakey and their associates on an island in Lake Victoria. It is not likely that exactly this form was ancestral to man, but it probably closely resembles our ancestors at that time: apelike (in fact definitely an ape in vernacular terms), small-brained, quadrupedal, not yet as specialized for arboreal life as are the living apes.

Later members of that complex, Pliocene in age and perhaps about 10 million years old, include *Ramapithecus* from India. It also has been known from fragments for many years, but its affinities have been disputed. It is now considered as a probable close ally or even a direct ancestor of man. This conclusion is supported in part by the most recent important discovery in this age span: a likewise early Pliocene creature found in Kenya by Leakey and called by him *Kenyapithecus*. It also has decidedly prehuman characteristics and may, indeed, prove to be the same as the Indian *Ramapithecus*. Unfortunately, these finds include only teeth and partial upper and lower jaws, so that they do not indicate much about the evolutionary level of our ancestors at that time. But they do strongly suggest that the lineage leading to man was separate from that of the great apes in the early Pliocene, at latest.

The next stage in human evolution is much better known. It is represented by the australopithecines, first discovered in South Africa in 1924. From complete skulls, jaws, and parts of skeletons found there, we can distinguish two species.[4] These creatures were bipedal, and in one

---

4 *Australopithecus africanus* and *Australopithecus robustus*. The latter is sometimes considered to represent a distinct genus, *Paranthropus*.

species the teeth are almost identical with those of modern man, but the size of the brain is still in the range of the living great apes. It thus appears—and this is quite understandable on evolutionary principles—that the brain was the last part of the body to acquire human status. The latest australopithecines were off the main line of descent, but some of the earliest forms are in or, unquestionably, very near that main line.

The Leakeys in 1959 discovered an australopithecine[5] in Olduvai (or Oldoway) Gorge, northern Tanganyika (now Tanzania). This discovery is important not so much for adding another specimen of this group as for placing this creature in its historical frame. The South African specimens were found helter-skelter in limestone fissures, but this one from East Africa was in an undisturbed stratigraphic sequence, containing a rich associated fauna, extremely crude tools perhaps made by this creature, and buried surfaces or living floors that it occupied. These beds also can be dated by radioactivity. The methods involved are still subject to large errors, and the dates are in dispute, but the results suggest that the East African australopithecines may have appeared there almost two million years ago. (They persisted over a long span of time, and the latest australopithecines are much younger.)

The most recent discoveries by the Leakeys in Olduvai Gorge (announced in 1964) include several fragmentary specimens of a distinct species contemporaneous with the previously known australopithecine. The Leakeys and some of their associates believe that this second species is so advanced that it should be placed in the same genus as modern man. Other authorities believe that it is another, somewhat more manlike australopithecine, comparable to the more manlike of the two South African species. The question cannot be settled until more complete specimens are found. In the meantime, the find confirms the opinion that at least two different manlike species existed at that early date (early Pleistocene in geological terms), only one of which was near or in man's own ancestry. There is some probability that it was the more recently discovered, more manlike species that made the crude artifacts found in the lowest stratigraphic levels of Olduvai Gorge. Some other recent discoveries (1965) by the Leakeys might indicate as many as three contemporaneous lines of early hominids, but the interpretation of these latest data is still dubious and disputed.

The next general stage of human evolution is represented by a large and far-flung group of specimens, the first of which was discovered in 1891-92 and is widely known as "Java man" or *"Pithecanthropus."* So-called Peking man, first clearly identified in 1927, is now generally agreed

---

5 This is the form widely publicized as *Zinjanthropus* or "zinj." Most students now place it in *Australopithecus*, and some believe that it belongs to the otherwise South African species *Australopithecus robustus.*

to belong to the same species. The most recent discoveries in this general group include jaws found in North Africa and a skull (not yet fully described or adequately classified) found in Olduvai Gorge at a level later than the definitely identified australopithecines there. There are more doubtful occurrences elsewhere which may or may not prove to belong in this group. Discoverers of fossil humans have a way of giving a new name to every find they make, whether or not a demonstrably new species or genus is represented, and a plethora of mostly invalid technical names has been proposed. The present consensus is that all these finds belong in the same genus as ourselves, *Homo*, and that most if not all of them belong to a single species, *Homo erectus*, immediately antecedent to our own, *Homo sapiens. Homo erectus* really differed little from us, but he had a heavier skull with massive brow ridges, no chin, and a distinctly lower average volume of brain.

The fossil record is notoriously incomplete, and there are still gaps that we would like very much to fill in. However, the main features of human descent are beginning to be adequately illustrated by fossils, and we can follow, even in considerable detail, the changes that led from an early placental mammal in the Cretaceous period, 75 million years or more ago, to ourselves today.

I t is obvious that *Homo sapiens* cannot have descended from any other species contemporaneous with us today. But it is also obvious that we are related in different degrees to all living animals and that our nearest living relatives are to be found among the Primates and almost certainly among the apes. Our relationship to other living animals makes possible still other approaches to the study of human evolution and affinities. Particularly active at present are studies of biochemical resemblances and differences, using the newest techniques of molecular biology.

Some studies refer to the chemical structure of complex, varying molecules, such as the widespread hemoglobins and the almost universal cytochromes, both families of molecules involved, in different ways, in the essential oxidation-reduction processes of organisms. For example, human and gorilla hemoglobins exhibit only a single, one-step difference in their chemical composition, and from this point of view, men and gorillas could be considered parts of a single population. (That is valid evidence of relationship, but other evidence shows that the total affinities are not all that close!)

Particularly interesting results have been obtained from serological or immunological studies. If serum (the liquid part of the blood) from one species A is injected into a second species B, proteins dissolved in the serum induce a defensive reaction in the blood of B. The result is the formation in B of specific antibodies, proteins inactivating the foreign proteins (antigens) introduced in the serum from A. The antibodies immunize the serum of B against that of A. If now the immune serum of B is mixed with the serum of A against which it is immune, a dense precipitate is formed. If the immune serum of B is mixed with serum from still a third species C, the amount of precipitate, if any, will depend on the resemblance between the serum proteins of that third species C and those of the first A (the one from which the original antigens came). Repetition of this procedure for the various combinations of species within a larger group provides quantitative estimates of the resemblances of serum proteins among all the species involved. It is reasonable to assume that these resemblances will usually tend to reflect the evolutionary relationships of the species.

Earlier studies, begun well over fifty years ago, gave only an approximate measure of overall resemblance among all the many proteins in sera. The results were interesting but not detailed or, it would seem, fully reliable as evolutionary evidence. Recent more complex methods distinguish among different families of serum proteins and thus give much more detailed and more precise evidence on relationships.

The biochemical evidence proves definitely that the earlier consensus was correct in concluding that the recent apes are the nearest living relatives of man. The biochemical evidence seems to show quite conclusively that, among the apes, man is much the most closely allied to the gorilla and the chimpanzee. This strongly suggests further important conclusions which, while not yet fully confirmed from the fossil evidence, are also not contradicted by it. The specifically human lineage apparently did not arise early and from the base of the ape family, but at a relatively late (Miocene?) date when the family already had split up into a number of different lineages of apes. Man clearly did not arise from the gibbon or orangutan lineages, but from the lineages of the gorilla and chimpanzee (which are closely related to each other and of quite late divergence), probably before the two species became separated. Thus our ancestors definitely were apes: they were proto-gorillas + chimps.

If man's anatomical and chemical makeup indicates close relationships with other primates, it is reasonable to suppose that basic elements of human behavior might also be elucidated by such comparisons. As with anatomy and chemistry, it is necessary to remember that each living species is the terminal point of a divergent line, specialized in its own way. One cannot simply extrapolate from monkeys or apes and say, "That is how our ancestors were." For example, the fact that gibbons are, on the whole, more primitive than man and of more ancient origin does not mean that our ancestors ever swung (brachiated) through the treetops as gibbons do. In fact, we know positively that such was not the case. That part of gibbon behavior and its anatomical basis arose far along in specifically gibbon history, a development in proto-gibbons already widely divergent from our ancestry. Nevertheless, judicious interpretation of nonhuman primate behavior can surely be expected to throw some light on the roots of our own behavior.

Such considerations have led to intense recent activity in the study of nonhuman primate behavior. Earlier observations in this field were for the most part either casual travelers' anecdotes or based on captive zoo or laboratory animals. Recently these have been supplemented, when not entirely replaced, by long, intensive study of the animals free in their native habitats. For example, studies of baboons in the London Zoo showed them most intensely and, it would appear, abnormally preoccupied with sexual activities. Later observations on free animals showed that sexual concerns are but part of a much wider range of behaviors. The zoo animals were simply neurotic in the absence of most of their normal interests. Such results are of exceptional interest, because baboons, as the studies of S. L. Washburn and Irven DeVore in Kenya have shown, possess a fairly complex organization of "tribal" society which may have been rather closely paralleled by proto-humans.

Other examples of important discoveries about primate behavior are provided by the work of Jane Goodall, a young British woman who has spent two years living with a group of chimpanzees in what is now Tanzania. For one thing, she found that chimpanzees not only use but also make rudimentary tools. It had long been believed that the making of tools was one respect in which the most primitive men differed absolutely from any other animals. Another unexpected observation is that chimpanzees, previously believed to be strict vegetarians, frequently pursue, capture, and eat other animals. This may help us to understand better the influence of food habits in the evolution of the australopithecines and earliest *Homo*.

Although laboratory studies may be misleading regarding the natural behavior of primates, or of any animals, they are indispensable for probing the nature and potentialities of animal intelligence, reactivity, and learning. Such studies are being intensified in this country, notably by setting up, with government support, a number of centers for primate research. Important results are already beginning to appear from them, but it is too soon to judge the extent of their eventual total contribution. Besides behavioral or comparative psychological experimentation, they provide material for biochemical, physiological, and anatomical (now especially microscopic) research.

We may find analogues and bases for human behavior in the behavior of other primate species, but the fact remains that human behavior differs vastly both in extent of repertory and in kind from that of any other species. Human culture is a phenomenon that surely arose slowly from prehuman social behavior, but it has become something unique, with an evolutionary potentiality of its own. Culture is the concern of anthropologists, psychologists, and sociologists from their several points of view, but it can also be considered as a biological phenomenon.[6] The biological and evolutionary roles of culture have not always been well understood and are worthy of renewed attention, which they are receiving.

That culture changes is an obvious fact, illustrated in a thousand ways, such as the contrast between the crude implements buried at the bottom of Olduvai Gorge and the artifacts on sale in a Woolworth's store. Nevertheless, the first attempts to study culture from an evolutionary point of view fell into disrepute for a time, mostly because some evolutionary anthropologists assumed that there is a single cultural sequence through which all cultural development has necessarily proceeded. In fact, cultures diverge, just as species do, and they are in the main adaptive to the conditions in which human groups live—conditions that vary radically from one time to another and from one place to another. The many ways in which, for example, Chinese culture differs from our own are not representative of any earlier stage through which our culture passed or of any later stage that we will reach. They are simply divergent, for the most part historically adaptive to the quite distinct Chinese milieu (both social and other). For another example, the culture of an uncivilized Indian tribe in the Amazon Basin is certainly simpler than ours (as the Chinese culture is not), and in some sense more primitive, but it is extremely unlikely that it closely resembles any cultural stage of our own ancestry.

It has frequently been claimed, usually by nonbiologists, that biological evolution has virtually ceased in man and has been replaced by cultural evolution. That is wrong on both counts: first, biological evolution has not ceased in man; and, second, cultural evolution is not an entirely separate process but is an outcome and, in the main, an extension of biological evolution. The most striking feature of biological evolution is that it is adaptive, it involves principally attainment, maintenance, and change of effective relationships between organisms and their environments. From this point of view, human culture is simply a biological adaptation, the broadest and most successful one that has yet evolved. Theodosius Dobzhansky, a leading student of these matters, has put the point as follows:

> The interrelations between the biological and the cultural components of human evolution may be brought out perhaps most clearly if we consider that they serve the same basic function—adaptation to and control of man's environments. . . . Adaptation of a living species to its environment

---

6 The word "culture" is an ambiguous one, defined in many different ways. As a biologist, I use it to refer to specifically human symbolization (especially language), artifacts (anything made by man), and the nongenetic (learned) components of human social behavior or interaction.

is the chief agency impelling and directing biological evolution. . . . The adaptation takes place through natural selection, which promotes the survival and reproduction of the carriers of some genetic endowments and inhibits others. The construction of man's body and the conformation of his intellect developed as they did because they made our species biologically highly successful. . . . The genetic basis of man's capacity to acquire, develop or modify, and transmit culture emerged because of the adaptive advantages which this capacity conferred on its possessors. . . .[7]

Those who consider biological evolution and cultural evolution entirely distinct processes, rather than interacting phases of one overall process, have introduced another fallacy. Since both are called "evolution," they have assumed that there is a close analogy between them and have tried to develop a theoretical structure for one in terms of the other. Biological evolution is much the better understood of the two, so that this fallacious approach has usually involved application of biological principles to cultural evolution. (Complications have been added when, as often happened, this procedure was followed by anthropologists and sociologists who did not understand the biological principles to begin with.)

In fact, there are such fundamental differences between biological evolution and the historical changes in culture that it is misleading to apply the same name to them. The processes of descent through the generations are totally different. Cultural "heredity" involves *only* "acquired" (learned) characters; biological descent includes *no* acquired characters. Biological characters are inherited only from the one or two parents of the immediately preceding generation; cultural elements may come from anyone on earth and directly from any time in recorded history. Genetic changes (mutations) arise without direct connection with needs or adaptations; cultural changes are often (although not necessarily) deliberately made with reference to a felt and usually to some extent adaptive need. Cultural "evolution" cannot be understood in this way. It becomes comprehensible when viewed as an adaptive sequence produced by and occurring within the sweep of biological evolution.

Finally, one can hardly summarize present knowledge of human evolution without touching on the subject of race. Reactions to this burning question are often so emotional, even among scientists, that they range from denial of the completely obvious fact that human races really do exist to the statement, even more absurd biologically, that human races are in fact distinct species, that they are at different levels of progress, and (wildest illogicality of all) that they differ in innate worth.

Races among humans are fully analogous to subspecies among other ani-

---

7 *Mankind Evolving* (New Haven: Yale University Press, 1962). *Heredity and the Nature of Man* (New York: Harcourt, Brace & World, Inc., 1964) is essentially a more popularized summary of Dobzhansky's earlier book.

mals. It might minimize emotion to consider them objectively as animal subspecies. There is not, in any species, a fixed and determinable number of subspecies. Subspecies all intergrade and are never clear-cut or fixed units persisting through the generations. All exchange genes marginally, and a "pure" race is a biological impossibility. Subspecies or other local populations differ in their average genetical makeup, perhaps occasionally because of chance genetic fluctuations, but usually and mainly because of adaptation to different environmental conditions. The origin of human races had a geographic background and was adaptive for the most part, if not completely. It thus makes sense to say of each race that it was "superior," that is, better adapted, where it originated, but it makes no sense to speak of overall "superiority" within the species. Furthermore, the geographic distributions have now been so greatly modified and cultural adaptation has so completely reduced bodily adaptation to insignificance that race has practically lost its original adaptive nature.

Racial differences in skin color and numerous other anatomical features, although never absolute, are obvious enough in extreme and even in average forms. It is natural to wonder whether differences might also exist in genetically influenced behavioral traits or in special abilities of various sorts, including mental. Many attempts have been made to find or define such possible differences. Some were not made in good faith, being undertaken either to indicate or to negate the presence of difference in ability. Others have been open to question on valid grounds. None is accepted by men of good faith as definitely showing racial differences in ability. Yet from what we know of the evolutionary processes involved, it would not be at all surprising if such differences did exist. But an *average* difference between races in *special* abilities would not warrant any biological value judgment of overall superiority or inferiority. Yet it takes a certain temerity for a biologist to make such a statement, because it is almost certain to call down a flood of abuse from biased colleagues. (Bias does not cease to be such because it is on the side of the angels.)

Anyway, even if we knew that some races are overall more intelligent than others—which we do *not* know and which is quite unlikely—that would have no adverse bearing on any race in a political or social sense. The political equality and social value of a human being are not canceled by the omnipresent genetical inequalities. We *are* all one species; we *are* all brothers; and we *are* our brothers' keepers.

THE PROCESSES OF ORGANIC EVOLUTION

Up to this point we have been mainly concerned with historical aspects of evolution, especially the earliest beginnings of life and one of the latest episodes, the origin of man. Tracing what has happened is one form of explanation and a major aim of scientific inquiry. It is not, however, complete or satisfying. We also want to delve more deeply into the processes that brought about the historical events and to understand their causes in a more profound and more explanatory way.

Any general theory and philosophy of biology must explain adaptation. Before Darwin, it was generally held, although with certain exceptions, that adaptation was inexplicable unless organisms were created just as they are and provided from the start with all the characteristics useful to them. A naturalistic explanation—one dependent only on objectively observable characteristics of the universe and eschewing supernatural intervention—was believed by most people, scientists and laymen alike, to be impossible. Nevertheless, J. B. Lamarck (1744-1829), one of the first to espouse a thoroughly evolutionary view of living nature, advanced two possibilities. First of all, he believed that all animals were constantly progressing from the lowest, spontaneously created every day, toward the highest, which of course was taken to be man. Such a view is naturalistic only in the sense that this progression was taken to be a characteristic of the universe. It explains nothing, because all it says is that evolution occurs because it is the nature of matter to evolve. As a subsidiary factor, Lamarck believed that organisms tend to deviate on their way to becoming men through being modified by their individual reactions to the environment—which modifications, or acquired characters, are inherited. As a hypothesis, this is both naturalistic and explanatory. The only thing against it, as we now know, is that it is not true. Lamarck's idea of constant progression of all animals toward man was equally untrue.

Lamarck's views were rejected by his contemporaries and immediate followers. Since those views were in fact incorrect, that rejection seems well justified, but adaptation was thereby still left without an evolutionary explanation. Darwin clearly saw that any evolutionary theory would remain incredible unless it accounted for adaptation. *The Origin of Species* (published in 1859) is at least as much concerned with explaining adaptation as with establishing that evolution has occurred.

Darwin proposed natural selection as the explanation not simply of the fact of evolution but also of its mainly adaptive course.[8] It is now virtually certain that this part of Darwin's views was correct as far as it went. (It has now been carried much further.) Darwin placed much less emphasis on other factors, but he also believed incorrectly that Lamarck had been right in supposing that effects of use and disuse of organs produced heritable results. Furthermore, he also considered, contrary to Lamarck, that effects of environmental conditions (such as stunting by cold) are heritable, and in this he was also wrong. Finally, he noted the existence of "variations which seem to us in our ignorance to arise spon-

8 Chapter IV of *The Origin of Species* is entitled "Natural Selection," in GBWW, Vol. 49, pp. 40–64.

taneously"—more or less what we now call mutations, although at that time true mutations could not be distinguished from some other sources of variation.

That Darwin's theories were incomplete was as manifest to him as to his followers. It also soon appeared that some of the comparatively unimportant parts of his complex of theories were probably incorrect. Thus, through the end of the nineteenth century and well into the twentieth, alternative and conflicting explanations of adaptation were advanced among biologists who agreed on the reality of evolution as an overall historical process. There thus arose several different schools of evolutionary theory, and it is instructive to outline briefly their theoretical tenets and their present status.

What became historically the most important anti-Darwinian school maintained that adaptation is caused by the inheritance of characters acquired either by use or disuse or by effects of the environment. Both of these two factors were also accepted by Darwin but considered unimportant by him. As it happens, they are also the only two points on which *The Origin of Species* was flatly wrong. Curiously enough, this school, once plausible but now clearly mistaken, came to be called Neo-Lamarckian outside of Russia. The curiosity is that the Neo-Lamarckian theory rejected the main feature of Lamarck's own theory and accepted factors flatly rejected by him. In Russia the theory of adaptation by inheritance of acquired characters was correctly recognized as stemming rather from Darwin than from Lamarck, although it was not officially recognized that it represented a minor and unsound part of Darwin's contribution. It was developed by I. V. Michurin, who seems to have been a sort of Russian Burbank—a successful empirical plant breeder whose knowledge of scientific principles was both slight and incorrect.

Michurin's views were developed into a more coherent theory and promoted by T. D. Lysenko, sometimes under the mildly comic name of "Soviet creative Darwinism." In 1948, Lysenko reported to the Lenin Academy that his theories had the support of Stalin and other Communist leaders. Lysenko thereupon became official czar of Russian biology, and numerous really capable Russian biologists went into obscurity or exile. We thus have the extraordinary phenomenon of a scientific theory, which incidentally happens to be wrong, made official by political means, and all others, including those that happen to be right, excluded from teaching or public hearing. Under Khrushchev, Lysenko apparently continued to dominate Russian biology, but there was some evidence that opposing views could be held, and perhaps even stated, with some degree of safety. After Khrushchev's downfall, Lysenko's position became untenable. In 1965, dispatches state that Lysenko is officially considered to have been in error and that all the textbooks must be rewritten once again. One reason for this is probably the fact that Lysenko's theories on heredity,

being in fact incorrect, failed to work out as a basis for practical agriculture. Still the suspicion lingers that a major factor is political and
that the scientific status of the rival theories is secondary.

In countries outside the Soviet Union it has long since been established
by open discussion, observation, and experimentation that so-called Neo-
Lamarckian theories, such as that of Lysenko, are scientifically invalid.

Another group of non-Darwinian theories, so diverse that it might be
misleading to call them a school, faintly echoes Lamarck to the extent that
it ascribes evolution to inexplicable inherent tendencies. These theories
are in general vitalistic: that is, most of them involve belief that life is in
essence something apart from or additional to the material and natural
universe. Some such theories are often frankly nonnaturalistic or super-
naturalistic and postulate what cannot be tested or concluded on
scientific grounds: that evolution follows a purposeful, foreordained
course. This course may or may not be conceived of as the pattern of
divine creation. Others eschew mention of divinity but still maintain that
the course is set a priori by some inherent vital factor and that evolution
proceeds orthogenetically: that is, in undeviating ways as if toward a
goal. In fact, the record of evolutionary history is now sufficient to
demonstrate that its course definitely has not been orthogenetic.

In scientific inquiry, vitalism, like Neo-Lamarckism, is now almost
entirely a thing of the past. This has come about not because vitalism has
been proved to be incorrect but just because it cannot be studied
scientifically one way or the other. Up to now vitalism has been a futile
and unnecessary hypothesis. Vitalism survives, when at all, as a theological or philosophical means of reconciling some religions with the facts
of evolution.

Around 1900, and for a generation or so thereafter, experimental
biologists were concerned mainly with what is now considered classical
or Mendelian genetics. The gene was to biology then what DNA has
been more recently: an exciting breakthrough, or the banner on a band-
wagon. Mutations were recognized, and we learned how to follow the
mutant forms of a gene (its alleles) or of chromosomes through their
effects on plants and animals bred in the laboratory. Although it was not
then known just what mutations are—and still is not completely known—
it became clear that they affect development and produce individuals with
new hereditary variations. Mutations were thus correctly recognized as
the basic materials for evolutionary change.

Such discoveries generate enthusiasm, and enthusiasts are all too
likely to become temporarily blinded. (The parallel with DNA is still
evident.) Some of the genetical enthusiasts decided that mutations are
not only materials for evolution but are, in themselves, the whole process.
They supposed that mutation produced new kinds of organisms, which
became new species either forthwith or by accumulation of further

mutations. Adaptation occurred when a mutation just happened to coincide with a possible way of life. Those early geneticists misunderstood and seriously underestimated the old problem of adaptation. Mutations are random, not in the sense that all kinds of change are possible and equally probable, but random in the sense of being adaptive only by chance, and a rare chance at that. They are seldom changes in the direction actually followed by evolution, and perhaps never are adaptively related to the cause (usually unknown) of the mutation. For example, heat can produce mutations, but these do not affect the heat tolerance of mutant individuals.

If adaptation arose from mutation alone, then adaptations would be due to an extremely improbable chance. But as the naturalists and field biologists well knew, that is impossible, and the experimentalists who advanced that hypothesis were plainly wrong. The astonishing complexities and complete universality of adaptation cannot possibly be accounted for by chance alone. Darwin was certainly right in seeking a nonrandom, antichance factor to account for adaptation. Selection is such a factor, as its very name indicates.[9] For these reasons, almost all the nongenetical biologists remained convinced that Darwinian selection is essential to adaptation; whether or not it is the only essential is another question. The Neo-Darwinian school of the turn of the century, with August Weismann (1834-1914) as an eminent example, discarded the so-called Neo-Lamarckian elements in Darwin's work. They ascribed adaptation entirely to natural selection, as Darwin had also done for the most part.

In retrospect, the Neo-Darwinians were right as far as they went, and they made an advance beyond their exemplar, Darwin himself. Yet even as regards natural selection, they did not fully grasp the essentials of the process, either in generalities or in specifics. They also had as yet no real understanding of the genetic system, the origin of variations, and the interaction of those factors with natural selection.

From about 1900 to about 1930 most geneticists, on one hand, and most organismic biologists, on the other, were advancing two apparently conflicting views on the causes of evolution, both of which were, in fact, correct for the most part, but each of which taken alone was a highly inadequate partial truth. Our present understanding of evolution, although ultimately indebted to Darwin, essentially began with realization that those views were not contradictory but complementary. When put together, to be sure, they still did not provide a complete explanation of adaptation or other aspects of evolution, but they did finally give a

9 This is now so obvious that one can only be amazed at the stupidity of some critics of Darwin. Certain of them, especially among the vitalists, attacked him on the grounds that natural selection—the preeminently *non*random element in evolution—depended solely on chance!

relatively complete base on which such an explanation can be built. The base was provided especially in a series of fundamental books published in the 1930's and 1940's by geneticists, biometricists, systematists, paleontologists, and other organismic biologists. The emerging theory, the work of so many hands, has no such simple eponym as "Darwinism" or "Lamarckism." It is commonly called the synthetic theory, because it arose as a literal synthesis of results in various different fields of biological research.[10]

Our understanding of adaptation and of other aspects of evolution is certainly not complete, but it has recently reached a remarkable level of reliability and profundity. That is well illustrated by two among the best recent books on both broad and detailed aspects of evolution. Verne Grant's *The Origin of Adaptations* is oriented on just the central problem we have been following. Ernst Mayr's *Animal Species and Evolution*, as its name indicates, is concerned in greater part with no less important problems of the nature and origin of species and the processes of speciation. The following exposition of our present knowledge of adaptation and speciation derives from those and many other studies, but it is here necessarily extremely abbreviated and put in different words.

A daptation is a relationship between organisms and their environments or, still more broadly, their whole ways of life. In an individual organism the basis for its adaptation must be an inherited developmental pattern and the reaction of that fixed but not inflexible pattern with the activities and surroundings of the organism throughout its life. Determinants for the inherited pattern must be in the cell—a fertilized egg or zygote in most plants and animals—from which the individual develops. In terms of communication theory (which, however, must be taken more metaphorically than literally), the zygote or other developing cell must contain information derived from one or more of its parents, and that information must specify the hereditary characteristics of its species as well as the hereditary individual variation, which is all but universal within species. It has long been known that the larger and more important part of that information is contained in the chromosomes of all organisms above the level of bacteria. Most recently, as noted at the outset of this discussion, it has been found more precisely that the information is in the conformation of DNA molecules within the chromosomes.

---

10 It has also been called "Neo-Darwinism," but that is misleading. Neo-Darwinism properly refers to a school of sixty or seventy years ago, which contributed to the present synthesis but was quite different in many respects. A recent suggestion that the present theory be called the "causal theory" is even more misleading, because all theories of adaptation (even that of special creation) and of evolution have been considered "causal" by their proponents.

The adaptation of a species, persisting through generations while individuals perish, depends on the hereditary information contained in the cells of all the reproducing members of the species, that is, in the genetic pool of the species. In modern terms, then, the problem of adaptation can be equated with the way that information is acquired and coded and becomes spread in the specific genetic pool. Evolutionary change entails, if it does not wholly consist of, the acquisition and spread of information not previously characteristic of the genetic pool. In the metaphor of communication, the process starts with the encoding of a modification in the genetic message, which is later communicated to increasing numbers of members of the reproducing population. Typically, at least, modification of the message means a change in the DNA code units. An adaptive hereditary message cannot, however, arise directly from such changes. In further communications metaphor, the DNA provides a language but does not determine what is said in that language. Chemical changes in the DNA are mutations, which, as previously noted, are not oriented by an adaptive organism–environment interaction.

Hereditary adaptation can be explained only if there is a circular or reciprocal connection between the organism–environment interaction and the developmental mechanism of individuals in the species. In cybernetic terms, there must be a feedback; the life-experiences and activities of members of a species, partly determined and wholly circumscribed by the genetic pool of that species, must in turn feed back in such a way as to affect that genetic pool. Although the matter was then put in entirely different words, that necessity was rather vaguely apprehended by Lamarck and quite clearly seen by the Neo-Lamarckians. The simplest feedback that could be postulated would be from the modification of an individual directly back to the genes in the germ cells of that individual. For example, such feedback would occur if larger stature due entirely to good nutrition, or smaller stature due entirely to bad nutrition, caused an individual's children to be larger or smaller by heredity, without reference to their own nutrition. That, however, is just what we now know does not happen, as we have learned from long observation and experimentation, and indeed cannot possibly happen, as we know from our understanding of the mechanisms of heredity.

Darwin, although he used quite different words, also clearly saw the necessity for feedback in the course of adaptation, and he correctly, although incompletely, identified it. In fact, this is the evolutionary role of natural selection, as we now see it. On the face of it, to look for the feedback within the individual was oversimplistic. It is not individuals but populations that evolve, and it is in populations, not individuals, that the feedback occurs. In all populations some individuals have more offspring than others. If on an average the individuals with more offspring differ genetically from those with fewer offspring, then the genetic characteristics of the more fecund group will spread in the population as the generations pass and will determine the direction of evolution. The differences in average fecundity may be very small and yet provide effective controls for evolution over the long periods of time actually involved. One additional point is that the effect depends not just on how many offspring are produced but on how many reproduce in their turn. Within a bird population, for example, this process may favor birds that lay fewer eggs but most of whose offspring also reproduce, rather than those laying more eggs but with hatchlings less successful in reproduction, because of early death or for any other reason.

Evidently what is favored by this process is effectiveness of reproduction over a sequence of generations. That is in itself adaptive: it obviously is beneficial for the species that it should be increasingly or maximally effective in reproducing itself continuously. However, it does not directly or, at least, obviously explain the innumerable anatomical, physiological, and behavioral adaptations not involved in actual reproduction. The explanation is completed and the feedback circle closed, so to speak, by the fact that any such adaptation, favorable to the individual's adjustment to its way of life, is also likely to improve its reproductive effectiveness. If that is not the case, then natural selection will favor the fittest *only* in the sense of the better reproducer, not in any other sense. For example, if it is true, as some students believe but without conclusive evidence, that genetically less well endowed humans tend on an average to have more grandchildren than those with a better genetic endowment, then they are *reproductively* more fit although selection is favoring evolution toward less fitness in other respects. The direction of selection must be stated in terms of grandchildren rather than of children, because the essential point is that more children reproduce (hence produce grandchildren) and not just that more children are born. (It is failure to allow for this fact that vitiates some of the data supposed to bear on the trend of human evolution.)

This modern understanding of natural selection is directly derived from Darwin's concept, but it is somewhat clearer and different in emphasis from strictly Darwinian, and especially from Neo-Darwinian, selection. Natural selection is now more definitely understood as a statistical effect in populations, providing feedback from organism–environment interaction to the genetic pool (not to the individual genetic system). Selection is thus a matter of continuing reproductive efficiency and not only of survival or mortality. Obviously mortality connected with genetic constitution will affect the reproduction of the next generation, but that is only a special case of a more general principle.

Selection may well occur without a differential in survival, and indeed that is its more important form in present human populations. If, to take the simplest possible example, one human group (genetically defined) averages two offspring per couple, both surviving and reproducing in turn, and another group averages ten offspring, only half surviving to reproduce, then survival is greater in the former (100 percent) than in the latter (50 percent), but natural selection strongly and decisively favors the latter (with two and one-half times as many descendants per generation).

The present concept also differs from earlier concepts of natural selection in the somewhat subtle but extremely important point that selection favors fitness in a general sense only if that promotes strictly reproductive fitness. As has been noted, the two usually coincide but this is not necessarily so. It is somewhat confusing and is, I think, unfortunate that most geneticists now define fitness as reproductive differential, whether or not it does in fact coincide with fitness in the general sense of adequate individual health, activity, and general adaptation.

The action of selection, of course, requires the existence of alternatives, that is, a genetic difference between the parts of a population with more offspring and those with fewer. Selection cannot operate in a genetically uniform population. Since only selection can produce and maintain adaptation in the face of inevitable environmental changes, it follows that a genetically homogeneous population would almost certainly fail to adapt and hence would become extinct—contrary to the opinions of some geneticists that genetic homogeneity, or what has been called a fixed "wild type" for a species, would be favored by selection and would be a general tendency of adaptive evolution. It has recently been found, in agreement with the current theoretical view, that a high degree of genetic heterogeneity is in fact characteristic of thriving, well-adapted, wild populations, which do not really have a "wild type" in the old sense.

The genetic variation that is in itself an adaptation and that provides the materials on which selection acts for increased or changing adaptation comes ultimately from mutations. "Mutation" is here meant in a broad sense, and it is now known to include several quite different phenomena, which cannot always be distinguished in objective examples. One is a so-called copying error, in which during the duplication of the information in the DNA a minimal element in the code is replaced by another in some way not yet understood. In other forms of mutation, parts of the message, in minimal code units or larger parts of the DNA molecule, may be dropped out. There may also be rearrangements of the message in a number of different ways, and these often affect the way the message is "read," so to speak. Finally, whole chromosomes, with their included information-bearing DNA, may be dropped out or duplicated.

Although mutation is necessarily (indeed, by definition) the ultimate source of any completely new factor in heredity, it is not the only or even the most important immediate source of variation. Most variation in

313

natural populations arises from the shuffling, or recombination, in each generation, of the genetic factors that had arisen by mutation in the sequence of earlier generations. This variation is especially important because it makes possible selection for whole sets of interacting genes or other factors of heredity. It is now known that selection seldom if ever acts on single genes as discrete elements. It acts on whole sets of genes in individual organisms and on the whole genetic pool of the population or species.

The whole interplay from genetic pool to mutation–recombination–natural selection–adaptation and back to genetic pool is more complex than was earlier realized, but it is now fairly well understood in its generalized form. The way in which it has operated and now operates specifically, in the millions upon millions of natural populations through all the changes of earth history, is endlessly complicated, and poses important problems for generations of evolutionary biologists yet to come.

While stressing adaptation as the most important aspect of evolution, we must not forget that there are other essential aspects, and that in the total evolutionary process all aspects interact simultaneously. Among these is the origin of species, the topic so curiously slighted in *The Origin of Species* but recently elucidated in much detail by Mayr, Dobzhansky, and many others. The essential phenomenon here is the splitting of one species into two or more, for which the German evolutionist Bernhard Rensch has proposed the term "cladogenesis."

One of the basic problems is whether, in Mayr's terms, speciation is normally sympatric or allopatric: that is, whether it occurs within a more or less continuous specific population or whether its initial phases occur in spatially separated populations. Without really clear discussion of the problem, which was of secondary importance at that time, Darwin and his immediate successors mostly assumed that sympatric speciation is usual. Most Darwinians believed that this could happen as a gradual result of ordinary natural selection, but it is more plausible as the possible result of single mutations within populations. This is still a common theme of science fiction (often, as here, far out of touch with current science), but it is no longer acceptable. The only mutationlike event that can produce a new sympatric species is polyploidy, the abrupt multiplication of the number of chromosomes. While not uncommon in plants, this is so rare in animals as to be almost negligible. There is no known example of an ordinary or gene mutation producing a species forthwith, and it is unlikely that such an event ever occurs in biparental organisms, at least. Furthermore, recent studies, especially by Mayr, again, make it virtually certain that sympatric speciation by natural selection acting on ordinary forms of intraspecific variation does not occur.

Speciation is, then, normally allopatric or geographic: it is preceded by spatial separation of two or more populations of a single ancestral species.

Such geographic isolation is in most cases a necessary condition for speciation, but it is never sufficient in itself. The isolation must continue over numerous generations, and the separate populations must diverge, that is, evolve in different ways usually by selection for different adaptations. Speciation is not definitive until the divergence is such that the two populations will not interbreed and fuse if they do again come in contact with each other. The differences that prevent such fusion are called isolating mechanisms, and they are highly diverse. Interbreeding may be reduced or eliminated by occupation of different habitats in the same region or by breeding at different times of the year or even of the day. Breeding may fail to occur unless it is stimulated by visual patterns, songs or calls, odors, or behavior characteristic for each species. The ultimate isolating mechanisms are, however, those that make the two species genetically incompatible so that fertile offspring would not be produced even if the two did attempt to interbreed. That is true of the vast majority of all species, and the question of isolating mechanisms hardly arises for existing species except for the relatively few cases of geologically recent speciation producing species still very closely related. For example, there is no other species on earth genetically compatible with *Homo sapiens,* and hybridization of man and any other animal is impossible.

THE FUTURE AND IMPACT OF EVOLUTIONARY BIOLOGY

Studies of evolution at the organismal and populational levels were never more active than at present. The traditional problems at these levels have not all been solved by a century of concentrated research. The main outlines do now seem to be within our grasp, but what remains are not only matters of detail. Particularly interesting at present is the outlook for further synthesis. The synthetic theory was in its inception a synthesis at organismal and higher levels. We are now reaching the point where molecular biology can be included to form a still more comprehensive synthesis.

Molecular and organismal biologists are now beginning a cooperation that will surely prove fruitful. Numerous efforts have been initiated in the last year or so to interpret molecular biology in evolutionary terms. It is too early to say just what the results will be, but they are certainly promising. It is somewhat surprising that the reciprocal contribution, that of molecular biology to an understanding of organismal evolution, has so far been slight and does not appear to be making great progress. Discovery of the role of DNA, the shape of its molecules, and the nature of its code has contributed virtually nothing as yet to principles of evolution beyond what was already known on the basis of the previously hypothetical or operational unit, the gene. It is certain that such a contribution is possible, and that is one of the most important vistas of the future for biology. We may look forward to a general theory much richer than we yet have, one which involves all levels of analysis in one interacting complex.

Knowledge of how evolution occurs brings the possibility of controlling its progress and direction within such limits as nature may impose. Not only is man the only animal who knows he evolves; he is the first who could guide his own future evolution. That statement has frequently been made of late, and usually in an optimistic frame of mind. It is true that our knowledge of evolution is already sufficient for the application of selection to mankind in such ways as to prevent biological degeneration and, within limits, to promote biological improvement. However, that hopeful fact is only one side of the matter. The actual application of biological knowledge in a desirable way goes well beyond biology itself. Application of selection to mankind and designation of desirable evolutionary goals require social comprehension and consent plus political wisdom and management. We do not seem as yet to be even approaching such levels of social and political capability.

We tend to ignore obstacles and to leap ahead in imagination. That is good as a spur to aspiration, but it may even impede progress by spreading quite unrealistic ideas of what in fact has been accomplished. For example, recent discoveries about DNA have led to many fantasies, presented in sober guise, such as that we are thus in a position to make genetic systems to order. We are not yet really in a position to judge whether that is possible, still less to start doing it. We do not know even so little as how a single real gene (DNA segment) is "written" in the genetic "code." If any immediate progress is possible, it will be on the basis of selection in existing genetic systems, not by the tailoring of new ones. T. M. Sonneborn has made this point well and authoritatively:

> There is . . . nothing yet in our knowledge of the new human genetics that provides a basis for seeing an early control of human hereditary constitution . . . There is still a long way to go. Tomorrow or 10 or 20 years hence there *may* be breakthroughs, but they cannot at present be foreseen . . . For the present and for the foreseeable future, sound application of genetic knowledge to the improvement of man—if it is to be done at all—will necessarily have to be restricted to the slower and less spectacular, but sound, methods based upon classical genetics.[11]

If optimism causes us to minimize or to deny the existence of unsolved problems, it delays their actual solution indefinitely.

11 "Implications of the New Genetics for Biology and Man," *Bulletin of the American Institute of Biological Sciences*, April, 1963, p. 26.

Knowledge of evolution is utilized in animal and plant breeding, which is evolution purposefully conducted by artificial selection. Its effective application to human evolution is not yet in sight. Nevertheless, it has had an incalculable effect on mankind in a less material way.

We are the products of descent with modification from other animals; we are animals ourselves; and we are, literally, physically related to all living things. The discovery of those facts profoundly altered man's image of himself. The psychological, philosophical, and religious re-orientation has been radical. It has been going on for over a century, and yet there are still numerous otherwise civilized people who not only have failed to adapt to it but also are actively opposed, in most cases on supposedly religious grounds. This is an appalling example of the human capacity for superstition and self-deception. Still, it is true that pre-dominant religious sects in the United States are not now dogmatically opposed to acceptance of the truth of evolution, although many of their communicants are.

The facts and the processes of evolution are neither ethical nor un-ethical. The questions of good or bad are simply irrelevant to this field, with the important reservation that evolution has produced a species, *Homo sapiens*, concerned with ethics. Denial of man's naturalistic origin and animal nature is flatly false, and any ethic based on such denial is invalid. Evolution controverts primitive creation myths, but it is consistent with higher values in the Judeo-Christian tradition and those in most now-current religions and philosophical systems. One need only think of the brotherhood of mankind—a biological fact, not only an ethical ideal.

Beyond such considerations as those, efforts to combine science and religion may be noble in intention but usually end up distorting or stultifying both. One of the most striking examples at present is the cult, as it may fairly be called, of Pierre Teilhard de Chardin. He preaches—necessarily posthumously, for the Roman Catholic Church suppressed his views during his life—a mystical Christianity ostensibly derived from evolutionary principles. But since the mysticism is primary, the evolutionary principles are distorted and downright falsified for seeming coherence with the nonscientific, nonnaturalistic premises. In turn, the mystical views advanced as having that false basis are thereby vitiated. The result (in my opinion) has been a disservice to true religion and to true science.

At the same time, no one can deny the purity of Father Teilhard's intentions or the correctness of his view that evolution and religious feeling should be considered congruent aspects of the nature of man. It is almost as irrational to deny evolution as to deny gravity. The management of life and the goals of aspiration, to be sane, must take account of all such truths of nature. They need not thereby become brutal or earthbound.

317

Biological Sciences

BIBLIOGRAPHY

1.   REORIENTATION IN BIOLOGY:

DOBZHANSKY, THEODOSIUS. "Biology, Molecular and Organismic." In *American Zoologist,* November, 1964, pp. 443-52.
DUBOS, RENÉ. "Biological Sciences and Medicine." In *The Great Ideas Today 1964,* pp. 224-71.
SIMPSON, G. G. *This View of Life.* New York: Harcourt, Brace & World Inc., 1964 (Chapters 5–6).
SONNEBORN, T. M. "Implications of the New Genetics for Biology and Man." In *Bulletin of the American Institute of Biological Sciences,* April, 1963, pp. 22-26.
VON BERTALANFFY, LUDWIG. *Problems of Life.* New York: Harper & Brothers, 1960.

2.   THE ORIGIN OF LIFE:

ALLEN, G. "Reflexive Catalysis, a Possible Mechanism of Molecular Duplication in Prebiological Evolution." In *American Naturalist,* March-April, 1957, pp. 65-78.
OPARIN, A. I. (editor). *Proceedings of the International Symposium on the Origin of Life on the Earth.* London: Pergamon Press, 1959.
WALD, GEORGE. "The Origins of Life." In *Proceedings of the National Academy of Sciences,* August, 1964, pp. 595-611.

3.   LIFE OUTSIDE THE EARTH:

ANDERS, EDWARD, et al. "Contaminated Meteorite." In *Science,* 146, November 27, 1964, pp. 1157-61.
CALVIN, M. "Communication from Molecules to Man." In *Bulletin of the American Institute of Biological Sciences,* October, 1962, pp. 29-44.
HAYATSU, RYOICHI. "Orgueil Meteorite: Organic Nitrogen Contents." In *Science,* 146, December 4, 1964, pp. 1291-93.
JACKSON, F. L., and MOORE, P. A. *Life in the Universe.* New York: W. W. Norton & Company, Inc., 1962.
SHIRK, JAMES S., HASELTINE, W. A., and PIMENTEL, G. C. "Sinton Bands: Evidence for Deuterated Water on Mars." In *Science,* 147, January 1, 1965, pp. 48-49.
SIMPSON, G. G. *This View of Life.* New York: Harcourt, Brace & World Inc., 1964 (Chapters 12–13).

4.   THE EVOLUTION OF MAN:

BUETTNER-JANUSCH, JOHN (editor). *The Relatives of Man.* New York: New York Academy of Sciences, 1962.
CLARK, W. E. LE GROS. *The Antecedents of Man.* Chicago: Quadrangle Books, Inc., 1960.
DE VORE, IRVEN (editor). *Primate Behavior: Field Studies of Monkeys and Apes.* New York: Holt, Rinehart & Winston, Inc., 1965.
DOBZHANSKY, THEODOSIUS. *Mankind Evolving.* New Haven: Yale University Press, 1962.
HOWELLS, W. W. *Mankind in the Making.* New York: Doubleday & Company, Inc., 1959.
LEAKEY, L. S. B., and LEAKEY, M. D. "Recent Discoveries of Fossil Hominids in Tanganyika: At Olduvai and Near Lake Natron." In *Nature,* 202, April 4, 1964, pp. 5-7. (*See* also articles on pp. 3 and 7 of same issue.)
LEAKEY, L. S. B., et al. *Olduvai Gorge.* Cambridge: Cambridge University Press, 1965.
ROE, ANNE, and SIMPSON, G. G. (editors). *Behavior and Evolution.* New Haven: Yale University Press, 1958.
SIMONS, ELWYN L. "A Critical Reappraisal of Tertiary Primates." In *Evolutionary and Genetic Biology of Primates,* ed. JOHN BUETTNER-JANUSCH. Vol. 1, 1963, pp. 65-129.
TAX, SOL (editor). *The Evolution of Man.* Chicago: University of Chicago Press, 1960.
WASHBURN, S. L. (editor). *Classification and Human Evolution.* Chicago: Aldine Publishing Company (Wenner-Gren Foundation for Anthropological Research), 1963.

5.   THE PROCESSES
     OF ORGANIC EVOLUTION:

DOBZHANSKY, THEODOSIUS. *Evolution, Genetics, and Man.* New York: John Wiley & Sons, Inc., 1955.
GRANT, VERNE. *The Origin of Adaptations.* New York: Columbia University Press, 1963.
HUXLEY, JULIAN S. *Evolution, the Modern Synthesis.* New York: Harper & Brothers, 1942.
MAYR, ERNST. *Animal Species and Evolution.* Cambridge: Harvard University Press, 1963.
RENSCH, BERNHARD. *Evolution Above the Species Level.* New York: Columbia University Press, 1960.
SIMPSON, G. G. *The Major Features of Evolution.* New York: Columbia University Press, 1953.
———. *This View of Life.* New York: Harcourt, Brace & World Inc., 1964 (especially Chapters 3–4).
TAX, SOL (editor). *The Evolution of Life.* Chicago: University of Chicago Press, 1960.

6.   THE FUTURE AND THE IMPACT
      OF EVOLUTIONARY BIOLOGY:

SIMPSON, G. G. "On the Remarkable Testament of the Jesuit Paleontologist Pierre Teilhard de Chardin." In *Scientific American*, 202, April, 1960, pp. 201-7.

———. *This View of Life*. New York: Harcourt, Brace & World Inc., 1964 (Chapters 4, 11).

———. "Organisms and Molecules in Evolution." In *Science*, 146, December 18, 1964, pp. 1535-38.

SONNEBORN, T. M. "Implications of the New Genetics for Biology and Man." In *Bulletin of the American Institute of Biological Sciences*, April, 1963, p. 26.

TEILHARD DE CHARDIN, PIERRE. *The Phenomenon of Man*. Translated by BERNARD WALL. New York: Harper & Brothers, 1959.

NOTE TO THE READER

In his essay Dr. Simpson reports the most recent developments in biology, and especially what is going on at the frontier of research in evolution. Readers interested in the history of evolution and the formation of many of its basic concepts will find material of interest in *Great Books of the Western World*. The great classic of evolutionary theory remains Darwin's *The Origin of Species* (GBWW, Vol. 49). Two of the most influential writers in the early controversy over evolution are represented in *Gateway to the Great Books*: T. H. Huxley, "On the Relations of Man to the Lower Animals" and "On a Piece of Chalk" (GGB, Vol. 8, pp. 155-222), and Sir Charles Lyell on "Geological Evolution" (GGB, Vol. 8, pp. 315-24).

In the *Syntopicon*, the idea of EVOLUTION is the subject of Chapter 24. Several of the areas in which Dr. Simpson describes recent advances provide the topics into which the chapter is divided. The question of primordial origins, that is, of the origin of all life, is discussed in the passages cited under EVOLUTION 4a; the question of the appearance of new species of living things is discussed in the passages under 4c. The geological record—the significance of fossil remains—is the subject of topic 6a. The geographical distribution of forms of life, and whether or not a new species appears within contiguous populations, is the subject of topic 6b.

On the evolution of man and his relation to other animals, the reader should consult Darwin's work, *The Descent of Man* (GBWW, Vol. 49) and the essay of Huxley in *Gateway*. What other *Great Books* authors say about this subject can be found by consulting the passages listed under EVOLUTION 7. Discussions of the various races of men will be found cited under MAN 7.

The problem of cultural change, which, as Dr. Simpson notes, is frequently referred to as cultural evolution, is analyzed in the texts cited under CUSTOM AND CONVENTION 2, 3, and 4 and PROGRESS 6.

In the course of his essay, and especially in his remarks on biology as a science, Dr. Simpson discusses the nature of science. Readers interested in this subject will find material in the discussions referred to under SCIENCE 4 on the nature of scientific knowledge and under SCIENCE 5 on scientific method. On this subject most of Volume 8 of *Gateway*, devoted to natural science, is also highly relevant.

In the final pages of his essay, Dr. Simpson touches upon two subjects that still arouse controversy, often of the most heated kind: one is the relation of science and religion; the other, man's place in the world. *Great Books* contains much on both subjects. SCIENCE 2a provides references to the discussion of science and religion. MAN 10 contains references on man's conception of himself and his place in the world. In the passages cited there, readers will find arguments on both sides of these controversies.

Physical and

JEREMY BERNSTEIN

"The ideas of modern science are so beautiful that I am convinced that anyone who understands some part of them will find himself enriched," writes Jeremy Bernstein, the first physicist to be on the staff of The New Yorker. *In 1963, he published in* The New Yorker *a series of essays on the world of the electronic computer which received wide comment. The essays were published as a book:* The Analytical Engine: Computers—Past, Present, and Future *(1964). In addition to being an Associate Professor of Physics at New York University, Dr. Bernstein spends his summers working and studying developments in physics at CERN, the international atomic laboratory—Centre Européen pour la Recherche Nucléaire—located in a suburb of Geneva, Switzerland. He enjoys mountain climbing and published three articles on the subject in* The New Yorker, March, 1965. *He was born in 1929 in Rochester, New York. For eight years he studied at Harvard University, from which he received his Doctorate in Physics in 1955. He then worked for two years as a research associate at the Harvard Cyclotron Laboratory, and two subsequent years at the Institute for Advanced Study at Princeton University. Dr. Bernstein has also been a physicist at Los Alamos and at Brookhaven National Laboratories. He serves as a consultant both to the General Atomics Corporation and the Rand Corporation. He lives in New York City.*

Sciences

Technology

INTRODUCTION: THIS YEAR IN PHYSICS

It is quite likely, although it is still too early to be certain, that this past year may turn out to have been a very decisive one for the physics of elementary particles and, hence, for all of physics. I say "hence for all of physics" because I think it can be argued that as elementary-particle physics goes, so goes all of physics. For that reason instead of surveying the most recent developments in the whole of physics, I am going to concentrate entirely on particle physics.

To put the matter very briefly, there appear to be two important advances. First, there is now good reason to believe (on the basis of work culminating this year) that there exist simple, very beautiful, and hitherto unsuspected connections among the elementary particles. Moreover, these connections have encouraged many physicists to believe that the elementary particles themselves may be built up—step by step —out of simple basic units in the same way that complex nuclei are built up step by step out of protons and neutrons—the nuclear "building blocks." It is now one of the most interesting tasks of the experimental physicists to find these basic units. The theory, as we shall see, suggests that they may exist, and it gives us hints as to what they are like. But until they are found this part of the theory remains a speculation. In that sense elementary-particle physics of today is like atomic physics in the 1920's before the discovery of the neutron and proton. It was generally conceded that nuclei were built out of simpler objects, but until they were actually pinned down no one could be sure what they were.

The second advance in elementary-particle physics this year is the product of experiments done at Brookhaven National Laboratory by J. H. Christenson, J. W. Cronin, V. L. Fitch, and R. Turlay, who were all at the time connected with Princeton University. It appears to show the breakdown of a symmetry that seemed to hold not only in the strong and electromagnetic interactions but also in the weak interactions, which up to the summer of 1964 most physicists had come to believe was actually the correct modified form of the old parity conservation that fell in 1956-57. This symmetry is called, for reasons that I will explain later, CP invariance, and, in the theories that have played a role in physics up to now, it is equivalent to another symmetry that has the esoteric-sounding name of "time-reversal" invariance. Physicists, at least many of us, had come to assume that time reversal invariance was a universal law that held for all forces. The new experiment, interpreted in the simplest fashion, seems to indicate that it is not so. This is a very exciting development because the lesson of the past is that whenever a "plausible" law of physics breaks down it can only mean progress.

ATOMIC PHYSICS: THEN AND NOW

I will first take up the elementary particles. It is something of a cliché to say that the Greeks invented the atomic theory of matter—*atomos* being the Greek word for "indivisible." The atomic theory of Democritus and his school was hardly scientific at all. It was really a philosophical prejudice—that matter could not be divided indefinitely but that there must be ultimately a finest division; and, moreover (in this Democritus made a basic innovation), that the complexities we observe in our everyday experience could be accounted for by the relatively simple behavior of the atoms. But both of these notions were purely hypothetical, since there was no way for Democritus to test either of them empirically. In fact, the atomic theory of matter remained purely a hypothesis until the twentieth century.[1]

Modern atomic theory arose in the beginning of the nineteenth century with chemistry. Chemists had long realized that there was a consistency in the way the elements combined to give compounds. For example, any sample of pure water, when analyzed into hydrogen and oxygen, always contains about eight times as much oxygen, in mass, as hydrogen. This is true no matter how large a sample of water one chooses to study, or indeed, how small a sample. This kind of regularity is true not only of water but of all chemical compounds. If one makes an analysis of any chemical compound, one finds that its constituents always combine in the same ratio by mass and that these ratios are very nearly the ratios

---

1 Democritus' theory of the atom is found in the poem of Lucretius, "On the Nature of Things," GBWW, Vol. 12, especially Books I-III, pp. 1-44.

of simple whole numbers—integers. From the atomic point of view this is a very simple regularity to explain: Water is conceived of as made up out of fundamental units—atoms, or as the chemists say, molecules—and each of these molecules has, in mass, eight times as much oxygen as hydrogen. Hence, any number of such molecules, that is, any sample of water, will have the same mass ratio. One cannot conclude from this that the hydrogen atom weighs an eighth of the oxygen atom because in a water molecule there are, in fact, two hydrogen atoms for each oxygen atom. This complexity of molecular structure goes under the general name of "valence," and it properly belongs in a discussion of chemistry rather than in this article. But certainly the constancy of the composition of chemical compounds suggests some kind of atomicity, and indeed, John Dalton, the English chemist of the early nineteenth century, was led to atoms by thinking along these lines.[2]

It must not be imagined that chemists and physicists of the nineteenth century took up the atomic theory as if it were a revelation. Not at all. Many of the best of them thought it was nonsense, and a few of them only accepted it at the turn of the century, more or less on their death-beds, after Einstein had succeeded in using it to explain Brownian movement.[3] (Brownian movement, named after the Scottish botanist Robert Brown, refers to the motion made by tiny, barely visible particles suspended in a liquid. They move in a random zigzag that Einstein explained by supposing that they were being continuously bombarded by the invisible atoms of the liquid.)

THE ATOM: SOME PROPERTIES

Just how small are the objects that chemists call atoms? The mere fact that liquids and solids do not look atomic already tells us that the wavelengths of ordinary visible light must be much larger than atomic sizes. To separate two closely spaced objects we must illuminate them with light whose wavelength is shorter than their separation. The eye is only optically sensitive to "visible" light whose wavelength is in the region of a hundred-thousandth of a centimeter. Hence, we can be confident that atomic sizes are smaller than that.

There are now many ways of estimating from experiment the size of the chemical atom. I will describe the principle of one of the simplest. If each atom in a sample of volume V is in the form of a little cube of side r, and if there are n atoms in the sample, then the volume V, if we

2 *See* Mendeleev on "The Periodic Law of the Chemical Elements," in GGB, Vol. 8, pp. 440–46.

3 For Einstein on the Brownian movement, *see* "The Rise and Decline of Classical Physics," in GGB, Vol. 8, pp. 526–28.

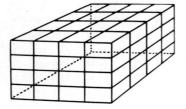

FIGURE 1

are discussing a solid where the atoms are tightly bunched together, is given by $V = nr^3$. If the same number of atoms is now spread out in a layer one atom thick, then the area of this layer is $A = nr^2$, since any one surface of each cube has area r^2 (*see* Fig. 1). A and V can be measured directly, although rather refined techniques are required to find A. Thus the ratio $\frac{V}{A}$, that is, $\frac{nr^3}{nr^2}$, gives a measure of r, $r = \frac{V}{A}$, and, hence, the size of the chemical atom. The result is that r is about one one-hundred-millionth of a centimeter—about a thousandth of the wavelength of visible light. (The common notation for one one-hundredth of a million is 10^{-8}, that is, $\frac{1}{100,000,000}$, and I shall use this notation in what follows.) This result is in agreement with a whole variety of other measurements obtained by using different techniques.

Now, is the chemical atom indivisible? Absolutely not. If one bombards it with radiation whose wavelength is of the order of 10^{-8} cm.

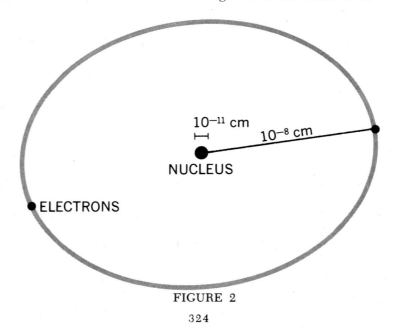

FIGURE 2

or less, X rays and γ rays, one can knock electrons off of it. (Electrons are light electrically charged particles that circulate around the atomic nucleus. *See* Particle Table, pp. 367–9, for more details of their properties.) And if the wavelength of the radiation is decreased to about 10^{-11} cm., the nucleus of the chemical atom itself breaks up (*see* Fig. 2). This releases the component parts: protons, neutrons, and sometimes combinations of these (e.g., helium nuclei). One may carry the process down to the lightest nucleus that exists, namely the proton—the nucleus of the hydrogen atom.

THE NEUTRON AND PROTON AND THE FORCES THAT ACT ON THEM

Much could be written about the proton. But at this point the thing I wish to stress is its stability. Of the literally dozens of particles that physicists have so far found, almost all of them are unstable. They spontaneously decay into lighter particles. Particles that decay are certainly not atoms in the sense of Democritus, since they break up even without applying external forces to them. But the proton just sits there. Protons, which have the same charge as the electron but of opposite sign, and neutrons, which have no charge, are the two lightest examples of what physicists call "baryons." Any particle that weighs about a billion electron volts or more (physicists conventionally give the mass of a particle in terms of energy units—electron volts) is called a "baryon." In contrast the electron, which weighs about a half million volts, is called a "lepton." It is an experimental fact that baryons cannot decay into leptons. If a baryon decays, some leptons may be produced, but along with them there must be produced at least one baryon. Since the proton is the lightest baryon, it cannot decay into anything.

Later we shall discuss why even the proton is not an atom—indivisible—in the sense of Democritus. Here it is useful to take up the question of the different forces that act on the particles—which sever and dissolve them.

Table of the Forces

1. *Strong forces*: these forces hold the nucleus together. In relative units we can say that these forces have strength 1.
2. *Electrical forces*: these forces are responsible for the chemical properties of the atoms. In the same units they have strength $1/137$.
3. *The weak forces*: these forces cause many of the elementary particles to decay.[4] They have a strength of about $1/10^5$.
4. *The gravitational forces*: these forces cause the planetary orbits around the sun. They are the weakest forces known and have a strength of about 10^{-39}.

---

4 Some, as we shall see, decay by the action of the strong and electromagnetic forces.

Let us first discuss the weak forces.

The reaction $n \rightarrow p + e^- + \bar{\nu}$, in which a neutron decays into a proton (p), an electron (e^-), and an antineutrino ($\bar{\nu}$),[5] is a prototype of the kind of "weak process" that is produced by the weak force. It is called a "weak process" because it takes a long time. The mean life of the neutron is about a thousand seconds. This means that in a sample of neutrons any given one is most likely to decay after a thousand seconds. Some will decay sooner and some later, but the average is about a thousand seconds. It is not clear whether this is a fast or slow time until it is compared with something. If we look at the Particle Table under the "mean life" column we see that most of the particles listed there decay in times of the order of a billionth or a ten-billionth of a second, so clearly a thousand seconds is very slow compared to this. But even a ten-billionth of a second is slow when compared to the time it takes some of the particles to decay. For example, the π^0 meson decays into two γ's a million times faster, and the so-called resonant states (*see* Particle Table and discussion, below) decay about a million times faster yet.

There appear to be three essential time ranges: from seconds to ten-billionths of a second, from ten-billionths of a second to ten-billion-billionths of a second, and then the still shorter times. The weaker the force the slower the decay process. Hence, these three time regions suggest that three different forces are at work causing the decays. Indeed, they are, in order of increasing strength: the weak force, the electromagnetic force, and the strong force. A glance at the different lifetimes of the various particles that fall into the weak force class might seem to suggest that there are many weak forces, since there is a great deal of variation even among the long lifetimes.

However, the differences among the lifetimes are really "accidental" in the following sense. According to the conservation of energy, a particle can decay into other particles only if the latter are lighter than the parent particle. One knows from the theory of relativity that mass and energy are interchangeable—a particle having mass m has a corresponding rest energy mc^2 (i.e., its energy when at rest). Thus, to conserve energy, the daughter particles in the decay must have a lighter total mass than the parent—the remaining energy, if any, goes into the kinetic energy of the daughters. Moreover, the theory of the weak decays, first worked out by the Italian physicist Enrico Fermi in the early 1930's, shows that the greater the difference in mass between the parent and the daughter

5 In this reaction the antineutrino is produced along with the electron. All particles in physics have antiparticle partners. The particles and antiparticles have the same mass and lifetimes but opposite electrical charges. Some of the neutral particles have antiparticles that are identical to them. In the case of the neutrino, however, which is a neutral particle, it and its antineutrino are distinct, and, hence, I have been careful to put an antiparticle in this reaction as that is what is observed to emerge.

the easier it is for the decay to take place. In fact, if there is no difference, the decay does not happen at all. Furthermore, for a three-body decay such as $n \rightarrow p + e^- + \bar{v}$ the Fermi theory predicts that the ratio of the lifetimes of two such decays goes as the fifth power of the mass difference between the daughters and the parents. The fifth power is a huge power—ten raised five times is 100,000—and, hence, there can be enormous variations in lifetimes just as a result of variations in mass differences.

For example, if we compare the process $n \rightarrow p + e^- + \bar{v}$, the familiar beta decay, with the process that is just now being studied,[6] $\Sigma^- \rightarrow \Lambda^\circ + e^- + \bar{v}$, we see that they are similar in form. We can neglect the masses of the electron and neutrino in computing the masses of the daughters since both are very light (the neutrino probably has no mass). Looking at the table, we find in the first case a mass difference of about 1 million electron volts, while in the second case there is a mass difference of about 70 million electron volts.[7] Now, 70 raised to the fifth power is about a billion and a half and, hence, the enormous observed difference in the lifetimes for these two processes is simply accounted for by the mass differences of the respective particles. Indeed, all the evidence we have is that the weak force is essentially universal (it is the same for all particles) and that lifetime differences can be accounted for, in first approximation, by accidental differences of the kind we have discussed. This universality of the weak force provides an analogy to the electromagnetic force. The electromagnetic force is absolutely universal in the sense that all particles with the same total electric charge have exactly the same electrostatic interactions.

ARE THE NEUTRON AND PROTON DIVISIBLE?

Since the neutron and proton are the nuclear "building blocks," and, since the proton is stable against decay, one might be tempted to think of the neutron and proton as the real indivisibles—the atoms. Yet, as we have just pointed out, the neutron decays spontaneously and therefore, so to speak, divides itself—or is divided by the weak force into a proton, an electron, and an antineutrino—the process $n \rightarrow e^- + \bar{v} + p$. It is true that proton decay, the process $p \rightarrow n + e^+ + v$, does not take place experimentally. However, according to the Fermi theory this is again an accident of mass. If the proton were heavier than the neutron, instead of vice versa (*see* Particle Table), the Fermi theory *would* predict the decay of the proton, that is, $p \rightarrow n + e^+ + v$. In fact, the theory *does* predict that the process $e^- + p \rightarrow n + v$ should take

6 The particles Σ and Λ are discussed more fully below.

7 $c^2(m_\Sigma - m_\Lambda) = 70$ mev

place, and this process—known as "electron K capture"—has been identified, especially in heavier nuclei where each nucleus consists of several
protons and neutrons.

Thus the weak interaction is capable of breaking up the building
blocks. But this is the least of it. Both the strong and electromagnetic
interactions break them up as well. Indeed, if the wavelength of electromagnetic radiation is reduced to a size of about 10^{-13} cm.,[8] collision
processes like $\gamma + p \rightarrow n + m^+$ occur (where m^+ stands for a meson
—a particle intermediate in mass between an electron and a baryon—
and γ stands for a light quantum, a photon). We shall have a good deal
to say about them in what follows.

By now the attentive reader will have remarked that the shorter the
wavelength of the radiation the more energetic it is. In fact, the energy
of a light quantum is given by $E = \dfrac{hc}{\lambda}$ where c is the velocity of light
in vacuum, λ is the wavelength of the light, and h is Planck's constant—
the universal quantum of action—whose value is $6.6256 \pm 0.0002 \times 10^{-27}$
erg second. As the velocity of light is $2.997925 \pm 0.000003 \times 10^{10}$ cm/sec
(I give these numbers with such precision because they show that while
physicists deal in a good deal of speculation, they can make precise
measurements), a fermi corresponds to about 100 million electron volts
worth of energy—100 mev—and hence a light quantum of such a wavelength is energetically capable of producing mesons with a mass of about
100 mev in the process $\gamma + p \rightarrow n + m^+$. This is an example of how
the electromagnetic interaction breaks up the proton.

But protons can also break each other up by means of the strong interaction. One may take a target composed of liquid hydrogen—protons
and electrons reduced to such a low temperature that they become
liquified—and hit it with a high energy beam of protons from an accelerator. It is then possible to photograph and obtain what are identified
as tracks of individual proton-proton collisions in which the protons
smash into each other and break up into all sorts of component parts,
mesons, and baryons.

THE STABILITY OF MATTER

With so much instability among the building blocks the reader
may well begin wondering whether all of matter is not really
a house of cards. Why is anything stable at all? The answer is twofold.
In the first place, the conservation of baryons prevents neutrons and
protons from disappearing outright. As we have remarked before, baryons
cannot turn themselves into leptons, so that processes like $p \rightarrow e^+ + e^-$

8 This is the unit of length known as a fermi.

$+ e^+$ are forbidden. However, that is only part of the answer. One can ask why all of the nuclei are not unstable since they consist of neutrons that *are* unstable. Of course, many nuclei are unstable. As everyone knows, the chemical properties of the atom are determined by the number of electrons around the nucleus which is, in turn, determined by the number of protons in the nucleus. Thus one may have several species of atom, all with the same chemical properties but differing in the number of neutrons in their individual nuclei. These other nuclei are called "isotopes" of the first one. In general, in any isotopic class only a small number of the isotopes are stable. The rest are radioactive. But some nuclei are perfectly stable against spontaneous decay—as stable as the proton itself. How can this be if the neutron is unstable?

To see what is involved let us take a specific example. A deuteron consists of one neutron and one proton. It is thus an isotope of ordinary hydrogen—"heavy" hydrogen. It is perfectly stable. What prevents the deuteron from breaking down into two protons, an electron, and an antineutrino, that is, the reaction $d \rightarrow p + p + e^- + \bar{v}$? The answer is the conservation of energy. The deuteron weighs less than the neutron and proton that make it up. The whole weighs *less* than the sum of its parts. This is again a consequence of the theory of relativity. The neutron and proton in the deuteron are stuck together by the nuclear force. To weigh each one separately we must get them apart and this requires energy, just as breaking a stick requires energy. But energy is mass, and, hence, the energy that goes into breaking them up gets converted into the mass of the final products, which therefore weigh more than the original nucleus. (The same thing is true of the stick, by the way, but the numbers involved are minuscule compared to the mass of the stick.) Indeed, the neutron and proton weigh together (*see* Particle Table) about 1,877.7 mev. The deuteron, on the other hand, weighs about 2.23 mev less. The 2.23 mev is what is known as the "binding energy" of the deuteron—the amount of energy that has to be supplied to take the deuteron apart. Two protons and an electron weigh 1,876.3 mev (the minimum possible energy for the four particle state, $p + p + e^- + \bar{v}$, in which the neutrino is assumed to have no energy and the electron is created at rest with no kinetic energy). It is clear from the numbers that this state weighs more than the original deuteron and, hence, the transition $d \rightarrow p + p + e^- + \bar{v}$ is energetically impossible.

The neutron and proton in the deuteron are what are called "virtual" particles—they do not have the same mass that they would have if they were free, since they have lost some of this mass in the binding process. In fact, one may observe the process $n + p \rightarrow d + \gamma$ in which this mass loss is released in the energy of the photon—a process called radiative neutron capture. But the mass loss of the neutron and proton in the deuteron is small—about 2.23 mev—compared to their actual mass of 939 mev or so. Hence, for many purposes one can think of the neutrons and protons in nuclei just as if they were free particles.

Since the particles that we are familiar with are not, in principle, indivisible, we may ask, can anything be indivisible if modern physics is right? I reason to a negative conclusion along the following lines. To study a particle at all we must assume that it can be produced. Let me call the particle that I want to study *s* and let us suppose that it is manufactured in some simple reaction like that of a photon (gamma) hitting a neutral particle, say *n*, and producing the *s* and some other particle called *m*: in formula, $\gamma + n = s + m$, and in a picture, *see* Figure 3. (In what follows I will assume that all the particles I discuss are identical with their antiparticles. This simplifies the details of the argument without changing its essentials.)

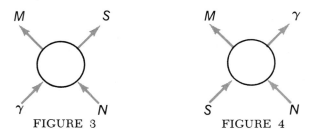

FIGURE 3　　　　　　FIGURE 4

Now it is a basic principle of our modern particle physics that if Figure 3 represents a possible reaction, then Figure 4 represents another possible reaction. The two reactions differ in that I have crossed the *s* and the gamma legs in the two diagrams. They are the "crossed" reactions of each other, and our physics tells us that whenever a reaction is allowed, so is its crossed reaction. But note that the crossed reaction represents the division of the particle *s* by the particle *n*. Hence, if a particle can be produced in a reaction then it can be divided in a suitable crossed reaction to the one that produced it. Thus, for contemporary particle physics, there are no atoms in the Democritean sense.

WHAT IS AN ELEMENTARY PARTICLE?

If this is so, then what is an elementary particle? This has been one of the most frequently discussed questions in contemporary physics, and there are almost as many answers to it as there are physicists. We might approach an answer by considering how classical physics conceived of a particle.[9] In classical physics the answer was clear. A particle

9 For Newton's conception of the atom, *see* his *Optics*, GBWW, Vol. 34, pp. 537–42.

is an object, like a billiard ball, that has mass, possible charge, and whose position can be determined. Of course, a billiard ball has a size and shape. For many purposes the size and shape of the classical particle was irrelevant, and, hence, an *idealized* classical particle was introduced: a mass point—an object with mass-charge, perhaps, but with no size. This is a very good model for the objects that make up a typical gas. The distances between the gas molecules are large compared to the size of the molecules themselves, and, hence, the molecular size can frequently be neglected. A gas molecule can be thought of as a dimensionless mass point unless effects of collisions among the molecules are taken into account.

When the subatomic constituents like the electron, the atomic nucleus, and, ultimately, the neutron and proton were discovered, it was natural to think of them as classical particles. This is an example of how analogy is used in physics when one encounters new phenomena. The first approximation is always to assume that the new phenomena are analogous to the old and to see how far one can get by simply taking over the old ideas. In the case of the particles of quantum physics, this works only up to a point. An electron, for example, does have a mass and charge. These can be determined by analogy with the way they would be determined for a billiard ball: by allowing the electron to come into contact with electric and magnetic fields and observing its reactions. Its resistance to acceleration, for example, determined its mass. A typical billiard ball has a mass of several grams. But the electron was discovered to have a rest mass of $9.1083 \pm 0.0003 \times 10^{-28}$ grams. Ten raised twenty-eight times is a fantastically large number—it is 10 million raised to the fourth power. To reach a mass the size of a billiard ball it would be necessary to put together at least this many electrons—if one wanted to make up a billiard ball out of electrons. These are typical numbers. A cubic centimeter of gas, for example, under ordinary conditions contains about 10^{23} gas molecules. One has every reason to wonder whether a particle with such a small mass really does behave like a classical billiard ball. The answer is, emphatically, that it does not.

As we have remarked, one of the attributes of an ordinary billiard ball is that its position can be determined at any instant of time and that its trajectory can be traced out. Before the discovery of quantum mechanics, in the 1920's, it was assumed that an electron going around the nucleus also had a definite trajectory that could be traced out, like that of a billiard ball. But how is one to determine the trajectory of an electron around a nucleus? One method that suggests itself is to "look at" the electron through a microscope. Of course, the electron must be fantastically small, much smaller than the chemical atom of which it is a part—if, indeed, it has any size at all. Hence, as we have seen earlier, we must illuminate it with "light" of a very small wavelength—a wavelength considerably smaller than the dimensions of the atom. But light carries energy in an amount that is inversely proportional to its wavelength. Light quanta also carry momentum. Indeed, the momentum is simply related to the energy by the formula $P = \dfrac{E}{c}$, where c is the velocity of light, and, hence, to the wavelength by $P = \dfrac{h}{\lambda}$. Thus, when the light quanta from our measuring instrument come in contact with the electron in the atom, they will collide with it. (If they did not then we would never "see" the electron, since we always look at something by reflecting light from it.) Yet, as is easily verified by substituting the appropriate numbers in the formula, if one were to locate an electron in an atom one would have to transfer so much momentum in each collision that the electron would be knocked clear out of the atom. Hence, in this arrangement one can never find the trajectory of the electron.

The best one can do is to take a great many atoms and determine one position of the electron in each of these atoms at a time. (In each of the atoms, after the measurement, its electron will have been knocked clear.) This will give us a kind of probability map of the positions of the electrons in the atom. In fact, the electron "orbits" around the nucleus —usually called Bohr orbits after the great Danish physicist Niels Bohr who first described them in modern terms—really represent those places around the atom where we are most likely to find the electron when we "look" for it by shining light on the atom.

The whole business is something like the following fantasy. Suppose we had a friend with a huge number of telephone numbers, each phone being at a different address. If he answered at one of his numbers, we would know, at that moment, where he was. We could map out his most likely positions by phoning all of his numbers at the same time of day each day and discovering which phone he was most likely to answer. This way we could predict only his most likely position, and we could say nothing, with certainty, about which phone he would answer the next time we tried.

Of course, it might be objected that the reason why we have not been able to determine the trajectory of the electron is that we have designed a silly experiment, that a better one could be used to determine it. However, all attempts to design such an experiment have failed, and this fact is summarized formally in terms of the Heisenberg uncertainty relations, which are cornerstones of the quantum theory. Unless the whole structure of modern physics is wrong, there is, in principle, no way of determining the trajectory of an electron in an atom, and, hence, there is no point in speaking of "trajectories." The same analysis applies to the billiard ball, but the uncertainty in the position that comes about in the process of illuminating the ball is negligible. In brief, an electron is not like a billiard ball, but a billiard ball is like an electron.

The nonclassical characteristics of the electron, and the other subatomic particles, are not confined to the Heisenberg uncertainty relations alone. They display properties for which there is simply no classical analogue at all. A classical mass point, at rest, can never have an angular momentum. The angular momentum measures the degree of spin or rotation of a particle, and classically speaking, an object without extension cannot rotate; there is nothing for it to rotate about. However, quantum-mechanical particles, even without extension, can, in a certain sense, spin. The spin acts like an angular momentum, except that it persists even if the particle is brought to rest. Spin is sometimes called the "intrinsic" angular momentum of the particle. There is no question that the electron has such a property. A particle in a uniform magnetic field has a coupling to that field that is proportional to its angular momentum. For the old-fashioned particles the only angular momentum a point particle could have was due to its orbital motion. This is a measure of the degree of its turning about some fixed point. (A ball being whirled about on a string has an orbital angular momentum about the center of the circle—the faster it is whirled the more orbital angular momentum it has.) Thus the classical particles have an interaction in a uniform magnetic field that depends only on their orbital angular momentum. However, the electron in a magnetic field has an additional magnetic interaction that depends on its spin or intrinsic angular momentum. This interaction has been measured countless times in very precise experiments. It behaves like an angular momentum but it simply has no classical analogue—it is a purely quantum-mechanical property. In fact, all of the "particles" of modern physics have a well-defined spin— if one allows that this spin is sometimes 0. These have been included in the Particle Table for those cases where they have been measured. Thus a quantum-mechanical particle is a system which has a well-defined mass and charge, and, in addition, may have other characteristics, like spin, which are collectively referred to as "quantum numbers" and which have no classical counterparts.

MORE PARTICLES

After the neutron and proton were discovered, it appeared, for a short while, that along with the electron, the neutrino, and the light quantum, they might be the only elementary particles. But in 1935, again using the method of analogy, the Japanese physicist Hideki Yukawa made a brilliant theoretical conjecture about the existence of new particles which not only turned out to be right but also opened Pandora's box and led, ultimately, to the discovery of the whole network of particles displayed in the table.

We can describe Yukawa's conjecture as follows. Two electrons (electrons are chosen here simply as examples of charge-bearing particles) interact with each other because they are electrically charged. In the simplest approximation this interaction is just the well-known Coulomb's Law. Coulomb's Law states that two charged particles have a mutual force between them that is proportional to the product of their charges and that gets weaker as the distance between them increases. In fact, the force is proportional to the inverse square power of the distance, or in algebraic language $F = \dfrac{e_1 e_2}{r^2}$. (This law is very similar in form to Newton's law of gravitation which states that $F = \dfrac{GmM}{r^2}$ where m and M are the masses of any two objects and G is the universal gravitational constant.)[10] In our modern quantum electrodynamics, this law has a more basic explanation, and the explanation is so typical of how present-day thinking in physics works that it is worth stating. In our current picture the two electrons do not interact directly with each other. Rather, each electron interacts directly with light quanta or, and this is really the same thing, with the electromagnetic field (*see* Fig. 5).

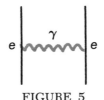

FIGURE 5

This avoids "action-at-a-distance," the idea that distant electrons interact with each other without some intermediary.[11] There is good evidence for the interaction of the electron with light quanta. When an electron is accelerated, it throws off light quanta which can be collected and studied, and the results can be compared with the calculations of quantum electrodynamics, with which they agree perfectly. Now two electrons, when they approach each other, can exchange light quanta; the light quanta thrown off by one can be caught by the other. Electrons playing this little game of catch influence each other's behavior in just such a way, it turns out, so as to give the Coulomb law as a first approximation. The higher approximations have been computed, and these, too, agree with experiment.

10 Newton's discussion of the law of gravitation may be located by consulting the GBWW *Syntopicon*, under MECHANICS 6d (1).

11 Discussion of action-at-a-distance may be found from the references cited under MECHANICS 6d (2) in the GBWW *Syntopicon*.

Now, Yukawa reasoned, if the nuclear force, the force that holds the nuclei together, is in any way analogous to the electrical one, it should result from the exchange of some particle among the components of the nucleus, the neutron and proton. At the first look one might suppose that the particle exchanged was the light quantum, just as it is for the electromagnetic force. This, however, Yukawa realized, was impossible. There are several reasons for this. In the first place, the nuclear force must be stronger than the electromagnetic one. After all, the protons in the nucleus, since they have like charges, repel each other electro-magnetically, and, hence, if the nuclear force were not stronger, the nucleus would simply fly apart. In the modern terminology, we would say that the number that measures the strength of the coupling of the nuclear quantum to the neutron or proton must be much greater than the number that measures the strength of the coupling of the electron to the light quantum. (*See* the *Table of Forces*, p. 325.) In fact, it turns out that the first number is a hundred to a thousand times larger than the second, which results in the rapid decays of unstable particles acted on by the strong force, to which we referred above. In the second place, the nuclear force is very "short range." This means that while the nuclear force is very strong, it comes into play only when the nuclear particles are very close to each other.

This can be seen experimentally as follows. When two charged par-ticles are made to collide, as, for example, in the famous experiments of Ernest Rutherford in 1911 in which helium nuclei (nuclei that consist of two positively-charged protons and two neutrons) were made to collide with other nuclei, also carrying positive charges, this collision (so long as the particle energies are low) is explicable essentially in terms of the electromagnetic forces alone. However, as the energy is increased, so that the colliding particles penetrate closer and closer to each other, one observes clear deviations from the electromagnetic pre-diction. These deviations are due to the nuclear force, and from such experiments one learns that its range does not extend out much farther than 10^{-13} cm., that is, a fermi.

In 1938, the Italian physicist Gian-Carlo Wick invented a beautiful argument that predicted the mass that the nuclear quanta must have. Wick's argument makes use of two points: the range of the nuclear force, which is 10^{-13} cm., and another of the Heisenberg uncertainty relations. This relation, which is, again, a cornerstone of the quantum theory, states that in no experiment that lasts a finite time can the energy of a system be measured precisely. In other words, the shorter the time a phenomenon takes to happen, the more uncertain—the less well determined—are the energies that characterize the process. Mathe-matically, we may express the relation by the formula $\Delta E \, \Delta t \sim h$ where Δt is the duration of time, ΔE is the uncertainty in energy and h is

Planck's constant. The occurrence of Planck's constant here means that we are dealing with a purely quantum-mechanical effect. We recover the classical physics by setting the constant equal to zero. In classical physics there are no uncertainties of this kind and the fact that the constant is so small, $h \sim 10^{-27}$ erg sec., explains why such phenomena never play a role in our ordinary daily experiences.

In Wick's argument, the uncertainty principle comes in as follows: When the neutron, or proton, emits the nuclear quantum, one would expect, according to classical physics, that it would weigh less after the emission than it did before—the mass loss being equal to the mass of the emitted quantum. This would be completely correct if we were considering the actual disintegration of the neutron or the proton. But in the processes that we are discussing, the neutron and proton do not lose their identity. A neutron and proton come together, exchange a nuclear quantum, and continue to be a neutron and a proton. This is possible in the quantum theory in view of the uncertainty principle discussed above; one does not expect energy to be exactly conserved in a process if it happens fast enough. If the nuclear quantum has a mass m, or an energy mc^2, then this is the amount of energy that would not be conserved in the emission process. But this is all right, as long as the particle is reabsorbed by another neutron or proton before a time $\Delta t \sim \dfrac{h}{mc^2}$. The particle, when it is emitted, will move at about the velocity of light. Hence, during its allowed time, it can move a distance away from the emitting particle that is about $c\,\Delta t \sim \dfrac{h}{mc}$. This is a famous length that is associated with any particle of mass m. It is known as the "Compton Wavelength" of the particle, after the American physicist Arthur Compton. The conclusion that Wick reached is that the range of the nuclear force is, by the uncertainty principle, about the size of the Compton wavelength of the nuclear quantum. Since we know the range, we can predict the Compton wavelength and, hence, the mass of the nuclear quantum. If the numbers are put in, one predicts, from the range, that the nuclear quantum should have a mass of about 100 mev.

Interestingly enough, at about this time, several physicists studying cosmic rays (showers of energetic particles that continually bombard the earth from outer space) discovered a particle that appeared to have all the properties of the nuclear quantum, including a mass close to the one predicted by Wick's argument. These objects have, in recent years, gone through some transformations in their nomenclature. From the beginning, names were given to them that reflected the fact that they were intermediate in mass between the 0.511006 ± 0.000007 mev of the electron and the 938.256 ± 0.01 mev of the proton. The name "meson" has stuck and all particles in this mass range are now called mesons.

Hence, before World War II, it appeared for a short time that the meson responsible for the nuclear forces had been discovered.

However, by 1947 it became apparent that this newly discovered meson was, in fact, the wrong meson. The reason that this became so clear was that the nuclear meson, by definition, must have very strong, short-range interactions with nuclei. Hence, when these mesons pass through matter they are very quickly absorbed by the neutrons and protons that constitute all matter. On the other hand, the meson that was first discovered was hardly absorbed at all by matter. To put the matter more accurately, it had essentially the same interactions with matter that an electron does—purely electromagnetic and, less importantly, weak interactions. The first meson discovered acted in all respects like a heavy electron and not like a nuclear quantum. This meson is now called the "mu meson" or "muon," and all the work done on it since the war has confirmed the fact that the muon is, essentially, a heavy electron. Indeed, one of the hardest problems in all of contemporary particle physics is to find an explanation of why nature has been so prodigal as to manufacture a light and a heavy electron.

STILL MORE PARTICLES

When physicists returned from the war they took up the puzzle of what had happened to the nuclear meson. In the late 1940's several things happened at once. On the theoretical side, H. A. Bethe and R. Marshak conjectured that the muon might be the product of the decay of the nuclear meson. In other words, the nuclear meson was there, all right, but it decayed so fast that all that was left when the cosmic rays finally arrived at the surface of the earth was its decay product, to wit the muon. At about the same time a number of physicists, especially C. F. Powell with C. G. Lattes and G. Ochiliani, renewed the experimental search in cosmic rays. It must be remembered that up until the late 1940's there were no large accelerators—accelerators capable of producing particles with a mass anything like 100 mev. To make good cosmic ray experiments it was necessary to go to higher altitudes where not so many cosmic ray particles were absorbed by the earth's atmosphere. In fact, many of the early cosmic-ray physicists were devoted mountain climbers, and some of the most active cosmic-ray laboratories could be found in the Andes and the Swiss and French Alps. But in addition to doing experiments at high altitudes—on mountains or in balloons—Powell was the principal developer of a new technique for detecting cosmic-ray particles. This was the photographic emulsion. Powell allowed a thick stack of photosensitive material to be the target of the particles, which then took their own pictures as they passed through the stack. These pictures look typically like Figure 6A.

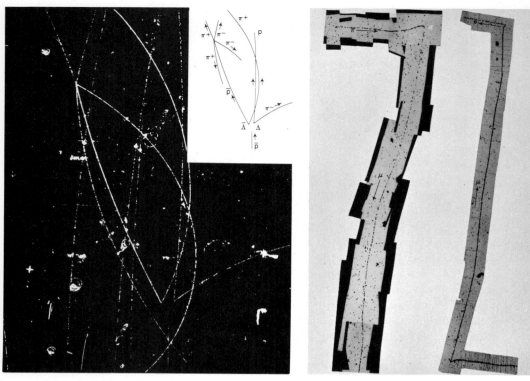

FIG. 6.—EARLY PHOTOGRAPHS OF ELEMENTARY PARTICLE TRACKS
Production and decay (A) of neutral lambda and antilambda pair in hydrogen bubble chamber as shown in photograph and diagram. The p from the decay annihilates forming four charged pions. Photographic emulsions (B) showing pion decay as observed in cosmic rays

In some of the photographic emulsions exposed in the Bolivian Andes, Powell found a set of tracks that looked like those in Figure 6B.

Of course, one such picture by itself would be hard to interpret. Only after one has accumulated many such photographs can one be confident that such a picture represents a real phenomenon and not some accident. In fact, all of the particles of modern physics leave very characteristic tracks, like fingerprints, in photographic emulsions. An electron, for example, leaves a light straight track which tends to curl up if the electron is left to slow down in the emulsion in the presence of a magnetic field; the field bends the electron and, hence, the track in a characteristic way. A proton leaves a wide superhighway of a track. The presence of a light quantum, which cannot be detected directly because it has no charge, shows up because the quanta produce electron-positron pairs that can be detected and have a special appearance familiar to experimental physicists. Also, the mass of a particle can be found, at least roughly, from the characteristics of the tracks, especially if the particle can be exposed in a region where there is a magnetic field. An experimental physicist can look at a photographic plateful of tracks and recite the history of the various particles depicted thereon, while to most of us, myself included, it has the look of the most obscure Jackson Pollock fantasy.

In these pictures, Powell and his collaborators found evidence for a particle with about the mass of the muon which decayed very quickly into at least one other particle—as it turned out, the muon—while the muon was observed to decay into at least an electron. Now, it is a consequence of the conservation of energy and momentum (not affected by the uncertainty relations, in this case) that a particle cannot simply decay into *one* other particle. The decay $A \rightarrow B$ is impossible. The two-particle decay $A \rightarrow B + C$ *is* possible and, hence, the new meson must have decayed into a muon plus something else, or perhaps plus several other things. The first question is, why did just the muon appear as a decay product on the photographic plate? The answer was clear. The other particle, or particles, must be electrically neutral, because an electrically neutral particle cannot show up directly in an emulsion, since it does not ionize the material composing the emulsion (which is how a particle photographs itself in the first place). Hence the new meson, now universally called a pi meson or pion, must have a decay of the form $\pi \rightarrow \mu + ?$, where the question mark represents some collection of neutral particles. But how many neutral particles were there?

To answer this question, we make use of the consequences of the conservation of energy and momentum in the decay. It turns out that energy-momentum conservation implies that, if there is only one missing particle, the muon will always be emitted in the pion decay with a unique, well-defined energy, while if there is more than one missing particle, the muon will be emitted with a whole spectrum of energies, the extra energies being shared among the neutrals. By measuring this energy and knowing the mass of the pi and the mass of the μ, one can determine the mass of the missing neutral. After studying this decay, the experimentalists were able to show that there could only be one missing neutral particle and that its mass must be very small. Indeed, all the properties of the missing particle were consistent with its being simply a neutrino. The neutrino was known to be emitted in nuclear beta decay, the other weak process that had been studied up to this time, and, hence, it was not implausible that it should make its appearance here as well. Thus the pion decay could be identified as the process $\pi \rightarrow \mu + \nu\mu$.

In writing this reaction I have been careful to write the symbol "$\nu\mu$" to make it clear that the neutrino emitted in this decay might be a different particle than the neutrino emitted along with the electron in beta decay which we may call ν_e. In fact, a series of remarkable experiments first done by a group of Columbia University physicists working on the large accelerator at Brookhaven in 1962, and recently repeated at CERN, show that these two neutrinos are different particles. The electron neutrino is known experimentally to have a mass less than 500 ev, and strong theoretical arguments suggest that it and the muon neutrino's mass are probably exactly zero, like that of the light quantum. The muon and its neutrino and the electron and its neutrino form a quartet of particles known collectively as "leptons."

At the time the pion was discovered, the first accelerators had just been built, energetic enough to produce pions in processes like $p + p \rightarrow p + n + \pi^+$ (where p stands for proton, n for neutron and π^+ for the positively charged pion). These accelerators produced pions more or less at the will of the experimenter—a modern machine can produce over a billion pions a second. This improved the experimental situation enormously since an experimenter no longer had to sit around waiting for a pion to show up in a cosmic-ray event so it could be studied.

Since the muon comes as the decay product of a pion, it, too, could be studied in detail. It was soon learned that the decay of the mu is actually given by $\mu^- \rightarrow e^- + \bar{v}_e + v_\mu$, where a muon neutrino and an electron antineutrino are emitted together with an electron or a positron depending on the charge of the mu. The mu, like the electron, comes in a positive and a negative version. It soon turned out that there were three kinds of pions: positive, negative, and neutral. This, too, was contained in Yukawa's theoretical proposal and its later modifications. The neutral particle is slightly lighter than the charged ones (*see* Particle Table for the exact masses), and it has the same interactions with neutrons and protons as the charged partners. The neutral pion, however, decays into two gammas (two light quanta) in the reaction $\pi^0 \rightarrow \gamma + \gamma$ which was also studied in great detail.

We can summarize the situation with respect to the particles as it stood in the late 1940's with a picture (*see* Fig. 7). (I have included in this picture the antineutrinos as well as the neutrinos.) It was quite a tidy diagram. One fully expected, at the time, that the antineutron and antiproton, with the same masses as the neutron and proton, would, sooner or later, be added to it as it was well known that every particle must have an antiparticle partner.

What had happened in the five years or so prior to 1955 is summarized in the right-hand half of the figure I drew up to describe the particle situation in the late forties. The right-hand table shows a set of new particles that simply turned up out of the blue, almost literally, since the first species showed up in cosmic-ray tracks of the type I have discussed in connection with the pion. (In the figure, I have given the positions of the masses of these new particles only roughly, and the reader can again consult the Particle Table to find out all the exact details). I think that it is entirely fair to say that no physicist of that time anticipated the arrival of these particles. In this respect, the situation was

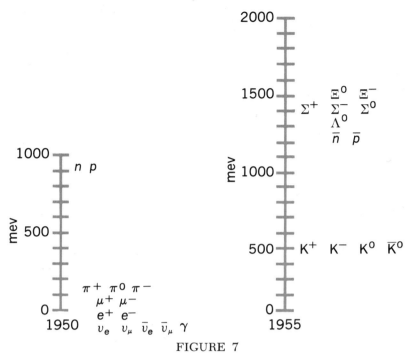

FIGURE 7

quite unlike that of the pion which had been brilliantly anticipated by
the work of Yukawa, but more like the situation of the muon that turned
up as a sort of uninvited guest preceding the arrival of the real guest
of honor, the pion. The new particles were so unexpected that they were,
almost at once, called "strange" particles, and, although they have by now
been very carefully studied and seem to us to be as normal as the pion,
they are still called strange particles.

AND STILL MORE PARTICLES

The new particles were first announced in 1947 by the English physicists G. D. Rochester and C. C. Butler. They used a device called
a "cloud chamber" to detect them. The cloud chamber can be expanded
and contracted. After the contraction, the heated water vapor in the
device is suddenly cooled by expansion of the chamber. The water vapor
is then put in a state of "supersaturation" in which the droplets composing it condense very easily around the ions produced by the passage
of charged particles through the chamber. These tracks of droplets were
illuminated and photographed by Rochester and Butler. If one looks at
these photographs, one sees among the many swirling, Jackson Pollock-
like lines showing the passage of presumably conventional particles, a

pair of tracks shaped like a "V" which appear to materialize from nowhere. There is an empty space in the chamber and then, suddenly, a "V" appears, indicating that two charged particles move off at high speed at an angle to each other. The natural interpretation of this event is that a neutral particle, unobservable in the chamber, has come along and decayed into the two charged particles. It is a consequence of the conservation of momentum that the two particles would be emitted in opposite directions to each other—they would fly away from each other along a straight line—if the emitting particle decayed at rest. The fact that the tracks were bent up in a "V" indicated that the decaying particle had been in motion when it decayed—the faster the motion, the more sharply the tracks are bent into the "V."

At the present time the object that Butler and Rochester found is called the lambda particle. Since it is heavier than the neutron and proton, it is given the generic name "hyperon," indicating that its mass lies beyond the neutron and proton, known generically as "nucleons." The lambda particle has no charged counterparts. It is known as an "isotopic singlet," indicating that it is the only particle to have its mass value—that is, there are no charged counterparts at about the same mass. The use of "isotopic" in this context has really nothing to do with the isotopes of the old-fashioned nuclear physics. The old sense of the word "isotope," as we have discussed above, has to do with the fact that adding a neutron to a nucleus produces a new nucleus, heavier than the first but with the same charge and, hence, the same chemical properties. The new use of "isotopic" refers to properties of the particles themselves. It is an empirical fact that at certain mass values there appear families of particles with very closely related properties. For example, at about 938 mev there are the neutron and proton. The neutron and proton have essentially the same nuclear interactions and seem to differ only in their electrical properties. The proton is charged, for example, and the neutron is neutral. Hence, in an imaginary world in which electricity and magnetism were somehow switched off, the neutron and proton would, one guesses, appear absolutely identical.

Borrowing from the language of atomic physics, where one frequently finds sets of electrons in shells around the nucleus all having about the same energy and where such similar energy levels are called "multiplets," one also calls these near degeneracies in energies among the particles multiplets; in this case, one calls them, traditionally, isotopic multiplets. The neutron and proton form an isotopic "doublet" since there are two of them. The three pions form an isotopic "triplet" since they come in charges of plus, minus, and zero, and the lambda, since it has no charged partners, is called an isotopic singlet. Soon after the lambda was discovered, a somewhat heavier isotopic triplet of hyperons was found and these were called the sigmas (*see* Fig. 7 and Particle Table). The decay of the charged sigmas is like that of the lambda. It goes into one nucleon and one pion with appropriate charges to conserve electric charge in the decay. The neutral sigma has an interesting decay mode. It goes into a lambda and a photon: $\Sigma^0 \rightarrow \Lambda^0 + \gamma$. This decay can only be seen after the photon has created an electron-positron pair and after the lambda has itself decayed into visible particles. But, by now, it has been extremely well studied.

At about the same time that the hyperons were found, an entirely new family of mesons was also discovered. These are now called "K" mesons, but for several years these objects and their nomenclature went through a period of extreme confusion. The reason is that the K mesons have several decay modes. The neutral K particles, for example, have at least five prominent modes (*see* Particle Table) and some remarkable rare ones that we shall want to discuss later.

APPROXIMATE CONSERVATION LAWS AND PARITY

In deciding this question (it finally turned out that the K mesons were a single particle with numerous decay modes), one of the most important discoveries in twentieth-century physics was made—I refer to the nonconservation of parity. Before discussing parity, a most difficult concept, let us discuss the concept of conservation laws in general. The conservation laws of classical physics were exact laws. The conservation of energy, momentum, charge—all classical concepts—hold exactly in any process in classical physics. As we have seen, with the quantum theory, the classical laws have to be somewhat modified to take into account the Heisenberg uncertainty principle. It makes no sense to say that something is conserved if it cannot be measured, and the uncertainty relations define the limitations on the measurements of quantum-mechanical systems. With the discovery of elementary particles, still a new type of conservation law began to appear in physics. These are the approximate conservation laws—laws that do not hold exactly but hold approximately, even taking into account the uncertainty principle.

In what follows we shall see some examples of these laws, but the general situation appears to be as follows. The strong interactions obey all the conservation laws. But as the interaction that is studied gets weaker—first the electromagnetic and then the weak interaction—many of the conservation laws that the strong interactions obey are violated. Since the weak interactions take the longest time, we might also restate this situation by saying that the longer the time scale of the interaction, the more it violates the conservation laws. Indeed, there is some question whether there might not be even weaker interactions which violate all the laws.

Parity is a perfect example of an approximate conservation law. To see

343

what it means let me note that, in classical physics, every system could be given two equivalent descriptions—a left-handed description and a right-handed description. This means a description in terms of left-handed coordinates and right-handed coordinates (*see* Fig. 8). Any

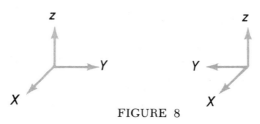

FIGURE 8

point in space can be located by measuring its distance from the axes in either of these systems, and all the laws of classical physics read exactly the same whether one uses a left-handed or a right-handed description. (Left and right hand here refer to the fact that one system can be formed out of the first three fingers of the left hand and the other out of the first three fingers of the right hand.) Naturally, the first guess was that quantum-mechanical systems had the same freedom of description. This has turned out to be true only so long as just the strong interactions are considered. For the weak interactions, the left- and right-handed descriptions are not equivalent.

This very remarkable fact first made its appearance with the K mesons. It turns out that elementary particles like the K meson and the pi meson have what is known as their "intrinsic" parity. This is a peculiar quantum-mechanical characteristic which describes how the mathematical description of the particle, when it is at rest, changes when one goes from a left-handed to a right-handed system. The intrinsic parity of the pi meson was determined not long after its discovery. Moreover, it was easy to show that two pions at rest and three pions at rest had to be in states of opposite parity. Hence, when it became clear, in 1955, that the K mesons decayed both into two and three pions, it looked as if the K meson must have both parities, which was impossible.

A way out of this impasse was to suppose that the K meson and the pi meson had the same parity, but that parity was violated in the decay mechanism itself, so that the decay could produce systems with opposite parities—that is, two and three pions. Following this lead, T.-D. Lee and C. N. Yang made an analysis of the whole question of parity conservation in the weak decays and found that at that time there was no experimental evidence for it. They suggested a number of experiments to test it, and when these were performed, they showed that parity was violated in all the weak decays and, hence, was, in general, only an approximate conservation law that held on very short time scales. Thus, the fact that the

K meson was a single particle with a mass of about 500 mev played a vital role in suggesting that parity symmetry and parity conservation were not exact laws.

STRANGENESS

The list of strange particles known in 1955 is completed by the xi particle which, like the nucleon, is a doublet system that exists in a neutral and a negatively charged version. All of the antiparticles to these strange particles have been discovered since then and they all have the properties that one would expect them to.

By 1955, accelerators had been built large enough to produce strange particles in reactions like $\pi^- + p \rightarrow \Sigma^- + K^+$. In studying these reactions, an absolutely striking fact began to appear. It was never possible to produce strange particles one at a time. A reaction like $\pi^+ + n \rightarrow K^+ + n$, in which a K meson is produced, alone, without another strange particle, has never been obtained. This fact acquired the name "associated production," indicating that strange particles were always produced in association with other strange particles. This, in itself, was curious enough, but to compound matters, the association rule was clearly violated in the decay of the strange particles. For example, the lambda was always produced in association with a K meson in reactions like $\pi^+ + n \rightarrow \Lambda^0 + K^+$, but when it decayed it decayed into, for example, $\Lambda^0 \rightarrow p + \pi^-$, and, here, there are no strange particles in the final state. It soon became clear that the two reactions, the production reaction and the decay reaction, were quite distinct. A glance at the Particle Table shows that the lambda is a relatively long-lived object, and, hence, its decay is caused by the weak force. On the other hand, lambdas are produced copiously in pion-nucleon collisions, and, hence, the production reaction is a strong reaction. The conclusion is that the strong reaction respects the associated production laws while the weak decays do not.

In 1953, the American physicist M. Gell-Mann and the Japanese physicist K. Nishijima, although independently, put forward a scheme that accommodated these new phenomena and predicted others as well. It has been an immensely fruitful notion. It is the concept of "strangeness." In the Gell-Mann-Nishijima scheme, each particle is given a new quantum number called its strangeness. This quantum number is something like the electric charge, and one can think of the strangeness as a new sort of charge (but having nothing to do with the electromagnetic field) that each particle carries. The conventional particles, the nucleon, photon, pion, mu meson, and the neutrinos are assigned 0 strangeness. In the Particle Table I have given the accepted assignment of strangeness to each of the strange particles. These assignments do not come out of thin air. They are determined by the rule that all strong interactions conserve the strangeness. This accounts for associated production. If the lambda has a negative strangeness it must be produced from pions and nucleons, which have no strangeness, in association with some particle that carries positive strangeness, the K^+ meson. The weak interactions do not conserve strangeness and, hence, one may have the decay $\Lambda^0 \rightarrow p + \pi^-$ in which there is a negative strangeness on the left side of the equation and a 0 strangeness on the right.

It is a remarkable experimental fact that when violations of strangeness occur, they are always in units of one at a time. There appear to be no cases where, for example, a weak force changes strangeness by two units. For example, there is no evidence for the decay of a xi zero into a proton and a pi minus, that is, $\Xi^0 \rightarrow p + \pi^-$, in which strangeness would change by two, while the decay $\Xi^0 \rightarrow \Lambda^0 + \pi^0$, in which strangeness changes by one, is a common decay mode of the xi particle. It is as if it costs nature something each time the strangeness is changed and that nature would have liked to conserve the strangeness exactly, but since this did not work, strangeness is violated by as little as possible.

The Gell-Mann-Nishijima scheme allows for particles that have strangeness as large as 3, and one of the most important recent discoveries, which we shall come back to, is the Ω^- particle which has a strangeness of -3.

THE RESONANCES

At this point the reader may be feeling a rising sense of despair over the complexity of the physics we have been describing. This despair was shared by many physicists at the time, and there were even more or less humorous suggestions that experimental work on elementary-particle physics be suspended until everyone had a chance to go home and think, or, more drastically, that people should be fined for any discoveries of new particles and so on. In a somewhat different context, the late Professor P. W. Bridgeman, a crusty New Englander and a Nobel Prize winner in Physics, once remarked, "Blame God, He put the facts there." In elementary-particle physics, it now begins to appear that the real underlying simplicity becomes apparent only after things seem to get much worse. It is just recently, after a whole universe of still newer particles has turned up, that some sort of a pattern is beginning to emerge from the chaos.

These new particles are typified by the first one of them that was found, the N^*, sometimes called the first excited state of the nucleon, or the first pion-nucleon resonance. The idea of resonances is familiar. A tuning fork absorbs energy from sound waves that strike it. This causes the metal to vibrate. However, at certain sound frequencies, which are determined by the material out of which the tuning forks are made, the absorption of energy is especially strong, and the vibration of the forks is increased dramatically. This is called a resonance.

A similar sort of phenomenon occurs in particle physics. This is usually studied in "scattering" processes, in which particles are made to collide with stationary targets. In a typical experiment, pions, of a fixed energy, made in an accelerator, are collimated into a narrow beam. (All of this is done with magnets that act to focus the charged mesons.) A typical modern target is a tank of liquid hydrogen, which is to say, a large collection of protons. (The electron is so far away from the proton and so loosely bound to it, when the collision occurs, that for all intents and purposes, one can forget that it is there.) The question of interest can be stated as follows: given that so many pions per second per unit area strike the target (or what is known as the "incident flux" of pions), what is the probability that a given pion will be reflected—scattered—from the target at a given angle? It may seem to the reader that this question is banal. But a few examples will show that in its answer are contained many keys to unraveling the nature of the forces that act between the particle and the target. An especially nice illustration is due to George Gamow. It concerns firing bullets—pions—into bales of cotton—a target. If there is just cotton in the bales then the bullets will go, almost undeflected, through the bales. This tells us that the target is "soft," meaning that the forces tending to repel the bullets are weak. On the other hand, if there are metal blocks in the bales, then some of the bullets will bounce off the metal blocks at wide angles. The presence of this wide-angle scattering tells us that there is a "hard" target—a target with strong, localized forces that tend to repulse the bullets.

Every force law produces its characteristic scattering, and, to test a force law, one of the best things that one can do is to compute the scattering that it would produce and to see if this fits the experimental data. In this way Lord Rutherford, in the experiments alluded to above, discovered that the atomic nucleus was confined to a small ball of positive charge, and, by further refinements in the experiment, learned that in addition to the Coulomb force, there also was a nuclear force. Scattering experiments can also show up resonances. At certain energies of the incident particle, the scattering becomes dramatically enhanced. In Figure 9 I have represented experimental curves for the scattering of π^+ mesons from protons as a function of the kinetic energy of the incoming pions. The kinetic energy of the pions is given in units of billions of electron volts—bev—on the side of Figure 9, while at the bottom the amount of scattering is given in somewhat arbitrary-looking units.

It is clear from the figure that in the neighborhood of 200 bev something very striking is going on. A careful study of the scattering in this region shows that there is a resonance and, further, that the resonance is confined to the state of the pion-nucleon system with angular momen-

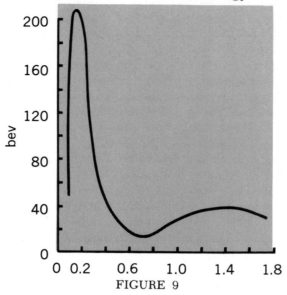

FIGURE 9

tum 3/2. One way of thinking about this resonance is to suppose that there is a particle with spin 3/2 but with the same quantum numbers as a pion and a nucleon, which is formed by the pion and nucleon when the incident pion has just the right energy. To explain the position of the resonance, this particle, it turns out, has a mass of 1,238 mev, and it decays, by the strong forces, into a pion and a nucleon. Thus, at resonance, the scattering looks like $\pi^+ + p \rightarrow N^\circ \rightarrow \pi^+ + p$. One interesting feature of this particle is that its mass is not quite well defined. The "1,238 Mev" refers to what might be thought of as its average mass. Actually, the N° has an uncertainty in its mass of about 100 mev, which reflects itself in the width of the resonance curve above. This is, in fact, to be expected. The strong interaction causes the N° to decay right away after it is formed, and, by the uncertainty principle, the uncertainty in the mass is related to the lifetime by the formula $\Delta mc^2 \sim \dfrac{h}{\tau}$ or $\tau \sim \dfrac{h}{\Delta mc^2}$. Putting in the numbers, we find that $\tau \sim 10^{-23}$ sec., so that the N° is very short-lived, indeed. The N° is doubly charged.

It seems something in the nature of a miracle that all of the particles we have discussed, and all that have been discovered, have electrical charges that are simple multiples of the charge of the electron or positron, or else 0. As we have noted, the nuclei all have charges that are simple multiples of the proton charge (which is identical to the charge of the positron). The explanation of this is, of course, that all the nuclei are made out of protons, and the charge of the nucleus is determined by the charges of the protons in it. On the basis of this analogy, one might speculate that all of the elementary particles are made up out of some basic units and that these basic units carry the charge of the electron. This would reduce the problem to that of finding these basic units and explaining why they have the charge of the electron, or some multiple thereof. Of this, more will be said later.

In fact, the N° is an isotopic quintet—there are five N°'s with charges 2, 1, 0, −1, −2. The other N°'s show up in pion-nucleon scattering when pions and nucleons of the appropriate charges are scattered.

Is the N° really a particle? In fact, the N° seems to be as much of a particle as anything else. It differs from the other objects we have discussed in that its decay goes very fast so that it has an observable spread in its mass. The other particles also have uncertainties in their masses, but these are relatively small, since the particles are rather long-lived.

Is this the end? By no means! After the N° was found, one resonance after another turned up. The energetic reader may turn to the Particle Table and see them listed in detail. Almost all our old friends, the pions, the K mesons, the nucleons, the strange hyperons, can, at certain energies, resonate with each other. It is a dazzling array, and there is no reason to think we have found anything like all of them.

THE LIGHT DAWNS

It is a source of continual amazement that some sort of order can now begin to be perceived in this almost fantastically complex situation. I will not trouble the reader with an account of all the false starts that the theorists made in coping with this situation. In this sense, theoretical physics is quite unlike experimental physics. A good experiment always has a value, since it has uncovered a piece of the truth. An unsuccessful theoretical speculation, or even a partially successful one, soon becomes a historical curiosity and is brushed aside as quickly as possible to make way for a better scheme. I will try to give a brief outline of the steps that have led to the present outlook.

In 1949, Fermi and Yang made the interesting observation that the pi meson has the same quantum numbers as a nucleon-antinucleon pair would have if they were stuck together in a state with no angular momentum. This is not to say that a pion meson *is* a nucleon-antinucleon pair, but rather that its quantum numbers such as charge, spin, and parity are the same as such a pair. We have a situation here that is somewhat analogous to that of regarding a nucleus as neutrons and protons stuck together. The great difference is that nuclei are relatively loosely bound systems so that the neutrons and protons retain, in the nucleus, many of the characteristics they have as free particles. On the other hand, in the Fermi-Yang model, the nucleon-antinucleon pair has a very strong bond. We can see this at once by considering the masses involved. The pion has a mass of 140 mev, while the nucleon-antinucleon pair has a mass of about 1,876 mev. Thus to bind them together requires a binding energy of 1,736 mev. This binding energy is enormous; it is larger than the mass of either nucleon. The theoretical study of systems with such large binding energies is still in its infancy, and it is by no means clear what sorts of problems such a study may reveal. It is quite clear, however, that, despite the huge binding energies, the composite system may be expected to retain some of the properties of the more elementary systems that compose it, including charge, parity, and so forth. This is a consequence of the assumption that the forces that cause the binding conserve these quantum numbers.

The real advantage of the Fermi-Yang model is that two particles, the pion and the nucleon, can be described for the price of one. It is natural to ask whether, in view of the many new particles that have been found, one could find a simple set of basic ones out of which to compose the rest in the same spirit that Fermi and Yang composed the pi meson out of nucleons and antinucleons. In making this attempt, one encounters two important conditions. In the first place, there must be at least one strange particle among the basic set. If there were only nonstrange particles, then no matter how they were combined, they could never make a strange particle. In the second place, there is a basic difference between baryons and the other particles that must be reckoned with. We have already emphasized that baryons never decay entirely into leptons. The most famous of all baryon decays, $n \rightarrow p + e^- + \bar{v}$, is typical in that, along with the two leptons in the final state, there is also a baryon, the proton. Baryons also never decay into mesons. The baryons always are conserved in the decays. If one starts with a baryon, there will always be a baryon left over. Thus, the number of baryons is a conserved quantity in any reaction. This number is called the baryon number. Each baryon is arbitrarily assigned a unit baryon number, and each antibaryon has baryon number -1. The fact that baryons and antibaryons have opposite baryon numbers is confirmed by the fact that a proton and antiproton which together have 0 baryon number can annihilate into only mesons and leptons while the proton itself which has unit baryon number is stable against decaying into them. All nonbaryons are given 0 baryon number.

From this analysis, it follows that the basic set of particles cannot all be mesons, since the mesons have 0 baryon number and can never be put together to make a baryon. A few years ago, the Japanese physicist S. Sakata noted that all particles (except the leptons, the electron, the mu meson, and the neutrinos, which do not have strong interactions and form a class apart) could be composed out of a basic set of three, namely the neutron, the proton, and the lambda, and their antiparticles. To see how this works for one of the strange particles, take the sigma minus which has negative charge, negative strangeness, and positive baryon number. In the spirit of Sakata, one may write the odd looking equation $\Sigma^- = \Lambda^0\,\bar{p}n$ which states that the sigma minus is made up of a lambda with 0 charge and negative strangeness, an antiproton with 0 strangeness and negative charge, and a neutron with 0 charge and no strangeness. It is easy to see that this system has unit baryon number like the sigma. In the same way, one can compose the other particles.

For some time after Sakata proposed his model, it was thought that it might account, in principle, for all that was known about the strange particles. Trouble appeared, however, on two fronts. The model, taken most simply, failed to describe some experiments involving proton-antiproton annihilation. The analysis is fairly complicated, and since, in light of present developments, the model has been abandoned, in its original form, there is not much point in going into the matter here.

More basically, there was the question of what many physicists call "particle democracy." Why, of all the observed particles, should the neutron, proton, and lambda really be the basic units instead of some other set? They do not appear to stand out in any special sense, and it is really quite arbitrary to make them the fundamental units. Hence, the idea began to gain ground that the fundamental units (if there are any) might consist of objects that had not as yet been discovered. Gell-Mann has given the name "quarks" to such objects in general, and the name has stuck. ("Quark" is a term that Gell-Mann cadged from James Joyce's *Finnegan's Wake* because these objects have been detected, at least up to now, only by their "palpitant piping, chirrup, croak, and quark.")

Before one dismisses out of hand the idea of accounting for the observed particles in terms of their being composites of objects as yet unobserved, it is important to recollect that this has been the history of atomic physics from the beginning. The real significance of Democritus' work is that he was the first scientist to attempt to explain the obviously very complicated patterns of experience by appealing to an underlying simple substratum of objects, the atoms, which were, in themselves, undetectable. As modern a subject as nuclear physics has operated along similar lines. It was held that all the complex nuclei were made up out of simpler units long before these units, the neutron and proton, were discovered. In fact, there were even proposals before the neutron was discovered that the basic components in the nucleus were simply the proton and the electron.

QUARKS AND UNITARY SYMMETRY

Hence, on to the quarks! I must warn the reader that what follows will take some special concentration on his part. I will make it as simple as I can, and anyone who bears with me will, I hope, come away with some of the sense of wonder that I feel myself that the scheme works.

The neutron, proton, and lambda, and the other strange particles appear at first glance to differ greatly from each other. In particular, it would appear as if there were an ineluctable difference between strange and nonstrange particles. But, ever since these particles were well established experimentally, physicists have been haunted by the idea that there was some connection among them. For example, it is an accident that there are just eight hyperons, n, p, Λ^0, Σ^+, Σ^0, Σ^-, Ξ^-, Ξ^0, or does this number eight reflect some deep underlying symmetry of the physics? Furthermore, these eight particles are not as different as all that. Experiments have now shown that they all have the same spin and parity. For quite awhile, it appeared as if the sigmas and the lambda might have opposite parities. This would have killed off any possibility of putting them together in some scheme in which the eight particles are somehow treated on the same footing. But now it is certain that all eight particles do have the same parities.

Not only are there eight hyperons that appear to have similar properties, apart from their electrical charges and strangeness, but there are two families of mesons, one a clear family of eight and another a mixed family of nine, that have among themselves very similar properties. The family of eight mesons includes the seven we have already discussed, namely the three pi mesons (π^+, π^-, π^0) and the four K mesons (K$^+$, K$^-$, K^0, $\overline{\text{K}}{}^0$). In addition, there is an eighth object known to physicists as the η ("eta") meson, which was discovered in 1962, a very short-lived particle with a mass of about 548 mev. It is neutral and decays into pi mesons and gamma rays in various combinations. Like the K meson and the pi, it has 0 spin and odd parity. The K meson and the eta have very similar masses and the pion is somewhat lighter. But here again is a group of eight particles, all with the same spin and parity, somewhat different masses and strangenesses, and the question arises again as to whether they could have something basic to do with each other.

The story is not over. There is still a third group of mesons—nine in number, or, for reasons that we shall explain later, eight-plus-one in number—again with properties similar to each other. These mesons are all very short-lived. They all have spin 1 this time, and they all have odd parity. For no very good reason, they are known by the names, in order of increasing mass, from the lightest, the ω at 757 mev, to the ϕ at 1,019 mev: ω^0, ρ^+, ρ^-, ρ^0, K^{*+}, K^{*-}, K^{*0}, $\overline{\text{K}}{}^{*0}$, ϕ. They come in assorted charges and strangenesses, but here again there is a striking overall similarity among them.

In fact, it begins to look as if we are in the presence of a conspiracy in which the number eight or eight-plus-one plays an important role.

It is remarkable that this property of the particles was anticipated, before the discovery of many of the resonances such as the eta, independently by Gell-Mann and by an Israeli physicist named Yuval Ne'eman. Their work was done in the early 1960's and has received brilliant confirmation during the past year. In viewing their work retrospectively, as we are doing, it appears much easier than it was. Now we see clearly why such family structures with magic numbers like eight or eight-plus-one might arise. But the reader should try to imagine what he would have made out of the chaos of incomplete experimental results that existed when this work was begun.

We have already noted that, following the analysis of the Sakata model, it was clear that all the observed particles could be regarded as being made up out of only three quarks. How would we make mesons out of quarks? That is easy. Suppose the quarks are baryons, as some of them must be if we are to make baryons out of them. Then a quark and an antiquark have together 0 baryon number just like a meson, so we just have to stick them together as in the Sakata model. Thus we can think of the mesons as quark-antiquark pairs being stuck together. But how many distinct pairs are there? That is also easy. We have three distinct quarks and three distinct antiquarks and they can be put together in any combination two at a time that we like. This makes nine pairs. But nine is eight plus one.

In view of the last paragraph, it must seem at least possible that the quark scheme can lead to definite groupings of the elementary particles that are made out of them. We must, of course, return to the question of where the ninth spin-0 meson is and why the spin-1 mesons fall into a closely knit eight-plus-one family, while the spin-0 mesons fall into a closely knit eight-member family. But, we can now begin to see why the families should exist—why sets of particles should be formed having very similar properties. Indeed, this similarity among the members of the families can be accounted for by supposing that the underlying quarks are similar. In genetic terms, if the quark and antiquark pairs combine to produce mesonic offspring, and if the parents are all very similar, then the offspring should also be quite similar. We may suppose, in first approximation, that the three parent quarks all have the same mass. At least one of them must be strange since the offspring include strange particles. At least one of them must be charged electrically since the offspring can carry charge. We can picture the three quarks which we might label S for strange neutral quark, N for nonstrange neutral quark, and P for positively charged nonstrange quark in terms of a little equilateral triangle (*see* Fig. 10). The two nonstrange quarks having the same mass constitute an isotopic doublet in our previous terminology, and the S, being the only strange member, is an isotopic singlet. The antiquarks can be pictured in terms of a quark triangle turned over

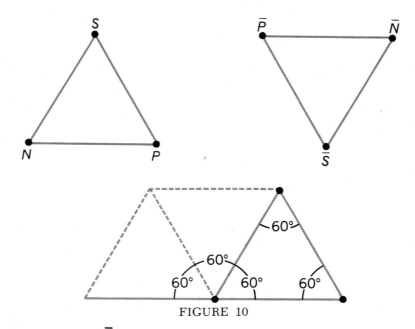

FIGURE 10

on its head. The $\overline{P}$, being the antiparticle of the P, will have negative charge if the P has positive charge, and the $\overline{N}$ and $\overline{S}$ are both neutral. If we give the S negative strangeness, then the $\overline{S}$ will have positive strangeness. Now we can see what kind of geometrical figures we can make up out of the equilateral quark-antiquark triangles. Equilateral triangles have equal angles, and since the total number of degrees in a triangle is 180, each angle is equal to 60 degrees. The equilateral triangles have a nice symmetry property which Figure 10 illustrates. If we rotate the triangle through 60 degrees about an end point, marked *0* in the figure, we rotate the quark triangle into the antiquark triangle, and if we rotate through another 60 degrees, we come back to a quark triangle. Thus, the quark and antiquark triangles are symmetric when rotated through 120 degrees. Such a rotation produces a figure identical to the original. Now, if we mate quarks with antiquarks, we might expect that the progeny, which we shall represent by geometric figures composed out of quark-antiquark triangles, will have the same properties—their geometrical figures will be symmetric under rotations of 120 degrees. Let us complete Figure 10 by continuing to rotate either the quark or antiquark triangles through 60-degree steps. We get a regular hexagon, which is symmetric under 120-degree rotations (*see* Fig. 11).

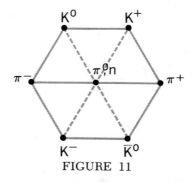

FIGURE 11

The reader will notice that we have identified the various vertices of the hexagon with mesons. In this case, we have represented the spin-0, odd-parity set of eight mesons on this diagram. Particles belonging to the same isotopic multiplet are on the same straight-line level on the diagram—viz., the three pions that run along the center straight line. The center point of the diagram is special in that there are two particles at the center. This degeneracy of particles is only possible for interior points in the diagram. Each edge point can represent only one particle.

By this time the reader, if he has any patience left, must be wondering if he is involved in some kind of confidence game. What do these diagrams really mean, and where do they come from, apart from their aesthetic appeal?

The symmetry among the three underlying quarks, which appears when their masses are set equal, is known, technically, as "unitary symmetry." The set of operations that leave the three quarks invariant is known, technically, as the "unitary group in three dimensions," and the three quarks form a representation of this group. The little triangle is a way of visualizing this representation. The three antiquarks form an antirepresentation or a conjugate representation, which we visualize with a triangle stood on its head. The process of making mesons out of quark-antiquark pairs preserves the unitary symmetry, assuming that the force that holds the pairs together is also symmetric. It can be thought of as combining together a three representation and an antithree representation to form a new representation of the group. It is a mathematical fact that this combination produces an eight representation, which we have diagrammed with the hexagon, and a representation containing just a single element which we would indicate by a point somewhere. This process is indicated by the mathematical equation $3 \cdot \overline{3} = 8 + 1$, and, in the technical jargon of the mathematicians, the eight and the one are "the irreducible representations in the decomposition of the product of the 3 and $\overline{3}$ representations."

The mathematicians can also prove something else about these product representations. As long as the three quarks and antiquarks have the same mass and the force that holds them together is sufficiently symmetric, all the members of the eight—the particles in the hexagon—must have exactly the same mass. This explains why there are families with nearly the same mass. Of course, it explains too much, since, in fact, the particles in the families do not have exactly the same mass—the K mesons weigh in at about 490 mev, while the pions weigh in at about 140 mev. But a slight refinement of the description given so far explains this, too, and tells us, in addition, what the real masses are or, at least, gives us relations among them. The representation with only one single particle—called the singlet or "trivial" representation—does not have to have the same mass as the eight. It can lie anywhere, and where it lies depends on the nature of the forces that hold the quarks and antiquarks together. For the spin-0 mesons, the pi, the K's, and the eta, the corresponding singlet, very probably, lies at a much higher mass. It has not yet been definitely identified, but there have been some candidates for it and it will, no doubt, be positively pinned down sooner or later.

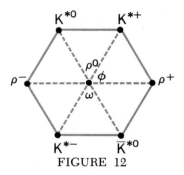

FIGURE 12

For the spin-1 mesons, the three rhos, the four K*'s, the phi, and the omega, we have a case in which the eight and the singlet lie very close together. In fact, they lie so closely together that it is impossible to say whether the phi or the omega belongs to the eight or the one. The K*'s and the rhos must belong to the eight, since, according to the theory, a meson carrying electrical charge can never be a singlet. In Figure 12, we have shown the spin-1 hexagon with the three neutral particles in the middle.

Suddenly, the existence of all these particles and resonances assumes quite a pleasant aspect; the more, the merrier. Let nature produce particles by the bushel. We can now think about them happily and try to fit them into pictures made up out of quark-antiquark triangles. This is why particle physicists have been so excited in the last year or so.

A final note about the mesons: it may appear somewhat odd that the same quarks and antiquarks can be put together to make both spin-1 and spin-0 mesons. This is easily accounted for if we assume that the quarks have spin 1/2 like the other baryons. Two spin-1/2 particles, when put together, can make a composite, in the simplest case, with either spin 1 or spin 0 (*see* Fig. 13); hence, the two types of mesons.

$$\uparrow + \uparrow = \uparrow \qquad\qquad \uparrow + \downarrow = \updownarrow$$

$$\tfrac{1}{2} + \tfrac{1}{2} = 1 \qquad\qquad \tfrac{1}{2} - \tfrac{1}{2} = 0$$

FIGURE 13

356

We began this discussion by observing that there were eight baryons with similar properties; that is, n, p, Σ^+, Σ^-, Σ^0, Λ^0, Ξ^-, Ξ^0. To make baryons out of quarks and antiquarks, we must stick them together to produce a final offspring that has baryon number 1. For this, there are two possibilities, broadly speaking. We can try to make baryons out of quarks alone, never resorting to antiquarks which have negative baryon number, or we can use both quarks and antiquarks in suitable combinations. Each of these possibilities has been explored by physicists, and each has its problems and rewards. Let us begin by supposing that we use only quarks and never antiquarks. The first thing to try is to stick two quarks together in the combination 3 × 3. Of course, the reader will see that if the quarks have the usual assignment of unit baryon number, then the offspring of this mating will have baryon number 2 and will not be the usual baryons which have only baryon number 1. But apart from this, the multiplication of two three's, unlike a three and an antithree, produces something quite different. Mathematically, we can represent these two cases with the following formulae:

$$3 \times \bar{3} = 1 + 8$$
$$\text{and}$$
$$3 \times 3 = \bar{3} + 6$$

Or, in terms of pictures:

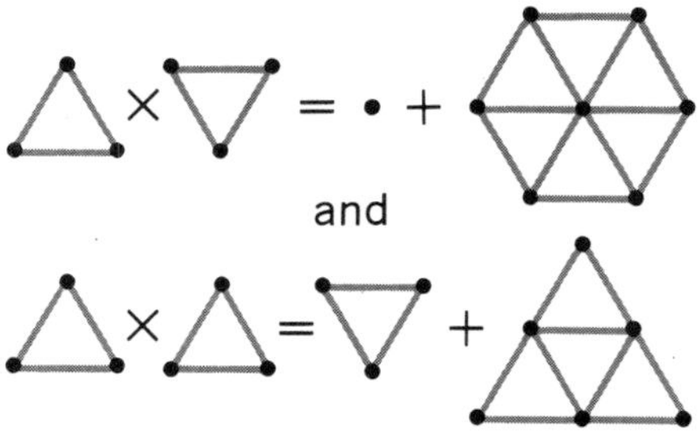

and

FIGURE 14

This is simply how the mathematical ball bounces. The latter case, the mating of two quarks, does not correspond to any structure that has as yet been seen. There are eight familiar baryons, and not six and three. Hence, if we adopt the first strategy, we are forced to make the baryons, or to try to make them, out of three quarks; we are led to consider the triple product 3 × 3 × 3. Here the mathematicians have something nice in store for us. In Figure 15 they show that

$$3 \times 3 \times 3 = 1 + 8 + 8 + 10$$
$$\text{or}$$

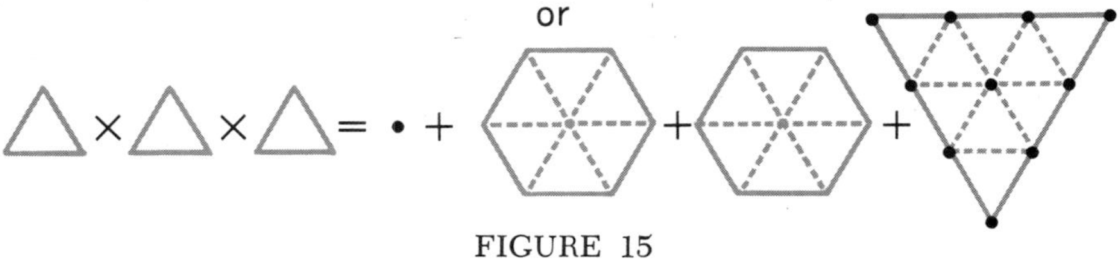

FIGURE 15

The last big triangle contains ten particles, so that out of the triple product of quarks we are led, besides the familiar eight's, to a new set of ten, and we might ask whether there are ten baryons somewhere that would fit into this triangle. In fact, the greatest triumph of the whole picture is that it led to the prediction that there would be a family of ten, and, during this past year, this has been decisively confirmed.

We can easily fit the set of eight on a hexagon with a double point in the middle, as with the mesons (*see* Fig. 16). The eight antibaryons can be fitted onto another hexagon, and the singlet baryon, which has not yet been identified, is, no doubt, floating around somewhere.

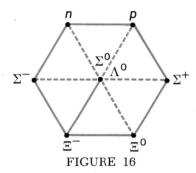

FIGURE 16

What are the ten's? We recall that after the strange particles were discovered, a new class of objects came in view, the first of which we labeled the N^*, or the nucleon resonant state. It has spin 3/2. But this is no obstacle to the quark scheme since if we compose a particle out of three spin-1/2 quarks the resulting system can have, it is easy to show, spin 1/2 or spin 3/2 (*see* Fig. 17).

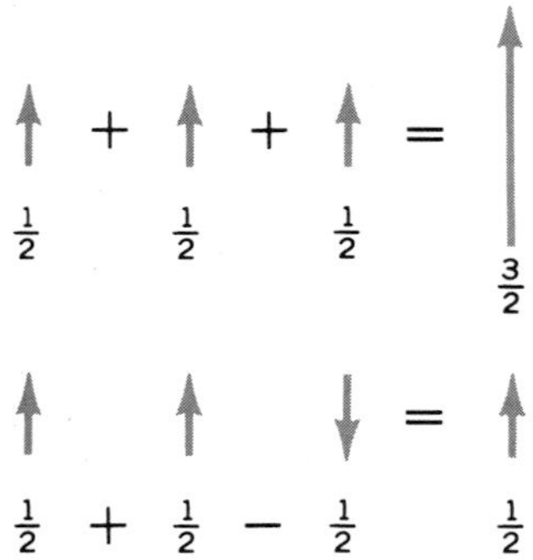

$$\uparrow + \uparrow + \uparrow = \Big|$$
$$\frac{1}{2} \quad \frac{1}{2} \quad \frac{1}{2} \qquad \frac{3}{2}$$

$$\uparrow \quad \uparrow \quad \downarrow = \uparrow$$
$$\frac{1}{2} + \frac{1}{2} - \frac{1}{2} \qquad \frac{1}{2}$$

FIGURE 17

Sometime after the N^* was found, several resonant states involving strange particles also began to appear. The first of these to show up is called the Y°. It appears to bear the same relation to the strange baryons as the N° bears to the nucleon. Namely, it has spin 3/2 and decays very quickly into strange particles and pions, just as the N° has spin 3/2 and decays very quickly into ordinary nucleons and pions. There are three Y°'s and they have similar masses, namely 1,382 mev, which is not very different from the N° mass of 1,237. Hence, to put the two of them together in a family is quite reasonable. In addition to the N° and the Y° particles there is also a Ξ°. The Ξ° bears the same relation to the Ξ as the N° bears to the N. It decays very quickly into a Ξ and a π, just as the N° decays into an N and a π. It also has spin 3/2 and it has a mass of 1,533 mev. It is a very striking fact that the different starred particles differ from each other in mass by about 150 mev, as the reader can verify by adding 150 mev to the N° mass and then 150 mev to the Y° mass to get nearly the Ξ° mass. The starred particles, so far mentioned, are nine in number; there are four N°'s, three Y°'s, and two Ξ°'s These fit very nicely on the triangle that represents the ten (*see* Fig. 18).

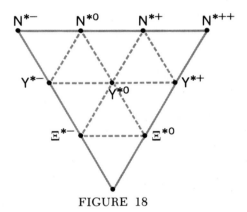

FIGURE 18

The reader will no doubt ask, "But where is the bottom point in the triangle?" In fact, this was *the* burning question in particle physics in 1963-64. The unitary scheme, as beautiful as it was as a piece of mathematics, was so bold that many physicists were not able to accept it without some sort of really decisive piece of evidence. The bottom particle conjectured to complete the ten triangle was given the name omega minus (Ω^-), and the great question in experimental particle physics in 1963-64 was, where was the Ω^-? A number of predictions about the Ω^- could be made. In the first place, if the 150 mev rule was obeyed, the mass of the Ω^- should be at about 1,680 mev. In the second place, the scheme demanded that the Ω^- have a strangeness of −3. Moving down the ten triangle we start with the N° with 0 strangeness, go to the Y° which has strangeness −1, and then the Ξ° which has strangeness -2. The next member must have strangeness -3. But a strangeness--3 particle with the mass of the Ω^- can only have extremely special decay modes. In fact, there turn out to be only three significant possible decay modes of the Ω^-: $\Omega^- \rightarrow \Xi^- + \pi^0$, $\Omega^- \rightarrow \Xi^0 + \pi^-$, or $\Omega^- \rightarrow \Lambda^0 + K^-$.

On December 14, 1963, a large group at Brookhaven National Laboratory, headed by W. Fowler and N. P. Samios, began the search for a particle with these properties. Fifty thousand pictures were obtained by January 30 and on January 31 the photograph shown in Figure 19 turned up. The analysis of this photograph showed that it was a negatively charged particle of mass 1,676 mev with the decay mode $\Xi^0 + \pi^-$, which is just the mass and the decay mode of the predicted Ω^-. The Brookhaven people had hit it lucky, because it was several weeks before another event like this was found. By now there are quite a few examples of Ω^- events, and physicists are convinced that there is something at the bottom of the triangle.

That the unitary scheme is essentially right is now generally agreed. But I have sloughed over a very basic point. In the scheme so far discussed, the eight's and the ten's were made out of three quarks in the combination $3 \cdot 3 \cdot 3$. But if each quark has baryon number 1, like an ordinary particle, then the resulting composite would have baryon number 3, which is not allowed, since, experimentally, these objects are known to have baryon number 1. Thus, Gell-Mann and, independently, another American physicist, G. Zweig, were led to propose the possibility that the quarks have baryon number 1/3. This is a very bold proposal, for no particle in quantum physics has ever had a baryon number that is a fraction.

Not only must the baryon number be a fraction, but the electric charge also must be a fraction. This is not hard to see, but we will spare the reader the analysis. In the Gell-Mann quark scheme, the strange quark is given charge $-1/3$ in units of electron charge, while the two nonstrange quarks have charges $-1/3$ and $2/3$. Such fractional charges, too, have never been known before in physics. These ideas lead to fascinating possibilities both for experiment and theory and are among the most active interests of our discipline. Several experiments have been suggested for "hunting the quark," but, so far, the quarks have not turned up. One is frustrated by the fact that the quarks must have a large mass—probably 5 to 10 bev, if they exist—since we stick them together to form particles which already have a large mass, and mass, as we have shown earlier, is always lost when particles are bound together to make other particles. There are no accelerators that exist that can make particles of such a mass, and the experimenters have been forced to go back to cosmic rays to hunt the quarks. But cosmic-ray experiments are slow and uncertain; what we really need are bigger machines.

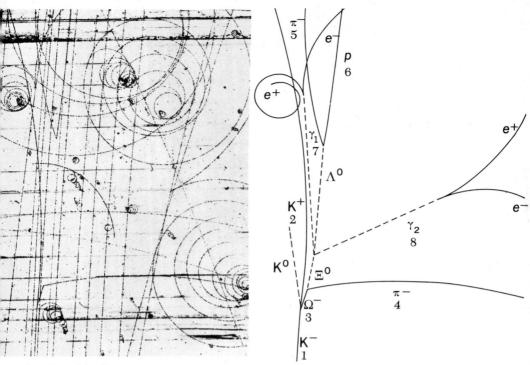

FIG. 19.—BUBBLE CHAMBER PHOTOGRAPH AND PARTICLE-TRACK SKETCH

Liquid hydrogen bubble chamber photograph showing the production of a negatively charged omega meson (Ω^-) by the interaction of a negative K^--meson (K^-) with a proton (a hydrogen nucleus in the bubble chamber). The sketch beside the photograph shows the proper assignments of a particle to each track. The paths of neutral particles, which produce no bubbles in the liquid hydrogen and therefore leave no tracks, are shown by dashed lines. The presence and properties of the neutral particles are established by the analysis of the tracks of their charged decay products or the application of the laws of conservation of mass and energy, or a combination of both. Track 1 is the incoming K^--meson which collides with an unseen, stationary proton in the liquid hydrogen with the resultant production of a neutral K-meson (K^0), a positive K-meson (K^+, track 2), and the negative omega meson (Ω^-, track 3). The Ω^- decays, after a lifetime of approximately one ten-billionth of a second, into a neutral cascade hyperon (Ξ^0) and a negative pi meson (π^-, track 4. The Ξ^0 decays into a neutral lambda hyperon (Λ^0) and a neutral pi meson (π^0), not shown, which immediately decays into two gamma rays (γ_1 and γ_2, tracks 7 and 8), which in turn each convert to a positron-electron pair (e^-, e^+). The neutral lambda hyperon (Λ^0) travels a few centimeters and then decays into a negative pi meson (π^-, track 5) and a proton (p, track 6)

In summary, the unitary symmetry scheme and its modifications have been successful in describing the gross features of the particles and even some of the more subtle features. It is a most spectacular triumph of theoretical physics. There are, at present, some attempts to go even farther, to unify baryons and mesons in still more elaborate schemes, and there have been suggestions for avoiding the fractional quark charges by introducing more than one basic set of three (*see* Fig. 20). While these look very promising, they are still too speculative to report on.

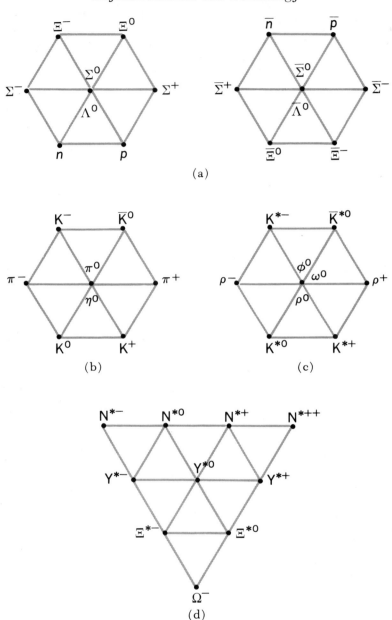

(a)

(b)　　　　　　　　　　　　(c)

(d)

FIGURE 20

FIG. 20.—PARTICLE CLASSIFICATIONS ACCORDING TO UNITARY SYMMETRY

(a) The baryons and antibaryons (an eightfold representation); (b) The spin-0 mesons (an eightfold representation with the antiparticles in the same representation as the particles); (c) the spin-1 mesons (an eight-plus-onefold representation); (d) The spin-3/2 hyperon resonances (a tenfold representation)

Jeremy Bernstein

TIME REVERSAL

The delightful thing about physics is that it is almost never dull. Just when physicists were settling back to enjoy the order brought about by the unitary symmetry, another experiment at Brookhaven, this one by the group from Princeton University, consisting of J. H. Christenson, J. W. Cronin, V. L. Fitch, and R. Turlay, and done in the summer of 1964, upset the apple cart. This experiment deals with the weak interactions. To appreciate its significance, we must discuss one of the most subtle symmetries—that of time reversal, which, until this experiment was done, was thought to be a property of all forces.

It is clear to everyone that events in the world show a natural flow of time. We age; indeed, the universe ages. Hence, the universe is certainly not symmetric between the past and the future. This lack of symmetry between past and future can come about even though the underlying equations of physics that predict the behavior of the universe *are* symmetric under the exchange of the past and future; they have the same form whether time runs from past to future or from future to past. A simple example of how symmetric equations can produce such a nonsymmetric behavior of a system as a whole can be found in the description of the way in which diffusion takes place.

Suppose I drop a little packet of colored powder into one tiny corner of a container of water. The powder will spread out through the whole container—will diffuse—and soon the water will appear altogether colored. It is, at first, paradoxical that this trend of diffusion can be accounted for by an assumption of perfect symmetry in the behavior of the molecules of the powder. If, at any given time, we assume that a powder molecule is as likely to move in one direction as in any other (and this is what is meant here by perfect symmetry), then it follows that, if we confine the powder initially to a corner of the water, it will spread out uniformly. The basic reason is that there is simply more likelihood of the powder molecule moving into a place where there is no powder than elsewhere. The diffusion is an "accident" of the initial conditions, which bunched all the powder into one corner. These conditions were so difficult to maintain that, when the powder was let free to move in the water, it quickly settled into a more probable configuration.

The equations of classical physics are all invariant with respect to past and future. This means that if some given path is a possible one for such a system, then the path in which the particles are all turned around and move backwards is also a possible one. We are not baffled by the apparent contradiction between this symmetry and the aging of the universe because we can think of the aging as a kind of diffusion process. In the beginning, the universe was in a very improbable initial configuration, and in time it has been diffusing toward more probable configurations. In this picture, aging and death are a trend toward more and more probable configurations. Life is a continual struggle against molecular chaos—a box full of gas molecules is one of the most disordered systems imaginable—a perfect chaos—while the organization of these molecules into a living being is one of the most ordered. Disorder is easy to achieve because it is so probable, and systems tend toward the probable.

Time-reversal symmetry can also be built into the equations of quantum mechanics, and it has been done. Indeed, all the experimental evidence involving the strong forces shows that this invariance holds for them in the quantum-mechanical setting. Furthermore, there is a remarkable connection between this invariance and another. The combined operations of parity and charge conjugation (C invariance) yield a new system, the mirror image of the first but a system involving antiparticles instead of particles. (C invariance refers to the fact that the equations of physics appear the same if particles are replaced by antiparticles. The experiments that showed that P conservation was violated by the weak forces also showed that C conservation was violated by them. However, it appeared as if the combined operation of charge conjugation C and parity P-CP—in which a left-handed system was replaced by a right-handed system and particles were exchanged for antiparticles—was still a good symmetry.) This combined operation is called "CP invariance." It was shown, some years ago, that under very general and plausible assumptions, CP invariance holds if time reversal holds, and vice versa. CP invariance is often simpler to test than time-reversal invariance, since it leads to predictions about the particles that can be readily examined in the laboratory. The strong forces seem to be CP invariant.

After the strong forces come the electromagnetic ones. As we have seen, these are perhaps a hundred times weaker, and produce all the familiar electrical phenomena. These forces also appear to show all of the symmetries of the strong forces, including CP invariance, except for one. In our discussion of the isotopic multiplets we have skipped over a basic point that I did not want to raise earlier in order not to burden the reader. We have supposed that all the particles in an isotopic multiplet really have the same mass. This is not exactly true experimentally as one can verify by looking at the Particle Table. For example, the π^+ and π^- have mass 139.58 mev, while the π^0 has a mass of 134.97. The neutron has a mass of 939.550 mev while the proton has a mass of 938.256 mev and so on. Thus, there is a mass splitting even in the isotopic multiplets, as well as a splitting between the multiplets. The strong force, being unitary symmetric, cannot induce such a splitting, but it is thought that the electromagnetic force, which slightly violates unitary symmetry, can account for the small splitting in the multiplets. The unitary symmetry scheme in its most refined versions even makes a prediction on how this happens quantitatively, and these predictions are also confirmed by experiment.

Next in order of weakness is the weak force, which, as we have noted, is about a thousand times weaker than the electromagnetic force. The weak force appears to respect the conservation of energy and momentum and electrical charge, but it violates strangeness conservation, the conservation of parity, and the charge conjugation symmetry.

But, until the summer of 1964, it appeared that the weak force, at least, respected time-reversal invariance or CP invariance. The C and P symmetries of gravitation have not yet been fully tested, although these are essentially built into the Einstein theory of gravitation, which accounts for the gravitational phenomena so far studied.

The Princeton experiment of 1964 (mentioned on p. 363) involved the neutral K^0 meson. The K^0 meson and its antiparticle partner, the $\overline{K^0}$, form a remarkable duo. If a K^0 meson is created, say, in the process $\pi^- + P \rightarrow K^0 + \Lambda^0$, it can convert into a $\overline{K^0}$ by means of the weak force. It needs the weak force to do this because the K^0 and the $\overline{K^0}$ have opposite strangeness and to convert them, a force is needed that does not conserve strangeness. A typical conversion process looks like Figure 21.

FIGURE 21

Thus the particle that actually decays is some mixture of the K^0 and K^0 which is produced by the conversion back and forth. It turns out that in the decay the K^0 and $\overline{K^0}$ are effectively replaced by two other particles, manufactured by the conversion, which we may call K_L^0 and K_S^0. K_S^0 is a very short-lived particle; it lives about one-ten-billionth of a second, while K_L^0 is a much longer lived particle. It lives nearly 600 times longer. These two new particles have almost completely different decay modes. From our point of view, the most important fact about them is that the short-lived one decays most of the time into two pi mesons, for example, $K_S^0 \rightarrow \pi^+ + \pi^-$, while the long-lived one decays into three pi mesons, viz., $K_L^0 \rightarrow \pi^+ + \pi^- + \pi^0$. The crucial point about these decay modes is their CP character. The two-pi mode always has CP = +1, while the three-pi mode usually has CP = −1. Thus, if CP is conserved, one should never see a two-pi decay coming from the long-lived mode. But this is exactly what was seen by the Brookhaven-Princeton group, alas! In a beautiful experiment they showed that, in small amounts, the long-lived K meson decays into two pions.

This has put physicists into a deep quandary. The simplest explanation is to say that there is yet another weak force, perhaps a hundred times weaker than the usual one, but a force that violates CP invariance or time reversal. There is nothing wrong with such an idea, but it means that none of the symmetries—C, P, CP—that only a few years ago were thought to be exact, really are.

The only symmetries that appear to be valid for all forces are the conservation of energy and momentum and angular momentum. These are symmetries that depend on the correctness of the special theory of relativity. As long as the special theory of relativity holds, one would expect these "last-ditch" symmetries to remain valid. The fact that all the other symmetries break down as the forces become weaker makes one think that perhaps the special theory of relativity, and its implications about momentum and energy conservation, should be very carefully explored to see how valid these implications really are.

Thus, the year 1964 has seen two major developments in the physics of elementary particles, both connected with symmetries. The overwhelming and, perhaps, unlooked-for success of the unitary symmetry has come as a pleasant surprise. I think no physicist would have thought, say five or six years ago, that nature would have chosen such a beautiful and subtle symmetry by means of which to display the patterns in the elementary particles. To see it, one needed just the right number of particles, and these have only been discovered very recently. On the other hand, even a year ago most physicists would have bet that CP invariance was a sacred principle and that the Princeton-Brookhaven experiment would simply have confirmed this fact once more. Indeed, as the strong interactions get clearer and more beautiful in their structure the weak interactions appear to retreat into obscurity and mystery. Why are all the symmetries violated by the weak interactions? Why has nature created the mu meson and the electron which differ only in their weak interactions? Why are there two neutrinos, one for the muon and one for the electron? And, finally, what, if anything, does the weakest and perhaps the most mysterious of all the forces, namely gravity, have to do with these questions? If one believes that all of nature is tied together by interconnecting simple universal laws, then one must believe that there are profound and intellectually satisfying answers to these questions. I wish I knew what they were.

THE PARTICLE TABLE

AN EXPLANATORY NOTE

In this table the reader will find the cast of characters in our drama with their *vitae* spelled out in detail. There are more particles known than appear here and there are, certainly, many as yet undiscovered particles that will appear. We have included only those mentioned in the text. Reading from left to right the entries have the following meanings:

Class: refers to whether a particle is a meson, a baryon, a resonance, etc.

Symbol: refers to the most common notation used by physicists for the object; e.g., n for neutron and p for proton, etc.

Spin: refers to the "intrinsic" angular momentum of a particle, as explained in the text. The spin of the known particles is, in the usual units, either 0, 1/2, 1, 3/2, although there are systems, not listed in the table, including heavy nuclei that have higher spin.

Strangeness: this concept has been discussed in the text and is something like an additional charge, not an electrical charge, that a particle has. The strong interactions conserve this "charge" as well as the electrical charge, while the weak interactions cause transformations among particles of different strangeness as well as electrical charge. The strangenesses of the known particles range from 0 to -3 while the strangenesses of the known antiparticles range from 0 to $+3$.

Mass: refers to the mass of the particles in Mev. Mev, million electron volts, is a unit of energy. But it is simply related to the mass by Einstein's formula $E = mc^2$, where c is the velocity of light. The mass in Mev is the "rest" energy of the particle, the amount of energy that would be available if the particle, at rest, were completely converted into energy. In giving these masses we have ignored the question of the "width" of the particles. As we have discussed in the text, the uncertainty principle between energy and time implies that a short-lived particle always has an undetermined rest energy. This manifests itself in a "width"—the rest energy when measured is spread around some central energy and it is this central energy that is quoted in the table. The width only becomes significant if the particle is very short-lived, indeed. In this case, "short-lived" means a lifetime of less than about 10^{-22} seconds. Hence, it is an important consideration for the pion and nucleon resonances—particles like the ρ which is a pion resonance, and the N^* which is a nucleon resonance. The exact value of the width, while very important to physicists, does not affect the general discussion given in the text, and we have not tabulated it here to avoid excessive complication.

Mean life: refers to the average length of time it takes a particle to decay. If one has a collection of unstable particles, then they will decay at different times; but, on the average, they will decay at the so-called mean lifetime. Quantum mechanics does not allow one to deduce which particle of a collection will decay at what time, but it does allow one to deduce the mean life and, hence, to predict the average behavior of an ensemble of particles. With four exceptions—the proton, the electron, the neutrino, the photon, and their antiparticles—all particles so far studied are unstable. For these four we have given infinity as their mean lives. The lifetimes are given in units of 10^{-10} seconds for convenience. This means that if the figure "1" appears in the table, the particle has a lifetime of 10^{-10} seconds and so on.

Common decay modes: refers to the particles that are generated when one of the unstable particles decays. It is often the case that more than one set of particles is produced by a given particle when it decays. We have listed several decay modes when these are common. In many cases there are rare decay modes of the particles which we have not listed to avoid complication in the table. If no decay modes are listed it means the particle is stable.

Baryon number: this, too, is a quantum number that each particle carries. It is an especially important quantity because all known interactions—strong, weak, electromagnetic—conserve this quantity exactly. In no process can baryon number be changed overall. Thus a process like $p \rightarrow e^+ + e^- + e^+$ is absolutely forbidden. This is why the proton is completely stable. No particle lighter carries a non-0 baryon number.

Hyperon resonances: hyperon refers to any particle that carries a non-0 baryon number (the Ω^- is the heaviest listed in the table, although heavier ones are known). The reader will find the so-called leptons listed. A lepton refers to any particle lighter than the pi meson These particles do not have strong interactions but only electromagnetic and weak interactions. They do not fit into the unitary scheme and, from a fundamental point of view, are the most mysterious objects in particle physics. One cannot claim to have a real understanding of the particles until one understands why there are exactly as many leptons as there are, no more and no less, and how they fit together with the heavy particles in some overall scheme.

The data in these tables were taken from a similar but more detailed table by Matts Roos and published in the journal *Nuclear Physics*, 52 (1964) pp. 1-24.

THE PARTICLE TABLE

Particle	
Ξ⁻	(xi minus)
Ξ⁰	(xi zero)
Σ⁻	(sigma minus)
Σ⁰	(sigma zero)
Σ⁺	(sigma plus)
Λ	(lambda)
n	(neutron)
p	(proton)
K⁰	(K zero)
K⁺	(K plus)
π⁺	(pi plus)
π⁰	(pi zero)
γ	(photon)
μ⁻	(mu minus)
e⁻	(electron)
ν	(neutrino)

Class	Symbol	Spin Js	Strangeness S	Mass (Mev)	Mean life (In units of one-ten-billionth of a second)	Common decay modes	Baryon number
Hyperons	Ξ^-	$\frac{1}{2}$	-2	1321.2 ± 0.2	1.75 ± 0.05	$\Lambda^0\pi^-$	1
	$\bar{\Xi}^+$		2				-1
	Ξ^0		-2	1315.2 ± 1.0	2.80 ± 0.26	$\Lambda^0\pi^0$	1
	$\bar{\Xi}^0$		2	1329 ± 19			-1
	Σ^-	$\frac{1}{2}$	-1	1197.6 ± 0.5	1.59 ± 0.05	$n\pi^-$	1
	$\bar{\Sigma}^+$		$+1$				-1
	Σ^0		-1	1193.2 ± 0.7	$0.17 > \tau > 10^{-12}$	$\Lambda^0\gamma$	1
	$\bar{\Sigma}^0$		$+1$				-1
	Σ^+		-1	1189.35 ± 0.15	0.78 ± 0.03	$p\pi^0$	1
	$\bar{\Sigma}^-$		$+1$			$n\pi^+$	-1
	Λ^0	$\frac{1}{2}$	-1	1115.38 ± 0.10	2.57 ± 0.30	$p\pi^-$	1
	$\bar{\Lambda}^0$		1	1115.44 ± 0.32	1.9 ± 1.0	$n\pi^0$	-1
Nucleons	n	$\frac{1}{2}$	0	939.505 ± 0.01	$1013 \pm 26 \times 10^{10}$	$pe^-\bar{\nu}_e$	1
	$\bar{n}$		0				-1
	p		0	938.211 ± 0.01	∞	(none)	1
	$\bar{p}$		0				-1
Mesons of spin 0	K^+	0	1	493.7 ± 0.3	122.7 ± 0.8	$\mu^+\nu_\mu$ $\pi^+\pi^0$	0
	K^-	0	-1			$\mu^+\pi^0\nu_\mu$ $\pi^+\pi^0\pi^0$	0
	K^0	0	1	497.9 ± 0.6	$K_S = 0.90 \pm 0.02$	$\pi^+\pi^-$ $\pi^0\pi^0$	0
	$\bar{K}^0$	0	-1		$K_L = 630 \begin{smallmatrix}+160\\-100\end{smallmatrix}$ (See text for the definition of K_S and K_L)	$\pi^+\pi^-\pi^0$ $\pi^0\pi^0\pi^0$ $\pi^+e^-\bar{\nu}_e$ $\pi^-e^+\nu_e$ $\pi^+\mu^-\bar{\nu}_\mu$ $\pi^-\mu^+\nu_\mu$ $\pi^+\pi^-$	0
	π^+	0	0	139.58 ± 0.05	254.7 ± 2.7	$\mu^+\nu_\mu$	0
	π^-	0	0	139.58 ± 0.05		$e^+\nu_e$	0
	π^0	0	0	134.97 ± 0.05	$1.05 \pm 0.18 \times 10^{-6}$	$\gamma\gamma$ γe^+e^-	0
	η^0	0	0	548.5 ± 0.6	$\geq 10^{-12}$	$\pi^+\pi^-\pi^0$ $\pi^+\pi^-\gamma$ $\pi^0\pi^0\pi^0$ $\pi^0\gamma\gamma$ $\gamma\gamma$	0
Mesons of spin 1	ρ^+	1	0	757 ± 5	$\sim 10^{-13}$	$\pi^+\pi^0$	0
	ρ^-	1	0			$\pi^-\pi^0$	0
	ρ^0	1	0	754 ± 5		$\pi^-\pi^0\pi^0$ $\pi^-\pi^+$	0
	ω^0	1	0	783 ± 2	$\sim 10^{-12}$	$\pi^+\pi^-\pi^0$ $\pi^0\gamma$ $\pi^+\pi^-$	0

Class	Symbol	Quantum numbers Spin J_s	Quantum numbers Strangeness S	Mass (Mev)	Mean life (In units of one-ten-billionth of a second)	Common decay modes	Baryon number
Mesons of spin 1	$K^{\circ-}$	1	-1	890.4 ± 1.2	$\sim 10^{-13}$	$\bar{K}^0\pi^-$	0
	$\bar{K}^{\circ 0}$	1	-1			$K^-\pi^0$	0
	$K^{\circ+}$	1	1			$K^-\pi^+$ $K^0\pi^0$	0
	$K^{\circ 0}$	1	1			$K^0\pi^+$ $K^+\pi^-$ $K^0\pi^0$	0
	ϕ^0	1	0	1019.5 ± 0.3	$> \sim 10^{-12}$	$\rho^+\pi^-$ $K^0\bar{K}^0$	0
Hyperon resonances	$N^{\circ-}$	$\frac{3}{2}$	0			$\pi^- n$	1
	$N^{\circ 0}$	$\frac{3}{2}$	0	1237	$\sim 10^{-13}$	$\pi^0 n$	1
	$N^{\circ+}$	$\frac{3}{2}$	0			$\pi^+ n$	1
	$N^{\circ++}$	$\frac{3}{2}$	0			$p\pi^+$	1
	$Y^{\circ+}$	$\frac{3}{2}$	-1	1382 ± 2	$\sim 10^{-13}$	$\Lambda^0\pi^+$	1
	$Y^{\circ-}$	$\frac{3}{2}$	-1			$\Lambda^0\pi^-$	1
	$Y^{\circ 0}$	$\frac{3}{2}$	-1			$\Lambda^0\pi^0$	1
	$\Xi^{\circ-}$	$\frac{3}{2}$	-2	1533 ± 3	$\sim 10^{-12}$	$\Xi^-\pi^0$ $\Xi^0\pi^-$	1
	$\Xi^{\circ 0}$	$\frac{3}{2}$	-2			$\Xi^-\pi^+$	1
	Ω^-	$\frac{3}{2}$	-3	~ 1680	~ 1	$\Xi^0\pi^-$ $\Xi^-\pi^0$ $\Lambda^0 K^-$	1
Leptons	μ^-	$\frac{1}{2}$	0	105.65	22040 ± 70	$e^-\bar{\nu}_e\nu_\mu$	0
	μ^+					$e^+\nu_e\bar{\nu}_\mu$	0
	e^-	$\frac{1}{2}$	0	0.510976 ± 0.000007	∞		0
	e^+				∞		0
	ν_μ	$\frac{1}{2}$	0	<2.5	∞		0
	$\bar{\nu}_\mu$				∞		0
	ν_e	$\frac{1}{2}$	0	<0.00025	∞		0
	$\bar{\nu}_e$				∞		0
Photon	γ	1	0	0	∞		0

Antiparticle

$\bar{\Xi}^+$	(antixi plus)
$\bar{\Xi}^0$	(antixi zero)
$\bar{\Sigma}^+$	(antisigma plus)
$\bar{\Sigma}^0$	(antisigma zero)
$\bar{\Sigma}^-$	(antisigma minus)
$\bar{\Lambda}$	(antilambda)
$\bar{n}$	(antineutron)
$\bar{p}$	(antiproton)
$\bar{K}^0$	(anti-K zero)
K^-	(K minus)
π^-	(pi minus)
π^0	(pi zero)
γ	(photon)
μ^+	(mu plus)
e^+	(positron)
$\bar{\nu}$	(antineutrino)

Physical Sciences and Technology

BIBLIOGRAPHY

BERNSTEIN, JEREMY. "A Question of Parity." In *The New Yorker*, May 12, 1962, pp. 49-104, where the work of T.-D. Lee and C. N. Yang and the problem of parity non-conservation are discussed.

BORN, MAX. *Atomic Physics*. New York: Hafner Publishing Company, 1962. The best introduction to atomic physics and the quantum theory of atoms for anyone with some background in physics and mathematics.

GELL-MANN, M., and NE'EMAN, Y. (eds.). *The Eightfold Way*. New York: W. A. Benjamin, Inc., 1964. A collection of papers which deal with the new symmetries from a technical point of view.

Scientific American. Almost every issue of this superb journal contains a first-rate article about high-energy and atomic physics. Of special interest to readers of this article are: CHEW, G., GELL-MANN, M., and ROSENFELD, A. H. "Strongly Interacting Particles." In *Scientific American*, February, 1964, p. 74; and FOWLER, W. B., and SAMIOS, N. P. "The Omega-Minus Experiment." *Scientific American*, October, 1964, p. 36.

SEGRÉ, E. *Nuclei and Particles*. New York: W. A. Benjamin, Inc., 1964. An extremely clear introduction to the subject for anyone with some background in physics.

YANG, CHEN NING. *Elementary Particles*. Princeton: Princeton University Press, 1962. A brief and excellently written introduction to the field for the general reader, which covers the period up to 1960.

NOTE TO THE READER

For the reader interested in following the historical development of atomic theory, there is a wealth of material in *Great Books of the Western World* and *Gateway to the Great Books*. Lucretius is the natural place to begin, since he provides the principal source of Democritus' theory (GBWW, Vol. 12, esp. pp. 1-44). The reader might turn next to "The Rise and Decline of Classical Physics" (in GGB, Vol. 8, pp. 485-560), where Einstein and Infeld review the history of physics from Newton down to Einstein himself. Their account provides an introduction to reading what Newton, Lavoisier, and Faraday have to say about atoms. Newton's main works are to be found in GBWW, Vol. 34; those of Lavoisier and Faraday, in Vol. 45.

Dr. Bernstein reports the latest developments in the theory of the basic elements of the material world. In the *Syntopicon*, Chapter 21 on ELEMENT is devoted to this subject. Two questions can be distinguished. One, the conceptual question, is whether matter is ultimately continuous or discrete, that is, composed of indivisible units. The other, the operational question, is whether the indivisibles, if such exist, can ever be reached or obtained. On the conceptual question, there is considerable material in *Great Books*, all of which is organized systematically and indexed under ELEMENT 5, on the theory of atomism. Dr. Bernstein discusses both questions; and, as the reader will see from consulting the passages cited under ELEMENT 5*b*, he sides with Aristotle against Democritus in favor of the infinite divisibility of matter.

Dr. Bernstein shows that physicists are particularly interested in the conservation laws of classical physics and the fact that they appear to be violated by the elementary particles. The consideration of these laws, as well as of the concept of force, can be found in the passages cited under MECHANICS 6, especially 6*c*-6*e*. The classical paper of Helmholz on the conservation of force is printed in GGB, Vol. 8, pp. 447-84.

One of the most fascinating developments in particle physics, as Dr. Bernstein's essay not only notes but also illustrates, is the marriage of mathematics with empirical observation. The idea that nature has a mathematical structure receives its classical expression in the *Timaeus* of Plato (GBWW, Vol. 7, pp. 442-77). Other material on this subject will be found cited under MATHEMATICS 5*b*.

PART FOUR

Additions to
the Great Books Library

Utopia (abridged): Sir Thomas More

Walden (selections): Henry David Thoreau

The Challenge of Democracy: John Strachey

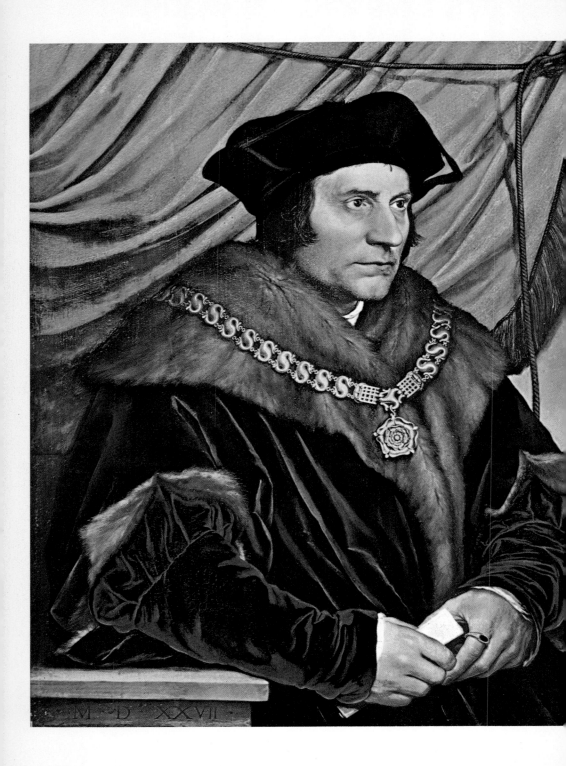

Sir Thomas More

Utopia

INTRODUCTION

Thomas More was, in the words of one of his contemporaries, "a man for all seasons." He earned a fortune as a lawyer and became the first layman to wear the Great Seal of the Lord Chancellor of England, but he was also the author of a book advocating a communistic ideal of common property and a scorn of wealth and political ambition. He was an urbane, witty scholar, the intimate of the most enlightened men of the early Renaissance, but he also practiced mortifications of the flesh in the manner of the Middle Ages and mercilessly persecuted and tortured religious heretics. He married twice and delighted in the love of a large family, but he also longed for a monastic and celibate life and put martyrdom above family.

The contradictions and lucidities of More's life are present in *Utopia*, the first and classic modern treatment of an ideal commonwealth. The book takes its place in the tradition of Utopian literature, which begins with Plato's *Republic*, and the fragmentary *Critias*, and extends through St. Augustine's *City of God* and Francis Bacon's *New Atlantis* down to modern Utopias like Edward Bellamy's *Looking Backward*, Samuel Butler's *Erewhon*, the innumerable Utopias of H. G. Wells, and anti-Utopias like Aldous Huxley's *Brave New World* and George Orwell's *1984*.

Scholars, philosophers, theologians, and statesmen—both Christian, secular, and Marxist—have advanced a multitude of conflicting interpretations of *Utopia* since it was published in 1516. Like most scholars' work of the time, the book was written in Latin; it was not translated into English until 1551. Because of the scholarly wit, irony, and occasional farce in the book, some critics have argued that *Utopia* is a *libellus festivus*, "an entertaining, merry handbook" intended by its author to amuse and delight his erudite friends, such as the celebrated humanist Desiderius Erasmus of Rotterdam. The title, for instance, means "nowhere" in Greek, "Hythlodaeus," the name of the philosophic traveler who describes Utopia, means "well-learned in nonsense," and the name of the main river in Utopia translates as "waterless."

Other interpretations emphasize the more sober, searching political and social criticism in the book. Here, too, are stimulating contradictions. Is More a political conservative? A revolutionary radical? A democrat or a communist? An orthodox Roman Catholic theologian or an ironic critic of organized religion? An impractical visionary or a practical social philosopher? He is probably all of these.

By using a dialogue form, More is able to explore all sides of his complex subject without, however, marking one as his own. When reading *Utopia* it is good to keep in mind that "More" is a literary character in the dialogue. Which of the points of view expressed represent the historical More is difficult to say. Probably he held all of them, in varying degrees.

Thomas More experienced firsthand not only the practical economic and political realities discussed in *Utopia* but also the happiness that comes from the freedom and culture of the intellect. Born in 1478 into the family of a successful lawyer from the burgeoning middle class, he received the best education available. As a youth he served as a page in the household of Lord Chancellor Cardinal Morton, who often said of him to guests: "This child here waiting at the table, whosoever shall live to see it, will prove a marvelous man." Cardinal Morton sent the promising boy to Oxford where the celebrated Greek scholar John Colet introduced him to the New Humanism which championed an enthusiastic study of Greek classics and an interpretation of Scripture stripped of the more ornate allegorical readings popular during the Middle Ages.

After studying at the Inns of Court, More became a lawyer in 1497. Continuing his humanistic studies while practicing the law, he lived for four years as a lay member of a Carthusian monastery in London. At twenty-seven he married, settling in a home in the heart of commercial London. In addition to raising three daughters and a son, More entertained humanists and wits like Erasmus, who wrote his scalding, brilliant *Praise of Folly* while a guest in the More household. As a young man More became one of the most successful and highly paid lawyers in the land. Appointed undersheriff of London in 1510, he soon attracted the attention of the young Henry VIII, who had ascended the throne the year before. The King employed More on embassies to the Low Countries and France and as a member of the King's Privy Council. Integrity, competency, and humanity distinguished his service. In 1521 he was knighted. The King cultivated his friendship and often enjoyed arriving unannounced for dinner. At fifty-one More succeeded Cardinal Wolsey as lord chancellor.

When his wife died, More remarried and later moved into a spacious home in the suburb of Chelsea. Warm accounts of the conviviality and intimacy of the More household—where his children and their spouses continued to live long after they had married—have come down from contemporaries, most notably in the first biography of More written by William Roper, the young lawyer who had married More's favorite daughter, Margaret. In spite of domestic felicities and political success, More continued the religious mortifications he had begun as a young man: he always wore a shirt of hair beneath his official robes, slept on a log block, and occasionally flogged himself in the privacy of his study.

Increasingly strident demands by Henry VIII that his subjects accept the legality and morality of his intention to divorce Queen Catherine and marry Anne Boleyn caused More, who supported the spiritual authority of the Pope, to resign as lord chancellor on the pretext of poor health. Although he was now a private citizen living in scholarly seclusion, his absence at the coronation of Anne Boleyn in 1533 was widely commented on. Henry VIII's displeasure with his former favorite expanded. Attempts were made to frame More on one trumped-up charge after another, all of which failed. But when More refused to take an oath accepting the King as head of the Church of England, he was imprisoned in the Tower of London. Perjured evidence helped to convict him of treason. On July 6, 1535, he was beheaded on Tower Hill; the severed head was stuck on a high pole erected on London Bridge.

With the same warm humanity with which he had lived More went to his death. To the executioner and attending officials he was courteous and generous. Neither did his wit desert him. As he laid his neck on the block, he "bade the executioner stay until he had removed aside his beard, saying that *that* had never committed any treason." Nor did dignity and sense of commitment fail him. Among his final words was the memorable statement that he was "the King's good servant, but God's first."

In 1935, four hundred years after his execution, he was canonized a saint by the Roman Catholic Church.

Yale University Press has undertaken to publish a critical edition of the complete works of St. Thomas More. Our text is from the 1964 Yale edition of *Utopia* newly translated and edited by Edward Surtz, S.J., Professor of English at Loyola University of Chicago. There is also available a 1965 edition containing the original Latin and full scholarly apparatus.

CONTENTS

UTOPIA

Thomas More to Peter Giles, Greetings. I am almost ashamed, my dear Peter Giles, to send you this little book about the state of Utopia after almost a year, when I am sure you looked for it within a month and a half. Certainly you know that I was relieved of all the labor of gathering materials for the work and that I had to give no thought at all to their arrangement. I had only to repeat what in your company I heard Raphael relate. Hence there was no reason for me to take trouble about the style of the narrative, seeing that his language could not be polished. It was, first of all, hurried and impromptu, and, secondly, the product of a person who, as you know, was not so well acquainted with Latin as with Greek. Therefore the nearer my style came to his careless simplicity the closer it would be to the truth, for which alone I am bound to care under the circumstances and actually do care.

I confess, my dear Peter, that all these preparations relieved me of so much trouble that scarcely anything remained for me to do. Otherwise the gathering or the arrangement of the materials could have required a good deal of both time and application even from a talent neither the meanest nor the most ignorant. If it had been required that the matter be written down not only accurately but eloquently, I could not have performed the task with any amount of time or application. But, as it was, those cares over which I should have had to perspire so hard had been removed. Since it remained for me only to write out simply what I had heard, there was no difficulty about it.

Yet even to carry through this trifling task, my other tasks left me practically no leisure at all. I am constantly engaged in legal business, either pleading or hearing, either giving an award as arbiter or deciding a case as judge. I pay a visit of courtesy to one man and go on business to another. I devote almost the whole day in public to other men's affairs and the remainder to my own. I leave to myself, that is to learning, nothing at all.

When I have returned home, I must talk with my wife, chat with my children, and confer with my servants. All this activity I count as business when it must be done—and it must be unless you want to be a stranger in your own home. Besides, one must take care to be as agreeable as possible to those whom nature has supplied, or chance has made, or you yourself have chosen, to be the companions of your life, provided you do not spoil them by kindness, or through indulgence make masters out of your servants.

Amid these occupations that I have named, the day, the month, the year slip away. When, then, can we find time to write? Nor have I spoken a word about sleep, nor even of food, which for many people takes up as much time as sleep—and sleep takes up almost half a man's life! So I get for myself only the time I filch from sleep and food. Slowly, therefore, because this time is but little, yet finally, because this time *is* something, I have finished *Utopia* and sent it to you, my dear Peter, to read—and to remind me of anything that has escaped me.

In this respect I do not entirely distrust myself. (I only wish I were as good in intelligence and learning as I am not altogether deficient in memory!) Nevertheless, I am not so confident as to believe that I have forgotten nothing. As you know, John Clement, my pupil-servant, was also present at the conversation. Indeed I do not allow him to absent himself from any talk which can be somewhat profitable, for from this young plant, seeing that it has begun to put forth green shoots in Greek and Latin literature, I expect no mean harvest some day. He has caused me to feel very doubtful on one point.

According to my own recollection, Hythlodaeus declared that the bridge which spans the river Anydrus at Amaurotum is five hundred paces in length. But my John says that two hundred must be taken off, for the river there is not more than three hundred paces in breadth. Please recall the matter to mind. If you agree with him, I shall adopt the same view and think myself mistaken. If you do not remember, I shall put down, as I have actually done, what I myself seem to remember. Just as I shall take great pains to have nothing incorrect in the book, so, if there is doubt about anything, I shall rather tell an objective falsehood than an intentional lie—for I would rather be honest than wise.

Nevertheless, it would be easy for you to remedy this defect if you ask Raphael himself by word of mouth or by letter. You must do so on account of another doubt which has cropped up, whether more through my fault or through yours or Raphael's I do not know. We forgot to ask, and he forgot to say, in what part of the new world Utopia lies. I am sorry that point was omitted, and I would be willing to pay a considerable sum to purchase that information, partly because I am rather ashamed to be ignorant in what sea lies the island of which I am saying so much, partly because there are several among us, and one in particular, a devout man and a theologian by profession, burning with an extraordinary desire to visit Utopia. He does so not from an idle and curious lust for sight-seeing in new places but for the purpose of fostering and promoting our religion, begun there so felicitously.

To carry out his plan properly, he has made up his mind to arrange to be sent by the pope and, what is more, to be named bishop for the Utopians. He is in no way deterred by any scruple that he must sue for this prelacy, for he considers it a holy suit which proceeds not from any consideration of honor or gain but from motives of piety.

Therefore I beg you, my dear Peter, either by word of mouth if you conveniently can or by letter if he has gone, to reach Hythlodaeus and to make sure that my work includes nothing false and omits nothing true. I am inclined to think that it would be better to show him the book itself. No one else is so well able to correct any mistake, nor can he do this favor at all unless he reads through what I have written. In addition, in this way you will find out whether he accepts with pleasure or suffers with annoyance the fact that I have composed this work. If he himself has decided to put down in writing his own adventures, perhaps he may not want me to do so. By making known the commonwealth of Utopia, I should certainly dislike to forestall him and to rob his narrative of the flower and charm of novelty.

Nevertheless, to tell the truth, I myself have not yet made up my mind whether I shall publish it at all. So varied are the tastes of mortals, so peevish the characters of some, so ungrateful their dispositions, so wrongheaded their judgments, that those persons who pleasantly and blithely indulge their inclinations seem to be very much better off than those who torment themselves with anxiety in order to publish something that may bring profit or pleasure to others, who nevertheless receive it with disdain or ingratitude.

Very many men are ignorant of learning; many despise it. The barbarian rejects as harsh whatever is not positively barbarian. The smatterers despise as trite whatever is not packed with obsolete expressions. Some persons approve only of what is old; very many admire only their own work. This fellow is so grim that he will not hear of a joke; that fellow is so

THOMAS MORE WRITING, WOODCUT BY AN ANONYMOUS ARTIST, FROM
Utopia, L'ANGELIER, PARIS, 1550
It remained for me only to write out simply what I had heard

insipid that he cannot endure wit. Some are so dull-minded that they fear all satire as much as a man bitten by a mad dog fears water. Others are so fickle that sitting they praise one thing and standing another thing.

These persons sit in taverns, and over their cups criticize the talents of authors. With much pontificating, just as they please, they condemn each author by his writings, plucking each one, as it were, by the hair. They themselves remain under cover and, as the proverb goes, out of shot. They are so smooth and shaven that they present not even a hair of an honest man by which they might be caught.

Besides, others are so ungrateful that, though extremely delighted with the work, they do not love the author any the more. They are not unlike discourteous guests who, after they have been freely entertained at a rich banquet, finally go home well filled without thanking the host who invited them. Go now and provide a feast at your own expense for men of such dainty palate, of such varied taste, and of such unforgetful and grateful natures!

At any rate, my dear Peter, conduct with Hythlodaeus the business which I mentioned. Afterward I shall be fully free to take fresh counsel on the subject. However, since I have gone through the labor of writing, it is too late for me to be wise now. Therefore, provided it be done with the consent of Hythlodaeus, in the matter of publishing which remains I shall follow my friends' advice, and yours first and foremost. Good-bye, my sweetest friend, with your excellent wife. Love me as you have ever done, for I love you even more than I have ever done.

Book I

*The Best State of a Commonwealth,
the Discourse of the Extraordinary
Character, Raphael Hythlodaeus, as
Reported by the Renowned Figure,
Thomas More, Citizen and Sheriff
of the Famous City of Great Britain,
London*

The most invincible King of England, Henry, the eighth of that name, who is distinguished by all the accomplishments of a model monarch, had certain weighty matters recently in dispute with His Serene Highness, Charles, Prince of Castile. With a view to their discussion and settlement, he sent me as a commissioner to Flanders—as a companion and associate of the peerless Cuthbert Tunstal, whom he has just created Master of the Rolls to everyone's immense satisfaction. Of the latter's praises I shall say nothing, not because I fear that the testimony of a friend should be given little credit but because his integrity and learning are too great for it to be possible, and too well known for it to be necessary, for me to extol them—unless I should wish to give the impression, as the proverb goes, of displaying the sun with a lamp!

We were met at Bruges, according to previous arrangement, by those men put in charge of the affair by the Prince—all outstanding persons. Their leader and head was the Burgomaster of Bruges, a figure of magnificence, but their chief speaker and guiding spirit was Georges de Themsecke, Provost of Cassel, a man not only trained in eloquence but a natural orator—most learned, too, in the law and consummately skillful in diplomacy by native ability as well as by long experience. When after one or two meetings there were certain points on which we could not agree sufficiently, they bade farewell to us for some days and left for Brussels to seek an official pronouncement from the Prince. Meanwhile, as my business led me, I made my way to Antwerp. While I stayed there, among my other visitors, but of all of them the most welcome, was Peter Giles, a native of Antwerp, an honorable man of high position in his home town yet worthy of the very highest position, being a young man distinguished equally by learning and character; for he is most virtuous and most cultured, to all most courteous, but to his friends so openhearted, affectionate, loyal, and sincere that you can hardly find one or two anywhere to compare with him as the perfect friend on every score. His modesty is uncommon; no one is less given to deceit, and none has a wiser simplicity of nature. Besides, in conversation he is so polished and so witty without offense that his delightful society and charming discourse largely took away my nostalgia and made me less conscious than before of the separation from my home, wife, and children to whom I was exceedingly anxious to get back, for I had then been more than four months away.

One day I had been at divine service in Notre Dame, the finest church in the city and the most crowded with worshipers. Mass being over, I was about to return to my lodging when I happened to see him in conversation with a stranger, a man of advanced years, with sunburned countenance and long beard and cloak hanging carelessly from his shoulder, while his appearance and dress seemed to me to be those of a ship's captain.

When Peter had espied me, he came up and greeted me. As I tried to return his salutation, he drew me a little aside and, pointing to the man I had seen him talking with, said:

"Do you see this fellow? I was on the point of taking him straight to you."

"He would have been very welcome," said I, "for your sake."

"No," said he, "for his own, if you knew him. There is no mortal alive today who can give you such an account of unknown peoples and lands, a subject about which I know you are always most greedy to hear."

"Well, then," said I, "my guess was not a bad one. The moment I saw him, I was sure he was a ship's captain."

"But you are quite mistaken," said he, "for his sailing has not been like that of Palinurus but that of Ulysses or, rather, of Plato.[1] Now this Raphael—for such is his personal name, with Hythlodaeus[2] as his family name—is no bad Latin scholar, and most learned in Greek. He had studied that language more than Latin because he had devoted himself unreservedly to philosophy, and in that subject he found that there is nothing valuable in Latin except certain treatises of Seneca and Cicero. He left his patrimony at home— he is a Portuguese—to his brothers, and, being eager to see the world, joined Amerigo Vespucci and was his constant companion in the last three of those four voyages which are now universally read of, but on the final voyage he did not return with him. He importuned and even wrested from Amerigo permission to be one of the twenty-four who at the farthest point of the last voyage were left behind in the fort. And so he was left behind that he might have his way, being more anxious for travel than about the grave. These two sayings are constantly on his lips: 'He who has no grave is covered by the sky,' and 'From all places it is the same distance to heaven.' This attitude of his, but for the favor of God, would have cost him dear. However, when after Vespucci's departure he had traveled through many

countries with five companions from the fort, by strange chance he was carried to Ceylon, whence he reached Calicut. There he conveniently found some Portuguese ships, and at length arrived home again, beyond all expectation."

When Peter had rendered this account, I thanked him for his kindness in taking such pains that I might have a talk with one whose conversation he hoped would give me pleasure; then I turned to Raphael. After we had greeted each other and exchanged the civilities which commonly pass at the first meeting of strangers, we went off to my house. There in the garden, on a bench covered with turfs of grass, we sat down to talk together.

He recounted how, after the departure of Vespucci, he and his friends who had stayed behind in the fort began by degrees through continued meetings and civilities to ingratiate themselves with the natives till they not only stood in no danger from them but were actually on friendly terms and, moreover, were in good repute and favor with a ruler (whose name and country I have forgotten). Through the latter's generosity, he and his five companions were supplied with ample provision and travel resources and, moreover, with a trusty guide on their journey (which was partly by water on rafts and partly over land by wagon) to take them to other rulers with careful recommendations to their favor. For, after traveling many days, he said, they found towns and cities and very populous commonwealths with excellent institutions.

To be sure, under the Equator and on both sides of the line nearly as far as the sun's orbit extends, there lie waste deserts scorched with continual heat. A gloomy and dismal region looms in all directions without cultivation or attractiveness, inhabited by wild beasts and snakes or, indeed, men no less savage and harmful than are the beasts. But when you have gone a little farther, the country gradually

---

1 On Palinurus, *see* Virgil *The Aeneid* v (GBWW, Vol. 13, pp. 209-210); on Ulysses, Homer *The Odyssey* ix-xii (GBWW, Vol. 4, pp. 229-254); and on Plato, *The Seventh Letter* (GBWW, Vol. 7, pp. 800 ff.).

2 Hythlodaeus: "expert in trifles" or "well-learned in nonsense." Raphael: "healing of God," possibly chosen because of his role as guide to Tobias in his travels.

UTOPIA CONVERSATION BETWEEN (LEFT TO RIGHT) JOHN CLEMENT, HYTHLO-
DAEUS, THOMAS MORE, PETER GILES. WOODCUT ATTRIBUTED TO AMBROSIUS
HOLBEIN, FROM THE 1518 EDITION OF *Utopia*, J. FROBEN, BASEL
There in the garden we sat down to talk

assumes a milder aspect, the climate is less fierce, the ground is covered with a pleasant green herbage, and the nature of living creatures becomes less wild. At length you reach peoples, cities, and towns which maintain a continual traffic by sea and land not only with each other and their neighbors but also with far-off countries.

Then they had opportunity of visiting many countries in all directions, for every ship which was got ready for any voyage made him and his companions welcome as passengers. The ships they saw in the parts first traveled were flat-bottomed and moved under sails made of papyrus or osiers stitched together and sometimes under sails made of leather. Afterward they found ships with pointed keels and canvas sails, in fact, like our own in all respects.

Their mariners were skilled in adapting themselves to sea and weather. But he reported that he won their extraordinary favor by showing them the use of the magnetic needle of which they had hitherto been quite ignorant so that they had hesitated to trust themselves to the sea and had boldly done so in the summer only. Now, trusting to the magnet, they do not fear wintry weather, being dangerously confident. Thus, there is a risk that what was thought likely to be a great benefit to them may, through their imprudence, cause them great mischief.

What he said he saw in each place would be a long tale to unfold and is not the purpose of this work. Perhaps on another occasion we shall tell his story, particularly whatever facts would be useful to readers, above all, those wise and prudent provisions which he noticed anywhere among nations living together in a civilized way. For on these subjects we eagerly inquired of him, and he no less readily discoursed; but about stale travelers' wonders we were not curious. Scyllas and greedy Celaenos and folk-devouring Laestrygones[3] and similar frightful monsters

3 For Scylla and Celaeno, *see* Virgil *The Aeneid* iii (GBWW, Vol. 13, pp. 153-154, 158b-159a); for the Laestrygones, Homer *The Odyssey* x (GBWW, Vol. 4, p. 237a-c).

are common enough, but well and wisely trained citizens are not everywhere to be found.

To be sure, just as he called attention to many ill-advised customs among these new nations, so he rehearsed not a few points from which our own cities, nations, races, and kingdoms may take example for the correction of their errors. These instances, as I said, I must mention on another occasion. Now I intend to relate merely what he told us of the manners and customs of the Utopians, first, however, giving the talk which drew and led him on to mention that commonwealth.

Raphael had touched with much wisdom on faults in this hemisphere and that, of which he found very many in both, and had compared the wiser measures which had been taken among us as well as among them; for he remembered the manners and customs of each nation as if he had lived all his life in places which he had only visited. Peter expressed his surprise at the man as follows:

"Why, my dear Raphael, I wonder that you do not attach yourself to some king. I am sure there is none of them to whom you would not be very welcome because you are capable not only of entertaining a king with this learning and experience of men and places but also of furnishing him with examples and of assisting him with counsel. Thus, you would not only serve your own interests excellently but be of great assistance in the advancement of all your relatives and friends."

"As for my relatives and friends," he replied, "I am not greatly troubled about them, for I think I have fairly well performed my duty to them already. The possessions, which other men do not resign unless they are old and sick and even then resign unwillingly when incapable of retention, I divided among my relatives and friends when I was not merely hale and hearty but actually young. I think they ought to be satisfied with this gen-erosity from me and not to require or expect additionally that I should, for their sakes, enter into servitude to kings."

"Fine words!" declared Peter. "I meant not that you should be in servitude but in service to kings."

"The one is only one syllable less than the other," he observed.

"But my conviction is," continued Peter, "whatever name you give to this mode of life, that it is the very way by which you can not only profit people both as private individuals and as members of the commonwealth but also render your own condition more prosperous."

"Should I," said Raphael, "make it more prosperous by a way which my soul abhors? As it is, I now live as I please, which I surely fancy is very seldom the case with your grand courtiers. Nay, there are plenty of persons who court the friendship of the great, and so you need not think it a great loss if they have to do without me and one or two others like me."

"Well," I then said, "it is plain that you, my dear Raphael, are desirous neither of riches nor of power. Assuredly, I reverence and look up to a man of your mind no whit less than to any of those who are most high and mighty. But it seems to me you will do what is worthy of you and of this generous and truly philosophic spirit of yours if you so order your life as to apply your talent and industry to the public interest, even if it involves some personal disadvantages to yourself. This you can never do with as great profit as if you are councillor to some great monarch and make him follow, as I am sure you will, straightforward and honorable courses. From the monarch, as from a never-failing spring, flows a stream of all that is good or evil over the whole nation. You possess such complete learning that, even had you no great experience of affairs, and such great experience of affairs that, even had you no learning, you would make an excellent member of any king's council."

"You are twice mistaken, my dear More," said he, "first in me and then in the matter in question. I have no such ability as you ascribe to me and, if I had ever so much, still, in disturbing my own peace and quiet, I should not promote the public interest. In the first place almost all monarchs prefer to occupy themselves in the pursuits of war—with which I neither have nor desire any acquaintance—rather than in the honorable activities of peace, and they care much more how, by hook or by crook, they may win fresh kingdoms than how they may administer well what they have got.

"In the second place, among royal councillors everyone is actually so wise as to have no need of profiting by another's counsel, or everyone seems so wise in his own eyes as not to condescend to profit by it, save that they agree with the most absurd saying of, and play the parasite to, the chief royal favorites whose friendliness they strive to win by flattery. To be sure, it is but human nature that each man favor his own discoveries most—just as the crow and the monkey like their own offspring best.

"If anyone, when in the company of people who are jealous of others' discoveries or prefer their own, should propose something which he either has read of as done in other times or has seen done in other places, the listeners behave as if their whole reputation for wisdom were jeopardized and as if afterward they would deserve to be thought plain blockheads unless they could lay hold of something to find fault with in the discoveries of others. When all other attempts fail, their last resource is a remark such as this: 'Our forefathers were happy with that sort of thing, and would to heaven we had their wisdom.' And then, as if that comment were a brilliant conclusion to the whole business, they take their seats—implying,

of course, that it would be a dangerous thing to be found with more wisdom on any point than our forefathers. And yet, no matter what excellent ideas our forefathers may have had, we very serenely bid them a curt farewell. But if in any situation they failed to take the wiser course, that defect gives us a handle which we greedily grab and never let go. Such proud, ridiculous, and obstinate prejudices I have encountered often in other places and once in England too."*

[Hythlodaeus resumed, saying,] "There is no room for philosophy with rulers."

"Right," I declared, "that is true—not for this academic philosophy which thinks that everything is suitable to every place. But there is another philosophy, more practical for statesmen, which knows its stage, adapts itself to the play in hand, and performs its role neatly and appropriately. This is the philosophy which you must employ. Otherwise we have the situation in which a comedy of Plautus is being performed and the household slaves are making trivial jokes at one another and then you come on the stage in a philosopher's attire and recite the passage from the *Octavia* where Seneca is disputing with Nero. Would it not have been preferable to take a part without words than by reciting something inappropriate to make a hodgepodge of comedy and tragedy? You would have spoiled and upset the actual play by bringing in irrelevant matter—even if your contribution would have been superior in itself. Whatever play is being performed, perform it as best you can, and do not upset it all simply because you think of another which has more interest.

"So it is in the commonwealth. So it is in the deliberations of monarchs. If you

---

* Hythlodaeus' account of his stay in England and of his criticism of contemporary conditions, amounting to some fifteen of our pages, has been omitted. (Ed.)

cannot pluck up wrongheaded opinions by the root, if you cannot cure according to your heart's desire vices of long standing, yet you must not on that account desert the commonwealth. You must not abandon the ship in a storm because you cannot control the winds.

"On the other hand, you must not force upon people new and strange ideas which you realize will carry no weight with persons of opposite conviction. On the contrary, by the indirect approach you must seek and strive to the best of your power to handle matters tactfully. What you cannot turn to good you must make as little bad as you can. For it is impossible that all should be well unless all men were good, a situation which I do not expect for a great many years to come!"

"By this approach," he commented, "I should accomplish nothing else than to share the madness of others as I tried to cure their lunacy. If I would stick to the truth, I must needs speak in the manner I have described. To speak falsehoods, for all I know, may be the part of a philosopher, but it is certainly not for me. Although that speech of mine might perhaps be unwelcome and disagreeable to those councillors, yet I cannot see why it should seem odd even to the point of folly. What if I told them the kind of things which Plato creates in his republic[4] or which the Utopians actually put in practice in theirs? Though such institutions were superior (as, to be sure, they are), yet they might appear odd because here individuals have the right of private property, there all things are common.

"To persons who had made up their minds to go headlong by the opposite road, the man who beckons them back and points out dangers ahead can hardly be welcome. But, apart from this aspect, what did my speech contain that would

not be appropriate or obligatory to have propounded everywhere? Truly, if all the things which by the perverse morals of man have come to seem odd are to be dropped as unusual and absurd, we must dissemble almost all the doctrines of Christ. Yet He forbade us to dissemble them to the extent that what He had whispered in the ears of His disciples He commanded to be preached openly from the housetops. The greater part of His teaching is far more different from the morals of mankind than was my discourse. But preachers, crafty men that they are, finding that men grievously disliked to have their morals adjusted to the rule of Christ and following I suppose your advice, accommodated His teaching to men's morals as if it were a rule of soft lead that at least in some way or other the two might be made to correspond. By this method I cannot see what they have gained, except that men may be bad in greater comfort.

"And certainly I should make as little progress in the councils of princes. For I should hold either a different opinion, which would amount to having none at all, or else the same, and then I should, as Mitio says in Terence, help their madness. As to that indirect approach of yours, I cannot see its relevancy; I mean your advice to use my endeavors, if all things cannot be made good, at least to handle them tactfully and, as far as one may, to make them as little bad as possible. At court there is no room for dissembling, nor may one shut one's eyes to things. One must openly approve the worst counsels and subscribe to the most ruinous decrees. He would be counted a spy and almost a traitor, who gives only faint praise to evil counsels.

"Moreover, there is no chance for you to do any good because you are brought among colleagues who would easily corrupt even the best of men before being reformed themselves. By their evil com-

---

4 For Plato's *Republic*, see GBWW, Vol. 7, pp. 295-441.

panionship, either you will be seduced yourself or, keeping your own integrity and innocence, you will be made a screen for the wickedness and folly of others. Thus you are far from being able to make anything better by that indirect approach of yours.

"For this reason, Plato by a very fine comparison shows why philosophers are right in abstaining from administration of the commonwealth. They observe the people rushing out into the streets and being soaked by constant showers and cannot induce them to go indoors and escape the rain. They know that, if they go out, they can do no good but will only get wet with the rest. Therefore, being content if they themselves at least are safe, they keep at home, since they cannot remedy the folly of others.[5]

"Yet surely, my dear More, to tell you candidly my heart's sentiments, it appears to me that wherever you have private property and all men measure all things by cash values, there it is scarcely possible for a commonwealth to have justice or prosperity—unless you think justice exists where all the best things flow into the hands of the worst citizens or prosperity prevails where all is divided among very few—and even they are not altogether well off, while the rest are downright wretched.

"As a result, when in my heart I ponder on the extremely wise and holy institutions of the Utopians, among whom, with very few laws, affairs are ordered so aptly that virtue has its reward, and yet, with equality of distribution, all men have abundance of all things, and then when I contrast with their policies the many nations elsewhere ever making ordinances and yet never one of them achieving good order—nations where whatever a man has acquired he calls his own private prop-

erty, but where all these laws daily framed are not enough for a man to secure or to defend or even to distinguish from someone else's the goods which each in turn calls his own, a predicament readily attested by the numberless and ever new and interminable lawsuits—when I consider, I repeat, all these facts, I become more partial to Plato and less surprised at his refusal to make laws for those who rejected that legislation which gave to all an equal share in all goods.

"This wise sage, to be sure, easily foresaw that the one and only road to the general welfare lies in the maintenance of equality in all respects. I have my doubts that the latter could ever be preserved where the individual's possessions are his private property. When every man aims at absolute ownership of all the property he can get, be there never so great abundance of goods, it is all shared by a handful who leave the rest in poverty. It generally happens that the one class preeminently deserves the lot of the other, for the rich are greedy, unscrupulous, and useless, while the poor are well behaved, simple, and by their daily industry more beneficial to the commonwealth than to themselves. I am fully persuaded that no just and even distribution of goods can be made and that no happiness can be found in human affairs unless private property is utterly abolished. While it lasts, there will always remain a heavy and inescapable burden of poverty and misfortunes for by far the greatest and by far the best part of mankind.

"I admit that this burden can be lightened to some extent, but I contend that it cannot be removed entirely. A statute might be made that no person should hold more than a certain amount of land and that no person should have a monetary income beyond that permitted by law. Special legislation might be passed to prevent the monarch from being overmighty and the people overweening; likewise,

---

5 Plato *The Republic* vi. 496, GBWW, Vol. 7, pp. 379d-380b.

that public offices should not be solicited with gifts, nor be put up for sale, nor require lavish personal expenditures. Otherwise, there arise, first, the temptation to recoup one's expenses by acts of fraud and plunder, and, secondly, the necessity of appointing rich men to offices which ought rather to have been administered by wise men. By this type of legislation, I maintain, as sick bodies which are past cure can be kept up by repeated medical treatments, so these evils, too, can be alleviated and made less acute. There is no hope, however, of a cure and a return to a healthy condition as long as each individual is master of his own property. Nay, while you are intent upon the cure of one part, you make worse the malady of the other parts. Thus, the healing of the one member reciprocally breeds the disease of the other as long as nothing can so be added to one as not to be taken away from another."

"But," I ventured, "I am of the contrary opinion. Life cannot be satisfactory where all things are common. How can there be a sufficient supply of goods when each withdraws himself from the labor of production? For the individual does not have the motive of personal gain and he is rendered slothful by trusting to the industry of others. Moreover, when people are goaded by want and yet the individual cannot legally keep as his own what he has gained, must there not be trouble from continual bloodshed and riot? This holds true especially since the authority of magistrates and respect for their office have been eliminated, for how there can be any place for these among men who are all on the same level I cannot even conceive."

"I do not wonder," he rejoined, "that it looks this way to you, being a person who has no picture at all, or else a false one, of the situation I mean. But you should have been with me in Utopia and personally seen their manners and customs as I did, for I lived there more than five years and would never have wished to leave except to make known that new world. In that case you unabashedly would admit that you had never seen a well-ordered people anywhere but there."

"Yet surely," objected Peter Giles, "it would be hard for you to convince me that a better-ordered people is to be found in that new world than in the one known to us. In the latter I imagine there are equally excellent minds, as well as commonwealths which are older than those in the new world. In these commonwealths long experience has come upon very many advantages for human life—not to mention also the chance discoveries made among us, which no human mind could have devised."

"As for the antiquity of commonwealths," he countered, "you could give a sounder opinion if you had read the historical accounts of that world. If we must believe them, there were cities among them before there were men among us. Furthermore, whatever either brains have invented or chance has discovered hitherto could have happened equally in both places. But I hold for certain that, even though we surpass them in brains, we are far inferior to them in application and industry.

"According to their chronicles, up to the time of our landing they had never heard anything about our activities (they call us the Ultra-equinoctials) except that twelve hundred years ago a ship driven by a tempest was wrecked on the island of Utopia. Some Romans and Egyptians were cast on shore and remained on the island without ever leaving it. Now mark what good advantage their industry took of this one opportunity. The Roman empire possessed no art capable of any use which they did not either learn from the shipwrecked strangers or discover for themselves after receiving the hints for investigation—so great a gain was it to

AMBROSIUS HOLBEIN'S INTERPRETATION OF THE ISLAND OF UTOPIA, SHOWING THE CAPITAL
CITY, AMAUROTUM, THE SOURCE OF THE RIVER ANDYRUS (FONS ANYDRI) AND THE
HARBOR OF ANYDRUS (OSTIUM ANYDRI)

Set forth in order the terrain, the rivers . . .

them that on a single occasion some persons were carried to their shores from ours.

"But if any like fortune has ever driven anyone from their shores to ours, the event is as completely forgotten as future generations will perhaps forget that I had once been there. And, just as they immediately at one meeting appropriated to themselves every good discovery of ours, so I suppose it will be long before we adopt anything that is better arranged with them than with us. This trait, I judge, is the chief reason why, though we are inferior to them neither in brains nor in resources, their commonwealth is more wisely governed and more happily flourishing than ours."

"If so, my dear Raphael," said I, "I beg and beseech you, give us a description of the island. Do not be brief, but set forth in order the terrain, the rivers, the cities, the inhabitants, the traditions, the customs, the laws, and, in fact, everything which you think we should like to know. And you must think we wish to know everything of which we are still ignorant."

"There is nothing," he declared, "I shall be more pleased to do, for I have the facts ready to hand. But the description will take time."

"In that case," I suggested, "let us go in to dine. Afterward we shall take up as much time as we like."

"Agreed," he replied.

So we went in and dined. We then returned to the same place, sat down on the same bench, and gave orders to the servants that we should not be interrupted. Peter Giles and I urged Raphael to fulfill his promise. As for him, when he saw us intent and eager to listen, after sitting in silent thought for a time, he began his tale as follows.

Holbein, among other things, shows merely one city on the island while More mentions 54. Holbein's Utopia is elliptical in shape; More describes it as crescent shaped.

Book II

The Best State of a Commonwealth, the Discourse of Raphael Hythlodaeus as Reported by Thomas More, Citizen and Sheriff of London

The island of the Utopians extends in the center (where it is broadest) for two hundred miles and is not much narrower for the greater part of the island, but toward both ends it begins gradually to taper. These ends form a circle five hundred miles in circumference and so make the island look like a new moon, the horns of which are divided by straits about eleven miles across. The straits then unfold into a wide expanse. As the winds are kept off by the land which everywhere surrounds it, the bay is like a huge lake, smooth rather than rough, and thus converts almost the whole center of the country into a harbor which lets ships cross in every direction to the great convenience of the inhabitants.

The mouth of this bay is rendered perilous here by shallows and there by reefs. Almost in the center of the gap stands one great crag which, being visible, is not dangerous. A tower built on it is occupied by a garrison. The other rocks are hidden and therefore treacherous. The channels are known only to the natives, and so it does not easily happen that any foreigner enters the bay except with a Utopian pilot. In fact, the entrance is hardly safe even for themselves, unless they guide themselves by landmarks on the shore. If these were removed to other positions, they could easily lure an enemy's fleet, however numerous, to destruction.

On the outer side of the island, harbors are many. Everywhere, however, the landing is so well defended by nature or by engineering that a few defenders can prevent strong forces from coming ashore.

As the report goes and as the appearance of the ground shows, the island once was not surrounded by sea. But Utopus,[6] who as conqueror gave the island its name (up to then it had been called Abraxa) and who brought the rude and rustic people to such a perfection of culture and humanity as makes them now superior to almost all other mortals, gained a victory at his very first landing. He then ordered the excavation of fifteen miles on the side where the land was connected with the continent and caused the sea to flow around the land. He set to the task not only the natives but, to prevent them from thinking the labor a disgrace, his own soldiers also. With the work divided among so many hands, the enterprise was finished with incredible speed and struck the neighboring peoples, who at first had derided the project as vain, with wonder and terror at its success.

The island contains fifty-four city-states, all spacious and magnificent, identical in language, traditions, customs, and laws. They are similar also in layout and everywhere, as far as the nature of the ground permits, similar even in appearance. None of them is separated by less than twenty-four miles from the nearest, but none is so isolated that a person cannot go from it to another in a day's journey on foot. From each city three old and experienced citizens meet to discuss the affairs of common interest to the island once a year at Amaurotum,[7] for this city, being in the very center of the country, is situated most conveniently for the representatives of all sections. It is considered the chief as well as the capital city.

The lands are so well assigned to the cities that each has at least twelve miles of country on every side, and on some sides even much more, to wit, the side on which the cities are farther apart. No city has any desire to extend its territory,

for they consider themselves the tenants rather than the masters of what they hold.

Everywhere in the rural districts they have, at suitable distances from one another, farmhouses well equipped with agricultural implements. They are inhabited by citizens who come in succession to live there. No rural household numbers less than forty men and women, besides two serfs attached to the soil. Over them are set a master and mistress, serious in mind and ripe in years. Over every group of thirty households rules a phylarch.[8]

Twenty from each household return every year to the city, namely, those having completed two years in the country. As substitutes in their place, the same number are sent from the city. They are to be trained by those who have been there a year and who therefore are more expert in farming; they themselves will teach others in the following years. There is thus no danger of anything going wrong with the annual food supply through want of skill, as might happen if all at one time were newcomers and novices at farming. Though this system of changing farmers is the rule, to prevent any individual's being forced against his will to continue too long in a life of rather hard work, yet many men who take a natural pleasure in agricultural pursuits obtain leave to stay several years.

The occupation of the farmers is to cultivate the soil, to feed the animals, and to get wood and convey it to the city either by land or by water, whichever way is more convenient. They breed a vast quantity of poultry by a wonderful contrivance. The hens do not brood over the eggs, but the farmers, by keeping a great number of them at a uniform heat, bring them to life and hatch them. As soon as they come out of the shell, the chicks

---

6 "No place," therefore, "ruler over no place."

7 "Darkling City," a term apt for foggy London.

---

8 "The Head of a Tribe."

follow and acknowledge humans as their mothers!

They rear very few horses, and these only high-spirited ones, which they use for no other purpose than for exercising their young men in horsemanship. All the labor of cultivation and transportation is performed by oxen, which they admit are inferior to horses in a sudden spurt but which are far superior to them in staying power and endurance and not liable to as many diseases. Moreover, it requires less trouble and expense to feed them. When they are past work, they finally are of use for food.

They sow grain only for bread. Their drink is wine or cider or perry, or it is even water. The latter is sometimes plain and often that in which they have boiled honey or licorice, whereof they have a great abundance.

Though they are more than sure how much food the city with its adjacent territory consumes, they produce far more grain and cattle than they require for their own use: they distribute the surplus among their neighbors. Whenever they need things not found in the country, they send for all the materials from the city and, having to give nothing in exchange, obtain it from the municipal officials without the bother of bargaining. For very many go there every single month to observe the holiday.

When the time of harvest is at hand, the agricultural phylarchs inform the municipal officials what number of citizens they require to be sent. The crowd of harvesters, coming promptly at the appointed time, dispatch the whole task of harvesting almost in a single day of fine weather.

THE CITIES, ESPECIALLY AMAUROTUM

The person who knows one of the cities will know them all, since they are exactly alike insofar as the terrain permits. I shall therefore picture one or other (nor does it matter which), but which should I describe rather than Amaurotum? First, none is worthier, the rest deferring to it as the meeting place of the national senate; and, secondly, none is better known to me, as being one in which I had lived for five whole years.

To proceed. Amaurotum is situated on the gentle slope of a hill and is almost four-square in outline. Its breadth is about two miles starting just below the crest of the hill and running down to the river Anydrus;[9] its length along the river is somewhat more than its breadth.

The Anydrus rises eighty miles above Amaurotum from a spring not very large; but, being increased in size by several tributaries, two of which are of fair size, it is half a mile broad in front of the city. After soon becoming still broader and after running farther for sixty miles, it falls into the ocean. Through the whole distance between the city and the sea, and even above the city for some miles, the tide alternately flows in for six whole hours and then ebbs with an equally speedy current. When the sea comes in, it fills the whole bed of the Anydrus with its water for a distance of thirty miles, driving the river back. At such times it turns the water salt for some distance farther, but above that point the river grows gradually fresh and passes the city uncontaminated. When the ebb comes, the fresh and pure water extends down almost to the mouth of the river.

The city is joined to the opposite bank of the river not by a bridge built on wooden pillars or piles but by one magnificently arched with stonework. It is situated in the quarter which is farthest from the sea so that ships may pass along the whole of that side of the city without hindrance.

_____
9 "Waterless."

They have also another river, not very large, but very gentle and pleasant, which rises out of the same hill whereon the city is built and runs down through its middle into the river Anydrus. The head and source of this river just outside the city has been connected with it by outworks, lest in case of hostile attack the water might be cut off and diverted or polluted. From this point the water is distributed by conduits made of baked clay into various parts of the lower town. Where the ground makes that course impossible, the rainwater collected in capacious cisterns is just as useful.

The city is surrounded by a high and broad wall with towers and ravelins at frequent intervals. A moat, dry but deep and wide and made impassable by thorn hedges, surrounds the fortifications on three sides; on the fourth the river itself takes the place of the moat.

The streets are well laid out both for traffic and for protection against the winds. The buildings, which are far from mean, are set together in a long row, continuous through the block and faced by a corresponding one. The house fronts of the respective blocks are divided by an avenue twenty feet broad. On the rear of the houses, through the whole length of the block, lies a broad garden enclosed on all sides by the backs of the blocks. Every home has not only a door into the street but a back door into the garden. What is more, folding doors, easily opened by hand and then closing of themselves, give admission to anyone. As a result, nothing is private property anywhere. Every ten years they actually exchange their very homes by lot.

The Utopians are very fond of their gardens. In them they have vines, fruits, herbs, flowers, so well kept and flourishing that I never saw anything more fruitful and more tasteful anywhere. Their zest in keeping them is increased not merely by the pleasure afforded them but by the keen competition between blocks as to which will have the best kept garden. Certainly you cannot readily find anything in the whole city more productive of profit and pleasure to the citizens. There is nothing which their founder seems to have cared so much for as these gardens.

In fact, they report that the whole plan of the city had been sketched at the very beginning by Utopus himself. He left to posterity, however, to add the adornment and other improvements for which he saw one lifetime would hardly suffice. Their annals, embracing the history of 1,760 years, are preserved carefully and conscientiously in writing. Here they find stated that at first the houses were low, mere cabins and huts, haphazardly made with any wood to hand, with mud-plastered walls. They had thatched the steeply sloping roofs with straw.

But now all the homes are of handsome appearance with three stories. The exposed faces of the walls are made of stone or cement or brick, rubble being used as filling for the empty space between the walls. The roofs are flat and covered with a kind of cement which is cheap but so well mixed that it is impervious to fire and superior to lead in defying the damage caused by storms. They keep the winds out of their windows by glass (which is in very common use in Utopia) or sometimes by thin linen smeared with translucent oil or amber. The advantage is twofold: the device results in letting more light in and keeping more wind out.

THE OFFICIALS

Every thirty families choose anually an official whom in their ancient language they call a syphogrant[10] but in their newer a phylarch. Over ten syphogrants with their families is set a person once

---

10 Derivation uncertain but possibly "Wise Old Man" or, better, "Silly Old Man."

called a tranibor[11] but now a protophylarch.[12] The whole body of syphogrants, in number two hundred, having sworn to choose the man whom they judge most useful, by secret balloting appoint a governor, specifically one of the four candidates named to them by the people, for one is selected out of each of the four quarters of the city to be commended to the Senate.

The governor holds office for life, unless ousted on suspicion of aiming at a tyranny. The tranibors are elected annually but are not changed without good reason. The other officials all hold their posts for one year.

The tranibors enter into consultation with the governor every other day and sometimes, if need arises, oftener. They take counsel about the commonwealth. If there are any disputes between private persons—there are very few—they settle them without loss of time. They always admit to the Senate chamber two syphogrants, and different ones every day. It is provided that nothing concerning the commonwealth be ratified if it has not been discussed in the Senate three days before the passing of the decree. To take counsel on matters of common interest outside the Senate or the Popular Assembly is considered a capital offense. The object of these measures, they say, is to prevent it from being easy, by a conspiracy between the governor and the tranibors and by tyrannous oppression of the people, to change the order of the commonwealth. Therefore whatever is considered important is laid before the assembly of the syphogrants who, after informing their groups of families, take counsel together and report their decision to the Senate. Sometimes the matter is laid before the Council of the whole island.

In addition, the Senate has the custom of debating nothing on the same day on which it is first proposed but of putting it off till the next meeting. This is their rule lest anyone, after hastily blurting out the first thought that popped into his head, should afterward give more thought to defending his opinion than to supporting what is for the good of the commonwealth, and should prefer to jeopardize the public welfare rather than to risk his reputation through a wrongheaded and misplaced shame, fearing he might be thought to have shown too little foresight at the first—though he should have been

---

11 Derivation doubtful but possibly "Plain Glutton."

12 "First among the Chiefs."

enough foresighted at the first to speak with prudence rather than with haste!

OCCUPATIONS

Agriculture is the one pursuit which is common to all, both men and women, without exception. They are all instructed in it from childhood, partly by principles taught in school, partly by field trips to the farms closer to the city as if for recreation. Here they do not merely look on, but, as opportunity arises for bodily exercise, they do the actual work.

Besides agriculture (which is, as I said, common to all), each is taught one particular craft as his own. This is generally either wool-working or linen-making or masonry or metalworking or carpentry. There is no other pursuit which occupies any number worth mentioning. As for clothes, these are of one and the same pattern throughout the island and down the centuries, though there is a distinction between the sexes and between the single and married. The garments are comely to the eye, convenient for bodily movement, and fit for wear in heat and cold. Each family, I say, does its own tailoring.

Of the other crafts, one is learned by each person, and not the men only, but the women too. The latter as the weaker sex have the lighter occupations and generally work wool and flax. To the men are committed the remaining more laborious crafts. For the most part, each is brought up in his father's craft, for which most have a natural inclination. But if anyone is attracted to another occupation, he is transferred by adoption to a family pursuing that craft for which he has a liking. Care is taken not only by his father but by the authorities, too, that he will be assigned to a grave and honorable householder. Moreover, if anyone after being thoroughly taught one craft desires another also, the same permission is given.

Having acquired both, he practices his choice unless the city has more need of the one than of the other.

The chief and almost the only function of the syphogrants is to manage and provide that no one sit idle, but that each apply himself industriously to his trade, and yet that he be not wearied like a beast of burden with constant toil from early morning till late at night. Such wretchedness is worse than the lot of slaves, and yet it is almost everywhere the life of workingmen—except for the Utopians. The latter divide the day and night into twenty-four equal hours and assign only six to work. There are three before noon, after which they go to dinner. After dinner, when they have rested for two hours in the afternoon, they again give three to work and finish up with supper. Counting one o'clock as beginning at midday, they go to bed about eight o'clock, and sleep claims eight hours.

The intervals between the hours of work, sleep, and food are left to every man's discretion, not to waste in revelry or idleness, but to devote the time free from work to some other occupation according to taste. These periods are commonly devoted to intellectual pursuits. For it is their custom that public lectures are daily delivered in the hours before daybreak. Attendance is compulsory only for those who have been specially chosen to devote themselves to learning. A great number of all classes, however, both males and females, flock to hear the lectures, some to one and some to another, according to their natural inclination. But if anyone should prefer to devote this time to his trade, as is the case with many minds which do not reach the level for any of the higher intellectual disciplines, he is not hindered; in fact, he is even praised as useful to the commonwealth.

After supper they spend one hour in recreation, in summer in the gardens, in winter in the common halls in which they have their meals. There they either play music or entertain themselves with conversation. Dice and that kind of foolish and ruinous game they are not acquainted with. They do play two games not unlike chess. The first is a battle of numbers in which one number plunders another. The second is a game in which the vices fight a pitched battle with the virtues. In the latter is exhibited very cleverly, to begin with, both the strife of the vices with one another and their concerted opposition to the virtues; then, what vices are opposed to what virtues, by what forces they assail them openly, by what stratagems they attack them indirectly, by what safeguards the virtues check the power of the vices, by what arts they frustrate their designs; and, finally, by what means the one side gains the victory.

But here, lest you be mistaken, there is one point you must examine more closely. Since they devote but six hours to work, you might possibly think the consequence to be some scarcity of necessities. But so far is this from being the case that the aforesaid time is not only enough but more than enough for a supply of all that is requisite for either the necessity or the convenience of living. This phenomenon you too will understand if you consider how large a part of the population in other countries exists without working. First, there are almost all the women, who constitute half the whole; or, where the women are busy, there as a rule the men are snoring in their stead. Besides, how great and how lazy is the crowd of priests and so-called religious! Add to them all the rich, especially the masters of estates, who are commonly termed gentlemen and noblemen. Reckon with them their retainers—I mean, that whole rabble of good-for-nothing swashbucklers. Finally, join in the lusty and sturdy beggars who make some disease an excuse for idleness. You will certainly find far less numerous than you had supposed those whose labor produces all the articles that mortals require for daily use.

Now estimate how few of those who do work are occupied in essential trades. For, in a society where we make money the standard of everything, it is necessary to practice many crafts which are quite vain and superfluous, ministering only to luxury and licentiousness. Suppose the host of those who now toil were distributed over only as few crafts as the few needs and conveniences demanded by nature. In the great abundance of commodities which must then arise, the prices set on them would be too low for the craftsmen to earn their livelihood by their work. But suppose all those fellows who are now busied with unprofitable crafts, as well as all the lazy and idle throng, any one of whom now consumes as much of the fruits of other men's labors as any two of the working-men, were all set to work and indeed to useful work. You can easily see how small an allowance of time would be enough and to spare for the production of all that is required by necessity or comfort (or even pleasure, provided it be genuine and natural).

The very experience of Utopia makes the latter clear. In the whole city and its neighborhood, exemption from work is granted to hardly five hundred of the total of men and women whose age and strength make them fit for work. Among them the syphogrants, though legally exempted from work, yet take no advantage of this privilege so that by their example they may the more readily attract the others to work. The same exemption is enjoyed by those whom the people, persuaded by the recommendation of the priests, have given perpetual freedom from labor through the secret vote of the syphogrants so that they may learn thoroughly the various branches of knowledge. But if any of these scholars falsifies the hopes entertained of him, he is reduced to the rank of workingman. On the other hand, not seldom does it happen

"BUILDING," FROM THE
GOITEIN EDITION OF 1925
*They promptly repair
any damage*

that a craftsman so industriously employs his spare hours on learning and makes such progress by his diligence that he is relieved of his manual labor and advanced into the class of men of learning. It is out of this company of scholars that they choose ambassadors, priests, tranibors, and finally the governor himself, whom they call in their ancient tongue Barzanes[13] but in their more modern language Ademus.[14]

Nearly all the remaining populace being neither idle nor busied with useless occupations, it is easy to calculate how much good work can be produced in a very few hours. Besides the points mentioned, there is this further convenience that in most of the necessary crafts they do not require as much work as other nations. In the first place the erection or repair of buildings requires the constant labor of so many men elsewhere because what a father has built, his extravagant heir allows gradually to fall into ruin. As a result, what might have been kept up at small cost, his successor is obliged to erect anew at great expense. Further, often even when a house has cost one man a large sum, another is so fastidious that he thinks little

13 "Son of Zeus."
14 "Peopleless."

of it. When it is neglected and therefore soon becomes dilapidated, he builds a second elsewhere at no less cost. But in the land of the Utopians, where everything has its proper place and the general welfare is carefully regulated, a new home on a new site is a rare event, for not only do they promptly repair any damage, but they even take care to prevent damage. What is the result? With the minimum of labor, buildings last very long, and masons and carpenters sometimes have scarcely anything to do, except that they are set to hew out timber at home and to square and prepare stone meantime so that, if any work be required, a building may the sooner be erected.

In the matter of clothing, too, see how little toil and labor is needed. First, while at work, they are dressed unpretentiously in leather or hide, which lasts for seven years. When they go out in public, they put on a cape to hide their comparatively rough working clothes. This garment is of one color throughout the island and that the natural color. Consequently not only is much less woolen cloth needed than elsewhere, but what they have is much less expensive. On the other hand, since linen cloth is made with less labor, it is more used. In linen cloth only whiteness, in woolen cloth only cleanliness, is considered. No value is set on fineness of thread. So it comes about that, whereas elsewhere one man is not satisfied with four or five woolen coats of different colors and as many silk shirts, and the more fastidious not even with ten, in Utopia a man is content with a single cape, lasting generally for two years. There is no reason, of course, why he should desire more, for if he had them he would not be better fortified against the cold nor appear better dressed in the least.

Wherefore, seeing that they are all busied with useful trades and are satisfied with fewer products from them, it even happens that when there is an abundance of all commodities, they sometimes take out a countless number of people to repair whatever public roads are in bad order. Often, too, when there is nothing even of this kind of work to be done, they announce publicly that there will be fewer hours of work. For the authorities do not keep the citizens against their will at superfluous labor since the constitution of their commonwealth looks in the first place to this sole object: that for all the citizens, as far as the public needs permit, as much time as possible should be withdrawn from the service of the body and devoted to the freedom and culture of the mind. It is in the latter that they deem the happiness of life to consist.

SOCIAL RELATIONS

But now, it seems, I must explain the behavior of the citizens toward one another, the nature of their social relations, and the method of distribution of goods. Since the city consists of households, households as a rule are made up of those related by blood. Girls, upon reaching womanhood and upon being settled in marriage, go to their husbands' domiciles. On the other hand, male children and then grandchildren remain in the family and are subject to the oldest parent, unless he has become a dotard with old age. In the latter case the next oldest is put in his place.

But that the city neither be depopulated nor grow beyond measure, provision is made that no household shall have fewer than ten or more than sixteen adults; there are six thousand such households in each city, apart from its surrounding territory. Of children under age, of course, no number can be fixed. This limit is easily observed by transferring those who exceed the number in larger families into those that are under the prescribed number. Whenever all the families of a city reach their full quota, the adults in excess of that number help to make up the deficient population of other cities.

And if the population throughout the island should happen to swell above the fixed quotas, they enroll citizens out of every city and, on the mainland nearest them, wherever the natives have much unoccupied and uncultivated land, they found a colony under their own laws. They join with themselves the natives if they are willing to dwell with them. When such a union takes place, the two parties gradually and easily merge and together absorb the same way of life and the same customs, much to the great advantage of both peoples. By their procedures they make the land sufficient for both, which previously seemed poor and barren to the natives. The inhabitants who refuse to live according to their laws, they drive from the territory which they carve out for themselves. If they resist, they wage war against them. They consider it a most just cause for war when a people which does not use its soil but keeps it idle and waste nevertheless forbids the use and possession of it to others who by the rule of nature ought to be maintained by it.

If ever any misfortune so diminishes the number in any of their cities that it cannot be made up out of other parts of the island without bringing other cities below their proper strength (this has happened, they say, only twice in all the ages on account of the raging of a fierce pestilence), they are filled up by citizens returning from colonial territory. They would rather that the colonies should perish than that any of the cities of the island should be enfeebled.

But to return to the dealings of the citizens. The oldest, as I have said, rules the household. Wives wait on their husbands, children on their parents, and generally the younger on their elders.

Every city is divided into four equal districts. In the middle of each quarter is a market of all kinds of commodities. To designated market buildings the products of each family are conveyed. Each kind of goods is arranged separately in storehouses. From the latter any head of a household seeks what he and his require and, without money or any kind of compensation, carries off what he seeks. Why should anything be refused? First, there is a plentiful supply of all things and, secondly, there is no underlying fear that anyone will demand more than he needs. Why should there be any suspicion that someone may demand an excessive amount when he is certain of never being in want? No doubt about it, avarice and greed are aroused in every kind of living creature by the fear of want, but only in man are they motivated by pride alone—pride which counts it a personal glory to excel others by superfluous display of possessions. The latter vice can have no place at all in the Utopian scheme of things.

Next to the market place that I have mentioned are the food markets. Here are brought not only different kinds of vegetables, fruit, and bread but also fish and whatever is edible of bird and four-footed beast. Outside the city are designated places where all gore and offal may be washed away in running water. From these places they transport the carcasses of the animals slaughtered and cleaned by the hands of slaves. They do not allow their citizens to accustom themselves to the butchering of animals, by the practice of which they think that mercy, the finest feeling of our human nature, is gradually killed off. In addition, they do not permit to be brought inside the city anything filthy or unclean for fear that the air, tainted by putrefaction, should engender disease.

To continue, each street has spacious halls, located at equal distance from one another, each being known by a special name of its own. In these halls live the syphogrants. To each hall are assigned thirty families, fifteen on either side, to take their meals in common. The managers of each hall meet at a fixed time in the market and get food according to the number of persons in their individual charge.

Special care is first taken of the sick who are looked after in public hospitals. They have four at the city limits, a little outside the walls. These are so roomy as to be comparable to as many small towns. The purpose is twofold: first, that the sick, however numerous, should not be packed too close together in consequent discomfort, and, second, that those who have a contagious disease likely to pass from one to another may be isolated as much as possible from the rest. These hospitals are very well furnished and equipped with everything conducive to health. Besides, such tender and careful treatment and such constant attendance of expert physicians are provided that, though no one is sent to them against his will, there is hardly anybody in the whole city who, when suffering from illness, does not prefer to be nursed there rather than at home.

After the supervisor for the sick has received food as prescribed by the physicians, then the finest of everything is distributed equally among the halls according to the number in each, except that special regard is paid to the governor, the high priest, and the tranibors, as well as to ambassadors and all foreigners (if there are any, but they are few and far between). Yet the latter, too, when they are in Utopia, have definite homes got ready for them.

To these halls, at the hours fixed for dinner and supper, the entire syphograncy assembles, summoned by the blast of a brazen trumpet, excepting persons who are taking their meals either in the hospitals or at home. No one is forbidden, after the halls have been served, to fetch food from the market to his home: they realize that no one would do it without good reason. For, though nobody is forbidden to dine at home, yet no one does it willingly since the practice is considered not decent and since it is foolish to take the trouble of preparing an inferior dinner when an excellent and sumptuous one is ready at hand in the hall nearby.

In this hall all menial offices which to some degree involve heavy labor or soil the hands are performed by slaves. But the duty of cooking and preparing the food and, in fine, of arranging the whole meal is carried out by the women alone, taking turns for each family. Persons sit down at three or more tables according to the number of the company. The men sit with their backs to the wall, the women on the outside, so that if they have any sudden pain or sickness, such as often happens to women with child, they may rise without disturbing the arrangements and go to the nurses.

The nurses sit separately with the infants in a dining room assigned for the purpose, never without a fire and a supply of clean water nor without cradles. Thus they can both lay the infants down and, when they wish, undo their wrappings and let them play freely by the fire. Each woman nurses her own offspring, unless prevented by either death or disease. When that happens, the wives of the syphogrants quickly provide a nurse and

find no difficulty in doing so. The reason is that women who can do the service offer themselves with the greatest readiness since everybody praises this kind of pity and since the child who is thus fostered looks on his nurse as his natural mother. In the nurses' quarters are all children up to five years of age. All other minors, among whom they include all of both sexes below the age of marriage, either wait at table on the diners or, if they are not old and strong enough, stand by—and that in absolute silence. Both groups eat what is handed them from the table and have no other separate time for dining.

The syphogrant and his wife sit in the middle of the first table, which is the highest place and which allows them to have the whole company in view, for it stands crosswise at the farthest end of the dining room. Alongside them are two of the eldest, for they always sit four by four at all tables. But if there is a temple in the syphograncy, the priest and his wife so sit with the syphogrant as to preside. On both sides of them sit younger people, and next to them old people again, and so through the house those of the same age sit together and yet mingle with those of a different age. The reason for this practice, they say, is that the grave and reverend behavior of the old may restrain the younger people from mischievous freedom in word and gesture, since nothing can be done or said at table which escapes the notice of the old present on every side.

The trays of food are not served in order from the first place and so on, but all the old men, who are seated in conspicuous places, are served first with the best food, and then equal portions are given to the rest. The old men at their discretion give a share of their delicacies to their neighbors when there is not enough to go around to everybody in the house. Thus, due respect is paid to seniority, and yet all have an equal advantage.

They begin every dinner and supper with some reading which is conducive to morality but which is brief so as not to be tiresome. Taking their cue from the reading, the elders introduce approved subjects of conversation, neither somber nor dull. But they do not monopolize the whole dinner with long speeches: they are ready to hear the young men too, and indeed deliberately draw them out that they may test each one's ability and character, which are revealed in the relaxed atmosphere of a feast.

Their dinners are somewhat short, their suppers more prolonged, because the former are followed by labor, the latter by sleep and a night's rest. They think the night's rest to be more efficacious to wholesome digestion. No supper passes without music, nor does the dessert course lack delicacies. They burn spices and scatter perfumes and omit nothing that may cheer the company. For they are somewhat too much inclined to this attitude of mind: that no kind of pleasure is forbidden, provided no harm comes of it.

This is the common life they live in the city. In the country, however, since they are rather far removed from their neighbors, all take their meals in their own homes. No family lacks any kind of edible inasmuch as all the food eaten by the city dwellers comes from those who live in the country.

UTOPIAN TRAVEL [ETC.]

Now if any citizens conceive a desire either to visit their friends who reside in another city or to see the place itself, they easily obtain leave from their syphogrants and tranibors, unless some good reason prevents them. Accordingly a party is made up and dispatched carrying a letter from the governor which bears witness to the granting of leave to travel and fixes the day of their return. A wagon is granted them with a public slave to conduct and see to the oxen, but, unless they have women in their company, they dispense with the wagon, regarding it as a burden and hindrance. Throughout their journey, though they carry nothing with them, yet nothing is lacking, for they are at home everywhere. If they stay longer than a day in any place, each practices his trade there and is entertained very courteously by workers in the same trade.

If any person gives himself leave to stray out of his territorial limits and is caught without the governor's certificate, he is treated with contempt, brought back as a runaway, and severely punished. A

"TRAVELLING," FROM THE GOITEIN EDITION OF 1925 *A wagon is granted them with a public slave to conduct and see to the oxen*

rash repetition of the offense entails the sentence of slavery.

If anyone is seized with the desire of exploring the country belonging to his own city, he is not forbidden to do so, provided he obtain his father's leave and his wife's consent. In any district of the country to which he comes, he receives no food until he has finished the morning share of the day's work or the labor that is usually performed there before supper. If he keep to this condition, he may go where he pleases within the territory belonging to his city. In this way he will be just as useful to the city as if he were in it.

Now you can see how nowhere is there any license to waste time, nowhere any pretext to evade work—no wine shop, no alehouse, no brothel anywhere, no opportunity for corruption, no lurking hole, no secret meeting place. On the contrary, being under the eyes of all, people are bound either to be performing the usual labor or to be enjoying their leisure in a fashion not without decency. This universal behavior must of necessity lead to an abundance of all commodities. Since the latter are distributed evenly among all, it follows, of course, that no one can be reduced to poverty or beggary.

In the Senate at Amaurotum (to which, as I said before, three are sent annually from every city), they first determine what commodity is in plenty in each particular place and again where on the island the crops have been meager. They at once fill up the scarcity of one place by the surplus of another. This service they perform without payment, receiving nothing in return from those to whom they give. Those who have given out of their stock to any particular city without requiring any return from it receive what they lack from another to which they have given nothing. Thus, the whole island is like a single family.

But when they have made sufficient provision for themselves (which they do not consider complete until they have provided for two years to come, on account of the next year's uncertain crop), then they export into other countries, out of their surplus, a great quantity of grain, honey, wool, linen, timber, scarlet and purple dyestuffs, hides, wax, tallow, leather, as well as livestock. Of all these commodities they bestow the seventh part on the poor of the district and sell the rest at a moderate price.

By this trade they bring into their country not only such articles as they lack themselves—and practically the only thing lacking is iron—but also a great quantity of silver and gold. This exchange has gone on day by day so long that now they have everywhere an abundance of these metals, more than would be believed. In consequence, they now care little whether they sell for ready cash or appoint a future day for payment, and in fact have by far the greatest amount out on credit. In all transactions on credit, however, they never trust private citizens but the municipal government, the legal documents being drawn up as usual. When the day for payment comes, the city collects the money due from private debtors and puts it into the treasury and enjoys the use of it until the Utopians claim payment.

The Utopians never claim payment of most of the money. They think it hardly fair to take away a thing useful to other people when it is useless to themselves. But if circumstances require that they should lend some part of it to another nation, then they call in their debts—or when they must wage war. It is for that single purpose that they keep all the treasure they possess at home: to be their bulwark in extreme peril or in sudden emergency. They use it above all to hire at sky-high rates of pay foreign mercenaries (whom they would jeopardize rather than their own citizens), being well aware that by large sums of money even their enemies themselves may be bought and sold or set to fight one another either by treachery or by open warfare.

For these military reasons they keep a vast treasure, but not as a treasure. They keep it in a way which I am really quite ashamed to reveal for fear that my words will not be believed. My fears are all the more justified because I am conscious that, had I not been there and witnessed the phenomenon, I myself should have been with difficulty induced to believe it from another's account. It needs must be almost always the rule that, as far as a thing is unlike the ways of the hearers, so far is it from obtaining their credence. An impartial judge of things, however, seeing that the rest of their institutions are so unlike ours, will perhaps wonder less that their use of silver and gold should be adapted to their way of life rather than to ours. As stated, they do not use money themselves but keep it only for an emergency, which may actually occur, yet possibly may never happen.

Meanwhile, gold and silver, of which money is made, are so treated by them that no one values them more highly than their true nature deserves. Who does not see that they are far inferior to iron in usefulness since without iron mortals cannot live any more than without fire and water? To gold and silver, however, nature has given no use that we cannot dispense with, if the folly of men had not made them valuable because they are rare. On the other hand, like a most kind and indulgent mother, she has exposed to view all that is best, like air and water and earth itself, but has removed as far as possible from us all vain and unprofitable things.

If in Utopia these metals were kept locked up in a tower, it might be suspected that the governor and the Senate—for such is the foolish imagination of the common folk—were deceiving the people by the scheme and they themselves were deriving some benefit therefrom. Moreover, if they made them into drinking vessels and other such skillful handiwork, then if occasion arose for them all to be melted down again and applied to the pay of soldiers, they realize that people would be unwilling to be deprived of what they had once begun to treasure.

To avoid these dangers, they have devised a means which, as it is consonant with the rest of their institutions, so it is extremely unlike our own—seeing that we value gold so much and are so careful in safeguarding it—and therefore incredible except to those who have experience of it. While they eat and drink from earthenware and glassware of fine workmanship but of little value, from gold and silver they make chamber pots and all the humblest vessels for use everywhere, not only in the common halls but in private homes also. Moreover, they employ the same metals to make the chains and solid fetters which they put on their slaves. Finally, as for those who bear the stigma of disgrace on account of some crime, they have gold ornaments hanging from their ears, gold rings encircling their fingers, gold chains thrown around their necks, and, as a last touch, a gold crown binding their temples. Thus by every means in their power they make gold and silver a mark of ill fame. In this way, too, it happens that, while all other nations bear the loss of these metals with as great grief as if they were losing their very vitals, if circumstances in Utopia ever required the removal of all gold and silver, no one would feel that he were losing as much as a penny.

They also gather pearls by the seashore and diamonds and rubies on certain cliffs. They do not look for them purposely, but they polish them when found by chance. With them they adorn little children, who in their earliest years are proud and delighted with such decorations. When they have grown somewhat older and perceive that only children use such toys, they lay them aside, not by any order of their parents, but through their own feeling of shame, just as our own children, when they grow up, throw away their marbles, rattles, and dolls.

What opposite ideas and feelings are created by customs so different from those of other people came home to me never more clearly than in the case of the Anemolian[15] ambassadors. They arrived in Amaurotum during my stay there. Because they came to treat of important matters, the three representatives of each city had assembled before their appearance. Now all the ambassadors of neighboring nations, who had previously visited the land, were well acquainted with the manners of the Utopians and knew that they paid no respect to costly clothes but looked with contempt on silk and regarded gold as a badge of disgrace. These persons usually came in the simplest possible dress. But the Anemolians, living farther off and having had fewer dealings with them, since they heard that in Utopia all were dressed alike, and in a homespun fashion at that, felt sure that they did not possess what they made no use of. Being more proud than wise, they determined by the grandeur of their apparel to represent the gods themselves and by their splendid adornment to dazzle the eyes of the poor Utopians.

Consequently the three ambassadors made a grand entry with a suite of a hundred followers, all in parti-colored clothes and most in silk. The ambassadors themselves, being noblemen at home, were arrayed in cloth of gold, with heavy gold necklaces and earrings, with gold rings on their fingers, and with strings of pearls and gems upon their caps; in fact, they were decked out with all those articles which in Utopia are used to punish slaves, to stigmatize evildoers, or to amuse children.

15 "Windy People," *i.e.*, "Vain, Conceited, Inconstant People."

It was a sight worth seeing to behold their cockiness when they compared their grand clothing with that of the Utopians, who had poured out into the street to see them pass. On the other hand, it was no less delightful to notice how much they were mistaken in their sanguine expectations and how far they were from obtaining the consideration which they had hoped to get. To the eyes of all the Utopians, with the exception of the very few who for a good reason had visited foreign countries, all this gay show appeared disgraceful. They therefore bowed to the lowest of the party as to the masters but took the ambassadors themselves to be slaves because they were wearing gold chains, and passed them over without any deference whatever.

Why, you might have seen also the children who had themselves discarded gems and pearls, when they saw them attached to the caps of the ambassadors, poke and nudge their mothers and say to them:

"Look, mother, what a big booby is still wearing pearls and jewels as if he were yet a little boy!"

But the mother, also in earnest, would say:

"Hush, son, I think it is one of the ambassadors' clowns."

Others found fault with the golden chains as useless, being so slender that a slave could easily break them or, again, so loose that at his pleasure he could throw them off and escape anywhere scot-free.

After spending one or more days there, the ambassadors saw an immense quantity of gold held as cheaply and in as great contempt there as in honor among themselves. They saw, too, that more gold and silver were amassed to make the chains and fetters of one runaway slave than had made up the whole array of the three of them. They then were crestfallen and for shame put away all the finery with which they had made themselves haughtily conspicuous, especially when, after familiar talk with the Utopians, they had learned their ways and opinions.

The Utopians wonder that any mortal takes pleasure in the uncertain sparkle of a tiny jewel or precious stone when he can look at a star or even the sun itself. They wonder that anyone can be so mad as to think himself more noble on account of the texture of a finer wool, since, however fine the texture is, a sheep once wore the wool and yet all the time was nothing more than a sheep.

They wonder, too, that gold, which by its very nature is so useless, is now everywhere in the world valued so highly that man himself, through whose agency and for whose use it got this value, is priced much cheaper than gold itself. This is true to such an extent that a blockhead who has no more intelligence than a log and who is as dishonest as he is foolish keeps in bondage many wise men and good men merely for the reason that a great heap of gold coins happens to be his. Yet if some chance or some legal trick (which is as apt as chance to confound high and low) transfers it from this master to the lowest rascal in his entire household, he will surely very soon pass into the service of his former servant—as if he were a mere appendage of and addition to the coins! But much more do they wonder at and abominate the madness of persons who pay almost divine honors to the rich, to whom they neither owe anything nor are obligated in any other respect than that they are rich. Yet they know them to be so mean and miserly that they are more than sure that of all that great pile of cash, as long as the rich men live, not a single penny will ever come their way.

These and similar opinions they have conceived partly from their upbringing, being reared in a commonwealth whose institutions are far removed from follies of the kind mentioned, and partly from instruction and reading good books.

Though there are not many in each city who are relieved from all other tasks and assigned to scholarship alone, that is to say, the individuals in whom they have detected from childhood an outstanding personality, a first-rate intelligence, and an inclination of mind toward learning, yet all children are introduced to good literature. A large part of the people, too, men and women alike, throughout their lives, devote to learning the hours which, as we said, are free from manual labor.

They learn the various branches of knowledge in their native tongue. The latter is copious in vocabulary and pleasant to the ear and a very faithful exponent of thought. It is almost the same as that current in a great part of that side of the world, only that everywhere else its form is more corrupt, to different degrees in different regions.

Of all those philosophers whose names are famous in the part of the world known to us, the reputation of not even a single one had reached them before our arrival. Yet in music, dialectic, arithmetic, and geometry they have made almost the same discoveries as those predecessors of ours in the classical world. But while they measure up to the ancients in almost all other subjects, still they are far from being a match for the inventions of our modern logicians. In fact, they have discovered not even a single one of those very ingeniously devised rules about restrictions, amplifications, and suppositions which our own children everywhere learn in the *Small Logicals*.[16] In addition, so far are they from ability to speculate on second intentions that not one of them could see even man himself as a so-called universal—though he was, as you know, colossal and greater than any giant, as well as pointed out by us with our finger.

They are most expert, however, in the courses of the stars and the movements

---

16 Authored by Peter of Spain.

of the celestial bodies. Moreover, they have ingeniously devised instruments in different shapes, by which they have most exactly comprehended the movements and positions of the sun and moon and all the other stars which are visible in their horizon. But of the agreements and discords of the planets and, in sum, of all that infamous and deceitful divination by the stars, they do not even dream.

They forecast rains, winds, and all the other changes in weather by definite signs which they have ascertained by long practice. But as to the *causes* of all these phenomena, and of the flow of the sea and its saltiness, and, in fine, of the origin and nature of the heavens and the universe, they partly treat of them in the same way as our ancient philosophers and partly, as the latter differ from one another, they, too, in introducing new theories disagree with them all and yet do not in all respects agree with fellow Utopians.

In that part of philosophy which deals with morals, they carry on the same debates as we do. They inquire into the good: of the soul and of the body and of external gifts. They ask also whether the name of good may be applied to all three or simply belongs to the endowments of the soul. They discuss virtue and pleasure, but their principal and chief debate is in what thing or things, one or more, they are to hold that happiness consists. In this matter they seem to lean more than they should to the school that espouses pleasure as the object by which to define either the whole or the chief part of human happiness.

What is more astonishing is that they seek a defense for this soft doctrine from their religion, which is serious and strict, almost solemn and hard. They never have a discussion of philosophy without uniting certain principles taken from religion as well as from philosophy, which uses rational arguments. Without these principles they think reason insufficient and weak by

itself for the investigation of true happiness. The following are examples of these principles. The soul is immortal and by the goodness of God born for happiness. After this life rewards are appointed for our virtues and good deeds, punishment for our crimes. Though these principles belong to religion, yet they hold that reason leads men to believe and to admit them.

Once the principles are eliminated, the Utopians have no hesitation in maintaining that a person would be stupid not to seek pleasure by fair means or foul, but that he should only take care not to let a lesser pleasure interfere with a greater nor to follow after a pleasure which would bring pain in retaliation. To pursue hard and painful virtue and not only to banish the sweetness of life but even voluntarily to suffer pain from which you expect no profit (for what profit can there be if after death you gain nothing for having passed the whole present life unpleasantly, that is, wretchedly?)—this policy they declare to be the extreme of madness.

As it is, they hold happiness rests not in every kind of pleasure but only in good and decent pleasure. To such, as to the supreme good, our nature is drawn by virtue itself, to which the opposite school alone attributes happiness. The Utopians define virtue as living according to nature since to this end we were created by God. That individual, they say, is following the guidance of nature who, in desiring one thing and avoiding another, obeys the dictates of reason.

Now reason first of all inflames men to a love and veneration of the divine majesty, to whom we owe both our existence and our capacity for happiness. Secondly, it admonishes and urges us to lead a life as free from care and as full of joy as possible and, because of our natural fellowship, to help all other men, too, to attain that end. No one was ever so solemn and severe a follower of virtue and hater of pleasure that he, while imposing on you labors, watchings, and discomforts, would not at the same time bid you do your best to relieve the poverty and misfortunes of others. He would bid you regard as praiseworthy in humanity's name that one man should provide for another man's welfare and comfort—if it is especially humane (and humanity is the virtue most peculiar to man) to relieve the misery of others and, by taking away all sadness from their life, restore them to enjoyment, that is, to pleasure. If so, why should not nature urge everyone to do the same for himself also?

For either a joyous life, that is, a pleasurable life, is evil, in which case not only ought you to help no one to it but, as far as you can, should take it away from everyone as being harmful and deadly, or else, if you not only are permitted but are obligated to win it for others as being good, why should you not do so first of all for yourself, to whom you should show no less favor than to others? When nature bids you to be good to others, she does not command you conversely to be cruel and merciless to yourself. So nature herself, they maintain, prescribes to us a joyous life or, in other words, pleasure, as the end of all our operations. Living according to her prescription they define as virtue.

To pursue this line. Nature calls all men to help one another to a merrier life. (This she certainly does with good reason, for no one is raised so far above the common lot of mankind as to have his sole person the object of nature's care, seeing that she equally favors all whom she endows with the same form.) Consequently nature surely bids you take constant care not so to further your own advantages as to cause disadvantages to your fellows.

Therefore they hold that not only ought contracts between private persons to be observed but also public laws for the distribution of vital commodities, that is to say, the matter of pleasure, provided they have been justly promulgated by a good king or ratified by the common consent of a people neither oppressed by tyranny nor deceived by fraud. As long as such laws are not broken, it is prudence to look after your own interests, and to look after those of the public in addition is a mark of devotion. But to deprive others of their pleasure to secure your own, this is surely an injustice. On the contrary, to take away something from yourself and to give it to others is a duty of humanity and kindness which never takes away as much advantage as it brings back. It is compensated by the return of benefits as well as by the actual consciousness of the good deed. Remembrance of the love and good will of those whom you have benefited gives the mind a greater amount of pleasure than the bodily pleasure which you have forgone would have afforded. Finally—and religion easily brings this home to a mind which readily assents—God repays, in place of a brief and tiny pleasure, immense and never-ending gladness. And so they maintain, having carefully considered and weighed the matter, that all our actions, and even the very virtues exercised in them, look at last to pleasure as their end and happiness.

By pleasure they understand every movement and state of body or mind in which, under the guidance of nature, man delights to dwell. They are right in including man's natural inclinations. For just as the senses as well as right reason aim at whatever is pleasant by nature—whatever is not striven after through wrongdoing, nor involves the loss of something more pleasant, nor is followed by pain—so they hold that whatever things mortals imagine by a futile consensus to be sweet to them in spite of being against nature (as though they had the power to change the nature of things as they do their names) are all so far from making for happiness that they are even a great hindrance to it. The reason is that they possess the minds of persons in whom they have once become deep-seated with a false idea of pleasure so that no room is left anywhere for true and genuine delights. In fact, very many are the things which, though of their own nature they contain no sweetness, nay, a good part of them very much bitterness, still are, through the perverse attraction of evil desires, not only regarded as the highest pleasures but also counted among the chief reasons that make life worth living.

In the class that follow this spurious pleasure, they put those whom I mentioned before, who think themselves the better men, the better the coat they wear. In this one thing they make a twofold mistake: they are no less deceived in thinking their coat better than in thinking themselves better. If you consider the use of the garment, why is wool of finer thread superior to that of thicker? Yet, as if it were by nature and not by their own mistake that they had the advantage, they hold their heads high and believe some extra worth attaches to themselves thereby. Thus, the honor which, if ill clad, they would not have ventured to hope for, they require as if of right for a smarter coat. If passed by with some neglect, they are indignant.

Again, does it not show the same stupidity to think so much of empty and unprofitable honors? What natural and true pleasure can another's bared head or bent knees afford you? Will this behavior cure the pain in your own knees or relieve the lunacy in your own head? In this conception of counterfeit pleasure, a strange and sweet madness is displayed by men who imagine themselves to be noble and plume themselves on it and applaud themselves because their fortune has been to be born of certain ancestors of whom the long succession has been counted rich—for that is now the only nobility—and especially rich in landed estates. They consider themselves not a whit less noble even if their ancestors have not left them a square foot or if they themselves have consumed in extravagant living what was left them.

With these persons they class those who, as I said, dote on jewels and gems and who think they become a species of god if ever they secure a fine specimen, especially of the sort which at the period is regarded as of the highest value in their country. It is not everywhere or always that one kind of stone is prized. They will not purchase it unless it is taken out of its gold setting and exposed to view, and not even then unless the seller takes an oath and gives security that it is a true gem and a true stone, so anxious are they lest a spurious stone in place of a genuine one deceive their eyes. But why should a counterfeited one give less pleasure to your sight when your eye cannot distinguish it from the true article? Both should be of equal value to you, even as they would be, by heaven, to a blind man!

What can be said of those who keep superfluous wealth to pleasure themselves, not with putting the heap to any use but merely with looking at it? Do they feel true pleasure, or are they not rather cheated by false pleasure? Or, what of those who have the opposite feeling and hide the gold, which they will never use and perhaps never see again, and who, in their anxiety not to lose it, thereby do lose it? What else but loss is it to deprive yourself of its use, and perhaps all other men too, and to put it back in the ground? And yet you joyfully exult over your hidden treasure as though your mind were now free from all anxiety. Suppose that someone removed it by stealing it and that you died ten years afterward knowing nothing of the theft. During the whole decade which you lived after the money was stolen, what did it matter to you whether it was stolen or safe? In either case it was of just as little use to you.

Among those who indulge such senseless delights they reckon dicers (whose madness they know not by experience but by hearsay only), as well as hunters and hawkers. What pleasure is there, they ask, in shooting dice upon a table? You have shot them so often that, even if some pleasure had been in it, weariness by now could have arisen from the habitual practice. Or what sweetness can there be, and not rather disgust, in hearing the barking and howling of dogs? Or what greater sensation of pleasure is there when a dog chases a hare than when a dog chases a dog? The same thing happens in both cases: there is racing in both if speed gives you delight.

But if you are attracted by the hope of slaughter and the expectation of a creature being mangled under your eyes, it ought rather to inspire pity when you behold a weak, fugitive, timid, and innocent little hare torn to pieces by a strong, fierce, and cruel dog. In consequence the Utopians have imposed the whole activity of hunting, as unworthy of free men, upon their butchers—a craft, as I explained before, they exercise through their slaves. They regard hunting as the meanest part of the butcher's trade and its other functions as more useful and more honorable, seeing that they do much more positive good and kill animals only from necessity, whereas the hunter seeks nothing but pleasure from the killing and mangling of a poor animal. Even in the case of brute beasts, this desire of looking on bloodshed, in their estimation, either arises from a cruel disposition or degenerates finally into cruelty through the constant practice of such brutal pleasure.

Although the mob of mortals regards these and all similar pursuits—and they are countless—as pleasures, yet the Utopians positively hold them to have nothing to do with true pleasure since there is nothing sweet in them by nature. The fact that for the mob they inspire in the senses a feeling of enjoyment—which seems to be the function of pleasure—does not make them alter their opinion. The enjoyment does not arise from the nature of the thing itself but from their own perverse habit. The latter failing makes them take what is bitter for sweet, just as pregnant women by their vitiated taste suppose pitch and tallow sweeter than honey. Yet it is impossible for any man's judgment, depraved either by disease or by habit, to change the nature of pleasure any more than that of anything else.

The pleasures which they admit as genuine they divide into various classes, some pleasures being attributed to the soul and others to the body. To the soul they ascribe intelligence and the sweetness which is bred of contemplation of truth. To these two are joined the pleasant recollection of a well-spent life and the sure hope of happiness to come.

Bodily pleasure they divide into two kinds. The first is that which fills the sense with clearly perceptible sweetness. Sometimes it comes from the renewal of those organs which have been weakened by our natural heat. These organs are then restored by food and drink. Sometimes it comes from the elimination of things which overload the body. This agreeable sensation occurs when we discharge feces from our bowels or perform the activity generative of children or relieve the itching of some part by rubbing or scratching. Now and then, however, pleasure arises, not in process of restoring anything that our members lack, nor in process of eliminating anything that causes distress, but from something that tickles and affects our senses with a secret but remarkable moving force and so draws them to itself. Such is that pleasure which is engendered by music.

The second kind of bodily pleasure they claim to be that which consists in a calm and harmonious state of the body. This is nothing else than each man's health undisturbed by any disorder. Health, if assailed by no pain, gives delight of itself, though there be no motion arising from pleasure applied from without. Even though it is less obvious and less perceptible by the sense than that overblown craving for eating and drinking, yet nonetheless many hold it to be the greatest of pleasures. Almost all the Utopians regard it as great and as practically the foundation and basis of all pleasures. Even by itself it can make the state of life peaceful and desirable, whereas without it absolutely no place is left for any pleasure. The absence of pain without the presence of health they regard as insensibility rather than pleasure.

They long ago rejected the position of those who held that a state of stable and tranquil health (for this question, too, had been actively discussed among them) was not to be counted as a pleasure because its presence, they said, could not be felt except through some motion from without. But on the other hand now they almost all agree that health is above all things conducive to pleasure. Since in disease, they query, there is pain, which is the bitter enemy of pleasure no less than disease is of health, why should not pleasure in turn be found in the tranquillity of health? They think that it is of no importance in the discussion whether you say that disease is pain or that disease is accompanied with pain, for it comes to the same thing either way. To be sure, if you hold that health is either a pleasure or the necessary cause of pleasure, as fire is of heat, in both ways the conclusion is that those who have permanent health cannot be without pleasure.

Besides, while we eat, say they, what is that but health, which has begun to be impaired, fighting against hunger, with food as its comrade in arms? While it gradually gains strength, the very progress to the usual vigor supplies the pleasure by which we are thus restored. Shall the health which delights in conflict not rejoice when it has gained the victory? When at length it has successfully acquired its former strength, which was its sole object through the conflict, shall it immediately become insensible and not recognize its own good? The assertion that health cannot be felt they think to be far wide of the truth. Who in a waking state, ask they, does not feel that he is in good health—except the man who is not? Who is bound fast by such insensibility or lethargy that he does not confess that health is agreeable and delightful to him? And what is delight except pleasure under another name?

To sum up, they cling above all to mental pleasures, which they value as the first and foremost of all pleasures. Of these the principal part they hold to arise from the practice of the virtues and the consciousness of a good life. Of those pleasures which the body supplies, they give the palm to health. The delight of eating and drinking, and anything that gives the same sort of enjoyment, they think desirable, but only for the sake of health. Such things are not pleasant in themselves but only insofar as they resist the secret encroachment of ill health. Just as a wise man should pray that he may escape disease rather than crave a remedy for it and that he may drive pain off rather than seek relief from it, so it would be better not to need this kind of pleasure rather than to be soothed by it.

If a person thinks that his felicity consists in this kind of pleasure, he must admit that he will be in the greatest happiness if his lot happens to be a life which is spent in perpetual hunger, thirst, itching, eating, drinking, scratching, and rubbing. Who does not see that such a life is not only disgusting but wretched? These pleasures are surely the lowest of all as being most adulterated, for they never occur unless they are coupled with the pains which are their opposites. For example, with the pleasure of eating is united hunger—and on no fair terms, for the pain is the stronger and lasts the longer. It comes into existence before the pleasure and does not end until the pleasure dies with it. Such pleasures they hold should not be highly valued and only insofar as they are necessary. Yet they enjoy even these pleasures and gratefully acknowledge the kindness of mother nature who, with alluring sweetness, coaxes her offspring to that which of necessity they must constantly do. In what discomfort should we have to live if, like all other sicknesses which less frequently assail us, so also these daily diseases of hunger and thirst had to be expelled by bitter poisons and drugs?

Beauty, strength, and nimbleness—these as special and pleasant gifts of nature they gladly cherish. Nay, even those pleasures entering by the ears, eyes, or nostrils, which nature intended to be peculiarly characteristic of man (for no other species of living creature either takes in the form and fairness of the world or is affected by the pleasantness of smell, except in choice of food, or distinguishes harmonious and dissonant intervals of sound)—these, too, I say, they follow after as pleasant seasonings of life. But in all they make this limitation: that the lesser is not to interfere with the greater and that pleasure is not to produce pain in aftermath. Pain they think a necessary consequence if the pleasure is base.

But to despise the beauty of form, to impair the strength of the body, to turn nimbleness into sluggishness, to exhaust the body by fasts, to injure one's health, and to reject all the other favors of nature, unless a man neglects these advantages to himself in providing more zealously for the pleasure of other persons or of the public, in return for which sacrifice he expects a greater pleasure from God—but otherwise to deal harshly with oneself for a vain and shadowy reputation of virtue to no man's profit or for preparing oneself

more easily to bear adversities which may never come—this attitude they think is extreme madness and the sign of a mind which is both cruel to itself and ungrateful to nature, to whom it disdains to be indebted and therefore renounces all her benefits.

This is their view of virtue and pleasure. They believe that human reason can attain to no truer view, unless a heaven-sent religion inspire man with something more holy. Whether in this stand they are right or wrong, time does not permit us to examine—nor is it necessary. We have taken upon ourselves only to describe their principles, and not also to defend them. But of this I am sure, that whatever you think of their ideas, there is nowhere in the world a more excellent people nor a happier commonwealth. They are nimble and active of body, and stronger than you would expect from their stature. The latter, however, is not dwarfish. Though they have not a very fertile soil or a very wholesome climate, they protect themselves against the atmosphere by temperate living and make up for the defects of the land by diligent labor. Consequently, nowhere in the world is there a more plentiful supply of grain and cattle, nowhere are men's bodies more vigorous and subject to fewer diseases. Not only may you behold the usual agricultural tasks carefully administered there, whereby the naturally barren soil is improved by art and industry, but you may also see how a whole forest has been uprooted in one place by the hands of the people and planted in another. Herein they were thinking not so much of abundance as of transport, that they might have wood closer to the sea or the rivers or the cities themselves. For it takes less labor to convey grain than timber to a distance by land.

The people in general are easygoing, good-tempered, ingenious, and leisure-loving. They patiently do their share of manual labor when occasion demands, though otherwise they are by no means fond of it. In their devotion to mental study they are unwearied. When they had heard from us about the literature and learning of the Greeks (for in Latin there was nothing, apart from history and poetry, which seemed likely to gain their great approval), it was wonderful to see their extreme desire for permission to master them through our instruction.

We began, therefore, to give them public lessons, more at first that we should not seem to refuse the trouble than that we expected any success. But after a little progress, their diligence made us at once feel sure that our own diligence would not be bestowed in vain. They began so easily to imitate the shapes of the letters, so readily to pronounce the words, so quickly to learn by heart, and so faithfully to reproduce what they had learned that it was a perfect wonder to us. The explanation was that most of them were scholars picked for their ability and mature in years, who undertook to learn their tasks not only fired by their own free will but acting under orders of the Senate. In less than three years they were perfect in the language and able to peruse good authors without any difficulty unless the text had faulty readings. According to my conjecture, they got hold of Greek literature more easily because it was somewhat related to their own. I suspect that their race was derived from the Greek because their language, which in almost all other respects resembles the Persian, retains some traces of Greek in the names of their cities and officials.

When about to go on the fourth voyage, I put on board, in place of wares to sell, a fairly large package of books, having made up my mind never to return rather than to come back soon. They received from me most of Plato's works, several of Aristotle's, as well as Theophrastus on plants, which I regret to say was mutilated in parts. During the voyage an ape found the book, left lying carelessly about, and in wanton sport tore out and destroyed several pages in various sections. Of grammarians they have only Lascaris, for I did not take Theodore with me. They have no dictionaries except those of Hesychius and Dioscorides. They are very fond of the works of Plutarch and captivated by the wit and pleasantry of Lucian. Of the poets they have Aristophanes, Homer, and Euripides, together with Sophocles in the small Aldine type. Of the historians they possess Thucydides and Herodotus, as well as Herodian.

In medicine, moreover, my companion Tricius Apinatus[17] had carried with him some small treatises of Hippocrates and the *Ars medica* of Galen, to which books they attribute great value. Even though there is scarcely a nation in the whole world that needs medicine less, yet nowhere is it held in greater honor—and this for the reason that they regard the knowledge of it as one of the finest and most useful branches of philosophy. When by the help of this philosophy they explore the secrets of nature, they appear to themselves not only to get great pleasure in doing so but also to win the highest approbation of the Author and Maker of nature. They presume that, like all other artificers, He has set forth the visible mechanism of the world as a spectacle for man, whom alone He has made capable of appreciating such a wonderful thing. Therefore He prefers a careful and diligent beholder and admirer of His work to one who like an unreasoning brute beast passes by so great and so wonderful a spectacle stupidly and stolidly.

Thus, trained in all learning, the minds of the Utopians are exceedingly apt in

---

17 The name is of course fictitious. Apina and Trica, little towns in Apulia, were so ignominiously overwhelmed by Diomedes that they became a symbol of ridiculous trifles.

"PRINTING," FROM THE GOITEIN EDITION OF 1925
No lack of books

the invention of the arts which promote the advantage and convenience of life. Two, however, they owe to us, the art of printing and the manufacture of paper—though not entirely to us but to a great extent also to themselves. When we showed them the Aldine printing in paper books, we talked about the material of which paper is made and the art of printing without giving a detailed explanation, for none of us was expert in either art. With the greatest acuteness they promptly guessed how it was done. Though previously they wrote only on parchment, bark, and papyrus, from this time they tried to manufacture paper and print letters. Their first attempts were not very successful, but by frequent experiment they soon mastered both. So great was their success that if they had copies of Greek authors, they would have no lack of books. But at present they have no more than I have mentioned, but by printing books they have increased their stock by many thousands of copies.

Whoever, coming to their land on a sight-seeing tour, is recommended by any special intellectual endowment or is acquainted with many countries through long travel, is sure of a hearty welcome, for they delight in hearing what is happening in the whole world. On this score our own landing was pleasing to them. Few persons, however, come to them in the way of trade. What could they bring except iron, or what everybody would rather take back home with him—gold and silver! And as to articles of export, the Utopians think it wiser to carry them out of the country themselves than to let strangers come to fetch them. By this policy they get more information about foreign nations and do not forget by disuse their skill in navigation.

SLAVERY [ETC.]

Prisoners of war are not enslaved unless captured in wars fought by the Utopians themselves; nor are the sons of slaves, nor anyone who was in slavery when acquired from some foreign country. Their slaves are either such as are enslaved in their own country for heinous crimes or such as have been condemned to death elsewhere for some offense. The greater number are of this latter kind. They carry away many of them; sometimes they buy

412

them cheaply; but often they ask for them and get them for nothing. These classes of slaves they keep not only continually at work but also in chains. Their own countrymen are dealt with more harshly, since their conduct is regarded as all the more regrettable and deserving a more severe punishment as an object lesson because, having had an excellent rearing to a virtuous life, they still could not be restrained from crime.

There is yet another class of slaves, for sometimes a hard-working and poverty-stricken drudge of another country voluntarily chooses slavery in Utopia. These individuals are well treated and, except that they have a little more work assigned to them as being used to it, are dealt with almost as leniently as citizens. If anyone wishes to depart, which seldom happens, they do not detain him against his will nor send him away empty-handed.

The sick, as I said, are very lovingly cared for, nothing being omitted which may restore them to health, whether in the way of medicine or diet. They console the incurably diseased by sitting and conversing with them and by applying all possible alleviations. But if a disease is not only incurable but also distressing and agonizing without any cessation, then the priests and the public officials exhort the man, since he is now unequal to all life's duties, a burden to himself, and a trouble to others, and is living beyond the time of his death, to make up his mind not to foster the pest and plague any longer nor to hesitate to die now that life is torture to him but, relying on good hope, to free himself from this bitter life as from prison and the rack, or else voluntarily to permit others to free him. In this course he will act wisely, since by death he will put an end not to enjoyment but to torture. Because in doing so he will be obeying the counsels of the priests, who are God's interpreters, it will be a pious and holy action.

Those who have been persuaded by these arguments either starve themselves to death or, being put to sleep, are set free without the sensation of dying. But they do not make away with anyone against his will, nor in such a case do they relax in the least their attendance upon him. They do believe that death counseled by authority is honorific. But if anyone commits suicide without having obtained the approval of priests and Senate, they deem him unworthy of either fire or earth and cast his body ignominiously into a marsh without proper burial.

PRISONER OF WAR. WOODCUT FROM THE L'ANGELIER EDITION OF 1550
Prisoners of war are not enslaved

Women do not marry till eighteen, men not till they are four years older. If before marriage a man or woman is convicted of secret intercourse, he or she is severely punished, and they are forbidden to marry altogether unless the governor's pardon remits their guilt. In addition, both father and mother of the family in whose house the offense was committed incur great disgrace as having been neglectful in doing their duties. The reason why they punish this offense so severely is their foreknowledge that, unless persons are carefully restrained from promiscuous intercourse, few will contract the tie of marriage, in which a whole life must be spent with one companion and all the troubles incidental to it must be patiently borne.

In choosing mates, they seriously and strictly espouse a custom which seemed to us very foolish and extremely ridiculous. The woman, whether maiden or widow, is shown naked to the suitor by a worthy and respectable matron, and similarly the suitor is presented naked before the maiden by a discreet man. We laughed at this custom and condemned it as foolish. They, on the other hand, marveled at the remarkable folly of all other nations. In buying a colt, where there is question of only a little money, persons are so cautious that though it is almost bare they will not buy until they have taken off the saddle and removed all the trappings for fear some sore lies concealed under these coverings. Yet in the choice of a wife, an action which will cause either pleasure or disgust to follow them the rest of their lives, they are so careless that, while the rest of her body is covered with clothes, they estimate the value of the whole woman from hardly a single handbreadth of her, only the face being visible, and clasp her to themselves not without great danger of their agreeing ill together if something afterward gives them offense.

All men are not so wise as to regard only the character of the woman, and even in the marriages of wise men bodily attractions also are no small enhancement to the virtues of the mind. Certainly such foul deformity may be hidden beneath these coverings that it may quite alienate a man's mind from his wife when bodily separation is no longer lawful. If such a deformity arises by chance after the marriage has been contracted, each person must bear his own fate, but beforehand the laws ought to protect him from being entrapped by guile.

This provision was the more necessary because the Utopians are the only people in those parts of the world who are satisfied with one wife and because matrimony there is seldom broken except by death, unless it be for adultery or for intolerable offensiveness of disposition. When husband or wife is thus offended, leave is granted by the Senate to take another mate. The other party perpetually lives a life of disgrace as well as of celibacy. But they cannot endure the repudiation of an unwilling wife, who is in no way to blame, because some bodily calamity has befallen her. They judge it cruel that a person should be abandoned when most in need of comfort and that old age, since it both entails disease and is a disease itself, should have only an unreliable and weak fidelity.

It sometimes happens, however, that when a married couple agree insufficiently in their dispositions and both find others with whom they hope to live more agreeably, they separate by mutual consent and contract fresh unions, but not without the sanction of the Senate. The latter allows of no divorce until its members and their wives have carefully gone into the case. Even then they do not readily give consent because they know that it is a very great drawback to cementing the affection between husband and wife if they have before them the easy hope of a fresh union.

Violators of the conjugal tie are punished by the strictest form of slavery. If both parties are married, the injured parties, provided they consent, are divorced from their adulterous mates and couple together, or else are allowed to marry whom they like. But if one of the injured parties continues to feel affection for so undeserving a mate, it is not forbidden to have the marriage continue in force on condition that the party is willing to accompany and share the labor of the other who has been condemned to slavery. Now and then it happens that the penance of the one and the dutiful assiduity of the other move the compassion of the governor and win back their liberty. Relapse into the same offense, however, involves the penalty of death.

For all other crimes there is no law prescribing any fixed penalty, but the punishment is assigned by the Senate according to the atrocity, or veniality, of the individual crime. Husbands correct their wives, and parents their children, unless the offense is so serious that it is to the advantage of public morality to have it punished openly. Generally the worst offenses are punished by the sentence of slavery since this prospect, they think, is no less formidable to the criminal and more advantageous to the state than if they make haste to put the offenders to death and get them out of the way at once. Their labor is more profitable than their death, and their example lasts longer to deter others from like crimes. But if they rebel and kick against this treatment, they are thereupon put to death like untamable beasts that cannot be restrained by prison or chain. If they are patient, however, they are not entirely deprived of all hope. When tamed by long and hard punishment, if they show such repentance as testifies that they are more sorry for their sin than for their punishment, then sometimes by the prerogative of the governor and sometimes by the vote of the people

their slavery is either lightened or remitted altogether.

To tempt another to an impure act is no less punishable than the commission of that impure act. In every crime the deliberate and avowed attempt is counted equal to the deed, for they think that failure ought not to benefit one who did everything in his power not to fail.

They are very fond of fools. It is a great disgrace to treat them with insult, but there is no prohibition against deriving pleasure from their foolery. The latter, they think, is of the greatest benefit to the fools themselves. If anyone is so stern and morose that he is not amused with anything they either do or say, they do not entrust him with the care of a fool. They fear that he may not treat him with sufficient indulgence since he would find in him neither use nor even amusement, which is his sole faculty.

To deride a man for a disfigurement or the loss of a limb is counted as base and disfiguring, not to the man who is laughed at but to him who laughs, for foolishly upbraiding a man with something as if it were a fault which he was powerless to avoid. While they consider it a sign of a sluggish and feeble mind not to preserve natural beauty, it is, in their judgment, disgraceful affectation to help it out by cosmetics. Experience itself shows them how no elegance of outward form recommends wives to husbands as much as probity and reverence. Some men are attracted only by a handsome shape, but no man's love is kept permanently except by virtue and obedience.

Not merely do they discourage crime by punishment but they offer honors to invite men to virtue. Hence, to great men who have done conspicuous service to their country they set up in the marketplace statues to stand as a record of noble exploits and, at the same time, to have the glory of forefathers serve their descendants as a spur and stimulus to virtue.

The man who solicits votes to obtain any office is deprived completely of the hope of holding any office at all. They live together in affection and goodwill. No official is haughty or formidable. They are called fathers and show that character. Honor is paid them willingly, as it should be, and is not exacted from the reluctant. The governor himself is distinguished from citizens not by a robe or a crown but by the carrying of a handful of grain, just as the mark of the high priest is a wax candle borne before him.

They have very few laws because very few are needed for persons so educated. The chief fault they find with other peoples is that almost innumerable books of laws and commentaries are not sufficient. They themselves think it most unfair that any group of men should be bound by laws which are either too numerous to be read through or too obscure to be understood by anyone.

Moreover, they absolutely banish from their country all lawyers, who cleverly manipulate cases and cunningly argue legal points. They consider it a good thing that every man should plead his own cause and say the same to the judge as he would tell his counsel. Thus there is less ambiguity and the truth is more easily elicited when a man, uncoached in deception by a lawyer, conducts his own case and the judge skillfully weighs each statement and helps untutored minds to defeat the false accusations of the crafty. To secure these advantages in other countries is difficult, owing to the immense mass of extremely complicated laws. But with the Utopians each man is expert in law. First, they have, as I said, very few laws, and, secondly, they regard the most obvious interpretation of the law as the most fair interpretation.

This policy follows from their reasoning that, since all laws are promulgated to remind every man of his duty, the more recondite interpretation reminds only very few (for there are few who can arrive at it) whereas the more simple and obvious sense of the laws is open to all. Otherwise, what difference would it make for the common people, who are the most numerous and also most in need of instruction, whether you framed no law at all or whether the interpretation of the law you framed was such that no one could elicit it except by great ingenuity and long argument? Now, the untrained judgment of the common people cannot attain to the meaning of such an interpretation nor can their lives be long enough, seeing that they are wholly taken up with getting a living.

These virtues of the Utopians have spurred their neighbors (who are free and independent since many of them were long ago delivered from tyrants by the Utopians) to obtain officials from them, some for one year and others for five years. On the expiration of their office they escort them home with honor and praise and bring back successors with them to their own country. Certainly these peoples make very good and wholesome provision for the commonwealth. Seeing that the latter's prosperity or ruin depends on the character of officials, of whom could they have made a wiser choice than of those who cannot be drawn from the path of honor by any bribe since it is no good to them as they will shortly return home, nor influenced by crooked partiality or animosity toward any since they are strangers to the citizens? These two evils, favoritism and avarice, wherever they have settled in men's judgments, instantly destroy all justice, the strongest sinew of the commonwealth. The nations who seek their administrators from Utopia are called allies by them; the name of friend is reserved for all the others whom they have benefited.

Treaties which all other nations so often conclude among themselves, break, and renew, they never make with any nation.

"What is the use of a treaty," they ask, "as though nature of herself did not sufficiently bind one man to another? If a person does not regard nature, do you suppose he will care anything about words?"

They are led to this opinion chiefly because in those parts of the world treaties and alliances between kings are not observed with much good faith. In Europe, however, and especially in those parts where the faith and religion of Christ prevails, the majesty of treaties is everywhere holy and inviolable, partly through the justice and goodness of kings, partly through the reverence and fear of the Sovereign Pontiffs. Just as the latter themselves undertake nothing which they do not most conscientiously perform, so they command all other rulers to abide by their promises in every way and compel the recalcitrant by pastoral censure and severe reproof. Popes are perfectly right, of course, in thinking it a most disgraceful thing that those who are specially called the faithful should not faithfully adhere to their commitments.

But in that new world, which is almost as far removed from ours by the Equator as their life and character are different from ours, there is no trust in treaties. The more numerous and holy the ceremonies with which a treaty is struck the more quickly is it broken. They find some defect in the wording, which sometimes they cunningly devise of set purpose, so that they can never be held by such strong bonds as not somehow to escape from them and break both the treaty and their faith. If this cunning, nay fraud and deceit, were found to have occurred in the contracts of private persons, the treaty makers with great disdain would exclaim against it as sacrilegious and meriting the gallows—though the very same men plume themselves on being the authors of such advice when given to kings.

In consequence men think either that all justice is only a plebeian and low virtue which is far below the majesty of kings or that there are at least two forms of it: the one which goes on foot and creeps on the ground, fit only for the common sort and bound by many chains so that it can never overstep its barriers; the other a virtue of kings, which, as it is more august than that of ordinary folk, is also far freer so that everything is permissible to it— except what it finds disagreeable.

This behavior, as I said, of rulers there who keep their treaties so badly is, I suppose, the reason why the Utopians make none; if they lived here, they would perhaps change their minds. Nevertheless they believe that, though treaties are faithfully observed, it is a pity that the custom of making them at all had grown up. The result (as though peoples which are divided by the slight interval of a hill or a river were joined by no bond of nature) is men's persuasion that they are born one another's adversaries and enemies and that they are right in aiming at one another's destruction except insofar as treaties prevent it. What is more, even when treaties are made, friendship does not grow up but the license of freebooting continues to the extent that, for lack of skill in drawing up the treaty, no sufficient precaution to prevent this activity has been included in the articles. But the Utopians, on the contrary, think that nobody who has done you no harm should be accounted an enemy, that the fellowship created by nature takes the place of a treaty, and that men are better and more firmly joined together by goodwill than by pacts, by spirit than by words.

MILITARY AFFAIRS

War, as an activity fit only for beasts and yet practiced by no kind of beast so constantly as by man, they regard with utter loathing. Against the usage of almost all nations they count

MILITARY AFFAIRS. WOODCUT FROM L'ANGELIER EDITION OF 1550
An activity fit only for beasts

nothing so inglorious as glory sought in war. Nevertheless men and women alike assiduously exercise themselves in military training on fixed days lest they should be unfit for war when need requires. Yet they do not lightly go to war. They do so only to protect their own territory or to drive an invading enemy out of their friends' lands, or, in pity for a people oppressed by tyranny, to deliver them by force of arms from the yoke and slavery of the tyrant, a course prompted by human sympathy.

They oblige their friends with help, not always indeed to defend them merely but sometimes also to requite and avenge injuries previously done to them. They act, however, only if they themselves are consulted before any step is taken and if they themselves initiate the war after they have approved the cause and demanded restitution in vain. They take the final step of war not only when a hostile inroad has carried off booty but also much more fiercely when the merchants among their friends undergo unjust persecution under the color of justice in any other country, either on the pretext of laws in themselves unjust or by the distortion of laws in themselves good.

Such was the origin of the war which the Utopians had waged a little before our time on behalf of the Nephelogetes[18] against the Alaopolitans.[19] The Nephelogetic traders suffered a wrong, as they thought, under pretense of law, but whether right or wrong, it was avenged by a fierce war. Into this war the neighboring nations brought their energies and resources to assist the power and to intensify the rancor of both sides. Most flourishing nations were either shaken to their foundations or grievously afflicted. The troubles upon troubles that arose were ended only by the enslavement and surrender of the Alaopolitans. Since the Utopians were not fighting in their own interest, they yielded them into the power of the Nephelogetes, a people who, when the Alaopolitans were prosperous, were not in the least comparable to them.

So severely do the Utopians punish wrong done to their friends, even in money matters—but not wrongs done to themselves. When they lose their goods any-

18 "Cloud-born."

19 "Peopleless citizens," *i.e.,* "citizens without a country" or "citizens in a city without people."

418

where through fraud, but without personal violence, their anger goes no further than abstention from trade with that nation until satisfaction is made. The reason is not that they care less for their citizens than their allies. They are more grieved at their allies' pecuniary loss than their own because their friends' merchants suffer severely by the loss as it falls on their private property, but their own citizens lose nothing but what comes from the common stock and what was plentiful and, as it were, superfluous at home—or else it would not have been exported. As a result, the loss is not felt by any individual. They consider it excessively cruel to avenge such a loss by the death of many when the disadvantage of the loss affects neither the life nor the subsistence of any of their own people.

If a Utopian citizen, however, is wrongfully disabled or killed anywhere, whether the plot is due to the government or to a private citizen, they first ascertain the facts by an embassy and then, if the guilty persons are not surrendered, they cannot be appeased but forthwith declare war. If the guilty persons are surrendered, they are punished either with death or with enslavement.

They not only regret but blush at a victory that has cost much bloodshed, thinking it folly to purchase wares, however precious, too dear. If they overcome and crush the enemy by stratagem and cunning, they feel great pride and celebrate a public triumph over the victory and put up a trophy as for a strenuous exploit. They boast themselves as having acted with valor and heroism whenever their victory is such as no animal except man could have won, that is, by strength of intellect; for, by strength of body, say they, bears, lions, boars, wolves, dogs, and other wild beasts are wont to fight. Most of them are superior to us in brawn and fierceness, but they are all inferior in cleverness and calculation.

Their one and only object in war is to secure that which, had it been obtained beforehand, would have prevented the declaration of war. If that is out of the question, they require such severe punishment of those on whom they lay the blame that for the future they may be afraid to attempt anything of the same sort. These are their chief interests in the enterprise, which they set about promptly to secure, yet taking more care to avoid danger than to win praise or fame.

The moment war is declared, they arrange that simultaneously a great number of placards, made more effective by bearing their public seal, should be set up secretly in the most prominent spots of enemy territory. Herein they promise huge rewards to anyone who will kill the enemy king. Further, they offer smaller sums, but those considerable, for the heads of the individuals whose names they specify in the same proclamations. These are the men whom, next to the king himself, they regard as responsible for the hostile measures taken against them. Whatever reward they fix for an assassin, they double for the man who brings any of the denounced parties alive to them. They actually offer the same rewards, with a guarantee of personal safety, to the persons proscribed, if they will turn against their fellows.

So it swiftly comes about that their enemies suspect all outsiders and, in addition, neither trust nor are loyal to one another. They are in a state of utter panic and no less peril. It is well known that it has often happened that many of them, and especially the king himself, have been betrayed by those in whom they had placed the greatest trust, so easily do bribes incite men to commit every kind of crime. They are boundless in their offers of reward. Remembering, however, what a risk they invite the man to run, they take care that the greatness of the peril is balanced by the extent of the rewards.

In consequence they promise and faithfully pay down not only an immense amount of gold but also landed property with high income in very secure places in the territory of friends.

This habit of bidding for and purchasing an enemy, which is elsewhere condemned as the cruel deed of a degenerate nature, they think reflects great credit, first on their wisdom because they thus bring to a conclusion great wars without any battle at all, and secondly on their humanity and mercy because by the death of a few guilty people they purchase the lives of many harmless persons who would have fallen in battle, both on their own side and that of the enemy. They are as sorry for the throng and mass of the enemy as for their own citizens. They know that the common folk do not go to war of their own accord but are driven to it by the madness of kings.

If this plan does not succeed, they sow the seeds of dissension broadcast and foster strife by leading a brother of the king or one of the noblemen to hope that he may obtain the throne. If internal strife dies down, then they stir up and involve the neighbors of their enemies by reviving some forgotten claims to dominion such as kings have always at their disposal. Promising their own assistance for the war, they supply money liberally but are very chary of sending their own citizens. They hold them so singularly dear and regard one another of such value that they would not care to exchange any of their own people for the king of the opposite party. As to gold and silver, since they keep it all for this one use, they pay it out without any reluctance, for they would live just as well if they spent it all. Moreover, in addition to the riches which they keep at home, they have also a vast treasure abroad in that many nations, as I said before, are in their debt.

With the riches, they hire and send to war soldiers from all parts, but especially from among the Zapoletans.[20] These people live five hundred miles to the east of Utopia and are fearsome, rough, and wild. They prefer their own rugged woods and mountains among which they are bred. They are a hard race, capable of enduring heat, cold, and toil, lacking all refinements, engaging in no farming, careless about the houses they live in and the clothes they wear, and occupied only with their flocks and herds. To a great extent they live by hunting and plundering. They are born for warfare and zealously seek an opportunity for fighting. When they find it, they eagerly embrace it. Leaving the country in great force, they offer themselves at a cheap rate to anyone who needs fighting men. The only trade they know in life is that by which they seek their death.

They fight with courage and incorruptible loyalty for those from whom they receive their pay. Yet they bind themselves for no fixed period but take sides on such terms that the next day when higher pay is offered them, even by the enemy, they take his side, and then the day after, if a trifle more is offered to tempt them back, return to the side they took at first.

In almost every war that breaks out there are many of them in both armies. It is a daily occurrence that men connected by ties of blood, who were hired on the same side and so became intimate with one another, soon afterward are separated into two hostile forces and meet in battle. Forgetting both kinship and friendship, they run one another through with the utmost ferocity. They are driven to mutual destruction for no other reason than that they are hired by opposing kings for a tiny sum of which they take such careful account that they are readily induced to change sides by the addition of a penny to their daily rate of pay. So have they

---

20 "Busy sellers," *i.e.*, sellers and resellers of their services.

speedily acquired a habit of avarice which nevertheless profits them not one whit. What they get by exposing their lives they spend instantly in debauchery and that of a dreary sort.

This people will battle for the Utopians against any mortals whatsoever because their service is hired at a rate higher than they could get anywhere else. The Utopians, just as they seek good men to use them, so enlist these villains to abuse them. When need requires, they thrust them under the tempting bait of great promises into greatest perils. Generally a large proportion never returns to claim payment, but the survivors are honestly paid what has been promised them to incite them again to like deeds of daring. The Utopians do not care in the least how many Zapoletans they lose, thinking that they would be the greatest benefactors to the human race if they could relieve the world of all the dregs of this abominable and impious people.

Next to them they employ the forces of the people for whom they are fighting and then auxiliary squadrons of all their other friends. Last of all they add a contingent of their own citizens out of which they appoint some man of tried valor to command the whole army. For him they have two substitutes who hold no rank as long as he is safe. But if he is captured or killed, the first of the two becomes as it were his heir and successor, and he, if events require, is succeeded by the third. They thus avoid the disorganization of the whole army through the endangering of the commander, the fortunes of war being always incalculable.

In each city a choice is made among those who volunteer. No one is driven to fight abroad against his will because they are convinced that if anyone is somewhat timorous by nature, he not only will not acquit himself manfully but will throw fear into his companions. Should any war, however, assail their own country, they put the fainthearted, if physically fit, on shipboard mixed among the braver sort or put them here and there to man the walls where they cannot run away. Thus, shame at being seen to flinch by their own side, the close quarters with the enemy, and the withdrawal of hope of escape combine to overpower their timidity, and often they make a virtue of extreme necessity.

Just as no one of the men is made to go to a foreign war against his will, so if the women are anxious to accompany their husbands on military service, not only do they not forbid them but actually encourage them and incite them by expressions of praise. When they have gone out, they are placed alongside their husbands on the battlefront. Each man is surrounded by his own children and relations by marriage and blood so that those may be closest and lend one another mutual assistance whom nature most impels to help one another. It is the greatest reproach for a husband to return without his wife or for a son to come back having lost his father. The result is that, when it comes to hand-to-hand fighting, if the enemy stands his ground, the battle is long and anguished and ends with mutual extermination.

As I have said, they take every care not to be obliged to fight in person as long as they can finish the war by the assistance of hired substitutes. When personal service is inevitable, they are as courageous in fighting as they were ingenious in avoiding it as long as they might. They are not fierce in the first onslaught, but their strength increases by degrees through their slow and hard resistance. Their spirit is so stubborn that they would rather be cut to pieces than give way. The absence of anxiety about livelihood at home, as well as the removal of that worry which troubles men about the future of their families (for such solicitude everywhere breaks the highest courage), makes their spirit exalted and disdainful of defeat.

Moreover, their expert training in military discipline gives them confidence. Finally, their good and sound opinions, in which they have been trained from childhood both by teaching and by the good institutions of their country, give them additional courage. So they do not hold their life so cheap as recklessly to throw it away and not so immoderately dear as greedily and shamefully to hold fast to it when honor bids them give it up.

While the battle is everywhere most hot, a band of picked youths who have taken an oath to devote themselves to the task hunt out the opposing general. They openly attack him; they secretly ambush him. They assail him both from far and from near. A long and continuous wedge of men, fresh comers constantly taking the place of those exhausted, keeps up the attack. It seldom happens, unless he look to his safety by running away, that he is not killed or does not fall alive into the enemy's hands.

If the victory rests with them, there is no indiscriminate carnage, for they would rather take the routed as prisoners than kill them. They never pursue the fleeing enemy without keeping one division all the time drawn up ready for engagement under their banners. To such an extent is this the case that if, after the rest of the army has been beaten, they win the victory by this last reserve force, they prefer to let all their enemies escape rather than get into the habit of pursuing them with their own ranks in disorder. They remember that more than once it has happened to themselves that, when the great bulk of their army has been beaten and routed and when the enemy, flushed with victory, has been chasing the fugitives in all directions, a few of their number, held in reserve and ready for emergencies, have suddenly attacked the scattered and straying enemy who, feeling themselves quite safe, were off their guard. Thereby they have changed the whole fortune of the

battle and, wresting out of the enemy's hands a certain and undoubted victory, have, though conquered, conquered their conquerors in turn.

It is not easy to say whether they are more cunning in laying ambushes or more cautious in avoiding them. You would think they contemplated flight when that is the very last thing intended; but, on the other hand, when they do determine to flee, you would imagine that they were thinking of anything but that. If they feel themselves to be inferior in number or in position, either by night they noiselessly march and move their camp or evade the enemy by some stratagem, or else by day they retire so imperceptibly and in such regular order that it is as dangerous to attack them in retreat as it would be in advance. They protect their camp most carefully by a deep and broad ditch, the earth taken out of it being thrown inside. They do not utilize the labor of the lowest workmen for the purpose, but the soldiers do it with their own hands. The whole army is set at work, except those who watch under arms in front of the rampart in case of emergencies. Thus, through the efforts of so many, they complete great fortifications, enclosing a large space, with incredible speed.

They wear armor strong enough to turn blows but easily adapted to all motions and gestures of the body. They do not feel any awkwardness even in swimming, for they practice swimming under arms as part of their apprenticeship in military discipline. The weapons they use at a distance are arrows, which they shoot with great strength and sureness of aim not only on foot but also on horseback. At close quarters they use not swords but battle-axes which, because of their sharp point and great weight, are deadly weapons, whether employed for thrusting or hacking. They are very clever in inventing war machines. They hide them, when made, with the greatest care lest, if made known before required by circumstances, they be rather a laughingstock than an instrument of war. In making them, their first object is to have them easy to carry and handy to pivot.

If a truce is made with the enemy, they keep it so religiously as not to break it even under provocation. They do not ravage the enemy's territory nor burn his crops. Rather, they do not even allow them to be trodden down by the feet of men or horses, as far as can be, thinking that they grow for their own benefit. They injure no noncombatant unless he is a spy. When cities are surrendered to them, they keep them intact. They do not plunder even those which they have stormed but put to death the men who prevented surrender and make slaves of the rest of the defenders. They leave unharmed the crowd of noncombatants. If they find out that any person recommended the surrender of the town, they give them a share of the property of the condemned. They present their auxiliaries with the rest of the confiscated goods, but not a single one of their own men gets any of the booty.

When the war is over, they do not charge the expense against their friends, for whom they have borne the cost, but against the conquered. Under this head they make them not only pay money, which they lay aside for similar warlike purposes, but also surrender estates, from which they may enjoy forever a large annual income. In many countries they have such revenues which, coming little by little from various sources, have grown to the sum of over seven hundred thousand ducats[21] a year. To these estates they dispatch some of their own citizens under the title of Financial Agents to live there in great style and to play the part of magnates. Yet much is left over to put into the public treasury, unless they prefer to give the conquered nation credit. They often do the latter until they need to use the money, and even then it scarcely ever happens that they call in the whole sum. From these estates they confer a share on those who at their request undertake the dangerous mission which I have previously described.

If any king takes up arms against them and prepares to invade their territory, they at once meet him in great strength beyond their borders. They never lightly make war in their own country nor is an emergency so pressing as to compel them to admit foreign auxiliaries into their island.

UTOPIAN RELIGIONS

There are different kinds of religion not only on the island as a whole but also in each city. Some worship as god the sun, others the moon, others one of the planets. There are some who reverence a man conspicuous for either virtue or glory in the past not only as god but even as the supreme god. But by far the majority, and those by far the wiser, believe in nothing of the kind but in a certain single being, unknown, eternal, immense, inexplicable, far above the reach of the human mind, diffused throughout the universe not in mass but in power. Him they call father. To him alone they attribute the beginnings, the growth, the increase, the changes, and the ends of all things as they have perceived them. To no other do they give divine honors.

In addition, all the other Utopians too, though varying in their beliefs, agree with them in this respect that they hold there is one supreme being, to whom are due both the creation and the providential government of the whole world. All alike call him Mithras in their native language, but in this respect they disagree, that he is looked on differently by different persons. Each professes that whatever that

---

21 About £327,000, with many times the present-day value.

"RAPHAEL PREACHING TO THE UTOPIANS." WOODCUT FROM THE GOITEIN EDITION OF 1925

They had heard from us the name of Christ

is which he regards as supreme is that very same nature to whose unique power and majesty the sum of all things is attributed by the common consent of all nations. But gradually they are all beginning to depart from this medley of superstitions and are coming to unite in that one religion which seems to surpass the rest in reasonableness. Nor is there any doubt that the other beliefs would all have disappeared long ago had not an untoward event, which chance brought upon one of their number when he was deliberating on a change of religion, been construed by fear as not having happened by chance but as having been sent from heaven—as if the deity whose worship he was forsaking were thus avenging an intention so impious against himself.

But after they had heard from us the name of Christ, His teaching, His character, His miracles, and the no less wonderful constancy of the many martyrs whose blood freely shed had drawn so many nations far and wide into their fellowship, you would not believe how readily disposed they, too, were to join it, whether through the rather mysterious inspiration of God or because they thought it nearest to that belief which has the widest prevalence among them. But I think that this factor, too, was of no small

weight, that they had heard that His disciples' common way of life had been pleasing to Christ and that it is still in use among the truest societies of Christians. But whatever it was that influenced them, not a few joined our religion and were cleansed by the holy water of baptism.

But because among us four (for that was all that was left, two of our group having succumbed to fate) there was, I am sorry to say, no priest, they were initiated in all other matters, but so far they lack those sacraments which with us only priests administer. They understand, however, what they are, and desire them with the greatest eagerness. Moreover, they are even debating earnestly among themselves whether, without the dispatch of a Christian bishop, one chosen out of their own number might receive the sacerdotal character. It seemed that they would choose a candidate, but by the time of my departure they had not yet done so.

Even those who do not agree with the religion of Christ do not try to deter others from it. They do not attack any who have made their profession. Only one of our company, while I was there, was interfered with. As soon as he was baptized, in spite of our advice to the contrary, he spoke publicly of Christ's religion with more zeal than discretion. He began to grow so warm in his preaching that not only did he prefer our worship to any other but he condemned all the rest. He proclaimed them to be profane in themselves and their followers to be impious and sacrilegious and worthy of everlasting fire. When he had long been preaching in this style, they arrested him, tried him, and convicted him not for despising their religion but for stirring up a riot among the people. His sentence after the verdict of guilty was exile. Actually, they count this principle among their most ancient institutions, that no one should suffer for his religion.

Utopus had heard that before his arrival the inhabitants had been continually quarreling among themselves. He had made the observation that the universal dissensions between the individual sects who were fighting for their country had given him the opportunity of overcoming them all. From the very beginning, therefore, after he had gained the victory, he especially ordained that it should be lawful for every man to follow the religion of his choice, that each might strive to bring others over to his own, provided that he quietly and modestly supported his own by reasons nor bitterly demolished all others if his persuasions were not successful nor used any violence and refrained from abuse. If a person contends too vehemently in expressing his views, he is punished with exile or enslavement.

Utopus laid down these regulations not merely from regard for peace, which he saw to be utterly destroyed by constant wrangling and implacable hatred, but because he thought that this method of settlement was in the interest of religion itself. On religion he did not venture rashly to dogmatize. He was uncertain whether God did not desire a varied and manifold worship and therefore did not inspire different people with different views. But he was certain in thinking it both insolence and folly to demand by violence and threats that all should think to be true what you believe to be true. Moreover, even if it should be the case that one single religion is true and all the rest are false, he foresaw that, provided the matter were handled reasonably and moderately, truth by its own natural force would finally emerge sooner or later and stand forth conspicuously. But if the struggle were decided by arms and riots, since the worst men are always the most unyielding, the best and holiest religion would be overwhelmed because of the conflicting false religions, like grain choked by thorns and underbrush.

So he made the whole matter of religion an open question and left each one free to choose what he should believe. By way of exception, he conscientiously and strictly gave injunction that no one should fall so far below the dignity of human nature as to believe that souls likewise perish with the body or that the world is the mere sport of chance and not governed by any divine providence. After this life, accordingly, vices are ordained to be punished and virtue rewarded. Such is their belief, and if anyone thinks otherwise, they do not regard him even as a member of mankind, seeing that he has lowered the lofty nature of his soul to the level of a beast's miserable body—so far are they from classing him among their citizens whose laws and customs he would treat as worthless if it were not for fear. Who can doubt that he will strive either to evade by craft the public laws of his country or to break them by violence in order to serve his own private desires when he has nothing to fear but laws and no hope beyond the body?

Therefore an individual of this mind is tendered no honor, is entrusted with no office, and is put in charge of no function. He is universally regarded as of a sluggish and low disposition. But they do not punish him in any way, being convinced that it is in no man's power to believe what he chooses, nor do they compel him by threats to disguise his views, nor do they allow in the matter any deceptions or lies which they hate exceedingly as being next door to actual wrongdoing. They forbid him to argue in support of his opinion in the presence of the common people, but before the priests and important personages they not only permit but also encourage it, being sure that such madness will in the end give way to reason.

There are others, too, and these not a few, who are not interfered with because they do not altogether lack reason for their view and because they are not evil men. By a much different error, these believe that brute animals also have immortal souls, but not comparable to ours in dignity or destined to equal felicity. Almost all Utopians are absolutely certain and convinced that human bliss will be so immense that, while they lament every man's illness, they regret the death of no one but him whom they see torn from life anxiously and unwillingly. This behavior they take to be a very bad omen as though the soul, being without hope and having a guilty conscience, dreaded its departure through a secret premonition of impending punishment. Besides, they suppose that God will not be pleased with the coming of one who, when summoned, does not gladly hasten to obey but is reluctantly drawn against his will. Persons who behold this kind of death are filled with horror and therefore carry the dead out to burial in melancholy silence. Then, after praying God to be merciful to their shades and graciously to pardon their infirmities, they cover the corpse with earth.

On the other hand, when men have died cheerfully and full of good hope, no one mourns for them, but they accompany their funerals with song, with great affection commending their souls to God. Then, with reverence rather than with sorrow, they cremate the bodies. On the spot they erect a pillar on which are inscribed the good points of the deceased. On returning home they recount his character and his deeds. No part of his life is more frequently or more gladly spoken of than his cheerful death.

They judge that this remembrance of uprightness is not only a most efficacious means of stimulating the living to good deeds but also a most acceptable form of attention to the dead. The latter they think are present when they are talked about, though invisible to the dull sight of mortals. It would be inconsistent with the lot of the blessed not to be able to travel freely where they please, and it would be ungrateful of them to reject absolutely all desire of revisiting their friends to whom they were bound during their lives by mutual love and charity. Freedom, like all other good things, they conjecture to be increased after death rather than diminished in all good men. Consequently they believe that the dead move about among the living and are witnesses of their words and actions. Hence they go about their business with more confidence because of reliance on such protection. The belief, moreover, in the personal presence of their forefathers keeps men from any secret dishonorable deed.

They utterly despise and deride auguries and all other divinations of vain superstition, to which great attention is paid in other countries. But miracles, which occur without the assistance of nature, they venerate as operations and witnesses of the divine power at work. In their country, too, they say, miracles often occur. Sometimes in great and critical affairs they pray publicly for a miracle, which they very confidently look for and obtain.

They think that the investigation of nature, with the praise arising from it, is an act of worship acceptable to God. There are persons, however, and these not so very few, who for religious motives eschew learning and scientific pursuit and yet allow themselves no leisure. It is only by keeping busy and by all good offices that they are determined to merit the happiness coming after death. Some tend the sick. Others repair roads, clean out ditches, rebuild bridges, dig turf and sand and stone, fell and cut up trees, and transport wood, grain, and other things into the cities in carts. Not only for the public but also for private persons they behave as servants and as more than slaves.

If anywhere there is a task so rough, hard, and filthy that most are deterred from it by the toil, disgust, and despair involved, they gladly and cheerfully claim it all for themselves. While perpetually engaged in hard work themselves, they secure leisure for the others and yet claim no credit for it. They neither belittle insultingly the life of others nor extol their own. The more that these men put themselves in the position of slaves the more are they honored by all.

Of these persons there are two schools. The one is composed of celibates who not only eschew all sexual activity but also abstain from eating flesh meat and in some cases from eating all animal food. They entirely reject the pleasures of this life as harmful. They long only for the future life by means of their watching and sweat. Hoping to obtain it very soon, they are cheerful and active in the meantime.

The other school is just as fond of hard labor, but regards matrimony as preferable, not despising the comfort which it brings and thinking that their duty to nature requires them to perform the marital act and their duty to the country to beget children. They avoid no pleasure unless it interferes with their labor. They, like flesh meat just because they think that this fare makes them stronger for any work whatsoever. The Utopians regard these men as the saner but the first-named as the holier. If the latter based upon arguments from reason their preference of celibacy to matrimony and of a

hard life to a comfortable one, they would laugh them to scorn. Now, however, since they say they are prompted by religion, they look up to and reverence them. For there is nothing about which they are more careful than not lightly to dogmatize on any point of religion. Such, then, are the men whom in their language they call by a special name of their own, Buthrescae,[22] a word which may be translated as "religious par excellence."

They have priests of extraordinary holiness, and therefore very few. They have no more than thirteen in each city—with a like number of churches—except when they go to war. In that case, seven go forth with the army, and the same number of substitutes is appointed for the interval. When the regular priests come back, everyone returns to his former duties. Then those who are above the number of thirteen, until they succeed to the places of those who die, attend upon the high priest in the meantime. One, you see, is appointed to preside over the rest. They are elected by the people, just as all the other officials are, by secret ballot to avoid party spirit. When elected, they are ordained by their own group.

They preside over divine worship, order religious rites, and are censors of morals. It is counted a great disgrace for a man to be summoned or rebuked by them as not being of upright life. It is their function to give advice and admonition, but to check and punish offenders belongs to the governor and the other civil officials. The priests, however, do exclude from divine services persons whom they find to be unusually bad. There is almost no punishment which is more dreaded: they incur very great disgrace and are tortured by a secret fear of religion. Even their bodies will not long go scot-free. If they do not demonstrate to the priests their speedy repentance, they are seized and punished

22 "Extraordinarily religious."

by the Senate for their impiety.

To the priests is entrusted the education of children and youths. They regard concern for their morals and virtue as no less important than for their advancement in learning. They take the greatest pains from the very first to instill into children's minds, while still tender and pliable, good opinions, which are also useful for the preservation of their commonwealth. When once they are firmly implanted in children, they accompany them all through their adult lives and are of great help in watching over the condition of the commonwealth. The latter never decays except through vices which arise from wrong attitudes.

The feminine sex is not debarred from the priesthood, but only a widow advanced in years is ever chosen, and that rather rarely. Unless they are women, the priests have for their wives the very finest women of the country.

To no other office in Utopia is more honor given, so much so that, even if they have committed any crime, they are subjected to no tribunal, but left only to God and to themselves. They judge it wrong to lay human hands upon one, however guilty, who has been consecrated to God in a singular manner as a holy offering. It is easier for them to observe this custom because their priests are very few and very carefully chosen.

Besides, it does not easily happen that one who is elevated to such dignity for being the very best among the good, nothing but virtue being taken into account, should fall into corruption and wickedness. Even if it does happen, human nature being ever prone to change, yet since they are but few and are invested with no power except the influence of honor, it need not be feared that they will cause any great harm to the state. In fact, the reason for having but few and exceptional priests is to prevent the dignity of the order, which they now reverence very highly, from being cheapened by communicating the honor to many. This is especially true since they think it hard to find many men so good as to be fit for so honorable a position for the filling of which it is not enough to be endowed with ordinary virtues.

They are not more esteemed among their own people than among foreign nations. This can easily be seen from a fact which, I think, is its cause. When the armies are fighting in battle, the priests are to be found separate but not very far off, settled on their knees, dressed in their sacred vestments. With hands outstretched to heaven, they pray first of all for peace, next for a victory to their own side—but without much bloodshed on either side. When their side is winning, they run among the combatants and restrain the fury of their own men against the routed enemy. Merely to see and to appeal to them suffices to save one's life; to touch their flowing garments protects one's remaining goods from every harm arising from war.

This conduct has brought them such veneration among all nations everywhere and has given them so real a majesty that they have saved their own citizens from the enemy as often as they have protected the enemy from their own men. The following is well known. Sometimes their own side had given way, their case had been desperate, they were taking to flight, and the enemy was rushing on to kill and to plunder. Then the carnage had been averted by the intervention of the priests. After the armies had been parted from each other, peace had been concluded and settled on just terms. Never had there been any nation so savage, cruel, and barbarous that it had not regarded their persons as sacred and inviolable.

They celebrate as holidays the first and the last day of each month and likewise of each year. The latter they divide into months, measured by the orbit of the moon just as the course of the sun rounds out the year. In their language they call the first days Cynemerni and the last days Trapemerni.[23] These names have the same meaning as if they were rendered "First Feasts" and "Final Feasts." Their temples are fine sights, not only elaborate in workmanship but also capable of holding a vast throng, and necessarily so, since only a very small number of the populace are priests. The temples are all rather dark. This feature is due not to an ignorance of architecture but to the deliberate intention of the priests. They think that excessive light makes the thoughts wander, whereas scantier and uncertain light concentrates the mind and conduces to devotion.

In Utopia, as has been seen, the religion of all is not the same, and yet all its manifestations, though varied and manifold, by different roads as it were, tend to the same end, the worship of the divine nature. Therefore nothing is seen or heard in the temples which does not seem to agree with all in common. If any sect has a rite of its own, it is performed within the walls of each man's home. Therefore no image of the gods is seen in the temple so that the individual may be free to conceive of God with the most ardent devotion in any form he pleases. They invoke God by no special name except that of Mithras. By this word they agree to represent the one nature of the divine majesty whatever it be. The prayers formulated are such as every man may utter without offense to his own belief.

On the evening of the Final Feasts, they gather in the temple, still fasting. They thank God for the prosperity they have enjoyed in the month or year of which

that holiday is the last day. Next day, which is the First Feast, they flock to the temples in the morning. They pray for good luck and prosperity in the ensuing year or month, of which this holiday is the auspicious beginning.

On the Final Feasts, before they go to the temple, wives fall down at the feet of their husbands, children at the feet of their parents. They confess that they have erred, either by committing some fault or by performing some duty carelessly, and beg pardon for their offense. Hence, if any cloud of quarrel in the family has arisen, it is dispelled by this satisfaction so that with pure and clear minds they may be present at the sacrifices, for it is sacrilegious to attend with a troubled conscience. If they are aware of hatred or anger against anyone they do not assist at the sacrifices until they have been reconciled and have cleansed their hearts, for fear of swift and great punishment.

When they reach the temple, they part, the men going to the right side and the women to the left. Then they arrange their places so that the males in each home sit in front of the head of the household and the womenfolk are in front of the mother of the family. They thus take care that every gesture of everyone abroad is observed by those whose authority and discipline govern them at home. They also carefully see to it that everywhere the younger are placed in the company of the elder. If children were trusted to children, they might spend in childish foolery the time in which they ought to be conceiving a religious fear toward the gods, the greatest and almost the only stimulus to the practice of virtues.

They slay no animal in their sacrifices. They do not believe that the divine clemency delights in bloodshed and slaughter, seeing that it has imparted life to animate creatures that they might enjoy life. They burn incense and other fragrant substances and also offer a great number of candles.

---

23 Derivation uncertain. The second element in both words is "day." *Cynemerni*, "Dog Days," or "Starting Days," or "Rogation Days." *Trapemerni*, "Turning Days" or "Closing Days."

They are not unaware that these things add nothing to the divine nature, any more than do human prayers, but they like this harmless kind of worship. Men feel that, by these sweet smells and lights, as well as the other ceremonies, they somehow are uplifted and rise with livelier devotion to the worship of God.

The people are clothed in white garments in the temple. The priest wears

Utopias

Although Utopia means "nowhere" in Greek, several outstanding attempts were made in America during the eighteenth and nineteenth centuries to create an ideal community in an imperfect society. The American Utopias were of two types: religious and secular. One of the most prominent of the religious Utopias was the Shaker Society founded in the 1770's near Albany, New York, and claiming the fulfillment of the Second Coming in the person of their leader, Mother Ann Lee, who believed that "through the agitation of the body" came the "gift of prophecy" (illustration below). A distinguished secular Utopia was the community established in the 1820's at New Harmony, In-

ENGRAVING SHOWING A NEW MALE RECRUIT AT ONEIDA, N.Y., A UTOPIA OF SORTS WHICH PRACTICED COMPLEX MARRIAGE OR FREE LOVE ("THE ULTIMATE SELFLESSNESS OF SHARING MATES"). FOUNDED IN 1847, IT ENDURED PUBLIC CRITICISM FOR SOME THIRTY YEARS, THEN BECAME A STOCK COMPANY

ENGRAVING SHOWING SHAKERS AT A MEETINGHOUSE IN NISKAYUNA, N.Y., PERFORMING THE SORT OF BODILY GYRATIONS WHICH THEY BELIEVED INSPIRED PROPHETIC "COMMUNICATIONS"

vestments of various colors, of wonderful design and shape, but not of material as costly as one would expect. They are not interwoven with gold or set with precious stones but wrought with the different feathers of birds so cleverly and artistically that no costly material could equal the value of the handiwork. Moreover, in these birds' feathers and plumes and the definite order and plan by which they are set

in America

diana, by British economist Robert Owen who sought a "perfect cooperative society" encompassing two thousand persons on as many acres. Neither the Shakers nor the Owenites were to achieve their Utopian ideals. The Shakers lost their zeal in time and, with it, their force as a community. New Harmony was envisioned by Owen as a massive structure (far right) but actually became little more than a village of rural dwellings. Other Utopias in America—like the religious society at Oneida, New York, and the secular Brook Farm near Boston, both of which flourished during the 1840's, and are shown here— fared no better, despite the fervor and energy of their beginnings.

New Harmony, Ind.: (top) the ideal plan conceived by Owen; (bottom) an 1831 sketch by Charles Lesueur of the actuality

Brook Farm, Mass., shown in this painting by J. Wolcott, was a Transcendentalist Utopia founded in 1841 by George Ripley. Aim was to provide time for "the production of intellectual goods" by accomplishing toil swiftly through common planning and shared labor. It failed and the community was abandoned in 1847

off on the priest's vestment, they say certain hidden mysteries are contained. By knowing the meaning as it is carefully handed down by the priests, they are reminded of God's benefits toward them and, in turn, of their own piety toward God and their duty toward one another.

As soon as the priest thus arrayed appears from the vestibule, all immediately fall on the ground in reverence. The silence all around is so deep that the very appearance of the congregation strikes one with awe as if some divine power were really present. After remaining awhile on the ground, at a signal from the priest they rise.

At this point they sing praises to God, which they diversify with musical instruments, largely different in shape from those seen in our part of the world. Very many of them surpass in sweetness those in use with us, but some are not even comparable with ours. But in one respect undoubtedly they are far ahead of us. All their music, whether played on instruments or sung by the human voice, so renders and expresses the natural feelings, so suits the sound to the matter (whether the words be supplicatory, or joyful, or propitiatory, or troubled, or mournful, or angry), and so represents the meaning by the form of the melody that it wonderfully affects, penetrates, and inflames the souls of the hearers.

At the end, the priest and the people together repeat solemn prayers fixed in form, so drawn up that each individual may apply to himself personally what all recite together. In these prayers every man recognizes God to be the author of creation and governance and all other blessings besides. He thanks Him for all the benefits received, particularly that by the divine favor he has chanced on that commonwealth which is the happiest and has received that religion which he hopes to be the truest. If he errs in these matters or if there is anything better and more approved by God than that commonwealth or that religion, he prays that He will, of His goodness, bring him to the knowledge of it, for he is ready to follow in whatever path He may lead him. But if this form of a commonwealth be the best and his religion the truest, he prays that then He may give him steadfastness and bring all other mortals to the same way of living and the same opinion of God—unless there be something in this variety of religions which delights His inscrutable will.

Finally, he prays that God will take him to Himself by an easy death, how soon or late he does not venture to determine. However, if it might be without offense to His Majesty, it would be much more welcome to him to die a very hard death and go to God than to be kept longer away from Him even by a very prosperous career in life.

After this prayer has been said, they prostrate themselves on the ground again. Then shortly they rise and go away to dinner. The rest of the day they pass in games and in exercises of military training.

Now I have described to you, as exactly as I could, the structure of that commonwealth which I judge not merely the best but the only one which can rightly claim the name of a commonwealth. Outside Utopia, to be sure, men talk freely of the public welfare—but look after their private interests only. In Utopia, where nothing is private, they seriously concern themselves with public affairs. Assuredly in both cases they act reasonably. For, outside Utopia, how many are there who do not realize that, unless they make some separate provision for themselves, however flourishing the commonwealth, they will themselves starve? For this reason, necessity compels them to hold that they must take account of themselves rather than of the people, that is, of others.

On the other hand, in Utopia, where everything belongs to everybody, no one doubts, provided only that the public granaries are well filled, that the individual will lack nothing for his private use. The reason is that the distribution of goods is not niggardly. In Utopia there is no poor man and no beggar. Though no man has anything, yet all are rich.

For what can be greater riches for a man than to live with a joyful and peaceful mind, free of all worries—not troubled about his food or harassed by the querulous demands of his wife or fearing poverty for his son or worrying about his daughter's dowry, but feeling secure about the livelihood and happiness of himself and his family: wife, sons, grandsons, great-grandsons, great-great-grandsons, and all the long line of their descendants that gentlefolk anticipate? Then take into account the fact that there is no less provision for those who are now helpless but once worked than for those who are still working.

At this point I should like anyone to be so bold as to compare this fairness with the so-called justice prevalent in other nations, among which, upon my soul, I cannot discover the slightest trace of justice and fairness. What brand of justice is it that any nobleman whatsoever, or goldsmith-banker, or moneylender, or, in fact, anyone else from among those who either do no work at all or whose work is of a kind not very essential to the commonwealth, should attain a life of luxury and grandeur on the basis of his idleness or his nonessential work? In the meantime, the common laborer, the carter, the carpenter, and the farmer perform work so hard and continuous that beasts of burden could scarcely endure it and work so essential that no commonwealth could last even one year without it. Yet they earn such scanty fare and lead such a miserable life that the condition of beasts of burden might seem far preferable. The latter do not have to work so incessantly nor is their food much worse (in fact, sweeter to their taste) nor do they entertain any fear for the future. The workmen, on the other hand, not only have to toil and suffer without return or profit in the present but agonize over the thought of an indigent old age. Their daily wage is too scanty to suffice even for the day: much less is there an excess and surplus that daily can be laid by for their needs in old age.

Now is not this an unjust and ungrateful commonwealth? It lavishes great rewards on so-called gentlefolk and banking goldsmiths and the rest of that kind, who are either idle or mere parasites and purveyors of empty pleasures. On the contrary, it makes no benevolent provision for farmers, colliers, common laborers, carters, and carpenters without whom there would be no commonwealth at all. After it has misused the labor of their prime and after they are weighed down with age and disease and are in utter want, it forgets all their sleepless nights and all the great benefits received at their hands and most ungratefully requites them with a most miserable death.

What is worse, the rich every day extort a part of their daily allowance from the poor not only by private fraud but by public law. Even before they did so it seemed unjust that persons deserving best of the commonwealth should have the worst return. Now they have further distorted and debased the right and, finally, by making laws, have palmed it off as justice. Consequently, when I consider and turn over in my mind the state of all commonwealths flourishing anywhere today, so help me God, I can see nothing else than a kind of conspiracy of the rich, who are aiming at their own interests under the name and title of the commonwealth. They invent and devise all ways and means by which, first, they may keep without fear of loss all that they have amassed by evil practices, and, secondly, they may then purchase as cheaply as possible and abuse the toil and labor of all the poor. These devices become law as soon as the rich have once decreed their observance in the name of the public—that is, of the poor also!

Yet when these evil men with insatiable greed have divided up among themselves all the goods which would have been enough for all the people, how far they are from the happiness of the Utopian commonwealth! In Utopia all greed for money was entirely removed with the use of money. What a mass of troubles was then cut away! What a crop of crimes was then pulled up by the roots! Who does not know that fraud, theft, rapine, quarrels, disorders, brawls, seditions, murders, treasons, poisonings, which are avenged rather than restrained by daily executions, die out with the destruction of money? Who does not know that fear, anxiety, worries, toils, and sleepless nights will also perish at the same time as money? What is more, poverty, which alone money seemed to make poor, forthwith would itself dwindle and disappear if money were entirely done away with everywhere.

To make this assertion clearer, consider in your thoughts some barren and unfruitful year in which many thousands of men have been carried off by famine. I emphatically contend that at the end of that scarcity, if rich men's granaries had been searched, as much grain could have been found as, if it had been divided among the people killed off by starvation and disease, would have prevented anyone from feeling that meager return from soil and climate. So easily might men get the necessities of life if that blessed money, supposedly a grand invention to ease access to those necessities, was not in fact the only barrier to our getting what we need.

Even the rich, I doubt not, feel that it would be a much better state of affairs to lack no necessity than to have abundance of superfluities—to be snatched from such numerous troubles rather than to be hemmed in by great riches. Nor does it occur to me to doubt that a man's regard for his own interests or the authority of Christ our Savior—Who in His wisdom could not fail to know what was best and Who in His goodness would not fail to counsel what He knew to be best—would long ago have brought the whole world to adopt the laws of the Utopian commonwealth, had not one single monster, the chief and progenitor of all plagues, striven against it—I mean, Pride.

Pride measures prosperity not by her own advantages but by others' disadvantages. Pride would not consent to be made even a goddess if no poor wretches were left for her to domineer over and scoff at, if her good fortune might not dazzle by comparison with their miseries, if the display of her riches did not torment and intensify their poverty. This serpent from hell entwines itself around the hearts of men and acts like the suckfish in preventing and hindering them from entering on a better way of life.

Pride is too deeply fixed in men to be easily plucked out. For this reason, the fact that this form of a commonwealth—which I should gladly desire for all—has been the good fortune of the Utopians at least, fills me with joy. They have adopted such institutions of life as have laid the foundations of the commonwealth not only most happily, but also to last forever, as far as human prescience can forecast. At home they have extirpated the roots of ambition and factionalism, along with all the other vices. Hence there is no danger of trouble from domestic discord, which has been the only cause of ruin to the well-established prosperity of many cities. As long as harmony is preserved at home and its institutions are in a healthy state, not all the envy of neighboring rulers, though it has rather often attempted it and has always been repelled, can avail to shatter or to shake that nation.

When Raphael had finished his story, many things came to my mind which seemed very absurdly established in the customs and laws of the people described—not only in their method of waging war, their ceremonies and religion, as well as their other institutions, but most of all in that feature which is the principal foundation of their whole structure. I mean their common life and subsistence—without any exchange of money. This latter alone utterly overthrows all the nobility, magnificence, splendor, and majesty which are, in the estimation of the common people, the true glories and ornaments of the commonwealth.

I knew, however, that he was wearied with his tale, and I was not quite certain that he could brook any opposition to his views, particularly when I recall his censure of others on account of their fear that they might not appear to be wise enough, unless they found some fault to criticize in other men's discoveries. I there-fore praised their way of life and his speech and, taking him by the hand, led him in to supper. I first said, nevertheless, that there would be another chance to think about these matters more deeply and to talk them over with him more fully. If only this were some day possible!

Meanwhile, though in other respects he is a man of the most undoubted learning as well as of the greatest knowledge of human affairs, I cannot agree with all that he said. But I readily admit that there are very many features in the Utopian commonwealth which it is easier for me to wish for in our countries than to have any hope of seeing realized.

The end of the afternoon discourse of Raphael Hythlodaeus on the laws and customs of the island of Utopia, hitherto known but to few, as reported by the most distinguished and most learned man, Mr. Thomas More, citizen and sheriff of London.

FINIS

"THE CONCLUSION OF THE DISCOURSE." WOODCUT FROM THE GOITEIN EDITION OF 1925
End of the afternoon

The ideal society described in *Utopia*, based on democratic election of rulers, a socialist economy, and happiness found in "the freedom and culture of the mind," is part of the literature of Utopia which begins with *The Republic* of Plato (GBWW, Vol. 7). Comparison also can be made between More's *Utopia*, inhabited by heathens, and the Christian ideal delineated in St. Augustine's *The City of God* (GBWW, Vol. 18), especially in Book XI which contrasts the earthly with the heavenly city, and in Book XXII which describes the City of God in its final form. Another book in the Utopian tradition is Francis Bacon's *New Atlantis* (GBWW, Vol. 30).

A merry satire on the more sober aspects of *Utopia* can be read in the description of life in the "Utopia" Abbey of Theleme, as told by Rabelais in *Gargantua and Pantagruel* (GBWW, Vol. 24, Bk. I, chaps. 52–57). Existence in More's commonwealth, which is based on reason and not on pride, covetousness, lust, anger, gluttony, envy, or sloth, can be compared with the rational life in the land of the Houyhnhnms, which Gulliver visits in Jonathan Swift's *Gulliver's Travels* (GBWW, Vol. 36, Part IV, pp. 135–184). The customs and opinions of a modern Utopia can be found in Samuel Butler's *Erewhon* (GGB, Vol. 2, pp. 483–506).

In reading such books, one of the first questions that many readers ask is: How does Utopia compare with an actual state or society? Distinctions between the practical and Utopian ideals of society can be found in the passages cited in GOVERNMENT 2*e* and STATE 6 in the *Syntopicon*. In addition, the introductory essay to the chapter on STATE explores the various political theories and traditions in the Western tradition with which the blueprint of a Utopia can be compared.

Utopia is devoted to the cultivation of happiness. Citizens use the time obtained from the elimination of superfluous labor for the freedom and culture of the mind. Happiness as a speculative activity is examined in passages cited under HAPPINESS 2*b* (7). A striking feature of More's Utopian happiness is the concept of the social aspect of happiness, involving a doctrine of the common good. This aspect of happiness is examined in the passages listed under HAPPINESS 5.

Economically, the Utopians have a socialist conception of the common good. References to passages describing the condition of the worker in a socialist economy are cited under LABOR 5*d*. Also, the antagonism between classes when wealth is distributed unequally —a condition which the Utopian economy sought to eliminate—is discussed in passages referred to under LABOR 7*c* (1). Passages cited under JUSTICE 8*a* explore another aspect of this economic condition; that is, private and public property: the just distribution of economic goods. The existence of slaves is the one fact in the Utopian economy that seems to be at odds with the ideal of socialist workers laboring for the common good. An entire chapter in the *Syntopicon* is devoted to the question of SLAVERY.

In the introductory note, it was suggested that the dialogue form of *Utopia* permitted the author to present and examine all sides of his complex subject without, however, marking one as his own. This form of the dialogue is also used by Plato in his *Dialogues* (GBWW, Vol. 7), where it is often difficult to ascertain which of the views being expressed belongs to the author. Much the same can be said of Shakespeare in his tragedies and comedies (GBWW, Vols. 26 and 27).

A radically different type of dialogue is that used by Galileo in *Dialogues Concerning the Two New Sciences* (GBWW, Vol. 28), where it is evident that the author favors one character in the dialogue and that the two other characters are merely foils advancing incorrect positions.

Should a philosopher become a counselor to a king? That question is debated in the first book of *Utopia*. Whether or not a philosopher should accept high political responsibility is discussed in passages cited under PHILOSOPHY 4*c*. Of particular interest will be *The Seventh Letter* of Plato (GBWW, Vol. 7). In it Plato recounts his disastrous experience as a philosopher at the court of Dionysius of Syracuse. Another philosopher who discusses a ruler is Machiavelli in *The Prince* (GBWW, Vol. 23, pp. 1–37). Macaulay's essay on Machiavelli and Machiavellian statesmanship, which More opposed in *Utopia*, can be read in *Gateway to the Great Books*, Vol. 7, pp. 295–329.

Sir Thomas More and Family

The *Utopia* of the preceding pages is built of considered ideas formed by a searching mind—an intellectual edifice existing merely in the imaginations of Sir Thomas and his readers. But there was in More's life a real, palpable Utopia of sorts: the family circle. Our introduction makes reference to this and the pen-and-ink sketch below shows the family members grouped around the solemnly benign Sir Thomas. The sketch is by Holbein, the Younger, and was rendered either in 1527 or 1528. It is now in the Kunstmuseum, Basel. Notes on the drawing were probably made by Nicolas Kratzer, who instructed More's daughter in astronomy and was a frequent visitor in the home. Left to right: Elizabeth Dauncey, More's daughter; Margaret Giggs, the family's ward; Sir John More (Sir Thomas' father); Anne Cresacre, who married More's son John; and Sir Thomas. Seated on his left: Cecily Heron and Margaret Roper (Sir Thomas' daughters); and Alice, his wife. Behind them: John More and More's jester, Henry Pattenson.

Henry David Thoreau

Walden

WALDEN POND, SUMMER, 1961

Walden is blue at one time and green at another, even from the same point of view. Lying between the earth and the heavens, it partakes of the color of both.

THOREAU PORTRAITS: (LEFT) A DAGUERREOTYPE MADE IN 1856 AT AGE 39 IN WORCHESTER, MASS., BY BENJAMIN D. MAXHAM; (CENTER) CRAYON DRAWING BY SAMUEL ROWSE IN 1854, THE EARLIEST AUTHENTIC PORTRAIT OF THOREAU; (RIGHT) AMBROTYPE BY E. S. DUNSHEE IN NEW BEDFORD, MASS., 1861

INTRODUCTION

Stubborn in his Yankee contempt for the business world, culture, manners, and religion of the nineteenth century, which he dismissed as "restless, nervous, bustling, trivial," Thoreau is the American Diogenes because of the independence of his convictions and way of life, his asceticism, prickly wit, and his chronic stinginess with human warmth. Frequently and fiercely he took his beliefs and life to the edge of eccentricity, as the great Greek Cynic had done. His discoveries of who he was and how best to conduct his life have captured the imagination of many men, including Tolstoy, Gandhi, Ramsay MacDonald, and Martin Luther King, Jr.

"My purpose in going to Walden Pond," Thoreau says, "was not to live cheaply nor to live dearly there, but to transact some private business with the fewest obstacles. . . ." What that business was is spelled out in the book's opening chapters, "Economy" and "Where I Lived, and What I Lived For," both of which are included in our selection. These chapters describe an experiment in living as simply and self-sufficiently as possible.

The physical act, then, of living day by day at Walden Pond is what gives the book authority. To live as a hermit or an adventurer in a wilderness, however, was never Thoreau's intention. Tranquillity and privacy were what he sought: not mortification or exploits. Critics who have satirized him for having been, at best, a bogus hermit who was hardly as primitive as he pretended, miss the essential point of his Walden experiment. Such criticism assumes, incorrectly, that Thoreau's purpose in living at Walden Pond was to seek solitude and cultivate independence.

Early in the spring of 1845, Thoreau, then twenty-seven, began to chop

440

down tall pines with which to build the foundations of his home on the shores of Walden Pond, a small glacial lake located two miles south of the village of Concord. Once settled, he restricted his diet for the most part to what fruit and vegetables he found growing wild and the beans he planted and hoed. When not busy weeding his bean rows and trying to protect them from hungry woodchucks, or occupied with fishing, swimming, or rowing, he spent long hours observing and recording the local flora and fauna, reading, and writing *A Week on the Concord and Merrimack Rivers* and an essay on Carlyle, and making entries in his *Journals* which later he would polish and include in *Walden.* Much time, too, was spent in meditation.

Out of such activity and thought came *Walden,* a series of eighteen essays describing his experiment in basic living and his effort to set time free for leisure. Since that experience provides another perspective on the meaning of work and leisure, discussed in the essays in Part One, we have selected six of the essays that are particularly relevant to this discussion. In the essays omitted, Thoreau describes the various realities of life at Walden Pond: his intimacy, for instance, with the moles in his cellar, the pickerel in the Pond, a wild mouse turned into a pet, and a happy-go-lucky Canadian lumberjack; the sounds, smells, and look of woods and water at various seasons; the music of wind in telegraph wires—in short, the felicities of learning how to fulfill his desire "to live deep and suck out all the marrow of life."

Then, in 1847, Emerson had to visit Europe, and, worried about his wife's illness, he invited Thoreau to take care of his family and house. Thoreau accepted, leaving Walden Pond for good on September 6, 1847. Deeper motives for deciding to leave are contained in the chapter "Conclusions," probably the most eloquent prose that Thoreau ever wrote.

His conclusions tend to be practical. He proved to his own satisfaction that he could pursue a happy and fruitful existence if he simplified his needs to the point where the little money he could earn easily as a handyman or surveyor would suffice, freeing his mind and spirit to pursue their destinies. A distinguished modern critic, Stanley Edgar Hyman, argues that the Walden experiment embodies a reenactment of one of the most ancient, universal, and seminal of myths: that of death and resurrection. James Russell Lowell viewed the experiment as a ritual of pompous exhibitionism, jeering that "this egotism of his is a Stylites pillar after all, a seclusion which keeps him in the public eye."

Whatever the significance of the Walden Pond experiment, it certainly supplied some concrete answers to the questions to which Thoreau addressed himself throughout his life: What can a man do with his life? What is the value of work? What is leisure? What is success? The answers that Thoreau found, embodied in their maturity in *Walden* (1854) and the essays "Civil Disobedience" (1849) and "Life Without Principle"

(1863), involved a defiant individualism, which occasionally took refuge in absolute nonresistence and nonparticipation.

His residence at Walden Pond was interrupted, for instance, by a day's imprisonment in Concord jail for refusal to pay a poll tax to a government which waged the Mexican War, a war that Thoreau considered a dishonest scheme by Southern slaveholders greedy to grab land. (He was released from jail when the tax was paid for him by his old Aunt Maria, disguised by a shawl so that Henry would not be cross at her for spoiling his gesture.) Above all, he came to believe in the right of each man to find how he wanted to live, holding that this right was given by a moral law superior to statutes and constitutions. But he offered no convenient rule of thumb by which others should live or pursue happiness. The essence as well as the boundary of his advice on how to live is contained in a stinging aphorism: "However mean your life is, meet it and live it; do not call it hard names. It is not so bad as you are."

J udged by conventional standards of success—judged, in fact, by any standard other than his own—Thoreau's life was a mean failure. Born July 12, 1817, in Concord into a family of French, Scottish, Quaker, and Puritan stock, he was graduated, without distinction, from Harvard College in 1837. Failures of several sorts plagued him in the years that followed. At first he tried his hand as a teacher—only to resign from his first position as schoolmaster in the Concord grammar school because he opposed the policy of flogging, and then to quit the school he established with his brother John, despite a waiting list of pupils. Haphazard jobs followed: fence builder, house painter, gardener, carpenter, surveyor, handyman, tutor, unpaid editorial assistant on the Transcendentalist periodical, the *Dial*, pencil maker in his unsuccessful father's small factory, and occasional lecturer at the Concord Lyceum.

At love he was also a failure. In 1839, he fell in love with Ellen Sewall, the sister of a Unitarian minister friend of the Thoreaus. Although she accepted his proposal, made a year later during a jaunt on the beach near her home in Scituate, Massachusetts, she immediately broke the engagement at the insistence of her parents. Thoreau died a bachelor.

In the years following his stay at Walden Pond, he earned what scant money he needed by becoming the village surveyor, by occasionally making pencils, by working as a handyman, or by selling odd essays to the *Dial* and *The Atlantic Monthly*. In contrast to Emerson, who commanded an ample income as a popular lecturer, Thoreau was seldom invited back to the Concord Lyceum or to any of the other New England Lyceums, despite the occasional success of his lectures on life at Walden Pond or on John Brown, whom he passionately defended against the more timid groups among the Abolitionists of New England.

In the one career he cared about—that of a man of letters—he was also a failure. Niggardly critical reception greeted the two volumes he published during his lifetime—*Walden* and *A Week on the Concord and Merrimack Rivers*—and sales were anemic.

Except for a few camping and hiking trips, Thoreau lived for the most part in the home of his parents in Concord, where, at the age of forty-four, he died of tuberculosis on May 6, 1862.

Over 150 editions of *Walden* have been published since the first one in 1854. Yet it was not until Professor Walter Harding produced *The Variorum Walden* in 1962 that Thoreau's own corrections and additions in his personal copy of the first edition came to be incorporated into the published text. Professor Harding, chairman of the English Department at the State University College, Geneseo, New York, is secretary of the Thoreau Society and author or editor of some eighteen books relating to Thoreau. Our selections are from his edition of *The Variorum Walden*, published by Twayne Publishers, Inc., of New York City.

CONTENTS

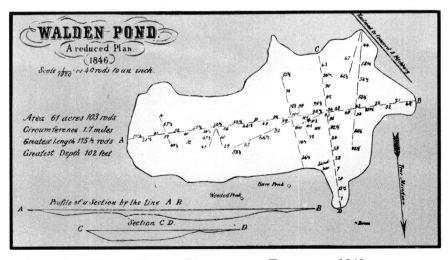

MAP OF WALDEN POND MADE BY THOREAU IN 1846

THE POND
I lived alone, in the woods

ECONOMY

When I wrote the following pages, or rather the bulk of them, I lived alone, in the woods, a mile from any neighbor, in a house which I had built myself, on the shore of Walden Pond, in Concord, Massachusetts, and earned my living by the labor of my hands only. I lived there two years and two months. At present I am a sojourner in civilized life again.

I should not obtrude my affairs so much on the notice of my readers if very particular inquiries had not been made by my townsmen concerning my mode of life, which some would call impertinent, though they do not appear to me at all impertinent, but, considering the circumstances, very natural and pertinent. Some have asked what I got to eat; if I did not feel lonesome; if I was not afraid; and the like. Others have been curious to learn what portion of my income I devoted to charitable purposes; and some, who have large families, how many poor children I maintained. I will therefore ask those of my readers who feel no particular interest in me to pardon me if I undertake to answer some of these questions in this book: In most books, the *I*, or first person, is omitted; in this it will be retained; that, in respect to egotism, is the main difference. We commonly do not remember that it is, after all, always the first person that is speaking. I should not talk so much about myself if there were anybody else whom I knew as well. Unfortunately, I am confined to this theme by the narrowness of my experience. Moreover, I, on my side, require of every writer, first or last, a simple and sincere account of his own life, and not merely what he has heard of other men's lives; some such account as he would send to his kindred from a distant land; for if he has lived sincerely, it must have been in a distant land to me. Perhaps these pages are more particularly addressed to poor students. As for the rest of my readers, they will accept such portions as apply to them. I trust that none will stretch the seams in putting on the coat, for it may do good service to him whom it fits.

I would fain say something, not so much concerning the Chinese and Sandwich Islanders as you who read these pages, who are said to live in New England; something about your condition, especially your outward condition or circumstances in this world, in this town, what it is, whether it is necessary that it be as bad as it is, whether it cannot be improved as well as not. I have traveled a good deal in Concord; and everywhere, in shops, and offices, and fields, the inhabitants have appeared to me to be doing penance in a thousand remarkable ways. What I have heard of Bramins sitting exposed to four fires and looking in the face of the sun; or hanging suspended, with their heads downward, over flames; or looking at the heavens over their shoulders "until it becomes impossible for them to resume their natural position, while from the twist of the neck nothing but liquids can pass into the stomach;" or dwelling, chained for life, at the foot of a tree; or measuring with their bodies, like caterpillars, the breadth of vast empires; or standing on one leg on the tops of pillars—even these forms of conscious penance are hardly more incredible and astonishing than the scenes which I daily witness. The twelve labors of Hercules were trifling in comparison with those which my neighbors have undertaken; for they were only twelve, and had an end; but I could never see that these men slew or captured any monster or finished any labor. They have no friend Iolaus to burn with a hot iron the root of the hydra's head, but as soon as one head is crushed, two spring up.

I see young men, my townsmen, whose misfortune it is to have inherited farms, houses, barns, cattle, and farming tools; for these are more easily acquired than got rid of. Better if they had been born in the open pasture and suckled by a wolf, that they might have seen with clearer eyes what field they were called to labor in. Who made them serfs of the soil? Why should they eat their sixty acres, when man is condemned to eat only his peck of dirt? Why should they begin digging their graves as soon as they are born? They have got to live a man's life, pushing all these things before them, and get on as well as they can. How many a poor immortal soul have I met well-nigh crushed and smothered under its load, creeping down the road of life, pushing before it a barn seventy-five feet by forty, its Augean stables never cleansed, and one hundred acres of land, tillage, mowing, pasture, and woodlot! The portionless, who struggle with no such unnecessary inherited encumbrances, find it labor enough to subdue and cultivate a few cubic feet of flesh.

But men labor under a mistake. The better part of the man is soon plowed into the soil for compost. By a seeming fate, commonly called necessity, they are employed, as it says in an old book, laying up treasures which moth and rust will corrupt and thieves break through and steal. It is a fool's life, as they will find when they get to the end of it, if not before. It is said that Deucalion and Pyrrha created men by throwing stones over their heads behind them—

Inde genus durum sumus, experiensque laborum,
Et documenta damus quâ simus origine nati.

Or, as Raleigh rhymes it in his sonorous way—

From thence our kind hard-hearted is,
  enduring pain and care,
Approving that our bodies of a stony
  nature are.

So much for a blind obedience to a blundering oracle, throwing the stones over their heads behind them, and not seeing where they fell.

Most men, even in this comparatively free country, through mere ignorance and mistake, are so occupied with the factitious cares and superfluously coarse labors of life that its finer fruits cannot be plucked by them. Their fingers, from excessive toil, are too clumsy and tremble too much for that. Actually, the laboring man has not leisure for a true integrity day by day; he cannot afford to sustain the manliest relations to men; his labor would be depreciated in the market. He has no time to be anything but a machine. How can he remember well his ignorance—which his growth requires—who has so often to use his knowledge? We should feed and clothe him gratuitously sometimes, and recruit him with our cordials, before we judge of him. The finest qualities of our nature, like the bloom on fruits, can be preserved only by the most delicate handling. Yet we do not treat ourselves nor one another thus tenderly.

Some of you, we all know, are poor, find it hard to live, are sometimes, as it were, gasping for breath. I have no doubt that some of you who read this book are unable to pay for all the dinners which you have actually eaten, or for the coats and shoes which are fast wearing or are already worn out, and have come to this page to spend borrowed or stolen time, robbing your creditors of an hour. It is very evident what mean and sneaking lives many of you live, for my sight has been whetted by experience; always on the limits, trying to get into business and trying to get out of debt, a very ancient slough, called by the Latins *aes alienum*, "another's brass," for

some of their coins were made of brass; still living, and dying, and buried by this other's brass; always promising to pay, promising to pay, tomorrow, and dying today, insolvent; seeking to curry favor, to get custom, by how many modes, only not state-prison offenses; lying, flattering, voting, contracting yourselves into a nutshell of civility, or dilating into an atmosphere of thin and vaporous generosity, that you may persuade your neighbor to let you make his shoes, or his hat, or his coat, or his carriage, or import his groceries for him; making yourselves sick, that you may lay up something against a sick day, something to be tucked away in an old chest, or in a stocking behind the plastering, or, more safely, in the brick bank; no matter where, no matter how much or how little.

I sometimes wonder that we can be so frivolous, I may almost say, as to attend to the gross but somewhat foreign form of servitude called Negro Slavery, there are so many keen and subtle masters that enslave both North and South. It is hard to have a Southern overseer; it is worse to have a Northern one; but worst of all when you are the slavedriver of yourself. Talk of a divinity in man! Look at the teamster on the highway, wending to market by day or night; does any divinity stir within him? His highest duty to fodder and water his horses! What is his destiny to him compared with the shipping interests? Does not he drive for Squire Make-a-stir? How godlike, how immortal, is he? See how he cowers and sneaks, how vaguely all the day he fears, not being immortal nor divine, but the slave and prisoner of his own opinion of himself, a fame won by his own deeds. Public opinion is a weak tyrant compared with our own private opinion. What a man thinks of himself, that it is which determines, or rather indicates, his fate. Self-emancipation even in the West Indian provinces of the fancy and imagination—what Wilberforce is there to bring that about? Think, also, of the ladies of the land weaving toilet cushions against the last day, not to betray too green an interest in their fates! As if you could kill time without injuring eternity.

The mass of men lead lives of quiet desperation. What is called resignation is confirmed desperation. From the desperate city you go into the desperate country, and have to console yourself with the bravery of minks and muskrats. A stereotyped but unconscious despair is concealed even under what are called the games and amusements of mankind. There is no play in them, for this comes after work. But it is a characteristic of wisdom not to do desperate things.

When we consider what, to use the catechism, is the chief end of man, and what are the true necessaries and means of life, it appears as if men had deliberately chosen the common mode of living because they preferred it to any other. Yet they honestly think there is no choice left. But alert and healthy natures remember that the sun rose clear. It is never too late to give up our prejudices. No way of thinking or doing, however ancient, can be trusted without proof. What everybody echoes or in silence passes by as true today may turn out to be falsehood tomorrow, mere smoke of opinion, which some had trusted for a cloud that would sprinkle fertilizing rain on their fields. What old people say you cannot do, you try and find that you can. Old deeds for old people, and new deeds for new. Old people did not know enough once, perchance, to fetch fresh fuel to keep the fire a-going; new people put a little dry wood under a pot, and are whirled round the globe with the speed of birds, in a way to kill old people, as the phrase is. Age is no better, hardly so well, qualified for an instructor as youth, for it has not profited so much as it has lost. One may almost doubt if the wisest man has learned anything of absolute value by living. Practically, the old have no very important advice to give the young, their own experience has been so partial, and their lives have been such miserable failures, for private reasons, as they must believe; and it may be that they have some faith left which belies that experience, and they are only less young than they were. I have lived some thirty years on this planet, and I have yet to hear the first syllable of valuable or even earnest advice from my seniors. They have told me nothing, and probably cannot tell me anything to the purpose. Here is life, an experiment to a great extent untried by me; but it does not avail me that they have tried it. If I have any experience which I think valuable, I am sure to reflect that this my Mentors said nothing about.

One farmer says to me, "You cannot live on vegetable food solely, for it furnishes nothing to make bones with"; and so he religiously devotes a part of his day to supplying his system with the raw material of bones; walking all the while he talks behind his oxen, which, with vegetable-made bones, jerk him and his lumbering plow along in spite of every obstacle. Some things are really necessaries of life in some circles, the most helpless and diseased, which in others are luxuries merely, and in others still are entirely unknown.

The whole ground of human life seems to some to have been gone over by their predecessors, both the heights and the valleys, and all things to have been cared for. According to Evelyn, "the wise Solomon prescribed ordinances for the very distances of trees; and the Roman praetors have decided how often you may go into your neighbor's land to gather the acorns which fall on it without trespass, and what share belongs to that neighbor." Hippocrates has even left directions how we should cut our nails; that is, even with the ends of the fingers, neither shorter nor longer. Undoubtedly the very tedium and ennui which presume to have exhausted the variety and the joys of life are as old as Adam. But man's capacities have never been measured; nor are we to judge of what he can do by any precedents, so little has been tried. Whatever have been thy failures hitherto, "be not afflicted, my child, for who shall assign to thee what thou hast left undone?"

We might try our lives by a thousand simple tests; as, for instance, that the same sun which ripens my beans illumines at once a system of earths like ours. If I had remembered this it would have prevented some mistakes. This was not the light in which I hoed them. The stars are the apexes of what wonderful triangles! What distant and different beings in the various mansions of the universe are contemplating the same one at the same moment! Nature and human life are as various as our several constitutions. Who shall say what prospect life offers to another? Could a greater miracle take place than for us to look through each other's eyes for an instant? We should live in all the ages of the world in an hour; ay, in all the worlds of the ages. History, Poetry, Mythology!—I know of no reading of another's experience so startling and informing as this would be.

The greater part of what my neighbors call good I believe in my soul to be bad, and if I repent of anything, it is very likely to be my good behavior. What demon possessed me that I behaved so well? You may say the wisest thing you can, old man —you who have lived seventy years, not without honor of a kind—I hear an irresistible voice which invites me away from all that. One generation abandons the enterprises of another like stranded vessels.

I think that we may safely trust a good deal more than we do. We may waive just so much care of ourselves as we honestly bestow elsewhere. Nature is as well adapted to our weakness as to our strength. The incessant anxiety and strain of some is a well-nigh incurable form of disease. We are made to exaggerate the importance of what work we do; and yet how much is not

done by us! or, what if we had been taken sick? How vigilant we are! determined not to live by faith if we can avoid it; all the day long on the alert, at night we unwillingly say our prayers and commit ourselves to uncertainties. So thoroughly and sincerely are we compelled to live, reverencing our life, and denying the possibility of change. This is the only way, we say; but there are as many ways as there can be drawn radii from one center. All change is a miracle to contemplate; but it is a miracle which is taking place every instant. Confucius said, "To know that we know what we know, and that we do not know what we do not know, that is true knowledge." When one man has reduced a fact of the imagination to be a fact to his understanding, I foresee that all men will at length establish their lives on that basis.

Let us consider for a moment what most of the trouble and anxiety which I have referred to is about, and how much it is necessary that we be troubled, or at least careful. It would be some advantage to live a primitive and frontier life, though in the midst of an outward civilization, if only to learn what are the gross necessaries of life and what methods have been taken to obtain them; or even to look over the old daybooks of the merchants, to see what it was that men most commonly bought at the stores, what they stored, that is, what are the grossest groceries. For the improvements of ages have had but little influence on the essential laws of man's existence: as our skeletons, probably, are not to be distinguished from those of our ancestors.

By the words, *necessary of life*, I mean whatever, of all that man obtains by his own exertions, has been from the first, or from long use has become, so important to human life that few, if any, whether from savageness, or poverty, or philosophy, ever attempt to do without it. To many creatures there is in this sense but one necessary of life, Food. To the bison of the prairie it is a few inches of palatable grass, with water to drink; unless he seeks the Shelter of the forest or the mountain's shadow. None of the brute creation requires more than Food and Shelter. The necessaries of life for man in this climate may, accurately enough, be distributed under the several heads of Food, Shelter, Clothing, and Fuel; for not till we have secured these are we prepared to entertain the true problems of life with freedom and a prospect of success. Man has invented not only houses but clothes and cooked food; and possibly from the accidental discovery of the warmth of fire, and the consequent use of it, at first a luxury, arose the present necessity to sit by it. We observe cats and dogs acquiring the same second nature. By proper Shelter and Clothing we legitimately retain our own internal heat; but with an excess of these, or of Fuel, that is, with an external heat greater than our own internal, may not cookery properly be said to begin? Darwin, the naturalist, says of the inhabitants of Tierra del Fuego that while his own party, who were well clothed and sitting close to a fire, were far from too warm, these naked savages, who were farther off, were observed, to his great surprise, "to be streaming with perspiration at undergoing such a roasting." So, we are told, the New Hollander goes naked with impunity, while the European shivers in his clothes. Is it impossible to combine the hardiness of these savages with the intellectualness of the civilized man? According to Liebig, man's body is a stove, and food the fuel which keeps up the internal combustion in the lungs. In cold weather we eat more, in warm less. The animal heat is the result of a slow combustion, and disease and death take place when this is too rapid; or for want of fuel, or from some defect in the draught, the fire goes out. Of course the vital heat is not to be confounded with fire; but so much for analogy. It appears, therefore, from the above list, that the ex-

pression, *animal life*, is nearly synonymous with the expression, *animal heat*; for while Food may be regarded as the Fuel which keeps up the fire within us—and Fuel serves only to prepare that Food or to increase the warmth of our bodies by addition from without—Shelter and Clothing also serve only to retain the *heat* thus generated and absorbed.

The grand necessity, then, for our bodies, is to keep warm, to keep the vital heat in us. What pains we accordingly take, not only with our Food, and Clothing, and Shelter, but with our beds, which are our nightclothes, robbing the nests and breasts of birds to prepare this shelter within a shelter, as the mole has its bed of grass and leaves at the end of its burrow! The poor man is wont to complain that this is a cold world; and to cold, no less physical than social, we refer directly a great part of our ails. The summer, in some climates, makes possible to man a sort of Elysian life. Fuel, except to cook his Food, is then unnecessary; the sun is his fire, and many of the fruits are sufficiently cooked by its rays; while Food generally is more various, and more easily obtained, and Clothing and Shelter are wholly or half unnecessary. At the present day, and in this country, as I find by my own experience, a few implements, a knife, an ax, a spade, a wheelbarrow, etc., and for the studious, lamplight, stationery, and access to a few books, rank next to necessaries, and can all be obtained at a trifling cost. Yet some, not wise, go to the other side of the globe, to barbarous and unhealthy regions, and devote themselves to trade for ten or twenty years, in order that they may live —that is, keep comfortably warm—and die in New England at last. The luxuriously rich are not simply kept comfortably warm, but unnaturally hot; as I implied before, they are cooked, of course *à la mode*.

Most of the luxuries, and many of the so-called comforts of life, are not only not indispensable, but positive hindrances to the elevation of mankind. With respect to luxuries and comforts, the wisest have ever lived a more simple and meager life than the poor. The ancient philosophers, Chinese, Hindu, Persian, and Greek, were a class than which none has been poorer in outward riches, none so rich in inward. We know not much about them. It is remarkable that *we* know so much of them as we do. The same is true of the more modern reformers and benefactors of their race. None can be an impartial or wise observer of human life but from the vantage ground of what *we* should call voluntary poverty. Of a life of luxury the fruit is luxury, whether in agriculture, or commerce, or literature, or art. There are nowadays professors of philosophy, but not philosophers. Yet it is admirable to profess because it was once admirable to live. To be a philosopher is not merely to have subtle thoughts, nor even to found a school, but so to love wisdom as to live according to its dictates, a life of simplicity, independence, magnanimity, and trust. It is to solve some of the problems of life, not only theoretically, but practically. The success of great scholars and thinkers is commonly a courtier-like success, not kingly, not manly. They make shift to live merely by conformity, practically as their fathers did, and are in no sense the progenitors of a nobler race of men. But why do men degenerate ever? What makes families run out? What is the nature of the luxury which enervates and destroys nations? Are we sure that there is none of it in our own lives? The philosopher is in advance of his age even in the outward form of his life. He is not fed, sheltered, clothed, warmed, like his contemporaries. How can a man be a philosopher and not maintain his vital heat by better methods than other men?

When a man is warmed by the several modes which I have described, what does he want next? Surely not more warmth of the same kind, as more and richer food, larger and more splendid houses, finer and more abundant clothing, more numerous, incessant, and hotter fires, and the like. When he has obtained those things which are necessary to life, there is another alternative than to obtain the superfluities; and that is, to adventure on life now, his vacation from humbler toil having commenced. The soil, it appears, is suited to the seed, for it has sent its radicle downward, and it may now send its shoot upward also with confidence. Why has man rooted himself thus firmly in the earth, but that he may rise in the same proportion into the heavens above?—for the nobler plants are valued for the fruit they bear at last in the air and light, far from the ground, and are not treated like the humbler esculents, which, though they may be biennials, are cultivated only till they have perfected their root, and often cut down at top for this purpose, so that most would not know them in their flowering season.

I do not mean to prescribe rules to strong and valiant natures, who will mind their own affairs whether in heaven or hell, and perchance build more magnificently and spend more lavishly than the richest, without ever impoverishing themselves, not knowing how they live—if, indeed, there are any such, as has been dreamed; nor to those who find their encouragement and inspiration in precisely the present condition of things, and cherish it with the fondness and enthusiasm of lovers—and, to some extent, I reckon myself in this number; I do not speak to those who are well employed, in whatever circumstances, and they know whether they are well employed or not, but mainly to the mass of men who are discontented, and idly complaining of the hardness of their lot or of the times, when they might improve them. There are some who complain most energetically and inconsolably of any, because they are, as they say, doing their duty. I also have in my mind that seem-

HILLTOP "OBSERVATORY"
Telegraph any new arrival

ingly wealthy, but most terribly impoverished class of all, who have accumulated dross, but know not how to use it, or get rid of it, and thus have forged their own golden or silver fetters.

If I should attempt to tell how I have desired to spend my life in years past, it would probably surprise those of my readers who are somewhat acquainted with its actual history; it would certainly astonish those who know nothing about it. I will only hint at some of the enterprises which I have cherished.

In any weather, at any hour of the day or night, I have been anxious to improve the nick of time, and notch it on my stick too; to stand on the meeting of two eternities, the past and future, which is precisely the present moment; to toe that line. You will pardon some obscurities, for there are more secrets in my trade than in most men's, and yet not voluntarily kept, but inseparable from its very nature. I would gladly tell all that I know about it, and never paint "No Admittance" on my gate.

I long ago lost a hound, a bay horse, and a turtledove, and am still on their trail. Many are the travelers I have spoken to concerning them, describing their tracks and what calls they answered to. I have met one or two who had heard the hound, and the tramp of the horse, and even seen the dove disappear behind a cloud, and they seemed as anxious to recover them as if they had lost them themselves.

To anticipate, not the sunrise and the dawn merely, but, if possible, Nature herself! How many mornings, summer and winter, before yet any neighbor was stirring about his business, have I been about mine! No doubt, many of my townsmen have met me returning from this enterprise, farmers starting for Boston in the twilight, or woodchoppers going to their work. It is true, I never assisted the sun materially in his rising, but, doubt not, it was of the last importance only to be present at it.

So many autumn, ay, and winter days, spent outside the town, trying to hear what was in the wind, to hear and carry it express! I well-nigh sunk all my capital in it, and lost my own breath into the bargain, running in the face of it. If it had concerned either of the political parties, depend upon it, it would have appeared in the Gazette with the earliest intelligence. At other times watching from the observatory of some cliff or tree, to telegraph any new arrival; or waiting at evening on the hill-tops for the sky to fall, that I might catch something, though I never caught much, and that, manna-wise, would dissolve again in the sun.

For a long time I was reporter to a journal, of no very wide circulation, whose editor has never yet seen fit to print the bulk of my contributions, and, as is too common with writers, I got only my labor for my pains. However, in this case my pains were their own reward.

For many years I was self-appointed inspector of snowstorms and rainstorms and did my duty faithfully; surveyor, if not of highways, then of forest paths and all across-lot routes, keeping them open, and ravines bridged and passable at all seasons, where the public heel had testified to their utility.

I have looked after the wild stock of the town, which give a faithful herdsman a good deal of trouble by leaping fences, and I have had an eye to the unfrequented nooks and corners of the farm; though I did not always know whether Jonas or Solomon worked in a particular field today; that was none of my business. I have watered the red huckleberry, the sand cherry and the nettle-tree, the red pine and the black ash, the white grape and the yellow violet, which might have withered else in dry seasons.

In short, I went on thus for a long time (I may say it without boasting), faithfully minding my business, till it became more and more evident that my townsmen would not after all admit me into the list of town officers, nor make my place a sinecure with a moderate allowance. My accounts, which I can swear to have kept faithfully, I have, indeed, never got audited, still less accepted, still less paid and settled. However, I have not set my heart on that.

Not long since, a strolling Indian went to sell baskets at the house of a well-known lawyer in my neighborhood. "Do you wish to buy any baskets?" he asked. "No, we do not want any," was the reply. "What!" exclaimed the Indian as he went out the gate, "do you mean to starve us?" Having seen his industrious white neighbors so well off—that the lawyer had only to weave arguments, and, by some magic, wealth and standing followed—he had said to himself: "I will go into business; I will weave baskets; it is a thing which I can do." Thinking that when he had made the baskets he would have done his part, and then it would be the white man's to buy them, he had not discovered that it was necessary for him to make it worth the other's while to buy them, or at least make him think that it was so, or to make something else which it would be worth his while to buy. I too had woven a kind of basket of a delicate texture, but I had not made it worth any one's while to buy them. Yet not the less, in my case, did I think it worth my while to weave them, and instead of studying how to make it worth men's while to buy my baskets, I studied rather how to avoid the necessity of selling them. The life which men praise and regard as successful is but one kind. Why should we exaggerate any one kind at the expense of the others?

Finding that my fellow-citizens were not likely to offer me any room in the courthouse, or any curacy or living anywhere else, but I must shift for myself, I turned my face more exclusively than ever to the woods, where I was better known. I determined to go into business at once, and not wait to acquire the usual capital, using such slender means as I had already got. My purpose in going to Walden Pond was not to live cheaply nor to live dearly there, but to transact some private business with the fewest obstacles; to be hindered from accomplishing which for want of a little common sense, a little enterprise and business talent, appeared not so sad as foolish.

I have always endeavored to acquire strict business habits; they are indispensable to every man. If your trade is with the Celestial Empire, then some small counting-house on the coast, in some Salem harbor, will be fixture enough. You will export such articles as the country affords, purely native products, much ice and pine timber and a little granite, always in native bottoms. These will be good ventures. To oversee all the details yourself in person; to be at once pilot and captain, and owner and underwriter; to buy and sell and keep the accounts; to read every letter received, and write or read every letter sent; to superintend the discharge of imports night and day; to be upon many parts of the coast almost at the same time—often the richest freight will be discharged upon a Jersey shore—to be your own telegraph, un-

weariedly sweeping the horizon, speaking all passing vessels bound coastwise; to keep up a steady dispatch of commodities, for the supply of such a distant and exorbitant market; to keep yourself informed of the state of the markets, prospects of war and peace everywhere, and anticipate the tendencies of trade and civilization—taking advantage of the results of all exploring expeditions, using new passages and all improvements in navigation—charts to be studied, the position of reefs and new lights and buoys to be ascertained, and ever, and ever, the logarithmic tables to be corrected, for by the error of some calculator the vessel often splits upon a rock that should have reached a friendly pier—there is the untold fate of La Pérouse—universal science to be kept pace with, studying the lives of all great discoverers and navigators, great adventurers and merchants, from Hanno and the Phoenicians down to our day; in fine, account of stock to be taken from time to time, to know how you stand. It is a labor to task the faculties of a man—such problems of profit and loss, of interest, of tare and tret, and gauging of all kinds in it, as demand a universal knowledge.

I have thought that Walden Pond would be a good place for business, not solely on account of the railroad and the

ICE FISHING
Ice in the Neva

ice trade; it offers advantages which it may not be good policy to divulge; it is a good port and a good foundation. No Neva marshes to be filled; though you must everywhere build on piles of your own driving. It is said that a floodtide, with a westerly wind, and ice in the Neva, would sweep St. Petersburg from the face of the earth.

As this business was to be entered into without the usual capital, it may not be easy to conjecture where those means, that will still be indispensable to every such undertaking, were to be obtained. As for Clothing, to come at once to the practical part of the question, perhaps we are led oftener by the love of novelty and a regard for the opinions of men, in procuring it, than by a true utility. Let him who has work to do recollect that the object of clothing is, first, to retain the vital heat, and secondly, in this state of society, to cover nakedness, and he may judge how much of any necessary or important work may be accomplished without adding to his wardrobe. Kings and queens who wear a suit but once, though made by some tailor or dressmaker to their majesties, cannot know the comfort of wearing a suit that fits. They are no better than wooden horses to hang the clean clothes on. Every day our garments become more assimilated to ourselves, receiving the impress of the wearer's character, until we hesitate to lay them aside without such delay and medical appliances and some such solemnity even as our bodies. No man ever stood the lower in my estimation for having a patch in his clothes; yet I am sure that there is greater anxiety, commonly, to have fashionable, or at least clean and unpatched clothes, than to have a sound conscience. But even if the rent is not mended, perhaps the worst vice betrayed is improvidence. I sometimes try my acquaintances by such tests as this—Who could wear a patch, or two extra seams only, over the knee? Most behave as if they believed that their prospects for life would be ruined if they should do it. It would be easier for them to hobble to town with a broken leg than with a broken pantaloon. Often if an accident happens to a gentleman's legs, they can be mended; but if a similar accident happens to the legs of his pantaloons, there is no help for it; for he considers not what is truly respectable but what is respected. We know but few men, a great many coats and breeches. Dress a scarecrow in your last shift, you standing shiftless by, who would not soonest salute the scarecrow? Passing a cornfield the other day, close by a hat and coat on a stake, I recognized the owner of the farm. He was only a little more weather-beaten than when I saw him last. I have heard of a dog that barked at every stranger who approached his master's premises with clothes on, but was easily quieted by a naked thief. It is an interesting question how far men would retain their relative rank if they were divested of their clothes. Could you, in such a case, tell surely of any company of civilized men which belonged to the most respected class? When Madam Pfeiffer, in her adventurous travels round the world, from east to west, had got so near home as Asiatic Russia, she says that she felt the necessity of wearing other than a traveling dress, when she went to meet the authorities, for she "was now in a civilized country, where . . . people are judged of by their clothes." Even in our democratic New England towns the accidental possession of wealth, and its manifestation in dress and equipage alone, obtain for the possessor almost universal respect. But they who yield such respect, numerous as they are, are so far heathen, and need to have a missionary sent to them. Beside, clothes introduced sewing, a kind of work which you may call endless; a woman's dress, at least, is never done.

A man who has at length found something to do will not need to get a new suit to do it in; for him the old will do, that has lain dusty in the garret for an indeterminate period. Old shoes will serve a hero longer than they have served his valet—if a hero ever has a valet—bare feet are older than shoes, and he can make them do. Only they who go to *soirées* and legislative halls must have new coats, coats to change as often as the man changes in them. But if my jacket and trousers, my hat and shoes, are fit to worship God in, they will do; will they not? Who ever saw his old clothes—his old coat, actually worn out—resolved into its primitive elements so that it was not a deed of charity to bestow it on some poor boy, by him perchance to be bestowed on some poorer still, or shall we say richer, who could do with less? I say, beware of all enterprises that require new clothes, and not rather a new wearer of clothes. If there is not a new man, how can the new clothes be made to fit? If you have any enterprise before you, try it in your old clothes. All men want not something to *do with* but something to *do*, or rather something to *be*. Perhaps we should never procure a new suit, however ragged or dirty the old, until we have so conducted, so enterprised or sailed in some way, that we feel like new men in the old, and that to retain it would be like keeping new wine in old bottles. Our molting season, like that of the fowls, must be a crisis in our lives. The loon retires to solitary ponds to spend it. Thus also the snake casts its slough, and the caterpillar its wormy coat, by an internal industry and expansion; for clothes are but our outmost cuticle and mortal coil. Otherwise we shall be found sailing under false colors, and be inevitably cashiered at last by our own opinion, as well as that of mankind.

We don garment after garment, as if we grew like exogenous plants by addition without. Our outside and often thin and fanciful clothes are our epidermis, or false skin, which partakes not of our life, and may be stripped off here and there without fatal injury; our thicker garments, constantly worn, are our cellular integument, or cortex; but our shirts are our liber, or true bark, which cannot be removed without girdling and so destroying the man. I believe that all races at some seasons wear something equivalent to the shirt. It is desirable that a man be clad so simply that he can lay his hands on himself in the dark, and that he live in all respects so compactly and preparedly that, if an enemy take the town, he can, like the old philosopher, walk out the gate empty-handed without anxiety. While one thick garment is, for most purposes, as good as three thin ones, and cheap clothing can be obtained at prices really to suit customers; while a thick coat can be bought for five dollars, which will last as many years, thick pantaloons for two dollars, cowhide boots for a dollar and a half a pair, a summer hat for a quarter of a dollar, and a winter cap for sixty-two and a half cents, or a better be made at home at a nominal cost, where is he so poor that, clad in such a suit, *of his own earning*, there will not be found wise men to do him reverence?

When I ask for a garment of a particular form, my tailoress tells me gravely, "They do not make them so now," not emphasizing the "They" at all, as if she quoted an authority as impersonal as the Fates, and I find it difficult to get made what I want, simply because she cannot believe that I mean what I say, that I am so rash. When I hear this sentence, I am for a moment absorbed in thought, emphasizing to myself each word separately that I may come at the meaning of it, that I may find out by what degree of consanguinity *They* are related to *me*, and what authority they may have in an affair which affects me so nearly; and, finally, I am inclined to answer her with equal mystery, and without any more emphasis of the "they"—"It is true, they did not make them so recently, but they do now." Of what use this measuring of me if she does not measure my character, but only the breadth of my shoulders, as it were a peg to hang the coat on? We worship not the Graces, nor the Parcae, but Fashion. She spins and weaves and cuts with full authority. The head monkey at Paris puts on a traveler's cap, and all the monkeys in America do the same. I sometimes despair of getting anything quite simple and honest done in this world by the help of men. They would have to be passed through a powerful press first, to squeeze their old notions out of them, so that they would not soon get upon their legs again; and then there would be some one in the company with a maggot in his head, hatched from an egg deposited there nobody knows when, for not even fire kills these things, and you would have lost your labor. Nevertheless, we will not forget that some Egyptian wheat was handed down to us by a mummy.

On the whole, I think that it cannot be maintained that dressing has in this or any country risen to the dignity of an art. At present men make shift to wear what they can get. Like shipwrecked sailors, they put on what they can find on the beach, and at a little distance, whether of space or time, laugh at each other's masquerade. Every generation laughs at the old fashions, but follows religiously the new. We are amused at beholding the costume of Henry VIII, or Queen Elizabeth, as much as if it was that of the King and Queen of the Cannibal Islands. All costume off a man is pitiful or grotesque. It is only the serious eye peering from and the sincere life passed within it which restrain laughter and consecrate the costume of any people. Let Harlequin be taken with a fit of the colic and his trappings will have to serve that mood too. When the soldier is hit by a cannonball, rags are as becoming as purple.

The childish and savage taste of men and women for new patterns keeps how many shaking and squinting through kaleidoscopes that they may discover the particular figure which this generation requires today. The manufacturers have learned that this taste is merely whimsical. Of two patterns which differ only by a few threads more or less of a particular color, the one will be sold readily, the other lie on the shelf, though it frequently happens that after the lapse of a season the latter becomes the most fashionable. Comparatively, tattooing is not the hideous custom which it is called. It is not barbarous merely because the printing is skin-deep and unalterable.

I cannot believe that our factory system is the best mode by which men may get clothing. The condition of the operatives is becoming every day more like that of the English; and it cannot be wondered at, since, as far as I have heard or observed, the principal object is not that mankind may be well and honestly clad but, unquestionably, that the corporations may be enriched. In the long run men hit only what they aim at. Therefore, though they should fail immediately, they had better aim at something high.

As for a Shelter, I will not deny that this is now a necessary of life, though there are instances of men having done without it for long periods in colder countries than this. Samuel Laing says that "the Laplander in his skin dress, and in a skin bag which he puts over his head and shoulders, will sleep night after night on the snow . . . in a degree of cold which would extinguish the life of one exposed to it in any woollen clothing." He had seen them asleep thus. Yet he adds, "They are not hardier than other people." But, probably, man did not live long on the earth without discovering the convenience which there is in a house, the domestic comforts, which phrase may have originally signified the satisfactions of the house more than of the family; though these must be extremely partial and occasional in those climates where the house is associated in our thoughts with winter or the rainy season chiefly, and two-thirds of the year, except for a parasol, is unnecessary. In our climate, in the summer, it was formerly almost solely a covering at night. In the Indian gazettes a wigwam was the symbol of a day's march, and a row of them cut or painted on the bark of a tree signified that so many times they had camped. Man was not made so large-limbed and robust but that he must seek to narrow his world, and wall in a space such as fitted him. He was at first bare and out-of-doors; but though this was pleasant enough in serene and warm weather, by daylight, the rainy season and the winter, to say nothing of the torrid sun, would perhaps have nipped his race in the bud if he had not made haste to clothe himself with the shelter of a house. Adam and Eve, according to the fable, wore the bower before other clothes. Man wanted a home, a place of warmth, or comfort, first of physical warmth, then the warmth of the affections.

We may imagine a time when, in the infancy of the human race, some enterprising mortal crept into a hollow in a rock for shelter. Every child begins the world again, to some extent, and loves to stay outdoors, even in wet and cold. It plays house, as well as horse, having an instinct for it. Who does not remember the interest with which, when young, he looked at shelving rocks, or any approach to a cave? It was the natural yearning of that portion of our most primitive ancestor which still survived in us. From the cave we have advanced to roofs of palm leaves, of bark and boughs, of linen woven and stretched, of grass and straw, of boards and shingles, of stones and tiles. At last, we know not what it is to live in the open air, and our lives are domestic in more senses than we think. From the hearth to the field is a great distance. It would be well, perhaps, if we were to spend more of our days and nights without any obstruction between us and the celestial bodies, if the poet did not speak so much from under a

CABIN IN THE WOODS
A little Yankee shrewdness

roof, or the saint dwell there so long. Birds do not sing in caves, nor do doves cherish their innocence in dovecots.

However, if one designs to construct a dwelling-house, it behooves him to exercise a little Yankee shrewdness, lest after all he find himself in a workhouse, a labyrinth without a clue, a museum, an almshouse, a prison, or a splendid mausoleum instead. Consider first how slight a shelter is absolutely necessary. I have seen Penobscot Indians, in this town, living in tents of thin cotton cloth, while the snow was nearly a foot deep around them, and I thought that they would be glad to have it deeper to keep out the wind. Formerly, when how to get my living honestly, with freedom left for my proper pursuits, was a question which vexed me even more than it does now, for unfortunately I am become somewhat callous, I used to see a large box by the railroad, six feet long by three wide, in which the laborers locked up their tools at night; and it suggested to me that every man who was hard pushed might get such a one for a dollar, and, having bored a few auger holes in it, to admit the air at least, get into it when it rained and at night, and hook down the lid, and so have freedom in his love, and in his soul be free. This did not appear the worst, nor by any means a despicable alternative. You could sit up as late as you pleased, and, whenever you got up, go abroad without any landlord or house-lord dogging you for rent. Many a man is harassed to death to pay the rent of a larger and more luxurious box who would not have frozen to death in such a box as this. I am far from jesting. Economy is a subject which admits of being treated with levity, but it cannot so be disposed of. A comfortable house for a rude and hardy race, that lived mostly out-of-doors, was once made here almost entirely of such materials as Nature furnished ready to their hands. Gookin, who was superintendent of the Indians subject to the Massachusetts

Colony, writing in 1674, says, "The best of their houses are covered very neatly, tight and warm, with barks of trees, slipped from their bodies at those seasons when the sap is up, and made into great flakes, with pressure of weighty timber, when they are green. . . . The meaner sort are covered with mats which they make of a kind of bulrush, and are also indifferently tight and warm, but not so good as the former. . . . Some I have seen, sixty or a hundred feet long and thirty feet broad. . . . I have often lodged in their wigwams, and found them as warm as the best English houses." He adds that they were commonly carpeted and lined within with well-wrought embroidered mats, and were furnished with various utensils. The Indians had advanced so far as to regulate the effect of the wind by a mat suspended over the hole in the roof and moved by a string. Such a lodge was in the first instance constructed in a day or two at most, and taken down and put up in a few hours; and every family owned one, or its apartment in one.

In the savage state every family owns a shelter as good as the best, and sufficient for its coarser and simpler wants; but I think that I speak within bounds when I say that, though the birds of the air have their nests, and the foxes their holes, and the savages their wigwams, in modern civilized society not more than one-half the families own a shelter. In the large towns and cities, where civilization especially prevails, the number of those who own a shelter is a very small fraction of the whole. The rest pay an annual tax for this outside garment of all, become indispensable summer and winter, which would buy a village of Indian wigwams, but now helps to keep them poor as long as they live. I do not mean to insist here on the disadvantage of hiring compared with owning, but it is evident that the savage owns his shelter because it costs so little, while the civilized man hires his commonly because he cannot afford to own it; nor can he, in the long run, any better afford to hire. But, answers one, by merely paying this tax the poor civilized man secures an abode which is a palace compared with the savage's. An annual rent of from twenty-five to a hundred dollars (these are the country rates) entitles him to the benefit of the improvements of centuries, spacious apartments, clean paint and paper, Rumford fireplace, back plastering, Venetian blinds, copper pump, spring lock, a commodious cellar, and many other things. But how happens it that he who is said to enjoy these things is so commonly a *poor* civilized man, while the savage, who has them not, is rich as a savage? If it is asserted that civilization is a real advance in the condition of man— and I think that it is, though only the wise improve their advantages—it must be shown that it has produced better dwellings without making them more costly; and the cost of a thing is the amount of what I will call life which is required to be exchanged for it, immediately or in the long run. An average house in this neighborhood costs perhaps eight hundred dollars, and to lay up this sum will take from ten to fifteen years of the laborer's life, even if he is not encumbered with a family—estimating the pecuniary value of every man's labor at one dollar a day, for if some receive more, others receive less— so that he must have spent more than half his life commonly before *his* wigwam will be earned. If we suppose him to pay a rent instead, this is but a doubtful choice of evils. Would the savage have been wise to exchange his wigwam for a palace on these terms?

It may be guessed that I reduce almost the whole advantage of holding this superfluous property as a fund in store against the future, so far as the individual is concerned, mainly to the defraying of funeral expenses. But perhaps a man is not required to bury himself. Nevertheless this points to an important distinction between the civilized man and the savage; and, no doubt, they have designs on us for our benefit, in making the life of a civilized people an *institution*, in which the life of the individual is to a great extent absorbed, in order to preserve and perfect that of the race. But I wish to show at what a sacrifice this advantage is at present obtained, and to suggest that we may possibly so live as to secure all the advantage without suffering any of the disadvantage. What mean ye by saying that the poor ye have always with you, or that the fathers have eaten sour grapes, and the children's teeth are set on edge?

As I live, saith the Lord God, ye shall not have occasion any more to use this proverb in Israel.

Behold all souls are mine; as the soul of the father, so also the soul of the son is mine: the soul that sinneth, it shall die.

When I consider my neighbors, the farmers of Concord, who are at least as well off as the other classes, I find that for the most part they have been toiling twenty, thirty, or forty years, that they may become the real owners of their farms, which commonly they have inherited with encumbrances, or else bought with hired money—and we may regard one-third of that toil as the cost of their houses—but commonly they have not paid for them yet. It is true, the encumbrances sometimes outweigh the value of the farm, so that the farm itself becomes one great encumbrance, and still a man is found to inherit it, being well acquainted with it, as he says. On applying to the assessors, I am surprised to learn that they cannot at once name a dozen in the town who own their farms free and clear. If you would know the history of these homesteads, inquire at the bank where they are mortgaged. The man who has actually paid for his farm with labor on it is so rare that every neighbor can point to him. I doubt if there are three such men in Concord. What has been said of the merchants, that a very large majority, even ninety-seven in a hundred, are sure to fail, is equally true of the farmers. With regard to the merchants, however, one of them says pertinently that a great part of their failures are not genuine pecuniary failures, but merely failures to fulfill their engagements, because it is inconvenient; that is, it is the moral character that breaks down. But this puts an infinitely worse face on the matter, and suggests, beside, that probably not even the other three succeed in saving their souls, but are perchance bankrupt in a worse sense than they who fail honestly. Bankruptcy and repudiation are the springboards from which much of our civilization vaults and turns its somersets, but the savage stands on the unelastic plank of famine. Yet the Middlesex Cattle Show goes off here with *éclat* annually, as if all the joints of the agricultural machine were suent.

The farmer is endeavoring to solve the problem of a livelihood by a formula more complicated than the problem itself. To get his shoestrings he speculates in herds of cattle. With consummate skill he has set his trap with a hairspring to catch comfort and independence, and then, as he turned away, got his own leg into it. This is the reason he is poor; and for a similar reason we are all poor in respect to a thousand savage comforts, though surrounded by luxuries. As Chapman sings,

> The false society of men—
> —for earthly greatness
> All heavenly comforts rarefies to air.

And when the farmer has got his house, he may not be the richer but the poorer for it, and it be the house that has got him. As I understand it, that was a valid objection urged by Momus against the house which Minerva made, that she "had not made it movable, by which means a bad neighborhood might be avoided"; and it may still be urged, for our houses are such unwieldy property that we are often imprisoned rather than housed in them; and the bad neighborhood to be avoided is our own scurvy selves. I know one or two families, at least, in this town, who, for nearly a generation, have been wishing to sell their houses in the outskirts and move into the village, but have not been able to accomplish it, and only death will set them free.

Granted that the *majority* are able at last either to own or hire the modern house with all its improvements. While civilization has been improving our houses, it has not equally improved the men who are to inhabit them. It has created palaces, but it was not so easy to create noblemen and kings. And *if the civilized man's pursuits are no worthier than the savage's, if he is employed the greater part of his life in obtaining gross necessaries and comforts merely, why should he have a better dwelling than the former?*

But how do the poor *minority* fare? Perhaps it will be found that just in proportion as some have been placed in outward circumstances above the savage, others have been degraded below him. The luxury of one class is counterbalanced by the indigence of another. On the one side is the palace, on the other are the almshouse and "silent poor." The myriads who built the pyramids to be the tombs of the Pharaohs were fed on garlic, and it may be were not decently buried themselves. The mason who finishes the cornice of the palace returns at night perchance to a hut not so good as a wigwam. It is a mistake to suppose that, in a country where the usual evidences of civilization exist, the condition of a very large body of the inhabitants may not be as degraded as that of savages. I refer to the degraded poor, not now to the degraded rich. To know this I should not need to look farther than to the shanties which everywhere border our railroads, that last improvement in civilization; where I see in my daily walks human beings living in sties, and all winter with an open door, for the sake of light, without any visible, often imaginable, woodpile, and the forms of both old and young are permanently contracted by the long habit of shrinking from cold and misery, and the development of all their limbs and faculties is checked. It certainly is fair to look at that class by whose labor the works which distinguish this generation are accomplished. Such too, to a greater or less extent, is the condition of the operatives of every denomination in England, which is the great workhouse of the world. Or I could refer you to Ireland, which is marked as one of the white or enlightened spots on the map. Contrast the physical condition of the Irish with that of the North American Indian, or the South Sea Islander, or any other savage race before it was degraded by contact with the civilized man. Yet I have no doubt that that people's rulers are as wise as the average of civilized rulers. Their condition only proves what squalidness may consist with civilization. I hardly need refer now to the laborers in our Southern States who produce the staple exports of this country, and are themselves a staple production of the South. But to confine myself to those who are said to be in *moderate* circumstances.

Most men appear never to have considered what a house is, and are actually though needlessly poor all their lives because they think that they must have such a one as their neighbors have. As if one were to wear any sort of coat which the tailor might cut out for him, or, gradually leaving off palm-leaf hat or cap of woodchuck skin, complain of hard times because he could not afford to buy him a crown! It is possible to invent a house still more convenient and luxurious than we have, which yet all would admit that man could not afford to pay for. Shall we always study to obtain more of these things, and not sometimes to be content with less? Shall the respectable citizen thus gravely teach, by precept and example, the necessity of the young man's providing a certain number of superfluous glow-shoes, and umbrellas, and empty guest chambers for empty guests, before he dies? Why should not our furniture be as simple as the Arab's or the Indian's? When I think of the benefactors of the race, whom we have apotheosized as messengers from heaven, bearers of divine gifts to man, I do not see in my mind any retinue at their heels, any carload of fashionable furniture. Or what if I were to allow—would it not be a singular allowance?—that our furniture should be more complex than the Arab's, in proportion as we are morally and intellectually his superiors! At present our houses are cluttered and defiled with it, and a good housewife would sweep out the greater part into the dust hole, and not leave her morning's work undone. Morning work! By the blushes of Aurora and the music of Memnon, what should be man's *morning work* in this world? I had three pieces of limestone on my desk, but I was terrified to find that they required to be dusted daily, when the furniture of my mind was all undusted still, and I threw them out the window in disgust. How, then, could I have a furnished house? I would rather sit in the open air, for no dust gathers on the grass, unless where man has broken ground.

It is the luxurious and dissipated who set the fashions which the herd so diligently follow. The traveler who stops at the best houses, so-called, soon discovers this, for the publicans presume him to be a Sardanapalus, and if he resigned himself to their tender mercies he would soon be completely emasculated. I think that in the railroad car we are inclined to spend more on luxury than on safety and convenience, and it threatens without attaining these to become no better than a modern drawingroom, with its divans, and ottomans, and sunshades, and a hundred other oriental things, which we are taking west with us, invented for the ladies of the harem and the effeminate natives of the Celestial Empire, which Jonathan should be ashamed to know the names of. I would rather sit on a pumpkin and have it all to myself than be crowded on a velvet cushion. I would rather ride on earth in an ox-cart, with a free circulation, than go to heaven in the fancy car of an excursion train and breathe a *malaria* all the way.

The very simplicity and nakedness of man's life in the primitive ages imply this advantage, at least, that they left him still but a sojourner in nature. When he was refreshed with food and sleep, he contemplated his journey again. He dwelt, as it were, in a tent in this world, and was either threading the valleys, or crossing the plains, or climbing the mountaintops. But lo! men have become the tools of their tools. The man who independently plucked the fruits when he was hungry is become a farmer; and he who stood under a tree for shelter, a housekeeper. We now no longer camp as for a night, but have settled down on earth and forgotten heaven. We have adopted Christianity merely as an improved method of *agri*-culture. We have built for this world a family mansion, and for the next a family tomb. The best works of art are the expression of man's struggle to free himself from this condition, but the effect of our art is merely to make this low state comfortable and that higher state to be forgotten. There is actually no place in this village for a work of *fine* art, if any had come down to us, to stand, for our lives, our houses and streets, furnish no proper pedestal for it. There is not a nail to hang a picture on, nor a shelf to receive the bust of a hero or a saint. When I consider how our houses are built and paid for, or not paid for, and their internal economy man-

aged and sustained, I wonder that the floor does not give way under the visitor while he is admiring the gewgaws upon the mantelpiece, and let him through into the cellar, to some solid and honest though earthy foundation. I cannot but perceive that this so-called rich and refined life is a thing jumped at, and I do not get on in the enjoyment of the *fine* arts which adorn it, my attention being wholly occupied with the jump; for I remember that the greatest genuine leap, due to human muscles alone, on record, is that of certain wandering Arabs, who are said to have cleared twenty-five feet on level ground. Without factitious support, man is sure to come to earth again beyond that distance. The first question which I am tempted to put to the proprietor of such great impropriety is, "Who bolsters you? Are you one of the ninety-seven who fail, or the three who succeed?" Answer me these questions, and then perhaps I may look at your baubles and find them ornamental. The cart before the horse is neither beautiful nor useful. Before we can adorn our houses with beautiful objects the walls must be stripped, and our lives must be stripped, and beautiful housekeeping and beautiful living be laid for a foundation: now, a taste for the beautiful is most cultivated out-of-doors, where there is no house and no housekeeper.

Old Johnson, in his "Wonder-Working Providence," speaking of the first settlers of this town, with whom he was contemporary, tells us that "they burrow themselves in the earth for their first shelter under some hillside, and, casting the soil aloft upon timber, they make a smoky fire against the earth, at the highest side." They did not "provide them houses," says he, "till the earth, by the Lord's blessing, brought forth bread to feed them," and the first year's crop was so light that "they were forced to cut their bread very thin for a long season." The secretary of the Province of New Netherland, writing in

Dutch, in 1650, for the information of those who wished to take up land there, states more particularly that "those in New Netherland, and especially in New England, who have no means to build farmhouses at first according to their wishes, dig a square pit in the ground, cellar fashion, six or seven feet deep, as long and as broad as they think proper, case the earth inside with wood all round the wall, and line the wood with the bark of trees or something else to prevent the caving in of the earth; floor this cellar with plank, and wainscot it overhead for a ceiling, raise a roof of spars clear up, and cover the spars with bark or green sods, so that they can live dry and warm in these houses with their entire families for two, three, and four years, it being understood that partitions are run through those cellars which are adapted to the size of the family. The wealthy and principal men in New England, in the beginning of the colonies, commenced their first dwelling-houses in this fashion for two reasons: firstly, in order not to waste time in building, and not to want food the next season; secondly, in order not to discourage poor laboring people whom they brought over in numbers from Fatherland. In the course of three or four years, when the country became adapted to agriculture, they built themselves handsome houses, spending on them several thousands."

In this course which our ancestors took there was a show of prudence at least, as if their principle were to satisfy the more pressing wants first. But are the more pressing wants satisfied now? When I think of acquiring for myself one of our luxurious dwellings, I am deterred, for, so to speak, the country is not yet adapted to *human* culture, and we are still forced to cut our *spiritual* bread far thinner than our fore-

fathers did their wheaten. Not that all architectural ornament is to be neglected even in the rudest periods; but let our houses first be lined with beauty, where they come in contact with our lives, like the tenement of the shell-fish, and not overlaid with it. But, alas! I have been inside one or two of them, and know what they are lined with.

Though we are not so degenerate but that we might possibly live in a cave or a wigwam or wear skins today, it certainly is better to accept the advantages, though so dearly bought, which the invention and industry of mankind offer. In such a neighborhood as this, boards and shingles, lime and bricks, are cheaper and more easily obtained than suitable caves, or whole logs, or bark in sufficient quantities, or even well-tempered clay or flat stones. I speak understandingly on this subject, for I have made myself acquainted with it both theoretically and practically. With a little

WALDEN TREES
*I cut down some
tall arrowy white pines.*

more wit we might use these materials so as to become richer than the richest now are, and make our civilization a blessing. The civilized man is a more experienced and wiser savage. But to make haste to my own experiment.

Near the end of March, 1845, I borrowed an ax and went down to the woods by Walden Pond, nearest to where I intended to build my house, and began to cut down some tall, arrowy white pines, still in their youth, for timber. It is difficult to begin without borrowing, but perhaps it is the most generous course thus to permit your fellow-men to have an interest in your enterprise. The owner of the ax, as he released his hold on it, said that it was the apple of his eye; but I returned it sharper than I received it. It was a pleasant hillside where I worked, covered with pine woods, through which I looked out on the pond, and a small open field in the woods where pines and hickories were springing up. The ice in the pond was not yet dissolved, though there were some open spaces, and it was all dark-colored and saturated with water. There were some slight flurries of snow during the days that I worked there; but for the most part when I came out on to the railroad, on my way home, its yellow sand-heap stretched away gleaming in the hazy atmosphere, and the rails shone in the spring sun, and I heard the lark and pewee and other birds already come to commence another year with us. They were pleasant spring days, in which the winter of man's discontent was thawing as well as the earth, and the life that had lain torpid began to stretch itself. One day, when my ax had come off and I had cut a green hickory for a wedge, driving it with a stone, and had placed the whole to soak in a pond-hole in order to swell the wood, I saw a striped snake run into the water, and he lay on the bottom, apparently without inconvenience, as long as I stayed there, or more than a quarter of an

hour; perhaps because he had not yet fairly come out of the torpid state. It appeared to me that for a like reason men remain in their present low and primitive condition; but if they should feel the influence of the spring of springs arousing them, they would of necessity rise to a higher and more ethereal life. I had previously seen the snakes in frosty mornings in my path with portions of their bodies still numb and inflexible, waiting for the sun to thaw them. On the 1st of April it rained and melted the ice, and the early part of the day, which was very foggy, I heard a stray goose groping about over the pond and cackling as if lost, or like the spirit of the fog.

So I went on for some days cutting and hewing timber, and also studs and rafters, all with my narrow ax, not having many communicable or scholar-like thoughts, singing to myself,

> Men say they know many things;
> But lo! they have taken wings—
> The arts and sciences,
> And a thousand appliances:
> The wind that blows
> Is all that anybody knows.

I hewed the main timbers six inches square, most of the studs on two sides only, and the rafters and floor timbers on one side, leaving the rest of the bark on, so that they were just as straight and much stronger than sawed ones. Each stick was carefully mortised or tenoned by its stump, for I had borrowed other tools by this time. My days in the woods were not very long ones; yet I usually carried my dinner of bread and butter, and read the newspaper in which it was wrapped, at noon, sitting amid the green pine boughs which I had cut off, and to my bread was imparted some of their fragrance, for my hands were covered with a thick coat of pitch. Before I had done I was more the friend than the foe of the pine tree, though I had cut down some of them, having become better acquainted with it. Sometimes a rambler in the wood was attracted by the sound of my ax, and we chatted pleasantly over the chips which I had made.

By the middle of April, for I made no haste in my work, but rather made the most of it, my house was framed and ready for the raising. I had already bought the shanty of James Collins, an Irishman who worked on the Fitchburg Railroad, for boards. James Collins' shanty was considered an uncommonly fine one. When I called to see it he was not at home. I walked about the outside, at first unobserved from within, the window was so deep and high. It was of small dimensions, with a peaked cottage roof, and not much else to be seen, the dirt being raised five feet all around as if it were a compost heap. The roof was the soundest part, though a good deal warped and made brittle by the sun. Doorsill there was none, but a perennial passage for the hens under the door-board. Mrs. C. came to the door and asked me to view it from the inside. The hens were driven in by my approach. It was dark, and had a dirt floor for the most part, dank, clammy, and aguish, only here a board and there a board which would not bear removal. She lighted a lamp to show me the inside of the roof and the walls, and also that the board floor extended under the bed, warning me not to step into the cellar, a sort of dust hole two feet deep. In her own words, they were "good boards overhead, good boards all around, and a good window," of two whole squares originally, only the cat had passed out that way lately. There was a stove, a bed, and a place to sit, an infant in the house where it was born, a silk parasol, gilt-framed looking-glass, and a patent new coffee-mill nailed to an oak sapling, all told. The bargain was soon concluded, for James had in the meanwhile returned. I to pay four dollars and twenty-five cents tonight, he to vacate at five tomorrow morning, selling to nobody else meanwhile: I to take possession at six. It were well, he said, to be there early, and anticipate certain indistinct but wholly unjust claims on the score of ground rent and fuel. This he assured me was the only encumbrance. At six I passed him and his family on the road. One large bundle held their all—bed, coffee-mill, looking-glass, hens—all but the cat; she took to the woods and became a wild cat, and, as I learned afterward, trod in a trap set for woodchucks, and so became a dead cat at last.

I took down this dwelling the same morning, drawing the nails, and removed it to the pond-side by small cartloads, spreading the boards on the grass there to bleach and warp back again in the sun. One early thrush gave me a note or two as I drove along the woodland path. I was informed treacherously by a young Patrick that neighbor Seeley, an Irishman, in the intervals of the carting, transferred the still tolerable, straight, and drivable nails, staples, and spikes to his pocket, and then stood when I came back to pass the time of day, and look freshly up, unconcerned, with spring thoughts, at the devastation; there being a dearth of work, as he said. He was there to represent spectatordom, and help make this seemingly insignificant event one with the removal of the gods of Troy.

I dug my cellar in the side of a hill sloping to the south, where a woodchuck had formerly dug his burrow, down through sumac and blackberry roots, and the lowest stain of vegetation, six feet square by seven deep, to a fine sand where potatoes would not freeze in any winter. The sides were left shelving, and not stoned; but the sun having never shone on them, the sand still keeps its place. It was but two hours' work. I took particular pleasure in this breaking of ground, for in almost all latitudes men dig into the earth for an equable temperature. Under the most splendid house in the city is still to be found the cellar where they store their roots as of old, and long after the super-structure has disappeared posterity remark its dent in the earth. The house is still but a sort of porch at the entrance of a burrow.

At length, in the beginning of May, with the help of some of my acquaintances, rather to improve so good an occasion for neighborliness than from any necessity, I set up the frame of my house. No man was ever more honored in the character of his raisers than I. They are destined, I trust, to assist at the raising of loftier structures one day. I began to occupy my house on the 4th of July, as soon as it was boarded and roofed, for the boards were carefully feather-edged and lapped, so that it was perfectly impervious to rain, but before boarding I laid the foundation of a chimney at one end, bringing two cartloads of stones up the hill from the pond in my arms. I built the chimney after my hoeing in the fall, before a fire became necessary for warmth, doing my cooking in the mean-while out of doors on the ground, early in the morning: which mode I still think is in some respects more convenient and agree-able than the usual one. When it stormed before my bread was baked, I fixed a few boards over the fire, and sat under them to watch my loaf, and passed some pleasant hours in that way. In those days, when my hands were much employed, I read but little, but the least scraps of paper which lay on the ground, my holder, or tablecloth, afforded as much entertain-ment, in fact answered the same purpose as the Iliad.

It would be worth the while to build still more deliberately than I did, consider-ing, for instance, what foundation a door, a window, a cellar, a garret, have in the nature of man, and perchance never raising any superstructure until we found a better reason for it than our temporal necessities even. There is some of the same fitness in

a man's building his own house that there is in a bird's building its own nest. Who knows but if men constructed their dwell-ings with their own hands, and provided food for themselves and families simply and honestly enough, the poetic faculty would be universally developed, as birds universally sing when they are so engaged? But alas! we do like cowbirds and cuckoos, which lay their eggs in nests which other birds have built, and cheer no traveler with their chattering and unmusical notes. Shall we forever resign the pleasure of construc-tion to the carpenter? What does architec-ture amount to in the experience of the mass of men? I never in all my walks came across a man engaged in so simple and natural an occupation as building his house. We belong to the community. It is not the tailor alone who is the ninth part of a man; it is as much the preacher, and the merchant, and the farmer. Where is this division of labor to end? and what object does it finally serve? No doubt another *may* also think for me; but it is not therefore desirable that he should do so to the ex-clusion of my thinking for myself.

True, there are architects so called in this country, and I have heard of one at least possessed with the idea of making architectural ornaments have a core of truth, a necessity, and hence a beauty, as if it were a revelation to him. All very well perhaps from his point of view, but only a little better than the common dilettant-ism. A sentimental reformer in architecture, he began at the cornice, not at the founda-tion. It was only how to put a core of truth within the ornaments, that every sugar-plum, in fact, might have an almond or caraway seed in it—though I hold that almonds are most wholesome without the sugar—and not how the inhabitant, the in-dweller, might build truly within and without, and let the ornaments take care of themselves. What reasonable man ever supposed that ornaments were something outward and in the skin merely—that the tortoise got his spotted shell, or the shell-fish its mother-o'-pearl tints, by such a contract as the inhabitants of Broadway their Trinity Church? But a man has no more to do with the style of architecture of his house than a tortoise with that of its shell: nor need the soldier be so idle as to try to paint the precise *color* of his virtue on his standard. The enemy will find it out. He may turn pale when the trial comes. This man seemed to me to lean over the cornice, and timidly whisper his half-truth to the rude occupants who really knew it better than he. What of architectural beauty I now see, I know has gradually grown from within outward, out of the necessities and character of the indweller, who is the only builder—out of some unconscious truthfulness, and nobleness, without ever a thought for the appearance; and whatever additional beauty of this kind is destined to be produced will be preceded by a like unconscious beauty of life. The most interesting dwellings in this country, as the painter knows, are the most unpretending, humble log huts and cottages of the poor commonly; it is the life of the inhabitants whose shells they are, and not any peculiarity in their surfaces merely, which makes them *picturesque*; and equally interesting will be the citizen's suburban box, when his life shall be as simple and as agreeable to the imagination, and there is as little straining after effect in the style of his dwelling. A great proportion of architectural ornaments are literally hollow, and a September gale would strip them off, like borrowed plumes, without injury to the substantials. They can do without *architecture* who have no olives nor wines in the cellar. What if an equal ado were made about the ornaments of style in literature, and the architects of our Bibles spent as much time about their cornices as the architects of our churches do? So are made the *belles-lettres* and the *beaux-arts* and their professors. Much it concerns a man, forsooth, how a few sticks are slanted over him or under him, and what colors are daubed upon his box. It would signify somewhat, if, in any earnest sense, *he* slanted them and daubed it; but the spirit having departed out of the tenant, it is of a piece with constructing his own coffin—the architecture of the grave—and "carpenter" is but another name for "coffin-maker." One man says, in his despair or indifference to life, take up a handful of the earth at your feet, and paint your house that color. Is he thinking of his last and narrow house? Toss up a copper for it as well. What an abundance of leisure he must have! Why do you take up a handful of dirt? Better paint your house your own complexion; let it turn pale or blush for you. An enterprise to improve the style of cottage architecture! When you have got my ornaments ready, I will wear them.

Before winter I built a chimney, and shingled the sides of my house, which were already impervious to rain, with imperfect and sappy shingles made of the first slice of the log, whose edges I was obliged to straighten with a plane.

I have thus a tight shingled and plastered house, ten feet wide by fifteen long, and eight-feet posts, with a garret and a closet, a large window on each side, two trap-doors, one door at the end, and a brick fireplace opposite. The exact cost of my house, paying the usual price for such materials as I used, but not counting the work, all of which was done by myself, was as follows: and I give the details because very few are able to tell exactly what their houses cost, and fewer still, if any, the separate cost of the various materials which compose them:

Boards $8.03½
   Mostly shanty boards.
Refuse shingles for roof and sides 4.00
Laths 1.25
Two second-hand windows with
   glass 2.43

One thousand old brick	4.00
Two casks of lime	2.40
That was high.	
Hair	0.31
More than I needed.	
Mantle-tree iron	0.15
Nails	3.90
Hinges and screws	0.14
Latch	0.10
Chalk	0.01
Transportation	1.40
I carried a good part on my back.	

In all	$28.12½

These are all the materials, excepting the timber, stones, and sand, which I claimed by squatter's right. I have also a small woodshed adjoining, made chiefly of the stuff which was left after building the house.

I intend to build me a house which will surpass any on the main street in Concord in grandeur and luxury, as soon as it pleases me as much and will cost me no more than my present one.

I thus found that the student who wishes for a shelter can obtain one for a lifetime at an expense not greater than the rent which he now pays annually. If I seem to boast more than is becoming, my excuse is that I brag for humanity rather than for myself; and my shortcomings and inconsistencies do not affect the truth of my statement. Notwithstanding much cant and hypocrisy—chaff which I find it difficult to separate from my wheat, but for which I am as sorry as any man—I will breathe freely and stretch myself in this respect, it is such a relief to both the moral and physical system; and I am resolved that I will not through humility become the devil's attorney. I will endeavor to speak a good word for the truth. At Cambridge College the mere rent of a student's room, which is only a little larger than my own, is thirty dollars each year, though the corporation had the ad-

vantage of building thirty-two side by side and under one roof, and the occupant suffers the inconvenience of many and noisy neighbors, and perhaps a residence in the fourth story. I cannot but think that if we had more true wisdom in these respects, not only less education would be needed, because, forsooth, more would already have been acquired, but the pecuniary expense of getting an education would in a great measure vanish. Those conveniences which the student requires at Cambridge or elsewhere cost him or somebody else ten times as great a sacrifice of life as they would with proper management on both sides. Those things for which the most money is demanded are never the things which the student most wants. Tuition, for instance, is an important item in the term bill, while for the far more valuable education which he gets by associating with the most cultivated of his contemporaries no charge is made. The mode of founding a college is, commonly, to get up a subscription of dollars and cents, and then, following blindly the principles of a division of labor to its extreme—a principle which should never be followed but with circumspection—to call in a contractor who makes this a subject of speculation, and he employs Irishmen or other operatives actually to lay the foundation, while the students that are to be are said to be fitting themselves for it; and for these oversights successive generations have to pay. I think that it would be *better than this*, for the students, or those who desire to be benefited by it, even to lay the foundation themselves. The student who secures his coveted leisure and retirement by systematically shirking any labor necessary to man obtains but an ignoble and unprofitable leisure, defrauding himself of the experience which alone can make leisure fruitful. "But," says one, "you do not mean that the students should go to work with their hands instead of their heads?" I do not mean that exactly, but I mean something which he might think a good deal like that; I mean that they should not *play* life, or *study* it merely, while the community supports them at this expensive game, but earnestly *live* it from beginning to end. How could youths better learn to live than by at once trying the experiment of living? Methinks this would exercise their minds as much as mathematics. If I wished a boy to know something about the arts and sciences, for instance, I would not pursue the common course, which is merely to send him into the neighborhood of some professor, where anything is professed and practiced but the art of life; to survey the world through a telescope or a microscope, and never with his natural eye; to study chemistry, and not learn how his bread is made, or mechanics, and not learn how it is earned; to discover new satellites to Neptune, and not detect the motes in his eyes, or to what vagabond he is a satellite himself; or to be devoured by the monsters that swarm all around him, while contemplating the monsters in a drop of vinegar. Which would have advanced the most at the end of a month: the boy who had made his own jackknife from the ore which he had dug and smelted, reading as much as would be necessary for this, or the boy who had attended the lectures on metallurgy at the Institute in the meanwhile, and had received a Rodgers penknife from his father? Which would be most likely to cut his fingers? . . . To my astonishment I was informed on leaving college that I had studied navigation!— why, if I had taken one turn down the harbor I should have known more about it. Even the *poor* student studies and is taught only *political* economy, while that economy of living which is synonymous with philosophy is not even sincerely professed in our colleges. The consequence is, that while he is reading Adam Smith, Ricardo, and Say, he runs his father in debt irretrievably.

As with our colleges, so with a hundred "modern improvements"; there is an illusion about them; there is not always a positive advance. The devil goes on exacting compound interest to the last for his early share and numerous succeeding investments in them. Our inventions are wont to be pretty toys, which distract our attention from serious things. They are but improved means to an unimproved end, an end which it was already but too easy to arrive at; as railroads lead to Boston or New York. We are in great haste to construct a magnetic telegraph from Maine to Texas; but Maine and Texas, it may be, have nothing important to communicate. Either is in such a predicament as the man who was earnest to be introduced to a distinguished deaf woman, but when he was presented, and one end of her ear trumpet was put into his hand, had nothing to say. As if the main object were to talk fast and not to talk sensibly. We are eager to tunnel under the Atlantic and bring the Old World some weeks nearer to the New; but perchance the first news that will leak through into the broad, flapping American ear will be that the Princess Adelaide has the whooping cough. After all, the man whose horse trots a mile in a minute does not carry the most important messages; he is not an evangelist, nor does he come round eating locusts and wild honey. I doubt if Flying Childers ever carried a peck of corn to mill.

One says to me, "I wonder that you do not lay up money; you love to travel; you might take the cars and go to Fitchburg today and see the country." But I am wiser than that. I have learned that the swiftest traveler is he that goes afoot. I say to my friend, Suppose we try who will get there first. The distance is thirty miles; the fare ninety cents. That is almost a day's wages. I remember when wages were sixty cents a day for laborers on this very road. Well, I start now on foot, and get there before night; I have traveled at that rate by the

FITCHBURG RAILROAD
*I learned that the swiftest
traveler is he that goes afoot*

the depot, and the conductor shouts "All aboard!" when the smoke is blown away and the vapor condensed, it will be perceived that a few are riding, but the rest are run over—and it will be called, and will be, "A melancholy accident." No doubt they can ride at last who shall have earned their fare, that is, if they survive so long, but they will probably have lost their elasticity and desire to travel by that time. This spending of the best part of one's life earning money in order to enjoy a questionable liberty during the least valuable part of it reminds me of the Englishman who went to India to make a fortune first, in order that he might return to England and live the life of a poet. He should have gone up garret at once. "What!" exclaim a million Irishmen starting up from all the shanties in the land, "is not this railroad which we have built a good thing?" Yes, I answer, *comparatively* good, that is, you might have done worse; but I wish, as you are brothers of mine, that you could have spent your time better than digging in this dirt.

Before I finished my house, wishing to earn ten or twelve dollars by some honest and agreeable method, in order to meet my unusual expenses, I planted about two acres and a half of light and sandy soil near it chiefly with beans, but also a small part with potatoes, corn, peas, and turnips. The whole lot contains eleven acres, mostly growing up to pines and hickories, and was sold the preceding season for eight dollars and eight cents an acre. One farmer said that it was "good for nothing but to raise cheeping squirrels on." I put no manure whatever on this land, not being the owner, but merely a squatter, and not expecting to cultivate so much again, and

week together. You will in the meanwhile have earned your fare, and arrive there sometime tomorrow, or possibly this evening, if you are lucky enough to get a job in season. Instead of going to Fitchburg, you will be working here the greater part of the day. And so, if the railroad reached round the world, I think that I should keep ahead of you; and as for seeing the country and getting experience of that kind, I should have to cut your acquaintance altogether.

Such is the universal law, which no man can ever outwit, and with regard to the railroad even we may say it is as broad as it is long. To make a railroad round the world available to all mankind is equivalent to grading the whole surface of the planet. Men have an indistinct notion that if they keep up this activity of joint stocks and spades long enough all will at length ride somewhere, in next to no time, and for nothing; but though a crowd rushes to

I did not quite hoe it all once. I got out several cords of stumps in plowing, which supplied me with fuel for a long time, and left small circles of virgin mold, easily distinguishable through the summer by the greater luxuriance of the beans there. The dead and for the most part unmerchantable wood behind my house, and the driftwood from the pond, have supplied the remainder of my fuel. I was obliged to hire a team and a man for the plowing, though I held the plow myself. My farm outgoes for the first season were, for implements, seed, work, etc., $14.72½. The seed corn was given me. This never costs anything to speak of unless you plant more than enough. I got twelve bushels of beans, and eighteen bushels of potatoes, beside some peas and sweet corn. The yellow corn and turnips were too late to come to anything. My whole income from the farm was:

$23.44
Deducting the outgoes 14.72½

There are left .... $ 8.71½,

beside produce consumed and on hand at the time this estimate was made of the value of $4.50—the amount on hand much more than balancing a little grass which I did not raise. All things considered, that is, considering the importance of a man's soul and of today, notwithstanding the short time occupied by my experiment, nay, partly even because of its transient character, I believe that that was doing better than any farmer in Concord did that year.

The next year I did better still, for I spaded up all the land which I required, about a third of an acre, and I learned from the experience of both years, not be-

ing in the least awed by many celebrated works on husbandry, Arthur Young among the rest, that if one would live simply and eat only the crop which he raised, and raise no more than he ate, and not exchange it for an insufficient quantity of more luxurious and expensive things, he would need to cultivate only a few rods of ground, and that it would be cheaper to spade up that than to use oxen to plow it, and to select a fresh spot from time to time than to manure the old, and he could do all his necessary farm work as it were with his left hand at odd hours in the summer; and thus he would not be tied to an ox, or horse, or cow, or pig, as at present. I desire to speak impartially on this point, and as one not interested in the success or failure of the present economical and social arrangements. I was more independent than any farmer in Concord, for I was not anchored to a house or farm, but could follow the bent of my genius, which

HIRED MAN AND TEAM
I held the plow myself

471

HOEING
*I got twelve
bushels of beans*

is a very crooked one, every moment. Beside being better off than they already, if my house had been burned or my crops had failed, I should have been nearly as well off as before.

I am wont to think that men are not so much the keepers of herds as herds are the keepers of men, the former are so much the freer. Men and oxen exchange work; but if we consider necessary work only, the oxen will be seen to have greatly the advantage, their farm is so much the larger. Man does some of his part of the exchange work in his six weeks of haying, and it is no boy's play. Certainly no nation that lived simply in all respects, that is, no nation of philosophers, would commit so great a blunder as to use the labor of animals. True, there never was and is not likely soon to be a nation of philosophers, nor am I certain it is desirable that there should be. However, *I* should never have broken a horse or bull and taken him to board for any work he might do for me, for fear I should become a horse-man or a herds-man merely; and if society seems to be the gainer by so doing, are we certain that what is one man's gain is not another's loss, and that the stable-boy has equal cause with his master to be satisfied? Granted that some public works would not have been constructed without this aid, and let man share the glory of such with

the ox and horse; does it follow that he could not have accomplished works yet more worthy of himself in that case? When men begin to do, not merely unnecessary or artistic, but luxurious and idle work, with their assistance, it is inevitable that a few do all the exchange work with the oxen, or, in other words, become the slaves of the strongest. Man thus not only works for the animal within him, but, for a symbol of this, he works for the animal without him. Though we have many substantial houses of brick or stone, the prosperity of the farmer is still measured by the degree to which the barn overshadows the house. This town is said to have the largest houses for oxen, cows, and horses hereabouts, and it is not behindhand in its public buildings; but there are very few halls for free worship or free speech in this county. It should not be by their architecture, but why not even by their power of abstract thought, that nations should seek to commemorate themselves? How much more admirable the Bhagavad Gita than all the ruins of the East! Towers and temples are the luxury of princes. A simple and independent mind does not toil at the bidding of any prince. Genius is not a retainer to any emperor, nor is its material silver, or gold, or marble, except to a trifling extent. To what end, pray, is so much stone hammered? In Arcadia, when I was there, I did not see any hammering stone. Nations are possessed with an insane ambition to perpetuate the memory of themselves by the amount of hammered stone they leave. What if equal pains were taken to smooth and polish their manners? One piece of good sense would be more memorable than a monument as high as the moon. I love better to see stones in place. The grandeur of Thebes was a vulgar grandeur. More sensible is a rod of stone wall that bounds an honest man's field than a hundred-gated Thebes that has wandered farther from the true end of life. The religion and civilization which are barbaric and heathenish build splendid temples; but what you might call Christianity does not. Most of the stone a nation hammers goes toward its tomb only. It buries itself alive. As for the Pyramids, there is nothing to wonder at in them so much as the fact that so many men could be found degraded enough to spend their lives constructing a tomb for some ambitious booby, whom it would have been wiser and manlier to have drowned in the Nile, and then given his body to the dogs. I might possibly invent some excuse for them and him, but I have no time for it. As for the religion and love of art of the builders, it is much the same all the world over, whether the building be an Egyptian temple or the United States Bank. It costs more than it comes to. The mainspring is vanity, assisted by the love of garlic and bread and butter. Mr. Balcom, a promising young architect, designs it on the back of his Vitruvius, with hard pencil and ruler, and the job is let out to Dobson & Sons, stonecutters. When the thirty centuries begin to look down on it, mankind begin to look up at it. As for your high towers and monuments, there was a crazy fellow once in this town who undertook to dig through to China, and he got so far that, as he said, he heard the Chinese pots and kettles rattle; but I think that I shall not go out of my way to admire the hole which he made. Many are con-

cerned about the monuments of the West and the East—to know who built them. For my part, I should like to know who in those days did not build them—who were above such trifling. But to proceed with my statistics.

By surveying, carpentry, and day-labor of various other kinds in the village in the meanwhile, for I have as many trades as fingers, I had earned $13.34. The expense of food for eight months, namely, from July 4th to March 1st, the time when these estimates were made, though I lived there more than two years—not counting potatoes, a little green corn, and some peas, which I had raised, nor considering the value of what was on hand at the last date —was:

Rice	$1.73½
Molasses	1.73
Cheapest form of the saccharine.	
Rye meal	1.04¾
Indian meal	0.99¾
Cheaper than rye.	
Pork	0.22
All experiments which failed.	
Flour	0.88
Costs more than Indian meal, both money and trouble.	
Sugar	0.80
Lard	0.65
Apples	0.25
Dried apple	0.22
Sweet potatoes	0.10
One pumpkin	0.06
One watermelon	0.02
Salt	0.03

Yes, I did eat $8.74, all told; but I should not thus unblushingly publish my guilt, if I did not know that most of my readers were equally guilty with myself, and that their deeds would look no better in print. The next year I sometimes caught a mess of fish for my dinner, and once I went so far as to slaughter a woodchuck which ravaged my bean-field—effect his transmigration, as a Tartar would say—and de-

WOODCHUCK
Ravaged my bean-field

vour him, partly for experiment's sake; but though it afforded me a momentary enjoyment, notwithstanding a musky flavor, I saw that the longest use would not make that a good practice, however it might seem to have your woodchucks ready dressed by the village butcher.

Clothing and some incidental expenses within the same dates, though little can be inferred from this item, amounted to:

	$8.40¾
Oil and some household utensils	2.00

So that all the pecuniary outgoes, excepting for washing and mending, which for the most part were done out of the house, and their bills have not yet been received —and these are all and more than all the ways by which money necessarily goes out in this part of the world—were:

House	$28.12½
Farm one year	14.72½
Food eight months	8.74
Clothing, etc., eight months	8.40¾
Oil, etc., eight months	2.00
In all	$61.99¾

I address myself now to those of my readers who have a living to get. And to meet this I have for farm produce sold:

	$23.44
Earned by day-labor	13.34
In all	$36.78,

which subtracted from the sum of the outgoes leaves a balance of $25.21¾ on the one side—this being very nearly the means with which I started, and the measure of expenses to be incurred—and on the other, beside the leisure and independence and health thus secured, a comfortable house for me as long as I choose to occupy it.

These statistics, however accidental and therefore uninstructive they may appear, as they have a certain completeness, have a certain value also. Nothing was given me of which I have not rendered some account. It appears from the above estimate, that my food alone cost me in money about twenty-seven cents a week. It was, for nearly two years after this, rye and Indian meal without yeast, potatoes, rice, a very little salt pork, molasses, and salt; and my drink, water. It was fit that I should live on rice, mainly, who loved so well the philosophy of India. To meet the objections of some inveterate cavilers, I may as well state, that if I dined out occasionally, as I always had done, and I trust shall have opportunities to do again, it was frequently to the detriment of my domestic arrangements. But the dining out, being, as I have stated, a constant element, does not in the least affect a comparative statement like this.

I learned from my two years' experience that it would cost incredibly little trouble to obtain one's necessary food, even in this latitude; that a man may use as simple a diet as the animals, and yet retain health and strength. I have made a satisfactory dinner, satisfactory on several accounts, simply off a dish of purslane (*Portulaca oleracea*) which I gathered in my cornfield, boiled and salted. I give the Latin on account of the savoriness of the trivial name. And pray what more can a reasonable man desire, in peaceful times, in ordinary noons, than a sufficient number of ears of green sweet corn boiled, with the addition of salt? Even the little variety which I used was a yielding to the demands of appetite, and not of health. Yet men have come to such a pass that they frequently starve, not for want of necessaries, but for want of luxuries; and I know a good woman who thinks that her son lost his life because he took to drinking water only.

The reader will perceive that I am treating the subject rather from an economic than a dietetic point of view, and he will not venture to put my abstemiousness to the test unless he has a well-stocked larder.

Bread I at first made of pure Indian meal and salt, genuine hoe-cakes, which I baked before my fire out of doors on a shingle or the end of a stick of timber sawed off in building my house; but it was wont to get smoked and to have a piny flavor. I tried flour also; but have at last found a mixture of rye and Indian meal most convenient and agreeable. In cold weather it was no little amusement to bake several small loaves of this in succession, tending and turning them as carefully as an Egyptian his hatching eggs. They were a real cereal fruit which I ripened, and they had to my senses a fragrance like that of other noble fruits, which I kept in as long as possible by wrapping them in cloths. I made a study of the ancient and indispensable art of bread-making, consulting such authorities as offered, going back to the primitive days and first invention of the unleavened kind, when from the wildness of nuts and meats men first reached the mildness and refinement of this diet, and traveling gradually down in my studies through that accidental souring of the dough which, it is supposed, taught the leavening process, and through the various fermentations thereafter, till I came to "good, sweet, wholesome bread," the staff of life. Leaven, which some deem the soul of bread, the *spiritus* which fills its cellular tissue, which is religiously preserved like the vestal fire—some precious bottleful, I suppose, first brought over in the Mayflower, did the business for America, and its influence is still rising, swelling, spreading, in cerealian billows over the land—this seed I regularly and faithfully procured from the village, till at length one morning I forgot the rules, and scalded my yeast; by which accident I discovered that even this was not indispensable—for my discoveries were not by the synthetic but analytic process—and I have gladly omitted it since, though most housewives earnestly assured me that safe and wholesome bread without yeast might not be, and elderly people prophesied a speedy decay of the vital forces. Yet I find it not to be an essential ingredient, and after going without it for a year am still in the land of the living; and I am glad to escape the trivialness of carrying a bottleful in my pocket, which would sometimes pop and discharge its contents to my discomfiture. It is simpler and more respectable to omit it. Man is an animal who more than any other can adapt himself to all climates and circumstances.

Neither did I put any sal-soda, or other acid or alkali, into my bread. It would seem that I made it according to the recipe which Marcus Porcius Cato gave about two centuries before Christ. *Panem depsticium sic facito. Manus mortariumque bene lavato. Farinam in mortarium indito, aquae paulatim addito, subigitoque pulchre. Ubi bene subegeris, defingito, coquitoque sub testu.* Which I take to mean, "Make kneaded bread thus. Wash your hands and trough well. Put the meal into the trough, add water gradually, and knead it thoroughly. When you have kneaded it well, mold it, and bake it under a cover," that is, in a baking-kettle. Not a word about leaven. But I did not always use this staff of life. At one time, owing to the emptiness of my purse, I saw none of it for more than a month.

Every New Englander might easily raise all his own foodstuffs in this land of rye and Indian corn, and not depend on distant and fluctuating markets for them. Yet so far are we from simplicity and independence that, in Concord, fresh and sweet meal is rarely sold in the shops, and hominy and corn in a still coarser form are hardly used by any. For the most part the farmer gives to his cattle and hogs the grain of his own producing, and buys flour, which is at least no more wholesome, at a greater cost, at the store. I saw that I could easily raise my bushel or two of rye and Indian corn, for the former will grow on the poorest land, and the latter does not require the best, and grind them in a hand-mill, and so do without rice and pork; and if I must have some concentrated sweet, I found by experiment that I could make a very good molasses either of pumpkins or beets, and I knew that I needed only to set out a few maples to obtain it more easily still, and while these were growing I could use various substitutes beside those which I have named. "For," as the Forefathers sang,

we can make liquor to sweeten our lips
Of pumpkins and parsnips and walnut-tree chips.

Finally, as for salt, that grossest of groceries, to obtain this might be a fit occasion for a visit to the seashore, or, if I did without it altogether, I should probably drink the less water. I do not learn that the Indians ever troubled themselves to go after it.

Thus I could avoid all trade and barter, so far as my food was concerned, and having a shelter already, it would only remain to get clothing and fuel. The pantaloons which I now wear were woven in a farmer's family—thank Heaven there is so much virtue still in man; for I think the fall from the farmer to the operative as great and memorable as that from the man to the farmer—and in a new country, fuel is an encumbrance. As for a habitat, if I were not permitted still to squat, I might purchase one acre at the same price for which the land I cultivated was sold—namely, eight dollars and eight cents. But as it was, I considered that I enhanced the value of the land by squatting on it.

There is a certain class of unbelievers who sometimes ask me such questions as, if I think that I can live on vegetable food alone; and to strike at the root of the matter at once—for the root is faith—I am accustomed to answer such, that I can live on board nails. If they cannot understand that, they cannot understand much that I have to say. For my part, I am glad to hear of experiments of this kind being tried; as that a young man tried for a fortnight to live on hard, raw corn on the ear, using his teeth for all mortar. The squirrel tribe tried the same and succeeded. The human race is interested in these experiments, though a few old women who are incapacitated for them, or who own their thirds in mills, may be alarmed.

My furniture, part of which I made myself—and the rest cost me nothing of which I have not rendered an account—consisted of a bed, a table, a desk, three chairs, a looking-glass three inches in diameter, a pair of tongs and andirons, a kettle, a skillet, and a frying-pan, a dipper, a wash-bowl, two knives and forks, three plates, one cup, one spoon, a jug for oil, a jug for molasses, and a japanned lamp. None is so poor that he need sit on a pumpkin. That is shiftlessness. There is a plenty of such chairs as I like best in the village garrets to be had for taking them away. Furniture! Thank God, I can sit and I can stand without the aid of a furniture warehouse. What man but a philosopher would not be ashamed to see his furniture packed in a cart and going up country exposed to the light of heaven and the eyes of men, a beggarly account of empty boxes? That is Spaulding's furniture. I could never tell from inspecting such a load whether it belonged to a so-called rich man or a poor one; the owner always seemed poverty-stricken. Indeed, the more you have of such things the poorer you are. Each load looks as if it contained the contents of a dozen shanties; and if one shanty is poor, this is a dozen times as poor. Pray, for what do we *move* ever but to get rid of our furniture, our *exuviae*; at last to go from this world to another newly furnished, and leave this to be burned? It is the same as if all these traps were buckled to a man's belt, and he could not move over the rough country where our lines are cast without dragging them—dragging his trap. He was a lucky fox that left his tail in the trap. The muskrat will gnaw his third leg off to be free. No wonder man has lost his elasticity. How often he is at a dead set! "Sir, if I may be so bold, what do you mean by a dead set?" If you are a seer, whenever you meet a man you will see all that he owns, ay, and much that he pretends to disown, behind him, even to his kitchen furniture and all the trumpery which he saves and will not burn, and he will appear to be harnessed to it and making what headway he can. I think that the man is at a dead set who has got through a knot-hole or gateway where his sledge load of furniture cannot follow him. I cannot but feel compassion when I hear some trig, compact-looking man, seemingly free, all girded and ready, speak of his "furniture," as whether it is insured or not. "But what shall I do with my furniture?" My gay butterfly is entangled in a spider's web then. Even those who seem for a long while not to have any, if you inquire more narrowly you will find have some stored in somebody's barn. I look upon England today as an old gentleman who is traveling with a great deal of baggage, trumpery which has accumulated from long housekeeping, which he has not the courage to burn; great trunk, little

CABIN INTERIOR
*None is so poor that he
need sit on a pumpkin*

trunk, bandbox, and bundle. Throw away the first three at least. It would surpass the powers of a well man nowadays to take up his bed and walk, and I should certainly advise a sick one to lay down his bed and run. When I have met an immigrant tottering under a bundle which contained his all —looking like an enormous wen which had grown out of the nape of his neck—I have pitied him, not because that was his all, but because he had all *that* to carry. If I have got to drag my trap, I will take care that it be a light one and do not nip me in a vital part. But perchance it would be wisest never to put one's paw into it.

I would observe, by the way, that it costs me nothing for curtains, for I have no gazers to shut out but the sun and moon, and I am willing that they should look in. The moon will not sour milk nor taint meat of mine, nor will the sun injure my furniture or fade my carpet; and if he is sometimes too warm a friend, I find it still better economy to retreat behind some curtain which nature has provided, than to add a single item to the details of housekeeping. A lady once offered me a mat, but as I had no room to spare within the house, nor time to spare within or without to shake it, I declined it, preferring to wipe my feet on the sod before my door. It is best to avoid the beginnings of evil.

Not long since I was present at the auction of a deacon's effects, for his life had not been ineffectual:

The evil that men do lives after them.

As usual, a great proportion was trumpery which had begun to accumulate in his father's day. Among the rest was a dried tapeworm. And now, after lying half a century in his garret and other dust holes, these things were not burned; instead of a *bonfire*, or purifying destruction of them, there was an *auction*, or increasing of them. The neighbors eagerly collected to view them, bought them all, and carefully transported them to their garrets and dust holes, to lie there till their estates are settled, when they will start again. When a man dies he kicks the dust.

The customs of some savage nations might, perchance, be profitably imitated by us, for they at least go through the semblance of casting their slough annually; they have the idea of the thing, whether they have the reality or not. Would it not be well if we were to celebrate such a "busk," or "feast of first fruits," as Bartram describes to have been the custom of the Mucclasse Indians? "When a town celebrates the busk," says he, "having previously provided themselves with new clothes, new pots, pans, and other household utensils and furniture, they collect all their worn out clothes and other despicable things, sweep and cleanse their houses, squares, and the whole town, of their filth, which with all the remaining grain and other old provisions they cast together into one common heap, and consume it with fire. After having taken medicine, and fasted for three days, all the fire in the town is extinguished. During this fast they abstain from the gratification of every appetite and passion whatever. A general amnesty is proclaimed; all malefactors may return to their town.

"On the fourth morning, the high priest, by rubbing dry wood together, produces new fire in the public square, from whence every habitation in the town is supplied with the new and pure flame."

They then feast on the new corn and fruits, and dance and sing for three days, "and the four following days they receive visits and rejoice with their friends from neighboring towns who have in like manner purified and prepared themselves."

The Mexicans also practiced a similar purification at the end of every fifty-two years, in the belief that it was time for the world to come to an end.

I have scarcely heard of a truer sacrament, that is, as the dictionary defines it, "outward and visible sign of an inward and spiritual grace," than this, and I have no doubt that they were originally inspired directly from Heaven to do thus, though they have no Biblical record of the revelation.

For more than five years I maintained myself thus solely by the labor of my hands, and I found that, by working about six weeks in a year, I could meet all the expenses of living. The whole of my winters, as well as most of my summers, I had free and clear for study. I have thoroughly tried schoolkeeping, and found that my expenses were in proportion, or rather out of proportion, to my income, for I was obliged to dress and train, not to say think and believe, accordingly, and I lost my time into the bargain. As I did not teach for the good of my fellow-men, but simply for a livelihood, this was a failure. I have tried trade; but I found that it would take ten years to get under way in that, and that then I should probably be on my way to the devil. I was actually afraid that I might by that time be doing what is called a good business. When formerly I was looking about to see what I could do for a living, some sad experience in conforming to the wishes of friends being fresh in my mind to tax

my ingenuity, I thought often and seriously of picking huckleberries; that surely I could do, and its small profits might suffice—for my greatest skill has been to want but little—so little capital it required, so little distraction from my wonted moods, I foolishly thought. While my acquaintances went unhesitatingly into trade or the professions, I contemplated this occupation as most like theirs; ranging the hills all summer to pick the berries which came in my way, and thereafter carelessly dispose of them; so, to keep the flocks of Admetus. I also dreamed that I might gather the wild herbs, or carry evergreens to such villagers as loved to be reminded of the woods, even to the city, by hay-cart loads. But I have since learned that trade curses everything it handles; and though you trade in messages from Heaven, the whole curse of trade attaches to the business.

As I preferred some things to others, and especially valued my freedom, as I could fare hard and yet succeed well, I did not wish to spend my time in earning rich carpets or other fine furniture, or delicate cookery, or a house in the Grecian or the Gothic style just yet. If there are any to whom it is no interruption to acquire these things, and who know how to use them when acquired, I relinquish to them the

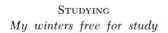
STUDYING
My winters free for study

pursuit. Some are "industrious," and appear to love labor for its own sake, or perhaps because it keeps them out of worse mischief; to such I have at present nothing to say. Those who would not know what to do with more leisure than they now enjoy, I might advise to work twice as hard as they do—work till they pay for themselves, and get their free papers. For myself I found that the occupation of a day-laborer was the most independent of any, especially as it required only thirty or forty days in a year to support one. The laborer's day ends with the going down of the sun, and he is then free to devote himself to his chosen pursuit, independent of his labor; but his employer, who speculates from month to month, has no respite from one end of the year to the other.

In short, I am convinced, both by faith and experience, that to maintain one's self on this earth is not a hardship but a pastime, if we will live simply and wisely; as the pursuits of the simpler nations are still the sports of the more artificial. It is not necessary that a man should earn his living by the sweat of his brow, unless he sweats easier than I do.

One young man of my acquaintance, who has inherited some acres, told me that he thought he should live as I did, *if he had the means*. I would not have any one adopt *my* mode of living on any account; for, beside that before he has fairly learned it I may have found out another for myself, I desire that there may be as many different persons in the world as possible; but I would have each one be very careful to find out and pursue *his own* way, and not his father's or his mother's or his neighbor's instead. The youth may build or plant or sail, only let him not be hindered from doing that which he tells me he would like to do. It is by a mathematical point only that we are wise, as the sailor or the fugitive slave keeps the polestar in his eye; but that is sufficient guidance for all our life. We may not arrive at our port within a calculable period, but we would preserve the true course.

Undoubtedly, in this case, what is true for one is truer still for a thousand, as a large house is not proportionally more expensive than a small one, since one roof may cover, one cellar underlie, and one wall separate several apartments. But for my part, I preferred the solitary dwelling. Moreover, it will commonly be cheaper to build the whole yourself than to convince another of the advantage of the common wall; and when you have done this, the common partition, to be much cheaper, must be a thin one, and that other may prove a bad neighbor, and also not keep his side in repair. The only cooperation which is commonly possible is exceedingly partial and superficial; and what little true cooperation there is, is as if it were not, being a harmony inaudible to men. If a man has faith, he will cooperate with equal faith everywhere; if he has not faith, he will continue to live like the rest of the world, whatever company he is joined to. To cooperate in the highest as well as the lowest sense, means *to get our living together*. I heard it proposed lately that two young men should travel together over the world, the one without money, earning his means as he went, before the mast and behind the plow, the other carrying a bill of exchange in his pocket. It was easy to see that they could not long be companions or cooperate, since one would not *operate* at all. They would part at the first interesting crisis in their adventures. Above all, as I have implied, the man who goes alone can start today; but he who travels with another must wait till that other is ready, and it may be a long time before they get off.

But all this is very selfish, I have heard some of my townsmen say. I confess that I have hitherto indulged very little in philanthropic enterprises. I have made some sacrifices to a sense of duty, and among others have sacrificed this pleasure also. There are those who have used all their arts to persuade me to undertake the support of some poor family in the town; and if I had nothing to do—for the devil finds employment for the idle—I might try my hand at some such pastime as that. However, when I have thought to indulge myself in this respect, and lay their Heaven under an obligation by maintaining certain poor persons in all respects as comfortably as I maintain myself, and have even ventured so far as to make them the offer, they have one and all unhesitatingly preferred to remain poor. While my townsmen and women are devoted in so many ways to the good of their fellows, I trust that one at least may be spared to other and less humane pursuits. You must have a genius for charity as well as for anything else. As for Doing-good, that is one of the professions which are full. Moreover, I have tried it fairly, and, strange as it may seem, am satisfied that it does not agree with my constitution. Probably I should not consciously and deliberately forsake my particular calling to do the good which society demands of me, to save the universe from annihilation; and I believe that a like but infinitely greater steadfastness elsewhere is all that now preserves it. But I would not stand between any man and his genius; and to him who does this work, which I decline, with his whole heart and soul and life, I would say, Persevere, even if the whole world call it doing evil, as it is most likely they will.

I am far from supposing that my case is a peculiar one; no doubt many of my readers would make a similar defense. At doing something—I will not engage that my neighbors shall pronounce it good—I do not hesitate to say that I should be a capital fellow to hire; but what that is, it is for my employer to find out. What *good* I do, in the common sense of that word, must be aside from my main path, and for the most part wholly unintended. Men

say, practically, "Begin where you are and such as you are, without aiming mainly to become of more worth, and with kindness aforethought go about doing good." If I were to preach at all in this strain, I should say rather, "Set about being good." As if the sun should stop when he had kindled his fires up to the splendor of a moon or a star of the sixth magnitude, and go about like a Robin Goodfellow, peeping in at every cottage window, inspiring lunatics, and tainting meats, and making darkness visible, instead of steadily increasing his genial heat and beneficence till he is of such brightness that no mortal can look him in the face, and then, and in the meanwhile too, going about the world in his own orbit, doing it good, or rather, as a truer philosophy has discovered, the world going about him getting good. When Phaeton, wishing to prove his heavenly birth by his beneficence, had the sun's chariot but one day, and drove out of the beaten track, he burned several blocks of houses in the lower streets of Heaven, and scorched the surface of the earth, and dried up every spring, and made the great desert of Sahara, till at length Jupiter hurled him headlong to the earth with a thunderbolt, and the sun, through grief at his death, did not shine for a year.

There is no odor so bad as that which arises from goodness tainted. It is human, it is divine, carrion. If I knew for certainty that a man was coming to my house with the conscious design of doing me good, I should run for my life, as from that dry and parching wind of the African deserts called the simoom, which fills the mouth and nose and ears and eyes with dust till you are suffocated, for fear that I should get some of his good done to me—some of its virus mingled with my blood. No, in this case I would rather suffer evil the natural way. A man is not a good *man* to me because he will feed me if I should be starving, or warm me if I should be freezing, or pull me out of a ditch if I should ever fall into one. I can find you a Newfoundland dog that will do as much. Philanthropy is not love for one's fellowman in the broadest sense. Howard was no doubt an exceedingly kind and worthy man in his way, and has his reward; but, comparatively speaking, what are a hundred Howards to *us*, if their philanthropy do not help *us* in our best estate, when we are most worthy to be helped? I never heard of a philanthropic meeting in which it was sincerely proposed to do any good to me, or the like of me.

The Jesuits were quite balked by those Indians who, being burned at the stake, suggested new modes of torture to their tormentors. Being superior to physical suffering, it sometimes chanced that they were superior to any consolation which the missionaries could offer; and the law to do as you would be done by fell with less persuasiveness on the ears of those who, for their part, did not care how they were done by, who loved their enemies after a new fashion, and came very near freely forgiving them all they did.

Be sure that you give the poor the aid they most need, though it be your example which leaves them far behind. If you give money, spend yourself with it, and do not merely abandon it to them. We make curious mistakes sometimes. Often the poor man is not so cold and hungry as he is dirty and ragged and gross. It is partly his taste, and not merely his misfortune. If you give him money, he will perhaps buy more rags with it. I was wont to pity the clumsy Irish laborers who cut ice on the pond, in such mean and ragged clothes, while I shivered in my more tidy and somewhat more fashionable garments, till, one bitter cold day, one who had slipped into the water came to my house to warm him, and I saw him strip off three pairs of pants and two pairs of stockings ere he got down to the skin, though they were dirty and ragged enough, it is true, and that he could afford to refuse the *extra* garments which I

offered him, he had so many *intra* ones. This ducking was the very thing he needed. Then I began to pity myself, and I saw that it would be a greater charity to bestow on me a flannel shirt than a whole slop-shop on him. There are a thousand hacking at the branches of evil to one who is striking at the root, and it may be that he who bestows the largest amount of time and money on the needy is doing the most by his mode of life to produce that misery which he strives in vain to relieve. It is the pious slave-breeder devoting the proceeds of every tenth slave to buy a Sunday's liberty for the rest. Some show their kindness to the poor by employing them in their kitchens. Would they not be kinder if they employed themselves there? You boast of spending a tenth part of your income in charity; maybe you should spend the nine-tenths so, and done with it. Society recovers only a tenth part of the property then. Is this owing to the generosity of him in whose possession it is found, or to the remissness of the officers of justice?

Philanthropy is almost the only virtue which is sufficiently appreciated by mankind. Nay, it is greatly overrated; and it is our selfishness which overrates it. A robust poor man, one sunny day here in Concord, praised a fellow-townsman to me, because, as he said, he was kind to the poor; meaning himself. The kind uncles and aunts of the race are more esteemed than its true spiritual fathers and mothers. I once heard a reverend lecturer on England, a man of learning and intelligence, after enumerating her scientific, literary, and political worthies, Shakespeare, Bacon, Cromwell, Milton, Newton, and others, speak next of her Christian heroes, whom, as if his profession required it of him, he elevated to a place far above all the rest, as the greatest of the great. They were Penn, Howard, and Mrs. Fry. Every one must feel the falsehood and cant of this. The last were not England's best men and women; only, perhaps, her best philanthropists.

I would not subtract anything from the praise that is due to philanthropy, but merely demand justice for all who by their lives and works are a blessing to mankind. I do not value chiefly a man's uprightness and benevolence, which are, as it were, his stem and leaves. Those plants of whose greenness withered we make herb tea for the sick serve but a humble use, and are most employed by quacks. I want the flower and fruit of a man; that some fragrance be wafted over from him to me, and some ripeness flavor our intercourse. His goodness must not be a partial and transitory act, but a constant superfluity, which costs him nothing and of which he is unconscious. This is a charity that hides a multitude of sins. The philanthropist too often surrounds mankind with the remembrance of his own cast-off griefs as an atmosphere, and calls it sympathy. We should impart our courage, and not our despair, our health and ease, and not our disease, and take care that this does not spread by contagion. From what southern plains comes up the voice of wailing? Under what latitudes reside the heathen to whom we would send light? Who is that intemperate and brutal man whom we would redeem? If anything ail a man, so that he does not perform his functions, if he have a pain in his bowels even—for that is the seat of sympathy—he forthwith sets about reforming—the world. Being a microcosm himself, he discovers—and it is a true discovery, and he is the man to make it—that the world has been eating green apples; to his eyes, in fact, the globe itself is a great green apple, which there is danger awful to think of that the children of men will nibble before it is ripe; and straightway his drastic philanthropy seeks out the Eskimo and the Patagonian, and embraces the populous Indian and Chinese villages; and thus, by a few years of philanthropic activity, the powers in the mean-

while using him for their own ends, no doubt, he cures himself of his dyspepsia, the globe acquires a faint blush on one or both of its cheeks, as if it were beginning to be ripe, and life loses its crudity and is once more sweet and wholesome to live. I never dreamed of any enormity greater than I have committed. I never knew, and never shall know, a worse man than myself.

I believe that what so saddens the reformer is not his sympathy with his fellows in distress, but, though he be the holiest son of God, is his private ail. Let this be righted, let the spring come to him, the morning rise over his couch, and he will forsake his generous companions without apology. My excuse for not lecturing against the use of tobacco is, that I never chewed it, that is a penalty which reformed tobacco-chewers have to pay; though there are things enough I have chewed which I could lecture against. If you should ever be betrayed into any of these philanthropies, do not let your left hand know what your right hand does, for it is not worth knowing. Rescue the drowning and tie your shoestrings. Take your time, and set about some free labor.

Our manners have been corrupted by communication with the saints. Our hymnbooks resound with a melodious cursing of God and enduring Him forever. One would say that even the prophets and redeemers had rather consoled the fears than confirmed the hopes of man. There is nowhere recorded a simple and irrepressible satisfaction with the gift of life, any memorable praise of God. All health and success does me good, however far off and withdrawn it may appear; all disease and failure helps to make me sad and does me evil, however much sympathy it may have with me or I with it. If, then, we would indeed restore mankind by truly Indian, botanic, magnetic, or natural means, let us first be as simple and well as Nature ourselves, dispel the clouds which hang over our own brows, and take up a little life into our pores. Do not stay to be an overseer of the poor, but endeavor to become one of the worthies of the world.

I read in the *Gulistan*, or "Flower Gar- den," of Sheikh Sa'di of Shiraz, that "they asked a wise man, saying: 'Of the many celebrated trees which the Most High God has created lofty and umbrageous, they call none azad, or free, excepting the cy-

Thoreau *vs.*

19TH-CENTURY AMERICAN PARLOR
Most luxuries are positive hindrances to the elevation of mankind

GOTHIC REVIVAL HOUSE, C. 1840
*Ornaments a September gale
would strip off*

19TH-CENTURY PRIVATE RAILROAD CAR
*I would rather ride on earth
in an ox-cart than go to heaven
in the fancy car of an excursion train*

press, which bears no fruit; what mystery is there in this?' He replied: 'Each has its appropriate produce, and appointed season, during the continuance of which it is fresh and blooming, and during their absence dry and withered; to neither of which states is the cypress exposed, being always flourishing; and of this nature are the azads, or religious independents.—Fix not thy heart on that which is transitory;

An Age's Frills

"BLOOMERISM—AN AMERICAN CUSTOM," *Harper's Weekly*, 1851
We worship not the Graces . . .

If Thoreau was radical in his ascetic tastes, which he was, numerous contemporaries were clearly as radical in their taste for frills in dress and design. The conspicuous cravats and bloomers, the rosettes and finials were the rage of the age but caused Thoreau to lament: "We worship not the Graces, nor the Parcae, but Fashion." One level-headed architect likened the expensive architectural frills to noodles "in a German soup," a judgment which Thoreau might have seconded as indicated by his cabin, which served, though it had no frills, and cost merely $28.12½ plain.

"VICISSITUDES OF THE CRAVAT," *Harper's Weekly*, 1859
. . . . *but Fashion*

for the Dijlah, or Tigris, will continue to flow through Bagdad after the race of caliphs is extinct: if thy hand has plenty, be liberal as the date tree; but if it affords nothing to give away, be an azad, or free man, like the cypress.'"

COMPLEMENTAL VERSES

THE PRETENSIONS OF POVERTY

Thou dost presume too much, poor needy wretch,
To claim a station in the firmament
Because thy humble cottage, or thy tub,
Nurses some lazy or pedantic virtue
In the cheap sunshine or by shady springs,
With roots and pot-herbs; where thy right hand,
Tearing those humane passions from the mind,
Upon whose stocks fair blooming virtues flourish,
Degradeth nature, and benumbeth sense,
And, Gorgon-like, turns active men to stone.
We not require the dull society
Of your necessitated temperance,
Or that unnatural stupidity
That knows nor joy nor sorrow; nor your forc'd
Falsely exalted passive fortitude
Above the active. This low abject brood,
That fix their seats in mediocrity,
Become your servile minds; but we advance
Such virtues only as admit excess,
Brave, bounteous acts, regal magnificence,
All-seeing prudence, magnanimity
That knows no bound, and that heroic virtue
For which antiquity hath left no name,
But patterns only, such as Hercules,
Achilles, Theseus. Back to thy loath'd cell;
And when thou seest the new enlightened sphere,
Study to know but what those worthies were.

T. CAREW

WHERE I LIVED, AND WHAT I LIVED FOR

At a certain season of our life we are accustomed to consider every spot as the possible site of a house. I have thus surveyed the country on every side within a dozen miles of where I live. In imagination I have bought all the farms in succession, for all were to be bought, and I knew their price. I walked over each farmer's premises, tasted his wild apples, discoursed on husbandry with him, took his farm at his price, at any price, mortgaging it to him in my mind; even put a higher price on it, took everything but a deed of it—took his word for his deed, for I dearly love to talk—cultivated it, and him too to some extent, I trust, and withdrew when I had enjoyed it long enough, leaving him to carry it on. This experience entitled me to be regarded as a sort of real-estate broker by my friends. Wherever I sat, there I might live, and the landscape radiated from me accordingly. What is a house but a *sedes*, a seat?—better if a country seat. I discovered many a site for a house not likely to be soon improved, which some might have thought too far from the village, but to my eyes the village was too far from it. Well, there I might live, I said; and there I did live, for an hour, a summer and a winter life; saw how I could let the years run off, buffet the winter through, and see the spring come in. The future inhabitants of this region, wherever they may place their houses, may be sure that they have been anticipated. An afternoon sufficed to lay out the land into orchard, woodlot, and pasture, and to decide what fine oaks or pines should be left to stand before the door, and whence each blasted tree could be seen to the best advantage; and then I let it lie, fallow perchance, for a man is rich in proportion to the number of things which he can afford to let alone.

My imagination carried me so far that I even had the refusal of several farms—the refusal was all I wanted—but I never got my fingers burned by actual possession. The nearest that I came to actual possession was when I bought the Hollowell place, and had begun to sort my seeds, and collected materials with which to make a wheelbarrow to carry it on or off with; but before the owner gave me a deed of it, his wife—every man has such a wife—changed her mind and wished to keep it, and he offered me ten dollars to release him. Now, to speak the truth, I had but ten cents in the world, and it surpassed my arithmetic to tell, if I was that man who had ten cents, or who had a farm, or ten dollars, or all together. However, I let him keep the ten dollars and the farm too, for I had carried it far enough; or rather, to be generous, I sold him the farm for just what I gave for it, and, as he was not a rich man, made him a present of ten dollars, and still had my ten cents, and seeds, and materials for a wheelbarrow left. I found thus that I had been a rich man without any damage to my poverty. But I retained the landscape, and I have since annually carried off what it yielded without a wheelbarrow. With respect to landscapes,

I am monarch of all I *survey*,
My right there is none to dispute.

I have frequently seen a poet withdraw, having enjoyed the most valuable part of a farm, while the crusty farmer supposed that he had got a few wild apples only. Why, the owner does not know it for many years when a poet has put his farm in rhyme, the most admirable kind of invisible fence, has fairly impounded it, milked it, skimmed it, and got all the cream, and left the farmer only the skimmed milk.

The real attractions of the Hollowell farm, to me, were: its complete retirement, being about two miles from the village, half a mile from the nearest neighbor, and separated from the highway by a broad field; its bounding on the river, which the owner said protected it by its fogs from frosts in the spring, though that was nothing to me; the gray color and ruinous state of the house and barn, and the dilapidated fences, which put such an interval between me and the last occupant; the hollow and lichen-covered apple trees, gnawed by rabbits, showing what kind of neighbors I should have; but above all, the recollection I had of it from my earliest voyages up the river, when the house was concealed behind a dense grove of red maples, through which I heard the house-dog bark. I was in haste to buy it, before the proprietor finished getting out some rocks, cutting down the hollow apple trees, and grubbing up some young birches which had sprung up in the pasture, or, in short, had made any more of his improvements. To enjoy these advantages I was ready to carry it on; like Atlas, to take the world on my shoulders—I never heard what compensation he received for that—and do all those things which had no other motive or excuse but that I might pay for it and be unmolested in my possession of it; for I knew all the while that it would yield the most abundant crop of the kind I wanted, if I could only afford to let it alone. But it turned out as I have said.

All that I could say, then, with respect to farming on a large scale—I have always cultivated a garden—was, that I had had my seeds ready. Many think that seeds improve with age. I have no doubt that time discriminates between the good and the bad; and when at last I shall plant, I shall be less likely to be disappointed. But I would say to my fellows, once for all, As long as possible live free and uncommitted. It makes but little difference whether you are committed to a farm or the county jail.

Old Cato, whose "De Re Rusticâ" is my "Cultivator," says—and the only translation I have seen makes sheer nonsense of the passage—"When you think of getting a farm turn it thus in your mind, not to buy greedily; nor spare your pains to look at it, and do not think it enough to go round it once. The oftener you go there the more it will please you, if it is good." I think I shall not buy greedily, but go round and round it as long as I live, and be buried in it first, that it may please me the more at last.

The present was my next experiment of this kind, which I purpose to describe more at length, for convenience putting the experience of two years into one. As I have said, I do not propose to write an ode to dejection, but to brag as lustily as chanticleer in the morning, standing on his roost, if only to wake my neighbors up.

When first I took up my abode in the woods, that is, began to spend my nights as well as days there, which, by accident, was on Independence Day, or the Fourth of July, 1845, my house was not finished for winter, but was merely a defense against the rain, without plastering or chimney, the walls being of rough, weather-stained boards, with wide chinks, which made it cool at night. The upright white hewn studs and freshly planed door and window casings gave it a clean and airy look, especially in the morning, when its timbers were saturated with dew, so that I fancied that by noon some sweet gum would exude from them. To my imagination it retained throughout the day more or less of this auroral character, reminding me of a certain house on a mountain which I had visited a year before. This was an airy and unplastered cabin, fit to entertain a traveling god, and where a goddess might trail her garments. The winds which passed over my dwelling were such as sweep over the ridges of mountains, bearing the broken strains, or celestial parts only, of terrestrial music. The morning wind forever blows, the poem of creation is uninterrupted; but few are the ears that hear it. Olympus is but the outside of the earth everywhere.

The only house I had been the owner of before, if I except a boat, was a tent, which I used occasionally when making excursions in the summer, and this is still rolled up in my garret; but the boat, after passing from hand to hand, has gone down the stream of time. With this more substantial shelter about me, I had made some progress toward settling in the world. This frame, so slightly clad, was a sort of crystallization around me, and reacted on the builder. It was suggestive somewhat as a picture in outlines. I did not need to go outdoors to take the air, for the atmosphere within had lost none of its freshness. It was not so much within-doors as behind a door where I sat, even in the rainiest weather. The Harivaṁśa says, "An abode without birds is like a meat without seasoning." Such was not my abode, for I found myself suddenly neighbor to the birds; not by having imprisoned one, but having caged myself near them. I was not only nearer to some of those which commonly frequent the garden and the orchard, but to those wilder and more thrilling songsters of the forest which never, or rarely, serenade a villager—the wood thrush, the veery, the scarlet tanager, the field sparrow, the whip-poor-will, and many others.

I was seated by the shore of a small pond, about a mile and a half south of the village of Concord and somewhat higher than it, in the midst of an extensive wood between that town and Lincoln, and about two miles south of that our only field known to fame, Concord Battle Ground; but I was so low in the woods that the opposite shore, half a mile off, like the rest, covered with wood, was my most distant horizon. For the first week, whenever I looked out on the pond it impressed me like a tarn high up on the side of a mountain, its bottom far above the surface of other lakes, and, as the sun arose, I saw it throwing off its nightly clothing of mist, and here and there, by degrees, its soft ripples or its smooth reflecting surface was revealed, while the mists, like ghosts, were stealthily withdrawing in every direction into the woods, as at the breaking up of some nocturnal conventicle. The very dew seemed to hang upon the trees later into the day than usual, as on the sides of mountains.

This small lake was of most value as a neighbor in the intervals of a gentle rainstorm in August, when, both air and water being perfectly still, but the sky overcast, midafternoon had all the serenity of evening, and the wood thrush sang around, and was heard from shore to shore. A lake like this is never smoother than at such a time; and the clear portion of the air above it being shallow and darkened by clouds, the water, full of light and reflections, becomes a lower heaven itself so much the more important. From a hilltop near by, where the wood had been recently cut off, there was a pleasing vista southward across the pond, through a wide indentation in the hills which form the shore there, where their opposite sides sloping toward each other suggested a stream flowing out in that direction through a wooded valley, but stream there was none. That way I looked between and over the near green hills to some distant and higher ones in the horizon, tinged with blue. Indeed, by standing on tiptoe I could catch a glimpse of some of the peaks of the still bluer and more distant mountain ranges in the northwest, those true-blue coins from heaven's own mint, and also of some portion of the village. But in other directions, even from this point, I could not see over or beyond the woods which surrounded me. It is well to have some water in your neighborhood, to give buoyancy to and float the earth. One value even of the smallest well is, that when you look into it you see that earth is not continent but insular. This is as important as that it keeps butter cool.

When I looked across the pond from this peak toward the Sudbury meadows, which in time of flood I distinguished elevated perhaps by a mirage in their seething valley, like a coin in a basin, all the earth beyond the pond appeared like a thin crust insulated and floated even by this small sheet of intervening water, and I was reminded that this on which I dwelt was but *dry land.*

Though the view from my door was still more contracted, I did not feel crowded or confined in the least. There was pasture enough for my imagination. The low shrub oak plateau to which the opposite shore arose stretched away toward the prairies of the West and the steppes of Tartary, affording ample room for all the roving families of men. "There are none happy in the world but beings who enjoy freely a vast horizon," said Damodara, when his herds required new and larger pastures.

Both place and time were changed, and I dwelt nearer to those parts of the universe and to those eras in history which had most attracted me. Where I lived was as far off as many a region viewed nightly by astronomers. We are wont to imagine rare and delectable places in some remote and more celestial corner of the system, behind the constellation of Cassiopeia's Chair, far from noise and disturbance. I discovered that my house actually had its site in such a withdrawn, but forever new and unprofaned, part of the universe. If it were worth the while to settle in those parts near to the Pleiades or the Hyades, to Aldebaran or Altair, then I was really there, or at an equal remoteness from the life which I had left behind, dwindled and twinkling with as fine a ray to my nearest neighbor, and to be seen only in moonless nights by him. Such was that part of creation where I had squatted—

There was a shepherd that did live,
  And held his thoughts as high
As were the mounts whereon his flocks
  Did hourly feed him by.

What should we think of the shepherd's life if his flocks always wandered to higher pastures than his thoughts?

Every morning was a cheerful invitation to make my life of equal simplicity, and I may say innocence, with Nature herself. I have been as sincere a worshipper of Aurora as the Greeks. I got up early and bathed in the pond; that was a religious exercise, and one of the best things which I did. They say that characters were engraven on the bathing tub of King Tching-thang to this effect: "Renew thyself completely each day; do it again, and again, and forever again." I can understand that. Morning brings back the heroic ages. I was as much affected by the faint hum of a mosquito making its invisible and unimaginable tour through my apartment at earliest dawn, when I was sitting with door and windows open, as I could be by any trumpet that ever sang of fame. It was Homer's requiem; itself an Iliad and Odyssey in the air, singing its own wrath and wanderings. There was something cosmical about it; a standing advertisement, till forbidden, of the everlasting vigor and fertility of the world. The morning, which is the most memorable season of the day, is the awakening hour. Then there is least somnolence in us; and for an hour, at least, some part of us awakes which slumbers all the rest of the day and night. Little is to be expected of that day, if it can be called a day, to which we are not awakened by our Genius, but by the mechanical nudgings of some servitor, are not awakened by our own newly acquired force and aspirations from within, accompanied by the undulations of celestial music, instead of factory bells, and a fragrance filling the air—to a higher life than we fell asleep from; and thus the darkness bear its fruit, and prove itself to be good, no less than the light. That man who does not believe that each day contains an earlier, more sacred, and auroral hour than he has yet profaned, has despaired of life, and is pursuing a descending and darkening way. After a partial cessation of his sensuous life, the soul of man, or its organs rather, are reinvigorated each day, and his Genius tries again what noble life it can make. All memorable events, I should say, transpire in morning time and in a morning atmosphere. The Vedas say, "All intelligences awake with the morning." Poetry and art, and the fairest and most memorable of the actions of men, date from such an hour. All poets and heroes, like Memnon, are the children of Aurora, and emit their music at sunrise. To him whose elastic and vigorous thought keeps pace with the sun, the day is a perpetual morning. It matters not what the clocks say or the attitudes and labors of men. Morning is when I am awake and there is a dawn in me. Moral reform is the effort to throw off sleep. Why is it that men give so poor an account of their day if they have not been slumbering? They are not such poor calculators. If they had not been overcome with drowsiness, they would have performed something. The millions are awake enough for physical labor; but only one in a million is awake enough for effective intellectual exertion, only one in a hundred millions to a poetic or divine life. To be awake is to be alive. I have never yet met a man who was quite awake. How could I have looked him in the face?

We must learn to reawaken and keep ourselves awake, not by mechanical aids, but by an infinite expectation of the dawn, which does not forsake us in our soundest sleep. I know of no more encouraging fact than the unquestionable ability of man to elevate his life by a conscious endeavor. It is something to be able to paint a particular picture, or to carve a statue, and so to make a few objects beautiful; but it is far more glorious to carve and paint the very atmosphere and medium through which we look, which morally we can do. To affect the quality of the day, that is the highest of arts. Every man is tasked to make his life, even in its details, worthy of the contemplation of his most elevated and critical hour. If we refused, or rather used up, such paltry information as we get, the oracles would distinctly inform us how this might be done.

I went to the woods because I wished to live deliberately, to front only the essential facts of life, and see if I could not learn what it had to teach, and not, when I came to die, discover that I had not lived. I did not wish to live what was not life, living is so dear; nor did I wish to practice resignation, unless it was quite necessary. I wanted to live deep and suck out all the marrow of life, to live so sturdily and Spartan-like as to put to rout all that was not life, to cut a broad swath and shave close, to drive life into a corner, and reduce it to its lowest terms, and, if it proved to be mean, why then to get the whole and genuine meanness of it, and publish its meanness to the world; or if it were sublime, to know it by experience, and be able to give a true account of it in my next excursion. For most men, it appears to me, are in a strange uncertainty about it, whether it is of the devil or of God, and have *somewhat hastily* concluded that it is the chief end of man here to "glorify God and enjoy him forever."

Still we live meanly, like ants; though the fable tells us that we were long ago changed into men; like pygmies we fight with cranes; it is error upon error, and clout upon clout, and our best virtue has for its occasion a superfluous and evitable wretchedness. Our life is frittered away by detail. An honest man has hardly need to count more than his ten fingers, or in extreme cases he may add his ten toes, and lump the rest. Simplicity, simplicity, simplicity! I say, let your affairs be as two or three, and not a hundred or a thousand; instead of a million count half a dozen, and keep your accounts on your thumb-nail. In the midst of this chopping sea of civilized life, such are the clouds and storms and quicksands and thousand-and-one items to be allowed for, that a man has to live, if he would not founder and go to the bottom and not make his port at all, by dead reckoning, and he must be a great calculator indeed who succeeds. Simplify, simplify. Instead of three meals a day, if it be necessary eat but one; instead of a hundred dishes, five; and reduce other things in proportion. Our life is like a German Confederacy, made up of petty states, with its boundary forever fluctuating, so that even a German cannot tell you how it is bounded at any moment. The nation itself, with all its so-called internal improvements, which, by the way, are all external and superficial, is just such an unwieldy and overgrown establishment, cluttered with furniture and tripped up by its own traps, ruined by luxury and heedless expense, by want of calculation and a worthy aim, as the million households in the land; and the only cure for it, as for them, is in a rigid economy, a stern and more than Spartan simplicity of life and elevation of purpose. It lives too fast. Men think that it is essential that the *Nation* have commerce, and export ice, and talk through a telegraph, and ride thirty miles an hour, without a doubt, whether *they* do or not; but whether we should live like baboons or like men, is a little uncertain. If we do not get out sleepers, and forge rails, and devote days and nights to the work, but go to tinkering upon our *lives* to improve *them*, who will build railroads? And if railroads are not built, how shall we get to Heaven in season? But if we stay at home and mind our business, who will want railroads? We do not ride on the railroad; it rides upon us. Did you ever think what those sleepers are that underlie the railroad? Each one is a man, an Irishman, or a Yankee man. The rails are laid on them, and they are covered with sand, and the cars run smoothly over them. They are sound sleepers, I assure you. And every few years a new lot is laid down and run over; so that, if some have the pleasure of riding on a rail, others have the misfortune to be ridden upon. And when they run over a man that is walking in his sleep, a supernumerary sleeper in the wrong position, and wake him up, they suddenly stop the cars, and make a hue and cry about it, as if this were an exception. I am glad to know that it takes a gang of men for every five miles to keep the sleepers down and level in their beds as it is, for this is a sign that they may sometime get up again.

Why should we live with such hurry and waste of life? We are determined to be starved before we are hungry. Men say that a stitch in time saves nine, and so they take a thousand stitches today to save nine tomorrow. As for *work*, we haven't any of any consequence. We have the Saint Vitus' dance, and cannot possibly keep our heads still. If I should only give a few pulls at the parish bell-rope, as for a fire, that is, without setting the bell, there is hardly a man on his farm in the outskirts of Concord, notwithstanding that press of engagements which was his excuse so many times this morning, nor a boy, nor a woman, I might almost say, but would forsake all and follow that sound, not mainly to save property from the flames, but, if we will confess the truth, much more to see it burn, since burn it must, and we, be it known, did not set it on fire—or to see it put out, and have a hand in it, if that is done as handsomely; yes, even if it were the parish church itself. Hardly a man takes a half-hour's nap after dinner, but when he wakes he holds up his head and asks, "What's the news?" as if the rest of mankind had stood his sentinels. Some give directions to be waked every half-hour, doubtless for no other purpose; and then, to pay for it, they tell what they have dreamed. After a night's sleep the news is as indispensable as the breakfast. "Pray tell me anything new that has happened to a man anywhere on this globe,"—and he reads it over his coffee and rolls, that a man has had his eyes gouged out this morning on the Wachito River; never dreaming the while that he lives in the dark unfathomed mammoth cave of this world, and has but the rudiment of an eye himself.

For my part, I could easily do without the post-office. I think that there are very few important communications made through it. To speak critically, I never received more than one or two letters in my life—I wrote this some years ago—that were worth the postage. The penny-post is, commonly, an institution through which you seriously offer a man that penny for his thoughts which is often safely offered in jest. And I am sure that I never read any memorable news in a newspaper. If we read of one man robbed, or murdered, or killed by accident, or one house burned, or one vessel wrecked, or one steamboat blown up, or one cow run over on the Western Railroad, or one mad dog killed, or one lot of grasshoppers in the winter, we never need read of another. One is enough. If you are acquainted with the principle, what do you care for a myriad instances and applications? To a philosopher all *news*, as it is called, is gossip, and they who edit and read it are old women over their tea. Yet not a few are greedy after this gossip. There was such a rush, as I hear, the other day at one of the offices to learn the foreign news by the last arrival, that several large squares of plate glass belonging to the establishment were broken by the pressure—news which I seriously think a ready wit might write a twelvemonth, or twelve years, beforehand with sufficient accuracy. As for Spain, for instance, if you know how to throw in Don Carlos and the Infanta, and Don Pedro and Seville and Granada, from time to time in the right proportions—they may have changed the names a little since I saw the papers—and serve up a bull-fight when other entertainments fail, it will be true to the letter, and give us as good an idea of the exact state or ruin of things in Spain as the most succinct and lucid reports under this head in the newspapers: and as for England, almost the last significant scrap of news from that quarter was the revolution of 1649; and if you have learned the history of her crops for an average year, you never need attend to that thing again, unless your speculations are of a merely pecuniary character. If one may judge who rarely looks into the newspapers, nothing new does ever happen in foreign parts, a French revolution not excepted.

What news! how much more important to know what that is which was never old! "Kieou-he-yu (great dignitary of the state of Wei) sent a man to Khoung-tseu to know his news. Khoung-tseu caused the messenger to be seated near him, and questioned him in these terms: "What is your master doing?" The messenger answered with respect: "My master desires to diminish the number of his faults, but he cannot come to the end of them." The messenger being gone, the philosopher remarked: "What a worthy messenger! What a worthy messenger!" The preacher, instead of vexing the ears of drowsy farmers on their day of rest at the end of the week—for Sunday is the fit conclusion of an ill-spent week, and not the fresh and brave beginning of a new one—with this one other draggle-tail of a sermon, should shout with thundering voice, "Pause! Avast! Why so seeming fast, but deadly slow?"

Shams and delusions are esteemed for soundest truths, while reality is fabulous. If men would steadily observe realities only, and not allow themselves to be deluded, life, to compare it with such things as we know, would be like a fairy tale and the Arabian Nights' Entertainments. If we respected only what is inevitable and has a right to be, music and poetry would resound along the streets. When we are unhurried and wise, we perceive that only great and worthy things have any permanent and absolute existence, that petty fears and petty pleasures are but the shadow of the reality. This is always exhilarating and sublime. By closing the eyes and slumbering, and consenting to be deceived by shows, men establish and confirm their daily life of routine and habit everywhere, which still is built on purely illusory foundations. Children, who play life, discern its true law and relations more clearly than men, who fail to live it worthily, but who think that they are wiser by experience, that is, by failure. I have read in a Hindu book, that "there was a king's son, who, being expelled in infancy from his native city, was brought up by a forester, and, growing up to maturity in that state, imagined himself to belong to the barbarous race with which he lived. One of his father's ministers having discovered him, revealed to him what he was, and the misconception of his character was removed, and he knew himself to be a prince. So soul," continues the Hindu philosopher, "from the circumstances in which it is placed, mistakes its own character, until the truth is revealed to it by some holy teacher, and then it knows itself to be *Brahme*." I perceive that we inhabitants of New England live this mean life that we do because our vision does not penetrate the surface of things. We think that that *is* which *appears* to be. If a man should walk through this town and see only the reality, where, think you, would the "Mill-dam" go to? If he should give us an account of the realities he beheld there, we should not recognize the place in his description. Look at a meeting-house, or a court-house, or a jail, or a shop, or a dwelling-house, and say what that thing really is before a true gaze, and they would all go to pieces in your account of them. Men esteem truth remote, in the outskirts of the system, behind the farthest star, before Adam and after the last man. In eternity there is indeed something true and sublime. But all these times and places and occasions are now and here. God himself culminates in the present moment, and will never be more divine in the lapse of all the ages. And we are enabled to apprehend at all what is sublime and noble only by the perpetual instilling and drenching of the reality that surrounds us. The universe constantly and obediently answers to our conceptions; whether we travel fast or slow, the track is laid for us. Let us spend our lives in conceiving then. The poet or the artist never yet had so fair and noble a design but some of his posterity at least could accomplish it.

Let us spend one day as deliberately as Nature, and not be thrown off the track by every nutshell and mosquito's wing that falls on the rails. Let us rise early and fast, or break fast, gently and without perturbation; let company come and let company go, let the bells ring and the children cry—determined to make a day of it. Why should we knock under and go with the stream? Let us not be upset and overwhelmed in that terrible rapid and whirlpool called a dinner, situated in the meridian shallows. Weather this danger and you are safe, for the rest of the way is down hill. With unrelaxed nerves, with morning vigor, sail by it, looking another way, tied to the mast like Ulysses. If the engine whistles, let it whistle till it is hoarse for its pains. If the bell rings, why should we run? We will consider what kind of music they are like. Let us settle ourselves, and work and wedge our feet downward through the mud and slush of opinion, and prejudice, and tradition, and delusion, and appearance, that alluvion which covers the globe, through Paris and London, through New York and Boston and Concord, through Church and State, through poetry and philosophy and religion, till we come to a hard bottom and rocks in place, which we can call *reality*,

and say, This is, and no mistake; and then begin, having a *point d'appui*, below freshet and frost and fire, a place where you might found a wall or a state, or set a lamp-post safely, or perhaps a gauge, not a Nilometer, but a Realometer, that future ages might know how deep a freshet of shams and appearances had gathered from time to time. If you stand right fronting and face to face to a fact, you will see the sun glimmer on both its surfaces, as if it were a scimitar, and feel its sweet edge dividing you through the heart and marrow, and so you will happily conclude your mortal career. Be it life or death, we crave only reality. If we are really dying, let us hear the rattle in our throats and feel cold in the extremities; if we are alive, let us go about our business.

Time is but the stream I go a-fishing in. I drink at it; but while I drink I see the sandy bottom and detect how shallow it is. Its thin current slides away, but eternity remains. I would drink deeper; fish in the sky, whose bottom is pebbly with stars. I cannot count one. I know not the first letter of the alphabet. I have always been regretting that I was not as wise as the day I was born. The intellect is a cleaver; it discerns and rifts its way into the secret of things. I do not wish to be any more busy with my hands than is necessary. My head is hands and feet. I feel all my best faculties concentrated in it. My instinct tells me that my head is an organ for burrowing, as some creatures use their snout and fore paws, and with it I would mine and burrow my way through these hills. I think that the richest vein is somewhere hereabouts; so by the divining-rod and thin rising vapors I judge; and here I will begin to mine.

SOLITUDE

This is a delicious evening, when the whole body is one sense, and imbibes delight through every pore. I go and come with a strange liberty in Nature, a part of herself. As I walk along the stony shore of the pond in my shirt-sleeves, though it is cool as well as cloudy and windy, and I see nothing special to attract me, all the elements are unusually congenial to me. The bullfrogs trump to usher in the night, and the note of the whip-poor-will is borne on the rippling wind from over the water. Sympathy with the fluttering alder and poplar leaves almost takes away my breath; yet, like the lake, my serenity is rippled but not ruffled. These small waves raised by the evening wind are as remote from storm as the smooth reflecting surface. Though it is now dark, the wind still blows and roars in the wood, the waves still dash, and some creatures lull the rest with their notes. The repose is never complete. The wildest animals do not repose, but seek their prey now; the fox, and skunk, and rabbit, now roam the fields and woods without fear. They are Nature's watchmen—links which connect the days of animated life.

When I return to my house I find that visitors have been there and left their cards, either a bunch of flowers, or a wreath of evergreen, or a name in pencil on a yellow walnut leaf or a chip. They who come rarely to the woods take some little piece of the forest into their hands to play with by the way, which they leave, either intentionally or accidentally. One has peeled a willow wand, woven it into a ring, and dropped it on my table. I could always tell if visitors had called in my absence, either by the bended twigs or grass, or the print of their shoes, and generally of what sex or age or quality they were by some slight trace left, as a flower dropped, or a bunch of grass plucked and thrown away, even as far off as the railroad, half a mile distant, or by the lingering odor of a cigar or pipe. Nay, I was frequently notified of the passage of a traveler along the highway sixty rods off by the scent of his pipe.

There is commonly sufficient space about us. Our horizon is never quite at our elbows. The thick wood is not just at our door, nor the pond, but somewhat is always clearing, familiar and worn by us, appropriated and fenced in some way, and reclaimed from Nature. For what reason have I this vast range and circuit, some square miles of unfrequented forest, for my privacy, abandoned to me by men? My nearest neighbor is a mile distant, and no house is visible from any place but the hill-tops within half a mile of my own. I have my horizon bounded by woods all to myself; a distant view of the railroad where it touches the pond on the one hand, and of the fence which skirts the woodland road on the other. But for the most part it is as solitary where I live as on the prairies. It is as much Asia or Africa as New England. I have, as it were, my

THE POND
*The rippling wind from
over the water*

own sun and moon and stars, and a little world all to myself. At night there was never a traveler passed my house, or knocked at my door, more than if I were the first or last man; unless it were in the spring, when at long intervals some came from the village to fish for pouts—they plainly fished much more in the Walden Pond of their own natures, and baited their hooks with darkness—but they soon retreated, usually with light baskets, and left "the world to darkness and to me," and the black kernel of the night was never profaned by any human neighborhood. I believe that men are generally still a little afraid of the dark, though the witches are all hung, and Christianity and candles have been introduced.

Yet I experienced sometimes that the most sweet and tender, the most innocent and encouraging society may be found in any natural object, even for the poor misanthrope and most melancholy man. There can be no very black melancholy to him who lives in the midst of nature and has his senses still. There was never yet such a storm but it was Aeolian music to a healthy and innocent ear. Nothing can rightly compel a simple and brave man to a vulgar sadness. While I enjoy the friendship of the seasons I trust that nothing can make life a burden to me. The gentle rain which waters my beans and keeps me in the house today is not drear and melancholy, but good for me too. Though it prevents my hoeing them, it is of far more worth than my hoeing. If it should continue so long as to cause the seeds to rot in the ground and destroy the potatoes in the low lands, it would still be good for the grass on the uplands, and, being good for the grass, it would be good for me. Sometimes, when I compare myself with other men, it seems as if I were more favored by the gods than they, beyond any deserts that I am conscious of; as if I had a warrant and surety at their hands which my fellows have not, and were especially guided and guarded. I do not flatter myself, but if it be possible they flatter me. I have never felt lonesome, or in the least oppressed by a sense of solitude, but once, and that was a few weeks after I came to the woods, when, for an hour, I doubted if the near neighborhood of man was not essential to a serene and healthy life. To be alone was something unpleasant. But I was at the same time conscious of a slight insanity in my mood, and seemed to foresee my recovery. In the midst of a gentle rain while these thoughts prevailed, I was suddenly sensible of such sweet and beneficent society in Nature, in the very pattering of the drops, and in every sound and sight around my house, an infinite and unaccountable friendliness all at once like an atmosphere sustaining me, as made the fancied advantages of human neighborhood insignificant, and I have never thought of them since. Every little pine needle expanded and swelled with sympathy and befriended me. I was so distinctly made aware of the presence of something kindred to me, even in scenes which we are accustomed to call wild and dreary, and also that the nearest of blood to me and humanest was not a person nor a villager, that I thought no place could ever be strange to me again—

Mourning untimely consumes the sad;
Few are their days in the land of the living,
Beautiful daughter of Toscar.

Some of my pleasantest hours were during the long rainstorms in the spring or fall, which confined me to the house for the afternoon as well as the forenoon, soothed by their ceaseless roar and pelting; when an early twilight ushered in a long evening in which many thoughts had time to take root and unfold themselves. In those driving northeast rains which tried the village houses so, when the maids stood ready with mop and pail in front entries to keep the deluge out, I sat behind my door in my little house, which was all entry, and thoroughly enjoyed its protection. In one heavy thunder-shower the lightning struck a large pitch pine across the pond, making a very conspicuous and perfectly regular spiral groove from top to bottom, an inch or more deep, and four or five inches wide, as you would groove a walking-stick. I passed it again the other day, and was struck with awe on looking up and beholding that mark, now more distinct than ever, where a terrific and resistless bolt came down out of the harmless sky eight years ago. Men frequently say to me, "I should think you would feel lonesome down there, and want to be nearer to folks, rainy and snowy days and nights especially." I am tempted to reply to such: "This whole earth which we inhabit is but a point in space. How far apart, think you, dwell the two most distant inhabitants of yonder star, the breadth of whose disk cannot be appreciated by our instruments? Why should I feel lonely? Is not our planet in the Milky Way? This which you put seems to me not to be the most important question. What sort of space is that which separates a man from his fellows and makes him solitary? I have found that no exertion of the legs can bring two minds much nearer to one another. What do we want most to dwell near to? Not to many men surely, the depot, the post-office, the bar-room, the meeting-house, the school-house, the grocery, Beacon Hill, or the Five Points, where men most congregate, but to the perennial source of our life, whence in all our experience we have found that to issue, as the willow stands near the water and sends out its roots in that direction. This will vary with different natures, but this is the place where a wise man will dig his cellar. . . ." I one evening overtook one of my townsmen, who has accumulated what is called "a handsome property"— though I never got a *fair* view of it—on the Walden road, driving a pair of cattle to market, who inquired of me how I could bring my mind to give up so many of the comforts of life. I answered that I was very sure I liked it passably well; I was not joking. And so I went home to my bed, and left him to pick his way through the darkness and the mud to Brighton—or Brighttown—which place he would reach some time in the morning.

Any prospect of awakening or coming to life to a dead man makes indifferent all times and places. The place where that may occur is always the same, and indescribably pleasant to all our senses. For the most part we allow only outlying and transient circumstances to make our occasions. They are, in fact, the cause of our distraction. Nearest to all things is that power which fashions their being. *Next* to us the grandest laws are continually being executed. *Next* to us is not the workman whom we have hired with whom we love so well to talk, but the workman whose work we are.

"How vast and profound is the influence of the subtile powers of Heaven and of Earth!

"We seek to perceive them, and we do not see them; we seek to hear them, and we do not hear them; identified with the substance of things, they cannot be separated from them.

"They cause that in all the universe men purify and sanctify their hearts, and clothe themselves in their holiday garments to offer sacrifices and oblations to their ancestors. It is an ocean of subtile intelligences. They are everywhere, above us, on our left, on our right; they environ us on all sides."

We are the subjects of an experiment which is not a little interesting to me. Can we not do without the society of our gossips a little while under these circumstances—have our own thoughts to cheer us? Confucius says truly, "Virtue does not remain as an abandoned orphan; it must of necessity have neighbors."

With thinking we may be beside ourselves in a sane sense. By a conscious effort of the mind we can stand aloof from actions and their consequences; and all things, good and bad, go by us like a torrent. We are not wholly involved in Nature. I may be either the driftwood in the stream, or Indra in the sky looking down on it. I *may* be affected by a theatrical exhibition; on the other hand, I *may not* be affected by an actual event which appears to concern me much more. I only know myself as a human entity; the scene, so to speak, of thoughts and affections; and am sensible of a certain doubleness by which I can stand as remote from myself as from another. However intense my experience, I am conscious of the presence and criticism of a part of me, which, as it were, is not a part of me, but a spectator, sharing no experience, but taking note of it, and that is no more I than it is you. When the play, it may be the tragedy, of life is over, the spectator goes his way. It was a kind of fiction, a work of the imagination only, so far as he was concerned. This doubleness may easily make us poor neighbors and friends sometimes.

I find it wholesome to be alone the greater part of the time. To be in company, even with the best, is soon wearisome and dissipating. I love to be alone. I never found the companion that was so companionable as solitude. We are for the most part more lonely when we go abroad among men than when we stay in our chambers. A man thinking or working is always alone, let him be where he will. Solitude is not measured by the miles of space that intervene between a man and his fellows. The really diligent student in one of the crowded hives of Cambridge College is as solitary as a dervish in the desert. The farmer can work alone in the field or the woods all day, hoeing or chopping, and not feel lonesome, because he is employed; but when he comes home at night he cannot sit down in a room alone, at the mercy of his thoughts, but must be where he can "see the folks," and recreate, and, as he thinks, remunerate himself for his day's solitude; and hence he wonders how the student can sit alone in the house all night and most of the day without ennui and "the blues"; but he does not realize that the student, though in the house, is still at work in *his* field, and chopping in *his* woods, as the farmer in his, and in turn seeks the same recreation and society that the latter does, though it may be a more condensed form of it.

Society is commonly too cheap. We meet at very short intervals, not having had time to acquire any new value for each other. We meet at meals three times a day, and give each other a new taste of that old

REVERIE AT WALDEN
I found solitude

musty cheese that we are. We have had to agree on a certain set of rules, called etiquette and politeness, to make this frequent meeting tolerable and that we need not come to open war. We meet at the post-office, and at the sociable, and about the fireside every night; we live thick and are in each other's way, and stumble over one another, and I think that we thus lose some respect for one another. Certainly less frequency would suffice for all important and hearty communications. Consider the girls in a factory, never alone, hardly in their dreams. It would be better if there were but one inhabitant to a square mile, as where I live. The value of a man is not in his skin, that we should touch him.

I have heard of a man lost in the woods and dying of famine and exhaustion at the foot of a tree, whose loneliness was relieved by the grotesque visions with which, owing to bodily weakness, his diseased imagination surrounded him, and which he believed to be real. So also, owing to bodily and mental health and strength, we may be continually cheered by a like but more normal and natural society, and come to know that we are never alone.

I have a great deal of company in my house; especially in the morning, when nobody calls. Let me suggest a few comparisons, that some one may convey an idea of my situation. I am no more lonely than the loon in the pond that laughs so loud, or than Walden Pond itself. What company has that lonely lake, I pray? And yet it has not the blue devils, but the blue angels in it, in the azure tint of its waters. The sun is alone, except in thick weather, when there sometimes appear to be two, but one is a mock sun. God is alone; but the devil, he is far from being alone; he sees a great deal of company; he is legion. I am no more lonely than a single mullein or dandelion in a pasture, or a bean leaf, or sorrel, or a horsefly, or a bumblebee. I am no more lonely than the Mill Brook, or a weathercock, or the north star, or the south wind, or an April shower, or a January thaw, or the first spider in a new house.

I have occasional visits in the long winter evenings, when the snow falls fast and the wind howls in the wood, from an old settler and original proprietor, who is reported to have dug Walden Pond, and stoned it, and fringed it with pine woods; who tells me stories of old time and of new eternity; and between us we manage to pass a cheerful evening with social mirth and pleasant views of things, even without apples or cider—a most wise and humorous friend, whom I love much, who keeps himself more secret than ever did Goffe or Whalley; and though he is thought to be dead, none can show where he is buried. An elderly dame, too, dwells in my neighborhood, invisible to most persons, in whose odorous herb garden I love to stroll sometimes, gathering simples and listening to her fables; for she has a genius of unequaled fertility, and her memory runs back farther than mythology, and she can tell me the original of every fable, and on what fact every one is founded, for the incidents occurred when she was young. A ruddy and lusty old dame, who delights in all weathers and seasons, and is likely to outlive all her children yet.

The indescribable innocence and beneficence of Nature—of sun and wind and rain, of summer and winter—such health, such cheer, they afford forever! and such sympathy have they ever with our race, that all Nature would be affected and the sun's brightness fade, and the winds would sigh humanely, and the clouds rain tears, and the woods shed their leaves and put on mourning in midsummer, if any man should ever for a just cause grieve. Shall I not have intelligence with the earth? Am I not partly leaves and vegetable mold myself?

What is the pill which will keep us well, serene, contented? Not my or thy great-grandfather's, but our great-grandmother

Nature's universal, vegetable, botanic medicines, by which she has kept herself young always, outlived so many old Parrs in her day, and fed her health with their decaying fatness. For my panacea, instead of one of those quack vials of a mixture dipped from Acheron and the Dead Sea, which come out of those long shallow black-schooner-looking wagons which we sometimes see made to carry bottles, let me have a draught of undiluted morning air. Morning air! If men will not drink of this at the fountainhead of the day, why, then, we must even bottle up some and sell it in the shops, for the benefit of those who have lost their subscription ticket to morning time in this world. But remember, it will keep quite till noonday even in the coolest cellar, but drive out the stopples long ere that and follow westward the steps of Aurora. I am no worshipper of Hygieia, who was the daughter of that old herb-doctor Asclepius, and who is represented on monuments holding a serpent in one hand, and in the other a cup out of which the serpent sometimes drinks; but rather of Hebe, cup-bearer to Jupiter, who was the daughter of Juno and wild lettuce, and who had the power of restoring gods and men to the vigor of youth. She was probably the only thoroughly sound-conditioned, healthy, and robust young lady that ever walked the globe, and wherever she came it was spring.

THE VILLAGE

After hoeing, or perhaps reading and writing in the forenoon, I usually bathed again in the pond, swimming across one of its coves for a stint, and washed the dust of labor from my person, or smoothed out the last wrinkle which study had made, and for the afternoon was absolutely free. Every day or two I strolled to the village to hear some of the gossip which is incessantly going on there, circulating either from mouth to mouth, or from newspaper to newspaper, and which, taken in homeopathic doses, was really as refreshing in its way as the rustle of leaves and the peeping of frogs. As I walked in the woods to see the birds and squirrels, so I walked in the village to see the men and boys; instead of the wind among the pines I heard the carts rattle. In one direction from my house

CONCORD
Every day I strolled to the village

VILLAGE STORES

I escaped wonderfully from these dangers

there was a colony of muskrats in the river meadows; under the grove of elms and buttonwoods in the other horizon was a village of busy men, as curious to me as if they had been prairie-dogs, each sitting at the mouth of its burrow, or running over to a neighbor's to gossip. I went there frequently to observe their habits. The village appeared to me a great news room; and on one side, to support it, as once at Redding & Company's on State Street, they kept nuts and raisins, or salt and meal and other groceries. Some have such a vast appetite for the former commodity, that is, the news, and such sound digestive organs, that they can sit forever in public avenues without stirring, and let it simmer and whisper through them like the Etesian winds, or as if inhaling ether, it only producing numbness and insensibility to pain —otherwise it would often be painful to hear—without affecting the consciousness. I hardly ever failed, when I rambled through the village, to see a row of such worthies, either sitting on a ladder sunning themselves, with their bodies inclined forward and their eyes glancing along the line this way and that, from time to time, with a voluptuous expression, or else leaning against a barn with their hands in their pockets, like caryatids, as if to prop it up. They, being commonly out of doors, heard whatever was in the wind. These are the coarsest mills, in which all gossip is first rudely digested or cracked up before it is emptied into finer and more delicate hoppers within doors. I observed that the vitals of the village were the grocery, the barroom, the post-office, and the bank; and, as a necessary part of the machinery, they kept a bell, a big gun, and a fire-engine, at convenient places; and the houses were so arranged as to make the most of mankind, in lanes and fronting one another, so that every traveler had to run the gauntlet, and every man, woman, and child might get a lick at him. Of course, those who were stationed nearest to the head of the line, where they could most see and be seen, and have the first blow at him, paid the highest prices for their places; and the few straggling inhabitants in the outskirts, where long gaps in the line began to occur, and the traveler could get over walls or turn aside into cow-paths, and so escape, paid a very slight ground or window tax.

Signs were hung out on all sides to allure him; some to catch him by the appetite, as the tavern and victualling cellar; some by the fancy, as the dry goods store and the jeweler's; and others by the hair or the feet or the skirts, as the barber, the shoemaker, or the tailor. Besides, there was a still more terrible standing invitation to call at every one of these houses, and company expected about these times. For the most part I

The Pond And

FITCHBURG R.R. TRAIN STEAMING PAST WALDEN
Trains of clouds rising higher, going to heaven
while the cars are going to Boston

escaped wonderfully from these dangers, either by proceeding at once boldly and without deliberation to the goal, as is recommended to those who run the gauntlet, or by keeping my thoughts on high things, like Orpheus, who, "loudly singing the praises of the gods to his lyre, drowned the voices of the Sirens, and kept out of danger." Sometimes I bolted suddenly, and nobody could tell my whereabouts, for I

The Village

CONCORD MAIN STREET, 19TH CENTURY
I went there frequently to observe their habits

CAIRN MARKING THOREAU'S CABIN SITE
The pond impressed me like a tarn high up on the side of a mountain

did not stand much about gracefulness, and never hesitated at a gap in a fence. I was even accustomed to make an irruption into some houses, where I was well entertained, and after learning the kernels and very last sieveful of news—what had subsided, the prospects of war and peace, and whether the world was likely to hold together much longer—I was let out through the rear avenues, and so escaped to the woods again.

It was very pleasant, when I stayed late in town, to launch myself into the night, especially if it was dark and tempestuous, and set sail from some bright village parlor or lecture room, with a bag of rye or Indian meal upon my shoulder, for my snug harbor in the woods, having made all tight without and withdrawn under hatches with a merry crew of thoughts, leaving only my outer man at the helm, or even tying up the helm when it was plain sailing. I had many a genial thought by the cabin fire "as I sailed." I was never cast away nor distressed in any weather, though I encountered some severe storms. It is darker in the woods, even in common nights, than most suppose. I frequently had to look up at the opening between the trees above the path in order to learn my route, and, where there was no cart-path, to feel with my feet the faint track which I had worn, or steer by the known relation of particular trees which I felt with my hands, passing between two pines for instance, not more than eighteen inches apart, in the midst of the woods, invariably, in the darkest night. Sometimes, after coming home thus late in a dark and muggy night, when my feet felt the path which my eyes could not see, dreaming and absent-minded all the way, until I was aroused by having to raise my hand to lift the latch, I have not been able to recall a single step of my walk, and I have thought that perhaps my body would find its way home if its master should forsake it, as the hand finds its way to the mouth without

assistance. Several times, when a visitor chanced to stay into evening, and it proved a dark night, I was obliged to conduct him to the cart-path in the rear of the house, and then point out to him the direction he was to pursue, and in keeping which he was to be guided rather by his feet than his eyes. One very dark night I directed thus on their way two young men who had been fishing in the pond. They lived about a mile off through the woods, and were quite used to the route. A day or two after one of them told me that they wandered about the greater part of the night, close by their own premises, and did not get home till toward morning, by which time, as there had been several heavy showers in the meanwhile, and the leaves were very wet, they were drenched to their skins. I have heard of many going astray even in the village streets, when the darkness was so thick that you could cut it with a knife, as the saying is. Some who live in the outskirts, having come to town a-shopping in their wagons, have been obliged to put up for the night; and gentlemen and ladies making a call have gone half a mile out of their way, feeling the sidewalk only with their feet, and not knowing when they turned. It is a surprising and memorable, as well as valuable experience, to be lost in the woods any time. Often in a storm, even by day, one will come out upon a well-known road and yet find it impossible to tell which way leads to the village. Though he knows that he has traveled it a thousand times, he cannot recognize a feature in it, but it is as strange to him as if it were a road in Siberia. By night, of course, the perplexity is infinitely greater. In our most trivial walks, we are constantly, though unconsciously, steering like pilots by certain well-known beacons and headlands, and if we go beyond our usual course we still carry in our minds the bearing of some neighboring cape; and not till we are completely lost, or turned round—for a man needs only to be turned round once with his eyes shut in this world to be lost—do we appreciate the vastness and strangeness of Nature. Every man has to learn the points of compass again as often as he awakes, whether from sleep or any abstraction. Not till we are lost, in other words not till we have lost the world, do we begin to find ourselves, and realize where we are and the infinite extent of our relations.

One afternoon, near the end of the first summer, when I went to the village to get a shoe from the cobbler's, I was seized and put into jail, because, as I have elsewhere related, I did not pay a tax to, or recognize the authority of, the State which buys and sells men, women, and children, like cattle, at the door of its senate-house. I had gone down to the woods for other purposes. But, wherever a man goes, men will pursue and paw him with their dirty institutions, and, if they can, constrain him to belong to their desperate odd-fellow society. It is true, I might have resisted forcibly with more or less effect, might have run "amok" against society; but I preferred that society should run "amok" against me, it being the desperate party. However, I was released the next day, obtained my mended shoe, and returned to the woods in season to get my dinner of huckleberries on Fair Haven Hill. I was never molested by any person but those who represented the State. I had no lock nor bolt but for the desk which held my papers, not even a nail to put over my latch or windows. I never fastened my door night or day, though I was to be absent several days; not even when the next fall I spent a fortnight in the woods of Maine. And yet my house was more respected than if it had been surrounded by a file of soldiers. The tired rambler could rest and warm himself by my fire, the literary amuse himself with the few books on my table, or the curious, by opening my closet door, see what was left of my dinner, and what

prospect I had of a supper. Yet, though many people of every class came this way to the pond, I suffered no serious inconvenience from these sources, and I never missed anything but one small book, a volume of Homer, which perhaps was improperly gilded, and this I trust a soldier of our camp has found by this time. I am convinced that if all men were to live as simply as I then did, thieving and robbery would be unknown. These take place only in communities where some have got more than is sufficient while others have not enough. The Pope's Homers would soon get properly distributed.

> *Nec bella fuerunt,*
> *Faginus astabat dum scyphus ante dapes.*

> "Nor wars did men molest,
> When only beechen bowls were in request."

"You who govern public affairs, what need have you to employ punishments? Love virtue, and the people will be virtuous. The virtues of a superior man are like the wind; the virtues of a common man are like the grass; the grass, when the wind passes over it, bends."

HIGHER LAWS

As I came home through the woods with my string of fish, trailing my pole, it being now quite dark, I caught a glimpse of a woodchuck stealing across my path, and felt a strange thrill of savage delight, and was strongly tempted to seize and devour him raw; not that I was hungry then, except for that wildness which he represented. Once or twice, however, while I lived at the pond, I found myself ranging the woods, like a half-starved hound, with a strange abandonment, seeking some kind of venison which I might devour, and no morsel could have been too savage for me. The wildest scenes had become unaccountably familiar. I found in myself, and still find, an instinct toward a higher, or, as it is named, spiritual life, as do most men, and another toward a primitive rank and savage one, and I reverence them both. I love the wild not less than the good. The wildness and adventure that are in fishing still recommended it to me. I like sometimes to take rank hold on life and spend my day more as the animals do. Perhaps I have owed to this employment and to hunting, when quite young, my closest acquaintance with Nature. They early introduce us to and detain us in scenery with which otherwise, at that age, we should have little acquaintance. Fishermen, hunters, woodchoppers, and others, spending their lives in the fields and woods, in a peculiar sense a part of Nature themselves, are often in a more favorable mood for observing her, in the intervals of their pursuits, than philosophers or poets even, who approach her with expectation. She is not afraid to exhibit herself to them. The traveler on the prairie is naturally a hunter, on the head waters of the Missouri and Columbia a trapper, and at the Falls of St. Mary a fisherman. He who is only a traveler learns things at second-hand and by the halves, and is poor authority. We are most interested when science reports what those men already know practically or instinctively, for that alone is a true *humanity*, or account of human experience.

They mistake who assert that the Yankee has few amusements, because he has not so many public holidays, and men and boys do not play so many games as they do in England, for here the more primitive but solitary amusements of hunting, fishing, and the like have not yet given place to the former. Almost every New England boy among my contemporaries shouldered a fowling-piece between the ages of ten and fourteen; and his hunting and fishing grounds were not limited, like the preserves of an English nobleman, but were more boundless even than those of a savage. No wonder, then, that he did not oftener stay to play on the common. But already a change is taking place, owing, not to an increased humanity, but to an increased scarcity of game, for perhaps the hunter is the greatest friend of the animals hunted, not excepting the Humane Society.

Moreover, when at the pond, I wished sometimes to add fish to my fare for variety. I have actually fished from the same kind of necessity that the first fishers did. Whatever humanity I might conjure up against it was all factitious, and concerned my philosophy more than my feelings. I speak of fishing only now, for I had long felt differently about fowling, and sold my gun before I went to the woods. Not that I am less humane than others, but I did not perceive that my feelings were much affected. I did not pity the fishes nor the worms. This was habit. As for fowling, during the last years that I carried a gun my excuse was that I was studying ornithology, and sought only new or rare birds. But I confess that I am now inclined to think that there is a finer way of studying ornithology than this. It requires so much closer attention to the habits of the birds, that, if for that reason only, I have been willing to omit the gun. Yet notwithstanding the objection on the score of humanity, I am compelled to doubt if equally valuable sports are ever substituted for these; and when some of my friends have asked me anxiously about their boys, whether they should let them hunt, I have answered, yes—remembering that it was one of the best parts of my education—*make* them hunters, though sportsmen only at first, if possible, mighty hunters at last, so that they shall not find game large enough for them in this or any vegetable wilderness—hunters as well as fishers of men. Thus far I am of the opinion of Chaucer's nun, who:

yave not of the text a pulled hen
That saith that hunters ben not holy men.

There is a period in the history of the

individual, as of the race, when the hunters are the "best men," as the Algonquins called them. We cannot but pity the boy who has never fired a gun; he is no more humane, while his education has been sadly neglected. This was my answer with respect to those youths who were bent on this pursuit, trusting that they would soon outgrow it. No humane being, past the thoughtless age of boyhood, will wantonly murder any creature which holds its life by the same tenure that he does. The hare in its extremity cries like a child. I warn you, mothers, that my sympathies do not always make the usual *philanthropic* distinctions.

Such is oftenest the young man's introduction to the forest, and the most original part of himself. He goes thither at first as a hunter and fisher, until at last, if he has the seeds of a better life in him, he distinguishes his proper objects, as a poet or naturalist it may be, and leaves the gun and fish-pole behind. The mass of men are still and always young in this respect. In some countries a hunting parson is no uncommon sight. Such a one might make a good shepherd's dog, but is far from being the Good Shepherd. I have been surprised to consider that the only obvious employment, except woodchopping, ice-cutting, or the like business, which ever to my knowledge detained at Walden Pond for a whole half-day any of my fellow-citizens, whether fathers or children of the town, with just one exception, was fishing. Commonly they did not think that they were lucky, or well paid for their time, unless they got a long string of fish, though they had the opportunity of seeing the pond all the while. They might go there a thousand times before the sediment of fishing would sink to the bottom and leave their purpose pure; but no doubt such a clarifying process would be going on all the while. The Governor and his Council faintly remember the pond, for they went a-fishing there when they were boys; but now they are too old and dignified to go a-fishing, and so they know it no more forever. Yet even they expect to go to heaven at last. If the legislature regards it, it is chiefly to regulate the number of hooks to be used there; but they know nothing about the hook of hooks with which to angle for the pond itself, impaling the legislature for a bait. Thus, even in civilized communities, the embryo man passes through the hunter stage of development.

I have found repeatedly, of late years, that I cannot fish without falling a little in self-respect. I have tried it again and again. I have skill at it, and, like many of my fellows, a certain instinct for it, which revives from time to time, but always when I have done I feel that it would have been better if I had not fished. I think that I do not mistake. It is a faint intimation, yet so are the first streaks of morning. There is unquestionably this instinct in me which belongs to the lower orders of creation; yet with every year I am less a fisherman, though without more humanity or even wisdom; at present I am no fisherman at all. But I see that if I were to live in a wilderness I should again be tempted to become a fisher and hunter in earnest. Beside, there is something essentially unclean about this diet and all flesh, and I began to see where housework commences, and whence the endeavor, which costs so much, to wear a tidy and respectable appearance each day, to keep the house sweet and free from all ill odors and sights. Having been my own butcher and scullion and cook, as well as the gentleman for whom the dishes were served up, I can speak from an unusually complete experience. The practical objection to animal food in my case was its uncleanness; and besides, when I had caught and cleaned and cooked and eaten my fish, they seemed not to have fed me essentially. It was insignificant and unnecessary, and cost more than it came to. A little bread or a few potatoes would have done as well, with less trouble and filth. Like many of my contemporaries, I had rarely for many years used animal food, or tea, or coffee, etc.; not so much because of any ill effects which I had traced to them, as because they were not agreeable to my imagination. The repugnance to animal food is not the effect of experience, but is an instinct. It appeared more beautiful to live low and fare hard in many respects; and though I never did so, I went far enough to please my imagination. I believe that every man who has ever been earnest to preserve his higher or poetic faculties in the best condition has been particularly inclined to abstain from animal food, and from much food of any kind. It is a significant fact, stated by entomologists—I find it in Kirby and Spence—that "some insects in their perfect state, though furnished with organs of feeding, make no use of them"; and they lay it down as "a general rule, that almost all insects in this state eat much less than in that of larvae. The voracious caterpillar when transformed into a butterfly . . . and the gluttonous maggot when become a fly" content themselves with a drop or two of honey or some other sweet liquid. The abdomen under the wings of the butterfly still represents the larva. This is the tidbit which tempts his insectivorous fate. The gross feeder is a man in the larva state; and there are whole nations in that condition, nations without fancy or imagination, whose vast abdomens betray them.

It is hard to provide and cook so simple and clean a diet as will not offend the imagination; but this, I think, is to be fed when we feed the body; they should both sit down at the same table. Yet perhaps this may be done. The fruits eaten temperately need not make us ashamed of our appetites, nor interrupt the worthiest pursuits. But put an extra condiment into your dish, and it will poison you. It is not worth the while to live by rich cookery. Most men would feel shame if caught preparing with their own hands precisely such a dinner,

whether of animal or vegetable food, as is every day prepared for them by others. Yet till this is otherwise we are not civilized, and, if gentlemen and ladies, are not true men and women. This certainly suggests what change is to be made. It may be vain to ask why the imagination will not be reconciled to flesh and fat. I am satisfied that it is not. Is it not a reproach that man is a carnivorous animal? True, he can and does live, in a great measure, by preying on other animals; but this is a miserable way —as any one who will go to snaring rabbits, or slaughtering lambs, may learn—and he will be regarded as a benefactor of his race who shall teach man to confine himself to a more innocent and wholesome diet. Whatever my own practice may be, I have no doubt that it is a part of the destiny of the human race, in its gradual improvement, to leave off eating animals, as surely as the savage tribes have left off eating each other when they came in contact with the more civilized.

If one listens to the faintest but constant suggestions of his genius, which are certainly true, he sees not to what extremes, or even insanity, it may lead him; and yet that way, as he grows more resolute and faithful, his road lies. The faintest assured objection which one healthy man feels will at length prevail over the arguments and customs of mankind. No man ever followed his genius till it misled him. Though the result were bodily weakness, yet perhaps no one can say that the consequences were to be regretted, for these were a life in conformity to higher principles. If the day and the night are such that you greet them with joy, and life emits a fragrance like flowers and sweet-scented herbs, is more elastic, more starry, more immortal, that is your success. All nature is your congratulation, and you have cause momentarily to bless yourself. The greatest gains and values are farthest from being appreciated. We easily come to doubt if they exist. We soon forget them. They are the highest reality. Perhaps the facts most astounding and most real are never communicated by man to man. The true harvest of my daily life is somewhat as intangible and indescribable as the tints of morning or evening. It is a little star-dust caught, a segment of the rainbow which I have clutched.

Yet, for my part, I was never unusually squeamish; I could sometimes eat a fried rat with a good relish, if it were necessary. I am glad to have drunk water so long, for the same reason that I prefer the natural sky to an opium-eater's heaven. I would fain keep sober always; and there are infinite degrees of drunkenness. I believe that water is the only drink for a wise man; wine is not so noble a liquor; and think of dashing the hopes of a morning with a cup of warm coffee, or of an evening with a dish of tea! Ah, how low I fall when I am tempted by them! Even music may be intoxicating. Such apparently slight causes destroyed Greece and Rome, and will destroy England and America. Of all ebriosity, who does not prefer to be intoxicated by the air he breathes? I have found it to be the most serious objection to coarse labors long continued, that they compelled me to eat and drink coarsely also. But to tell the truth, I find myself at present somewhat less particular in these respects. I carry less religion to the table, ask no blessing; not because I am wiser than I was, but, I am obliged to confess, because, however much it is to be regretted, with years I have grown more coarse and indifferent. Perhaps these questions are entertained only in youth, as most believe of poetry. My practice is "nowhere," my opinion is here. Nevertheless I am far from regarding myself as one of those privileged ones to whom the Veda refers when it says, that "he who has true faith in the Omnipresent Supreme Being may eat all that exists," that is, is not bound to inquire what is his food, or who prepares it; and even in their case it is to

be observed, as a Hindu commentator has remarked, that the Vedant limits this privilege to "the time of distress."

Who has not sometimes derived an inexpressible satisfaction from his food in which appetite had no share? I have been thrilled to think that I owed a mental perception to the commonly gross sense of taste, that I have been inspired through the palate, that some berries which I had eaten on a hillside had fed my genius. "The soul not being mistress of herself," says Thseng-tseu, "one looks, and one does not see; one listens, and one does not hear; one eats, and one does not know the savor of food." He who distinguishes the true savor of his food can never be a glutton; he who does not cannot be otherwise. A puritan may go to his brown-bread crust with as gross an appetite as ever an alderman to his turtle. Not that food which entereth into the mouth defileth a man, but the appetite with which it is eaten. It is neither the quality nor the quantity, but the devotion to sensual savors; when that which is eaten is not a viand to sustain our animal, or inspire our spiritual life, but food for the worms that possess us. If the hunter has a taste for mud-turtles, muskrats, and other such savage tidbits, the fine lady indulges a taste for jelly made of a calf's foot, or for sardines from over the sea, and they are even. He goes to the mill-pond, she to her preserve-pot. The wonder is how they, how you and I, can live this slimy, beastly life, eating and drinking.

Our whole life is startlingly moral. There is never an instant's truce between virtue and vice. Goodness is the only investment that never fails. In the music of the harp which trembles round the world it is the insisting on this which thrills us. The harp is the traveling patterer for the Universe's Insurance Company, recommending its laws, and our little goodness is all the assessment that we pay. Though the youth at last grows indifferent, the laws of the universe are not indifferent, but are forever on the side of the most sensitive. Listen to every zephyr for some reproof, for it is surely there, and he is unfortunate who does not hear it. We cannot touch a string or move a stop but the charming moral transfixes us. Many an irksome noise, go a long way off, is heard as music, a proud, sweet satire on the meanness of our lives.

We are conscious of an animal in us, which awakens in proportion as our higher nature slumbers. It is reptile and sensual, and perhaps cannot be wholly expelled; like the worms which, even in life and health, occupy our bodies. Possibly we may withdraw from it, but never change its nature. I fear that it may enjoy a certain health of its own; that we may be well, yet not pure. The other day I picked up the lower jaw of a hog, with white and sound teeth and tusks, which suggested that there was an animal health and vigor distinct from the spiritual. This creature succeeded by other means than temperance and purity. "That in which men differ from brute beasts," says Mencius, "is a thing very inconsiderable; the common herd lose it very soon; superior men preserve it carefully." Who knows what sort of life would result if we had attained to purity? If I knew so wise a man as could teach me purity I would go to seek him forthwith. "A command over our passions, and over the external senses of the body, and good acts, are declared by the Veda to be indispensable in the mind's approximation to God." Yet the spirit can for the time pervade and control every member and function of the body, and transmute what in form is the grossest sensuality into purity and devotion. The generative energy, which, when we are loose, dissipates and makes us unclean, when we are continent invigorates and inspires us. Chastity is the flowering of man; and what are called Genius, Heroism, Holiness, and the like, are but various fruits which succeed it.

Man flows at once to God when the channel of purity is open. By turns our purity inspires and our impurity casts us down. He is blessed who is assured that the animal is dying out in him day by day, and the divine being established. Perhaps there is none but has cause for shame on account of the inferior and brutish nature to which he is allied. I fear that we are such gods or demigods only as fauns and satyrs, the divine allied to beasts, the creatures of appetite, and that, to some extent, our very life is our disgrace.

> How happy's he who hath due place assigned
> To his beasts and disafforested his mind!
>
> .　　.　　.　　.　　.
>
> Can use his horse, goat, wolf, and ev'ry beast,
> And is not ass himself to all the rest!
> Else man not only is the herd of swine,
> But he's those devils too which did incline
> Them to a headlong rage, and made them worse.

All sensuality is one, though it takes many forms; all purity is one. It is the same whether a man eat, or drink, or cohabit, or sleep sensually. They are but one appetite, and we only need to see a person do any one of these things to know how great a sensualist he is. The impure can neither stand nor sit with purity. When the reptile is attacked at one mouth of his burrow, he shows himself at another. If you would be chaste, you must be temperate. What is chastity? How shall a man know if he is chaste? He shall not know it. We have heard of this virtue, but we know not what it is. We speak conformably to the rumor which we have heard. From exertion come wisdom and purity; from sloth ignorance and sensuality. In the student sensuality is a sluggish habit of mind. An unclean person is universally a slothful one, one who sits by a stove, whom the sun shines on prostrate, who reposes without being fatigued. If you would avoid uncleanness, and all the sins, work earnestly, though it be at cleaning a stable. Nature is hard to be overcome, but she must be overcome. What avails it that you are Christian, if you are not purer than the heathen, if you deny yourself no more, if you are not more religious? I know of many systems of religion esteemed heathenish whose precepts fill the reader with shame, and provoke him to new endeavors, though it be to the performance of rites merely.

I hesitate to say these things, but it is not because of the subjects—I care not how obscene my *words* are—but because I cannot speak of them without betraying my impurity. We discourse freely without shame of one form of sensuality, and are silent about another. We are so degraded that we cannot speak simply of the necessary functions of human nature. In earlier ages, in some countries, every function was reverently spoken of and regulated by law. Nothing was too trivial for the Hindu law-giver, however offensive it may be to modern taste. He teaches how to eat, drink, cohabit, void excrement and urine, and the like, elevating what is mean, and does not falsely excuse himself by calling these things trifles.

Every man is the builder of a temple, called his body, to the god he worships, after a style purely his own, nor can he get off by hammering marble instead. We are all sculptors and painters, and our material is our own flesh and blood and bones. Any nobleness begins at once to refine a man's features, any meanness or sensuality to imbrute them.

John Farmer sat at his door one September evening, after a hard day's work, his mind still running on his labor more or less. Having bathed, he sat down to recreate his intellectual man. It was a rather cool evening, and some of his neighbors were apprehending a frost. He had not attended to the train of his thoughts long when he heard some one playing on a flute, and that sound harmonized with his mood. Still he thought of his work; but the burden of his thought was, that though this kept running in his head, and he found himself planning and contriving it against his will, yet it concerned him very little. It was no more than the scurf of his skin, which was constantly shuffled off. But the notes of the flute came home to his ears out of a different sphere from that he worked in, and suggested work for certain faculties which slumbered in him. They gently did away with the street, and the village, and the state in which he lived. A voice said to him, "Why do you stay here and live this mean moiling life, when a glorious existence is possible for you? Those same stars twinkle over other fields than these." But how to come out of this condition and actually migrate thither? All

FLUTE PLAYER
Sound harmonized with mood

that he could think of was to practice some new austerity, to let his mind descend into his body and redeem it, and treat himself with ever increasing respect.

CONCLUSION

To the sick the doctors wisely recommend a change of air and scenery. Thank Heaven, here is not all the world. The buckeye does not grow in New England, and the mockingbird is rarely heard here. The wild goose is more of a cosmopolite than we; he breaks his fast in Canada, takes a luncheon in the Ohio, and plumes himself for the night in a southern bayou. Even the bison, to some extent, keeps pace with the seasons, cropping the pastures of the Colorado only till a greener and sweeter grass awaits him by the Yellowstone. Yet we think that if rail fences are pulled down, and stone walls piled up on our farms, bounds are henceforth set to our lives and our fates decided. If you are chosen town clerk, forsooth, you cannot go to Tierra del Fuego this summer: but you may go to the land of infernal fire nevertheless. The universe is wider than our views of it.

Yet we should oftener look over the taffrail of our craft, like curious passengers, and not make the voyage like stupid sailors picking oakum. The other side of the globe is but the home of our correspondent. Our voyaging is only great-circle sailing, and the doctors prescribe for diseases of the skin merely. One hastens to southern Africa to chase the giraffe; but surely that is not the game he would be after. How long, pray, would a man hunt giraffes if he could? Snipes and woodcocks also may afford rare sport; but I trust it would be nobler game to shoot one's self.

> Direct your eye right inward, and you'll find
> A thousand regions in your mind
> Yet undiscovered. Travel them, and be
> Expert in home-cosmography.

What does Africa—what does the West stand for? Is not our own interior white on the chart, black though it may prove, like the coast, when discovered? Is it the source of the Nile, or the Niger, or the Mississippi, or a Northwest Passage around this continent, that we would find? Are these the problems which most concern mankind? Is Franklin the only man who is lost, that his wife should be so earnest to find him? Does Mr. Grinnell know where he himself is? Be rather the Mungo Park, the Lewis and Clark and Frobisher, of your own streams and oceans; explore your own higher latitudes, with shiploads of preserved meats to support you, if they be necessary; and pile the empty cans sky-high for a sign. Were preserved meats invented to preserve meat merely? Nay, be a Columbus to whole new continents and worlds within you, opening new channels, not of trade, but of thought. Every man is the lord of a realm beside which the earthly empire of the Czar is but a petty state, a hummock left by the ice. Yet some can be patriotic who have no *self*-respect, and sacrifice the greater to the less. They love the soil which makes their graves, but have no sympathy with the spirit which may still animate their clay. Patriotism is a maggot in their heads. What was the meaning of that South-Sea Exploring Expedition, with all its parade and expense, but an indirect recognition of the fact that there are continents and seas in the moral world to which every man is an isthmus or an inlet, yet unexplored by him, but that it is easier to sail many thousand miles through cold and storm and cannibals, in a government ship, with five hundred men and boys to assist one, than it is to explore the private sea, the Atlantic and Pacific Ocean of one's being alone.

Erret, et extremos alter scrutetur Iberos.
Plus habet hic vitae, plus habet ille viae.

"Let them wander and scrutinize the outlandish Australians.

I have more of God, they more of the road."

It is not worth the while to go round the world to count the cats in Zanzibar. Yet do this even till you can do better, and you may perhaps find some "Symmes' Hole" by which to get at the inside at last. England and France, Spain and Portugal, Gold Coast and Slave Coast, all front on this private sea; but no bark from them has ventured out of sight of land, though it is without doubt the direct way to India. If you would learn to speak all tongues and conform to the customs of all nations, if you would travel farther than all travelers, be naturalized in all climes, and cause the Sphinx to dash her head against a stone, even obey the precept of the old philosopher, and *Explore thyself*. Herein are demanded the eye and the nerve. Only the defeated and deserters go to the wars, cowards that run away and enlist. Start now on that farthest western way, which does not pause at the Mississippi or the Pacific, nor conduct toward a worn-out China or Japan, but leads on direct, a tangent to this sphere, summer and winter, day and night, sun down, moon down, and at last earth down too.

It is said that Mirabeau took to highway robbery "to ascertain what degree of resolution was necessary in order to place one's self in formal opposition to the most sacred laws of society." He declared that "a soldier who fights in the ranks does not require half so much courage as a footpad,"—"that honor and religion have never stood in the way of a well-considered and firm resolve." This was manly, as the world goes; and yet it was idle, if not desperate. A saner man would have found himself often enough "in formal opposition" to what are deemed "the most sacred laws of society," through obedience to yet more sacred laws, and so have tested his resolution without going out of his way. It is not for a man to put himself in such an attitude to society, but to maintain himself in whatever attitude he find himself through obedience to the laws of his being, which will never be one of opposition to a just government, if he should chance to meet with such.

I left the woods for as good a reason as I went there. Perhaps it seemed to me that I had several more lives to live, and could not spare any more time for that one. It is remarkable how easily and insensibly we fall into a particular route, and make a beaten track for ourselves. I had not lived there a week before my feet wore a path from my door to the pondside; and though it is five or six years since I trod it, it is still quite distinct. It is true, I fear, that others may have fallen into it, and so helped to keep it open. The surface of the earth is soft and impressible by the feet of men; and so with the paths which the mind travels. How worn and dusty, then, must be the highways of the world, how deep the ruts of tradition and conformity! I did not wish to take a cabin passage, but rather to go before the mast and on the deck of the world, for there I could best see the moonlight amid the mountains. I do not wish to go below now.

I learned this, at least, by my experiment: that if one advances confidently in the direction of his dreams, and endeavors to live the life he has imagined, he will meet with a success unexpected in common hours. He will put some things behind, will pass an invisible boundary; new, universal, and more liberal laws will begin to establish themselves around and within him; or the old laws be expanded, and interpreted in his favor in a more liberal sense, and he will live with the license of a higher order of beings. In proportion as he simplifies his life, the laws of the universe will appear less complex, and solitude will not be solitude, nor poverty poverty, nor weakness weakness. If you have built castles in the air, your work need not be lost; that is where they should be. Now put the foundations under them.

It is a ridiculous demand which England and America make, that you shall speak so that they can understand you. Neither men nor toadstools grow so. As if that were important, and there were not enough to understand you without them. As if Nature could support but one order of understandings, could not sustain birds as well as quadrupeds, flying as well as creeping things, and *hush* and *who*, which Bright can understand, were the best English. As if there were safety in stupidity alone. I fear chiefly lest my expression may not be *extra-vagant* enough, may not wander far enough beyond the narrow limits of my daily experience, so as to be adequate to the truth of which I have been convinced. *Extra vagance!* it depends on how you are yarded. The migrating buffalo, which seeks new pastures in another latitude, is not extravagant like the cow which kicks over the pail, leaps the cowyard fence, and runs after her calf, in milking time. I desire to speak somewhere *without* bounds; like a man in a waking moment, to men in their waking moments; for I am convinced that I cannot exaggerate enough even to lay the foundation of a true expression. Who that has heard a strain of music feared then lest he should speak extravagantly any more forever? In view of the future or possible, we should live quite laxly and undefined in front, our outlines dim and misty on that side; as our shadows reveal an insensible perspiration toward the sun. The volatile truth of our words should continually betray the inadequacy of the residual statement. Their truth is instantly *translated;* its literal monument alone remains. The words which express our faith and piety are not definite; yet they are significant and fragrant like frankincense to superior natures.

Why level downward to our dullest perception always, and praise that as common sense? The commonest sense is the sense of men asleep, which they express by snoring. Sometimes we are inclined to class those who are once-and-a-half-witted with the half-witted, because we appreciate only a third part of their wit. Some would find fault with the morning red, if they ever got up early enough. "They pretend," as I hear, "that the verses of Kabir have four different senses; illusion, spirit, intellect, and the exoteric doctrine of the Vedas"; but in this part of the world it is considered a ground for complaint if a man's writings admit of more than one interpretation. While England endeavors to cure the potato-rot, will not any endeavor to cure the brain-rot, which prevails so much more widely and fatally?

I do not suppose that I have attained to obscurity, but I should be proud if no more fatal fault were found with my pages on this score than was found with the Walden ice. Southern customers objected to its blue color, which is the evidence of its purity, as if it were muddy, and preferred the Cambridge ice, which is white, but tastes of weeds. The purity men love is like the mists which envelop the earth, and not like the azure ether beyond.

Some are dinning in our ears that we Americans, and moderns generally, are intellectual dwarfs compared with the ancients, or even the Elizabethan men. But what is that to the purpose? A living dog is better than a dead lion. Shall a man go and hang himself because he belongs to the race of pygmies, and not be the biggest pygmy that he can? Let every one mind his own business, and endeavor to be what he was made.

Why should we be in such desperate haste to succeed and in such desperate enterprises? If a man does not keep pace with his companions, perhaps it is because he hears a different drummer. Let him step to the music which he hears, however measured or far away. It is not important that he should mature as soon as an apple tree or an oak. Shall he turn his spring into summer? If the condition of things which we were made for is not yet, what were any reality which we can substitute? We will not be ship-wrecked on a vain reality. Shall we with pains erect a heaven of blue glass over ourselves, though when it is done we shall be sure to gaze still at the true ethereal heaven far above, as if the former were not?

There was an artist in the city of Kouroo who was disposed to strive after perfection. One day it came into his mind to make a staff. Having considered that in an imperfect work time is an ingredient, but into a perfect work time does not enter, he said to himself, It shall be perfect in all respects, though I should do nothing else in my life. He proceeded instantly to the forest for wood, being resolved that it should not be made of unsuitable material; and as he searched for and rejected stick after stick, his friends gradually deserted him, for they grew old in their works and died, but he grew not older by a moment. His singleness of purpose and resolution, and his elevated piety, endowed him, without his knowledge, with perennial youth. As he made no compromise with Time, Time kept out of his way, and only sighed at a distance because he could not overcome him. Before he had found a stick in all respects suitable the city of Kouroo was a hoary ruin, and he sat on one of its mounds to peel the stick. Before he had given it the proper shape the dynasty of the Candahars was at an end, and with the point of the stick he wrote the name of the last of that race in the sand, and then resumed his work. By the time he had smoothed and polished the staff Kalpa was no longer the pole-star; and ere he had put on the ferrule and the head adorned with precious stones, Brahma had awoke and slumbered many times. But why do I stay to mention these things? When the finishing stroke was put to his work, it suddenly expanded before the eyes of the astonished artist into the fairest of all the creations of Brahma. He had made a new system in making a staff, a world with full and fair proportions; in which, though the old cities and dynasties had passed away, fairer and more glorious ones had taken their places. And now he saw by the heap of shavings still fresh at his feet, that, for him and his work, the former lapse of time had been an illusion, and that no more time had elapsed than is required for a single scintillation from the brain of Brahma to fall on and inflame the tinder of a mortal brain. The material was pure, and his art was pure; how could the result be other than wonderful?

No face which we can give to a matter will stead us so well at last as the truth. This alone wears well. For the most part, we are not where we are, but in a false position. Through an infirmity of our natures, we suppose a case, and put ourselves into it, and hence are in two cases at the same time, and it is doubly difficult to get out. In sane moments we regard only the facts, the case that is. Say what you have to say, not what you ought. Any truth is better than make-believe. Tom Hyde, the tinker, standing on the gallows, was asked if he had anything to say. "Tell the tailors," said he, "to remember to make a knot in their thread before they take the first stitch." His companion's prayer is forgotten.

However mean your life is, meet it and live it; do not shun it and call it hard names. It is not so bad as you are. It looks poorest when you are richest. The fault-finder will find faults even in paradise. Love your life, poor as it is. You may perhaps have some pleasant, thrilling, glorious hours, even in a poorhouse. The setting sun is reflected from the windows of the almshouse as brightly as from the rich man's abode; the snow melts before its door as early in the spring. I do not see but a quiet mind may live as contentedly there, and have as cheering thoughts, as in a palace. The town's poor seem to me often to live the most independent lives of any. Maybe they are simply great enough to receive without misgiving. Most think that they are above being supported by the town; but it oftener happens that they are not above supporting themselves by dishonest means, which should be more disreputable. Cultivate poverty like a garden herb, like sage. Do not trouble yourself much to get new things, whether clothes or friends. Turn the old; return to them. Things do not change; we change. Sell your clothes and keep your thoughts. God will see that you do not want society. If I were confined to a corner of a garret all my days, like a spider, the world would be just as large to me while I had my thoughts about me. The philosopher said: "From an army of three divisions one can take away its general, and put it in disorder; from the man the most abject and vulgar one cannot take away his thought." Do not seek so anxiously to be developed, to subject yourself to many influences to be played on; it is all dissipation. Humility like darkness reveals the heavenly lights. The shadows of poverty and meanness gather around us, "and lo! creation widens to our view." We are often reminded that if there were bestowed on us the wealth of Croesus, our aims must still be the same, and our means essentially the same. Moreover, if you are restricted in your range by poverty, if you cannot buy books and newspapers, for instance, you are but confined to the most significant and vital experiences; you are compelled to deal with the material which yields the most sugar and the most starch. It is life near the bone where it is sweetest. You are defended from being a trifler. No man loses ever on a lower level by magnanimity on a higher. Superfluous wealth can buy superfluities only. Money is not required to buy one necessary of the soul.

I live in the angle of a leaden wall, into whose composition was poured a little alloy of bell-metal. Often, in the repose of my mid-day, there reaches my ears a confused *tintinnabulum* from without. It is the noise of my contemporaries. My neighbors tell me of their adventures with famous gentlemen and ladies, what notabilities they met at the dinner-table; but I am no more interested in such things than in the contents of the Daily Times. The interest and the conversation are about costume and manners chiefly; but a goose is a goose still, dress it as you will. They tell me of California and Texas, of England and the Indies, of the Hon. Mr. ——— of Georgia or of Massachusetts, all transient and fleeting phenomena, till I am ready to leap from their court-yard like the Mameluke bey. I delight to come to my bearings, not walk in procession with pomp and parade, in a conspicuous place, but to walk even with the Builder of the universe, if I may, not to live in this restless, nervous, bustling, trivial Nineteenth Century, but stand or sit thoughtfully while it goes by. What are men celebrating? They are all on a committee of arrangements, and hourly expect a speech from somebody. God is only the president of the day, and Webster is his orator. I love to weigh, to settle, to gravitate toward that which most strongly and rightfully attracts me; not hang by the beam of the scale and try to weigh less, not suppose a case, but take the case that is; to travel the only path I can, and that on which no power can resist me. It affords me no satisfaction to commence to spring an arch before I have got a solid foundation. Let us not play at kittly-benders. There is a solid bottom everywhere. We read that the traveler asked the boy if the swamp before him had a hard bottom. The boy replied that it had. But presently the traveler's horse sank in up to the girths, and he observed to the boy, "I thought you said that this bog had a hard bottom." "So it has," answered the latter, "but you have not got half way to it yet." So it is with the bogs and quicksands of society; but he is an old boy that knows it. Only what is thought said or done at a certain rare coincidence is good. I would not be one of those who will foolishly drive a nail into mere lath and plastering; such a deed would keep me awake nights. Give me a hammer, and let me feel for the furring. Do not depend on the putty. Drive a nail home and clinch it so faithfully that you can wake up in the night and think of your work with satisfaction, a work at which you would not be ashamed to invoke the Muse. So will help you God, and so only. Every nail driven should be as another rivet in the machine of the universe, you carrying on the work.

Rather than love, than money, than fame, give me truth. I sat at a table where were rich food and wine in abundance, and obsequious attendance, but sincerity and truth were not; and I went away hungry from the inhospitable board. The hospitality was as cold as the ices. I thought that there was no need of ice to freeze them. They talked to me of the age of the wine and the fame of the vintage; but I thought of an older, a newer, and purer wine, of a more glorious vintage, which they had not got, and could not buy. The style, the house and grounds and "entertainment" pass for nothing with me. I called on the king, but he made me wait in his hall, and conducted like a man incapacitated for hospitality. There was a man in my neighborhood who lived in a hollow tree. His manners were truly regal. I should have done better had I called on him.

How long shall we sit in our porticoes practicing idle and musty virtues, which any work would make impertinent? As if one were to begin the day with long-suffering, and hire a man to hoe his potatoes; and in the afternoon go forth to practice Christian meekness and charity with goodness aforethought! Consider the China pride and stagnant self-complacency of mankind. This generation inclines a little to congratulate itself on being the last of an illustrious line; and in Boston and London and Paris and Rome, thinking of its long descent, it speaks of its progress in art and science and literature with satisfaction. There are the Records of the Philosophical Societies, and the public Eulogies of *Great Men!* It is the good Adam contemplating his own virtue. "Yes, we have done great deeds, and sung divine songs, which shall never die,"—that is, as long as *we* can remember them. The learned societies and great men of Assyria—where are they? What youthful philosophers and experimentalists we are! There is not one of my readers who has yet lived a whole human life. These may be but the spring months in the life of the race. If we have had the seven-years' itch, we have not seen the seventeen-year locust yet in Concord. We are acquainted with a mere pellicle of the globe on which we live. Most have not delved six feet beneath the surface, nor leaped as many above it. We know not where we are. Beside, we are sound asleep nearly half our time. Yet we esteem ourselves wise, and have an established order on the surface. Truly, we are deep thinkers, we are ambitious spirits! As I stand over the insect crawling amid the pine needles on the forest floor, and endeavoring to conceal itself from my sight, and ask myself why it will cherish those humble thoughts, and hide its head from me who might, perhaps, be its benefactor, and impart to its race some cheering information, I am reminded of the greater Benefactor and Intelligence that stands over me the human insect.

There is an incessant influx of novelty into the world and yet we tolerate incredible dullness. I need only suggest what kind of sermons are still listened to in the most enlightened countries. There are such words as joy and sorrow, but they are only the burden of a psalm, sung with a nasal twang, while we believe in the ordinary and mean. We think that we can change our clothes only. It is said that the

British Empire is very large and respectable, and that the United States are a first-rate power. We do not believe that a tide rises and falls behind every man which can float the British Empire like a chip, if he should ever harbor it in his mind. Who knows what sort of seventeen-year locust will next come out of the ground? The government of the world I live in was not framed, like that of Britain, in after-dinner conversations over the wine.

The life in us is like the water in the river. It may rise this year higher than man has ever known it, and flood the parched uplands; even this may be the eventful year, which will drown out all our musk-rats. It was not always dry land where we dwell. I see far inland the banks which the stream anciently washed, before science began to record its freshets. Every one has heard the story which has gone the rounds of New England, of a strong and beautiful bug which came out of the dry leaf of an old table of apple-tree wood, which had stood in a farmer's kitchen for sixty years, first in Connecticut and afterward in Massachusetts—from an egg deposited in the living tree many years earlier still, as appeared by counting the annual layers beyond it; which was heard gnawing out for several weeks, hatched perchance by the heat of an urn. Who does not feel his faith in a resurrection and immortality strengthened by hearing of this? Who knows what beautiful and winged life, whose egg has been buried for ages under many concentric layers of woodenness in the dead dry life of society, deposited at first in the alburnum of the green and living tree, which has been gradually converted into the semblance of its well-seasoned tomb, heard perchance gnawing out now for years by the astonished family of man, as they sat round the festive board,

SUNRISE

The sun is but a morning star

may unexpectedly come forth from amidst society's most trivial and handseled furniture, to enjoy its perfect summer life at last!

I do not say that John or Jonathan will realize all this; but such is the character of that morrow which mere lapse of time can never make to dawn. The light which puts out our eyes is darkness to us. Only that day dawns to which we are awake. There is more day to dawn. The sun is but a morning star.

NOTE TO THE READER

W*alden* describes the experiment of one man trying to discover how best to find and know happiness. What Thoreau discovered about happiness can be compared with the conclusions of other great thinkers in the Western tradition. An entire chapter in the *Syntopicon*, for example, is devoted to the idea of HAPPINESS. Of particular interest is the introductory essay delineating some of the views held concerning the definition of happiness and its attainability. Passages most relevant to Thoreau among authors of the *Great Books of the Western World* can be found cited under HAPPINESS 1 and 2, and in particular under 2*a*, 2*b*(1), and 2*b*(7).

One of Thoreau's most searching conclusions about happiness—contained in the chapter "Economy"—is his indictment of conventional opinions and prejudices about the good life. Most of all, he assails as blinding or crippling the effect of custom and convention upon the individual. References to other descriptions of the influence of custom on the liberty of the individual can be found under CUSTOM AND CONVENTION 7*d*. Additional discussion of the social and political significance of public opinion is indicated under OPINION 7.

Among the conventional opinions of the good life that Thoreau attacks vigorously and at length is the tacit belief that money and luxuries are beneficial. References to authors examining the moral aspects of wealth and poverty can be found under WEALTH 10—in particular, WEALTH 10*a* on the nature of wealth as a good.

Questions about the nature and value of work and the uses of leisure are also raised by the experiment in living at Walden Pond. The spectrum of attitudes concerning the nature of work is reviewed in the introductory essay to the chapter LABOR. Of especial interest to readers of *Walden* will be references to passages on labor in human life and the nature

of work under LABOR 1 and 2. Also of interest will be Thoreau's belief that contemplation is the most fruitful and useful activity. References to this discussion involving action and contemplation can be found under LABOR 1*b*.

Thoreau's attitude about the uses of leisure can be compared with other authors who discuss labor, leisure, and happiness by consulting the references cited under LABOR 1*b*. Descriptions of the myth of the golden age where labor was unnecessary—reference to these passages are cited under MAN 9*a*—might provide another perspective on the implications of the Walden experience.

Learning apart from teachers and books is still another aspect of the experiment at Walden Pond. Passages relevant to this experience are cited under EDUCATION 5*f*, as well as under EXPERIENCE 4*b*, which treats of experience as the ultimate criterion of truth.

Thoreau is best known, however, for his experience of Nature. His description of that experience can be compared with the discussion of the personification and worship of nature and that of nature and grace in human life found in the passages under NATURE 6*a* and 6*b*. Due to his intimacy with natural life, Thoreau has been called the first American ecologist. References to ecology in *Great Books of the Western World* can be found in the Inventory of Terms at the end of Volume II of the *Syntopicon*.

Finally, the beauty that Thoreau discovered in Nature can be put into perspective by consulting references to passages examining the natural as providing a canon of beauty cited under NATURE 5*d*.

The social and political implications of the Walden Pond experiment are explored more extensively by Thoreau in two essays, "Civil Disobedience" and "A Plea for Captain John Brown," both of which will be found in Volume 6 of *Gateway to the Great Books*.

John Strachey

The Challenge

of Democracy

INTRODUCTION

Few men in our century have been as well qualified as John Strachey to diagnose not only the challenge of democracy but also the decadence of the Communist ideal of "a working-class democracy" and the impact of the reality of nuclear warfare on political thinking and policy. From the time he graduated from Oxford in the early 1920's, Strachey took an active and often passionate part as a political theorist in the various and changing forms of democracy in Great Britain, particularly as practiced by the British Labour party. From 1945 until his death in 1963 at the age of 61, he experienced at firsthand the realities of practical democracy, not only as a member of the House of Commons but also as a minister in various responsible positions in the Labour governments during the 1950's. Shortly before his death, the *London Times* commended him as "the most mature ideological thinker in the Labour movement."

Strachey knew Communism from the inside. Throughout the 1920's and 1930's, he professed himself a Communist, although he never officially joined the party. During those years, he published several influential books expounding Marxist theories of society and the state, and he was considered "the most brilliant apologist for the party line in the English-speaking world." But he broke violently with Communism in 1939, and became one of its most relentless and informed critics.

Born in 1901 into a distinguished English family, John Strachey was the son of John St. Loe Strachey, the eminent Tory editor of *The Spectator*. Brilliant, vitriolic Lytton Strachey was his cousin. After educaton at Eton and Magdalen College, Oxford, Strachey joined the Independent Labour party in 1924. He became one of British Labour's "wild young men" and served a term in the House of Commons as a Labourite in the late 1920's.

During the next decade, Strachey experienced a series of political conversions which were to carry him as far to the left in politics as he was ever to move. Breaking with the Independent Labour party in 1930, he became private secretary to Sir Oswald Mosley, who had left the Labour party to found his own political organization. When Mosley began to move in the direction of what was soon to become the British Union of Fascists, known as the Black Shirts, Strachey left his party and devoted himself to political writing. One of the most influential books among the radical young during the 1930's was his *The Coming Struggle for Power* (1932). The book was an anthology of Marxist positions: capitalism was doomed, imperialism and fascism were last-ditch defenses against socialism, Social Democratic parties were traitors to the working-class cause, a sound society was rising in Soviet Russia and revolution in the rest of the world was both inevitable and imminent.

Throughout the 1930's, Strachey continued to expound Marxist theories of society and the state. With Harold J. Laski, his close associate in the Labour party, he was a member of the selection committee of the influential Left Book Club which successfully propagated British socialism during that decade.

When the Hitler-Stalin pact of nonaggression and neutrality was signed in 1939 and Russia invaded Finland that same year, Strachey denounced Communism in the strongest terms, an action that received considerable attention in the press in England and the United States. Strachey continued to develop his political philosophy in *A Programme for Progress* (1940), in which he explored the internal contradictions of capitalism and the possibility of keeping capitalism active through governmental control of saving and investment. Critic Max Lerner described the book as being "the most striking blend of Marxism and Keynesism in our literature," and while he praised the author's development as an economist, he claimed that Strachey had yet to develop as a political realist.

During the next decade, Strachey gained considerable experience in politics as a minister in several prominent positions in the Labour governments that came into power after World War II. After a distinguished career as a staff officer in the Royal Air Force during the war, he was elected a member of Parliament for Dundee, Scotland, in 1945, and he was then appointed, successively, Undersecretary of State for Air, Minister of Food, and Secretary of State for War. At one time during the Attlee governments, he was widely considered as a future prime minister. He became one of the best informed leaders in England on the nature of nuclear strategy. After the Labour government fell in the early 1950's, Strachey continued to serve as representative from West Dundee, Scotland, until his death, July 15, 1963.

Strachey's mature political philosophy was expressed in *Contemporary Capitalism* (1956), *The End of Empire* (1959), and *On the Prevention of War* (1962). His dissection of the rise and decadence of Communism in *The Strangled Cry* (1962), *The Great Awakening* (1961), and *The Challenge of Democracy* (1963) brought him wide acclaim.

The Challenge of Democracy was first published in 1963 as a pamphlet by *Encounter*, the English monthly of political and literary thought, edited by Stephen Spender and Melvin J. Lasky. The text was originally broadcast by the author over Radio Free Europe.

I. THE WORLD DEBATE

There is a continuous many-sided debate going on in the world today, conducted between those who support the Western, and those who support the Communist societies. These lectures are part of that debate.

The debate covers the whole field of human affairs: both the political and the economic aspects of these two rival systems; their achievements and their failures; the way they organize production and the way they organize their political lives —it covers everything.

The existence of this worldwide debate is an excellent thing, for it means that for the first time in history an attempt is being made to secure the conscious participation of the whole population of the world in human affairs. This attempt, however, has not come about because of idealistic determination that such participation would be "a good thing," in the abstract. On the contrary, the world debate has come about by way of a competitive process in the course of which each side has had to try to win the minds of as many people as possible. Both the Western governments and the Communists have had to try to win the minds of, first, their own peoples, second, the peoples of the rival societies across the great world divide; and, third, and above all, they have had to try to win over that largest section of the world's population which is still uncommitted to one side or the other.

All this is splendid. I cannot say however that *the way* the debate is conducted is at all splendid; in fact, much of it could hardly be worse conducted. Hitherto much of it has consisted in mere mutual abuse. Again, much of the efforts of some governments has consisted in attempts to prevent people on their own side from even hearing the case of the other side. It may be just my Western prejudice but, on the whole, I am bound to say that the Communist side seems to me even more reprehensible than the Western side in this respect. The systematic attempt to prevent the West stating its case to the people of the Communist world—for instance, jamming these broadcasts—strikes one as not only fundamentally wrong, but also as an unmistakable sign of weakness. On the other hand, some sections of opinion in the West are almost as bad; for, though they may listen if they like to Communist broadcasts, or read Communist books, yet they have become mentally deaf and blind to any case but their own. I must say that Americans and some Western Europeans, in particular, strike me like this. Moreover it is worth noting that this is true not only, and not even especially, of well-to-do or "bourgeois" Americans and Western Europeans, but of many American and Western European manual workers also.

This last point is something which Communist propagandists ought, in their own interest, to take carefully into account. If they think about its implications it will, I believe, show them that something very unexpected is happening in the world. In any case, this mutual deafness, blindness, and incomprehension naturally makes a large part of the world debate rather empty and boring. The debaters never really come to grips with each other's arguments. Still, the great world debate goes on and unless we blow ourselves up—as we may— it is bound to continue. Surely such a debate, on however low a level of argument, is a great deal better than blowing ourselves up.

We All Say We Are Democrats

What especially concerns us here is democracy. The first thing to notice is the curious fact that both sides claim that they are democracies and that both deny that the societies on the other side of the great divide are democracies. One can deduce something from this peculiar fact. Since both sides claim to be democracies everybody must agree that democracy is a highly important and highly desirable thing: otherwise both sides would not claim it for themselves and deny it to their opponents. It is evident that everybody regards democracy—whatever it is—as something which human societies ought to possess. But evidently also each side defines democracy quite differently, for both the economic and political systems of each side have very different characteristics. They can hardly *both* be democratic under any one definition of democracy.

The approach of these lectures will be to examine the claims and counterclaims of the West and the Communists in this world debate. Now I am a practical, working politician, not a professor of political theory; so if you expect a learned discussion on the history of democracy, on democracy in the ancient world, on the Greek city-states, for instance, or again on Rousseau's theory of the general will, you will be disappointed. I am concerned with what we in the middle of the twentieth century mean when we talk about democracy.

After all we must mean *something*, for we are all continually saying that this country is a democracy and that country is not. But we in the West on the one hand, and the Communists on the other hand, claim the title of democracy for quite different countries. Well then, what *do* we mean by this word democracy which we all bandy about?

I can tell you what I mean when I call a country a democracy. I mean that in a democratic country the adult citizens attempt—let me repeat that word, *attempt*—to govern themselves instead of being governed by some authority over which they have no control.

The first thing I want to say about that definition is that for a people to govern itself is an exceptionally difficult thing. Indeed I am going to put it to you that it has only proved possible, hitherto at any rate, for people in large, complex, modern communities, such as ours, to govern themselves in an indirect way. They have only been able to govern themselves in the sense of being able to choose the kind of government they want. And even this indirect form of self-government needs the establishment of careful and subtle political and social arrangements. But I am also going to put it to you that to achieve even this degree of indirect self-government, which is all anybody has achieved so far, is immensely important. As a matter of fact I have come to believe that the establishment, preservation, and development of democracy in this sense, rather than the question of what kind of economic system is best, has now become the main question in the public life of the world.

Representative Government

What I have just defined as democracy is, of course, what is usually called "representative government." And you may quickly object that representative government is only one feature of democracy. I quite agree. Nevertheless, representative government is the all-important core of democracy as a whole. All the other, and in themselves equally valuable, features of democracy depend on this central feature: how freedom of speech, freedom of assembly, freedom of association, the rule of law, etc., are dependent in the long run for their very existence on representative government.

Let us try and get behind these rather abstract phrases. What I mean by representative government is that the adult citizens of a country should be able to choose between different kinds of governments, offering themselves at freely conducted elections: that they should be able to dismiss at a subsequent election a government which they had previously chosen, and that they should have at any rate a certain amount of control over the actions of their government even when they have chosen it. Representative government, in this sense, has turned out to be the only way in which we can assure such extremely practical and important things in our daily lives as whether we are able to combine with our fellow citizens in order to bargain on how much we are paid for our work (that is, freedom of association); as whether or not we risk arbitrary arrest without the right of public trial by our fellow citizens (that is, the rule of law); as whether we are able to say and write and publish what we like within broad limits (that is, freedom of speech). In practice it has turned out that there is no way of assuring these desperately important rights except by securing this other, underlying, right of choosing the kind of government which is to rule the country.

The Antidemocratic Case

Let us note the antidemocratic view. Why should it be so important for a people as a whole to be able to choose the kind of government which it wants, to dismiss that government at stated intervals, and to control its actions to some extent? Why do those precious rights and liberties depend upon the principle of representative government? Why is it not better to leave the management of society to experts, to full-time professional rulers? Won't they do it much better if they are left free and uncontrolled than if they are hampered at every turn by the often confused, and sometimes contradictory, wishes of the people? Aren't the experts better educated, far more experienced, far wiser than the hundreds of millions of ordinary people who, because of the condition of their lives, find it difficult to spare time for the consideration of public affairs?

Well, we have had plenty of experience to guide us when we attempt to answer such questions. For leaving the government to full-time, uncontrolled, professional rulers is the way in which human societies have, in fact, been run in the vast majority of cases from time immemorial. Kings, priests, nobles, landowners, merchants, capitalists, officials—call them what you will—have until very recently always ruled. The mass of the population has simply obeyed without any right or ability to control their rulers, or to get rid of them and get different ones. We have ample experience of *undemocratic* societies, and if there is any fatal objection to them, it ought to have become fully apparent by now.

There is such a fatal objection to them, and it has become fully apparent. Undemocratic societies have sometimes worked comparatively well though more often they have worked, from the point of view of their populations, extremely badly. But whether they have worked well or badly, they have all had one thing in common. To a greater or lesser degree their rulers—kings, priests, nobles, landowners, merchants, capitalists, officials—have exploited the peoples over whom they ruled. And when I use the word "exploited" I mean simply that they have ruled to a greater or lesser extent in their own interests rather than in the interests of their peoples. This is the fatal objection to undemocratic societies, and I should have thought that it is something on which we could all agree, from the most orthodox Communist theoretician to the most ardent Western democrat. But if you do agree with this conclusion, you will be driven to two further conclusions.

The first is that if a people wants to be well-ruled, in the sense of ruled in its own interests, it will have to find a way of doing the job itself. For no one will do the job for it. In a word, there is no satisfactory substitute for self-government. For government by somebody else always, in the end, turns into government in the interest of somebody else. If you leave the task of government to a single man or, more often, to a single class of men, he, or they, will always exploit you. So, however difficult it is to achieve workable arrangements by which a people may rule themselves, even if only indirectly, that will prove, in the end, the only tolerable political arrangement. For now that people have become sufficiently developed to understand what their own interests are, they will not indefinitely tolerate being ruled in other people's interests.

Democracy Is Brand New

The second conclusion which you will be driven to accept is that democracy, of which the core is the establishment of representative government, is an extremely new and extremely bold, even revolutionary, experiment in the conduct of human affairs. The development of democracy, in this sense of the attempt at a significant degree of self-rule by large communities, is by far the most important and challenging thing which is happening in the world today. It is not certain to succeed; but on the success or failure of this attempt the fate of the world will turn.

After all, the attempt to establish democracy in this sense has been going on for less than two hundred years. For I have never been able to count the Greek city-states of the ancient world as democracies. Even Athens at her zenith was, in fact, an oligarchy. The only people who had the vote were free male citizens of Athenian parents of two generations on both sides. The slaves, alone, formed something like nine-tenths of the population, and then there were a great many foreigners. The actual voters must have been much

under one-tenth of even the total male population: that is oligarchy, not democracy.

No, democracy in the sense that I am talking about is something which only began to evolve and develop about two hundred years ago. The decisive events, to my mind, were the American Revolution of 1776, the French Revolution of 1789, and the great Reform Bill in England in 1832. None of these events in themselves secured what I am talking about, namely free elections in which the whole adult population chose the kind of government it wanted; all that those events did was to start the process by which this system of society has eventually come into being. Actually the coming into being of anything which I would be willing to call democracy is very recent. I would say that in the case of my country, Britain, it was really impossible to call her a democracy in this sense until 1918. (For that matter the final extension of the franchise did not occur till 1929.) Parts of America and the whole of France, were, from time to time, more democratic in the second half of the nineteenth century than Britain. But even there, genuinely working democratic institutions at the center, *i.e.*, representative government, only really got going in our own time.

Moreover, I would be the last to claim that even now, the democratic institutions of my own country, or of America, or of France, or of Western Germany, or of any of the democracies of the world, were complete or perfect. They are still being evolved; we are still experimenting with them; they are still being perfected. And, what is more, they are still vulnerable and may suffer setbacks or even catastrophies. Nevertheless the fact remains that the original three major modern democracies, America, France, and Britain, have been at any rate sufficiently successful in evolving democratic institutions for them to be very widely imitated.

The Spread of Democracy

It is an undeniable fact that all over the world today—right through the five continents—attempts are being made to set up democracies. Country after country is attempting to set up governments which can be chosen, dismissed, and to some extent controlled, by their peoples. That is a most remarkable thing. I do not for a moment say that all these attempts to set up democracies will succeed: on the contrary it is quite clear that many of them will fail. Nevertheless it does appear that democratic institutions are something which people desperately want. They may or may not be capable of establishing them and working them, for that, I repeat, is a very difficult thing to do; but they evidently feel that democratic institutions are extremely valuable.

Thus the most important thing which is happening in the world today will probably be seen by future historians to be this attempt to spread democratic institutions throughout the world. It will turn out that this is a more significant thing than the competitive struggle between the two different kinds of economic systems which is also going on. This is not because the question of what is the best economic system is unimportant; on the contrary, it is essential to establish a workable economic system. Unless you can do that you cannot even consider your political institutions; you will simply starve. Therefore I agree completely that no political system, whether it be democratic, dictatorial—or whatever kind it is—is any good unless it has a workable economic foundation on which to rest. But the fact is that both the major economic systems, the Communist and the Western, which exist in the world today, will, I forecast, prove capable of working fairly well. I will discuss the way in which each of them is working today later on. But, broadly, it is becoming apparent that it is possible for an advanced industrial society to order its economic life in either the Communist or in the Western way, and to succeed well, at any rate to avoid economic breakdown. In fact, I am inclined to think that in twenty or thirty years' time we shall find that these two economic systems are, on the whole, giving a rather similar result in terms of material welfare.

This may seem a strange conclusion to the citizens of countries where either one system or the other is at present working very badly, for example to the citizens of China or of East Germany on the Communist side, or of, say, one of the worse-run South American republics on the Western side. In those cases economic breakdown is still the main concern in people's minds because they are still directly menaced by it. But in the big, decisive countries on each side, in Russia, in America, and in Western Europe, I shall be surprised if the systems do not slowly and unevenly, but unmistakably, give a rising standard of life. And if this is so, their people's attention will be increasingly concentrated, not on the way their economic systems work, or fail to work, but on the development of really effective democratic institutions. Thus in the second half of our century, people's attention will shift from the economic issues to the political arrangements under which the public life of their communities are organized. In particular their attention will shift to this question of whether their society has made workable arrangements for the choice, dismissal, and control of its government by its people. This is the core of democracy.

II. THE WESTERN SOCIETIES

I have said that a government which is responsible to the population as a whole is, in my view, the thing on which all other aspects of democracy depend. When I say a responsible government, I mean that there should be some effective working mechanism, such as freely conducted elections, by which all the adult citizens of the community can choose their government out of several practical alternatives. Second, there must exist a working mechanism by which they can dismiss such a government, after not too long an interval and without fear of civil war and bloodshed, and replace it by another. Third, there must exist a mechanism by which they can exercise some degree of control over their government while it is in power. This is a representative government. It does not make a decisive difference whether it is practiced under the British parliamentary system or under the American presidential and congressional system, or under one or other of the systems which the French, for example, have tried out in recent times: each of these are forms of representative government.

But, of course, contemporary Western democracy consists in much more than representative government. In fact representative, responsible government may be thought of as the mechanism by means of which the existence of several things, which are, in daily life, much more precious to the people than the right to vote at elections, is ensured.

Representative government is, in this sense, *the way* in which political freedom is preserved. And that takes us to this great word "Freedom." Now freedom is a fundamental but also a subtle conception which it will be necessary to discuss a good deal in what follows. At this point I shall merely try to break down that word, which has such a ring to it, but which has often been used too hypocritically and falsely, into certain definite limited *freedoms*, in the plural. For the purpose of representative, responsible government is to ensure four major freedoms, each of which is exceedingly important in the contemporary world.

Freedom of Association

First, I take freedom of association. Today this means, above all, the freedom of the wage earners, who form the immense majority of the populations of highly developed Western societies, to form themselves into trade unions. Such trade unions, experience has shown, are indispensable to wage earners for the purpose of bargaining with their employers over their wages, their hours of work, and their conditions of employment generally. I do not think that any Communist would question that it is vitally important for wage earners in Western capitalist societies to possess this freedom. We can surely agree on that. Exhaustive experience has shown that unless the workers do possess this freedom, they will be miserably exploited: they will get, that is to say, a miserably small portion of all the values that they create by their work. But, as I shall show, if they *do* possess this freedom of association, the wage earners of the Western societies can, and do, get a much higher proportion of the wealth that they produce.

So far, surely, we are all agreed. But I believe this ability to form trade unions, which are controlled only by themselves, is—or would be if it existed—a very precious freedom for wage earners in Communist societies also. This assertion will be disputed by all Communists, so it will be worth looking for a moment at the history of Communist thinking on the question of trade unions in Communist countries.

There was a full-dress debate on the role of trade unions in socialist or Communist societies directly after the Russian Revolution. Some of the original Russian Communist leaders took the, at first sight, quite logical view that in a socialist society there was "no need" or "function" for trade unions. For, they said, with whom were the trade unions to bargain, once the capitalists had been abolished and the people themselves owned all the means of production? After all, they said, "one does not have to bargain with oneself. . . ."

But Lenin and the majority of the Russian Communist party came to agree that, in practice, it was important that trade unions should exist even when all the means of production had become publicly owned. Unfortunately, however, they did not agree, in practice at any rate, that these trade unions should be free, in the sense of being independent of the government; and of course, as everyone knows, trade unions in the Communist world are *not* free in this sense. On the contrary, they are a part of the general governmental machine. Therefore they can exercise very little independent pressure on their employers who are also part of that governmental machine. In particular they cannot (and do not) use the sanction of the withdrawal of their members' labor—the right to strike—as the ultimate sanction in their negotiations with the employing organizations.

The consequence is that the wage earners of Communist societies *are* gravely exploited, in the sense that they get only a small proportion of the value which they produce. (They may—or may not—be consoled by the fact that the rest of the value which they produce goes, not to individuals in the form of private profit, but to the state, to be reinvested, or spent on armaments, or on education, or on something else as the state decides.)

From this experience of our own times I deduce that this particular freedom, namely the freedom of association, is an immensely important thing for wage earners whether their employer is the state or a private company. For without this freedom the wage earners are unable to exercise much influence on the very things which concern them most of all, namely their wages, hours, and conditions of work.

Freedom of Speech

The second freedom which responsible, representative government is designed to ensure is freedom of speech, and it is in fact indissolubly associated with that form of government itself. Unless it exists, it is clearly impossible for the electorate genuinely to choose between the political parties, which are potential governments and which are competing for its votes. These competing would-be governments, which are, in practice, political parties, must be able to speak and write freely in their efforts to persuade the people to support them. But, of course, freedom of speech and of writing go much further than this. The whole intellectual life of the community depends, in my opinion, on there being the widest practical degree of freedom in this respect. I say advisedly the words "widest practical degree" because this can never be an absolute freedom. It is perfectly true that in all communities there must be things people are not free to say or write. For example, no civilized community could tolerate an incitement in speech or writing to murder some particular individual; therefore, freedom of speech is a question of degree. But it is a fundamental error in political thinking to suppose that a freedom is unimportant because it has to be limited in practice.

Freedom of Assembly

The third freedom is freedom of assembly. This is the freedom for people to get together in public meetings to discuss, to agitate for, what they think is the right course in public affairs. This used to be one of the most important of all freedoms. Modern techniques of communication by broadcasting, television, daily newspapers, and the like, have made it less important but, nevertheless, one can hardly imagine a free community without this right.

The Rule of Law

The fourth freedom may be called the rule of law. Broadly, under the rule of law, a man or woman is free to do anything which is not specifically forbidden by the laws of his or her community. This is one of the oldest and simplest freedoms; but it has turned out to be one of the most precious. It has turned out that if and when governments infringe this freedom and start imprisoning, arresting, torturing, and killing people at their own sweet will, without regard to the public laws of the community, every other kind of freedom becomes impossible. For obviously people will not be able to organize trade unions, to speak and write freely, or to meet freely in public assemblies if they are in danger of arrest, imprisonment, and torture, if the government does not like what they are doing.

Moreover, the rule of law has turned out to be dependent upon carefully thought-out arrangements for the administration of the laws. Laws are simply the rules for the community which are made from time to time; but someone has to apply those rules to particular cases. Once again, if the government is free to apply these rules as it thinks fit, in practice the citizens will be at the mercy of that government. Therefore, it is crucially important that there should be law courts which are, to the greatest practicable extent, independent of the government, which apply the laws fairly and impartially, and are strong and bold enough to deny the government the right arbitrarily to imprison or persecute a citizen if he has not broken the law.

Once again, nobody will, I think, deny the importance of this freedom in Western capitalist societies. But we now know that the rule of law is exceedingly important in Communist societies also. For sad experience has shown that in practice (and contrary to Communist theory) the government of Communist societies becomes a massive institution, separated from the population: therefore clear-cut rules or laws are desperately needed to prevent it tyrannizing over its own citizens. As a matter of fact, while this need for the rule of law is still inadequately recognized in Communist theory, it is now beginning to be rather better recognized in Communist

PROSECUTOR VISHINSKY (CENTER) AT THE MOSCOW PURGE TRIALS OF THE 1930's
One of the most terrible examples of governmental lawlessness

practice. After all, one of the strongest criticisms of Stalin's regime which Mr. Khrushchev made at the Twentieth and Twenty-second Party Congresses, was that Stalin had violated the rule of law in Russia. Stalin certainly had. The purges of the thirties were one of the most terrible examples of governmental lawlessness which we have seen in our times.

It is worth noting what a modest freedom "the rule of law" actually is. It is not a question of good laws or bad laws. The aspiration to be governed by "good laws" is a more ambitious aspiration altogether. All we are talking about at this stage is that there shall be definite, comprehensible laws administered by honest courts, and that a citizen shall not be punished unless the state can prove in open court that he or she has broken one of these laws. Unless at least this freedom has been established democratic institutions cannot function—for everybody is at the mercy of the whim of the government.

Is "The Free World" Really Free?

These four freedoms constitute the main pillars of a free society. The question is: to what extent are these freedoms realized in practice in various parts of the world of the 1960's? Many people refer to what I have called, for short (and inaccurately), "the West" as "the free world." To do that is to beg the question which we are discussing; so I do not, as you may notice, use the term. But nevertheless these four freedoms, resting on responsible, representative government, do appear to me to be more nearly realized in the more highly developed states of the Western (or non-Communist) world than elsewhere.

However, I may be asked whether they constitute "real freedom." I may be told that all this, in practice, may mean for the wage earners only "the freedom to starve." There was force in that jeer in the past,

but I do not think that there is much force in it today. In any case I am afraid that it is perfectly possible to starve in jail as well as in freedom. The fact is that even though freedom does not necessarily and in itself guarantee economic security and a decent standard of life, its opposite, servitude, far from guaranteeing these material benefits, makes their attainment almost impossible.

Therefore what I would claim is that these four particular freedoms, which I have listed, if they are substantially achieved, constitute the greatest degree of freedom which human societies have yet been able to establish. It may be that it is a very imperfect freedom; but it is incomparably better than servitude. It is the best humanity has been able to do so far.

This kind and degree of freedom is, then, what contemporary Western democracy is attempting to achieve. This is the objective of what the Communists call "bourgeois democracy." The question remains, what is it worth?

Lenin's Criticism

I now come to the Communist criticism of the Western or "bourgeois" democracy—call it what you will—which I have just defined.

What the Communists say is broadly this. They say that the class divisions in Western societies make "bourgeois democracy" into a sham. They say that in such societies as these the population is divided into those who own the means of production and those who work: into, that is to say, employers and employed. And (the Communists continue) this basic division of society spoils and nullifies all the claims which Western societies make to freedom and democracy. Lenin, as usual, put the matter with perfect clarity. In *The State and Revolution*, that extremely important pamphlet which he published on the very eve of the Russian Revolution, in August 1917, Lenin wrote these words on "bourgeois democracy":

> . . . this democracy is always restricted by the narrow framework of capitalist exploitation, and consequently always remains, in reality, a democracy for the minority, only for the possessing classes, only for the rich. Freedom in capitalist society always remains about the same as it was in the ancient Greek republics: freedom for the slave-owners. Owing to the conditions of capitalist exploitation, the modern wage-slaves are also so crushed by want and poverty that "they cannot be bothered with democracy," "they cannot be bothered with politics"; in the ordinary peaceful course of events the majority of the population is debarred from participating in social and political life.

The essence of Lenin's criticism of "bourgeois democracy" is contained in the last sentences. He is saying that the wage earners in societies such as those of the West today are so poor and badly educated that they cannot make use of the democratic freedom which they nominally possess: that they are, in practice, "debarred from participating in social and political life" by poverty and ignorance. Therefore, according to Lenin (and all Communist theory), the fact that they can nominally elect what government they like, dismiss that government and elect another, and that they possess, to a lesser or greater degree, the four freedoms we have just listed is all a sham. The Communists say that the wage earners in the Western societies only possess these things on paper; for they are too "crushed by want and poverty" to be able to exercise these freedoms in practice.

What are we to make of this basic Communist criticism of "bourgeois democracy"? Only someone who is ignorant of history would deny that it had force in the early stages of capitalism. Moreover, it still has force in certain places in the non-Communist world even today. Nevertheless, as one rereads those words of Lenin's, one cannot but be struck by how inappropriate they have become to the highly developed capitalist societies of the 1960's, such as North America, Britain, Western Europe, Australia, New Zealand, and some others.

No one who, like myself, is a working politician in one or other of these highly developed societies can believe for one moment that today the wage earners are "debarred from participating in social and political life" by poverty and ignorance. The fact is that they participate very actively in Western political life. For instance, I could not possibly have been elected to the British Parliament over the past twenty years unless they had done so. Of course it is true that the fact that the wage earners' education is still inferior to that of the rich is a handicap to them. Of course it is true that it is harder for a party depending on the wage earners, like the British Labour party, to raise funds than it is for a party depending upon the upper classes. For the wage earners are poorer than the upper possessing classes. But such handicaps as these have been, and are being, increasingly overcome. In a word, this fundamental Communist criticism of Western democracy has become, obviously and undeniably, out of date.

The "Thought Control" Criticism

However, this is not the only Communist criticism of "bourgeois democracy." It is also said by the Communists that "the ownership of the means of production" by the rich in bourgeois societies gives them, in practice, control of everything else as well. According to this view, the capitalist ownership of the means of production includes ownership of what might be called "the means of production of opinion"—directly or indirectly, control of the educational system of the country, the press, broadcasting, television, and the other extremely powerful modern methods for the production of mass opinion. In a word, it is suggested that it is possible for the owners of the means of production to control the opinions of the wage earners, even if the wage earners are now well enough educated and well enough off to take part in public life. According to this theory, the wage earners will never get the chance to want to escape from their exploitation: for what is called "thought control" will be exercised over them.

This is a much more up-to-date criticism. And, once again, no one who is, like me, a working politician in a "bourgeois democracy" will deny that there is some truth in it. But, again, experience shows that it is no longer true on balance. Of course the owners of the means of production do use all these powerful "means for the production of opinion" in their own interests. But they are not particularly successful in controlling the thoughts of the wage earners. On the contrary, the wage earners' own distinctive point of view begins, more and more, to color and condition the thinking, and after that the policies, of our Western societies. (I shall subsequently describe this long-drawn-out, somewhat subtle, but all-important process.)

Lenin Believed in Democracy

But do notice that the Communists, in making the above criticisms of "bourgeois democracy," fully agree as to the immense importance of democracy and freedom in themselves. Lenin, for example, writes again and again that democracy and freedom are supremely important. In *The State and Revolution*, he did not so much promise as assume—entirely sincerely in my view—that there would be perfect democracy for the wage earners after the revolution. His three conditions for establishing this perfect democracy for the wage earners were:

1. The election of all officials.
2. The principle of recall, by which the wage earners could freely and at any time dismiss an official whom they had elected and put another in his place.
3. The principle that the salaries for these officials should be "reduced to the level of the wages of the average worker"—(these last are Lenin's own words).

When once these three conditions had been fulfilled by the revolution, there would be, Lenin said, a much more complete form of democracy for the wage earners than any which we know in the West.

It is important to realize that this extreme, or "primitive" (as Lenin did not hestitate to call it), form of democracy constituted the political institutions which Lenin wanted to see established after the revolution. In my opinion he really did want to see all officials freely elected, subject to recall, and paid the same salaries as the workers. The one qualification to complete democracy which he always made was that *only* the wage earners would be allowed to vote at the elections of these governing officials. For he always contemplated that a government founded on this form of "primitive" democracy would be used to coerce the minority of ex-property owners.

Here we come to the very core of the Communists' idea of democracy. In Lenin's opinion there was not, and never could be, any such thing as comprehensive democracy in class-divided societies. If one class of persons owned "the means of production" and another class of persons worked for them for "wages," then there could be democracy among the owners and for the owners; or, after the revolution, there could be democracy among the wage earners and for the wage earners. But there could be no such thing as democracy comprising both the owners and the wage earners.

Thus Lenin thought that "bourgeois democracy" was the concealed coercion of the majority by the minority. On the other hand, the kind of democracy in which he believed would be the coercion of the minority of expropriated owners by the majority of wage earners. After the revolution there was to be, within the wage-earning class, a more complete degree of freedom than had ever been attained in human societies before.

We will discuss below how this original Leninist theory of post-revolutionary democracy has, in practice, turned into its opposite. It has turned into a dictatorship, not of the majority of wage earners over the minority of expropriated owners, but into the almost entirely uncontrolled dictatorship of a few officials over the whole of the rest of the Russian people. This is the supreme tragedy of our times.

But before we begin to examine it, we must deal in much greater detail with these two Communist criticisms of bourgeois democracy. I have said that I know from personal experience that it is false to allege that the wage earners in the contemporary Western societies are, in Lenin's words, "so crushed by want and poverty" that they are "debarred from participating in social and political life." But it is extremely important to show why and how this allegation of Lenin's has turned out to be mistaken. We must trace the complex process by which the wage earners of the Western societies have undeniably begun to make a reality of our Western form of democracy.

III. WHAT WESTERN DEMOCRACY HAS ACHIEVED

The Communists say, flat out, that democracy in the Western sense (or "bourgeois democracy" as they term it) is a sham. Is it? What tests can one apply to political institutions in order to see whether they are real or sham? Once again, I shall not try to answer this question by an appeal to abstract political theory. What I want to say is that Western democracy is real in the sense that it is usable. The political institutions, freedoms, or powers exercised by the people have turned out to be real in the precise sense of usable.

For these freedoms, or rights, have been used, are being used, and will continue

LENIN AT MAY DAY RALLY, MOSCOW, 1918
Post-revolutionary democracy has, in practice, turned into its opposite

increasingly to be used, and *particularly* to be used, by the wage-earning masses of the populations of the Western societies. Moreover, they have been used effectively by the wage earners to get themselves real, tangible, material benefits. That is not the only use of these democratic institutions and freedoms; there are other things in life which matter as well as material benefits. Nevertheless, material benefits are very important and, in actual practice, Western democracy has proved itself capable of getting substantial material benefits for the Western wage earners. All this does not mean that Western democratic institutions are perfect; or that it is easy for the wage earners to use them effectively. On the contrary, Western democracy is undoubtedly imperfect and its use by the wage earners is made difficult by just those considerations which the Communists mention. It has been true at some times and in places (and is still true at certain times and in certain places, though decreasingly) that the wage earners are too poor, ignorant, and generally oppressed to make intelligent use of democratic institutions, even when they exist. But Lenin made his critique of Western democracy nearly half a century ago, and the wage earners of the West have learned during that half-century to use their democratic institutions much more effectively than he supposed would ever be possible.

Look, first of all, at what might be called the economic consequences of democracy. Communists will recall that Marx predicted that the wage earners of capitalist societies were bound to sink into "ever increasing misery." It is sometimes denied that this is what he predicted, but there is really no doubt about it. Let me give just two quotations, one from the first great statement of Marx's world-outlook, made in his youth in the *Communist Manifesto* itself. And then I will quote from the great work of Marx's maturity, from Volume I of *Das Kapital*. The *Manifesto* reads:

> The modern labourer . . . instead of rising with the progress of industry, sinks deeper and deeper below the conditions of existence of his own class. He becomes a pauper and pauperism develops more rapidly than population and wealth.[1]

Now from *Das Kapital*, in what is, in effect, the summing up of his first volume:

> While there is thus a progressive diminution in the number of the capitalist magnates (who usurp and monopolize all the advantages of this transformative process) there occurs a corresponding increase in the mass of poverty, oppression, enslavement, degeneration and exploitation. . . .[2]

Now it is perfectly true that Marxist scholars can find other passages in his works (and in those of Friedrich Engels) which qualify this prediction of ever increasing misery to some extent. Nevertheless I do not think that anyone can really doubt, in view of those two authoritative statements, that Marx thought that the standard of life of the wage earners of capitalist societies was bound either to remain at subsistence level, or actually to sink further.

Nor was there anything foolish or far-fetched about making such a prediction, either in 1848 when Marx first made it in the *Communist Manifesto*, or even when he made it in the 1860's in Volume I of *Das Kapital*. Undoubtedly it must have looked as if things were bound to go that way. It was not, of course, that Marx denied that capitalism was developing the means of production and, indeed, was increasing production itself. But he was sure that all of the fruits of this increased productivity would go to the owners of the means of production and none of them to the wage earners. This is not what hap-

---

1 GBWW, Vol. 50, p. 425a.
2 GBWW, Vol. 50, p. 378c.

pened. For whatever reasons, the un-questionable fact is that in all of the major and more successful Western democracies, the standard of life of the wage earners has risen substantially, instead of falling, in the one hundred years which have elapsed since Marx made his prediction.

How Much Better Off?

It is difficult, indeed probably impossible, to measure with statistical accuracy the degree to which the standard of life of the wage earners in, for example, Britain, has risen since the 1850's or 1860's. But all the statisticians and economists who have studied the matter have come broadly to the same conclusion, that British wage earners can, on the average, in the 1960's, purchase between two and three times as many commodities as they could purchase one hundred years ago. Therefore, instead of ". . . the mass of poverty, oppression, en-slavement, degeneration, and exploitation . . ." having grown, it has substantially diminished.

This is true not only of Britain but, I repeat, of the other advanced Western capitalist democracies also. In the case of the United States, it is estimated that the standard of life of the American wage earners has increased even more rapidly than that of the British wage earners; and this, I think, would also be true of Sweden. The standard of life has not risen so much in the Western European democracies but nevertheless it has risen—indeed in the last two decades it has risen substantially. All statistical investigation, combined with common observation, leaves no doubt whatever about this.

I am laboring this point because every-thing turns upon it. I need not, surely, emphasize to Communists that a reversal of direction in the movement of the stan-dard of life of the mass of the population in a society alters everything. If the standard of life of the wage earners rises where a fall

has been expected, every other expectation changes also; the whole social and political outlook of the wage earners becomes different. It is indispensable, above all for Marxists, to revise their prognosis as to what will happen. Because this is such a cardinal point, on which a great deal of the rest of my argument must turn, I must take up two further and related questions before leaving this strictly economic part.

The Wage Earners' Share

There is, first, the question of the dis-tribution of the national income. It is sometimes said—indeed it was said by one school of Marxists, the Austrian Marxists—that although the standard of life of the wage earners was undeniably rising, yet this was merely because of the enormous general increase in productivity and wealth, and that the wage earners' share in this rising total was falling. Therefore (they said) it remained true that the wage earn-ers were being increasingly exploited in the sense that the distribution of the na-tional income was becoming more and more unfair. Here the figures, up till about twenty years ago, are, in my opinion, in-conclusive. In some countries I think it was true that the share of the wage earners did not rise and may even have dropped. But recently in, for example, both Britain and America, the share in the national income of the wage earners, as well as the absolute amount which they receive, has undoubtedly risen. Their share has not risen at all fast in Britain, but it has risen. For example, Colin Clark has made an effort in his work *Conditions of Economic Progress* (Macmillan, 1940, revised 1957) to compute "labour's share of the net pro-duct" at various periods and in various countries. He puts this share in the United Kingdom at 63 percent in 1843. It actually fell between then and 1911, when it was 59.5 percent but then has risen slowly up

19TH-CENTURY FEMALE
LABOR IN ENGLISH MINE
*Beyond the limits
of human endurance*

till 1953, when it was 74.4 percent. In the United States, Clark has more recent figures. Labor's share was (he writes) 71.9 percent in 1919 and 80.1 percent in 1953; and this tendency for a slow rise is general throughout the Western societies. I would not ask you to rely on these figures being exact, for this is a very difficult thing to calculate, but I think that they probably do show what the general tendency is.

Again, Professor John Kenneth Galbraith, the American economist, in his well-known book *The Affluent Society*, gives recent figures for the distribution of the national income for the United States which have been very carefully assembled.

In 1928 disposable income, *i.e.*, income after taxes, of the 1 per cent of the individuals with the highest income was estimated to account for 19 per cent of all income. By 1946 it accounted for a little less than 8 per cent. In 1928 the 5 percent with the highest incomes received over a third of all income; by 1946 their share was about 18 per cent. The war and post-war years, especially, were a time of rapid improvement for those in the lower bracket. Between 1941 and 1950 the lowest fifth had a 42 per cent increase in income; the second lowest fifth had an increase of 37 per cent.

It will be seen from these figures that there can be no doubt that the distribution of income in the United States has become markedly less unequal than it was some thirty years ago. More than this I would not claim; but this is enough to show that

even the revised version of the theory of ever increasing misery—what the Austrian Marxists called "relative immiseration"—has not turned out to be correct.

Moreover, the actual amount of purchasing power received by the wage earners, either absolutely or relatively, is not, of course, the whole matter. There is the almost equally important question of hours of work, vacations with pay, access to education, health services, and the like. All these things make up an important part of the wage earners' "standard of life." And here the improvement over the last one hundred years is even more impossible to deny than in the case of purchasing power itself. Marx laid heavy emphasis on the greedy thirst of the capitalists of his day for increasing the hours of work of the wage earners, up to, and even beyond, the limits of human endurance. Once again he was quite right that such a dreadful tendency did exist in his day. You have only to reread the chapter in Volume I of *Kapital* in which he attacks, with magnificent vigor, the theory of "Senior's Last Hour." Senior was a contemporary British economist (he was my great-grandfather, as a matter of fact) who put out a pamphlet on behalf of the manufacturers of his day, seeking to prove that any reduction in the appallingly long working hours of the British wage earners of that time would destroy the whole profitability of British industry.

Marx, quite rightly, ridiculed Senior for his pretentious and inhuman nonsense. But I often think that Marx would be even more astonished today by the reduction in working hours than by the increase in wage earners' purchasing power. The fact that somehow or other the wage earners, while still under capitalist relations of production, have managed to get relatively short hours of work per day, that they have got two whole days off a week, and that they get annual vacations with pay, would, I think, greatly astonish him. And then again, the elaborate (though still in my opinion quite insufficient) educational system which is open to the wage earners of all the advanced Western democracies, by which they all get at any rate a primary education, and a steadily increasing minority of them get the opportunity for secondary and university education, is a transformation in their situation which neither Marx nor Engels nor anyone else could have forseen one hundred years ago.

How Have the Wage Earners Done It —Imperialism?

How and why has all this happened? I must first deal with an explanation put forward by Communists. They say, in effect, that insofar as these improvements in the standards of the wage earners of the Western democracies have occurred, it is due, not to any difference in the way in which the capitalist system has been working, but to the superprofits of imperialism. For, they say, some of the superprofits of imperialism have filtered down to the wage earners of the West. This is a very important question and one which deserves detailed treatment. (As a matter of fact I have written a whole book on this particular issue called *The End of Empire*.) I have no space to prove to you here that this Communist contention is mistaken, although I am quite sure, myself, that it is mistaken. But consider at least the following undoubted fact. During the last twenty or thirty years—in those same years, that is to say, in which the improvement in the

standard of life of the wage earners in the Western democracies has been most marked—every one of the great empires has been dissolved. For example, even twenty years ago we in Britain ruled over no less than 600 million people outside the United Kingdom. Today that number has dwindled to less than 25 million, and in a few years more will have gone down to a very small figure, if not to zero. Therefore it is an impossible argument to say that the increase in the standard of life of the Western wage earners is all due to "imperialist exploitation," since that increase has been most marked just while the empires were being dissolved.

However, the Communists have a counterargument to that also. They say, in effect, that these empires have not been dissolved: that a form of "neocolonialism" (as they call it) has been introduced, by which the exploitation of all these ex-colonial people is being continued in a new way. Surely this is not the case in, for example, far the biggest instance, that of Britain's relations with India. It is quite utterly untrue that we in Britain have any longer an opportunity to exploit the present independent India, even if we wished to do so. But, in any case, I do not see how it can be argued that the remains of imperialist exploitation—and I agree that there are such remains—can have *increased* imperialist gains to a higher amount than they were before the empires were dissolved. To say this would be like saying that the remains of something were more important than the thing itself. It does not really make sense; the "neocolonialist" argument simply won't do.

Democracy Has Done It

One must look for some other explanation of the fact that, especially in the last twenty years, the standard of life, in the broadest sense of the word, of the wage earners in the Western societies has incontrovertibly gone up, not down. Well, what is the explanation? Why is it that Marx's prophecy of ever increasing misery, which must have seemed thoroughly reasonable and sensible when he made it, turned out to be wrong? I have no hesitation in saying that the explanation is to be found in the increasingly effective use of their democratic institutions by the mass of the wage earners of the Western societies. It is democracy which has done it. The Western capitalist employers have not had a change of heart; they still work, and must work, their industries in order to make the maximum amount of profit. They do not like paying higher wages to their workers, or working these shorter hours. By and large they have been impelled to do these things by the wage earners themselves. It is the fact that the wage earners in the democracies have been able to organize themselves, both politically and industrially, that has done the trick.

I will discuss below the question of exactly how democracy has enabled the wage earners to increase their standard of life, and the extent to which it has been the right to vote and to choose the kind of governments which they preferred as against the extent to which it has been the right to organize in trade unions, which has enabled them to do this. On the whole, the direct instrument has been trade unions. It is trade-union pressure—collective bargaining—which has pushed up wages much above that subsistence level beyond which Marx believed they could not go. But, on the other hand, I do not think that we ought to underestimate the importance of the right to vote. For the trade-union instrument could never have been used—the trade unions would have remained small, weak, helpless bodies—unless the workers had had the power to vote into office governments which would recognize the trade unions and make their work possible.

There is another very important factor

in the rise in the standard of life of the wage earners: taxation. Slowly, but in the end inexorably, the pressure of the wage earners has driven the governments of the Western democracies to undertake a substantial redistribution of the national income by means of taxation. A few British figures. In Marx's day, over one hundred years ago, there was no such thing as income tax. In his old age there was an income tax of 6*d*. in the £1. Today that tax is 7*s*. 9*d*. in the £1, with a much higher rate on all incomes over £5,000 a year.[3] Again, in his day, the rich man in Britain could leave all his money to his children. Today, the really rich man, the millionaire, has to pay some 80 percent of his fortune when he dies to the government (although there are a good many ways of avoiding some, though not all, of this tax). Again, companies' profits were not taxed in Marx's day. Today every company in Britain has to pay almost exactly one-half of its profits to the government. These rates of taxation really do make an appreciable difference to the way income is distributed—for out of the money thus collected, quite a lot (though not all) of those social services, pensions, insurances, national health services, and the like, which are today a most important part of the wage earners' real incomes, are paid.

Are They "Wage Slaves"?

I have been stressing the material benefits which the wage earners of the West have got out of their democratic institutions because the Communists are accustomed to stress material benefits very heavily too. But of course material benefits are not everything. A critic of the Western democracies might object that even though he had to admit that the wage earners of the Western democracies were now com-

---

3 Sixpence is 2.5 percent of a pound; 7*s*. 9*d*. is 34.6 percent of a pound.

paratively well-fed "wage slaves," they were still "wage slaves." He might re-iterate Lenin's criticism of "bourgeois democracy" and say that the wage earners did not obtain an appreciable degree of true freedom from it. No doubt there is something in this criticism. It is true that by and large there still exists a governing class in the Western democracies which retains a power and influence which is quite disproportionate to its numbers. As a matter of fact this is a good deal truer of my own country, Great Britain, than for example of the United States; but it is also true, in varying degrees, of most of the Western democracies.

There are two considerations here which ought, surely, to be taken into account. Primarily the wage earners have used their democratic institutions to obtain for them-selves the above material benefits. But as they succeed in obtaining those benefits, they become increasingly able to use their democratic institutions. They they can, in turn, get themselves a greater degree of true freedom and this in turn enables them to get more material benefits; and so on, in action and reaction between material progress and an increasing amount of political and social freedom. Communists surely ought to understand this process for it is a dialectical interplay between the economic base and the political super-structure. As I shall show, there is ab-solutely no doubt about it that the West-ern wage earners are becoming slowly, un-evenly, and with many setbacks, but still undeniably, more free as well as more prosperous. They are becoming more free in the specific sense that they are getting more and more say in the way in which their countries are run.

Democracy Is So New

The second consideration which must be taken into account here is that Democracy in the sense in which I am describing it is a far more recent thing than is usually supposed. Britain is often thought of as "one of the oldest democ-racies in the world"; and it is true that some democratic institutions, such as the rule of law, a fair amount of freedom of speech, and some others, go back a good many years into British history. But real democracy, in the sense of a universal franchise by which all of the adult popula-tion of the country choose the kind of government they want, is a far more recent thing. As a matter of fact it has been finally established within my own political lifetime. One whole half of the British population, the women, were, after all, only given votes in 1918, an election which I remember quite well. And the younger women were, as a matter of fact, only given votes in 1929 during the election in which I was first elected to the British Parlia-ment. Moreover, British trade unions have only become really powerful in the past twenty years. Democracy, in the sense in which I am using the word, is, then, a very recent thing, even in Britain. We have only just begun to feel its full conse-quences. I cannot tell you what those con-sequences will ultimately be; but I am quite sure of this, they will be far reaching. Assuming that the present British demo-cratic institutions are preserved—and the vast majority of the British people is de-termined that they should be preserved—they will by, say, the end of this century have transformed British society. The wage earners will have asserted themselves to an ever increasing degree in every sphere of national life. Well within the next forty years we shall have in Britain a society which has been remodeled according to the desires of the British wage earners.

IV. HOW DEMOCRACY HAS DONE IT

In describing the economic consequences of democracy, we saw that democratic institutions have been put to highly practical use by the wage earners of the West: in short, they have used democracy to make themselves better off.

For my part I think that these material advantages are extremely important. People really are more free when they are prosperous than when they are not. It is worth saying this because it is rather the fashion to sneer at the recent material progress of the wage earners of the West. People talk about "mere TV freedom," about "motorcar freedom," "washing-machine freedom." It is the fashion to sneer at all the gadgets which the wage earners are coming to possess. People suggest that this "Affluent Society," as it is called, and which is undeniably coming into existence in the West, is a vulgar, garish sort of thing, not worth much to anyone.

I have very little sympathy with this point of view. Personally I like having a TV set, a motorcar, a washing machine, and the other gadgets of a contemporary home in Western society. For that matter the high standard of life which is being achieved in one Western society after another consists in many other things as well as gadgets: it consists in things like decent housing, more leisure, and a good education for one's children. I want such things, don't you?

The truth is, of course, that these things are enormously important to every wage earner's family. What we can agree is that there is something low and limited about caring *only* for material benefits. If democracy brought *only* washing machines, TV sets, and motorcars, or even good houses, it would be a limited thing. For once one has got these material benefits, one has to learn to use them wisely, and that is even more difficult than getting them. One has to learn that, in the end, their real use is to increase one's freedom to develop as a human being. That is why I suggested that there is a dialectical inter-play between the use of their democratic

institutions which the wage earners of the West have been making to get themselves material benefits, and the deeper, and in the end even more important, use of those institutions to increase human freedom.

Some spokesmen of the Communist point of view still go on trying to deny that there has been any real improvement in the conditions of the wage earners in the West. For instance, only eight years ago, in 1955, the Communist-dominated French trade unions—the CGT—solemnly debated Marx's theory of ever increasing misery. They debated, not whether the theory had turned out to be true—it was taken for granted that it was true. What they debated was how, in that case, they were to get the French workers to take an interest in trade-union activity. How were they to make the French workers struggle to raise wages, shorten hours, and improve conditions, when it was inevitable that they would sink into ever increasing misery whatever they did? The Communists debated every possible way of solving this obviously insoluble problem. For none of them could permit himself to face the simplest fact that his trade-union work was, in fact, helping to raise the standard of life of the French wage earners appreciably! To face *that* fact would have involved recognizing that Marx's theory of ever increasing misery had proved to be wrong.

Blinded by Theory

This is what I call being blinded by theory. I am not against political and economic theory. On the contrary it is indispensable to form the best theories which we possibly can about the way in which our societies work: otherwise we shall have no guide as to how to change and improve them. But it is essential to recognize that even the most brilliant theories are simply hypotheses designed to account for the observable facts of social life—hypotheses which must be scrapped the moment that these observable facts no longer fit the theories. What oceans of misery the world would have been saved if only the Communists—and everyone else too for that matter—had borne that simple principle in mind. Instead, everybody tends to cling desperately to the theories he has learned. The Communists have carried this common human error to an extreme: they have been, and remain, "blinded by theory" to the point where in some cases they take no account of the real world at all. The results are disastrous, not only for them, but for all of us, and the greatest example of all is the clinging to the dogma that the wage earners of the Western democracies are sinking into ever increasing misery, when quite obviously their standard of life is steadily rising.

Lenin on "Bourgeois Democracy"

What I want to discuss at this point is the question of *how* the wage earners of the West have used their democratic institutions to improve their standard of life; and then how, in turn, on the basis of that improved standard of life, they have further strengthened their democratic institutions. For the connection between voting every few years at a general election for this candidate rather than that, and getting a higher wage, shorter hours, and better conditions of work, is by no means obvious. Yet in the long run, there has proved to be such a connection.

In order to see *how* democracy has improved, and continues to improve, the people's standard of life, we must look at the origins and the workings of the democratic institutions of the West. As a matter of fact, the man who had least faith in these institutions—Lenin—described their original form very accurately. In *The State and Revolution*, Lenin (quoting Marx) said that in a "bourgeois democracy" a general

election is a process by which, every four or five years, the workers choose *which* members of the governing class are to rule over them.

I agree at once that that is a very good description of what, say, a late-nineteenth-century British election was like. It is quite true that at that time the British workers could only *in practice* choose between that section of the British governing class which was represented by the Conservative party—on the whole, the land-owning section—and that section of the governing class represented by the Liberal party—on the whole, the manufacturers' section. But Marx and Lenin, when they had pointed out this fact, thought that they had exposed "bourgeois democracy" as a sham and a deception. What good would it do the wage earners to choose a Liberal rather than a Conservative, or a Conservative rather than a Liberal, to rule over them? They would be just as much exploited by one as by the other, said Marx and Lenin.

But this plausible view has turned out to be mistaken. Because they were fundamentally uninterested in the workings of democratic institutions, both Marx and Lenin overlooked the fact that, once the wage earners had won the vote, they were bound to begin to get some of their own interests attended to. For naturally as they, by their votes, came more and more to decide *which* section of the governing class should be in power, the representatives of these sections could not resist the temptation of bidding against each other for the workers' votes. At any rate, that is what happened in Britain.

Trade-Union Voting Power

A substantial part of the British wage earners got the vote for the first time by the Reform Act of 1867. In the same period, an extremely hard-fought struggle for the other basic democratic right, the right to form genuinely free trade unions, was going on. During the 1860s, the unions, which had been legal in Britain since 1824, began to get strong enough to inconvenience the British employers. Immediately a series of enactments, investigating commissions, and administrative measures designed to remove, in fact, if not in form, the legality of trade-union activity were introduced by the Liberal government which was then in office. It looked as if the right of collective bargaining was going to be lost as soon as it was beginning to be effective.

But in 1874 there had to be a general election. The British trade unions made a supreme effort to win back, with the newly acquired votes of their members, the right to collective bargaining, which they were fast losing. And they succeeded in doing so. For the candidates of the Conservative party, hungry for office, pledged themselves to make trade-union activity legal again if they were elected. They were elected, and they did re-legalize trade unionism by what are called the "Cross Acts" of 1875.

True, that was by no means the end of the story. At the turn of the century in 1901, a new obstacle to trade unionism was contrived by the lawyers of the employers. It was decided, in what was called the "Taff Vale Decision," that a trade union could be fined the whole of the cost which had been inflicted upon the employers in a strike. This obviously made organized strike action impossible. But once again the British trade unionists used their voting power to get this decision reversed. They did so, this time, partly by supporting the Liberal party against the Conservatives, and partly by starting a new party of their own, the Labour party. By these means the Taff Vale Decision was reversed by the Trade Union Act of 1906. But still the struggle went on. In 1909, in what is

LONDON TENEMENTS, *Harper's Weekly*, 1872
Illustrates the ability of the wage earners . . .

CONTEMPORARY WORKERS' HOUSING, LONDON
. . . to push up their standard of life above subsistence level

called the "Osborn Judgment," the courts ruled that all political activity on the part of the trade unions was illegal. This judgment also had to be got rid of by means of the unions' voting power; and in fact it was overridden in 1913. Then, in my own political lifetime, after the General Strike of 1926, the Tory government of the day passed an act once again restricting trade-union political activity, though this time by no means completely. This final restriction on trade-union freedom was got rid of by means of the great Labour electoral victory of 1945. For one of the first acts of the Labour government was to abolish it.

The Pattern Elsewhere

It has been worthwhile to make this brief résumé of the British development over the past one hundred years because it illustrates so vividly the interplay between political democracy and the ability of wage earners to push up their standard of life above subsistence level. *This* is how democracy has done it. Of course the story has been different in timing and in detail

in each of the other Western democratic societies. But the end result has been, in general, much the same. By means of using their votes, the wage earners have in the end—and after prolonged and severe struggles—established their right to form organizations which can effectively bargain with the employers on rates of wages, and hours and conditions of work.

The specific pattern has usually been the same in one major respect at any rate. At first the wage earners have used their votes by means of supporting that "governing class" political party which promised freedom of trade-union action, and opposing that "governing class" party which opposed it. But at a certain point of development this method has always, on this side of the Atlantic at any rate, been found unsatisfactory, and the wage earners have set about organizing and financing a political party of their own. The apparent exception to this rule is the United States. There the trade unions for many decades (indeed right up to 1932) switched their votes between the Republicans and Democratic parties according to which of them seemed to offer them the better terms. But

MAULDIN CARTOON: "BY TH' WAY,
WHAT'S THAT BIG WORD?"
Disenfranchise the Negroes

since the great Roosevelt governments of the New Deal in the 1930's, the American trade unions have become (permanently, I think) associated with the Democratic party. This will· in time mean, I believe, that the Democrats will become, in effect, the party of the American wage earners, not so very different, in spite of their very different origins, from the Labor or Social Democratic parties of Western Europe.

Naturally, freedom for their trade unions to act effectively is not the only thing which the wage earners have got by using their voting powers (although it is, on the whole, the most important single thing). On the contrary, all the other freedoms which I have listed—both the material and the nonmaterial freedoms—are bound up with this power to choose and dismiss governments.

An American Example

Let me give a quite different example from the United States. Take the acute and terrible issue of social equality for the 10 percent of American citizens who are Negroes. The dreadful cases of race discrimination which take place in the Southern states of America are often given by Communists as instances of their main argument that "bourgeois democracy" is a sham. But in fact this struggle for racial equality which is being fought out in the United States today supports just the opposite conclusion. It illustrates the fact that it is impossible in a contemporary advanced society to discriminate against a particular and substantial body of citizens, *unless you can deny them the vote.* For it is precisely by means of denying the vote in practice, though not in theory, to Negro voters that the hard core, which is now down to four or five states of the "Old South," is enabled to carry on its vicious policy of race discrimination. By the threat of violence, or by imposing a prohibitive poll tax on the voters, these states disenfranchise the Negroes, and, by so doing, are enabled to deny them, in practice, most of the other freedoms such as access to education, trade-union rights, equality under the law.

If the Negroes had the vote in these states, it would be quite impossible for the whites to do this. This is proved by the fact that gradually the Negroes in most of even the Southern states are acquiring the right to vote. Backed by the federal government, which is at last beginning to perform its duties to the Negroes in the South, the Negroes of one Southern state after another are beginning actually to use their vote; and in one Southern state after another, as they do so, the most atrocious and blatant forms of race discrimination have to be abolished.

All this is not being accomplished without heroic and desperate struggles on the part of the American Negroes, just as the struggles of the British workers for trade-union recognition were of a prolonged and obdurate character. But the thing is being done. There is now only a small corner of the United States where Negroes, by using the votes which they have won for themselves, cannot help to dismiss any government which discriminates against them, and help to choose a government which will give them legal equality of status. Wise, though exceedingly firm, leaders of the American Negroes like Dr. Martin Luther King, with whom I have discussed this matter, are perfectly confident that, in a few years from now, they will have captured these last strongholds of white racial discrimination. And it is of the utmost significance that they are concentrating on winning the right to vote as the key to everything else.

My conclusion is that Lenin's and Marx's scoffing at "bourgeois democracy" has turned out to be singularly ill-founded. Far from it being valueless for the wage earners to acquire the right "to choose every few years which member of the governing class is to rule over them," precisely this has proved the gateway to their acquiring more and more political power. For even before they have organized political parties of their own, before they have been able to get invaluable rights, such as the legality of trade-union bargaining and strike action, by forcing the rival governing class parties to bid for their votes. Moreover, when they have come to the much more developed stage of political activity represented by the formation of organized political parties of their own, they have come more and more to influence, and in the end even in a measure to control, the governments of their own countries.

This is not because the political parties—call them Labor parties, or Social Democratic parties, or what you will—which the wage earners of the West have organized have always been particularly successful in winning a majority of the voters and forming governments. They have done this from time to time, and here and there, as we did in Britain in 1945 for example. But

Dr. Martin Luther King in Montgomery, Ala., 1965
Concentrating on winning the right to vote

547

the only case in which such a party, founded by the wage earners and their trade unions, has been almost continuously in office over long periods has been in the small state of Sweden. Nevertheless, it would be a profound error to think that these huge political efforts of the wage earners in forming their own parties have been a waste of time. On the contrary, they mark a new state of maturity in the wage earners' efforts to use democracy and in particular in that process of bidding competitively for the wage earners' votes which I described above. For in practice the formation of a wage earners' political party by no means ends that process.

How Will the Process End?

I have seen the thing working out in my own country of Great Britain during my own political lifetime, in which there have been three Labour governments, that of 1924, that of 1929, and that of 1945. These Labour governments have done a great deal to improve the wage earners' conditions in Britain. But, looking back on this nearly forty years of political experience, I am inclined to say that even more has been accomplished by means of the effect upon the rival parties, based on the governing class, which the existence and pressure of the Labour party has had. The fact is that the British Conservative party has pretty well had to turn itself inside out in order to prevent the whole of the British wage earners from voting Labour! More often than not, it has succeeded in retaining about one-third of the British wage earners' vote for the Conservatives. It has, therefore, continued to win more general elections than it has lost. But it has only done this at the cost to itself of an immense modification both of its program and even of the actual measures which it enacts. For example, the sort of persecution of the trade unions which I described above, and which went on, though in a diminishing

degree, right up to 1945, is not even discussed in the Conservative party today. Successive Conservative governments now deal with the British trade unions as one of the acknowledged and established powers of the state. They do not like doing so and they sometimes grumble about "trade-union power." But they know perfectly well that if they ever attack the unions again by anything remotely resembling the Taff Vale Decision or the Osborn Judgment or even the Trade Union Act of 1927, they would have little chance of winning an election.

What has happened is that, slowly but surely, the ever increasing use made by the wage earners of their voting power has transformed not this party or that, but the whole of the British political scene.

How it will end I do not know any better than you, of course. But unless some catastrophe intervenes, it seems to me quite inevitable that each and all of the British political parties will continue to adapt themselves to the overwhelming pressure of the wage earners' voting power. And when that has happened, power itself will have passed into the wage earners' hands. But all this is, of course, flatly contrary to what is supposed to be possible in Communist political theory. If I am right that this is what is actually happening, it must mean that that theory has proved to be defective. Therefore, our next task will be to examine Communist political theory, and in particular Lenin's theory of the state.

V. THE THEORY OF COMMUNIST SOCIETY

I have alluded from time to time to Lenin's theory of the state. It is time to set it out. Lenin states it himself, with all his incomparable clarity of exposition, in his famous pamphlet *The State and Revolution* which he wrote in August and September 1917, just a few weeks before the Bolshevik seizure of power. Indeed his text, as we have it, is unfinished. Lenin was going on, he tells us, to analyze "the experience of the Russian Revolutions of 1905 and 1917," when he was interrupted by the outbreak of the October, or Bolshevik, Revolution. "Such an interruption," he dramatically adds, "can only be welcome. It is more pleasant and useful to go through the experience of a Revolution than to write about it." However, the part of *The State and Revolution* which Lenin did complete is a definitive statement of what he thought about the nature of political power.

The first thing to realize is that for Lenin, as for Marx, the division of society in social classes is everything. And when I say "everything," I mean that phrase almost literally. For the Leninist, even more than for the Marxist, nothing in human life really counts compared with this division into social classes. Politics is

the struggle for power between these social classes, and power is the power of the state. The state is simply an engine of coercion by the use of which any class which is at the moment in power controls by physical force the class or classes which are not in power. This whole conception derives directly, of course, from Marx's and Engels' formulation of the matter in the *Communist Manifesto* where they wrote that the state is "the executive committee of the ruling class."

Let us agree to discuss the matter in these Leninist terms. For my part, I think that this Leninist theory of political power is an oversimplification of the real situation. Nevertheless, I think it has got a very great deal of truth in it. Indeed, unless one has seen that the essence of politics is a struggle for power between social classes, whether conducted by peaceful, parliamentary, and democratic means, or by

HAROLD WILSON ADDRESSING LABOUR PARTY CONFERENCE, 1963
Bidding for the wage earners' votes

violence and revolution, one has understood very little about politics.

Let us also agree, at any rate for the sake of argument, that the state in the Western democracies is "the executive committee of the ruling class." Very well then: but what *is* the ruling class, in my own country of Britain today, for example? In some ways, of course, it is quite true that the old ruling sections of the population, the landlords and capitalists in the classic Marxist sense, are still the ruling class. They still enjoy, not by any means all their previous privileges, but yet great privileges and great wealth compared with everyone else. Nevertheless, does it really make sense to say that the existing British state is their "executive committee"?

Despite the blank incredulity which every Communist will feel at the following proposition, the evidence shows that the British state today cannot possibly be regarded as the executive instrument of the old ruling classes, to be used for the suppression of the other classes of British society. The plain fact is that, because of the process of democratic pressure which I have described previously, the British state today acts almost as often in the interests of the wage earners as in the interests of the old ruling classes. I do not see how anyone who is aware of the realities of contemporary British political life can deny this proposition. The proof that the British state is no longer the executive committee of the old ruling classes is that that class has become extremely hostile to state action.

The really reactionary forces in Britain today spend almost their whole time in attempting to circumscribe, limit and, if possible, restrict, the activities of the state. Why on earth should they do this if it were *their* state? If they were still in secure control of the British state surely they would wish that state to be as strong as possible and to interfere in Britain's economic and social life as frequently as possible, for they would know that it would always interfere on their side. But just the contrary is the case. They wish to prevent the state from, for example, levying heavy taxation, because they know that a great deal of that taxation will fall on them. They wish to prevent big schemes of state pensions and state health insurance because, again, they know that they will have to pay a large part of them. They wish to prevent the state interfering in industry because they know that, more often than not, state control will be exercised in favor of the wage earners rather than the employers. Is not all this positive proof that our British ruling classes feel that control of the state is slowly but inexorably slipping out of their hands? And of course they are right. They are slowly losing control of the British state, and nothing but an antidemocratic counterrevolution on their part could regain it.

Therefore, even if we accept (as, I repeat, I do in part, accept) Lenin's and Marx's general theory of the state, one must immediately add that contemporary Leninists have failed to apply that theory in any way realistically to contemporary Western society. What they have failed to realize is that over the decades in well-entrenched, solidly based democracies, such as those of Britain and America, state power can begin to slip out of the hands of one class into the hands of another. Of course no one can prove that this process will continue peacefully until the wage earners are in complete control of the state. All one can say is that the process has gone a long way already, and that if democracy is preserved, there is no reason to suppose that it will not go a great deal further.

The New Workers' State

However, let us return to Lenin's theory of the state. As I have stated it so far, it is almost pure Marxism. But then

Lenin added a new proposition to which, though it is contained in the later writings of Marx himself (notably in *The Civil War in France*, his account of the Paris Commune of 1870), he gives a quite new emphasis. Lenin's new proposition was this: the existing state, he wrote, was the executive committee of the ruling, bourgeois class. Moreover, he added, it was quite impossible for the wage earners to take over this particular engine of power which had been built up by their class enemies. Its whole design and construction was totally unsuitable for the wage earners' ends. Lenin would have laughed to scorn the idea that over the decades the wage earners could gradually possess themselves of more and more influence over such states as these, for he had no understanding of Western democratic processes or their consequences. But he went much further than this. In his view, the objective of the wage earners must be, not to capture the existing state, but to destroy (to "break to pieces," as he put it) the existing capitalist state apparatus, and then to build up a quite differently designed and constructed state apparatus of their own.

What then was to be the purpose of this new kind of state? It was, Lenin writes, to hold down and coerce, if necessary by physical force, the old governing classes. Just as the real purpose of the old capitalist state had been, in his view, to hold down the wage earners by physical force, since all the trappings of bourgeois democracy were a sham, so the new workers' state must use physical force to hold down the remnants of the old governing classes so long as these remnants continued to exist. This was what Lenin meant by "the dictatorship of the proletariat."

Does all this mean that Lenin never intended to build a new kind of democracy, that he foresaw and would have approved the arbitrary and dictatorial kind of rule that exists in all the Communist states to-

day? It means nothing of the sort. On the contrary, I am quite sure that Lenin in 1917 would have been sincerely horrified if anyone had suggested that the state that he and the Russian Bolsheviks were about to construct would not be, in his sense, democratic. Indeed he would have claimed —and did claim—that it would be incomparably more democratic than any state which had gone before it. Nor, he would have added, did this contradict the fact that the new workers' state would be arbitrary and coercive toward the remnants of the old ruling classes. Lenin would have claimed—and did claim—that the state which he was to build would be ultrademocratic for the masses, that is to say for the Russian workers and peasants who formed perhaps 95 percent of the total Russian population.

Again, he would have taken the analogy of the old capitalist society which he was overthrowing. He would have agreed, I think, that the old capitalist society was, in the West—though not in Russia— genuinely democratic *for the ruling classes*. Within these classes people really did exercise a free choice as between one kind of government and another. But this bourgeois democracy was, he would have maintained, in practice a dictatorship over the wage earners. In just the same way he claimed that his new state was going to be a democracy for the wage earners and peasants, while being an iron dictatorship over the old governing classes.

Moreover, Lenin claimed (again sincerely, I think) that his state was going to be a far more direct and literal kind of democracy for the masses than the bourgeois state had been for the old governing classes. And I repeat that he advocated the three main measures which he was convinced would ensure this ultrademocratic form of society for the masses. He reiterates in *The State and Revolution* that these three principles will be applied unhesitatingly by the workers when they come to power:

All officials, without exception, elected and subject to recall *at any time*, their salaries reduced to the level of "workmen's wages"—these simple and "self-evident" democratic measures, while completely uniting the interests of the workers and the majority of the peasants, at the same time serve as the bridge between capitalism and socialism.

What Went Wrong?

How on earth did this vision of Lenin's turn into almost its exact opposite? How did this state which was to be democratic to a fault, so far as 95 percent of the population was concerned at any rate, turn into one of the tightest and most arbitrary dictatorships that the world has ever seen? When I say that the present Soviet government is one of the tightest and most arbitrary dictatorships that the world has ever seen, I do not mean that it is one of the worst governments that the world has ever seen. On the contrary, it has important achievements to its credit. It is much more creative than most of the arbitrary and dictatorial governments of history. Especially in the short run, democracy is not the *only* important thing: an arbitrary government can sometimes, and in some respects, be a good government. I am not denying that. What I am asserting is that democratic institutions are the sole way so far discovered of making governments conform, broadly, to the will of the governed.

And in this sense the Soviet government is one of the least democratic governments in the world. It is one of the least democratic governments in the world in the specific sense that the Russian people have, on the whole, less means of influencing their own government than almost any other well-developed people. They have no such power as we have been discussing, of choosing which kind of government they went, and of dismissing the kind of government they have got, and replacing it by another kind. I do not see how anyone can

possibly deny that simple fact. Nor will the Russian people ever be possessed of such a power until and unless they are permitted to choose freely between several different candidates at freely contested elections. As it is, each of Lenin's principles for working-class democracy has been totally violated. For Russian officials are not elected by free vote; they are not subject to recall by a free vote of the body which elected them; and they are paid for more than a skilled workman's wages.

How has this extraordinary reversal of the sincerely held intentions of Lenin and the other Bolshevik leaders come about? There are many reasons, but I believe that one of them, which is often overlooked, is this. The Communists believed that once the Revolution had taken place—that once, *i.e.*, the means of production had been taken out of the hands of the capitalists and landlords, and class distinctions thus, they believed, abolished—political life would become quite a simple matter. As a matter of fact, Lenin has a strange passage in *The State and Revolution* in which he says just this:

> Capitalist culture has *created* large-scale production, factories, railways, the postal service, telephones, etc., and *on this basis* the great majority of functions of the old "state power" have become so simplified and can be reduced to such simple operations of registration, filing, and checking that they can be easily performed by every literate person, and it will be possible to perform them for "workmen's wages," which circumstances can (and must) strip those functions of every shadow of privilege, of every semblance of "official grandeur."

Poor Lenin! It would be comic, if it were not tragic, to contrast Soviet society as it is today with this vision of state power "reduced to such simple operations of registration, filing, and checking. . . ." Think of the glittering Soviet marshals; of the hordes of bemedaled, gorgeously uniformed officers of all the Soviet armed services;

think of the tremendous army of Soviet high officials with their almost omnipotent powers, and their very considerable salaries, who rule Russia today; think of the vast apparatus of direct coercion represented by the secret police in all its forms (now a less monstrous growth than in Stalin's time but still incomparably greater than anything in the West). These dignitaries are not engaged in "simple operations of registration, filing, and checking"! They are engaged in ruling Russia, and I, for my part, find it impossible to deny that they constitute a ruling class, though, undoubtedly a different kind of ruling class to that of the West.

As a matter of fact, I do not particularly blame the Soviet government for having set up an enormous "bureaucratic-military state machine," as Lenin well called the state apparatus of the bourgeois societies of his day. I do not think that at the present state of human development, human societies can be run without some such "bureaucratic-military state machine" as this. It is by no means the case that either before or after the Revolution political life can be reduced to "simple operations of registration, filing, and checking." It is by no means the case that it is possible to get the difficult and complex functions of government, of military command, and of the management of great industries performed in return for the payment of wages no higher than the wages of a skilled worker.

But what does seem to me tragic is that the Russian Bolsheviks have set up a bureaucratic-military state machine, not merely as large, as privileged, as splendid, and as highly paid as, but far larger, more splendid, and more highly paid than the bureaucratic-military state machines of the old ruling classes of the West!

The Hypertrophy of the State

This raises the famous question of the "withering away of the state." As we all know, the final vision of Marx and Lenin is that even those simple and ultrademocratic forms of state organization which Lenin recommended would ultimately become unnecessary. Then there would be no state apparatus in the sense of an engine for the suppression and coercion of any section of the population; there would simply be experts to administer the productive process. The state itself would have withered away. Now, it is silly and unfair to sneer at the Soviet government because the Soviet state has not yet withered away. As a matter of fact Lenin was very careful to say that he had no idea how long this withering-away process would take. He wrote in *The State and Revolution* that we

have a right to speak only of the inevitable withering-away of the state; we must emphasize the protracted nature of this process . . . we leave the question of length of time . . . quite open.

But the Soviet state, far from even beginning to wither away, has become incomparably the largest, most complex state apparatus in the world, which seeks to control (and does control) the lives of its citizens in far greater detail, and far more arbitrarily, than any other state in the world. It is this hypocrisy of the state that we must deplore in the Soviet Union.

However, the real point to my mind is not the failure of the Russian state to wither away, or even its present monstrous growth. It may well be that in the first forty-five years of the new economic system, an enormous state apparatus was indispensable; I am inclined to think that it was. The real point is that if such a vast state apparatus was indispensable, then it was one hundred times more important than ever before that elaborate democratic institutions should be set up for the popular control of this huge and otherwise monstrous engine. I believe that even with its vast state apparatus, Russia could have

Yet Russian society now cries out for some mechanism by which the Russian people can choose the kind of governments they want, and dismiss the governments they do not want. The Russian people are now quite well educated enough to be able to work such a system effectively. The provision of mass popular education, and of extremely wide secondary and university education, is by far the greatest positive achievement of the Russian government. But it is an achievement which makes their present political arrangements hopelessly out of date. When and how will the Russian people establish the democratic institutions which I have no doubt they would now operate effectively?

Nothing less than the survival of the world may well depend, in my opinion, upon their establishing democratic institutions, of one kind or another, in the not too distant future.

VI. THE TRAGEDY OF COMMUNIST SOCIETIES

The conclusion of the last chapter was that the Communist societies of the present day desperately need some mechanism by which their people would be able to choose, dismiss, and broadly control their rulers. Goodness knows, we exercise these three fundamental democratic rights imperfectly enough in the West; but, by and large, we do exercise them. No government in any of the Western democracies can depart too far from the general point of view of the majority of its population. If it does, it gets dismissed, and another, more amenable, government is put in its place.

I am convinced that the main tragedies which have beset the Communist world over the last forty years have arisen from lack of any effective political mechanism of this kind. In the abstract and in theory, of course, the need for such a mechanism is recognized by the Communists; otherwise

become a very effective and progressive society if only she had created some mechanism for the democratic control of her governments. Ordinary, effective, democratic institutions are what she now tragically lacks.

Such democratic institutions might not necessarily have taken the particular forms which we have worked out in the West. They need not have either parliamentary or presidential democracy as I have defined those terms previously. The original Soviet form of democracy by indirect election from the factories, though abandoned under the Stalinist constitution, has always seemed to me an attractive democratic form, which might have been well worth experimenting with. But of course it was never given a chance to function. For the Russian Communist party never allowed any candidates but their own to be put up at elections. Therefore there were not, and never have been, any real elections at all in Soviet Russia.

they would not go through the form of holding elections. But their mechanism of political control by means of elections does not, in fact, work: and this for the simple reason that (as everybody knows) only candidates approved by the Communist party are allowed even to seek election. Indeed, when it comes to the point, only one candidate is nominated so that there is no choice at all before the electorate. As my old leader, Clement Attlee, expressed it: "A Communist election is a horse race with only one horse."

Khrushchev Unfair to Stalin?

The forty years of experience which we now have of societies ruled by Communist governments amply confirm the view that some political mechanism for democratic elections is almost a necessity for the government of highly complicated, advanced, industrial communities. For, on the whole, the troubles of the Communist world have not arisen from the fact that the Communist rulers have been either stupid or wicked. In fact most Communist rulers have ruled their respective countries to the best of their abilities. Some of them no doubt have been scrupulous, some of them exceedingly unscrupulous, men. But all that is true, of course, of the rulers in Western societies also. And for that matter, many of the Communist rulers have been men of far above average ability. That is true, for example, even of the now most infamous, but once most adulated, of them all—of Joseph Stalin himself. No serious student of Stalin can doubt that he was a man of enormous political ability. Nor, as a matter of fact, do I altogether agree with Mr. Khrushchev as to the nature of Stalin's motivation. Stalin murdered, lied, pillaged, and tortured; nobody can contradict Khrushchev when he says this. Indeed he ravaged his native land of Russia by doing these things on a scale unparalleled, except by Hitler, in the contemporary world. But I

sometimes get the impression from Khrushchev's denunciations of Stalin that he is suggesting that Stalin murdered, lied, pillaged, and tortured for his own pleasure, or simply to keep himself in power. This is what many an arbitrary ruler in the past has done, of course; they have had no particular social purpose; they have merely wanted to stay in power and terrorize anyone whom they thought could conceivably threaten their position.

But this was not the situation with Stalin. I think that Stalin sincerely believed that all the purges, horrors, and nightmares of Russian life under his regime were indispensable to his purpose of industrializing his country and making it a world power. Moreover, he almost certainly believed that unless he succeeded in doing this in a very short space of years, he would be attacked and destroyed by one or more of his capitalist neighbors. Both these beliefs were almost certainly false. But I am inclined to think that, except in the last few years, when he does seem to have become more and more purely pathological, they were the mainspring of Stalin's actions.

Be the case of Stalin as it may, I do not think there is any serious doubt that the terrible things, which, do not let us forget, Lenin also did, were done in almost perfect purity of motive. This purity of motive made Lenin all the more relentless, no doubt. Indeed I do not think he could possibly have done some of the things he did unless he had been totally convinced that they were right and necessary. For of course Lenin was an incomparably more civilized man than Stalin.

The Party as an Idol

And yet we should not forget that the relentless coercion, of even that section of the Russian people who had been the most passionate supporters of the Bolshevik regime, began under Lenin himself. Most

CHINESE WORKERS PARADING, NATIONAL DAY, 1950
The endowment of "the Party" with divine right . . .

historians are now agreed that it was the suppression of the revolt of the sailors of the Red fleet—the very heroes of the October Revolution—at Kronstadt in 1921 which marked the turning point in Bolshevik practice. It is true that a civil war was raging. There had been wholesale (if mainly ineffective) intervention by the capitalist states. Thus it would be ridiculous to blame Lenin for fighting to retain power. Nevertheless, once he had used the Red Army, and the whole Russian apparatus of physical coercion, not against the West, not against the remnants of the old ruling class, but against the very spearhead of the Russian proletariat itself, against the sailors of the Red fleet, the whole elaborate theory of Communist democracy, which, as we have seen, he had put out just a few years before in *The State and Revolution*, received a fatal blow.

I call it a fatal blow because from that time onward—from Kronstadt down to today—there has been no moment at which the Soviet government has not been using its arbitrary coercive power, not, I repeat, against anything which could conceivably be called the remnants of the old ruling classes, but against important sections of the Russian masses themselves. The Communists are accustomed to explain this by saying that these sections of the Russian masses had been "misled." This explanation is significant for it reveals an underlying cause of the tragedies of the Communist world. The fact is that Communists are absolutely convinced that *they* always know best; that they know much better than the masses themselves what are their true interests. But history shows that they do not.

It is this Communist cocksureness, this terrible conviction that they can do no wrong, which has caused the Communists to do such abominable things over the past forty years. It is strange indeed that these men, claiming, and originally not without some justification, to be in the vanguard of human progress, have erected "the Party" into one of those absolutes with which men have often tortured their imaginations, and in the name of which some of the darkest deeds of human history have been done. Monarchy, of course, was another of those absolutes. For "the divine right of kings" was also a claim that the monarch could do no wrong. These fundamentally irrational absolutes arise, I think, when a particular institution, the Monarch, "the Party," or what you will, really has a major historical function to perform. Just as monarchy certainly had a genuine historical function, of centralization and organization, to perform in the Western world five hundred years or so ago, so now either a monopolistic party *or* an effective democratic institution has an indispensable function of economic integration to perform. Seeing this function the Communists have made out of the human artifact, "the Party," a positive idol. They have en-

dowed "the Party" with divine right, so that in their eyes it literally can do no wrong. But "the Party" is in fact merely a collaboration of men and women just as fallible as the rest of us: and it both can and does do wrong, and that most terribly.

For history will show that the Party is not the only way of performing the historical function which genuinely is necessary in our time, namely the satisfactory organization of economic and social life in advanced industrial communities. The Communist way of performing this function is merely one of the ways of doing the job, and it is by no means the best way. Hence the endowment of "the Party" with divine right has become a genuine historical monstrosity. It has led, and still leads, to crimes and disasters seemingly without end.

HUNGARIANS DEMONSTRATING, BUDAPEST, 1956
. . . has become a historical monstrosity

SOVIET OFFICERS IN BUDAPEST, OCTOBER, 1956
A mistake to try "to make people happy by force"

The Export of Communism

This does not mean, I repeat, that the Communist societies have no achievements to their credit. They have great achievements and I will discuss these fully. But this endowment of "the Party," and hence of their governments, with divine right does mean that these achievements are punctuated by major crimes and disasters. More than that, Communist cocksureness—Communist conviction that the Party is always right—leads to an even more serious difficulty, which may yet destroy the world. This is because the Communists have quite forgotten one of the remarks of the founders of Marxism. Engels, in his mellow old age, said that it was always a mistake to try "to make people happy by force." "To make people happy by force," to export what the Communists, in their delusion, genuinely think is their infallible recipe for human happiness, and so force it upon unwilling peoples, has, unfortunately, as everyone in Eastern Europe knows only too well, been done by them again and again.

As it happened, I had the opportunity to witness at first hand one of these attempts

by the Russian government to impose on a neighbor its exact conception of the way in which a country should be run. For I was in Warsaw during the three weeks of the so-called October Days of the Russian-Polish crisis in 1956. Let me say at once that this was an example—unfortunately almost a unique example—in which the Russian government did, in the end, draw back, compromise, and allow a little variety or deviation on the part of another government which it controlled. But I am afraid that the Polish case was an instance of an exception which proves, or illustrates, the general rule. After all, the new Polish government, which came into power during those three weeks in Warsaw, was still a Communist government. Indeed it was, and is, in the main, as it has shown, a basically orthodox Communist government, with many of the prejudices and delusions, as I see them, of other Communist governments.

The new Polish government had no inclination to break its close military alliance with—indeed military dependence upon—Russia, or to displace the Russian troops garrisoned on Polish soil. It merely wished to do two things, first to stop the forced collectivization of the Polish peasants (which was ruining Polish agriculture), and, second, to give Polish Communism a generally Polish instead of a Russian accent. All the Poles wanted was to enjoy a certain amount of freedom to do things in a Polish instead of a Russian way—for instance, to carry out the industrialization program according to the plans of the exceedingly able and sophisticated Polish economists, and, perhaps above all, in cultural life, to enjoy a certain amount of "Polishness."

Yet even these exceedingly modest Polish demands were met by furious Russian resistance. While I was there, Mr. Khrushchev, Marshal Koniev, and most of the then Russian government arrived in a large Russian airplane in Warsaw and demanded that the Poles should do as they were told. More important, the two Russian divisions in Poland were set in motion and began to advance on Warsaw. The Poles, with extraordinary nerve, combined with the utmost wisdom and moderation, refused on the one hand to give in, or on the other to break with Russia, though they did make it perfectly clear that if the Russians resorted to armed force, they would fight. I myself saw the preparations being made in Warsaw to do so. In the end the Russians—and let me say at once that it was greatly to their credit—did come to terms, as we all know. They allowed the new Polish regime of Mr. Gomulka to take power. There was no crushing of the Polish resistance, and a mildly revisionist form of Communism has existed in Poland ever since.

But when we look at the record as a whole, we must regard this Polish episode as the exception which proves the rule. And for that matter, was it not monstrous that the Poles had to go to the very brink of desperate, indeed suicidal, war in order to be allowed slightly to modify their Communist regime? For it is clear that only extraordinary political skill, and per-

haps good luck, enabled the Poles to achieve the very limited success which they did achieve.

All this, of course, was proved only too vividly in the next week of 1956 by the opposite outcome of the Hungarian revolution. Millions of words have been written about the Hungarian tragedy but, at the end of the day, it seems to me that its real essence lay in the genuine inability of the Russians to conceive it possible that they had been mistaken. They could not bring themselves to allow the Hungarian people to develop their own kind of regime. I feel sure that the Soviet government of the day genuinely saw no alternative to crushing the revolt of the Hungarian workers under the tank tracks of several Soviet armored divisions. As a matter of fact, it is clear from the record that they were loath to do so. For they hesitated several times before using their armored divisions. But in the end they gave full rein to their fatal conviction of infallibility. They were sure that whatever they did they were furthering the "real interests" of the Hungarian workers—even if they had to do it by killing them! This Communist conviction of infallibility has become purely mystical. I came across one example of this mysticism in a quotation from the Soviet press soon after the Hungarian tragedy. It was a sentence written by a Colonel Federor on March 22, 1957, in *Krasnaia Zvezda:*

> Trained by the Communist Party, the armed forces of the U.S.S.R. live up to their international duty. This was demonstrated by the aid they gave to the working people of Hungary. . . .

I expect that the worthy colonel saw no irony in what he wrote. He believed in the principle that the Party could do no wrong: therefore, when the Party shot down the workers of Budapest, it was genuinely bringing them aid and support.

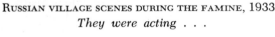

Russian village scenes during the famine, 1933
They were acting . . .

To such lengths can what I have called "blinding by theory" be taken.

Before continuing with these examples of the tragedies caused by the Communist delusion of infallibility, and by the absence of any democratic institutions which can correct this delusion, let me say at once that I am not suggesting that Western rulers are immune from making similar mistakes or committing similar crimes. They are not. What I am suggesting is that, because we—the West—have a mechanism, however crude and imperfect, for the control of our rulers: because above all we can hire and fire them at regular intervals, the errors and crimes of Western governments are kept within relatively narrow limits.

Collectivization

As a matter of fact, the most expensive errors of the Communist governments have not been their coercion by physical force of other peoples, such as the Poles or the Hungarians. I cannot doubt that history will say that by far their most expensive errors have been internal. And the greatest of these internal errors has been the policy of agricultural collec-

tivization. Very broadly speaking, I think that one can say that, regarded from a strictly economic standpoint, Communist economies have been a success industrially and an appalling failure agriculturally.

The forced collectivization of Russian agriculture was not only the root cause of the terrible crisis, famine, and purges of the thirties but it continues, in my opinion, gravely to set back the development of the Russian economy. The failure in agriculture is an appalling drag on Russia's economic progress as a whole. But it is in China, I think, that the consequences of forced collectivization will prove most serious. In conditions far less suitable for collectivization than Russia, the Chinese Communists have pushed through a yet more extreme form of the policy. The results speak for themselves. We do not know the extent of the Chinese famines, but there can be no doubt that they have taken place, for the Chinese government itself has announced that they exist. Moreover, the Chinese government has bought millions of tons of wheat on the world market; and they would not have dreamed of spending their precious foreign exchange on anything except capital goods for in-

560

dustrialization unless they had had to, because even the essential categories of their population would otherwise have starved. Thus Chinese economic development which, by all accounts was going spectacularly well up till about 1958, has suffered the most serious setback because of this agricultural catastrophe.

The adoption of the policy of forced collectivization by all the orthodox Communist governments has been due to two things. In the first place, it has been due to the unshakable Communist conviction that they always knew best; that they were acting in the real interests of the peasants even if they had to use extremes of physical coercion to make them pool their land. Second, it has been due to the lack of even the rudiments of a democratic mechanism by which the will of the majority of the people could make itself felt upon its government. For, of course, forced collectivization could not possibly have been pursued if there had been any way by which the peoples of the countries concerned had been able to control, or even influence, their governments. There cannot be the slightest doubt that the overwhelming majority of the peoples of these countries, including the whole of their peasantry, has been passionately opposed to it.

The Nature of the Tragedy

All the governments in the whole of human history have made errors, and very few of them have avoided committing crimes. In history, many a government has been as arbitrary, and as vicious—if not as thorough—as contemporary Communist governments have sometimes been. And these old tyrannies committed their crimes without the justification which the Communists undoubtedly have, that at least they thought they were serving the high purpose of human development. The old tyrannies were, it is true, a good deal milder than Stalin's government was at its worst; but they were purposeless, while no one at any rate can accuse the Communists of being that. And then, of course, there have been the fascist tyrannies of our own times which have committed, in the case of Hitler's Nazism at any rate, crimes which have never been surpassed or even equaled. And again, the twentieth-century fascist governments tortured and murdered without any real purpose, except the crude, old, futile purpose of attempting to conquer the world by military force.

For these reasons the Communist governments have been, in my opinion, of a different kind from either the old, historical, tyrannies or the criminal fascist govern-

COMMUNE SCENES, RED CHINA, 1964
. . . in the real interests of the peasants

ments of the twentieth century. For the motives, the intentions, of the Communist governments were good; but, unfortunately, as Marxists are the first to say, motives and intentions count for little in history. Indeed the gulf which has opened between what the Communists intended and what they have done is the essence of this tragedy.

All this leads me back to the conclusion, which I stated at the outset, namely that the new, crucial, and overwhelmingly important issue in the world today is *not* that of Communism versus Capitalism. The really important issue is raised by the contemporary attempt to run large, modern, highly developed communities under a democratic system. The fate of the world will hang upon the success or failure of the attempt to give the people of such societies control over their governments.

I expect that few of those who are following these remarks have themselves been ministers in a government. I have been a minister. And I can testify from personal experience how much even the best-intentioned governments need the restraining and correcting hand of ultimate popular control. Even ministers (indeed, especially ministers) who are sure that they are right, who have the best interests of the people at heart, and who are convinced that they can bring them enormous benefits, need desperately the restraining knowledge that if they do things that the people of their country object to, they will lose their power. If ministers have that knowledge there is genuine popular control of the government; if not, not. That is democracy. It is the hope of the human race.

VII. THE ACHIEVEMENTS OF COMMUNIST SOCIETIES

It is thought that the creation of a great industrial state in Russia, since the Revolution, is a sort of miracle; that it proves that Communism can do things which no other form of society can rival. On the whole, I think that this particular achievement of Russian Communism, though real enough, is greatly overpraised. Of course it is a great achievement to have dragged Russia out of the semibackward, semi-industrialized condition, in which she was in 1917, into the position of one of the leading industrial powers of the world. But where people go wrong is in thinking that this is in any way a unique achievement. A more careful reading of recent economic history would show that, on the contrary, a number of nations, under differing economic systems, have made, or are making, this same transition from peasant backwardness to industrialization.

Nor as a matter of fact is there anything unique about the pace at which Russia has done the job. Forty-five years is about the time which it usually takes to get from the sort of conditions which prevailed in Russia in 1917—and, remember, Russia was by no means completely backward in 1917 —to those which prevail today. Japan is perhaps the most striking example of another nation which has made the same transition in about the same time, but under a very different economic system. Japan is also an example which meets another point often made by those who are overimpressed with Russian economic progress. They point out that Russia has made this remarkable progress in spite of two appalling wars. But this applies to Japan also. It is true, of course, that Japan suffered far less than Russia in World War I; but, on the other hand, unlike Russia, she suffered total defeat in World War II. Moreover, the Japanese economy was subjected to the very considerable strain of an attempted conquest of China during the greater part of the period between the two wars. In spite of all this, the actual rate of Japanese economic progress, as measured by the growth of what the economists call the "gross national product," has been faster, even, than that of Russia.

However, I am not going to bore you with figures on these issues because, frankly, I do not trust them in detail. The economists make valiant efforts to measure the rate of economic progress made by different countries, and it is very important that we should have some sort of measuring rod for this purpose. But the truth is that these gross national product figures are far more approximate than they are usually supposed to be.

Japan is not the only case in point. Mexico, as a matter of fact, is another country which has come along at a sharp pace during the same period. I believe there have been years in which, at any rate on the economists' scale of measurement, Mexico has been growing faster than any other country in the world.

Then again, Western Europe, to everybody's astonishment, in the seventeen years since World War II, has recovered at an extraordinarily fast pace. This is, of course, a rather difficult story, in that her stage of development was much higher than Russia's was in 1917. And then, of course, both British and American development, though uneven and sometimes disappoint-

JAPANESE SHIPYARD, 1952
Growth faster, even, than Russia

ing, has, at any rate compared with any-thing which has ever happened before in the world, been very fast over the past seventeen years.

And now India, though still at an early stage in the process of economic develop-ment, is going ahead at a steady 4 percent rate of growth a year, again according to the economists' figures, and hopes soon to raise her rate to 6 percent. Once again, though you may think that slow in terms of the claimant needs of the Indian popula-tion, it is breathtakingly fast compared to any development which has ever before taken place on the Indian subcontinent.

One could give many more instances of countries, with many different kinds of economic systems, developing at, broadly, the same sort of pace that Russia has de-veloped since the October Revolution. The conclusion which one is driven to by a study of these facts is that once a country, by one means or another, can get its feet planted on the road of industrialization, it can go ahead far faster than human so-cieties have ever done before. And this is true, almost irrespective of whether the country in question possesses a predom-inantly capitalist, free-enterprise, market-economy system; a Communist economic system; or, like India, an economic system which is a compromise between the two. Of course the kind of economic system which a country possesses makes a differ-ence; there are advantages and disad-vantages in each kind of system. But ex-perience shows that it makes far less difference than I, for one, used to think that it would.

Does Gross National Product Matter?

But what, I shall be asked, about all those dazzling prophecies which the Russians are accustomed to make—as, for instance, that the Russian gross national product will overtake that of the Americans in 1970 or 1980 or some such time? Well,

it is perfectly true that if you extend the curves on the graph paper of the rising rate of growth of the two economies, you will get some such forecast as this. Whole teams of both Russian and American economists study these figures and come out with results which, while they vary fairly widely, all point in this direction. But again, in my opinion, this conclusion is a far less sensational one than most people suppose. It is quite possible for a latecomer in the industrial race to catch up, in terms of physical output at any rate, with a country of earlier industrializa-tion, by means of forced marches, such as Russia has undertaken. But once you get to the standard of affluence of America, or even of the West generally today, these figures of total physical output become extremely approximate as a measure of general development.

At the risk of going into some economics, let me illustrate this. As I understand it, the Russian and Western economists reckon the "gross national product" in very different ways. The Russians, true to what they suppose is the Marxist tradition, reckon only the physical product of indus-try and agriculture and the economic sys-tem generally: so many tons of steel, so many tons of wheat, so much aluminum, so many pairs of boots and shoes, so many machine tools, etc., etc. They take no ac-count of what we call "the service trades," that is to say, of wholesale and retail dis-tribution and the production of nonma-terial things—such as hairdos for women, for example—or the effect of better or worse service in shops.

There is no doubt that the Russian economists, in thus looking at the gross national product as a gigantic heap of ma-terial commodities, think that they are be-ing true to the Marxist tradition. And so, in some respects, they are. For Marx wrote in *Kapital* that wholesale and retail dis-tribution, and trading generally, added no value to the product. This conclusion followed naturally from Marx's way of reckoning value according to the socially necessary Labor Time expended—from the Labor theory of value which Marx had inherited, and adapted, from Ricardo. But Marx was a very profound man and he knew very well that commodities were not necessarily material things. As a matter of fact he says so on the very first page of Volume I of *Das Kapital*. He there defines a commodity as something which satisfies a want—which want, he writes, may arise either "in the stomach or in the imagination."

And the fact is that, as countries get richer, more and more of the wants which their production system attempts to satisfy arise, not in the stomachs of their populations, but in their imaginations. This is natural and inevitable, for until the belly is satisfied we cannot attend to other things. But once it is, all sorts of elaborate wants and desires begin to come into our heads which can often be satisfied, not by material objects but by services of one kind or another. We then begin to be willing to pay out money for such services. Some of these nonmaterial wants may be no "higher" in the sense of more intellectual or "spiritual," than the simple ache of the belly for food; some, on the other hand—and they are expensive wants to satisfy—may be for seats at the opera or at symphony concerts, or for opportunities to appreciate the most beautiful things which human hands have made during the centuries.

Therefore, in the case of highly developed, comparatively rich communities, it really will not do to think of commodities as a heap of material things. Take again my example of hairdos for women. According to the changes of fashion, in one decade women wear hats; in the next decade they abandon their hats and spend even more money on having their hair dressed in hairdressers' shops. Both these wants arise "in the imagination" rather than in the stomach. And the activities necessary to satisfy them use up a proportion of the available productive resources of the community, either on the production of hats in hat factories, or in the services of hairdressers in hairdressers' shops. Yet if we stick to what I would call the mechanically material definition of commodities for the purpose of reckoning up the gross national product, we shall count only those resources devoted to the production of hats but exclude those resources devoted to the production of hairdos. This is obviously illogical and makes one reach a false conclusion. It is merely one example of what happens increasingly when countries reach a high standard of life. More and more of their economic effort goes into what we call the service trades, providing conveniences, and easing the life of the people, rather than providing additional material commodities.

I have gone into all this to show how doubtful and relative it is to think of there being some particular moment at which Russian economic production will overtake American as Mr. Khrushchev so frequently prophesies. Maybe Russia will one day make more millions of tons of steel a year than America. But if she does, what of it? It won't make very much difference. It may well be that by that time the production of some other metal, say aluminum, will be a more important factor in economic development. Or, more likely, what will really matter will be the number and quality of the highly skilled designers, engineers, and craftsmen that a country possesses. The fact is that at a high level of development, the comparison of gross national products, of standards of life and of economic progress generally, becomes a very difficult and doubtful business. This is not to say that economic progress is not extremely important: it is, especially of course where the standard of life is still pretty low. But what I am doing is simply to attempt to get all this business of economic comparisons into some sort of perspective.

Russian Military Power

The second Russian achievement which enormously and naturally impresses people is her military power. Here there is little doubt about the facts. Russia has given most convincing proof by her *sputniks,* her rockets, her multimegaton nuclear explosions, and her spectacular military displays, of possessing great military power, based on the latest scientific techniques. I should be the last to dismiss or try to minimize the extent of this achievement.

But what it shows, I think, is this. If you specialize sufficiently—if, that is to say, you devote a big enough part of your total resources, of your skilled and unskilled labor, a sufficient number of your best scientists, a sufficient number of your ablest men in every walk of life, to producing military power—in a word, if you give military power an almost absolute priority, as the Russians have done, you can achieve these wonders.

It is not difficult to understand why the Russians have done this. During the whole period since the Revolution they have felt themselves to be inhabiting a besieged fortress. They have believed that their very existence depended on their military strength. Therefore they put it above every other consideration. Moreover, for a long time, the rest of the world, in its folly, gave them very good reason to think this. There were the interventions against the infant Bolshevik Republic at the end of World War I, and there was Hitler's attack on them in the middle of World War II. This concept of a besieged fortress still dominates Russian priorities. The question is whether it is any longer sensible or necessary?

Well, no one expects the Russians to disarm themselves; no nation-state, Com-munist or capitalist, feudal, peasant, or what you will, has ever done that in the face of the existence of other armed states in the rest of the world. It may be that it is idle for us to expect that nation-states ever will. Nevertheless, there is a special frenzy about the degree to which the Russians devote their resources to armaments. To go back to those economists' figures which I was criticizing just now (but which do give at any rate the best available guide to what is happening), it is usually reckoned that we in Britain, for example, are devoting about 7 percent of our gross national product (*i.e.,* of all our economic resources) to armaments. America is, on the other hand, devoting about 10 percent. The Russians are devoting at least 15 percent; and 15 percent is a lot, especially in a country like Russia which still faces acute economic problems of development. The truth is that while Russian military achievement is certainly most impressive, and while there are fully comprehensible historical reasons behind it, what finally confronts us is not some miracle, but simply a nation-state behaving very much as other nation-states have always behaved, only a bit more so! All nation-states have indulged in the arms race, but Russia indulges in it a little more wholeheartedly than anyone else.

Has It All Been Worthwhile?

So far our conclusion must be that in the economic and military fields the achievements of the Russian Communist government are real and substantial, but by no means unique. They are similar in kind to the achievements of other nation-states with different economic systems at similar stages in their development. What can be said is that the Russians have pressed on with the development of heavy industry and of military power more whole-heartedly, perhaps, than any other government has ever done.

But here we must ask two questions. First, is such wholeheartedness desirable and, second, what has it to do with the main question we are discussing in these pages, namely, democratic institutions? Personally, I answer the first of these questions in the negative. I do not believe that it has been desirable, either for Russia herself or for the world, that she has concentrated with such positively manic determination on the development of heavy industry and upon armaments. Take heavy industry first. I do not believe that Russian development would necessarily have been slower, over all, if there had been, in the forty-five years since the Revolution, less concentration on heavy industry and more attention both to light industry, producing consumer goods, and above all to agriculture. This is not the place to enter into a detailed economic argument, but, in my opinion, Russia's economy might actually be stronger, because better balanced, today, if she had done this. She would not be producing so much steel, so many machine tools perhaps, but she might be producing a great deal more wheat, meat, milk, shoes, and the like. I venture to think that that would have been better for everybody.

More than that, I do not really agree with the answer which I think the Russian Communists would make to this suggestion. They would say that that was all very well, but that they could not possibly have eased their concentration on heavy industry because that would have diminished their military strength. In the first place I repeat that I do not think that, at any rate since the end of World War II, they have needed as much military strength as they have developed. Second, I am inclined to think that, before World War II, when they certainly did need great military strength, the alternative policy would have given greater rather than less powers of resistance.

After all, the fact is that the Russian Army in 1941 suffered the most appalling initial military disaster at the hands of Hitler. Something like one hundred Russian divisions were destroyed with all their tanks and equipment in the initial weeks

RED ARMY DAY, MOSCOW, 1964
Russia indulges a little more wholeheartedly than anyone else

of the German advance. No doubt this was partly due to Stalin's military errors which Mr. Khrushchev has now denounced so vehemently. But it was also due, I think, to the frenzy of Stalin's concentration on heavy industry and armaments. For the consequent neglect of light consumer goods industry, and of agriculture, led to the famines and crises of the 1930's. Those famines and crises, in turn, led to the purges. They led to something between ten and twenty million Russians being sent to concentration camps. They led to the decimation of the Russian Communist party itself, and, in particular, to the appallingly drastic purge of the Officer Corps of the Red Army. Can there be any doubt that the frightful strains and stresses to which Russian society was subjected lessened the *will* of the Red Army to fight far more than the extra firepower provided by the extra units of heavy industry increased its *ability* to fight? Can we doubt that there was a net loss of fighting capacity? If the Russian Army had not possessed quite so many vehicles and heavy armaments in 1941, but had not gone through the ghastly process of having its whole Officer Corps destroyed down to the rank of colonel in the preceding five or six years, it would not, I am convinced, have had to suffer so frightfully in those terrible first months of Hitler's attack, when the Nazi *Panzers* reached the suburbs of Moscow.

What It Has to Do with Democracy

But what, you may be asking, has all this got to do with democracy? It has got this to do with it: the policies that the Russian government actually pursued, the policies of superconcentration on heavy industry and armaments, would have been totally impossible in a democracy. You could never conceivably have got the Russian people freely to vote for the degree of sacrifice which Stalin's policies in the 1930's, or even Khrushchev's in the 1950's, imposed on them. If the Russian people had had that fundamental right of choosing the kind of government which they wanted, they would unquestionably have insisted on a slower pace of industrial development, less armaments, and more food and clothing and housing for themselves.

They might have been right or wrong, rash or wise, in doing so, but this is what they would have done. Therefore, the fact is that the particular course of Russian development was based on the power of the Russian government physically to coerce the Russian people—to make them do what the government wanted by means of applying sheer brute force to them. On the whole, I think the verdict of history must be that this degree of coercion of a people by its government is not only a crime, but also a mistake. It is improbable that, on balance, it even increases the military power of the state, taking both material and *morale* factors into account. And it produces the most terrible symptoms of *degeneration*—I use the word advisedly—in any society which resorts to it.

The Wall

The inevitable consequences of the Communists' resort to the unrestrained physical coercion of their peoples can be seen not only in Russia itself, but also in the East European Communist satellites, and above all in the least successful of those satellites, namely, in East Germany.

Have you ever seen the Berlin Wall? I do not expect that many of those who are reading these remarks have had a chance to do so. I wish you could all see it. Not that the Berlin Wall is an impressive sight. It is a mean little wall, badly and hurriedly built of breeze blocks, only about breast high in most places and with a few rusty strands of barbed wire along the top of it. It would be easy enough to scale, or even to knock down, if it were not for the sentries of the East German police stationed every fifty yards along it, with their loaded rifles.

The impression which the Wall makes on you is out of all proportion to its height or strength. You suddenly realize that here is a wall not built, like any of the great walls of history—the Great Wall of China, for example, or the Roman Emperor Hadrian's Wall across the north of Britain—to keep the invaders out. Whether the governments which built these great walls of history were good or bad or indifferent, they were at least trying to protect their own peoples—to keep potential enemies out. These were walls which faced outward. The terrible thing about the Berlin Wall is that it faces inward, toward its own people. It is not a fortification. It is a prison wall, built to keep people in. It has been built, not to protect the people of East Germany from outside enemies, but to prevent them escaping from East Germany.

Somehow or other, all this is apparent in the physical look of the Wall. At some places it is not really a wall at all; it follows the line of houses down one side of the street. And these houses, which form the border of East Berlin, have had all their windows bricked up. As you walk along beneath them, in the last few yards of West Berlin, they look down on you like dozens of blinded eyes. On the pavement are little heaps of fading flowers to mark the places where people have jumped from the roofs of those blinded houses, and been killed in their efforts to get out of East Germany.

Propaganda, you may say. Well, yes, it is rather difficult *not* to make propaganda out of such a situation. But the situation itself— the Wall itself—has arisen quite naturally as it were, as the inevitable consequence of the determination of the Communist governments to apply any degree of coercion to their peoples. That is the ultimate denial of democracy. In the end, if you do that, you must build a wall round your country or your people will escape. And when you build such a wall, you turn your country into a prison.

VIII. THE LILIES

The main achievement of the Communist societies does not lie in either their massive economic development or in their military strength. Russia is strong, but there is nothing particularly remarkable about the achievement of this degree of strength by a major country in forty-five years of development. No, in my opinion much the greatest achievement of the Russian government, and to a less extent of the other Communist governments, lies in the field of education. I do not know what percentage of the gross national product the Russians are devoting to education, but it must be considerably higher than the Western nations. We in Britain, for instance, are devoting between 3 and 4 percent of our gross national product to education. It is not enough; it is not enough on any reckoning.

Education used to be thought of as a sort of luxury. The government spent what it could afford on it after it had seen to all the things it considered really important, like defense, or roads, or the physical development of the country. But this is a hopelessly mistaken attitude. As a matter of fact even from a narrowly economic point of view—even if you are thinking only of increasing a country's wealth and power at the fastest possible rate—money spent on education is probably more important than anything else. And whatever other mistakes the Communist governments have made they have understood this fact. They are educating more of their citizens, and probably on the whole doing it more thoroughly, than any countries have ever done before. It will stand them in good stead. In fact I do not think it is too much to say that in the long run it may make up for many of their terrible mistakes. I would go further and say that if the non-Communist countries do not do likewise, the Communists' devotion to education will give their countries, in spite of everything, a commanding position in the world.

The Glory and the Gravedigger

Here a paradox is involved. The genuine mass education which is going on in the Communist countries will only give them a commanding position in the world if it, in the end, corrects all their other ghastly mistakes. I believe that in the end it will do so. For well-educated men and women will not, in the end, tolerate living under the now unnecessary constraints and hardships of the present-day Communist countries. Above all, well-educated men and women will not tolerate indefinitely the lack of personal and political liberty which there prevails. They will insist on establishing political institutions which will give them some ultimate control of their governments: and this will be democracy.

So we arrive at the paradoxical conclusion that by far the greatest Communist achievement, namely genuine mass education, may well on the one hand outweigh all their errors and crimes but, on the other hand, will only do so by means of changing fundamentally the character of the Communist regimes as we know them. If the Western countries do not greatly step up their educational effort, the Communists may yet win world leadership. But, they will only do so by means which will in the end convert the Communist regimes into democracies: and once that has been done I, for one, shall have no objection to their becoming the most powerful societies on earth.

(LEFT) GREAT WALL OF CHINA; (RIGHT) HADRIAN'S WALL IN ENGLAND
To keep invaders out

ASPECT OF BERLIN WALL, 1962
To keep people in

Thus the Communists' great educational programs will prove, I foretell, at once the glory and the disruption of the Communist societies as we know them today. Marxists, after all, should find nothing strange in such paradoxes as these. For they are dialectical paradoxes. There is a dialectical interplay between economic development, mass education, and the development of democratic institutions. Marx, it will be recalled, said that capitalism in producing the proletariat was producing above all its own gravediggers.

The Way to the Classless Society

What, then, will be the future of the Communist countries? Will they in fact develop into the "classless societies" which their spokesmen hold before them as the goal to be aimed at? I myself believe in the goal of a classless society as strongly as

ever I did. It still seems to me that the organization of an economic and social system which does not result in men being separated from each other by the barriers of class—peasants from landlords, wage earners from the owners of the means of production, educated from uneducated, rich from poor—would be the greatest step forward that humanity could take. That is why I am and remain a socialist.

Moreover, I am convinced that if we do not blow each other up meanwhile, all advanced human societies are in fact on the way to becoming classless. And I think that this is true of the existing Communist societies also. What I have been saying in these pages is that the Communist societies, because they have destroyed, or failed to develop, genuine democratic institutions, are still much further away from the goal of classlessness than they pretend. In fact it no longer seems probable

RUSSIAN STUDENTS PREPARING FOR EXAMS
Producing its own gravediggers

that they will get there first. Several of the more advanced non-Communist countries, in spite of the fact that they have economic systems which look at first sight less rational and logical than the Communist economies, may well "beat them to it." For their political institutions are much superior, precisely in this respect of ensuring further advances upon the road to classlessness.

The fact is that democratic political institutions are proving an even more important factor in socialist development than the ownership of the means of production. Do not misunderstand me. Both factors are extremely important. It matters a great deal who owns the means of production. At *certain* stages in social development this is the decisive factor. It was, for instance, the decisive factor in Britain in Marx's day. In the absence of democratic institutions which could be used by the wage earners, the nineteenth-century British capitalists' and landlords' ownership of the means of production did give them almost complete control of society as a whole. But today, one hundred years later, in the advanced industrialized societies in which there is universal literacy (and so an ability to participate in political life), democratic political institutions are proving decisive. For they will in turn decide the ownership—or rather, perhaps, the command and control—of the means of production.

I do not mean by this that in each and all of the Western democracies the people will use their votes to nationalize some or all of the means of production and so expropriate their present owners. In some they may; in others they may not. But in one way or another, the people of the advanced democratic socities will arrange the distribution of the national income to suit themselves. Experience shows that they can do this in a number of ways. The most obvious of these ways is so to arrange the tax structure that the main fruits of production do not go to the owners but are shared, directly or indirectly, with the mass of the population. This is actually being done on a significant scale in the more politically advanced Western societies.

I would put the issue like this. Compare the position of a wage earner in a factory which is owned by a Western-type, private, profit-making, joint-stock company, but who possesses full democratic voting and trade-union rights, with the position of a wage earner in a Communist-type state-owned factory, without the right to choose either the kind of government which he prefers or to organize a political party of his choice, or to form his own trade union, or to strike for better pay if he thinks he can get it. Which of the two men has the better chance of getting for his own consumption a high proportion of the values which he produces? I have no doubt that experience has now shown that the wage earner with democratic rights, even if he works in a privately owned factory operated for profit, has the better chance.

Political Parties

We in the West do not think that the decisive democratic institution, namely the right to "hire and fire" governments, is in practice usable without the right to organize *more than one* political party. In nothing does Western and Communist political theory disagree more completely than on this issue of the nature and importance of rival political parties. Let us first state the Communist theory.

The Marxist view of political parties is that they are each the representative, "the executive" as it were, of a distinct social class, or sometimes of a subdivision of a class. Thus in Britain in the early nineteenth century the Tory party was the "executive committee" of the landowners, the Liberal party was the "executive committee" of the manufacturers, while the Chartists were a first, unsuccessful attempt to organize an "executive committee" for the British wage earners. Stated in a sentence like this, the Marxist theory of the

nature of political parties is inevitably an oversimplification. But broadly it is, in my opinion, true, for if you study present-day political parties you will be able to detect their class origins. There are farmers' parties, peasant parties, wage earners' parties, lower-middle-class parties, etc., etc. No doubt the big parties, in countries like Britain and America, in which the electoral system is such that only big parties can have a real chance of success, are bound to be coalitions of the interests of several classes or subclasses. This is true of the British Conservative and Labour parties and of the American Republican and Democratic parties. But even in these cases, the class roots are there if you dig deep enough for them.

"Well then," the Communists go on, "if that is so, and if after our revolution there is only one class left in society, namely the wage earners, what need is there for more than one political party? One class, one party. That is why we maintain the monopoly of the Communist party. All this Western demand for the peoples of the Communist countries to organize more than one political party is so much ignorant chatter."

This Communist argument has one fatal flaw in it. The argument that each class organizes only one party leads to the conclusion that in a society with only one class, there will be no tendency or desire on the part of anyone to organize more than one party. But if so, what possible need will there be to *prohibit* the organization of rival political parties? Why prohibit, with the most extreme pains and penalties, something which you have just proved that no one will want to do anyway? If the Communist theory of political parties is correct, there can be not the slightest need for the Russian government to forbid the Russian people to organize political parties other than the Communist party.

Yet if the Russian people were free to organize rival political parties, which could contest the seats for the Supreme Soviet against the candidates of the Communist party, everybody knows that they would promptly do so. This would be partly because Russia is by no means yet a one-class society. What would happen, for example, is that the Russian farmers would immediately organize a party, probably, I should think, with a one-plank political program, namely the de-collectivization of the Russian land. As the peasants still form 50 percent of the Russian population they would probably get sufficient power to have their way—with, in my opinion, immensely beneficial effects upon Russian economic development. The chronic food shortages would become a thing of the past, just as they have in Poland where they have apparently given up the attempt to collectivize the land.

The Russians, however, if they had the right to do so, would, in my opinion, almost certainly organize rival political parties, even if they really had become a one-class, or classless, society. For experience is showing that it is a huge oversimplification to suppose that political parties are only, or exclusively, the expression of particular social classes. On the contrary, it would surely turn out that even among the Russian wage earners, there would be sufficient differences of opinion to cause the appearance of more than one political party.

What would be the character and programs of the rival political parties which would be likely to appear in one-class or classless societies? What would such parties disagree about? The answer is that they would have plenty to disagree about. The Communist view that the only things which make people disagree with each other are class differences is so huge an oversimplification as to be fatally misleading as a guide to action. Social reality is much more complex than this.

It is true that in acutely divided class societies—societies founded upon chattel slavery, for example—the interests of the different classes are so diametrically opposed that it is impossible for them to show enough mutual toleration to enable democratic political institutions to function. Even in the relatively much less acutely class-divided societies of the present day, political differences, founded on opposing class interests, are sometimes so intractable and so violent that it is difficult to reconcile them by means of the compromises which are indispensable if democratic institutions are to work. But to jump from this truth to the conclusion that no differences at all would be left in a classless society is utterly wrong.

On the contrary, I believe that the future will show that it is precisely when class divisions have been reduced to relatively unimportant dimensions, or better still got rid of altogether, that political differences will become sufficiently mild and soluble to enable democratic institutions to function really well. It will be precisely when rival political parties represent, not social classes, but bodies of citizens who for one reason or another happen to be like-minded, that democracy will finally come into its own.

What would be the probable character of the differences which would divide the political parties of a society which was both democratic and classless (which no major society in human history has yet been)? Perhaps one may catch a hint of what they might be from a remark which an eminent Indian official made to me the other day. He said that in present-day India what they needed was a "6 percent party" and "an 8 percent party." What he meant was that the true issue in Indian public life today was the speed at which India should push forward her economic development. Should she aim at raising her gross national product by say 6 percent a year or by 8 percent a year? This was the really crucial issue. For involved in these simple figures were immense political and social decisions which would profoundly affect the life of every Indian. If the goal of the faster rate were adopted, painful sacrifices in immediate standards and major disturbances in Indian traditional ways of life would have to be accepted. If the slower rate of growth was considered sufficient, there need be fewer sacrifices and disturbances now—but also much less would have been achieved in ten years' time. The enthusiasts, the zealots for progress, should have a party pressing for the higher rate; the conservative and cautious should form a party advocating the slower rate. Out of their electoral contests and debates would emerge not merely the right rate to aim at—which my friend put at about 7 percent —but also, and above all, a nationwide understanding of the real tasks which faced the Indian people.

This is the sort of economic issue over which rival political parties in a classless society would contend, once they were free to do so. But economic issues are not everything. Indeed in the highly developed societies they will be increasingly overshadowed by other issues. Such issues will be such things as these: how much education are our children to have, and what is to be its character—predominantly humanistic or predominantly scientific, or in practice, of course, what blend of the two? Or again, what is to be the attitude of the state to organized religion, favorable, hostile, or neutral? Is complete national independence and sovereignty to be maintained at all costs or should there be federations and mergers with other suitable nation-states? Or finally, how much control from a world organization can be accepted? The moment one thinks of it, one sees that there will be plenty for rival parties to dispute about in classless societies.

The Verdict of History

What will be the verdict of history upon the Communist societies of the mid-twentieth century? They will be credited with major, but not unique, achievements in the economic and military fields. Above all they will be credited with having been the first important human societies to give a really adequate priority to mass education. But their undoubted achievements, history will say, were spoiled by the ruinous degree of physical coercion which these societies found necessary to apply to their citizens. In particular Russia, for a time in the 1930's, as Khrushchev has himself described, became a sort of vast torture chamber, in which some of the most terrible crimes of which a government has ever been guilty were perpetrated under Stalin's direction. Even now, in the 1960's, the worst of the Communist governments, such as that of East Germany, have to build walls round their territories in order to prevent their citizens from fleeing, even at the risk of their lives, from the prison house which their country has become.

Moreover, in the 1960's, the second major Communist country, China, appears to be making such hideous mistakes in its agricultural policy that hundreds of millions of its people have been brought to the edge—or have gone over the edge—of famine.

These are ghastly disasters. But, make no mistake about it, they are disasters for all of us, disasters for the whole human race, not merely for the Communists. For they tend to make the Communist governments desperate and reckless, and to intensify enormously the horror, partly justified, partly unjustified, with which many of the peoples of the advanced

Western societies regard Communism. Thus they enormously increase that world tension which in the nuclear age may yet mean the destruction of human civilization. These disasters have come about in the last analysis because of the lack of democratic institutions in the Communist countries. If governments will not give their people the basic freedoms, they must drive them: and experience shows that they drive them through a series of disasters.

It is true that the major Communist society, Russia, has survived all her disasters and is now on the way to becoming a successful and flourishing nation-state. Is it unfair, then, to complain so bitterly at the staggering price which the Russian people have had to pay for this ultimate achievement? It is not unfair. For the achievement is not outstanding. It can be matched, taking one thing with another, by the achievement of several developing non-Communist nation-states. What has been accomplished—outside of the outstanding achievement of mass education—is no more than the creation of one more large and powerful industrialized country. For that the price has been too high. As I have said, the means which the Communists have used have been terrible: their results, in the main, commonplace.

There is something more. History will judge the Communists by a higher standard than it will apply to many other governments, and inevitably so. For the Communists' own claims have been uniquely high. The Communists started out with incomparably the highest aspirations which have ever motivated any government in human history. They called themselves "the heaven-storming Bolsheviks." They must expect to be judged more strictly than the ordinary run of more or less purposeless, mediocre governments which have governed human societies at most times and in most places. It is the fate of the Communists to have produced the great disillusionment of the twentieth century. The fact that they have committed follies and crimes does not distinguish them from the rest of us. What makes it hard for our generation to forgive them is that they were once the hope of the world. Shakespeare put it, "lilies that fester smell far worse than weeds. . . ."

IX. DEMOCRACY NO CURE-ALL

I have attributed many of the tragedies of our century to the lack of democratic institutions in the Communist countries. But I should not like it to be supposed that I thought that democracy was a sort of cure-all for the ills of human life. Unfortunately that is far from being the case; and that for a number of reasons.

In the first place, democratic institutions do not appear to be workable in all countries. The truth is that many of the peoples of the world are not yet politically sophisticated enough to be able to work democratic institutions effectively. That is a very unpopular thing to say, for it hurts the feelings of many of the new nations, which are coming into being all over the world today. Nevertheless incontrovertible evidence is emerging almost every month which shows that it is true.

Mind you, I am not saying that the ex-colonial peoples are incapable of governing themselves. On the contrary many of them are doing so quite effectively. But for the most part they are doing so in the older, simpler way, living under essentially undemocratic governments, which can only be changed by unconstitutional, violent methods. This does not mean that it was wrong to yield to those peoples' demand for independence. After all, all peoples have lived under arbitrary governments for nearly the whole of recorded history. But it does mean that we cannot, yet awhile, expect that democratic institutions can become universal.

Two Kinds of Self-Government

It is necessary to say this because this argument as to the immaturity of many peoples, and their incapacity to work democratic institutions, is often used as an excuse by supporters of the lingering elements of colonialism which still exist here and there in the world. The white settlers in various parts of Africa, for instance, use this argument in order to perpetuate their own rule, and their own exploitation, of the Africans. But the fact that a people is not likely to be able to rule itself democratically does not mean that it is right for another people to exploit it. Unfortunately that does not alter the fact that when colonial rule is ended, as it has been over by far the greater part of the old colonial empires, the peoples concerned show, in many cases, that they are not yet able to work the democratic institutions which they usually establish in the first instance upon becoming independent.

This means that many of the peoples of Asia and Africa can achieve self-government in the sense of government by their own nationals. But it will not be self-government in the sense that the people as a whole control their governments, even in the indirect way in which we do so in the developed democracies. The real choice before most, though not all, of the new countries is, experience shows, between the continuance of arbitrary government imposed by one of the old colonial powers, and arbitrary government imposed by some leader of their own. Naturally, and rightly in my opinion, these peoples are choosing arbitrary government by one of their own leaders. Such a government is often less efficient than the arbitrary government of one of the old colonial powers. But it is their own; and the efficiency of the old colonial governments was used, in most cases, for the benefit of the white minority in the country and not for the people as a whole.

"Sheikh or Landlord Democracy"

Here, then, is one of the main limitations of democracy. Experience shows that this system of government cannot yet be applied over a large part of the world. The necessary preconditions have not been established. This fact has been demonstrated in numerous instances and in two different ways. I repeat that as soon as new countries become independent, or even in some cases during the last phase of colonial rule, democratic institutions are often established in the new countries. But if these countries have not established the preconditions for successfully working these institutions, the results usually prove extremely bad. One of two things has been apt to happen. In the case of some of the Middle Eastern countries, for example, what I would call "sheikh democracy" or "landlord democracy" resulted when universal suffrage was established. Everybody was given the vote, but as the mass of the population consisted of poor and illiterate peasants, who had not the faintest idea of what to do with the vote, they simply obeyed their sheikhs or landlords. It was not so much that they voted, as that they "were voted" by the landlord and feudal classes. In this way democratic institutions actually proved in these countries a fatal obstacle to progress. For many of these countries have developed relatively efficient and progressive middle classes which are burning with a desire to modernize them. But they were quite unable to win power against the landlords in democratic elections.

Egypt is a particularly good example of this. I have no doubt that Nasser's military dictatorship is proving a far better and more progressive government than the Egyptian governments founded on universal suffrage which preceded it. For these governments were not really democratic at all, even though they held contested elections. Their electors were the mere playthings of the landlord class.

"Chief Enemy"

In other instances, in the newer countries, democratic institutions break down in a still simpler way. It is not so much that any particular landlord class gets control of the voters as that no suitable or effective government results from the elective process. The political parties have not yet learned how to conduct either government or opposition in a democratic way with all the restraints that this involves.

The insuperable difficulties which face many newly independent peoples in establishing democratic institutions were brought home to me during a recent visit to Africa. I was told that the only translation into many African languages of the phrase "the leader of the opposition" was *"chief enemy"*! As so often, language here conditions thought, and thought language. How can there be that subtle interplay of real opposition, combined with cooperation in maintaining the ordered government of the country, which is necessary for the effective functioning of democracy, when the man at the head of the political party which does not agree with the government can only be called "chief enemy"? Compare that with our British phrase "the Leader of Her Majesty's Loyal Opposition"! The leader of the political party to which I belong is, as it happens, in that position today—and incidentally he receives, very rightly in my view, a salary *from* the government for performing the function of leading the opposition *to* the government. But if anyone supposes that this means that the leader of the opposition is not really, genuinely, and indeed passionately opposed to many of the policies of the present (1963) British Conservative government, they will be very much mistaken. What all of us in the Labour

party are loyal to are not the policies of the Conservatives: on the contrary, we shall reverse most of them as soon as we get the chance: what we are loyal to, and shall protect and preserve, is the system of British democracy.

All this does require, I think you will agree, a rather high degree of political sophistication, which can only grow gradually and over a long period. Experience seems to show that it is impossible for many of the peoples of the less developed countries to conceive of an opposition to the government which is less than total. But total opposition means revolutionary opposition; and revolutionary opposition has to be prosecuted by conspiratorial and violent means. Accordingly, in only too many cases, all opposition in these countries turns sooner rather than later to conspiracy and violence, while the government turns to suppression. Chaos begins to grow, and sooner rather than later, a strong man emerges who takes over and rules more or less arbitrarily, even if he preserves a facade of democracy. This is the sort of thing that has happened in, for example, Ghana and Pakistan.

I think we should be quite wrong to sneer at the countries in which these events have taken place, or to suppose that it means that it was wrong to give them their independence, as we British have done over so vast an area of the world in the past twenty years. Some of the arbitrary governments which have taken over after the failure of democratic institutions in these new countries are proving quite progressive and efficient. We should be thankful that these countries have found *some* way of governing themselves. All that has been proved, I repeat, is that for the time being these countries have not developed the necessary preconditions for working *democratic* institutions. In their case, what Lenin thought was true about all peoples under capitalism, everywhere and at all times, really is true. Lenin's opinion has turned out to be wrong in the case of the advanced, highly developed capitalisms: the British, American, and Western European wage earners can and do use their democratic institutions effectively. Naturally they do not use them perfectly; they are not always wise; they make mistakes and choose governments which prove unacceptable from time to time. Nevertheless, they do work these institutions; it is simply blinding oneself with theory to say that they do not. But this is because, quite contrary to what Lenin supposed would happen, the wage earners of these advanced capitalisms have got richer and better educated instead of poorer and generally more wretched and poverty stricken. Where people are still wretched and poverty stricken or simply illiterate and uneducated, they usually (though not always—there are exceptions) prove incapable of working democratic institutions.

The Preconditions of Democracy

What then are the preconditions for democracy? What makes a country capable of working democratic institutions? We shall find that this is a very difficult question to answer. Experience, which is now worldwide, shows that there is no one thing which one can point to as making a country capable of running democratic institutions. You might think, for example, that it was indispensable that the majority of the voters should be literate, or that they should have more than such-and-such an amount of per capita income. Yet, as a matter of fact, there is one major country which does succeed in running democratic institutions, in which some two-thirds of the population is illiterate, and in which per capita income is very low indeed, namely India. On the other hand, there are examples in South America of quite highly developed countries—such as

the Argentine, for example—with much higher rates of literacy and a much higher per capita income, which seem incapable, for some reason, of working democratic institutions, though they have nominally had these institutions for almost a century now.

Or again, there are countries which are divided by ghastly conflicts between races. It is quite impossible for instance to imagine the successful application of democratic institutions in South Africa, which is practicing *apartheid*.

All one can really say is that a certain level of general civilization seems to be necessary in order to enable a people to work democratic institutions. I think that it is this which enables India to do so. Although the mass of the Indian people are so poor, and although so many of them cannot read or write, yet they are in a very real sense highly civilized. Moreover, India does possess a quite large, highly literate and highly intelligent middle class which participates in public life effectively and actively; and India possessed, at the moment of independence, a framework of democratic political institutions. Although we British had ruled her arbitrarily, in the sense that ultimate power had resided in British hands (and was often used with total disregard of Indian wishes), yet we had long established some of the most important institutions of democracy: *e.g.*, a first-rate legal system of independent law courts in which people really could get impartial judgments. There were schools and universities which had turned out a well-educated middle class. Trade-union activity was permitted (although grudgingly). Finally, in the last decades of British rule, just enough political freedom was established to enable a major political party, the Congress party, to come into existence and agitate for Indian independence. It is quite true that Congress was persecuted from time to time, and that its leaders were put into prison; but it was never suppressed, and gradually the machinery for democratic voting was established, first in the Indian provinces and then, to a certain extent, in the central government.

Therefore when, in 1947, power finally came into Indian hands, the mechanism of a democratic political system was ready to hand. You may think that all this is a typically self-complacent British view. Perhaps it is. It is hard for me to be a judge of that. Nevertheless it does seem to me significant that among a dozen failures to work democratic institutions, the Indian success stands out. This is mainly, of course, to the credit of the Indians, but I also think the British legacy has contributed.

Be all that as it may, I cannot think that we can deny that there is some level of general civilization above which democratic institutions are workable and below which Lenin's opinions are correct. I have elsewhere expressed it in this way. Along the sides of all the ships of the world a line is drawn. This is called the "Plimsoll Line" —after an English M.P., Mr. Plimsoll, who in the nineteenth century got a bill passed making it compulsory to mark ships in this way and making it illegal, under heavy pains and penalties, to load the ships so heavily that this line sank below the water. This was because the greedy shipping capitalists of the day were constantly overloading their ships and endangering, and often destroying, the lives of the sailors by so doing, since the overloaded ships foundered in storms.

What I am now suggesting is that there is an invisible "Plimsoll Line" to be drawn along the sides of all the countries of the world today. If the ship of state floats with that line above water, democratic institutions are workable; if the ship of state is so overloaded with difficulties that the line is submerged, democracy is not there possible. In countries below a level of general development, marked by this line, any attempt to establish democratic institutions will be at best futile, and will be, more often, actually harmful. In these cases, some form of arbitrary government, with all its disadvantages, is inevitable. We are simply wasting our breath when we criticize countries overloaded by their difficulties for having established arbitrary governments. But, on the other hand, for any country which is above the Plimsoll Line of development—which, that is to say, is no longer so overloaded with illiteracy, poverty, racial division, or any other of the terrible burdens which only too many peoples of the world must bear—democratic institutions will prove of inestimable benefit.

Again, democracy is not all of a piece. A country does not have to have it or not have it. That is why I have spoken, usually, not of democracy, but of specific democratic institutions. I have spoken of the rule of law, of freedom of expression, freedom of trade-union organization, freedom to form competing political parties, and to vote freely. It is these institutions which add up to what we call democracy and it is true that they are in the long run interdependent. But, for important periods, a country may possess and work some of these institutions without the others. A country may have established the rule of law quite effectively, for example, without having much freedom of expression, without having established governments effectively chosen by universal suffrage. Several of the new states, *viz.* Pakistan and Ghana, have managed to preserve a certain degree of the rule of law while being quite unable to work political, electoral democracy.

Historically, the best-established, the oldest and most complete democracies in the world, such as those of Western Europe and America, only developed their democratic institutions gradually and one by one. For centuries Britain, for example, had a pretty effective rule of law with nothing like universal franchise. Or, again,

I have described the long struggle which took place in Britain, all within the last one hundred years, for the establishment of effective trade-union freedom. Therefore, it would ill-become anyone from the highly developed democracies to sneer at the state of things in some of the new countries. We should be only too thankful if they manage to establish *any* democratic elements in their life.

One should consider, in the light of all this, the situation in the Communist countries. The tragedy is that in all the European Communist countries, at any rate, the preconditions of workable democratic institutions undoubtedly exist. It would be ridiculous and insulting to say that the Poles, the Hungarians, the Czechs, Rumanians, Bulgarians, or the Russians are not now well enough educated, sufficiently literate, sufficiently civilized in general, to work democratic institutions. Of course they are. They are some of the most talented and intelligent peoples in the world. It is tragic that their whole social development is distorted and held back by Communist dogma, which forbids them freedom to choose the kind of political, social, and economic institutions which they themselves want.

Will Democracy Spread?

Well then, can democracy succeed in spreading throughout the world? I have conceded that democracy is not yet applicable in many parts of the world, but does this mean that democracy is only a passing phase of certain countries, mainly round the Atlantic seaboard, of countries which have had a particular historical development? Does it mean that democracy can never spread throughout the world? It does not.

For democracy *is* succeeding in, precisely, the decisive countries of the world. It is in the advanced, most highly developed, and therefore most powerful countries that democracy is proving a workable institution. This is the guarantee that democracy is the political system of the future.

I repeat that sooner or later as they become more and more highly developed, and above all as their peoples become better and better educated, the Communist countries themselves will adopt some form or other of democratic institutions. Neither they nor the undeveloped non-Communist countries will necessarily adopt what is often called "the Westminster model," namely the system of parliamentary democracy as we know it in Britain. Nor will they necessarily adopt what may be called "the Washington model" of presidential democracy, such as they use in the U.S.A. It may well be—I think it will be—that new types of democratic political institutions will be worked out. As I have said, the original Russian Communist intention —for I think it was a real intention—of basing genuine democratic elections, not on geographical areas, but on factories and farms, on the productive units, was a most interesting idea and well worth trying. In the event not only that form, but all forms, of genuine democracy were scrapped by the Communists. But when real democracy, which means real choice, begins to be exercised by the Russian people, it seems to me quite possible that they will go back to that original Soviet idea.

What I am saying is that the forms of democracy are various. It may well be that the one or two forms which have so far been evolved in the West are by no means the last word: no one is in a position to say that one form is inherently better than another. What matters is the fact of free popular choice.

A Conclusion

My conclusion is, then, that while democracy is no cure-all, it will prove to be the political system of the future. It is no cure-all, first because it is not yet applicable to large parts of the world and, second, because, even if it were, it would still fail, in itself, to solve some of the more acute problems of our period.

Nevertheless, democracy is the political system of the future, because it is by far the best way—in the long run the only tolerable way—of managing complex, highly developed societies made up of well-educated people, capable of taking part in public affairs. As these societies are the most powerful and influential, they will set the pace for the rest of the world.

But this is to look at democracy in a utilitarian, cold-blooded sort of way. Democracy is not only the most practical way of running up-to-date communities. It is much more than that. It is the only political system which recognizes the ultimate worth of every human being: which gives expression to the conviction that behind and beyond all the enormous inequalities, in education, in opportunity, and perhaps in innate ability, which today distinguish one man from another, there is yet an ultimate equivalence between all men, as men. Democracy gives expression to the conviction that no one of us, and certainly no government, is fit to say that one man is inherently better than another. In a word, democracy is a political system for free men instead of slaves.

X. WORLD DEMOCRACY

Democracy is simply the best way yet discovered of arranging the affairs of advanced modern societies. It is not a potential solution to the human problem, for there is none. For we had better learn to be modest in the demands we make on human institutions. One of my favorite quotations on democracy is a saying of Churchill: "Democracy," he used to say, stumping his way down the lobbies of the House of Commons, "democracy is the worst form of government in the world,

except for all the others. . . ."

There is another reason why democracy is not in itself a cure-all. Even if all the existing states in the world could become effectively functioning democracies, which they can't, this would not in itself be enough. This is because a world of a hundred or more democratic states would still be a world of *states*; a world of *sovereign* states; and it is my considered opinion that sovereign states will not do in the nuclear age. This form of human organization will not secure the survival of the human race in the desperate epoch in which we live.

This raises the whole question of democracy and war. War—the prevention of war—is the supreme question of our epoch. This is a far more urgent issue than whether we should organize our economic life on capitalist or socialist lines. After all, experience is showing that peoples can survive under either capitalism or social-

ism; but they cannot survive under nuclear war.

Writing as a lifelong socialist, I must say that there is no question on which, looking back, we socialists have suffered more disillusion than on this question of war. I think that all socialists, whether of the left or the right, whether crusty old Social Democrats like myself or active Communists, once believed, to a greater or lesser extent, that the essential cause of war lay in the economic rivalries of capitalist states. From this diagnosis of the causes of war arose the belief that once capitalism had been abolished and society organized on a socialist basis, the cause of war would have been removed and the establishment of world peace would be easy enough. I do not see how this argument can be maintained any longer.

We have now had forty-five years' experience of the world policies of a major socialist society, the Soviet Union. And

now we have had fourteen years' experience of the behavior of another vast country, organizing its economic life on ultra-socialist lines, China. What is their record on this supreme issue of peace and war? I am not one of those who allege that the socialist countries have been more warlike or aggressive than the capitalist countries. I think it is wrong to assert that Russia is determined to make the world Communist by means of military conquest. What is true is that the Russian government believes that one day the whole world will be Communist; and it also believed, at any rate until recently, that war was by no means a thing of the past. But what is more important than the exact belief of the men who form governments is the record of what they do. And, by and large, I would say that the record of the Communist countries, since they have come into existence, is neither worse nor better than the rest of us in the matter of peace and

(LEFT) PHILIPPINE PRESIDENTIAL CAMPAIGN, 1957; (RIGHT) CAMPAIGN SIGN OF THE PRAJA SOCIALIST PARTY IN INDIA, 1962
"Democracy is the worst form of government in the world, except for all the others. . . ."

war. Russia has often been aggressive, in Finland, in Hungary, in annexing the Baltic states and on other occasions. But so have we in the West: at Suez, for example, in the case of my own country, Britain.

But this, for a socialist, is a profoundly depressing conclusion. It suggests that there is no solution for our overwhelmingly important problem of the maintenance of peace in the nuclear age by means of transforming our societies along socialist lines. Socialism is desirable in itself: I am convinced that it is. But there is no evidence that it will solve the problem of peace and war. China was recently engaged in a most wanton aggression against India, a Communist country attacking a semisocialist country. It is really no longer open to socialists to claim that they have found the solution to the problem of the maintenance of peace. If they do so, they make a laughingstock of themselves.

The Economic Causes of War

What was wrong, then, with the socialist diagnosis of the economic causes of war? I am still as convinced as ever I was that the original purpose of wars of conquest was predominantly economic. In the ancient world, in the world of the great slave empires—Assyria, Egypt, Rome, and the like—the purpose of conquest was essentially to enslave the conquered peoples and then exploit their labor. Either you physically took them and transported them to your own country as slaves and set them to work, as the Romans did on their great landed estates, or you left them in their own country and then, by one device or another, you took away from them almost everything they produced above subsistence.

After all, in the ancient world with its very low level of productivity, the only way in which the leisured class could live in luxury was to acquire an abundant supply of slave (or semislave) labor by

means of conquest. However, that was all a long time ago. Nevertheless, socialists believed that by a different mechanism, the wars of capitalist society were still essentially economic. Lenin put forward his theory of the causation of war in his book *Imperialism*. He believed that capitalist societies must attack each other in order to expand and secure markets and spheres of investment. If they did not do so, they would stifle in their own "plethora of capital" and overproduced consumer goods. Every major capitalist society, Lenin taught, was a sort of pressure cooker which sooner or later must burst out on the rest of the world or stifle.

Now I still believe that this thesis of Lenin's had a very large measure of truth in it, at any rate for the type of capitalism which existed when he wrote in 1917. It was true that this kind of capitalism, of which the essential characteristic was that the wage-earning masses were held down at near subsistence level, could only expand into the outside world. It had to seek its markets and its fields of investment outside itself because its own internal market was so limited by the poverty of the vast majority of its people. But all this is demonstrably no longer true of contemporary capitalist society. As I have noted previously, there is no doubt at all about the fact that they are able to, and actually have, raised steadily the standard of life of their wage-earning masses. And this of course has provided them with an ever expanding internal market which has made external expansion unnecessary.

Lenin's Opinion

Curiously enough, Lenin noticed this possibility. But he dismissed it as something which, if it could be done, would no doubt solve the problem, but which capitalism was inherently incapable of doing. In a little-noticed passage in chapter 4 of his book *Imperialism* Lenin said quite clearly that *if* capitalism *could* raise the standard of life of the wage-earning masses and develop agriculture, then the outward pressure toward limitless expansion would be relieved. The capitalist powers would no longer need to collide with each other in bloody war.

Now there is no denying the fact that during the last twenty years, capitalism has done precisely these two things. It *has* developed agriculture and it *has* raised the standard of life of the masses in the capitalist countries. It is still doing both of these things. Therefore, according to Lenin's argument, it is no longer capitalism. In fact there are economists who say that the economic system as it exists in the Western countries today has been so greatly changed by the reforms and modifications of the last twenty years that it cannot any longer really be called "capitalist." I think this is wrong; I think that the Western countries are still most conveniently classified as capitalist societies. What has been shown is that with limited, but important, changes, capitalism can do precisely the two things which Lenin said it could never do. (As you will note we are back by another road at the fundamental question of Marx's forecast of the ever increasing misery of the wage earners. It is the fact that this forecast has been disproved which changes everything.)

No Inevitabilities

I conclude from all this that war is no longer inevitable between capitalist societies; they can manage all right while keeping the peace. But unfortunately this does not mean that they necessarily will keep the peace. Socialist societies, of course, are under no necessity to undertake aggression and expansion; they can occupy themselves indefinitely in raising the standard of life of their peoples, and with development in general. But, equally, experience shows that this is no guarantee

that they *will*, in fact, abstain from aggression. For what are the Chinese armies doing on the southern slopes of the Himalayas? China, surely, on any rational calculation, should be devoting every ounce of her energies and resources to her desperate task of internal development. But, on the contrary, she sent some fourteen divisions to attack India.

From this I conclude that all one can say about the causes of war is something simpler and more general than we socialists had supposed. The cause of war seems to be simply the existence of separate sovereign states, whether capitalist, socialist, feudal, or any other kind. It is the fact that the world is organized, or rather disorganized, into over one hundred sovereign states that is the cause of war.

Are Democracies Pacific?

I have gone into this whole question of the disillusionment which socialists have suffered on this issue of the economic causes of war in order to avoid a new disillusionment that I think democrats may well suffer unless they take care. Democrats are often accustomed to argue that the cause of war lies in tyrannies, autocracies, or other forms of arbitrary dictatorship, and that if only all the states of the world would become democracies, all governments would be pacific and there would be no danger of war. I am afraid that experience will show, if such a state of things as a world of democratic states ever comes into existence, that this belief in the inherent pacifism of democracies is also an illusion. I do indeed believe that democracies are, on the whole, rather less aggressive and bellicose than tyrannies, autocracies, or other forms of arbitrary government. A government which is responsible to its electors does, from time to time at any rate, experience pressures for peace. But I am afraid that it is far from true that democracies are always and completely pacific. On the contrary, a majority of democratic electors sometimes suffers moods in which it is unreasonable and bellicose. If we study the history of, say, the last one hundred years, in which alone we can find states with democratic governments in the sense in which I have been using the words, it will not, alas, be difficult to find examples in which undoubtedly democratic states have been aggressive and bellicose. You will readily call to mind examples of this in the case of Britain. Most left-wing people, at any rate, consider that the United States today is a rather aggressive country. Yet undoubtedly the United States government is one of the most effectively functioning democracies in the world. I do not myself think that America is specially aggressive but I agree that she is not absolutely, or even particularly, pacific either.

No, a world of democratic states would still be a world subject to war. The most that we can claim for such a world would be that it would be less likely to go to war than a world of states ruled by arbitrary, autocratic governments. Unless we face these unpleasant facts we shall, I think, suffer an analogous disillusionment with democracy to that which socialists have suffered over this question of peace and war.

Is War Inevitable?

War, then, would still be possible in a world of democratic states. In fact I am afraid that I must go further than this and say that, in the long run, war would be inevitable in a world of separate sovereign, democratic states. It might be postponed for a long time. Indeed I believe that the series of crises through which the world is passing at the present time—Cuba, Berlin, Vietnam, the Indo-Chinese conflict, to name a few—are by no means so immediately dangerous as many people think. I do not think that it is at all likely that, say, the next, or the next but one, of these crises will precipitate us into a world nuclear war and so blot us out. Nevertheless how can we deny that if the world goes on living like this: if crisis succeeds crisis in endless succession, sooner or later one of them *will* erupt into world nuclear war?

After all, we are living in an international anarchy. There is no power whatever superior to the sovereign state today. That is the essence of sovereignty. And anarchy

DETAIL OF CARTOON FROM
Judge, 1898
*Inherent pacifism of
democracies is an illusion*

has its own laws. They are statistical laws and for that very reason they are not subject to human control, but they are subject to human calculation and forecast. So we can forecast only too confidently that if you leave a state of anarchy in existence indefinitely, it will, sooner or later, erupt into conflict—or else all historical experience is at fault.

I conclude, therefore, that something more than a world of separate democratic states is necessary for the survival of man in the nuclear age. If mankind had not developed these fantastic powers of destruction, a world of separate sovereign democratic states might have been a possible and a tolerable world. No doubt there would have been periodic wars; but then there always have been periodic wars throughout human history and, somehow or other, civilization has survived them. The development of nuclear weapons has changed all that. I do not see how we can possibly escape the conclusion that full-scale nuclear war is incompatible with the maintenance of human civilization.

World Unity

What is necessary and indispensable for human survival is not merely the spread of democracy from one country to another until the world consists of democratic states. What is necessary, on the contrary, is *world democracy*. And I mean by this nothing less than the unification of the world under one democratic government. I cannot see how, in the long run, human civilization can survive unless within a few generations it somehow produces a government which is both worldwide in extent and responsible directly or indirectly to a world electorate. By "responsible" I mean that it must be possible for the peoples of the world, by one means or another, to hire and fire that government. And that means that it must be possible for them to choose between differ-

ent kinds of government; and it must be possible for them at least to influence their government while it is in power. In a word, those essential institutions of democracy, which I defined earlier in respect of any particular state, must be applied on a worldwide scale.

Of course all this is a long distance off. It cannot possibly come into existence immediately. But many of you I am sure will go much further in skepticism than this and say that world democracy can never come into existence; or at any rate that it is extremely unlikely. Well, maybe. If you say that, what you are really saying is that human survival in the nuclear age is very unlikely. You may well be right. But I should like to hear of any other aim, goal, cause, or ideal which can offer mankind the hope of survival in the nuclear age. I think that it is world democracy or nothing. After all, the fact that a goal is distant and difficult of attainment has never prevented man from giving his allegiance to it.

If you ask me for details of how a world unity might come about I cannot give them. It may be that the only way to the achievement of world unity soon enough to prevent world destruction will prove to be a very undemocratic way. It may be that, initially, it will have to be done by a virtual dictatorship of the major nuclear powers. Nevertheless that would not be tolerable in the long run. A unified world would have in the end to become a world democracy. Nor do I think it particularly important to try and imagine how a world democracy would be organized. I suppose that, for many decades, it might be organized indirectly upon the basis of the election of a world government by national governments (no doubt on some weighted system) which were themselves democratically elected.

But surely in the end it must be voted for directly by the peoples of the world. I regard the United Nations as a precious expression of man's aspirations toward some sort of world government, rather than as anything closely resembling a world government itself. The United Nations is a forum of debate and discussion and as such indispensable. But it is not in any sense a government. A world democratic government must have two characteristics —responsibility and power: the United Nations by its very nature can have neither.

A General Conclusion

In the light of twentieth-century experience, I may conclude that countries may have many sorts of economic systems, ranging from decidedly capitalist systems to completely socialist systems. With good luck and skill, any or all of these systems can be made to work tolerably well— though in my opinion the more socialistic systems will prove much the more satis-

WAR MINISTER JOHN STRACHEY VISITING WEST BERLIN
"Unite or perish!"

factory. Two things, therefore, have become even more important than the exact way in which we organize our economies. The first is whether or not we organize the political life of our nations upon a democratic basis. The second is the search for that worldwide unity of the human race without which we are all bound to perish in the nuclear age. The political arrangements which we establish within our own countries matter vitally, because experience shows that unless they are democratic, all sorts of injustices, instabilities, and outright disasters occur. Our capacity to unite the world matters more vitally still because the lesson of the nuclear age is this: "Unite or perish!"

NOTE TO THE READER

All of the major subjects discussed in *The Challenge of Democracy*—democracy, communism, and the ideal of a world government—receive prominent attention in the works of many of the authors of *Great Books of the Western World*. An entire chapter in the *Syntopicon* is devoted to democracy, and the introductory essay examines the long history of democracy in the literature of political thought and discusses the various meanings given to this political concept. Of particular relevance to readers of Strachey's essay will be the passages referred to under DEMOCRACY 4: the praise of democracy: the ideal state.

Freedom is fundamental to democracy, according to Strachey, and especially freedom of association, freedom of speech, freedom of assembly, and the rule of law, which Strachey claims is a form of freedom. For the discussion of freedom of association, the reader can consult the references cited under CONSTITUTION 7b, DEMOCRACY 4b, LIBERTY 1g, and TYRANNY 5a. Freedom of speech and of assembly are discussed in the passages referred to under LIBERTY 2a, PROGRESS 6e, CONSTITUTION 7b, DEMOCRACY 4b, EDUCATION 8c, and LIBERTY 1g. Texts dealing with the rule of law are referred to under DEMOCRACY 4a. A general discussion of the historical significance of freedom in the development of Western societies can be found in the essay by François Guizot, "Civilization" (GGB, Vol. 6, pp. 302–317).

Although strong in his defense of democracy, Strachey is also sensitive to the imperfections of democracy in practice. The infirmities of democracy and the reforms or remedies of these defects is the subject of DEMOCRACY 4c.

One of the crucial reasons why democracy has succeeded in Western societies, Strachey argues, is that the working class has become active and influential in politics during the 19th and 20th centuries. Extensive discussion of the working class can be found in the introductory essay on LABOR in the *Syntopicon*. Further analysis of labor and its problems can be found in the passages referred to under LABOR 7 and under PROGRESS 3b, STATE 5d, JUSTICE 8c (1), SLAVERY 4c, and LIBERTY 2d and 6b. Once the working class gains freedom from economic pressures, Strachey predicts that many laborers will shift attention "from economic issues to the political arrangements under which the public life of their communities are organized." Economic freedom is the subject of DEMOCRACY 4a and 4a(2), LABOR 7f, JUSTICE 6–6e, LIBERTY 1–2d, SLAVERY 4–6d, and PROGRESS 3b.

One of the goals of a democracy, in Strachey's opinion, is the eventual establishment of a classless society. Passages in which a classless society is examined can be found under STATE 5e and REVOLUTION 5c.

Contributions to the dialogue on democracy are also made by authors in *Gateway to the Great Books*. Aspects of democracy in the United States are described by Jean de Crèvecoeur in "The Making of Americans" (GGB, Vol. 6, pp. 546–559) and by Alexis de Tocqueville in "Observations on American Life and Government" (GGB, Vol. 6, pp. 564–690).

Strachey's analysis of communism contrasts the Marxist ideal of a "working-class democracy" with the contemporary realities in Soviet Russia. The foundation of communist doctrine is contained in the two works by Karl Marx in Volume 50 of GBWW: *Capital*, and *Manifesto of the Communist Party*, written by Marx and Engels. Additional discussion of communism can be found in the passages cited under

LABOR 5*d*, 7*b*, *c*, and *f*, REVOLUTION 1*a*, 4*b*, and 5*c*, STATE 5*e*, WEALTH 6*a* and 8*a*, DEMOCRACY 4*a* (2), JUSTICE 8*a*, and PROGRESS 3*b*. Discussion of the class war can be found in the passages listed under LABOR 7. The proletariat as a revolutionary class is the subject of LABOR 7*c*(3).

The third major subject in *The Challenge of Democracy* is the eloquent appeal at the end of the essay for world government, founded on democratic principles. Discussion of world government and universal peace can be read in works in *Gateway to the Great Books*: Dante's *On World Government*, Vol. 7, pp. 383-399; Jean Jacques Rousseau's *A Lasting Peace Through the Federation of Europe*, Vol. 7, pp. 405-436; Immanuel Kant's *Perpetual Peace*, Vol. 7, pp. 441-475. For further examination of world government, the reader can consult the texts indicated under LOVE 4*c*, STATE 10*f*, and WAR AND PEACE 11*d*. The idea of world citizenship—the political brotherhood of man—is discussed in the passages referred to under CITIZEN 8.

This book was adapted from the original design for the 1961 volume by William Nicoll of Edit, Inc., Chicago. It is set in Caledonia, a typeface created by the late W. A. Dwiggins. The type was set by SSPA Typesetting, Inc., Carmel, Indiana, and the book was printed and bound by Rand McNally & Co., Inc.

Authors

in Great Books of the Western World

Homer	Nicomachus
Aeschylus	Ptolemy
Sophocles	Marcus Aurelius
Herodotus	Galen
Euripides	Plotinus
Thucydides	Augustine
Hippocrates	Thomas Aquinas
Aristophanes	Dante
Plato	Chaucer
Aristotle	Machiavelli
Euclid	Copernicus
Archimedes	Rabelais
Apollonius	Montaigne
Lucretius	Gilbert
Virgil	Cervantes
Plutarch	Francis Bacon
Tacitus	Galileo
Epictetus	Shakespeare
	Kepler